Understanding

Capitalism

4′ c³

Understanding

Capitalism

COMPETITION, COMMAND, AND CHANGE

Third Edition

Samuel Bowles
Santa Fe Institute

Richard Edwards
University of Nebraska–Lincoln

Frank Roosevelt
Sarah Lawrence College

New York   Oxford
OXFORD UNIVERSITY PRESS
2005

Oxford University Press

Oxford   New York
Auckland Bangkok Buenos Aires Cape Town Chennai
Dar es Salaam Delhi Hong Kong Istanbul Karachi Kolkata
Kuala Lumpur Madrid Melbourne Mexico City Mumbai
Nairobi São Paulo Shanghai Taipei Tokyo Toronto

Published by Oxford University Press, Inc.
198 Madison Avenue, New York, New York 10016
www.oup.com

Library of Congress Cataloging-in-Publication Data

Bowles, Samuel.
   Understanding capitalism : competition, command, and change / Samuel Bowles, Richard
Edwards, and Frank Roosevelt.—3rd ed.
       p. cm.
   Includes bibliographical references and index.
   ISBN-13: 978-0-19-513864-1 (cloth)—ISBN-13: 978-0-19-513865-8 (pbk.)
   ISBN 0-19-513864-3 (cloth)—ISBN 0-19-513865-1 (pbk.)
   1. Economics. 2. Capitalism. 3. United States—Economic conditions. I. Edwards,
Richard, 1944- II. Roosevelt, Frank, 1938- III. Title.
   HB171.5.B6937 2005
   330.12′2—dc22   2004024955

Printing number: 9 8 7 6 5 4 3 2 1

Printed in the United States of America
on acid-free paper

TO LIBBY, CAROLYN, AND JINX

CONTENTS

FIGURES AND TABLES

PREFACE

*U*nderstanding Capitalism: Competition, Command, and Change is an introduction to economics that explains how capitalism works, why it sometimes does not work as well as we would like, and how over time it not only changes its own functioning but also revolutionizes the world around us. The book does not assume that the reader has any prior knowledge of economics.

The *three-dimensional approach* to economics offered in this book focuses not just on market *competition,* as highlighted in conventional economics textbooks, but also on relationships of *command*—the exercise of power in firms, among nations, and between social groups—and on processes of historical *change*. The approach is multidisciplinary, making extensive use of examples from history, anthropology, and the other behavioral sciences as well as economics.

The core idea uniting the three dimensions of competition, command, and change is the pursuit of profits by firms. Using this central idea, we analyze competition among firms, the search for profits as the driving force of investment and technical change, and profit seeking as a source of conflict among owners, workers, governments, employers, and consumers.

The book covers the standard topics of supply and demand, market competition, imperfect competition, aggregate demand, inflation, and unemployment. In addition, we give special attention to the extraordinary dynamism and material productivity of the capitalist economy, the psychological foundations of human behavior and the importance of Adam Smith's invisible hand, technical change and the new information-based economy, global economic integration and its impact on national economies, and inequality both within and among nations. We also provide a critical evaluation of the tenets of neoclassical economics and a clear introduction to contract theory as well as to new research in behavioral, institutional, and information economics.

We titled the book *Understanding Capitalism* (rather than, say, *Understanding Economics*) to stress that our subject matter is a real economic system—not just the ideas and models of economists. Considered in this way, economic theory is a body of knowledge that, along with history, politics, sociology, and the other social sciences, can help us understand capitalism.

STRUCTURE OF THE BOOK

Part 1, "Political Economy," introduces the three-dimensional approach to economics, explains its relationship to other approaches, develops its fundamental concepts, and summarizes some of the pertinent facts relating to life in a capitalist economy.

Part 2, "Microeconomics," develops the theory of the firm and of markets, including the labor market, and analyzes technological change using a Schumpeterian model of dynamic monopolistic competition. Most important, it develops the analysis of profits and the profit rate that provides the integrating principle of three-dimensional economics and establishes the link between micro- and macroeconomics.

Part 3, "Macroeconomics," deals with the workings of the economy as a whole. To provide a foundation for our study of macroeconomics, we examine inequality both within and among nations, focusing in particular on uneven development on a global scale. Here we introduce the concepts of aggregate demand and aggregate supply and explain why unemployment is a more-or-less permanent feature of capitalist labor markets. This part of the book ends with chapters on inflation and on the government's role in the economy.

In Part 4, we conclude the book with a challenging chapter on "The Future of Capitalism," raising questions about the adequacy of today's institutions to address tomorrow's problems, including environmental degradation, global inequality, and intellectual property rights and incentives in the new information-based economy.

Teachers using the book in a microeconomics course may want to assign Chapters 1–14 and Chapter 20. Those using it in a macroeconomics course might want to focus on Chapters 1–7, 10, and 14–20. For a one-semester course, Chapters 1–10 and 20 might be appropriate, while other chapters could be included as time and student interest permit.

CHANGES IN THE THIRD EDITION

This third edition of *Understanding Capitalism* is essentially a new book. The data and examples have been updated, and three entirely new chapters have been added. We take into account developments through the early years of the third millennium, including changes in economic thought as well as in global politics and economics. We list here the most important changes.

- A completely revised and expanded first chapter presents a dramatic picture of the revolutionary changes associated with capitalism over the past three centuries. Global warming and other environmental problems are given greater attention.
- As our cover suggests, the scope of the book is more global, with increasing attention given to economic forces operating on a world scale. In recognition of the fact that the U.S. is now part of a global economy, we dropped the "in the U.S. Economy" that appeared in the subtitle of the second edition.
- A new chapter addresses the behavioral foundations of economics, showing that the selfishness of the conventionally assumed "economic man" leaves out the important

role of more social motives and explaining how individuals' tastes and values evolve in response to their experiences.

- Inequality—especially its growth in the U.S.—is a more central focus of the book. A new chapter deals with the increasing inequality of income and wealth along lines of race and gender. We also document the way that economic success (and poverty) is passed on from parents to children.
- The information revolution and the importance of technological change in general are given greater attention in this edition. In the final chapter we ask whether the growing role of information in the economy is generating pressure for change in the institutions of the capitalist economy.

PEDAGOGICAL AIDS AND SUPPLEMENTS

The glossary, the definitions of terms placed in the text margins, and the captions under each figure will assist readers in mastering the basic language and analytical tools of economics. The boxes in the text present additional facts about the economy and raise issues that can be the basis of classroom discussions.

The "Sources of Economic Information" section near the beginning of the book can help readers locate economic information from official and other sources, both in print and online.

THREE-DIMENSIONAL ECONOMICS AND THE NEOCLASSICAL PARADIGM

When the first edition of this book was published in 1985, many thought of it as an "alternative text" and welcomed it as a counterpoint to the neoclassical paradigm that was the dominant approach to economics at the time. Since that time, economics has changed in significant ways. Many of the themes central to this book are now addressed by many economists as well as by other social scientists. In recent years economists have turned their attention to the problem of inequality, the importance of ethical values and unselfish motives in economic behavior, the exercise of power, the way that history shapes economic events, and how the economy shapes who we are as individuals and as people in societies and cultures. The rapid pace of economic, scientific, political, and other developments in today's world has forced economists to face the issue of change.

Since the first edition of *Understanding Capitalism* was published, the Nobel Prize in Economics has been awarded to many of the economists who have inspired our own work. Among them are Amartya Sen and Ronald Coase (whose ideas are featured in Chapter 4), as well as George Akerlof, Joseph Stiglitz, Robert Fogel, Douglass North, Daniel Kahneman, Vernon Smith, John Nash, and others.

Of course, economics remains a controversial topic. There is, however, no longer a single dominant school but rather many distinct approaches, each with its own merits and shortcomings. All of the Nobel Prize winners listed above have been sharp critics of some aspects of the neoclassical approach (while endorsing others). Unfortunately, the teaching of economics to undergraduates has lagged behind what is widely understood by leading economists. The conventional "neoclassical" model is still taught, often as if it were the only approach to the field. For this reason this book may still be thought of as an "alternative text" because it focuses on questions largely ignored in the standard textbooks and develops concepts and ideas that are at variance with—or not even mentioned in— conventional textbooks. In Chapter 4 we explain how our approach relates to the history of economic thought.

Samuel Bowles, *Santa Fe, New Mexico*

Richard Edwards, *Lincoln, Nebraska*

Frank Roosevelt, *New York, New York*

ACKNOWLEDGMENTS

U nderstanding Capitalism presents an approach to teaching about economics and the
economy that we have developed, along with colleagues too numerous to mention,
in our introductory economics courses over three and a half decades at Harvard
University, the University of Massachusetts at Amherst, and Sarah Lawrence College. To
the thousands of students and dozens of teaching assistants whose criticisms, suggestions,
enthusiasm, and (sometimes) indifference have guided us, we owe special thanks.

Jillian Porter and Jinx Roosevelt edited the entire text, bringing their formidable writing skills to bear on our prose. Arjun Jayadev provided the research for most of the empirical figures and suggested numerous improvements in the book based on his classroom
experience with an early draft of this edition. To these three close collaborators we are
greatly indebted.

Many colleagues have used previous editions of this book in their classes—or read
and used drafts of the present one—and given us the kind of feedback and advice only out-
standing teachers and researchers can offer. In this regard, we especially thank Frank
Thompson at the University of Michigan; Martin Hart-Landsberg at Lewis and Clark
College; Manuel Pastor at the University of California at Santa Cruz; Mehrene Larudee at
DePaul University; Bob Pollin and David Kotz at the University of Massachusetts at
Amherst; Jim Devine at Loyola Marymount University; Eric Nilsson at California State
University at San Bernardino; Fritz Efaw at the University of Tennessee at Chattanooga;
Eric Schutz of Rollins College; and Jeffrey Carpenter at Middlebury College. Their detailed
comments and suggestions have made this a much better book.

We also thank Ed Ford at the University of South Florida and Rachel Balkom at Santa
Fe Prep, who used one or another version of the book in their classes and, citing their students' responses, passed along helpful comments.

We are especially grateful to the following individuals who offered their expertise on
particular sections: Dominique Alhéritière (Food and Agriculture Organization of the
United Nations), Bob Allen (Oxford University), David Belkin (Independent Budget
Office of the City of New York), Lourdes Beneria (Cornell University), Mike Buckner
(United Mine Workers of America), Nancy Folbre (University of Massachusetts at
Amherst), Victor Lippit (University of California at Riverside), Jamee Moudud (Sarah
Lawrence College), Gordon Pavy (AFL-CIO), Michael Reich (University of California at
Berkeley), Peter Rosset (Institute for Food and Development Policy), Juliet Schor (Boston

College), Joe Von Fischer (Princeton University), Jim Weeks (ATL International), and Edward Wolff (New York University).

Kate Boyd scanned the entire second edition of the book so that the authors could begin their work on this edition with an electronic copy of the previous one; Bae Smith at the Santa Fe Institute helped us locate many sources of information; the librarians at the Santa Fe Institute, especially Margaret Alexander and Tim Taylor, provided invaluable assistance; and Scott Gillam proofread every page of the book and offered many helpful suggestions in the weeks before it went to press.

A number of people provided other kinds of assistance at various stages of our work. For this help we specifically thank Michael Arons, Allyce Bess, John Boettiger, Mark Brenner, Marcus Feldman, Christina Fong, Sarah Knutson, Bill Mayher, Jennifer McCharen, Richard Pollak, Kenneth Pomeranz, Nick Roosevelt, and Ray Seidelman.

Last but not least, we thank the following professionals at Oxford University Press who made possible the publication of this book: Jeffrey House, our original (1998) contact with the press; the late Kenneth MacLeod, our acquiring editor; Paul Donnelly, who had faith in us over the long haul; Terry Vaughn, our very supportive and patient editor in the final year and a half; and Leslie Anglin, who shepherded the book through the process of its production.

Of course, the authors retain responsibility for any remaining errors.

Samuel Bowles, *Santa Fe, New Mexico*

Richard Edwards, *Lincoln, Nebraska*

Frank Roosevelt, *New York, New York*

SOURCES OF
ECONOMIC INFORMATION

Most of the facts in this book are taken from the following sources. Many of the information sources listed here provide extensive discussions of the data and suggestions as to where to look for further information. They are generally available online as well as in libraries.

Council of Economic Advisors, *Economic Report of the President* (Washington, D.C.: U.S. Government Printing Office, annual, available at http://www.whitehouse.gov/cea/pubs.html; past reports are at http://gpoaccess.gov/eop/download.html).

U.S. Bureau of the Census, *Statistical Abstract of the United States* (Washington, D.C.: U.S. Government Printing Office, annual, current edition available at http://www.census.gov/statab/www).

U.S. Bureau of the Census, *Historical Statistics of the United States: Colonial Times to 1970* (Washington, D.C.: U.S. Government Printing Office, 1975).

United Nations Development Programme, *Human Development Report* (New York: Oxford University Press, annual, latest edition available at http://hdr.undp.org/reports/global/2003/).

The World Bank, *World Development Report* (New York: Oxford University Press, annual, available at http://econ.worldbank.org/wdr/).

International Monetary Fund, *International Financial Statistics Yearbook: 2002* (Washington, D.C.: International Monetary Fund, 2002).

Organization for Economic Cooperation and Development, *The State of the Environment* (Paris: OECD, 1991).

Economic Policy Institute, *The State of Working America* (Ithaca, NY: ILR Press, an imprint of Cornell University Press, biannual, see link at http://movingideas.org/).

WorldWatch Institute, *The State of the World* (Washington, D.C.: WorldWatch Institute, annual).

In addition, a number of newspapers and periodicals provide extensive reporting on economics and the economy. Among the more informative are the *Wall Street Journal,* the *New York Times,* the *Washington Post,* the *Los Angeles Times, Financial Times, Challenge, Dollars and Sense, The Economist,* the *Milken Institute Review, The American Prospect, Business Week, Fortune,* and *Forbes.*

More information is contained in the fact-filled reports regularly published by the following government agencies and private organizations located in Washington, D.C.: the Congressional Budget Office, the Bureau of Economic Analysis of the U.S. Department of

Commerce, the Census Bureau of the U.S. Department of Commerce, the Bureau of Labor Statistics of the U.S. Department of Labor, the Center on Budget and Policy Priorities, the Economic Policy Institute, the Institute for Women's Policy Research, and the Urban Institute.

The Center for Popular Economics in Amherst, Mass. (www.populareconomics.org) offers both week-long courses during the summer and weekend courses at other times of the year for anyone interested in obtaining economic information and developing the skills necessary for applying economic analysis to current economic and political issues.

With the growth of the World Wide Web, there are many online sources of economic information. We provide here a selected list of Web sites where such information may be found. Because Web sites do not always have long lives, some of the sites listed may have changed their addresses or ceased to exist.

http://www.oecd.org

The Organization for Economic Cooperation and Development (OECD) provides data from the statistical agencies of its 20 member countries. It also develops and promotes international statistical standards and coordinates statistical activities with other international agencies.

http://www.worldbank.org/data/onlinedatabases/onlinedatabases.html

The World Bank offers multiple databases online, some free of charge and some on an annual subscription basis. Free access is available to a 5-year, 54-indicators segment of the World Development Indicators (WDI) database.

http://www.imf.org/external/country/index.htm

The International Monetary Fund (IMF) provides country-specific data, from Afghanistan to Zimbabwe.

http://www.helsinki.fi/WebEc/webecc8d.html

Based in Helsinki, Finland, this is a master economic data source that provides links to a great number of Web sites both within the U.S. and internationally.

http://www.census.gov/econ/www/

This is the Web site of the U.S. Census Bureau, a subdivision of the U.S. Department of Commerce. It provides demographic as well as economic data.

http://www.bea.gov/

This is the Web site of the U.S. Bureau of Economic Analysis (BEA), a subdivision of the U.S. Department of Commerce. It provides a wealth of data on the U.S. economy, from gross domestic product (GDP) to U.S. investment abroad.

http://www.bls.gov/

This is the Web site of the U.S. Bureau of Labor Statistics (BLS), a subdivision of the U.S. Department of Labor. Information about employment, unemployment, and the unemployment rate may be found here.

http://www.nber.org/data

This is the Web site of the (U.S.) National Bureau of Economic Research, a private organization that is often identified as if it were an agency of the U.S. government. It offers individual-level data, industry data, and macroeconomic data (including dates for the beginnings and ends of U.S. recessions).

http://pwt.econ.upenn.edu/

The Penn World Tables, developed at the University of Pennsylvania, provide economic data on about 100 countries, in most cases covering the last 50 years.

http://rfe.org/

"Resources for Economists" is the creation of Bill Goffe, a professor of economics at the State University of New York (SUNY) at Oswego. Regularly updated, this Web site provides (as of this writing) 1,487 links (organized in 97 sections and subsections) to nearly every source of economic information on the Internet.

http://www.economics.ltsn.ac.uk/links/data_free.htm

This Web site presents data on the British economy.

http://movingideas.org/

This is the Web site of the "Electronic Policy Network" (EPN) sponsored by the *American Prospect* magazine. It provides links to dozens of U.S. policy-oriented organizations, from "Americans for Democratic Action" to "TomPaine.com."

http://www.economagic.com/

This Web site has more than 100,000 data files, with Excel files and charts for series from such sources as the U.S. government, the Federal Reserve Bank, the Internal Revenue Service, and the European Central Bank.

http://www.lib.umich.edu/govdocs/stats.html

This Web site, based at the University of Michigan, has links to economics data sets on U.S. business and industry, labor, finance, price indexes and the cost of living, federal and state finances, foreign and international economics, foreign trade, gross domestic product, gross state product, and gross city product.

http://www.economy.com/dismal/toolkit_landing.asp (requires subscription)

This Web site offers daily, weekly, monthly, and quarterly economic indicators for the U.S. economy as well as for states, metropolitan areas, and zip code districts. It provides GDP figures for 176 countries, all 50 U.S. states (plus Washington, D.C., and Puerto Rico), and 318 U.S. metropolitan areas, with tables summarizing economic information broken down by geographic area. In addition, the site offers a stock market calculator as well as a way to estimate the probability of recessions in states and selected metropolitan areas.

http://utip.gov.utexas.edu/

This Web site, based at the University of Texas, provides data on economic inequality.

http://www.econdata.net/

This Web site provides U.S. regional data on demographics, employment, occupations, income, output, prices, economic assets, quality of life, industry sectors, and firm listings. It draws on numerous sources for this data, including the U.S. Bureau of Labor Statistics, the U.S. Bureau of Economic Analysis, the U.S. Census Bureau, and other government and private sources.

http://www.csufresno.edu/Economics/econ_EDL.htm

This Web site, based at California State University at Fresno, offers data sets on productivity, the labor force, income distribution, profits ("earnings"), and other variables.

PART **1**

Political Economy

CHAPTER 1

Capitalism Shakes the World

For more than four decades following World War II, Germany was divided: East Germany was a dictatorship, while West Germany was a democracy. The economic systems of the two Germanys were as different as their systems of government. In the East, the economy, like just about everything else, was run by the Communist Party. Decisions about who should produce what, how, when, and for whom were made by the government and carried out under orders. Communism was not simply a form of government, it was also an economic system based on centralized direction of economic decisions. By contrast, West Germany had what is termed a capitalist economy. West Germans for the most part made economic decisions independently, guided in most cases by what they needed to do to turn a profit, to get and keep a decent job, or to have a particular kind of lifestyle given their means.

In October 1989 the general secretary of the East German Communist Party, Erich Honecker, grandly celebrated the founding of Communist East Germany 40 years earlier. He proclaimed that it had been both a "historical necessity" and a "turning point in the history of the German people." Parades and demonstrations commemorated the anniversary. But 12 days after the celebration, Honecker suddenly stepped down as prodemocracy demonstrations broke out first in the East German city of Leipzig and then spread throughout the country. A million and a half Germans participated in these demonstrations in October, and twice that number attended them in November.

Less than a month after Honeker's resignation, East and West Germans danced together on the Berlin Wall and then dismantled it. Less than a year after the grandiose celebration of its 40th anniversary, East Germany passed out of existence, its territory joined with that of West Germany, and the combined parts becoming once again simply Germany. As a result, the citizens of the former Communist nation passed from one economic system to another, from communism to capitalism. At about the same time, prodemocracy demonstrators

3

toppled their Communist rulers in the Soviet Union, Poland, Czechoslovakia, Hungary, and, indeed, in all of the remaining Communist-ruled countries except Cuba, Vietnam, Laos, North Korea, and China. The demonstrators rejected not only Communist dictatorships but also the centralized organization of their economies. All adopted some form of capitalist economic system.

Like communism, other economic systems had earlier fallen to the capitalist onslaught. An economic system based on slavery in the U.S. South ended with the victory of the Union troops in the Civil War and Lincoln's emancipation of the slaves. As a result the South ceased to be a slave economy and became capitalist. Similarly, the simple economics of hunting and gathering—what most humans did to make a living for most of our time on earth—has been abandoned in most parts of the world, to be replaced by other economic systems, and eventually, in most parts of the world, by capitalism. And the process continues. Capitalism is on a roll and has been since its birth.

Nevertheless, capitalism is new, having been a moving force in world history for only the past five centuries or so—less than 1 percent of the time that humans have inhabited the earth. During this relatively short period, however, the world has changed more quickly, more constantly, and more profoundly than during any earlier period of human history. And now the pace of change appears to be quickening, so even greater transformations will most likely occur in our lifetimes.

> **Capitalism** is an economic system in which employers, using privately owned capital goods, hire wage labor to produce commodities for the purpose of making a profit.

> The **capitalist epoch** began in some parts of Europe around AD 1500, when capitalist organization of labor processes first appeared. It continues to the present in most of the world.

Capitalism, as we will see in detail later, is an economic system in which employers hire workers to produce goods and services that will be marketed with the intention of making a profit. Wherever capitalism has taken root, it has left no aspect of society unchanged. It has brought with it unprecedented advances in scientific and other kinds of knowledge, astonishing developments in technology, previously unimaginable ways of sharing information, and rising standards of consumption, health, and education in most of the world. It has also led to fundamental realignments of power and redistributions of wealth, the abolition of slavery and other archaic forms of bondage, and radical changes in family life, ideals, and beliefs.

Since we have lived with rapid change all of our lives, we tend to think of it as normal, even natural. Yet from a historical perspective, rapid and relentless transformation of the social and physical world is anything but normal. Far from being driven by change, earlier economic systems were bound by inertia. The *capitalist epoch* began in Europe around AD 1500. The capitalist organization of work—employers hiring people for wages to make a profit—first appeared in parts of England, the Netherlands, Belgium, and Italy. Initially the new way of organizing production affected few people, even in the countries where it first appeared, but as it spread and became stronger, the transformative power of capitalism also grew. It would eventually revolutionize the world.

Capitalism's development and the social changes accompanying it occurred at different times in different places, and its impact was highly uneven. In some places capitalist development occurred quickly, in other places very slowly, and in some regions of the world, capitalism is only now replacing other economic systems.

EUROPE AT THE DAWN OF THE SECOND MILLENNIUM

A mere handful of folk—unending emptiness stretching so far west, north, and east that it covers everything—fallow land, fens, and wandering rivers, heaths, woods and pastureland, every conceivable type of erstwhile forest leaving behind it brush fires and the woodburners' furtive sowing—clearings here and there, wrested from the forest but still only half-tamed; shallow pitiful furrows that wooden implements drawn by scrawny oxen have scratched in the unyielding soil . . . huts of stone, mud or branches, clustered in hamlets surrounded by thorn hedges and a belt of gardens; sparsely scattered towns, streets in ruins, fortifications haphazardly repaired, stone structures dating back to the Roman Empire that have been turned into churches or strongholds.

Such is the Western world in the year 1000. Compared with Byzantium, compared with Cordoba, it seems rustic, very poor and defenseless. A wild world ringed round by hunger, its meager population is in fact too large. The people struggle almost bare-handed, slaves to intractable nature and to a soil that is unproductive because it is poorly worked. No peasant who sows one grain of wheat expects to harvest much more than three—if it is not too bad a year that means bread to eat until Easter time.

From Georges Duby, *The Age of the Cathedrals* (Chicago: University of Chicago Press, 1981), p. 3.

To see more clearly the changes that have come with capitalism, consider what life was like in Europe before the dawn of the capitalist age. In the year 1000, people there had short life spans; they had almost no experience with people or places farther away than the nearest town; and they depended on the food and other things they could produce by their own efforts, supplementing their consumption with only a few items available in local markets.

During most of human history, people lived in societies that had not changed much since the time of their parents, grandparents, or earlier ancestors. For generation after generation, sons made their livings in much the same ways as had their fathers before them, and daughters also followed in their mothers' footsteps. Tools and utensils, stories and beliefs were passed on from parents to children, just as they had been a century, or even a millennium, before. Good years and bad alternated with the weather, but continuous, rapid, and systematic change would not become an ordinary fact of life until the emergence of capitalism.

Around the world societies were organized in many different ways, but most people were only dimly aware of this diversity because their horizons did not extend beyond the small communities in which they lived. By the beginning of the 15th century, however, Europeans began to explore other continents and "discovered" what they called the "New World." Before long, traders and colonists, often financed by investors seeking fabulous riches, were intruding on indigenous peoples in areas located in what is now Virginia, Peru, Barbados, South Africa, and India. The dynamism unleashed by the advent of capitalism in Europe soon began to impinge on the rest of the world.

THE PERMANENT TECHNOLOGICAL REVOLUTION

It is hard to know which came first, capitalism or the great spurt of technical change that came along with it. Whatever the truth may be, the continuous, rapid, and far-reaching scientific discoveries and technological innovations that are now accepted as a permanent feature of modern life emerged more or less simultaneously with capitalism. And, of course, these discoveries and innovations made possible the remarkable economic advances of the last five centuries.

In 1500 goods were made almost entirely by hand, using simple tools. Power machinery consisted of such devices as the water wheel that turned a miller's grinding stone. People's understanding of the physical world was so rudimentary that births, deaths, and harvests, whether abundant or meager, were frequently interpreted with recourse to magic, superstition, or reference to God's will.

As late as 1800 traditional craft-based techniques, using skills that had been handed down from generation to generation, still prevailed in most production processes. But the new era brought new ideas, new discoveries, new methods, and new machines in every field of endeavor, making old ideas and old tools obsolete. And the new ways were in turn quickly made obsolete by even newer ones. As technical change revolutionized production, it reduced the amount of time required to produce most products.

The most important increases in labor productivity were those that occurred in the agricultural sector. As fewer people were required to produce the same or greater amounts of food, more labor could be devoted to the production of other things, particularly in the manufacturing sector. Thus, increases in agricultural productivity had to be achieved before the Industrial Revolution could take place. To illustrate the rapidity with which farm output has increased during the capitalist era, Figure 1.1 shows the growth of productivity in U.S. agriculture during the past two centuries.

There have also been dramatic improvements in methods of transportation during the past five centuries. In 1500 people either walked or used wagons to get themselves and their possessions or freight from one place to another on land. Wagons were pulled either by people or by animals, and the movement of people or freight overland was arduous, costly, slow, and sometimes dangerous. For all but a very few wealthy people, travel beyond a short distance from home was virtually impossible, and shipping freight was so expensive that it did not pay to send anything but very valuable and lightweight goods such as spices and silks.

Water transport on rivers and along coasts was easier, but ships were small, slow, and unsafe. In 1500 there had been few advances in maritime technology beyond what was available to the Romans 1,000 years earlier. Within a century, however, sea transport was greatly improved. Ships began regularly crossing the Atlantic or rounding the Cape of Good Hope en route to the East Indies. By 1800 clipper ships raced from China to London

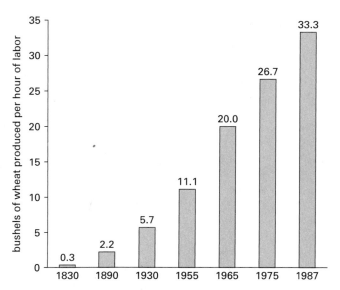

FIGURE 1.1   **Productivity increases in U.S. agriculture, 1830–1987.**   Focusing specifically on the production of wheat, this figure shows how labor productivity in U.S. agriculture has risen during the past two centuries. In the 18th century American farmers used crude wooden plows drawn by horses or oxen. They sowed seeds by hand, cultivated them with hoes, cut the wheat with sickles, and harvested their grain from the wheat using manual threshing devices called flails. Iron plows were introduced early in the 19th century, but as late as 1830 it still took about 300 hours of labor to produce 100 bushels of wheat on a five-acre farm. In the middle of the 19th century farmers began to use chemical fertilizers, and they also came to rely more and more on factory-made agricultural machinery. Over the next century agricultural productivity rose dramatically. By 1987 on a large, highly mechanized American farm, 100 bushels of wheat could be produced with only 3 hours of labor on 3 acres of land, 100 times more output per hour than could be produced in 1830.

Source: U.S. Department of Agriculture, "A History of American Agriculture, 1776–1990," available at http://www.usda.gov/history2/text4.htm.

in 80 days and from New York to San Francisco in 22 days. At the same time, sailing across the Atlantic became almost routine.

By 1900 steam power replaced sails, and the construction of the Suez Canal (and soon thereafter the Panama Canal) greatly shortened world trade routes. Before the end of capitalism's fifth century, oil tankers, each carrying 2,500 times the cargo of Columbus's ships, clogged the shipping arteries of the world and became too large to enter all but the largest and deepest harbors. Until the Concorde was grounded for economic reasons in 2003, those who could pay the $9,000 required for a reservation on this aircraft could travel from London to New York in three hours, moving at twice the speed of sound, overtaking the sun, and arriving "earlier" than when they had left.

Land transport was revolutionized as well. First, inland canals were dug—one of the most famous being the 365-mile (579 km) Erie Canal in New York State, constructed between 1817 and 1825—and barge traffic through canals greatly reduced the cost of overland haulage. Soon railroads would increase the speed and cut the cost of moving goods and people even more. In the U.S., the transcontinental railroad was completed in 1867, and by the end of the 19th century tracks would crisscross all the world's industrial areas and penetrate the Canadian Rockies, the East African highlands, the Chinese hinterland, the vast Russian steppes, and the plain of northern India as well. Yet all this was but a prelude to the great 20th-century land transport revolution based on automobiles, trucks, and highways. When air travel and transport, major innovations of the last century, were added to the mix, the role of railroads in global shipping and travel, although remaining important and appealing to travelers in some areas, became relatively diminished.

The technological advances in transportation were matched by equally significant developments in medicine, agriculture, and communications. Improvements in health care and agricultural productivity made possible the population explosion and urbanization discussed later in this chapter. Moreover, the communications revolution has been central to the process of globalization, also to be discussed later in this chapter.

Less beneficial were certain advances in weaponry and the discovery and production of toxic chemicals and biological agents. Today, chemical, biological, and nuclear weapons, sometimes referred to as weapons of mass destruction, are powerful enough to destroy the entire population of the world. Whether in production techniques, in transportation, in medicine, in agriculture, in communications, or in nuclear, chemical, and biological warfare, technical change has occurred with a speed and pervasiveness that is unprecedented in human history.

THE ENRICHMENT OF MATERIAL LIFE

The technological changes of the past five centuries have been accompanied by significant increases in people's consumption standards. Before the capitalist epoch, living conditions improved or deteriorated with changes in the weather, epidemics, and other natural phenomena, because most people made their livings by farming, herding, or hunting and gatherering. But wherever and whenever capitalism took hold, people's incomes and consumption levels began to rise in a sustained way. Although the rises were sometimes followed by declines, over a long period there have been—and continue to be—substantial improvements in living standards. Figure 1.2 shows the sharp upturn in real wages experienced by one group of workers following the emergence of capitalism as the dominant economic system in Great Britain in the 19th century.

While Britain was the first capitalist country, the new economic system soon spread to other countries, producing comparable increases in average living standards wherever it went. In the U.S., for example, the buying power of the average income in 2002 was 32 times what it was in 1789 (the year the U.S. Constitution was adopted). This does not mean, of course, that Americans are now 32 times happier than they were in 1789, but it does indicate an unprecedented growth in the availability of material goods. With the increase in material abundance, changes occurred in such things as diets (meats are now eaten more frequently) and housing (bigger homes are built and kept at warmer temperatures in the winter).

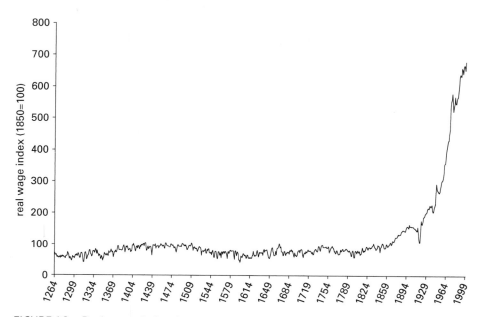

FIGURE 1.2   **Real wages in London over seven centuries.**   This figure shows the average real wage of skilled construction workers in London between 1264 and 1999. The term "real" means that the monetary wage in each year has been corrected for any price inflation that occurred. Thus, the real wage is the real buying power of the monetary wage in any particular year. The data are presented here in the form of an *index.* They show what the average real wage was in each year *relative to* what it was in some other year. For this chart the year 1850 was chosen as the *base year* for which the index is set to equal 100. Thus, whatever the actual wage was in 1850, it is recorded here as being equal to 100. Then the real wage in any other year is recorded as a percentage of what it was in 1850. For example, if the real wage in some other year was twice what it was in 1850, it is recorded here as being 200; if it was half of what it was in 1850, it is 50 here. While the data are subject to error, they nevertheless tell an interesting story. Prior to the full development of capitalism, real wages did not rise consistently. Fluctuations in the real wage before 1800 were often the result of changes in the size of the population. For example, the relatively brief increase after 1370 occurred because of a shortage of labor associated with the general depopulation of Great Britain caused by a catastrophic bubonic plague that spread from Asia to Europe in the 14th century. Gains made between 1300 and 1500 were eroded after 1500 by the rapid increase in prices resulting from the sudden inflow of gold to Europe from the Americas. Since money wages then would buy fewer and fewer goods, real wages generally declined between 1500 and 1800. After 1800, however, and particularly since 1900, increased productivity of labor and greater bargaining power of some workers led to dramatic increases in real wages for people such as the skilled construction workers represented in this figure. Since 1800 the demand for such labor has tended to outpace its supply, and employers have found themselves competing with one another for scarce workers. Real wages rose because employers had to offer significantly higher wages to attract particular workers to their enterprises.

Source: Robert Allen, "Wages, Prices and Living Standards: The World Historical Perspective," available at http://www.econ.ox.ac.uk/Members/robert.allen/WagesPrices.htm.

WHY DID THE ENGLISH ECONOMY TAKE OFF? COMPETITION, COAL, OR COLONIES?

No historical event has shaped the modern world more than the fact that in the 18th and 19th centuries it was parts of Europe (especially England) that took off economically, rather than parts of China. The outcome was a gap in incomes between Europe and everywhere else, and combined with Europe's population explosion, this gap led to a Euro-centered world (see Figures 1.3 and 1.4). Most of the rest of the world lagged behind economically and fell under the domination of Europeans and people of European descent in the U.S.

At first glance England, and Europe generally, had no special advantages that primed these economies to make the leap. Before the "European miracle" Chinese scientific knowledge surpassed that of Europe in many fields and rivaled it in most. Moreover, the areas of science in which Europe was ahead bore little relationship to the technological advances that were to propel the industrial revolution there. The more advanced economic areas of China such as the Chang River delta were not poorer than the advanced areas of Britain and Europe.

Economists sometimes suggest that British economic institutions made the difference. They have in mind an absence of governmental interventions such as price and wage setting, official monopolies, and confiscations of property. But recent historical research shows that an individual's pursuit of economic gain was probably freer from governmental fetters in the Chang delta in the 18th century than it was in England or other parts of Europe. Neither scientific preeminence, nor prior affluence, nor or a laissez-faire environment explains why capitalism took hold in England rather than in some other small corner of the earth, propelling some other people to world dominance.

The chief disadvantage of the Chang delta was a paucity of natural resources. Unlike England, the Chang delta had no rich coal deposits and little water power. And it lacked access to a natural resource–rich hinterland that could feed the voracious appetite for raw materials generated by an expanding economy.

By contrast, British military prowess, honed in centuries of Continental warfare, gave England cheap access to the raw materials of the New World, especially following the defeat of France in the Seven Years War (1756–1763). Sugar flowed in from Barbados, Jamaica, and the other British Caribbean colonies to provide more than a tenth of the calories of the rapidly expanding British industrial workforce. The slave plantations of Virginia and Georgia fed raw cotton to the booming textile mills of Manchester. All the agricultural land of Great Britain would not have been enough to produce domestically the sugar consumed by British workers and the fibers used to make British cloth (wool from sheep farms). Without the colonies economic expansion would have driven up the price of cotton, sugar, and other raw materials. The high cost of raw materials would have driven profits down and prematurely grounded the British takeoff.

On the eve of its economic takeoff, England's advantage was not that its institutions resembled the modern-day mainstream economist's ideal of secure individual property, effective competition, and limited government. A leading historian suggests a different view: England and the rest of Europe did indeed have institutional advantages, writes Kenneth Pomeranz, "but they seem applicable to very few endeavors in the pre-1800 world besides war, armed long-distance trade and colonization."

Source: Kenneth Pomeranz, *The Great Divergence: China, Europe, and the Making of the Modern World Economy* (Princeton: Princeton University Press, 2000). The quote is from p. 166.

Figure 1.3 shows how the rise of productivity in Europe eventually helped to lift output per person in the world as a whole. The main part of the figure shows that the dramatic increase in output per person, averaged for the world as a whole, did not occur until after 1820, while the smaller (inserted) chart shows in detail the relative contributions of different regions to the world's total output during the past five centuries. To simplify this chart, the nations of the world have been divided into three groups. The first group, called "Western world," includes western Europe and the nations originally "settled" by western Europeans—the U.S., Canada, Australia, and New Zealand. The second group includes all of Asia, including China, India, and Japan. The third group consists of all the nations in Africa, Latin America, and eastern Europe, including Russia.

It can be seen that the "Western world" was responsible for most of the growth of world output between 1500 and the early 1900s, its share of world output increasing from less than 20 percent in 1500 to more than 55 percent in 1950. But, as the chart shows, its relative share has been falling since 1950.

While the West's share of world output was increasing, that of Asia was moving in the opposite direction—downward. This was due in part to the fact that the absolute amount of output being produced in the West was growing much faster than the amounts being produced in other regions, so the *percentage* of world output attributable to the other regions had to be falling. Because Asia produced most of the world's output in 1500, it was the region with the most to lose. Most of the decline in Asia's share was due to the spectacular economic success of Europe and North America. But there were other reasons for the precipitous decline in Asia's share of world output between 1820 and 1950. For one thing, the effect of British imperialism on the productivity of India, a major contributor to Asia's output, was devastating. Whereas India had had a strong and diversified economy in 1800, by the middle of the 19th century the British rulers of India had begun to cripple that nation's cotton textile industry in order to gain the entire Indian market for their own cotton textile products. At the same time India was forced to specialize in the production of (less valuable) raw cotton for export to English textile factories.

The upturn in Asia's share of world output since 1950—and the simultaneous decline in the West's share during this period—is the result, in large measure, of economic expansion in Japan and China. Measured by total output, Japan is the world's second-largest

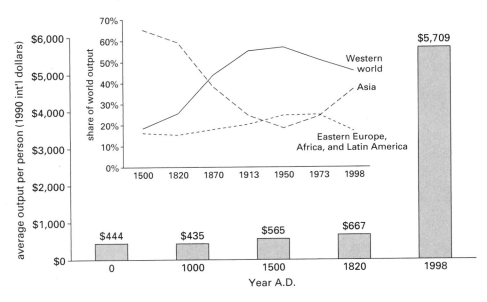

FIGURE 1.3 Two millennia of world GDP per capita. The larger chart in this figure presents inflation-adjusted estimates of output per person (GDP per capita) for the world as a whole during the last two millennia. These estimates are the result of more than half a century of empirical research conducted by Angus Maddison, one of the world's foremost scholars of global population size, technical change, and productivity growth. According to Maddison, the world's output per person remained at relatively low levels until 1820, with increases in output being largely absorbed by corresponding increases in the world's population. In the period since 1820, however, the technical changes associated with the rise of capitalism have allowed for a dramatic expansion of output per person. Although the data in the main chart show output per person averaged for the world as a whole, the insert shows how the productivity increases of the past few centuries have been generated disproportionately, and enjoyed unequally, by the various regions of the world. Since the vertical distances in the smaller chart represent percentages of total world output, and since all the regional shares thus represented must add up to 100 percent, the movements of any one region's output may seem exaggerated since any change in output in one part of the world must be offset by an opposite movement in at least one other part. In any case, the smaller chart reveals striking changes in shares of world output that are not shown in the larger chart.

Sources: Angus Maddison, *Monitoring the World Economy, 1820–1992* (Paris: OECD, 1995), p. 19, Table 1-1(a), and *The World Economy: A Millennial Perspective* (Paris: OECD, 2001), p. 28, Table 1-2.

economy (after the U.S.), and China (officially the People's Republic of China) has one-fifth of the world's population and has been racking up record-setting double-digit economic growth rates annually since the late 1970s. Also important is the contribution of the Asian "tigers"—South Korea, Taiwan, Thailand, and Singapore—all of which have been achieving exceptionally high rates of economic growth in recent decades.

India, the second-most-populous nation, has also experienced rapid increases in output since 1980.

One can also see from the insert in Figure 1.3 that the nations of Africa, Latin America, and eastern Europe started out with the smallest share of world output in 1500, increased their share slightly between 1820 and 1950, but ended up again (in 1998) with the smallest share. The recent decline here is mostly a result of the huge fall in output associated with the difficult transition from central planning to capitalism after the upheavals of 1989 to 1991 in eastern Europe and Russia. Another factor has been very slow economic growth or even declines in output in Latin America and (especially) Africa.

The data presented in Figures 1.2 and 1.3 showing vast increases in wages and output in much of the world over the past few centuries may actually *understate* the associated improvements in living standards. The reason is that the *quality* of goods has increased dramatically, and these increases in quality are not adequately accounted for when we measure prices and output.

Qualitative improvements can be seen most strikingly in the production of light, starting with the campfires of our distant ancestors and then moving on, with the passage of time, to oil lamps, candles, kerosene lamps, and, ultimately, to modern lighting technologies such as filament and fluorescent light bulbs. Among the changes that have come with these advances is an almost unbelievable increase in the efficiency of light production. Engineers define lighting efficiency with reference to how much light, measured in units called "lumens," can be produced using a certain amount of energy (measured in watts).

Figure 1.4 charts the advance of lighting technology from 1700 to the present, showing the lumens per watt of each new lighting source. Not shown in the chart is the fact that the lighting power of a campfire is between .002 and .003 lumens per watt. By 1800 a light source, the tallow candle, had been developed that was more than 32 times as efficient as a campfire: it emitted light at nearly .076 lumens per watt. With the coming of electric power in the late 19th century, lighting technology began to improve rapidly. By 1900 an "advanced" carbon filament lamp could light up a room (or a street) at 3.7 lumens per watt, and a century later a 100-watt tungsten filament lamp—the standard 100-watt commercial light bulb—could emit light at a rate of more than 14 lumens per watt. (See the source of this information cited in the caption for Figure 1.4.)

The biggest single advance in lighting technology so far has come with the development of the "compact" fluorescent light bulb. *Consumer Reports* tested this new light source in 1992 and found that it was capable of producing 68.3 lumens of light per watt, making it about 29,000 times more efficient than a campfire. The point is that our typical measures of improvements in standards of living—real wage increases and growth of real gross domestic product (GDP) per capita—do not account for the fact that we often get proportionally more of something, in this case illumination, than increases in our spending on it would indicate. These types of measurement issues have become increasingly important in the past century and a half as the rate of technical progress—stimulated by capitalism—has accelerated.

Capitalism is not unique in its capacity to promote rapid increases in material well-being. The Soviet Union, with a Communist government and a centrally planned non-market economy, achieved very high rates of economic growth between the late 1920s

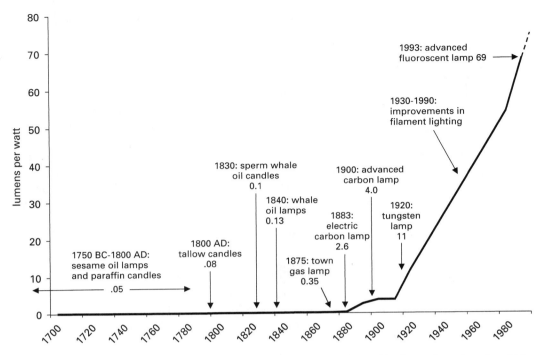

FIGURE 1.4   Improvements in lighting technology, 1700 to the present.   This figure shows how the efficiency of lighting technology (measured in lumens per watt on the vertical axis) has increased over the past three centuries. A "lumen" is a unit indicating a certain intensity of light, and a "watt" is a unit measuring the power of a source of energy.
Source: William D. Nordhaus, "Do Real-Output and Real-Wage Measures Capture Reality? The History of Lighting Suggests Not," in Timothy F. Bresnahan and Robert J. Gordon, eds., *The Economics of New Goods,* National Bureau of Economic Research Studies in Income and Wealth, vol. 58 (Chicago: University of Chicago Press, 1996), pp. 29–66.

and the mid-1980s. And, as we have just seen, over the past three decades China, also under Communist rule, has maintained rates of increase in total output unparalleled by any of the world's capitalist economies, supporting extraordinary improvements in living standards. But these cases of rapid economic growth under systems other than capitalism are atypical.

GROWING INEQUALITY

The material abundance that has come with capitalism is not evenly distributed. As capitalism has enhanced the generation of wealth in some parts of the world, it has also led to glaring global inequalities. Before the rise of capitalism, most of the world's population lived quite simply, without the material goods that the majority of people in rich countries now take for granted. But as capitalism developed, the gap between rich and poor became

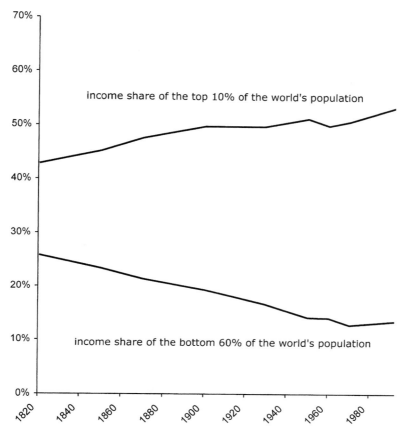

FIGURE 1.5   Growing world inequality, 1820–1992.   This figure charts the growing income gap between the top 10 percent and the bottom 60 percent of the world's population. Since the emergence of capitalism in Europe and its gradual spread throughout the world, the fortunes of the rich and the rest have diverged. This occurred because there was a rapid expansion of output in Europe and North America, where capitalism first flourished, but no such rapid expansion occurred in the rest of the world. Although inequality has been reduced considerably *within* many countries, increases in inequality *between* nations has resulted in a more unequal world. Since 1960 the increase in global inequality has slowed and by some measures even has been reversed because of the rapid economic growth of the two largest poor countries in the world—India and China.

Source: François Bourguignon and Christian Morrisson, "Inequality Among World Citizens: 1820–1992," *American Economic Review,* vol. 92, no. 4, September 2002, pp. 727–744.

a chasm (see Figure 1.5). Today many people in the world still do not have clean drinking water, while the wealthiest individuals possess their own jet planes. According to recent research the poorest 10 percent of Americans are richer on average than two-thirds of the people in the world, and four-fifths of the world's population lives below what is defined as the poverty line in North America and Europe.

The Population Explosion and the Growth of Cities

Along with capitalism's technical progress and rising standards of living, there has been a global population explosion. As Figure 1.6 shows, the population of the world grew very slowly from 10,000 BC to the 18th century AD. But since then, as the sharp upturn in the curve indicates, the rate of growth of the world's population has increased dramatically. From AD 1 to 1750 the population grew at a slow rate (0.56 per thousand annual growth); at that rate it took 1,200 years for the population to double. Between 1750 and 1950 it grew at a faster rate (about 5.7 per thousand), one that doubled the population every 120 years.

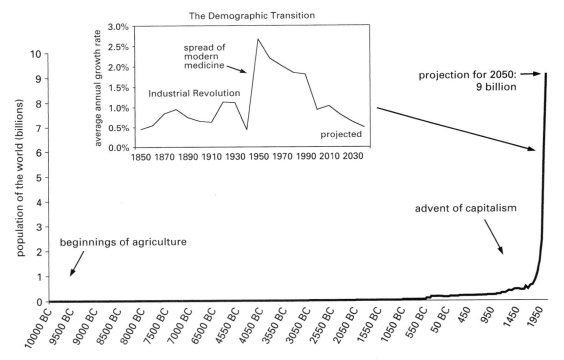

FIGURE 1.6   Capitalism and the population explosion.   This figure charts the population of the world from 10,000 BC to the end of the 20th century. For most of the last 12,000 years, the total population of the world grew slowly, if at all, with periods of increase in good years followed by intervals of decline in response to climatic adversity and other calamities. There are about 20 cities in the world today whose populations exceed the entire population of the world—which was probably less than 10 million—11,000 years ago, when agriculture began displacing hunting and gathering. Population started growing rapidly in a few countries two centuries ago, but the world's population really exploded in the 20th century with the development of modern medicine and its spread throughout the world. While the number of people in the world continues to grow, the pace of growth is slowing (see insert). Demographers predict that the population of the world will stabilize at about 11 billion around the middle of the 22nd century.

Sources: United Nations Development Programme, *World Population From Year 0 to Stabilization* (United Nations, 1996); U.S. Bureau of the Census, *Historical Estimates of World Population* (1995) available at http://www.census.gov/ipc/www/worldpop.html; U.S. Bureau of the Census, *Total Midyear Population for the World: 1950–2050* (1995, updated 2/28/98), available at http://www.census.gov/ipc/www/worldpop.html.

Since 1950 the world's population has been growing so quickly (about 17.1 per thousand) that it will double every 40 years.

The rapid population growth of the past 250 years is a radical departure from the previous trend. This population explosion is a new social phenomenon seen only in the capitalist epoch. However, population growth has slowed in the United States, Europe, Japan, China, and some other parts of the world. Hence, it seems, as the insert in Figure 1.6 suggests, that the population explosion may soon be over.

While the recent spurt in the world's total population has been dramatic, there have also been important movements of people from one part of the world to another. In places such as North and South America and Australia, for example, entirely new populations came in, overwhelming and virtually eliminating the indigenous peoples. At the same time a large number of people found themselves being involuntarily transported from their places of birth in Africa to unfamiliar lands.

Many of the indigenous Indian populations of North and South America were decimated, with their remnants relocated to remote territories. Millions of Africans—conservative estimates suggest at least 10 million, others say perhaps 100 million—were transported in chains across the Atlantic Ocean, having been forcibly taken from their communities to become slaves in the Americas. However, perhaps as many as half of the captives did not survive the crossing and went to watery graves instead of being sold to plantation owners. Numerous Chinese and (Asian) Indians, recruited to work under conditions little different from slavery, were shipped to faraway places—the Chinese to build railroads in North America, the Indians to build them in East and Southern Africa.

Other populations migrated long distances when their traditional livelihoods were destroyed by changes in their homelands. Germans, for example, had to leave their country when they were subjected to political repression. Italians left when declining grain prices made farming no longer a viable way of life. Others emigrated when they found their traditional crafts made obsolete by new capitalist factories. A large number of Irish people found it necessary to emigrate when the potato crop, their main source of nutrition, was wiped out by blight in the middle of the 19th century. For similar reasons Poles, Greeks, Jews, Hungarians, and Russians all found that they needed to move. It matters little whether we say that they moved because of the "pull" of opportunities in new places or whether we attribute their migration to the "push" of circumstances at home that became intolerable. What is important is that they experienced fundamental changes in their lives, saw old routines disrupted, and pursued alternative opportunities in new lands.

Along with the migrations of people from one area of the world to another came significant changes in occupations. For example, in 1800 the overwhelming majority of Americans were food producers of one sort or another: independent farmers, food-producing slaves, or fishermen. Today only 2 percent of the U.S. population lives and works on farms, while another 3 percent works in the food processing and food service industries. This small fraction of the population (5 percent) is able to grow, process, and serve enough food to meet the needs of the whole country while at the same time producing a surplus that is exported.

As people left farming, another change became apparent, namely, *urbanization* and the growth of cities. Before the emergence of capitalism, most people lived in the countryside, not in urban areas. In the last few centuries, however, people have been drawn, or in some cases pushed, into cities. In 1800 only 6 percent of Americans lived in towns or cities with more than 2,500 people. Today three-quarters of the U.S. population lives in such urban areas.

FIGURE 1.7 Cities of the world with more than a million inhabitants in 2002. Each of the dots in this figure represents a city of more than 1 million people (but not all cities of more than a million people are represented in the figure). Increasing concentration of people in cities—urbanization—has all along been an important consequence of the spread of capitalism. By 1850, three cities had grown to a size of more than 1 million people: London, Paris, and Beijing (the three arrows in this map pinpoint their locations). By 2002, as a result of rapid population growth and the expansion of capitalism throughout the world, there were 405 such cities (only some of which are shown in this figure).

Source: Tertius Chandler, Four Thousand Years of Urban Growth: An Historical Census (Lampeter, Wales, U.K.: St. David's University Press, 1987). Map generated by Deepta Sateesh.

London's population, only 70,000 in 1500, grew to 600,000 by 1700 and approached three-quarters of a million in 1800, making it then the largest English-speaking city in the world. Today, London has a population of 11 million, the New York metropolitan area, 17 million, and Mexico City, 18 million. Tokyo, the world's biggest urban area, is home to 28 million people.

The process of urbanization is not limited to the United States, England, Mexico, or Japan. Urbanization happens wherever industrialization takes place. As the economic historian Eric Hobsbawm argued in *The Age of Capital: 1848–1875,* capitalist economic development propels an exodus from rural areas to cities, pushes people to migrate from one region to another, and drives them to move from one town to another. In 1900, 9 of the 10 largest cities in the world were in Europe or North America, with Tokyo as the exception. Today, with the global spread of capitalism, 8 of the 10 are now in Asia, Africa, or Latin America, with New York and Los Angeles as the exceptions. In 1850 there were only 3 cities with populations exceeding 1 million people—London, Paris, and Beijing—but as Figure 1.7 shows, by 2002 there were cities of this size in all parts of the world.

Urbanization happened without anyone *planning* for it to happen: it occurred because individuals chose, for one reason or another, to leave their homes in the countryside and move to cities. Thus, the urbanization of the past few centuries is a prime example of how free markets can foster fundamental changes in society based on individual decisions.

In the waning years of the 20th century, Bill Gates, the founder of Microsoft and the richest man in the world (see Chapter 6), embarked on a program of offering free computers to all libraries in poor neighborhoods in the U.S., most of which were in rural areas. He imagined—and intended—that his program would halt the process of urbanization, since people in rural areas would now have access through the computers in their local libraries to most of what is available to denizens of urban areas. A story in the *New York Times* reported on this as follows: "Bill Gates predicted in 1995 that the Internet would help rural people stay put, in part because they would have the same advantages as city slickers in the virtual world." Having offered this prophecy in his 1995 book, *The Road Ahead,* Gates recently revisited "the land of no stoplights" and had to concede that "the road ahead was full of blind curves." The fact was that the introduction of computers had done nothing to halt, or even to slow down, the exodus of people from rural America. Indeed, many rural Americans used the new computers to help them find jobs in urban areas. Gates concluded: "I thought digital technology would eventually reverse urbanization, and so far that hasn't happened."

THE CHANGING NATURE OF WORK

The way people earn their livelihoods has changed as well. At the dawn of the capitalist era, most families consumed only what they themselves produced or what they could obtain by selling their own products. Except for slaves, most families owned the tools they needed to make a living. With the rise of capitalism, people have become increasingly dependent on employment, that is, on getting a job working for someone else. At the same time, they have become subject to the dangers and hardships of unemployment. When there is not a sufficient amount of employment available (not enough jobs to go around), unemployment leaves families and even whole regions destitute and desperate. It becomes a capitalist form of plague, potentially affecting everyone except the independently wealthy and thus threatening almost everyone with insecurity.

Rapid change in the workplace makes even the most skilled workers vulnerable to unemployment as technological change renders their skills obsolete. Before capitalism, the son of a blacksmith could be confident that the skills learned in his father's shop would be a secure source of his livelihood. Under capitalism, a worker may spend arduous years learning specific skills, but new production processes can make them useless almost overnight. Ironworkers in the 19th century, for instance, completed long apprenticeships, learning exactly how much to heat the iron and how to process it. But when steelmaking rather abruptly replaced iron manufacture, the skilled ironworkers became obsolete, their distress written off as part of the social costs to be paid for technological progress.

The changes also transformed working conditions. As time went on workers found employment in huge factories and mills, in circumstances where dangerous machinery, poor lighting, intense heat, long hours, and the pressure to produce quickly combined to make such jobs hazardous and exhausting. Before the passage of protective legislation in the past century and a half, the number of people wounded in industrial accidents multiplied like casualties on a battlefield.

Nothing has been left untouched by the expansion of the capitalist economic system. Even people's experience of time itself has changed. Precapitalist lives tended to follow natural time, marked by the passing of the seasons and the movement of the sun and moon across the sky. Individual work tasks were performed irregularly, with periods of high work effort alternating with periods of rest. The work pattern could follow the natural rhythms of the worker, or it might be dictated by the natural rhythms of the weather. But in capitalist employment labor is paid for by the hour, and work tasks are defined with reference to how much time they take to perform. Starting and stopping time, lunch, coffee breaks, and even bathroom breaks are often measured in minutes. Clock time has supplanted natural time. Clocks can now be seen on public buildings, in schoolrooms, at factory gates, and on people's wrists. "Time is money," Benjamin Franklin said more than 200 years ago, previewing what was to come.

In recent years the trend toward working outside the home has reversed for some as modern communications technology has made it possible for people who do certain kinds of jobs—mostly well-paid writers, lawyers, professionals in finance, and others working for themselves—to work at home, "meeting" with clients and collaborators and selling their services over the internet.

THE TRANSFORMATION OF THE FAMILY

Social and family life has also been transformed in the capitalist era. Although families remain important to our emotional lives and procreation, the household has been entirely reshaped and, as a productive unit, nearly eliminated. Before the advent of capitalism, a family of three generations and several married couples often lived within a stone's throw of one another or even under the same roof, sharing tasks and meals. By the mid-20th century in Western societies, the typical household had been reduced to a nuclear family (a family unit consisting of a mother and father and their children), with grandparents living in a nursing or retirement home and aunts and uncles scattered throughout the country. By the end of the

20th century, divorce, improved birth control, abortion, greater longevity, and increasing numbers of couples choosing not to get married had taken us even further from the traditional household. Households are much smaller now, consisting on average of fewer than three people; by 2000 unmarried couples constituted nearly 1 out of 10 of the 60 million U.S. households that were headed by couples.

At the same time, many of the customary functions of the family have been removed from the family's domain. Activities such as making clothes and preparing and preserving food that were once carried on at home are now performed mostly in factories or other market-oriented enterprises. The people engaged in such work outside the home today are often the very women (or their grandchildren) who once worked in their own kitchens or at the home loom. Much of the work of rearing children, providing education and medical care to family members, and accomplishing other tasks in the home has also been entrusted to outside professionals.

Finally, today's family finds itself in a greatly changed social network. Once, families tended to live in the same community from generation to generation, with skills and occupations being passed from parents to children and each family having an acknowledged and often hierarchically ordered place in that community. Today, few families remain in one spot from generation to generation. Many have to move in search of work. Indeed, it is common now for families to move several times in one generation, making it difficult to sustain their ties to any particular community. As a result, families cannot rely as much as they used to on a local network for support or assistance. This further contributes to people's use of purchased services and government assistance. The day care center and the babysitter have taken over for the grandmother or the older children. For many people today the idea of a neighborhood as a community of families lives on only as a source of nostalgia.

THREATS TO THE ECOSYSTEM

In 1984 the name of a city in India, Bhopal, came to symbolize environmental destruction because an accidental discharge of poisonous vapor from a Union Carbide chemical plant there killed at least 2,000 people and permanently injured many more. In the years since the Bhopal disaster, many more environmental crises have occurred, and people have become increasingly aware of the threats facing the earth's ecosystem.

As population and production have soared, so too have the use and degradation of our natural environment. With the development of capitalism, elements of the ecological system such as air, water, soil, and weather have been altered more radically than they have ever been before in human history. CO_2 now being released into the atmosphere is creating a "greenhouse effect," and we are now experiencing global warming as a result. The consequences are far-reaching: possible melting of the polar ice caps, rising sea levels that may put large coastal areas under water, and potential changes in climates and rain patterns that may destroy some of the world's prime food-growing areas.

Figure 1.8 presents evidence showing that human activities such as those that involve the use of fossil fuels—coal, oil, and gasoline—have profoundly affected our natural environment. Increasing emissions of carbon dioxide into the air during the past century have not only resulted in measurably larger amounts of CO_2 in the earth's atmosphere but have also brought about perceptible increases in Northern Hemisphere average temperatures.

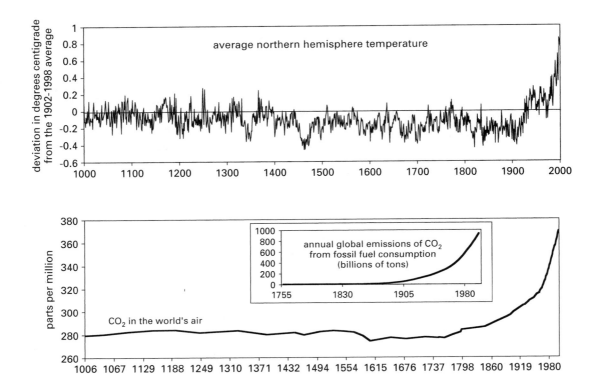

FIGURE 1.8   Fossil fuels, CO_2 emissions, CO_2 in the air, and global warming.   For most of the past 1,000 years Northern Hemisphere temperatures and amounts of CO_2 in the world's air remained more or less constant. However, the growing use of fossil fuels such as coal and petroleum products in the 20th century is associated with amplified CO_2 emissions and more intense concentrations of CO_2 in the world's air. Indeed, the smallest of the three charts shows that CO_2 emissions from fossil fuel consumption have risen exponentially over the past two and a half centuries. These changes have in turn generated more "greenhouse gases"—gases that trap heat and prevent it from escaping—thereby causing global temperatures to rise. The end result is what is referred to as "global warming." The data on which the charts are based come from estimates of past temperatures based on studies of tree fossils, centuries-old ice, and other phenomena.

Sources: Michael Mann, Raymond Bradley, and Malcolm Hughes, "Global-Scale Temperature Patterns and Climate Forcing over the Past Six Centuries," *Nature,* no. 391, April 1998, pp. 779–87, data available at http://www.people.virginia.edu/~mem6u/mbh99.html; G. Marland, T. A. Boden, and R. J. Andres, "Global, Regional, and National CO_2 Emissions," in *Trends: A Compendium of Data on Global Change* (Oak Ridge, Tennessee, Carbon Dioxide Information Analysis Center, Oak Ridge National Laboratory, U.S. Department of Energy, 2002), available at http://cdiac.esd.ornl.gov/trends/emis/em_cont.htm; World Resources Institute, *World Resources Institute Annual Report, 2001* (World Resources Institute, 2002). Joe Von Fischer of Princeton University and the Santa Fe Institute assisted in the creation of this diagram.

Average temperatures of the earth fluctuate from decade to decade under the influence of many factors, including reduced sunlight due to various factors including variations in solar radiation and volcanic events such as the massive Tambora eruption in 1815 and the Krakatau explosion in 1883. The Tambora volcano spewed forth so much ash in 1815 that 1816 became known as the "year without a summer." In that year frost covered the southern United States on the Fourth of July. The 1883 Krakatau eruption produced an ash cloud

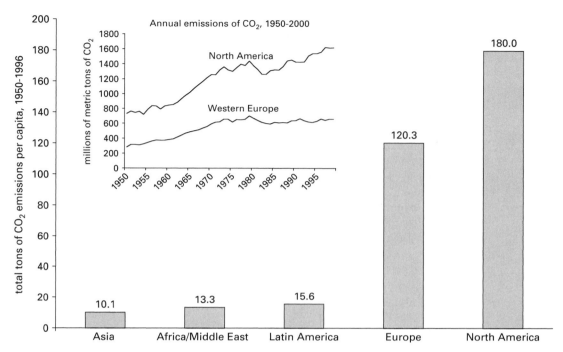

FIGURE 1.9   Cumulative CO_2 emissions per capita, 1950 to 1996.   This figure shows that the rich countries in North America and Europe were responsible for most of the CO_2 emissions that polluted the earth's atmosphere between 1950 and 1996. Cumulatively over the last half century, North America (mostly the U.S.) was responsible for about half and Europe for about a third of the world's emissions of CO_2. The bars show that, on a per capita basis, North America and Europe put nearly 10 times more CO_2 into the atmosphere than did the poorer nations in Asia, Africa, the Middle East, and Latin America combined. The smaller chart indicates that annual emissions from North America have continued to rise in the last 20 years, while those from Europe have leveled off.

Sources: G. Marland, T. A. Boden, and R. J. Andres, "Global, Regional, and National CO_2 emissions," in *Trends: A Compendium of Data on Global Change* (Oak Ridge, Tennessee, Carbon Dioxide Information Analysis Center, Oak Ridge National Laboratory, U.S. Department of Energy, 2002), available at http://cdiac.esd.ornl.gov/trends/emis/em_cont.htm; World Resources Institute, *World Resources Institute Annual Report, 2001* (World Resources Institute, 2002).

that circled the world for more than two years and, as a consequence, reduced the earth's temperature. During the last century, however, average temperatures have risen in response to increasingly high levels of greenhouse gas concentrations. These have resulted from the CO_2 emissions associated with the burning of fossil fuels. As shown in Figure 1.8, the decade of the 1990s was by far the hottest in the past 1,000 years.

Figure 1.9 shows the environmental effects of different lifestyles and government policies. It demonstrates that responsibility for CO_2 emissions lies more heavily with the rich industrial nations in Europe and North America than with less developed countries in Asia, Africa, the Middle East, and Latin America. The smaller chart within Figure 1.9 shows that because of more energy-using lifestyles and a paucity of conservation-oriented government policies, North America (primarily the U.S.) emits CO_2 at a considerably faster—and faster growing—rate than does western Europe. In per-capita terms the U.S. is, in fact, the biggest polluter in the world: in 2001 Americans accounted for more than 20 tons of CO_2 emissions per person, while Norway and Switzerland, countries with about the same levels of income per capita as the U.S., accounted for 7 and 5 tons per person, respectively. Looking at the data another way, the U.S. by itself emitted two and a half times as much CO_2 during the second half of the 20th century as did China and India combined, two nations that have a combined population of about eight times that of the U.S.

The list of fundamental environmental changes taking place in our times seems endless. The atmosphere's ozone layer, which protects us from the cancer-causing ultraviolet rays of the sun, is being depleted. Acid rain is destroying forests and killing life in lakes. Nuclear wastes, which must be stored "safely" for hundreds of thousands of years, are routinely produced. Tropical forests, which help to maintain the balance between oxygen and CO_2 in the earth's atmosphere, are being cut down. Many of the world's rivers are being polluted. With oil spills, the dumping of toxic and radioactive chemicals, and routine discharges from tankers and industrial plants, even the oceans are being spoiled. Toxic chemicals are leaking into the earth's groundwater, the last major source of pure drinking water. The destruction of natural habitats is causing the extinction of increasing numbers of animal and plant species. Insecticides and herbicides are poisoning prime farming soils, and vast areas of farmland are being destroyed by urban development. These changes in our physical world, especially when taken all together, threaten destruction on a scale that we cannot now even begin to calculate.

Just as people responded to economic insecurity in the 19th and early 20th century by demanding that governments assist them in times of need, pressures have been mounting in the last few decades for protective environmental policies. Some of these have been very effective, resulting in cleaner air and water in many parts of the U.S. and a greatly reduced use of energy in much of Europe. The main lesson is that environmental problems often cannot be addressed without cooperation among nations. The successful international effort to reverse the depletion of the ozone layer is an example of the kind of cooperation that is needed.

Other international efforts to reduce pollution have been less successful, however. In 1997 many nations came together in Kyoto, Japan, to work out a plan to reduce emissions of CO_2 on a worldwide basis. The meeting, organized by the United Nations, was called the United Nations Framework Convention on Climate Change, and the plan that came out of it is referred to as the Kyoto Protocol. By 2003, 111 nations, including all the member states of the European Union, had ratified the Kyoto Protocol, agreeing to reduce their CO_2 emissions by specified amounts each year. But the governments of a number of countries that are major CO_2 polluters—including China and the United States—have refused to sign on to it. As a result, the Kyoto Protocol regulates only 44 percent of the world's emissions of CO_2.

NEW ROLES FOR GOVERNMENT

Government and people's relations to government have also been altered since the rise of capitalism. In 1500 much of what was to become the capitalist world was ruled by some type of despot, with kings and emperors basing their claims to authority on God's will, hereditary right, or simply brute force. There were few ways in which ordinary people could protect themselves from the arbitrary powers of such rulers. But governments played a minor role in most people's daily lives; tax collection was typically nonexistent or ineffective, while compulsory schooling, permanent police forces, and standing armies did not become common until the 19th century.

Hereditary rulers were challenged by the British revolutions of the 17th century and by the American and French Revolutions of the 18th century. These revolutions established the important principle of governing with the consent of the governed, although only property-owning freeborn (nonslave) males gained the right to vote. But in Europe and the U.S. these revolutions placed important limitations on absolute rulers, and eventually they were followed by written constitutions, the abolition of slavery, widespread male suffrage, elimination of property qualifications for voting, and the extension of the franchise to women and minorities. In the 19th and 20th centuries, largely as a result of intense and lengthy struggles by workers, antislavery groups, suffragists, and others, all the major capitalist countries participated in the growth of democratic government. As governments became more democratic, they came to play a major role in providing such services as public education for the young and income support and health care for the elderly.

In the late 19th century in Europe and later in North America and other parts of the world, governments increasingly also took responsibility for providing assistance to the unemployed and those unable to work. Today, in western Europe and to a lesser degree in the United States, many people expect governments to provide something like a social safety net, especially during periods of economic decline. Moreover, governments have become major employers as well.

But while government in most countries has become more democratically accountable, everywhere it has also become more intrusive. In the past century governments have attained increased powers to invade the privacy and influence the sentiments of the citizenry. Television and other modern communications media give heads of state enormous influence in shaping people's opinions, while modern information technology allows government easy access to our location, private messages, and economic activity.

GLOBALIZATION

The finale of Warner Brothers' blockbuster Matrix film trilogy, *The Matrix Revolutions,* opened simultaneously on November 5, 2003, on 10,013 screens in more than 50 countries and in 43 languages. On that day at precisely the same moment—6 a.m. in Los Angeles, 9 a.m. in New York, 5 p.m. in Moscow, 11 p.m. in Tokyo, and so on—moviegoers watched the title shots appear on the screen as this first ever global debut of a film began.

The president of Warner Brothers Entertainment, Alan Horn, called it "showmanship." "It's theatrical, it's fun, it's exciting," Horn said about the megaopening. He also explained that by making the film available in theaters around the world he hoped to limit the profits of film pirates, who copy a film and distribute it globally (as they often do if a film opens in one country but cannot be seen in theaters in other countries until much later). Like many others, Horn understands that globalization means that many aspects of our life, from our entertainment to the enforcement of property rights, are no longer local or even national matters; they are global.

Capitalism has accomplished what not even the most powerful rulers in the past were able to do: it has brought the entire world into a single all-encompassing system. Alexander the Great conquered much of the world in the fourth century BC, expanding the reach of Greek civilization as far as India, but he soon retreated, leaving only traces of Greek culture behind. The Roman Empire at its height extended from the British Isles to the Middle East, at most a few thousand miles. In the two centuries following Muhammad's death in AD 632, his influence expanded well beyond Arabia, and Islam became the dominant force in a swath of loosely affiliated states stretching from Spain to what is now Indonesia—a third of the way around the world. But none of these empires touched more than parts of the globe. Only the capitalist economy, with a built-in tendency to expand and with the help of the 20th-century revolution in communications technology, has reached entirely around the world, obliterating distances, spawning common languages and appetites, and bringing most of the world's peoples into a single interdependent system.

Look at the cover of this book. The two women pictured in the upper photograph are from Bangalore, India, and they are responding to customer service inquiries placed via 800 numbers to companies such as General Electric, Dell Computer, America Online, and British Airways. But they are not living in the U.S. or England. Rather, they are in their hometown working at a "call center." They and others like them are doing back-office work for global corporations that, in order to cut costs, are "outsourcing" tasks such as customer service to India, where English is spoken and people are willing to work for a fraction of what American workers are paid. To facilitate the growth of this type of employment, the Indian government has recently installed reliable high-capacity telephone lines that make it possible for a person working in an Indian call center to communicate with customers overseas without sounding any different from a person working in the same country as the corporation being called.

To remove any suspicions that the person responding to a service call from the U.S. might be a foreigner, the young Indian women in the cover photograph were trained to sound just like Americans. To accomplish this they watched old episodes of *Friends* and *Ali McBeal* on videotape and learned that "Bimmer" refers to a BMW. In addition, the women have adopted American-sounding names. According to the story in the *New York Times* for which the photograph of the two women served as an illustration, they have assumed the names "Naomi Morrison" and "Susan Sanders" and, with accents one might hear at Wrigley Field, they have also begun pretending that they are residents of Chicago.

There are 60,000 call centers in the U.S. employing at least 3.5 and perhaps as many as 6 million people, three out of four of whom are women, most accepting relatively low wages. The number of people employed in U.S. call centers is roughly the same as the number of people working as truck drivers, assembly-line workers, or public school teachers. But the number of people employed in U.S. call centers is not likely to grow because competition impels companies to try to cut costs, and one good way of cutting costs these days is to outsource customer service tasks to a country such as India, where the average annual income per person is $500 and many people are happy to work for the $200 per month they can earn working in a call center.

The picture on the bottom half of the cover is a shot of the port of Hamburg, Germany, showing cargo containers that are about to be, or have just been, loaded onto or unloaded from the container ships that are also visible in the photograph. "Containerized shipping," as it is called, accounts for 90 percent of the world's trade (by value), and there are about 8,000 container ships currently in service around the world. Container traffic is measured on the basis of "twenty equivalent units," or TEUs, with each 20-foot-long container being counted as one TEU and each 40-foot long container (the only other size) as two TEUs. In 2001 Hamburg was the ninth-busiest container shipping port, accounting for 4.6 million of the 360 million TEUs that passed through the world's ports in that year. The particular containers shown in the cover photograph are filled with goods coming into or being exported from Germany and other European nations.

The fact that there is now a single world market for goods and services of all kinds means that producers depend on buyers worldwide for their livelihood. When the U.S. economy is booming and American wages are on the rise, automobile workers in South Korea prosper. The globalization of the economy also means that Indian software developers are constantly looking for ways to edge out competitors in Silicon Valley (and vice versa), and highly trained Indian radiologists (many of them having earned their MDs in American medical schools) are now providing interpretations of electronic images (X-rays and the like) at a fraction of the price usually charged by comparably trained American doctors (see box, '"Radiology Sweatshops"?' on next page.).

Similarly, the clothing worker stitching shirts in the U.S. is looking for ways to stay ahead of the competition in Sri Lanka, where the stitchers are paid less than one-tenth of what a comparable U.S. worker makes. Most large companies now consider the entire world not only as the market for their products but also as offering potential locations for production units. And, as readers of this book may already know, American students seeking admission to colleges or graduate schools now face competition from students from all over the world. The same is true for many jobs in the rapidly expanding information-based sectors of the U.S economy.

Trading over long distances has been integral to the functioning of capitalism since its inception. The huge market fairs in Europe from the 15th to the 17th centuries attracted merchants from hundreds of miles away and even from beyond Europe. They often brought with them lightweight luxuries such as spices and precious metals. However, long-distance trade in other goods was relatively insignificant. As noted earlier, transportation costs for heavier products were very high, and other difficulties blocking the transport of goods over long distances included brigandage, piracy, and the many local transit taxes levied by the rulers of the small kingdoms and principalities that then made up Europe. In the last half-century, however, there has been a dramatic increase in long-distance trade. In 1950 only 8 percent of the world's output was exported to other nations; now the comparable figure is almost 30 percent.

It now makes sense to think of the entire world system of investing, buying, and selling as a single global economy. National boundaries still matter, of course, but much less so than in the past: goods, money, information, and, to a lesser extent, people pass with only minor impediments from country to country. The process of globalization has challenged national governments, for it makes them more interdependent. Decisions made by the U.S. government or by the European Central Bank have ripple effects that extend throughout the world. The inability of Mexican or Russian borrowers to service their foreign debt can send shock waves through Wall Street and from there to the U.S. Treasury Department.

Globalization, as we have said, concerns the international movement of money, goods, and even people in search of a better livelihood. But globalization is not simply economic: it concerns languages, political rights and movements, what people value and admire, how people worship, what they eat and dance to, and the arts. The Indian women at the call center in Bangalore are able to imitate Chicago accents and discuss recent Chicago Bulls games because they see the Bulls on TV and hear Chicagoans on the radio.

"RADIOLOGY SWEATSHOPS"?

Who's afraid of globalization? Call-center employees. Auto and garment industry workers. Computer programmers. Data-entry personnel. People who compete with poorly paid workers in the rest of the world. How about doctors?

When a doctor at Massachusetts General Hospital began using radiologists in India to read X-rays and MRI scans in the fall of 2002, high-priced doctors started talking like auto workers. It's a "nail in the coffin of the job market" wrote one (anonymously) on the radiologists' website, AuntMinnie.com. Another asked: "Who needs to pay us $350,000 a year if they can get a cheap Indian radiologist for $25,000?" Still others talked about the "radiology sweatshops."

There is an acute shortage of radiologists in the U.S. Advertised vacancies rose from less than 100 per month in the mid 1990s to well over 500 a month in 2001, and the chairman of the board of chancellors at the American College of Radiology said of the shortage: "It's almost of crisis proportions." But there are many well-trained English-speaking radiologists in India. Add to this the fact that it is difficult to get U.S. radiologists to work nights, and nighttime in the U.S. is daytime in India.

X-ray, MRI, and other images can be beamed to medical centers in India instantaneously. The Indian radiologists are not licensed to do diagnosis, but they can perform nondiagnostic tasks such as converting two-dimensional images from scans into the three-dimensional images that surgeons find more informative. Arjun Kalyanpur is a doctor who had been on the faculty at Yale and moved back to India. He and a partner read about 100 scans a day, including some from the Centre Community Hospital in State College, Pennsylvania. The staff radiologist at the community hospital is entirely happy with Dr. Kalyanpur's work, but he did not know where it was done. "Is he actually in India?" the doctor asked when told that Kalyanpur worked in Bangalore.

Other areas of medical practice will also be globalized. Specialized firms in Ireland, India, and other countries have long handled billing and the processing of insurance claims for U.S. hospitals. But now images of tissue can be transmitted electronically, to be analyzed by specialists at remote sites. Robotic microscopes allow a doctor or technician to be oceans away from the slide under the microscope. Even the monitoring of patients in intensive care units can now be performed at remote sites. While this off-site monitoring is currently done within the U.S., there is no technical reason why it could not be done anywhere in the world where there is the necessary expertise.

U.S. medical institutions not only buy radiology and other services from the rest of the world, they sell, too. "I think the opportunities for U.S. health care internationally probably are very large," said Dr. Ronald Weinstein, head of pathology at the University of Arizona College of Medicine, where plans are underway to market diagnostic and other services around the world.

Sources: Andrew Pollack, "Who's Reading Your X-ray? Jobs in Medical Care, Too, Can Be Outsourced Overseas," *New York Times,* Sunday, November 16, 2003, Section 3, p. 1; www.AuntMinnie.com.

Globalization, like technical change, is a source of affluence for many, but it can quickly make a once cutting-edge industry or job skill obsolete, causing unemployment and financial hardship for the people involved. The citizens of most democratic nations have pressed their governments for protection against the vagaries of the global marketplace, in some cases seeking to limit the extent of global exchange. In some democracies, especially those in western Europe, governments have implemented extensive unemployment insurance and offered subsidies for retraining and relocation to workers in declining industries. These programs are expensive, of course, and many governments are reluctant to raise the taxes necessary to fund them for fear that higher taxes will induce some businesses to relocate to other (lower-tax) nations, which would only increase economic insecurity. Many fear that globalization increases economic insecurity while at the same time diminishing the power of governments to implement programs that might make people more secure.

Underlying such fears is a simple fact: the economy is now global while government is still local. The global economy is thus interconnected, while the power to coordinate it is dispersed among more than 200 national governments, a handful of international bodies, and a few thousand large corporations. Power in the global economy is not distributed among individual citizens and consumers. Rather, it is held by a small number of powerful institutions. For example, the World Trade Organization, which regulates the terms on which nations exchange goods and services, is deliberately structured to limit input from ordinary citizens.

The heads of the world's 1,000 largest corporations, producing 80 percent of the globe's industrial output, could all fit into a medium-sized concert hall, for example, Alice Tully Hall at Lincoln Center in New York City. About 2,000 corporate leaders, along with a few government officials, actually do come together annually at a ski resort in the small town of Davos, Switzerland. Calling themselves the "World Economic Forum," this exclusive group has been assembling there for more than 30 years, but these days extraordinary security measures are adopted to protect the participants from antiglobalization protesters, among others: the airspace over Davos is closed during the week-long conference, hundreds of police officers surround the hotels where the attendees meet, and 6,000 Swiss soldiers are on patrol nearby.

Some observers have hoped that global leaders such as those who meet in Davos would work together to regulate the world economy in ways that would protect both people and the environment from the social costs generated by multinational capitalist enterprises. However, the fact is that corporations have at least as much interest in competing as in cooperating, while their interest in protecting society and the environment from the consequences of global profit seeking is tempered by their opposition to restrictions on their own profit making. And in the absence of anything resembling a world government, all international cooperation must come about through negotiations among independent governments, but, of course, any government can refuse to participate in such negotiations.

CONCLUSION

To lay the foundations for an understanding of capitalism, this chapter has focused on the technological revolution, increasing material well-being, the population explosion, the growth of cities, the transformation of work and the family, threats to the ecosystem, new roles for government, and globalization. The list of changes that have come with capitalism could be expanded, but the set of transformations discussed here establishes the basic point of the chapter: capitalism generates perpetual change.

It could be argued that the rise of capitalism was not so much the cause as it was the effect of the changes outlined in this chapter. Might not advances in science and technology have led to the development of capitalism? Or could the population explosion have been the cause and capitalism the consequence?

Science and population growth are undoubtedly important, but before capitalism they did not have cumulative effects. Scientific knowledge and technology were more advanced in the Islamic world and China, for example, than they were in Europe before 1500. But neither Islamic science and mathematics nor the Chinese inventions of gunpowder, magnetic compasses, cast iron, moveable type, canal locks, and machines for keeping time led to sustained technological progress or industrial development. It is also true that periods of rapid population growth have accompanied short periods of economic expansion throughout the 100,000 or so years of human existence, but as Figure 1.6 shows, it was not until the advent of capitalism that rapid population growth became the rule rather than the exception.

In the last 500 years virtually all traditional patterns of life and livelihood have been disrupted and reconstructed. The world and the world's peoples have been shaken up and remade. In the chapters to follow we discuss the reasons why capitalism is such a powerful source of change and why it affects not only the economy but also politics, beliefs, and many other dimensions of social life.

SUGGESTED READINGS

James K. Boyce, *The Political Economy of the Environment* (Cheltenham, U.K.: Edward Elgar, 2002).

Fernand Braudel, *Capitalism and Material Life 1400–1800* (New York: Harper & Row, 1967).

William Cronon, *Changes in the Land: Indians, Colonists, and the Ecology of New England* (New York: Hill & Wang, 1983).

Jared Diamond, *Guns, Germs, and Steel: The Fates of Human Societies* (New York: W.W. Norton, 1999).

Maurice Dobb, *Studies in the Development of Capitalism* (New York: International Publishers, 1947).

Bill Gates, *The Road Ahead* (New York: Viking Penguin, 1995), especially Chapter 8, "Friction-Free Capitalism" (pp. 157–183).

Eban Goodstein, *Economics and the Environment* (New York: Simon & Schuster, 1999).

John Gray, *False Dawn: The Delusions of Global Capitalism* (New York: New Press, 1999).

Eric Hobsbawm, *The Age of Capital: 1848–1875* (New York: Vintage Books, 1996).

Intergovernmental Panel on Climate Change (IPCC), *Climate Change 1995: The Science of Climate Change*, ed. by J. T. Houghton et al. (Cambridge: Cambridge University Press, 1996).

David Landes, *The Wealth and Poverty of Nations: Why Some Are So Rich and Some So Poor* (New York: W.W. Norton, 1999).

Joel Mokyr, *The Lever of Riches: Technological Creativity and Economic Progress* (New York: Oxford University Press, 1990).

Barrington Moore, *The Social Origins of Dictatorship and Democracy* (Boston: Beacon Press, 1966).

George Soros, *The Crisis of Global Capitalism: Open Society Endangered* (New York: PublicAffairs™, a member of the Perseus Books Group, 1998), especially Chapter 6, "The Global Capitalist System" (pp. 101–134).

Eric Wolf, *Europe and the People Without History* (Berkeley: University of California Press, 1982).

CHAPTER 2

People, Preferences, and Society

Parents everywhere are sometimes late in picking up their children at day care centers, thereby inconveniencing the staff. An experiment, carried out in Haifa, Israel, was designed to find a solution to the problem of tardy parents. At six randomly chosen centers a fine was imposed for lateness, and a few other centers were selected to serve as a "control group" (nothing was changed at these centers). Staff at the centers with the newly instituted fines expected that punctuality would improve. Contrary to these expectations, however, there was an *increase* in tardiness when the fines were imposed: the number of parents picking up their kids late more than doubled. Even more striking was the fact that when the fines were revoked, the parents' higher rate of tardiness persisted. Meanwhile, the amount of parental lateness at the centers in the control group did not change.

The economists who designed the Haifa experiment were quite surprised by the results. Most economists assume that people seek monetary gain and try to avoid losses. From this perspective, the day care centers' fines should have given the parents an incentive to be more punctual. But the plan backfired. After analyzing the results, the designers of the experiment concluded that the imposition of the fines must have unintentionally suggested to the parents a new way of thinking about their behavior. Whereas before the experiment lateness had been seen as a violation of a *moral obligation* (to pick up the kids on time), after the imposition of the fines being late could be viewed as a *choice* between picking up the kids on time and paying a price (the fine) for being late. And under the new system many parents were apparently willing to pay the price. The designers of the experiment titled their report "A Fine Is a Price." Their main finding was that imposing the fines had signaled to the parents that they were now in a marketlike relationship to the day care staff—one in which they could *buy* lateness. Once the fines had been

31

introduced, revoking them could not restore the initial situation; it just lowered the "price of lateness" to zero.[1]

Why were the economists who designed the day care experiment surprised by its results? It was because they took it for granted, as have most economists until very recently, that people care little about others, act only to promote their self-interest, always seek opportunities for personal gain, even at the expense of others, and abide by the moral standards of their community only when it serves their own purposes.

> **Economic man** *(Homo economicus)* refers to the assumption that human beings are calculating, amoral, and self-interested.

> **Self-interest** refers to a disposition to consider only how one's actions will affect oneself, not how they may affect others.

The assumption that people are calculating, amoral, and governed by a self-interested predisposition is referred to as the *Homo economicus,* or "economic man," assumption. To say that people are governed by a *self-interested* disposition means that they consider only how their actions will affect themselves, not how their actions will affect others.

One of the truly radical ideas in economics is the idea that given the right laws and institutions, individual selfishness can be harnessed to serve the public good. The accompanying box contains statements by Adam Smith, the founder of economics, and his influential 18th-century contemporary, David Hume, expressing this hopeful thought (see box, "A Constitution for Knaves").

The economic man assumption, of course, leaves out a lot. While it is certainly true that selfish behavior is common, so are acts of compassion, selflessness, and altruism. People show concern for their friends' well-being, volunteer for military duty, care for their infants or aged parents, risk their lives for strangers, and forgo opportunities to steal even when no one is looking. When such acts are motivated by a concern for others—or for what happens to others—they are not self-interested acts. We might better call them *other-regarding* because they are motivated by a regard for others. (Self-interested behaviors are, of course, *self-regarding.*)

The key to whether an act is self-interested is its motivation. The deciding factor is whether the act is motivated by a concern for others, not whether it produces happiness in the actor. For example, many generous people take pleasure in helping others in need. But this pleasure does not make them selfish people: since they act from unselfish motives they are *not* self-interested. Not all other-regarding acts are as admirable as helping others and obeying moral codes, however. Hurting another person out of spite, jealousy, or intolerance of his or her religion or race is also other-regarding. Such an act is intended (based on a motive) to make something bad happen to someone else, just as generous actions seek good outcomes for others.

Also left out of the economic man assumption is the fact that people change. *Homo economicus* is believed to be a "natural" phenomenon, and, accordingly, the type of (self-interested) behavior associated with it is assumed to have been prevalent in every kind of society, unchanging across the entire span of human history, and sure to be characteristic of any future economic system.

---

[1] Uri Gneezy and Aldo Rustichini, "A Fine Is a Price," *Journal of Legal Studies,* vol. 29, no. 1, 2000, pp. 1–17.

A CONSTITUTION FOR KNAVES

The great 18th-century philosopher-economists Adam Smith and David Hume thought that the key to a well-ruled society was not to deny self-interest (which they thought to be impossible) but to find a way to harness selfish motives to serve socially valued objectives:

It is not from the benevolence of the butcher, the brewer, or the baker that we expect our dinner, but from their regard to their own interest.

—Adam Smith, *The Wealth of Nations* (1776), book I, chapter II

Political writers have established it as a maxim, that in contriving any system of government . . . every man ought to be supposed to be a knave and to have no other end, in all his actions, than his private interest. By this interest we must govern him, and, by means of it, make him, notwithstanding his insatiable avarice and ambition, cooperate to public good.

—David Hume, *Essays: Moral, Political and Literary* (1742)

It is well known, however, that people frequently change as a result of experiences they have in the economy. For example, a long but unsuccessful job search can turn a confident and happy person into a depressed and violent threat to his or her family or community. Even a whole group's culture can change when its way of making a living is altered. For example, when the sons and daughters of farmers become office or factory workers, it is quite likely that they will develop new patterns of behavior, discover new wants, and be guided by different values.

In this chapter we consider various ways in which economists attempt to explain individual behavior. A common starting point is that people make choices and do things for reasons—even if not always for good reasons, and even if their reasoning does not always correctly anticipate the outcomes of their actions. Thus, behavior is seen as intentional, or goal seeking.

The main idea of this chapter is that *while the intentional view of behavior is essential to understand why people do what they do, economic man is a fictional character. Real humans are diverse (some selfish, others generous) and versatile (sometimes brave, other times cowardly), and their values, tastes, habits, and beliefs are very much the product of their upbringing, work experience, and national, ethnic, and cultural backgrounds.* This main idea is expressed in five key points.

1. Explaining behavior requires taking into consideration an individual's *constraints* (limits on his or her actions), *preferences* (evaluations of outcomes), and *beliefs* (understandings of how particular actions may bring about specific outcomes).

2. Laboratory experiments as well as ordinary observations of daily life show that selfishness is but one of our motives. We are also generous, even toward those we do not know, and we are willing to reward those who treat us well and to punish those who treat us or others badly, even if such actions are costly to us in terms of lost income or missed opportunities for personal gain.

3. People are similar in many respects the world over, reflecting our common genetic inheritance, and these commonalities are sometimes termed *human nature*. But in other respects our behaviors differ greatly, reflecting differences in the things we have learned from others in our society; such differences are termed *cultural differences*.

4. Families, schools, neighborhoods, and workplaces all play a part in the processes by which we come to have our particular values, desires, and beliefs.

5. All animals *compete* with other members of their species, but humans are unique in the extent to which we can also *cooperate* with those to whom we are not related. We have become the "cooperative species" because throughout history cooperative people prospered, and their cooperative behaviors were copied by others, in part because groups that succeeded in cooperating survived and grew, eclipsing groups that did not.

> **Aggregate, or population-level, outcomes** refer to the economic totals, averages, and relationships that are generally studied by economists.

Economics is about *totals* (the output of an economy or the number of unemployed people, for instance) and *averages* (per capita income, for example). It is also about *relationships*—the power of employers over workers, the price of bread relative to the typical wage, the distribution of income between rich and poor, and so on. These totals, averages, and relationships are sometimes called *aggregate, or population-level, outcomes.*

Economics is not about what particular individuals do, but economists need to know how individuals behave in order to explain totals, averages, and relationships. In most cases it is difficult to understand aggregate, or population-level, outcomes without understanding why people do what they do. Hence, individual behavior comes in as part of an explanation of the larger picture.

CONSTRAINTS, PREFERENCES, AND BELIEFS

To explain why people do what they do, economists make use of three terms: *constraints, preferences,* and *beliefs.* An example will elucidate the meaning of each of these terms. Imagine that you are planning to drive across the country and are going to purchase a used car for the trip. You will need to pick out the car, decide how long you want to spend on the road, and select the kind of accommodations you will stay in while traveling.

> **Constraints** are the limits on the actions that an individual or a society can take.

Constraints put limits on the various actions available for you to take. Such constraints might include physical limitations (one cannot travel in a car from Massachusetts to California in less than two days);

your own capacities (you cannot drive for more than 12 hours at a stretch without going to sleep); your social relationships to others (the availability of friends you might ask to go with you); facts about institutions or your own ethical rules (you may not want to buy your car from a dealer you know is corrupt); and your wealth and capacity to borrow (you have a limited bank account and possess little that might serve as collateral in return for a loan). Constraints will limit your actions in such a way that you will face what is called a *trade-off:* achieving more of one thing means getting less of something else. Given your budget—limited by your wealth plus what you can borrow—you can buy a better car if you are willing, say, to give up staying at upscale motels.

Preferences are the relative values you place on various outcomes that your actions might bring about. For instance, as you plan your car trip to California you might assign

> **Preferences** are the relative values one places on the various outcomes that one's actions might bring about.

different degrees of importance to comfortable nights in upscale accommodations, fatigue from all-nighters on the road, ownership of a decent car at the end of the trip, and arrival in California by a certain date.

Your *beliefs* are your understandings of the actions necessary to bring about a particular outcome. (Note that this is a particular usage of the term *belief,* the broader definition of which refers to a conviction regarding the truth of something.) For example, you may believe that getting to California without a breakdown requires buying a better car.

> **Beliefs** are one's understandings of the actions necessary to bring about particular outcomes.

Information about constraints, preferences, and beliefs is generally sufficient to explain why a particular set of actions was taken. Continuing the road trip example: You bought a seven-year-old Honda Civic because you could not afford an Accord and you believed that the Civic would probably get you there. Also, you asked a friend to join you so that you could drive straight through, enjoy his company, and surprise your parents by getting home early.

In sum, individuals make choices to take various actions (within their constraints); they seek to bring about the outcomes they desire (according to their preferences); and they base their choices on their understandings (beliefs) about how certain actions may bring about the desired outcomes. The important thing to note here is that behavior involves choosing. The choices that the driver in the above example made may have been quite limited due to constraints such as a lack of wealth, but that does not mean that the actions taken were not choices. It may also be that the choices made were bad choices (the seven-year-old Civic might not have been adequate to get her all the way to California), but, in any case, choices were made.

We stress the element of choice because some views of behavior see choice as unimportant or even nonexistent. Such views are based either on the argument that individuals are not free (their constraints dictate a particular action) or that they are creatures of habit or conformity. There certainly are situations in which we are not free: the choice between "your money or your life!" is not much of a choice. It may also be the case that we sometimes repeat our past actions (out of habit) or copy (conform to) the actions of others without considering alternative possibilities. Habit and conformity certainly play a part in our behavior: just think of what you ate for breakfast this morning or what you wore to the last social event you attended. But views of behavior as coerced, habitual, or conformist fail to recognize the important elements of choice in most of what we do.

The constraints, preferences, and beliefs approach to understanding human behavior has therefore been widely accepted, not only in economics but in other social sciences as well. However, no theory can explain anything by itself. To explain behavior we need to know facts about the particular constraints, preferences, and beliefs pertaining to a given situation, and such facts will differ from person to person and among groups. Men and women face different constraints, for example, as do members of different classes, races, ethnic groups, and nationalities.

Moreover, two important aspects of the constraints, preferences, and beliefs approach have not yet been mentioned. The first is that preferences are not necessarily selfish: there is no reason to say that people must always be self-interested. The person driving across the country in our earlier example may have wanted to arrive early not for selfish reasons but to please her parents. Second, we have not said anything about where preferences come from. Was her concern for her parents' happiness an expression of "human nature"—an expression of a genetically transmitted trait? Or was it the result of her happy childhood? Was her lack of status consciousness (indicated by her purchase of the seven-year-old Civic) derived from a considered decision not to throw money away, or was it the result of a vague awareness that her cash-strapped friends would have frowned on the purchase of as nice a car as an Accord?

The view of preferences adopted in this book is fundamentally different from the one that prevails in the neoclassical school of economics, an approach to understanding the economy that appears in many textbooks and is discussed in detail in the next chapter. Neoclassical economists build their theories on the *Homo economicus* assumption that people have entirely self-interested preferences. They assume that people care about outcomes that involve themselves but not those that affect others. They also assume that everyone is this way and that everyone knows that everyone is this way: everyone is an economic man and everyone knows that everyone is an economic man.

In addition, neoclassical economists generally do not ask where preferences come from. Rather, they take preferences as "given," meaning that the preferences that guide economic decision making are thought to be simply there, possibly as an expression of human nature, or possibly due to advertising, socialization, or other factors that are of no concern to economists. Moreover, neoclassical economists usually view preferences as being *exogenously* determined, formed by forces *outside* the economy.

Because the neoclassical approach is out of line with many scientifically determined and widely known facts regarding human behavior, we take a different view. As we have said, in our understanding of the economy preferences are not necessarily selfish. More important, we do not assume that preferences are exogenously determined. Rather, we view them as *endogenously* determined, that is, determined mostly by processes *internal* to the economy. In the next section we set forth our reasons for doubting the assumption that preferences are entirely selfish. Later in the chapter we explore the question of where preferences come from.

"ECONOMIC MAN" RECONSIDERED

Nobody would pick *Homo economicus* for a housemate, a spouse, a friend, or (if we could choose them) a parent or a child. The economics Nobel Laureate Amartya Sen (see Chapter 4) has called economic man a "rational fool." But the implications of the concept are actually worse than Sen suggests: mental health professionals use the term *sociopath* to refer to a person whose behavior is governed entirely by calculation of self-interest. Sociopaths have no sense of right and wrong, and they lack any concern for the well-being or pain of others.

It is not surprising, then, that since the inception of neoclassical economics in the late 19th century, even its adherents have sometimes had difficulty with the assumption that human beings are motivated solely by self-interest. A founder of the neoclassical approach, F. Y. Edgeworth, wrote: "The first principle of economics is that every agent is actuated only by self-interest." In his next sentence, however, he cautioned that this "first principle" is strictly applicable only in situations of "contract and war."[2] With regard to war, Edgeworth was not entirely right: bravery under fire often is not based exclusively on self-interest. And with regard to contracts, sometimes a handshake is a handshake, even if one party could benefit by violating the unwritten contract.

Just how wrong the assumption of universal selfishness is has recently been revealed in a series of what are called behavioral experiments. Subjects, usually students, often economics or business majors, are invited to volunteer to play a game in which they can win real money. They are anonymously paired for a single interaction. One (usually chosen randomly) is termed the "proposer," the other, the "responder." The proposer is provisionally awarded some money referred to as the "pie," the amount of which is known to both participants. The game is explained to both participants in advance as follows: The proposer is to decide how much of the pie to share with the responder; the proposer then offers a certain proportion of the pie to the responder, and the responder decides whether to accept or to reject the offer. If the responder accepts, the responder gets the offered portion, and the proposer keeps the rest. If the responder rejects the offer, both get nothing. The pie is often a small sum, such as $10, but the game has been played in the U.S. for $100 and in Indonesia with a pie equal to three months' salary. This experiment is called the "ultimatum game," the proposer's offer being the ultimatum that can be either accepted or rejected.

How would "economic man" play this game? As the proposer, he would reason that the responder (assumed also to be an economic man) would accept *any* offer greater than zero, for rejecting an offer of even one penny would deprive the responder of a penny. For an economic man a penny is better than nothing, no matter how it is acquired. This being the case, the proposer would decide to offer a penny (or the smallest amount possible), anticipating that it will be accepted.

But this is not what usually happens when the ultimatum game is played with real people for real money. Before we tell you what *does* happen, however, think about what you would offer if you were a proposer with $100 to share, in some proportion, with a responder. Also try to imagine the lowest offer you would accept if you were the responder.

The ultimatum game has been played in hundreds of experiments with university students as subjects in all parts of the world. Few play the game as economic man would. In experiments conducted with students in the U.S., Japan, Israel, Germany, Russia, Slovakia, Slovenia, Indonesia, and many other countries, the vast majority of proposers offer between 40 and 50 percent. The most common offers are typically half of the pie. Equally striking is the fact that offers of 25 percent or less are frequently rejected.

---

[2] F. Y. Edgeworth, *Mathematical Psychics: An Essay on the Application of Mathematics to the Moral Sciences* (London: C. Kegan Paul, 1881), p. 104.

COKE VS. THE "JUST PRICE"

The Coca-Cola Company has tested a vending machine that automatically raises the price of a soda on hot days. Doing this does not require rocket science, just a thermostat and a computer chip. The company's chairman and chief executive at the time, M. Douglas Ivester, noting that the desire for a cold drink goes up with the temperature, concluded: "So it's fair that it should be more expensive." Airlines charge more when the demand is high, so why should Coke not do the same? "The machine will simply make this process automatic," Ivester explained.

Not everyone agrees. A Pepsi spokesman, no doubt seeking a competitive edge, took the high road: "We believe that machines that raise prices in hot weather exploit consumers who live in warm climates." Another beverage executive wondered: "What's next? A machine that X-rays people's pockets to find out how much change they have and raises the price accordingly? . . . It's another reason to move to Sweden!"

Apparently the price of a Coke—or that of any other commodity—is not, for some people at least, only something to be left to the market (or to the influence of large corporations). Economics Nobel Prize winner Daniel Kahneman (a psychologist by training) and his collaborators asked consumers if they thought it was fair for stores to raise the price of snow shovels during winter storms. The answer: they did not.

The Coca-Cola Company's new machine strikes at least some people as unfair because they think that when two parties engage in a mutually beneficial exchange—one, say, that increases a company's profits while quenching a consumer's thirst—the distribution of the benefits and burdens should not violate ethical norms. This idea can be traced to Thomas Aquinas, the medieval Catholic philosopher, and his concept of a "just price." Most economists think the idea of a just price is a nonsensical expression—like a "yellow logarithm." They would side with Coke. But judging from the reception that Coke received, they have not persuaded everyone yet.

Source: Constance Hayes, "Coke Tests Vending Unit That Can Hike Prices in Hot Weather," *New York Times,* October 28, 1999.

These experiments show that neither the proposers nor the responders behave like economic man. A responder is often willing to pay a price, rejecting a low offer and ending up with nothing, to punish a proposer who makes an unacceptably low offer. Many have interpreted this behavior as evidence of a *preference for reciprocity*—a tendency to be generous toward another person as long as you are treated well by the other person but a willingness to pay good money to punish someone who has crossed or insulted you, even if you will never see that person again.

While the responders' behavior is understood as reciprocity, the behavior of proposers seems to be more complex than a simple preference for reciprocity would suggest. It is possible that their high offers could reflect unconditional generosity toward the responders or a concern for their well-being irrespective of any behavior on the responders' part. If this is the correct interpretation, the proposers can be said to have *altruistic* preferences—preferences that lead them to act to benefit others at some cost to themselves (even with no expectation that reciprocal benefits will be received later).

An alternative interpretation is that a proposer could have well-informed beliefs and be motivated by selfish preferences. Suppose the proposer believes that the responder will not play the game like an economic man, one willing to accept a penny. If the proposer believes that the responder will reject low offers, then making a 50–50 offer could be nothing more than self-interest guided by prudence.

All we can say for sure in interpreting the most frequent outcomes of the ultimatum game is that neither the proposers nor the responders behave like economic man. Even the self-interested but prudent proposer just described does not believe that the responder is an economic man. And in virtually all cases the proposers assume that the responders will depart from the assumption of perfect selfishness.

Violations of the selfishness assumption are not confined to these experiments, and neither are they limited to such dramatic but exceptional examples as heroism in warfare. Most people do not steal or cheat on their taxes even when they are sure they can get away with it. And in all of the richest nations in the world (Canada, the U.S., and the European countries, for example), large majorities vote for income transfers to the poor, knowing that these programs require higher taxes on most income-earners. Even in the U.S., where such programs are relatively unpopular, there is substantial support for income transfers to the poor, even among rich and upwardly mobile people who will probably never be able (or have the need) to benefit directly from such transfers.

However, we cannot conclude from our recitation of the above facts that people are not selfish. What is probably true is something like Abraham Lincoln's assertion about people being fooled: being selfish is what some of the people are all of the time and what all of the people are some of the time. But the rest of the people, the rest of the time, are sometimes altruistic, sometimes reciprocal, sometimes spiteful, occasionally vengeful, and so on. To reiterate the key point: when students or others participate in experiments such as the ultimatum game, the fraction of players that consistently act selfishly is quite small; it is almost always less than a half and often as low as a quarter.

HUMAN NATURE AND CULTURAL DIFFERENCES

One undeniable lesson from the experiments—not a terribly surprising one—is that people differ. This lesson is important because it reinforces what we know from our own observations, namely, that assuming everyone is selfish (or generous, or spiteful, for that matter) ignores the facts. Not only do people differ one from another; their behavior differs (again, not surprisingly) from one society to another. To some extent this is due to the particular requirements of making a living in each society—people in Kansas farm, people in Iceland fish. But does the extent to which people resemble economic man vary from one society to another?

One of us (Bowles) and a team of anthropologists and economists designed a set of experiments to explore the connections (if any) between how people make their living and their preferences. We conducted our experiments in 15 societies in Africa, Asia, and Latin America where people live in sharply contrasting ways. In some, hunters and gatherers live in ways not very different from the ways in which our early human ancestors lived before the domestication of animals and plants. In others, herders and farmers use technologies that have been in use thousands of years to make a living from their animals and plants. Most of the groups we studied live in inaccessible places such as the New Guinea highlands and the Peruvian part of the Amazon, and they have very limited connections with modern governments or the world of markets. None of the groups we studied was large; most were settlements of less than 100 people and had had little contact with the outside world. For this reason, and because they have so little else in common, we call them "small-scale societies."[3]

The results of the experiments surprised us. When the ultimatum game was played among the Au and Gnau peoples in Papua, New Guinea, for example, offers of more than half of the pie were common. (Such offers were almost never encountered in experiments conducted with American students.) Even more interesting was the observation that in these societies high and low offers were rejected with equal frequency. (Most 50–50 offers were accepted.) This unusual result probably occurred because competitive gift-giving is a means of establishing status in these and many other New Guinea societies. We reasoned that proposers making high offers (offering more than half) may have been seeking to enhance their status, while those rejecting these offers were simply refusing (albeit at a high price) to accept a lower status. The frequent rejection of low offers was probably due to a sense that accepting them would mark the responders as already being of a low status.

In contrast, when the game was played among the Machiguenga forest agriculturalists in Amazonian Peru, the average offer was 27 percent of the pie. Nearly three-fourths of all the Machiguenga offers were less than 25 percent, and only one offer was rejected! This was a pattern strikingly different from the results of the other experiments we conducted. We were left wondering: if the Machiguenga were really so stingy (as suggested by the frequency of low offers and the infrequent rejection of them), why did they offer more than a penny?

Analysis of our experiments in the 15 small-scale societies led us to the following conclusions. First, and most important, is that typical behaviors vary significantly from group to group. The subjects in some groups were much more generous (and willing to punish stinginess) than were American, European, and other students, and some were much less so. Second, in no group did we find "economic man" behavior to be typical. Third, variations in behavior from one group to another seemed to reflect differences in how people in each group make their living. For example, the Aché people in Paraguay acquire some kinds of food (meat and honey) by hunting and gathering, and these foods are shared equally among

---

[3] Joe Henrich, Robert Boyd, Samuel Bowles, Ernst Fehr, and Herbert Gintis, *Foundations of Human Reciprocity: Economic Experiments and Ethnographic Evidence in 15 Small-scale Societies* (Oxford: Oxford University Press, 2004).

all group members. When playing the ultimatum game, almost all Aché proposers offered about half of the pie, and *none* of their offers was rejected. (This behavior differs, of course, from that of the Machiguenga and other groups such as American students.)

Another example of how a particular group's economic circumstances affect its typical behavior comes from Indonesia. There the Lamalera whale hunters need to hunt in large crews, and they divide their catch according to strict sharing rules (see p. 547 in Chapter 20). When they played the ultimatum game, the average offer was 58 percent of the pie.

Why do people play the ultimatum game so differently from one society to another? We know that the players in each society, from Orma herders in Kenya to Aché hunters in Paraguay, face the same constraints in the experiments. Therefore, the answer must be either that the players' beliefs vary or that their preferences differ. If it is their preferences, where do the differences come from?

Some of our preferences are influenced by our genes and are hence thought of as reflecting our "nature." Thus, we sometimes say that a certain person is generous or stingy (or something else) "by nature." To take another example, the taste for sweet or fatty foods seems universal and is probably genetically transmitted. But most food tastes vary greatly among countries, and genetic differences between human populations are not great enough to account for such variations. Spain, Italy, and France are famous for their distinctive national cuisines, but the crops grown in each of these countries can be grown in others, and there are no relevant genetic differences between their populations. Why do the Italians eat pasta while the French prefer bread or potatoes? These tastes are not inherited genetically. Rather, they are *learned* from parents, neighbors, and others.

Preferences that are learned from others—passed on from parents, elders, teachers, heroes, competitors, neighbors, or friends rather than being genetically transmitted just from parents—are part of what is called *culture*. We define culture as aspects of behavior that we learn from others.

As noted earlier, beliefs influence our behavior because our choices of actions to take are based in part on our understandings (beliefs) regarding cause-and-effect relationships. Since our beliefs are either learned from others or gathered from our own experiences, they, too (like preferences), are part of our culture. Similarly, learned skills, transmitted to us by parents, schools, friends, neighbors, and others, are part of the culture in which we are situated.

Culture and *human nature* have long been controversial terms: is it "nature" or "nurture" that explains why some people lead and others follow? Is it "genes" or "environment" that make some rich and others poor?

What is not controversial is that people do not differ much genetically from group to group. *Within* any group, of course—whether it is citizens of the U.S., the Aché people of Paraguay, or Italians—the genetic differences are very large. Researchers have found, however, that such within-group differences are much greater than the differences between a typical person in a certain group and one in some other group. For example, if you were to pick two Americans at random, even ones who share the same skin color or height, the genetic differences between them would most likely be huge in comparison to the differences, say, between the average American and the average Aché.

Behaviors, however, are another matter. People behave very differently in different societies. (Recall the varying results of the ultimatum game played in different societies.) Behaviors differ mainly because cultures are very different from one country or group to another: what we learn from others as we grow up and even when we are adults varies greatly from place to place. That is why the preferences and beliefs of the peoples studied by the authors differ so much. The culture of Lamalera whale hunters (who on average offered more than half of the pie) is different from that of the Machiguenga forest agriculturalists (who offered barely more than a quarter), which in turn is different from that of the Tanzanian Hadza hunter-gatherers (who rejected almost half of low offers)—and all of these cultures are different from that of the Ecuadorian forest people, the Tsimane (who rejected none). Why do people learn such different things from one culture to another?

THE ECONOMY PRODUCES PEOPLE

As explained in Chapter 5, the economy produces more than just goods and services; it also produces people. We call the creation of goods and services "production" and the production of people "reproduction" (see Figure 5.1). The term *reproduction* comprises not only biological procreation but also all the processes entailed in the formation of an individual, including what happens in families, schools, and all the other institutions in which parents, teachers, caregivers, spouses, and others combine their labor with other inputs to raise and support each new generation. Societies accomplish the tasks of reproduction in various ways, and some of the differences in methods of reproduction result from differences in the way people make their livings (production). This is what we mean when we say that the economy produces people.

As we have seen, ultimatum game experiments can provide information about the relationship between an economy and a culture. In our small-scale society experiments individual choices appeared to reflect everyday life, especially the way people made their living. For example, we saw that the Aché, who acquire much of their food by hunting and gathering and then share it, tended to divide the pie equally, sometimes offering more than half of it to the responders in our experiments.

Similar information can be gathered using other types of experiments. Among the Orma herders and throughout Kenya there is an important cultural institution they call the *harambee system*. With this system it is customary to collect money to build a school or repair a road by assessing each herder a certain amount, expecting him to make a contribution that varies with the size of his herd. We asked the Orma to play a different game called the "public goods game."

A public goods game is also explained to each player beforehand, and, like the ultimatum game, it is played anonymously and for real money. But in this game individuals play in groups rather than with a single partner, and they are asked to contribute to a common pot for the benefit of all. Once all the contributions are made, the amount in the pot is doubled and the total is then distributed in equal amounts to all the players. In this game, each player benefits from *the others* contributing, but each would personally gain the most by contributing nothing.

In the public goods game an Orma herder with a large herd who contributed one Kenyan shilling—quite a lot of money among his people—would see his contribution to the common pot doubled and then divided and distributed equally among the players in the game. Suppose there are five players. Then, the share distributed to the herder as a result of his contribution would be, say, 2/5 of a shilling, less than his original one, so he would have been better off remaining on the sidelines and just holding on to his shilling. Despite the fact that self-interest would prescribe contributing nothing, however, the herders in fact contributed generously—and those with large herds contributed more than those with smaller ones.

We wondered if the similarity between the local customs and the experimental play of such groups as the Aché hunters in Paraguay and the Orma herders in Kenya comes about because preferences are affected by a particular group's social institutions and norms of fairness. The large differences in institutions and norms in our sample allowed us to address this question. Accordingly, we ranked each society with reference to two aspects of its economic institutions and then sought to use the rankings to predict the results we achieved in the ultimatum games.

FIFTY-FIFTY: THE IMPORTANCE OF NORMS

On January 11, 1886, Fenner Powell, a former slave in Wade County, North Carolina, placed his X next to the signature of his landlord, W. S. Mial. Powell thereby agreed to "do all manner of work . . . as directed, and to be respectful in manners and comportment to said Mial . . . and to give to said Mial one half of all crops raised." There was nothing unusual about this contract, and that is why it is remarkable: it is exactly the same crop share that free-born white farmers in Wade County and throughout the South agreed to pay their landlords. Why would a former slave—illiterate, excluded from voting, and subject to denigration and lynching—be allowed to keep the same share as free-born farmers whose social status and bargaining power were much greater? Finding an answer will take us far from the post–Civil War U.S. South.

In Illinois today, growing corn is big business. Using capital-intensive technologies and computer-generated business plans, some farmers cultivate 1,000 acres or more, much of it on plots rented from multiple owners. In the mid-1990s more than half the contracts between farmers and owners were sharecropping agreements, and more than four-fifths of these contracts stipulated a fifty-fifty division of the crop. In the southern part of the state, where the soil tends to be less fertile, there are counties where most of the contracts allocate two-thirds of the crop to the tenant and one-third to the owner, despite considerable variation in land quality within these counties.

Rice cultivation in West Bengal in the mid-1970s seems light years away from Illinois. In West Bengal, poor illiterate farmers eked out a bare living on plots that averaged just two acres; they resided in villages without any electronic communication, isolated by impassable roads much of the year. There was one similarity with Illinois, however: the division of the crop between sharecroppers and owners was fifty-fifty in more than two-thirds of the contracts. Ibn Battuta, the famous Arab geographer who visited Bengal, India, in 1347, had recorded exactly the same division of the crop six centuries earlier. (Of course, if each landlord had 20 sharecroppers, contracts providing for fifty-fifty crop sharing would not mean

Continued . . .

that the owners and the farmers would have equal incomes: each landlord's income would be 20 times that of the typical farmer.)

John Stuart Mill, the 19th-century English philosopher and economist, noted both the widespread pattern of equal sharing of crops and local conformity to other proportions where fifty-fifty was not the rule. Mill's explanation: "The custom of the country is the universal rule." But why fifty-fifty as opposed to fifty-two to forty-eight? Why did the Bengalis and the Americans come up with the same proportion? Even more puzzling is the question: why do fifty-fifty or two-thirds to one-third persist when the owners could make huge profits if they were only to offer lower shares on higher-quality land? And when the shares do change, as happened in West Bengal in the 1980s and 1990s, why do they all change at once?

Fifty-fifty crop shares are social *norms*—widespread practices that are followed because violating them would bring criticism, retaliation, or ostracism. Norms play an important role in all economies, placing limits on the extent to which people can simply pursue their self-interest. Often norms become values in their own right, adhered to not to avoid sanction but because people would not feel right doing otherwise.

Sources: Samuel Bowles, *Microeconomics: Behavior, Institutions, and Evolution* (Princeton: Princeton University Press, 2004), Ch. 3; Roger L. Ransom and Richard Sutch, *One Kind of Freedom: The Economic Consequences of Emancipation* (Cambridge: Cambridge University Press, 1977); Peyton Young and Mary Burke, "Competition and Custom in Economic Contracts: A Case Study of Illinois Agriculture," *American Economic Review,* vol. 91, no. 3, 2001, pp. 559–73; Pranab Bardhan, *Land, Labor and Rural Poverty: Essays in Development Economics* (New York: Columbia University Press, 1984); John Stuart Mill, *Principles of Political Economy with Some of Their Applications* (London: Longmass, Green, Reader, and Diver, 1867 [1848]).

The first basis for ranking, *cooperation,* is a measure of the extent to which the local ecology allows for a more productive use of labor when many work together. The Lamalera whale hunters were ranked first because successful whaling requires large numbers of hunters to work together, and the dispersed Machiguenga forest agriculturalists were ranked last because their production is more individualized and they gain little by collective production activities. We speculated that in groups that cannot benefit much from cooperative production there would be few norms of sharing. We also guessed that in groups such as the Lamelera, whose livelihood depends on large-scale cooperation, ways of sharing would be well developed, and these would affect how the Lamalera played our games.

The second basis for ranking, *market integration,* is a measure of the fraction of a people's livelihood that is acquired through market exchange. The rationale for this measure is as follows: the more frequently people experience market transactions, the more they will also experience beneficial sharing of the gains made possible by trading with strangers. Historically, it is a fact that before markets became widespread, most interactions with strangers were potentially dangerous, often providing occasions for violent confrontation, theft, or worse. As markets developed they habituated us to the benefits of regular interactions with strangers in which both parties can benefit as long as they follow certain rules

DOES A CONSTITUTION FOR KNAVES MAKE KNAVES OF US?

Unlike Adam Smith and David Hume, the English conservative Edmund Burke, the German revolutionary Karl Marx, and the French liberal Alexis de Tocqueville feared that harnessing self-interest, or (to use Hume's phrase) living under a constitution designed for knaves, would turn us into knaves.

. . . the age of chivalry is gone. That of sophisters, economists, and calculators has succeeded . . . Nothing is left which engages the affections . . . so as to create in us love, veneration, admiration or attachment.

—Edmund Burke, *Reflections on the Revolution in France* (1790)

Finally, there came a time when everything that men had considered as inalienable became an object of exchange, of traffic, and could be alienated. This is the time when the very things which till then had been communicated, but never exchanged; given, but never sold; acquired, but never bought—virtue, love, conviction, knowledge, conscience, etc.—when everything, in short, passed into commerce. It is the time of general corruption, of universal venality.

—Karl Marx, *The Poverty of Philosophy* (1847)

Each [person] . . . is a stranger to the fate of all the rest . . . his children and his private friends constitute to him the whole of mankind; as for the rest of his fellow citizens, he is close to them but he sees them not . . . he touches them but he feels them not; he exists but in himself and for himself alone.

—Alexis de Tocqueville, *Democracy in America* (1830)

(you pay at the checkout, you do not take the groceries and run). Our speculation was that such experiences would give rise to societal sharing norms and that these would be reflected in the results of the experimental games.

Using the measures of cooperation and market integration we sought to explain both a group's average ultimatum game offer and its frequency of low offer rejection. We found that the two measures—cooperation and market integration—enabled us to predict the results of ultimatum game play in most of our societies. In societies with more cooperation or greater market integration, proposers made higher offers (on average), and low offers were more likely to be rejected. The great 18th- and 19th-century thinkers Karl Marx, Edmund Burke, and Alexis de Tocqueville might be surprised to find that exposure to markets leads to higher offers (greater sharing with others) and a greater tendency to reject unfair offers. (See the box, "Does a Constitution for Knaves Make Knaves of Us?")

Our ability to predict behavior in experiments that were entirely novel situations for our subjects on the basis of our two measures of economic structure suggests that economic institutions influence preferences. Our values, likes, dislikes, and morals seem to be affected by living within a particular set of institutions—sharing food like the Aché, cooperating in acquiring food like the Lamalera, pitching in voluntarily to build a school like the Orma, or, for that matter, competing for a job following graduation. How does this come about?

A plausible answer is that people acquire their preferences, in part, through the way they are brought up, and child-rearing practices stress values and skills that are important in a society's way of life. To test this idea, three anthropologists categorized 79 mostly nonliterate societies (similar to our 15 "small-scale" societies) according to their prevalent form of livelihood (animal husbandry, agriculture, hunting, and fishing) and their related capacity for food storage or other wealth accumulation. Food storage is common in agricultural societies but not among hunters and gatherers. These researchers also collected evidence on forms of child rearing, including obedience training ("compliance") and the degree to which self-reliance, independence, and taking responsibility ("assertion") were encouraged. They found significant variations of child-rearing practices, and they also found that these variations were correlated with differences in economic structure. They concluded, "Knowledge of the economy alone would enable one to predict with considerable accuracy whether a society's socialization pressures were primarily toward compliance or assertion."[4]

We do not need to confine our attention to anthropological studies of exotic societies to find evidence that economic institutions influence preferences. Over a period of three decades, a social psychologist, Melvin Kohn, and his collaborators have studied a number of individuals, focusing on the relationship between these individuals' positions in the authority structure of their workplaces and the extent to which they value obedience and discipline or self-direction and independence both in themselves and in their children. The hypothesis was that people who routinely take orders on the job value obedience and discipline, while those who give orders value autonomy. Kohn's collaborative study of Japan, the U.S., and Poland (when it was still ruled by a Communist government) found that in all three countries people who exercise self-direction on the job also value self-direction in other realms of their life (including child rearing and leisure activities) and are less likely to exhibit fatalism, distrust, and self-deprecation. Kohn and his coauthors argued that ". . . social structure affects individual psychological functioning mainly by affecting the conditions of people's own lives,"[5] and they concluded that ". . . the experience of occupational self-direction has a profound effect on people's values, orientation, and cognitive functioning."[6]

The facts presented above suggest that the way goods are produced and distributed in any society conditions what one must be or do to make a living. Hunters must be independent-minded and physically fit, industrial workers and clerical staff must be willing to take orders, and entrepreneurs must be self-motivated. Economic institutions thus impose characteristic patterns of interaction on the people who make up a society, affecting who meets whom, on what terms, to perform which tasks, and with what expectations of rewards. These patterns, in turn, influence the process by which people mature and change over their lifetimes, forming their personalities, habits, tastes, identities, and values—in short, their preferences.

---

[4] Herbert Barry III, Irvin L. Child, and Margaret K. Bacon, "Relation of Child Training to Subsistence Economy," *American Anthropologist,* vol. 61, 1959, pp. 51–63.

[5] Melvin L. Kohn, *Class and Conformity: A Study in Values* (Homewood, Ill.: Dorsey Press, 1969), p. 189.

[6] Melvin L. Kohn and Kazimierz M. Slomcyński, *Social Structure and Self-direction: A Comparative Analysis of the United States and Poland* (Cambridge, Mass.: B. Blackwell, 1990), p. 967.

Economic institutions shape people's preferences in part because institutions determine what kinds of individuals will be successful, and people try to copy the successful, either in their own likes, dislikes, and values or in raising their children. But in most societies the job of socializing young people is not left entirely to parents. Schools, religious institutions, and other organizations play a major part in bringing up the next generation.

If you look at the curriculum of a school, you might get the impression that its only objective is to teach skills such as reading, writing, math, and the ability to use a computer. But a closer look at what goes on in the classroom and how rewards are distributed among students shows that schools do something else, too: they teach children how to behave. The fact is that getting a good grade requires more than knowledge of the subject, and there is a study that proves this. It shows that to get good grades one also has to develop certain personality traits. (Many students already know this.) More surprising, however, is the study's additional finding that the personality traits rewarded with high grades in the classroom are the same as those rewarded with favorable rankings by supervisors in the workplace.

Here is the study. One of us (Edwards) used a peer-rated set of personality measures to predict supervisors' ratings of workers in both private and public employment. Peer-rated personality measures are based on how individuals are seen by people similar to, or in the same situation as, themselves. Such measures are expressed in words such as *tactful, creative,* and *punctual.* One of Edwards's collaborators, Peter B. Meyer, used the same peer-rated personality variables to predict differences in high school students' grade point averages from what would be predicted on the basis of their SAT and IQ scores.

Edwards found that certain peer-defined personality traits—perseverance, dependability, consistency, punctuality, tactfulness, and being able to "identify with work" and "empathize with others"—were highly correlated with positive supervisors' ratings, whereas to be judged by one's peers as being creative or independent meant receiving poor ratings from supervisors.[7] Meyer found virtually identical results for the high school students in his grading study: the correlations between their grade point averages and 12 personality traits are nearly the same as the correlations observed in Edwards's study of employees.[8] Thus, both teachers and employers reward the same personality traits. The conclusion: schools teach more than skills, and they also cultivate (or at least they reward) the kinds of personality traits that employers prefer.

All human societies have developed elaborate ways of teaching the preferences and beliefs required for normal functioning as an adult. In many hunter-gatherer societies children accompanied their parents as they stalked game and searched for fruits and nuts, learning the skills necessary to live by these means. Before the emergence of capitalism, most production took place within families—in small workshops, on farms, and the like—and a person could learn most of what was necessary to function in the economy from parents and relatives. Also, the skills required did not change much from generation to generation.

---

[7] Richard C. Edwards, "Personal Traits and 'Success' in Schooling and Work" (*Educational and Psychological Measurement,* spring 1977) and "Individual Traits and Organizational Incentives: What Makes a 'Good' Worker?" *Journal of Human Resources,* winter 1976.

[8] Samuel Bowles, Herbert Gintis, and Peter Meyer, "The Long Shadow of Work: Education, the Family, and the Reproduction of the Social Division of Labor," *The Insurgent Sociologist,* summer 1975.

Capitalism changed all this. It created huge workplaces in which thousands of strangers come into contact with one another, and rapid technological change may now render the skills of one's parents obsolete even before retirement becomes an option for them. As capitalism has become the preeminent economic system, schools have come to play an essential role in the socialization process. Moreover, the personality traits that schools foster—dependability, consistency, punctuality—now make it possible for large numbers of strangers to work together even if the bonds of kinship, loyalty, and affection are absent.

CONCLUSION: THE COOPERATIVE SPECIES

Humans are unique among animals in that large numbers of unrelated people cooperate to produce the goods and services we require. We also cooperate in pursuing other projects such as raising the next generation and engaging in warfare.

All animals compete: for food, for survival, for reproductive success. Some animals exchange goods and services. For example, fish called "cleaner fish" remove parasites from the skin and mouths of larger fish, providing health services in return for a good meal. The Greek scholar Herodotus described a similar exchange more than two and a half millennia ago:

> Because [the crocodile] spends its life in water, its mouth is filled with leeches. With the exception of the sandpiper, all other birds and animals run away from it. The sandpiper, however, is on good terms with it because it [the sandpiper] is of use to the crocodile. When the crocodile climbs out of the water and onto land, it yawns widely . . . and then the sandpiper slips into its mouth and swallows the leeches. This does the crocodile good and gives it pleasure, so it does not harm the sandpiper.[9]

Some animals even respect property rights. Spiders do not intrude onto the webs occupied by other spiders (unless the intruder is much bigger). A male Hamadryas baboon does not attempt to steal food that is in the possession of another one.

But in no other species but *Homo sapiens* do thousands of unrelated individuals work together to accomplish a common project, whether it be building cars, providing medical insurance for citizens, or making war. (Ants, bees, and some other so-called eusocial insects cooperate on a grand scale, but it is all in the family: the members of a hive or nest, even if they number in the thousands, are mostly relatives.) How do we do it?

In part, these feats of cooperation are accomplished because, distinct from other animals, we are able to devise laws and organizations that go beyond the family, such as governments and firms. These often provide the incentives and constraints that induce people to work together effectively, even if they are entirely self-interested.

Self-interested behavior is not characteristic of successful organizations, however. The soldier who goes to war may do it for the money or because he was drafted and had no choice. But as any officer knows, such motives do not inspire people to become good soldiers.

---

[9] Herodotus, *The Histories* (New York: Oxford University Press, 1998), p. 122.

All forms of human cooperation, including those capable of winning in warfare, are best understood by considering motives other than self-interest. These include envy or spite toward others as well as concern for others and the aspiration to see certain principles upheld. The success of humans as cooperators is much less puzzling once one realizes that economic man is just one kind of human, and not a very common one at that. Far more common are people who, at least some of the time, are reciprocators or altruists and, for better or worse, care about others. Humans are cooperative on a scale unmatched by any other animal because we have preferences that lead us to act in cooperative ways.

Our last question: how did we get this way? Part of the answer concerns human nature. We have the intellectual capacity to devise general ethical rules to live by, and we also have the linguistic capacity to communicate these rules among ourselves, to report violations of the rules, and to coordinate the punishment of those who break them. In addition, we are acutely sensitive to praise and blame, experiencing such *moral emotions* as shame, which serve as powerful incentives to avoid wrongdoing. It is worth noting that Adam Smith titled his first book *The Theory of Moral Sentiments* and devoted it to the analysis of exactly this aspect of human life. The moral emotions as well as the intellectual and linguistic capacity to devise and enforce social norms are part of human nature. They are not part of cat nature, or spider nature, or baboon nature.

The content of ethical rules—just what it is that they bid us to do and not do—is also, to some extent, a matter of human nature. Incest evokes disgust and shame among most humans, irrespective of the culture they grow up in, as do a number of unhealthy practices such as living with personal uncleanliness or ingesting unhealthy substances. But most of the content of our ethical norms is learned: it comes from culture, not nature.

People in most societies actively teach the value of curbing our selfish desires and behaving in altruistic or reciprocal ways under appropriate circumstances. For most people (but not, of course, for sociopaths), acting in accordance with such teachings becomes an objective that is embedded in our preferences, becoming thus more than just an external constraint. That is why most of us, most of the time, do not steal even when we could get away with it.

But what about those who, like *Homo economicus,* are clever enough and immoral enough to steal when they *can* get away with it? Why do they not succeed in taking advantage of and eventually outcompeting their more ethical neighbors for the goods necessary for survival? If this happened, would not the ethical ones have to respond by becoming like the immoral ones? We hear of cases of unethical behavior being rewarded and going unpunished all the time.

The answer is that a group made up of economic man types would not function successfully as a unit. Who would come to the defense of the group in an attack by an external enemy or help out during a drought or other ecological crisis? Not economic man. In his second great book, *The Descent of Man* (the first was his better-known *The Origin of Species*), Charles Darwin, the founder of the modern theory of biological evolution, came to the following conclusion:

> When two tribes of primeval man, living in the same country, came into competition, if . . . one tribe included a great number of courageous, sympathetic and faithful members, who were always ready to warn each other of danger [and] to aid and defend each other, this

tribe would succeed better and conquer the other. . . . Selfish and contentious people will not cohere, and without coherence nothing can be effected.[10]

The point of Darwin's statement is clear: in competitions among groups, those whose members have learned how to cooperate—that is, *not to compete* with one another—often win. Think of team sports. Darwin spoke of tribes as groups that would benefit from having a preponderance of cooperative members. The same reasoning applies to firms, neighborhoods, ethnic groups, and nations.

Thus, it is not that our good cultures beat out our bad nature. Rather, our cultures and our nature work together to make *Homo sapiens* the uniquely cooperative species that we are. The fact that we are cooperative means that nice guys do not always finish last. The reasoning that explains why nice guys do not always finish last also makes clear that neoclassical economists sometimes overrate the value of competition as a source of progress. Cooperation is also necessary.

SUGGESTED READINGS

Samuel Bowles, *Microeconomics: Behavior, Institutions, and Evolution* (Princeton: Princeton University Press, 2004).

Samuel Bowles and Herbert Gintis, *Schooling in Capitalist America: Educational Reform and the Contradictions of Economic Life* (New York: Basic Books, 1976).

Robert H. Frank, *Passions within Reason: The Strategic Role of the Emotions* (New York: Norton, 1988).

Bruno S. Frey, *Not Just for the Money: An Economic Theory of Personal Motivation* (Cheltenham, U.K.: Edward Elgar Publishing, 1997).

Herbert Gintis, Samuel Bowles, Robert Boyd, and Ernst Fehr, eds., *Moral Sentiments and Material Interests: The Foundations of Cooperation in Economic Life* (Cambridge, Mass.: Massachusetts Institute of Technology Press, 2004).

Uri Gneezy and Aldo Rustichini, "A Fine Is a Price," *Journal of Legal Studies,* vol. 29, no. 1, 2000, pp. 1–17.

Joe Henrich, Robert Boyd, Samuel Bowles, Ernst Fehr, and Herbert Gintis, *Foundations of Human Reciprocity: Economic Experiments and Ethnographic Evidence in 15 Small-scale Societies* (Oxford: Oxford University Press, 2004).

Albert O. Hirschman, *The Passions and the Interests: Political Arguments for Capitalism before Its Triumph* (Princeton: Princeton University Press, 1977).

Daniel Kahneman and Amos Tversky, *Choices, Values and Frames* (Princeton: Princeton University Press, 2000).

Robert E. Lane, *The Market Experience* (Cambridge: Cambridge University Press, 1991).

Peter Richerson and Robert Boyd, *Not By Genes Alone* (Chicago: University of Chicago Press, 2004).

William F. Whyte, *Money and Motivation* (New York: Harper & Row, 1955).

---

[10] Charles Darwin, *The Descent of Man* (Amherst, N.Y.: Prometheus Books, 1997 [1871]), Ch. 5, "On the Development of the Intellectual and Moral Faculties During Primeval and Civilized Times."

CHAPTER 3

A Three-Dimensional Approach to Economics

U nderstanding capitalism has become essential for anyone who reads the newspaper, watches the nightly news, listens to political candidates, or simply wonders why it is so hard to find a good job or get enough free time. Since capitalism is an economic system, understanding capitalism requires some knowledge of economics. But what *kind* of economics? We call the approach presented in this book *three-dimensional economics,* and we often refer to it simply as *political economy.*

> **Political economy** is a term we use for a theory that analyzes capitalism in terms of the three dimensions of competition, command, and change.

Until the beginning of the 20th century the term *political economy* was used to refer to all of economics, and the field itself encompassed most of what is now divided up among the social sciences: anthropology, sociology, psychology, and political science, as well as economics. But around 1900 the term *political economy* was replaced by *economics,* and the boundaries of the discipline were narrowed: the study of markets became its primary focus. Inquiries into politics, psychology, history, and other aspects of society were then left to the other social sciences. Thus, it is no accident that anthropology, sociology, psychology, and political science came into existence as separate fields at about this time.

We prefer to use the older term *political economy* (rather than *economics*) to describe our approach because one cannot understand contemporary societies very well unless politics, economics, psychology, and the other social science disciplines are all brought together to study the complexities of modern life. Another way of describing the *political economy* approach, then, is to say that it is *interdisciplinary.*

Many people believe that the approach presented here makes more sense and is a more useful way of understanding our economy than what is sometimes called *neoclassical economics*—the "conventional" approach that is set forth in most economics textbooks. Ultimately, however, everyone who seeks to understand capitalism needs to consider a number of approaches to economics and decide which one, or which combination, makes the most sense and is the most useful.

What is certain is that no one should accept a particular approach to economics just because it is what some experts believe. Each person must make a choice for herself or himself, asking: "Does this make sense to me?" "Does this help me understand things that I have experienced and believe to be true?" Of course, not all opinions about economics are equally valid. A useful approach to economics, whether it be political economy or some other approach, must be logically sound, internally consistent, and helpful in explaining what is known about economic reality ("the facts").

The main idea of this chapter is that *political economy considers all three dimensions of economic life*: *competition, command, and change.* The main points of the chapter are:

---

1. Capitalism is an *economic* system.

2. Every economic system can be analyzed in terms of three dimensions: a horizontal dimension (*competition*), a vertical dimension (*command*), and a time dimension (*change*).

3. Economics is about *values* (what ought to be) as well as *facts* (what is). It is useful to make values—and their role in any particular economic analysis—explicit. The values adopted in this book are simple: an economy should provide all members of a society with an equal opportunity to lead a flourishing life, and this objective is more likely to be achieved if the economy is *efficient, fair,* and *democratic*.

The fundamental concepts introduced in this chapter will be used throughout the book and will be further developed in later chapters.

ECONOMIC SYSTEMS AND CAPITALISM

Over the span of human history people have organized their economic activities in many different ways. The variety of economic systems runs the gamut from tribal commonwealths, slavery, and feudalism to self-sufficient households, capitalism, and state socialism.

What all these systems have in common—what makes them *economic* systems—is that they are all *ways of organizing the human labor needed in every society to produce the goods and services that support life.* No matter what type of society it is situated in, an economic system will determine *what* work is done, *how* it is done and *by whom,* and *to whom the resulting products are distributed.*

> An **economic system** is a set of relationships among people that organizes the labor processes all societies need to sustain life.

Economic systems are *relationships among people.* These relationships may be direct, face-to-face relationships, such as the interaction that occurs when you buy an orange from a grocer. At the other end of the spectrum, they may be relationships between people in different parts of the globe, for example the Iowa farmer producing grain that will later appear as bread on a table in Egypt. The relationships that make up economic systems may also be embodied in customs, laws, constitutions, political parties, or business corporations.

Economic relationships are shaped in important ways by the physical things and technologies used in production as well as by other factors such as geography, customs, religion, and whether production is primarily agricultural, industrial, or postindustrial (knowledge-based). Nevertheless, the *social relationships* among the various economic actors—producers and consumers, slave owners and slaves, feudal lords and serfs, employers and employees, borrowers and lenders—are the defining qualities of an economic system. Thus, the distinguishing features of any economic system may be seen in the social interactions among the economic players, and these interactions may be, in varying degrees, cooperative or competitive, altruistic or avaricious, equal or unequal, democratic or authoritarian.

How human work is organized differs from one economic system to another. To understand how work is organized in any particular society one must examine its economic system. The economic system that is the focus of this book, capitalism, is the one that prevails, in one way or another, throughout most of the world today.

Capitalism is quite familiar to most of us. In various forms it is the economic system not only of the United States but also of Great Britain, Japan, Chile, France, Russia, Mexico, Brazil, Germany, South Africa, and, indeed, more than 100 other countries. Thus, we can study capitalism directly because we experience it every day of our lives.

In a capitalist economic system most goods and services are produced at the direction of employers (businesspeople, entrepreneurs, capitalists, or managers of firms) who seek to make profits by selling the produced goods and services in markets. Most people in capitalist economies work for someone else (their employers) and receive a wage or salary in return. So work is organized for the purpose of making a profit; the employer, or his or her appointed manager, is the boss at the workplace; and goods, services, and people's capacity to work—their labor time—are all exchanged through markets.

To understand capitalism one must find answers to a number of questions. How is work organized? How do markets operate? How much of the output when sold will go to profits, how much to wages, and what will determine the relative magnitudes of these two types of income? Why do some workers get paid more than others? Who decides what technologies will be used, and on what basis will such decisions be made? How does our capitalist economy affect the way we develop as human beings? How does it condition our culture, influence our political system, and alter our natural environment? And, in turn, what reverberations will all these effects have on the capitalist economy itself?

THREE-DIMENSIONAL ECONOMICS

In this book the complex relationships of a capitalist economy are examined, taking into account all three dimensions of an economic system: competition, command, and change.

Competition

Competition, or the horizontal dimension in economics, refers to aspects of economic relationships in which voluntary exchange and choice among a large number of possible buyers and sellers play the predominant role.

The first dimension is called "competition," and it refers to that aspect of an economic system in which exchanges of one sort or another play the most important part. In capitalism, of course, competition and exchange occur primarily in markets. For example, when a motorist chooses to buy gasoline at a particular gas station, it is obvious that he or she is making a choice between competing suppliers.

The competition dimension of the economy is a *horizontal* one: it can be thought of as involving a relative equality of power among those offering the choices, engaging in exchanges, and competing with one another. In the gas station example, for instance, the sellers of gasoline must compete with one another to entice the motorist to come to their pumps. In the contest for customers, the gas suppliers are equal in the following sense: none can dictate to any other—or to the motorist—where the motorist will buy gasoline.

Political economy shares with conventional economics the view that an analysis of how competition works is essential to any attempt at understanding the economy. (As we point out in Chapter 11, however, political economy differs from the conventional approach on how competition actually takes place in a capitalist economy.) When, as in capitalism, much of economic life is organized in markets—not based, say, on ancient customs or on decisions imposed by central planners—markets are the terrain on which most of the competition is carried on and where most of the choices are made by individuals and firms.

Command

Command, or the vertical dimension in economics, refers to aspects of economic relationships in which power plays the predominant role.

The second dimension is called "command," and it refers to those aspects of economic relationships that involve power, coercion, hierarchy, subordination, or authority. In capitalist (and many other) societies, command is a central aspect of the workplace, the household, and the government. It concerns relations among nations, classes, races, men, women, and other groups in society as well.

The command dimension is regarded as *vertical* because it necessarily involves people or groups who are unequal, some being "higher up" in a hierarchy than others. One person or group is "dominant," while the others are "subordinate."

It is not always easy to distinguish command from choice. Suppose a thief points a gun at someone and demands, "Your money or your life!" This is *literally* a choice. The victim could presumably choose to surrender either the money or his or her life, yet the thief's threat is easily recognizable as *in fact* a command to hand over the money.

A less extreme example would be a situation in which a boss asks a worker to do something and the alternative to carrying out the boss's request is to get fired. It may seem here that the worker has the choice of doing or not doing what the boss has asked, but, in reality, the boss's request is a command.

Although the prospect of getting fired is not comparable to the possibility of losing one's life, for many people the loss of a job will cause financial disaster. This, in turn,

A has **power** over B if by imposing costs on B (or threatening to do so) A can cause B to act in a way that is to A's advantage.

will make it difficult to put food on the table, make the mortgage payments, or land another job.

One form of command is what we call "power." We define power as follows. A has power over B if by imposing costs on B (or threatening to do so) A can cause B to act in a way that is to A's advantage. The employer has power over the employee in this sense.

Command may be exercised, however, without threats and costs being imposed. It may just be that one party influences or shapes the conditions under which another party will be making a choice. Thus, corporations often use their financial resources to alter the conditions under which consumers make choices. If, for example, an aspirin producer's television commercials can convince consumers that its product is "stronger," works "faster," or is "recommended by most doctors," people going to the store in search of relief for headaches will tend to choose this product more frequently.

The point of the aspirin commercial example is that command is not only the ability to impose costs on others. It is also the ability of one person or group to control others' information, playing upon their fears, hopes, insecurities, or other emotions and thereby influencing their actions in order to promote the interests of the powerful person or group. Thus, in the case of advertising, command is often used in subtle—and sometimes not so subtle— ways to shape or condition choice.

Command is used in many other ways to influence outcomes. Examples of such influence include corporations making campaign contributions to sway the voting patterns of legislators or other politicians, companies hiring recent immigrants to work long hours for low wages in unsafe or unhealthy workplaces because such people have few other employment opportunities, and other circumstances in which money and power give one person or organization the ability to influence the actions of another. As we observe in later chapters, many economic relationships involve both choice and command, with neither one operating exclusively.

Change

Change, or the time dimension in economics, refers to the historical evolution of people and economic systems.

The third dimension of economic systems is called "change." It concerns the passage of time and the ways in which, over time, the operation of an economic system will change the system itself. In capitalism, change occurs because big profits can be made by changing the existing conditions—by building new and better machines, by designing novel products to meet previously unknown needs, by expanding production, or by building factories in distant corners of the world.

Central to the changefulness of capitalism is the system of investment for profit that creates an inexorable tendency for the economy to expand. With its expansionary drive, capitalism alters the conditions in which it operates—and within which people live and die. Capitalism's continuous expansion also transforms the ways in which the system itself actually works.

Change is called the "time" dimension because change always occurs through time. Thinking about change necessarily involves using concepts such as "before" and "after," "old" and "new," or "early" and "late."

Emphasizing the change dimension of economics reminds us that each economic system works differently at different points in time. It also brings out the fact that people participating in an economic system develop over time.

Each economic system has a history, and the way each system functions at any particular point in time will depend, in part, on its history. For example, American capitalism works differently in the 21st century from the way it worked in the 19th and 20th centuries, and although it is still capitalism, an analysis of how it works in the present must be informed by a consideration of the ways in which it has changed. Similarly, American capitalism today differs from, say, German capitalism, in part because the 19th- and 20th-century histories of these two countries differed.

Any economic system will undergo further change in the future. The present and even the future will become the past: what *is* today will *not be* tomorrow. Indeed, as noted in Chapter 1, capitalism is the most dynamic—or "changeful"—economic system yet to be observed in history.

Of course, many factors other than the normal, everyday functioning of the economic system may cause economic and social changes. A list of noneconomic change-inducing events might include wars, plagues, new discoveries, climate change, religious upheavals, or new scientific breakthroughs. In some cases the economic analysis presented in this book may help to explain why these events occur. However, this analysis is mainly concerned with change as it emerges from the routine and persistent operation of the economic system. Similarly, with regard to human development the concern here is with how people adopt new tastes, values, ways of life, and even religions at least partially in response to their changing experiences of working and making a living.

The emphasis it gives to change is one of the qualities that distinguish political economy from neoclassical economics. This and other differences are summarized in the table at the end of this chapter.

ECONOMICS, POLITICS, AND HISTORY

Economics is the study of *how people interact with one another, with nature, and with the other things they require in order to produce their livelihoods.* The three-dimensional approach to economics takes the view that, as important as they are, the processes of competition and market exchange on which conventional economics focuses are only part of the story. Processes of competition and market exchange are important. Indeed, they are the first dimension referred to in the triad of "competition, command, and change" that defines three-dimensional economics. However, the other two dimensions, command and change, are just as important.

The vertical dimension of political economy, command, takes the existence of power relationships into account. Conventional economists do not include these relationships in their analyses; instead, they leave power to be studied by political scientists. Abba Lerner, a prominent conventional economist, once commented that economics had become the "queen" of the social sciences by focusing only on those political problems that had already been solved. When political problems—such as a society's choice of a particular framework of laws or a system for the administration of justice—have already been solved, the ensuing relations can be conducted solely on the basis of contracts and market exchange.

Three-dimensional economics does not limit itself to the study of solved political problems. Focusing on command as one of the most important aspects of human social life, it sees the economy as a place where power plays a decisive role and where there have been—and continue to be—endless and often bitter struggles between workers and their employers, between buyers and sellers, and among giant corporations. Thus, one reason for the presence of the word *political* in *political economy* is the recognition of the fact that power relationships are an important aspect of any economy.

The third dimension of three-dimensional economics, change, suggests that studying economics also means studying history. The process of change in society cannot be understood without considering the past and how it changed, eventually becoming the present. Change in political economy may be contrasted with the static approach of conventional economics that freezes time at a moment. Economic reality, according to political economy, is better represented dynamically—as a process of change rather than a frozen state of affairs. It is a movie compared to the neoclassical snapshot.

From the standpoint of political economy, the usual distinctions among the disciplines in the social sciences—history, political science, economics, sociology, anthropology, and psychology—are quite arbitrary. These distinctions divide social reality into parcels that reflect the traditional boundaries among university departments, but they obscure our understanding of how the economy works.

NEOCLASSICAL ECONOMICS

The neoclassical (or conventional) approach to economics, mentioned in both this chapter and the previous one, sees capitalism as a system of markets. The label *neoclassical* is given to conventional economics because this approach presents an updated version of some of the ideas of 18th- and 19th-century "classical" economics, the founder of which, Adam Smith, will be discussed in the next chapter. Neoclassical economics is thus primarily an explanation of how markets and market systems work.

Neoclassical, or **conventional, economics** is an economic theory emphasizing the horizontal dimension of markets and voluntary exchange.

Neoclassical economics is mainly about competitive markets, that is, markets with many buyers and sellers, and it offers explanations of how economic systems made up of many competitive markets function. While understanding markets is essential to understanding capitalism, the neoclassical approach is founded on three very restrictive assumptions. The first, "economic man" (*Homo economicus*), was discussed in the previous chapter.

The second assumption underpinning the neoclassical approach is that when studying a market transaction, all essential aspects of it are covered in a contract. Accordingly, all other aspects and consequences of the exchange are treated as being of secondary importance.

> A **contract** is an agreement, either written (explicit) or unwritten (implicit), that commits two or more parties to taking certain actions, such as making payments and delivering goods or services.

The concept of a *contract* is significant not only in economic analysis but also in many other areas, for example, the law. It is defined as an agreement, either written (explicit) or unwritten (implicit), that commits two or more parties to taking certain actions, such as making payments and delivering goods or services.

Neoclassical economists assume that contracts are *complete* in the sense that the *prices* resulting from them take into account everything that is important about a particular transaction. This is sometimes referred to as the *complete contracting assumption.* A *complete contract* is one that fully specifies, in ways that the courts will enforce, everything that each party to the contract is to do as a result of the contract.

> A **complete contract** is one that fully specifies—in ways that the courts will enforce—everything that each party to the contract is to do as a result of the contract.

In making the assumption that all market transactions are based on complete contracts, neoclassical economists take for granted that the contracts into which we enter, explicitly or implicitly, whenever we buy or sell something are "complete" in the sense that (a) they cover everything of interest to both parties to an exchange, and (b) they can be enforced at no significant cost to either party. In contrast, an *incomplete contract* between two parties is one that leaves out certain aspects of an exchange and requires or imposes, upon one party or the other, significant enforcement costs.

> An **incomplete contract** is an agreement between two or more parties that leaves out certain aspects of an exchange and requires or imposes, upon one party or another, significant enforcement costs.

When a new car is purchased the contract is quite complete: the specifications of the car are described, the price is given, the payment plan is made clear, the warranty is spelled out, the limits on the liabilities of the producer are stated, and so on. When an employer hires a worker, however, the contract does not even mention some of the most important aspects of the bargain, such as the exact task (or tasks) the employee may be assigned to do or how hard he or she will be expected to work. The incompleteness of employment contracts is one of the most important issues given attention in the political economy approach. (Credit contracts are incomplete, too, but for a different reason: the exact amount the borrower is to repay is clearly specified, but the contract may be unenforceable if the borrower is broke when the time comes to repay.)

In making the complete contracting assumption, conventional economists picture a world in which exchanges are *voluntary* (the very idea of a contract implies that both parties have voluntarily agreed to it). Coercive—"command"—relationships are not in the picture because if everything that matters in an exchange has already been settled by contract, there is nothing for the exercise of power to be *about.* As the example of the employment contract makes clear, however, what is left out of an incomplete contract may have to be resolved by command. Moreover, when an employer issues an order to an employee, it may be necessary to hire a supervisor to make sure that the order is obeyed. In this case, the salary paid to the supervisor is a cost to the employer of having the contract enforced.

If the price paid for something in a market exchange *did* reflect all relevant aspects of the exchange, one could say "you get what you pay for," and vice versa. Thus, in the neoclassical economists' world, the things you might enjoy but do not have to pay for (such as the love of a friend or your neighbor's beautiful garden) are assumed to be either unimportant or the subject matter of some other discipline. Similarly, the things we get but would rather not get and are not paid to accept (such as a difficult supervisor or environmental pollution) are not given much attention.

> **Externalities** occur when some of the effects of a market exchange are not reflected in the price and are thus "external" to the participants in the exchange.

Side effects on people other than those directly involved in a transaction are termed "external effects," or *externalities*. They are called this because they are said to be "external" to the transaction itself. For example, the price one pays for gasoline does not reflect the costs imposed on others as a result of its consumption—carbon monoxide emissions, smog, health costs, traffic congestion—so all such effects are externalities of the purchase and consumption of the gasoline. Economists generally agree that externalities are a fact of life in any modern economy. But in practice they are taken to be the exception, not the rule. The issues are: How widespread are they? And what should be done about them? Externalities are discussed at length in Chapter 9 of this book.

The third important assumption of neoclassical economics is that *increasing returns to scale* generally do not occur. The term *increasing returns to scale* refers to a situation in which expanding the rate of output—or the *scale*—of a productive activity makes possible a reduction in the average cost of producing a unit of output. In this situation, enlarging the scale of production will have the effect of *increasing* the *return* (net profit) per unit as additional units are produced (since the average cost of producing each unit will be falling).

Neoclassical economists assume that, beyond a modest scale of production, increasing returns are rare enough to ignore for most purposes. This in turn allows them to say that, in general, the average cost of producing a unit of a good will rise (or at least will not fall) as the rate of output is increased. This assumption flies in the face of the facts, namely, the prevalence in modern economies of large-scale production that allows many goods and services to be turned out at lower and lower costs per unit. (Think of music, drugs, and this book.) The significance of the widespread presence—and growing importance—of increasing returns in modern economies is discussed at length in Chapters 9 and 20.

Why is the assumption of *nonincreasing returns* essential to neoclassical theory? If the assumption is false and increasing returns prevail, competition among many small- or medium-sized firms cannot be the normal state of the economy. Smaller firms will find it impossible to survive because larger firms will be able to produce at lower cost. When this is the case the larger firms will be able to drive the smaller firms out of the market, and there will tend to be more monopoly than competition—and the economics of competitive markets will be of little interest.

There is an additional reason why increasing returns may make the competitive markets of neoclassical economics the exception rather than the rule. The outcomes of competition will often depend not just on which firm delivers a better product at lower cost. Market success may also depend on a firm's political influence, its ability to get a head start and enter a market first, or just the luck of being in the right place at the right time. Whatever the reason, if a firm gets to be a certain size before others do, it will have the advantage of being able to produce at a lower cost than its (actual or potential) competitors. Its greater size—and the cost advantage flowing from increasing returns—will enable it to leave the competition behind.

The three assumptions that underpin and define neoclassical economics can best be understood as part of a worldview dating from the 17th-century physics of Isaac Newton. From the standpoint of this worldview, all social and physical phenomena involve knowable and predictable motions of atomlike particles. Thus, the complete contracting assumption is a way of limiting an observer's view of the interactions among the particles so that these interactions may be seen as obeying a few simple laws. Similarly, the economic man assumption establishes the principle of motion of each particle. Finally, the nonincreasing returns assumption eliminates the advantages of head starts and accidents, so the past history of the interacting particles does not influence their current relationship. The end result, in neoclassical theory, is that the economy is viewed as a smoothly running machine, not one with the sometimes harmonious but more often conflict-ridden and sporadically chaotic human interactions that actually occur in a capitalist economy.

The neoclassical approach may be summarized in three interrelated points. First, the economic machine, as seen by a neoclassical economist, operates continuously and indefinitely into the future without any change in its basic design. It may need repair or replacement parts from time to time, but the machine itself—the economy—is relatively trouble free and not very accident prone. Its few problems, such as recessions or technological unemployment, can easily be taken care of.

Second, change does not occur as a result of the workings of the economic system itself. If something in the economy should happen to change, it will do so only as a result of an *external* influence, such as a major technological innovation or the spontaneous emergence of a new fad in consumer tastes. The development of the Internet, with its corresponding expansion of electronic communication or the sudden proliferation of peoples' desires for running shoes and designer clothing might be seen as examples of such "external" influences. In fact, however, such innovations and changes in consumer tastes do not occur entirely as a result of forces external to the economy. Rather, they are most often brought about by capitalism's drive to increase profits, expand markets, and sell more products.

Finally, since the economy remains unaffected by its own operation, it does not have a history. It does not, in itself, have a past, present, or future. Thus, neoclassical economics presents only a "static" analysis of the economy—static (or "stationary") in the sense that it is not "dynamic." When this shortcoming is considered along with its (previously discussed) lack of interest in power (command) relationships, one may conclude that the conventional approach offers only a one-dimensional analysis of capitalism, focusing exclusively on competition and exchange on the supposedly level playing field of the market.

VALUES IN POLITICAL ECONOMY

Most people with an interest in economics care not only about how our economy works (or does not work), but also about what is good or bad about it and how it might be made to work better. The economy is the subject of much controversy and debate. It used to be said that if you wanted to avoid an argument, stay away from politics or religion. Today, better advice might be: don't mention economics.

Debate in economics is not only about "what is"; it is also about "what should be." This is sometimes referred to as the difference between "positive" (or "scientific") economics and "normative" (or "policy-oriented") economics, but, in fact, the boundary is not always clear. The "what is" question has to do not only with facts but also with their *interpretation*. Thus, differences arise when people disagree about what the facts are—*and what they mean.* The question "what should be," on the other hand, cannot even be addressed without explicit reference to *values*. In this case differences arise when people disagree about which situations are better and which are worse.

Getting the facts and their interpretation right is an essential task for *any* approach to economics. The facts regarding "what is" must be determined with enough accuracy that people with varying points of view can agree on them. Statements about how the economy works are either true or false, however difficult it may be to determine which, and one's judgment of their truth or falsity should not depend on one's values.

When one is choosing to examine a particular aspect of "what is," however, the choice will usually be strongly influenced by one's view of "what should be." If one places a high value on individual freedom of choice and less on fairness, one might be more interested in studying the way that markets and governments may affect one's freedom than in figuring out why women are generally paid less than men. This last topic would be of greater interest to someone who attaches a higher value to fairness. Nobody can be equally interested in all aspects of the economy, and your values will help you decide which economic questions you would most like your economic investigations to illuminate. You need to have some idea about where your lost car keys are in order to know where to point your flashlight.

Values also provide a basis for judging whether we think an economic system is good or bad, or, more specifically, what processes or outcomes of an economic system are better or worse. If you value democracy highly you probably have a very negative opinion of dictatorial regimes such as the ones that prevailed in the former Communist countries. But if you care a lot about increasing the amount of material goods available in a society, you have to be impressed by the record-setting increases in output achieved by Communist-ruled China in the last quarter of the 20th century. There are, of course, a number of different values, or criteria, on the basis of which one may, explicitly or implicitly, evaluate an economic system.

We evaluate economic systems on the basis of how well or how poorly they organize economic activities so as to provide opportunities for all their participants to lead flourishing lives. Our use of the biological term *flourish* is deliberate: plants flourish—as long as they have enough water, sunlight, and nutrients. In Chapter 14 we discuss some of the elements that people need in order to flourish. But certainly they cannot flourish when they lack adequate food and health care, when they are not free or are denied opportunities for learning, or when they are not respected both as individuals and as members of groups.

The most basic question regarding an economy is how does it affect people. And while each individual may have his or her own definition of "the good life," an economy that provides more people with more opportunities to lead flourishing lives is judged to be better than an economy that provides fewer people with fewer such opportunities. An economy is thus evaluated on more than just "economic" outcomes—individuals' incomes, for example. It is assessed on *all* of the ways it affects its participants.

How, then, are we to determine what is needed for a flourishing life? Can we say that one person's passion for opera is such a need, while another's craving for a BMW is not? In fact, though, judgements are not hard to make about many of the important issues to which our evaluation criteria may be applied. Imagine a child starving in a country where large quantities of grain are fed to cattle on their way to becoming steaks. Most people would not regard this as a good allocation of grain, even though this conclusion requires making a judgment about the value of a steak to one person relative to the value of enough nutrition to produce a healthy child to another. The world as we know it—sadly—poses many more problems similar to the steak vs. the hungry child than to the BMW vs. the opera.

An economy can provide the means for a flourishing life, or it can hinder the achievement of one. Of course, whether individuals actually do lead happy and free lives will be influenced by many more variables than how the economy is organized. To a significant degree, the achievement of a flourishing life will depend on the choices one makes. But economies can create conditions favorable to the achievement of a flourishing life, or they can generate conditions that make it difficult to live with dignity, freedom, and happiness.

An economy will impede the achievement of flourishing lives if jobs are mind-numbing or unsafe, if children die young of easily preventable diseases, if people remain illiterate or are not free to speak their minds or practice the religion of their choice, if malnutrition is common, if people are stigmatized because of their race, sex, or sexual orientation, or if other conditions that limit opportunities are generated. An economy is better to the extent that it reduces or does not create such conditions—not just for a few people but for everyone and to the greatest possible extent.

Whether an economy contributes to a flourishing life for all the members of a society will depend on a number of aspects of the way the economy works. Among these are its efficiency, its fairness, and the degree to which it is democratic.

Efficiency

> The term **efficient** is applied to a labor process if the effort, time, intelligence, creativity, raw materials, natural environment, information, and machinery used in it are applied in a way that enhances people's well-being by equipping them with the things and the free time needed to lead a flourishing life.

One criterion for evaluating an economic system is that it should be *efficient*. There are many definitions of efficiency in economics (see box, "Efficiency, Profitability, and 'Pareto Optimality'"). We use the term to mean that labor and inputs are used well rather than wasted. Inputs include effort, time, intelligence, creativity, raw materials, the natural environment, and machinery. Using these inputs well (rather than wasting them) means using them to enhance people's well-being by equipping them with the things and the free time needed to lead a full life. An economic system that uses its resources more efficiently than another is, according to this criterion, a better economic system. It is better because it increases people's freedom to use their time and energy for noneconomic ends such as leisure, play, and learning.

EFFICIENCY, PROFITABILITY, AND "PARETO OPTIMALITY"

Like much else, "efficiency" is a debated topic in economics. Our definition is: *Efficiency* requires that the effort, time, intelligence, creativity, information, raw materials, natural environment, and machinery used in production should be so devoted as to enhance people's well-being by equipping them with the things and the free time needed to lead a flourishing life.

This is not to be confused with *profitability,* which occurs when a firm's sales revenues exceed its costs, taking account of all the inputs paid for by the firm. In Chapters 13 and 20 we give examples of why profitability and efficiency are not the same thing.

Engineers think of efficiency as a relationship between physical inputs and outputs. A production process is said to be *technically efficient* if, given the existing technology, the output of it cannot be increased without using more of at least one of the inputs.

Pareto optimality, named after the economist Vilfredo Pareto (Pa-RAY-toh), who first thought it up about a century ago, is the definition of efficiency preferred by many economists. An outcome is a Pareto optimum (sometimes called *Pareto efficient*) if there exists no *other* outcome (using available resources and technologies) that would make at least one person better off without making anyone worse off.

If there is some alternative use of inputs and outputs that has the win-win quality that some could be made better off and none worse off, the outcome is said to be *Pareto inefficient.* Notice two things, however. First, there are a very large number of Pareto (efficient) optima, each with a different distribution of goods among the members of society. Second, even if some people are starving while others feed caviar to their cats, the result will be Pareto efficient if there is no way of redistributing the goods that makes the poor better off *without making the rich worse off* (the cats do not count).

Efficiency refers to the production of *useful* goods and services. The production of goods and services that are not useful should be left out of the efficiency calculation. For instance, the production of advertising (beyond the extent to which it simply informs the consumer) is highly profitable—this is why it is produced—but it is not useful. The same may be said of some forms of military goods production during peacetime.

All inputs used in the production of useful goods and services, whether they are paid for or not, must be entered into the efficiency calculation. One input that is often not taken into account is the natural environment. A profitable factory that uses up clean water by adding toxic wastes to it may, in fact, be inefficient when all of its inputs are considered. This is because in addition to the inputs it pays for, the factory is also using up (consuming or destroying) a part of the natural environment.

Still another input that is frequently ignored is household labor. When we consider all the useful inputs and outputs of an economic system, we include work in the home as well as the labor that is organized in factories and elsewhere.

Another input that is often overlooked is labor effort. This is not the same as the *time* that a worker spends "at work." An assembly line that speeds up production may increase a company's profits, but it may not be efficient if the increased output is made possible only by an even larger increase in the employees' work effort, leaving them with greater fatigue at the end of the day and increased susceptibility to health problems. One way of thinking about this aspect of efficiency is to consider people and their health not only as inputs in the production process but as outputs of it as well.

Fairness

> **Fairness** means that people in an economic system suffer the burdens and enjoy the benefits of that economic system equitably.

A second criterion for evaluating an economic system is *fairness,* which involves the distribution of the system's burdens and benefits. Burden refers to sacrifices such as the work necessary to produce goods and services; benefit refers primarily to the use of what is produced. Who does how much work? And who consumes the products of the work that is done? Just as in evaluating the efficiency of an economy, all the costs of—and gains from—production need to be included.

A fair economic system would be one in which its burdens and benefits were distributed *equitably.* When judged according to this criterion of fairness, an economic system that distributes its burdens and benefits more equitably than another does is a better economic system. It is better because it recognizes the equal worth of all human beings. When each person is valued equally, the pleasures of each are equally worthy of being promoted, and the pains of each are equally worthy of being avoided. Thus, though each of us is different, we are the same with regard to our right to enjoy pleasures and avoid pain.

The belief in the equality of human worth as an ethical benchmark may be seen as coming from a variety of sources. Virtually every religion considers each human being to be equal in the eye of whatever god is held to be supreme in the particular religious faith. The authors of the U.S. Declaration of Independence proclaimed in 1776: "We hold these truths to be self-evident, that all men are created equal, that they are endowed by their Creator with certain unalienable Rights."

Many, possibly most, people would agree with the framers of the U.S. Constitution: people should have equal rights to participate in governing their societies and to be respected as individuals. But *what else* should be equal? Hardly anyone would argue that every individual should have exactly the same things, for this would not respect differences among people with regard to what they like and dislike. Some people work hard and long because they value material things, while others value leisure or nonmaterial pleasures more and therefore work less; it does not seem fair that both sets of people should receive the same quantity of material goods. Thus, while equality is a value endorsed in this book, it is important to be able to answer the question: *equality of what?*

The answer offered here—and one that is widely shared not only in the U.S. but also throughout the world—is that people should have an *equal opportunity* to live a good life, however they may conceive of this objective. Equal opportunity requires that, insofar as it is possible, people should be equally free of impediments to fashioning for themselves the kind of life they want, as long as the exercise of their freedom does not limit or otherwise impinge on the pursuit of a good life by others.

Of course, there will always be impediments to doing what we would like to do. For example, it sometimes happens, as it did to one of the authors of this book, that a person dreams of becoming a musician, but falling short on talent, has to settle for going through life as an economist! Equal opportunity simply means that people should be equally free of those impediments that are within our power to remove.

Some violations of equality of opportunity are obvious, as when employers or landlords discriminate against people on the basis of their race, sex, or age. But there are many less blatant forms of inequality, and they are to be found in most societies. When some children attend well-equipped schools and are taught by outstanding teachers while other children do not have comparable facilities or teachers, opportunity is unequal. When poor people must pay more for groceries because, for example, lacking a car they must shop at small neighborhood stores, or when people must pay higher interest rates to borrow money because of their race, sex, or where they live, opportunity is unequal. If some young people start off life with an expensive college education and a trust fund while others have only debts that have been passed on to them by their parents, opportunity is unequal. When, as a result of different starting points, some hard-working people earn only the minimum wage while other people, working no harder, take home hundreds or even thousands of dollars per hour of labor, opportunity is unequal.

Unlike the idea of *equal outcomes,* the objective of *equal opportunity* often requires people to have access to different things or to be treated in different ways. For example, people with health problems need more medical attention than do those without them. Children with dyslexia or other learning disabilities need more attention at school to have the same learning opportunities as do others. Children of parents who cannot or will not help them with their homework may also need more help at school if equality of opportunity is to be achieved.

The criterion of fairness will always be controversial. Should it apply equally to everyone in the world? Or should it be applied only within a single nation? If the answer is that it should be applied worldwide, then we say that it is unfair that a child growing up in a particular part of India will, as a result of poor living conditions, live 20 years less than a child of the same age growing up in Norway.

A final question: to what extent is it fair to give people second or third chances? If certain people drink their way through college and, as a result, end up poor and unemployed, does fairness require that they be temporarily supported while they undergo job training?

Democracy

The third criterion for assessing an economic system is *democracy*. One important part of this criterion questions the extent to which the economic system promotes (or hinders) the democratic functioning of the government. Another part asks whether the system allows for the accountability of power when it is exercised in the economy. An economic system that promotes democracy in both areas is better than one that does not. It is better because the ability to influence a decision that has an effect on you gives you greater control over your life.

> **Democracy** is a process with three characteristics: the exercise of power is accountable to those affected by it, civil rights and personal liberties are guaranteed, and citizens have relatively equal access to political resources and influence.

Democracy is a process that has three characteristics: accountability of power, respect for civil liberties and other guarantees of individual choice, and equal opportunity for effective political participation. First, decision makers (whether in the government or elsewhere) must be held accountable to the people affected by their decisions. This requires periodic review and possible replacement of public officials by means of democratic elections. Those who wield power in the economy—owners of firms, for example—can be held accountable by similar means. Democratic governmental bodies can regulate the actions of firms. If there is competition among many firms, consumers can hold sellers accountable for bad products by switching to other sellers—"voting with their pocketbooks"—and firms failing to serve consumers well will be eliminated.

Second, there must exist guarantees for the exercise of the civil rights and personal liberties that are commonly associated with democratic citizenship. The rights to freedom of speech and assembly, for instance, are essential for democratic decision making.

Third, the citizens in a democratic polity must have approximately the same amount of resources with which to participate in the democratic process; this is necessary if citizens are to have roughly equal opportunity to influence how decisions are made. A system in which everyone can vote but a few people—campaign contributors, for example—have more political influence than everyone else is not democratic.

Democracy does not mean that all decisions have to be made through voting. Individuals should be free independently to make any decisions that will have consequences entirely or mainly felt only by the individuals themselves. For example, the choice of which food to consume for dinner is almost always a decision that affects only the eater or the eater's family.

When a decision imposes unavoidable effects on many people, however, democracy requires that individual choice give way to collective democratic decision making. For example, the choice between closing down or modernizing an old factory will affect many people: the investors, the workers, the consumers of the product, the people who live near the plant and may be bothered by its noise or pollution, the community that depends on the property taxes on the plant, and so forth. In this case, the democracy criterion holds that individual choice—for instance, the plant owner's right to choose whether to close the plant—is undemocratic. If this criterion is applied, all those affected by the decision must be able to participate in the decision-making process.

Of course, to call the owner's decision undemocratic does not mean that the value of democracy should trump the values of efficiency or fairness. Either or both of these may recommend against a democratic decision. In the plant-closing example, for instance, it is not easy to see how the competing claims of the consumers, neighbors, workers, owners, and others could all be accommodated. Should each be given one vote? Or should plant closings be regulated by democratic national governments to minimize their adverse effects?

Some economists would think it odd to suggest that a private firm should be run democratically. Conventional textbooks ignore the exercise of power in the economy and treat organizations such as corporations simply as pass-through structures: inputs go in one side and products come out the other. If no power is exercised, there is nothing to democratize. Moreover, the right of people to participate in a decision-making process, the outcome of which affects their entire community, is not considered to be a problem that falls within the purview of economics.

Democracy and command are not necessarily inconsistent, although a command can certainly be undemocratic. For instance, orders issued by dictators or rules imposed by employers will be undemocratic if the people affected by the orders or rules have had no influence in the processes that led to their issuance or imposition. But a command may also be a means of carrying out a democratic decision. Take, for example, a national environmental protection law that was formulated with popular participation and then voted on and passed by a democratically elected legislature. To enforce this law, a governmental agency, backed by a federal court, may have to order polluters to stop polluting. In a different kind of situation, the command given to a worker by a democratically chosen manager in a worker-owned and worker-run cooperative would be another example of a democratic command. Implementing and enforcing democratic decisions requires commands.

Economic systems may be judged according to how well they meet the criteria of efficiency, fairness, and democracy. Some systems may be evaluated more favorably according to one or two of these standards, while other systems perform well in relation to one or more of the other criteria. For example, slavery was efficient—at least in the production of some crops—but it was unfair and undemocratic. In contrast, production by independent producers (for instance, independent farmers who owned their own land in colonial New England) was probably less efficient than slavery, but it was fairer and more democratic. It is also possible that the ability of an economic system to perform well in relation to the standards of efficiency, fairness, and democracy will change over time as the economic system itself changes.

Moreover, it may be difficult for any economic system to make consistent progress toward meeting all three criteria simultaneously or with the same speed. For example, the efficiency criterion may conflict with the democracy standard in the following way: the achievement of efficiency—say, production of the greatest possible amount of useful goods and services with limited quantities of inputs—may require intense competition and a high degree of mobility of labor and capital, while these very same elements may make it difficult for worker-owned (or otherwise democratically controlled) enterprises or stable, democratically governed communities to survive.

Necessarily, then, our evaluations of economic systems will result in more complex judgments than simply "good" or "bad," "better" or "worse." Also, it is highly unlikely that everyone will agree on all of the issues involved. Each person's conclusions will depend on his or her own values, and as long as we remain autonomous individuals our values and the conclusions we reach on the basis of them will inevitably differ. To the

TABLE 3.1   Contrasting Perspectives on the Economy

Neoclassical Economics	Political Economy
The main social relationships studied involve competition among self-interested people or between the firms in which they work.	The social relationships studied are cooperative as well as competitive, and generosity and reciprocity are considered along with self-interest.
Most economic interactions take the form of complete contracts.	Many economic interactions are not governed, or governed completely, by contracts.
Economic outcomes are determined by market forces. Power is exercised only by monopolies and governments.	The exercise of power is an important determinant of economic outcomes, even in competitive markets. Many economic outcomes are determined through bargaining between the parties or agents involved.
Constancy is the rule; change occurs only in response to forces outside the economic system.	Change is the rule, constancy the exception. Change, both in economic systems and in people, takes place through the workings of the economic system itself.
People's tastes and needs are determined largely by human nature or by other influences outside the economic system.	People's tastes and needs change and are strongly influenced by the economic system.
Knowledge and science evolve outside the economic system, governed by noneconomic forces.	Knowledge and science are strongly influenced by the economic system and by the exercise of power within it.
Economic inequality is given little attention and is measured by a single scale: income inequality.	Economic inequality is many-sided, encompassing differences of race, gender, status, property ownership, authority, income, political rights, and citizenship.
Economies are evaluated according to how well they do in relation to a limited view of efficiency.	Economies are evaluated according to how well they foster everyone's chance to lead a flourishing life; economic efficiency, fairness, and democracy can support the achievement of this goal.
Increasing returns to scale (costs declining as output expands) are absent or may be ignored.	Increasing returns are common in modern economies and therefore must be taken seriously.

degree that diversity and debate are good indicators of a healthy democratic society, such differences are to be welcomed.

In this book the values of efficiency, fairness, and democracy are not explicitly brought into the description and analysis of how capitalism works. Indeed, our analysis of capitalism should stand or fall without regard to a particular reader's values. The important question is whether the political economy approach offers a more fruitful way of understanding capitalism than that provided by neoclassical economics. We conclude this chapter with Table 3.1 summarizing the differences between the two approaches.

The contrast in Table 3.1 between neoclassical economics and political economy is of course not the only way one can subdivide economics. Indeed the subject is usually broken down into *microeconomics,* which is concerned with what individuals, families, and firms do (and why), and

> **Microeconomics** deals with what individuals, families, and firms do (and why).

> **Macroeconomics** is about how the decisions of individuals, families, firms, and governments produce outcomes—such as economic progress or stagnation, inflation or unemployment—for society as a whole.

macroeconomics, which is about how decisions of the same individuals, families, and firms, together with government policies, determine outcomes for society as a whole. In Part 2 of this book—"Microeconomics"—we look at how buyers and sellers interact in markets, how firms seek to increase their profits, and how conflicts between employers and their employees regarding wages and work are resolved. In Part 3—"Macroeconomics"—we examine the interactions of individuals, firms, and governments, asking how they result in economy-wide outcomes affecting such things as incomes and opportunities, wealth and poverty, growth and stagnation, employment, unemployment, and inflation.

Having introduced the basic concepts of three-dimensional economics in this chapter, we proceed in the next chapter to review the contributions of six great economists to the development of this approach.

SUGGESTED READINGS

Robert A. Dahl, *Democracy and Its Critics* (New Haven, Conn.: Yale University Press, 1989).

Nancy Folbre, *The Invisible Heart: Economics and Family Values* (New York: New Press, 2001).

Robert Heilbroner, *Behind the Veil of Economics: Essays in the Worldly Philosophy* (New York: Norton, 1988).

Robert Nozick, *Anarchy, State, and Utopia* (New York: Free Press, 1974).

Louis Putterman, *Dollars and Change: Economics in Context* (New Haven, Conn.: Yale University Press, 2001).

John Rawls, *Justice as Fairness: A Restatement* (Cambridge, Mass.: Harvard University Press, 2001).

John Roemer, *Free to Lose: An Introduction to Marxist Economic Philosophy* (Cambridge, Mass.: Harvard University Press, 1988).

Amartya Sen, *Development as Freedom* (New York: Knopf, 1999).

Philippe van Parijs, *Real Freedom for All: What (If Anything) Can Justify Capitalism?* (New York: Oxford University Press, 1998).

CHAPTER 4

Political Economy, Past and Present

"Practical men, who believe themselves to be quite exempt from any intellectual influences, are usually the slaves of some defunct economist. Madmen in authority, who hear voices in the air, are distilling their frenzy from some academic scribbler of a few years back." Thus did John Maynard Keynes (rhymes with "rains"), one of the great 20th-century economists, conclude his major work, *The General Theory of Employment, Interest, and Money.* He was careful to warn that economic ideas are often powerful whether they are right or wrong. He might have added that economic ideas can have a great impact even when their author's major works are so dense that they are impenetrable except to specialists in economics.

So it was with Keynes. His book was read by few and understood by fewer. And yet, less than a decade after Keynes wrote his *General Theory,* "Keynesianism" had become a battle cry of social movements, or an epithet to hurl at opponents, depending on one's opinions. So, too, had it been with Adam Smith, the prophet of capitalism, and Karl Marx, capitalism's great critic. In neither case were their major works well understood by many of their contemporaries, but in both cases their writings became controversial and had great impacts on the course of history.

Thus, economics was born in controversy and has grown in controversy. Someone once quipped that if you laid all the economists in the world end to end, they would not reach a conclusion. But because it is about the most ordinary and the most important of our daily activities, earning a livelihood, economics is hardly an irrelevant pursuit, even in the hands of those whom Keynes labeled "academic scribblers."

Near the beginning of the last chapter we warned against accepting any particular economic opinion as true without careful scrutiny. In this chapter we underline this warning by introducing six of the all-time great economists, each of whom has contributed to what we call the three-dimensional approach to economics. Had they met (they did not), they would have agreed on some things and strongly disagreed on others. But as you will see, they had complex ideas, and they often respected points of view that were at odds with their own; none of them was simply grinding an ax or trying to sell his own point of view. Marx, you may be surprised to find, lavishly praised capitalism for its massive increases in material output. And Smith worried greatly about what capitalism was doing to those who worked in its factories.

The crux of this chapter is that *political economy (three-dimensional economics) is a way of understanding capitalism that has evolved and changed along with capitalism itself.* This idea is expressed in the following points:

1. The primary contributors to political economy grappled not only with abstract theoretical issues but also with the concrete economic reality around them.

2. Adam Smith showed how markets can work as a system of coordination of private economic decisions.

3. Karl Marx contributed an understanding of classes, class conflict, and how economic systems change over time.

4. Joseph Schumpeter ("shum PAY ter") taught that innovation and technical change lead both to economic instability and to growth in living standards.

5. John Maynard Keynes explained why unemployment is a persistent problem and what the government might do about it.

6. Ronald Coase (rhymes with "snows") showed that bargaining among private individuals can sometimes solve problems that governments fail to address, and that firms are political as well as economic organizations.

7. Amartya Sen challenged the idea that people are entirely selfish, stressing the importance of ethical values in people's behaviors.

8. None provided wholly satisfactory answers to the questions they raised. Economists continue to seek new answers and to face entirely new questions as capitalism continues to evolve.

As long as there has been human life on earth, there have been *economies,* for the process of producing one's livelihood is a precondition for life itself. But *economics,* the study of economies, is relatively new, having originated barely 300 years ago. Like urbanization, technological change, population growth, mass migrations, increasing material abundance, and the other revolutionary changes of the modern era, economics came along with capitalism.

To help the reader relate the developments in economics (political economy) traced in this chapter to some of the major events in modern political, economic, and social history, we include here a timeline connecting the history of economists and their ideas with the broader history of the 18th, 19th, and 20th centuries. (See Figure 4.1.)

Before the capitalist epoch, the production of one's livelihood was so much an integral part of the rest of one's life that it did not seem separate enough to be studied on its own.

ECONOMICS / POLITICAL ECONOMY

1723: Adam Smith born in Scotland

1759: Adam Smith publishes the "Theory of Moral Sentiments"

1776: Adam Smith publishes "The Wealth of Nations"

1790: Adam Smith dies

1818: Karl Marx born in Trier, Germany

1800–1840s: The classical economics of David Ricardo, Thomas Malthus and John Stuart Mill flourishes in England, spreads beyond

1848: Marx and Engels publish "The Communist Manifesto"

1867: Marx publishes the first volume of "Capital".

1870s: Birth of neoclassical economics

1883: Marx dies; John Maynard Keynes born in Cambridge, England; Joseph Schumpeter born in Moravia (now part of Czech Republic)

1910: Ronald Coase born in Middlesex, England

1911: Schumpeter publishes the "Theory of Economic Development"

1933: Amartya Sen born in British India

1936: Keynes publishes "The General Theory"

1937: Coase publishes "The Nature of the Firm"

1942: Schumpeter publishes "Capitalism, Socialism, and Democracy"

1940s: Keynes and others create IMF and World Bank, Keynes dies

1960: Coase publishes "The Problem of Social Cost"

1965–present: Sen publishes works on famine, poverty, and democracy

1990s: Coase and Sen win Nobel Prizes

Timeline years: 1700, 1720, 1740, 1760, 1780, 1800, 1820, 1840, 1860, 1880, 1900, 1920, 1940, 1960, 1980, 2000

ECONOMY AND SOCIETY

mid–1700s: "Enlightenment" intellectuals in Europe challenge the divine right of rulers, question tradition, promote science

late 1700s: First Industrial Revolution and the the full development of capitalism in England, later in France and Germany

1776: United States "Declaration of Independence"

1789: French Revolution: "Declaration of the Rights of Man" and decline of aristocracy and autocratic rule in France

1820s–1840s: Voting rights extended to freeborn males in U.S.; Chartist movement seeks to expand voting rights in England; England adopts "free trade" and factory acts protecting workers

1848: Year of revolutionary ferment by urban workers, craftsmen, and intellectuals in Europe

1860–1864: Civil War in the United States; Emancipation Act ends slavery

1870s–1890s: Era of the "robber barons" in the U.S.; increase in agrarian protest; birth of the labor movement

1914–1918: First World War decimates Europe; Bolsheviks sieze power in Russia

1929: Great Depression begins in capitalist nations except fascist Germany and Japan

1933: Franklin Roosevelt introduces "New Deal" in U.S.

1939–1945: Second World War

1943: Great Bengal Famine kills two million people in India

1949: Chinese Revolution ushers in Communist rule in China

1948–1980s: End of European colonial empires; Cold War; Keynesian economic policies implemented in the capitalist nations; central planning in the Communist-ruled nations;

1980s–1990s: Berlin Wall falls; Soviet Union ends; Communist rule is terminated in Eastern Europe; information revolution accelerates; global warming becomes recognized problem

FIGURE 4.1 Timeline of society and political economy.

Most production, for example, took place in or near one's home and involved all the grown members of a family and usually children as well. Family and economy were not distinct. In fact, economic activities were just a part of family life and had little existence outside families. Markets, to take another example, were as much meeting places and sites for (sometimes raucous) entertainment as they were opportunities to buy and sell. Certainly they were not the specialized institutions for the exchange of goods that economists write about. How and when one worked, who one exchanged goods with, and at what price the exchange was made were affected by, or even dictated by, ancient customs, social values, and religious and governmental decrees.

> **Embedded economy** is a description of the economy of the precapitalist epoch, which was so fully integrated into the whole society that it did not have a separate or specialized existence.

The anthropologist Karl Polanyi expressed the integration of the economy in the whole social order by saying that the precapitalist economy was *embedded* in society. Not surprisingly, at the time people did not regard "the economy" as a separate realm. They did not see economic activities as separate from other activities. The economy was there, of course, but people did not see it.

For economics to be recognized as distinct, the economy would have to become both more separate from society and more specialized. Work would have to be done in places specialized for work—factories, offices, plantations. Buying and selling would have to become the sole functions of markets. And the pursuit of economic gain—more than custom, moral scruple, or religious dictate— would have to become the guiding principle of economic life.

Capitalism brought about all three changes, and as a result the economy became *disembedded.* It was still part of society, but it had become separate enough and specialized enough to warrant a distinct type of investigation. The birth of economics awaited only minds creative enough to sense the new realities. In the 18th century a number of thinkers moved in this direction, but Adam Smith turned out to be the most perceptive.

ADAM SMITH

The first in the lineage of political economy is Adam Smith, whose great book, *The Wealth of Nations,* was published in 1776, the same year as the U.S. Declaration of Independence.

> **Laissez-faire** is an approach to economic policy that advocates a very limited role for the government, confining its activities to national defense and the enforcement of laws and contracts.

The Wealth of Nations is the most influential book on economics ever written. In it Smith expounds the idea that rather than to try to direct the economy, the government should leave well enough alone. This is roughly the meaning of the French expression *laissez-faire,* which has ever since been associated with Smith's thinking.

Adam Smith was a pioneer in understanding markets and in studying how whole economies composed of many markets work as integrated systems. Since every school of economics regards the workings of markets as important, Smith is widely regarded as the founding father of the discipline. Smith and the leading economists in the two generations that followed him are called the "classical economists." Three of Smith's ideas are key to the development of political economy.

First, Smith identified the basic challenge of economics: how can society *coordinate* the independent activities of large numbers of economic actors—producers, transporters, sellers, consumers—often unknown to one another and widely scattered across the world? This problem of coordination arises because no person is self-sufficient: everyone's livelihood requires a multiplicity of goods and services produced by others. Thus, Smith focused his attention on the *division of labor,* the fact that in all economic systems some people produce certain things while others produce different things, all the different outputs being necessary for the livelihood of all and everyone being economically interdependent with everyone else.

Second, Smith developed the idea—a very radical position to take in his day—that society could leave the coordination of the division of labor up to the individual self-interest of the economic actors themselves. This idea was radical because it asserted that a rational order might arise without any person or institution consciously attempting to create or maintain order. Earlier philosophers such as Thomas Hobbes, an English writer a century before Smith, had advocated a powerful government as the only means by which the self-seeking activities of large numbers of people could result in order rather than chaos. Smith argued that markets, or rather systems of markets, could do the job as long as two conditions were in place. Property rights would have to be well defined, so as to make it clear who owned—and therefore could exchange—what. Also, there would have to be enough competition among the many economic actors that no market was monopolized. We will explore his reasoning on these points in later chapters.

Third, Smith explained how a system of competitive markets could translate the self-interested actions of individuals into results beneficial for society. This was, again, a truly radical departure since it came at a time when selfish behavior was regarded as immoral. Smith argued that while the self-interested activity of the farmer or the barber may be based on greed, the pursuit of that greed will—under the right conditions—benefit all. Thus, socially beneficial results will be produced by well-defined property rights and competitive markets behind the backs of the people who make up the economy, even if most people care little or nothing for the well-being of their neighbors. Smith coined the phrase *the invisible hand* to refer to the tendency of markets to guide the economy toward the best use of its human and natural resources.

In Smith's view, then, markets would regulate the economy and harness self-interest to achieve material progress for the whole society. He warned the government against taking on inappropriate tasks, in particular the direction of individuals in their economic activities.

Smith's idea of limiting government's role in the economy was far from one-sided, however. He repeated the usual arguments that government should protect the nation from external enemies and assure internal justice with police and a system of courts; he also advocated government investments in bridges, roads, canals, and other "public works" (such as free education for all children) and proposed the imposition of taxes on alcohol to discourage drunkenness.

In other words, Smith saw that there were many valid exceptions to his general argument for minimal government intervention in the economy. He was also acutely concerned with the sometimes negative human consequences of the pursuit of economic gain. He worried, for example, that England might turn into a country of mindless robots if something were not done to alleviate the oppressive and mind-numbing conditions in its factories.

Moreover, Smith often took the side of the poor against the rich. In his chapter on wages in *The Wealth of Nations,* he wrote: "No society can surely be flourishing or happy, of which the far greater part of the members are poor and miserable. It is but equity, besides, that they

ADAM SMITH: PROPHET OF CAPITALISM (1723–1790)

There was nothing particularly routine or normal about Adam Smith's life. At age four he was kidnapped by gypsies (and later returned to his family). At age 14 he enrolled at the University of Glasgow. It is said that he once left home sleepwalking in his pajamas and traveled 15 miles before waking up. Another time he fell into a tanning vat while walking with a colleague, deep in conversation.

What was most unusual about Smith, however, was the range of his intelligence and his bent for radical ideas. He held the chair of moral philosophy at the University of Glasgow and lectured his students on "natural theology, ethics, jurisprudence, and expediency," in that order, the latter being his term for economics. While earlier philosophers had attempted to tame the selfish side of people, Smith sought to put their self-interest to good use: "It is not from the benevolence of the butcher, the brewer, or the baker, that we expect our dinner," he wrote, "but from their regard to their own interest."

Though his advocacy of laissez-faire has made Smith quite popular today, contemporary proponents of business-friendly policies often neglect to mention Smith's criticisms of capitalism. The advice of businessmen to governments, he warned, "ought always to be listened to with great precaution, and ought never to be adopted till after having been long and carefully examined . . . with the most suspicious attention. It comes from an order of men, whose interest is never exactly the same with that of the public, who have generally an interest to deceive and even to oppress the public." Moreover, the pursuit of self-interest does not always benefit society as a whole: "People of the same trade seldom meet together," he wrote, "but the conversation ends in a conspiracy against the public."

Perhaps most telling was Adam Smith's concern that the rise of the factory system, which he hoped would lead to a more affluent future, might, in fact, bring about the degradation of human labor. Pointing out that division of labor results in specialization of tasks, and noting that peoples' intellectual capacities "are necessarily formed by their ordinary employments," Smith concluded as follows: "The man whose whole life is spent in performing a few simple operations . . . has no occasion to exert his understanding. . . . He naturally loses, therefore, the habit of such exertion, and generally becomes as stupid and ignorant as it is possible for a human creature to become."

Sources: Robert Heilbroner, *The Worldly Philosophers* (New York: Simon & Schuster, 1999), Ch. III; Andrew S. Skinner, "Adam Smith" in John Eatwell et al., eds., *The New Palgrave: A Dictionary of Economics* (London: Macmillan, 1987); Emma Rothschild, *Economic Sentiments: Adam Smith, Condorcet, and the Enlightenment* (Cambridge, Mass.: Harvard University Press, 2001); Adam Smith, *The Wealth of Nations* (New York: Random House, 1937), Book I, Chs. II, VIII, X, XI; Book IV, Ch. IX; Book V, Ch. I.

who feed, clothe and lodge the whole body of the people should have such a share of the produce of their own labor as to be themselves tolerably well fed, clothed and lodged." However, in another part of the book he observed: "Wherever there is great property, there is great inequality. For one very rich man, there must be at least five hundred poor, and the affluence of the few supposes the indigence of the many." Not one to shy away from hard facts, Smith went on to say: "Civil government, so far as it is instituted for the security of property, is in reality instituted for the defense of the rich against the poor."

KARL MARX

The second major contributor to political economy was the 19th-century economist and philosopher Karl Marx. If Smith was capitalism's prophet, Marx was its critic. His contribution was to reformulate the classical economists' theories in such a way as to provide the original version of what in this book is called the three-dimensional approach to economics, or political economy.

Marx first mastered the theories of the classical economists—Adam Smith, David Ricardo, and others—and then developed a criticism of their ideas and an alternative way of looking at capitalism. While the classical economists writing at the time of the birth of capitalism had believed that the emerging capitalist economy would work for the benefit of all, Marx and his frequent coauthor, Friedrich Engels, had seen enough of the real history of capitalism to have a different view. They saw the immense productivity of modern industry juxtaposed with the grinding poverty and economic insecurity of England's new industrial towns. Marx argued that there were three elements that needed to be emphasized in, or added to, the classical economists' models.

First, there is conflict as well as harmony when it comes to economic interests. When two individuals trade with each other in a voluntary exchange, both benefit—otherwise why would they trade? This is the lesson of neoclassical economics, for which economics is mostly the study of exchange (or competition). But not all exchanges result in equal benefits for all the parties to them. Marx noted that the conditions under which people make trades—remember the robber's terms, "Your money or your life!"—affect the outcomes of those trades. He argued, moreover, that the exercise of power, coercion, and force (what we call "command") is a significant factor in most economic systems.

With regard specifically to capitalism, Marx observed that some people (employers) own the productive assets such as land, factories, and office buildings, while most people (workers) do not own these types of assets. The result is that there are differences in power as well as income, and these differences shape the economic relationships among the different classes of people in a capitalist economy.

Second, Marx expanded on Adam Smith's ideas about self-interest by observing that groups as well as individuals may act together to defend and advance their interests. Conventional economic textbooks focus on competitive market relations and on individual economic actors or agents. But people often act cooperatively in groups, and an approach that focuses exclusively on individual competitive behavior will miss this important aspect of human interaction.

KARL MARX: CRITIC OF CAPITALISM (1818–1883)

Few scholars have been as revered or as hated as Karl Marx. Though he was born in Germany and began his career as a journalist there, he spent a good part of his early years on the run. His newspaper, *Rheinische Zeitung,* was closed by the government because in it he advocated freedom of the press and other democratic rights unpopular with the autocratic rulers of the day. Seeking a more tolerant environment, he moved to Paris but was soon expelled for writing articles exposing poverty and economic injustice and advocating radical solutions to these problems. In 1848 he moved to London with his wife and family, often barely making a living by writing articles for such newspapers as the *New York Daily Tribune.* (His mother once commented, "Karl, I wish you would *make* some capital instead of just writing about it.") He remained in England, writing *Capital* and working with his friend and sometime coauthor, Friedrich Engels, until his death in 1883.

Capitalism, according to Marx, is an economic system that constantly expands the potential of society to harness science and human labor so as to meet the needs of people. In *The Communist Manifesto*—probably the most widely read pamphlet ever published—Marx and Engels wrote: "The bourgeoisie [meaning the capitalist class], during its rule of scarce[ly] one hundred years, has created more massive and more colossal productive forces than have all preceding generations together."

Marx dedicated the latter half of his life to a study of the capitalist economy. But he believed that an alternative to capitalism—he called it communism—could continue or even speed up the growth of the economy's productive potential while at the same time making better use of this potential. However, of the thousands of pages that Marx wrote, only a handful outlined his vision of a post-capitalist society. His main interest was in understanding how capitalism worked, not in designing an alternative to it

Marx advocated democratic reforms that were considered radical at the time, including the direct election of political leaders by universal suffrage, and he termed the American Civil War and the end of slavery "the one great event of contemporary history." But as Marxism became the official dogma of communism following Marx's death, these democratic ideas fell by the wayside. The leaders of the Soviet Union, China, and other Communist nations imposed forms of dictatorship far more oppressive than those Marx had criticized as a young journalist. As these countries abandoned their Communist systems starting in the late 1980s, the official dogmas bearing Marx's name fell into disuse. In spite of this

Continued . . .

(or perhaps because of it), many of Marx's ideas, including the importance of the economy as a factor in historical change, the division of societies into classes, and the contribution that conflict sometimes makes to progress, have become widely accepted even by people who might be surprised to know the origin of their ideas.

Sources: David McLellan, *Karl Marx: His Life and Thought* (New York: Harper & Row, 1973); John Cassidy, "The Return of Karl Marx," *The New Yorker,* October 20/27, 1997, pp. 248–259.

Of course, there exist many different groups, and these groups may be of different sizes, may have overlapping memberships, may be tightly or loosely organized, and may have different purposes. Thus, there are football fans, steel manufacturers, corn farmers, blacks, and Catholics, to mention just a few examples. Marx emphasized the importance of *economic classes* such as workers and employers or slaves and slave owners. Within such classes, he argued, people often act together to promote their common interests while also taking care of, or possibly even advancing, their own individual interests. We define and flesh out the concept of class in the chapters that follow.

Marx argued that capitalism itself is an obstacle to the full development of a society's productive potential. This is because, in his view, the conflictual owner-worker relationship at the heart of a capitalist economy blocks the adoption of many advances in technology and knowledge that, even though they would increase productivity, would also reduce the rate of profit of certain companies or eliminate jobs in a particular industry and would therefore be resisted by the companies involved or the unions representing the workers who would be displaced. Examples of these problems might include the opposition by oil companies to the development of alternative energy sources, the resistance (in the past) of dockworkers' unions to the introduction of container shipping technology, and music companies' attempts to design "copy-proof" systems of sound reproduction. More generally, in a capitalist society the pursuit of private economic gain, in Marx's view, consumes human intelligence and energy that might otherwise be directed toward meeting human needs.

Third, Marx emphasized that economic systems change over time, especially in response to their own operations. Rather than thinking of an economic system as a fixed set of relationships (for example, competitive markets and voluntary exchange), he insisted that the operation of an economic system itself tends to change the conditions within which economic activity is carried on. Marx argued specifically that capitalism fuels economic change, leads to the growth of cities, propels increases in material abundance, induces global migrations, fosters changes in family life, and will ultimately bring about its own destruction.

JOSEPH SCHUMPETER

A third great contributor to political economy was Joseph A. Schumpeter, an early 20th-century lawyer, financier, businessman, and economist who was born in what is now the Czech Republic, spent much of his life in the European academic and business worlds, and, from 1932 until his death in 1950, was a distinguished professor of economics at Harvard University. Schumpeter tackled the big problems in economics. The title of his most

JOSEPH SCHUMPETER: ADVOCATE OF "CREATIVE DESTRUCTION" (1883–1950)

The aristocratic and the modern were inextricably combined in Joseph Schumpeter. The paradoxes of this great economist, who also served as minister of finance in the post–World War I government of Austria, are suggested by the fact that at his first teaching post, he challenged the university librarian to a duel to win freer access to books for the students.

Perhaps Schumpeter was attracted to the big issues because he himself witnessed drastic changes in society. He was raised in pre–World War I Vienna, a city dominated by a glittering aristocracy made rich by the immense wealth of triumphant late 19th-century capitalism. The city was a center of splendorous art, music, opera, palaces, and balls. Yet there was an air of impending doom in Viennese high society. The propertied classes were imbued with a sense that this privileged and beautiful life could not last. Poor working people crowded the industrial districts of the city, and the whole Austrian empire, of which Vienna was the capital, tottered. Bourgeois life seemed like an overripe fruit ready to drop as soon as the tree was shaken. Although Schumpeter identified with the aristocracy and valued its culture, he could see that capitalism was an enormously dynamic system, one that was continually changing society and disrupting established (and by Schumpeter cherished) institutions.

Although Schumpeter was a staunch defender of capitalism, he had a gloomy view of its future. Just after World War II and a year before his death, he warned the American Economic Association of what he termed "the march into socialism." He believed that capitalism would solve the production problems of society, but he also thought that its success would sow the seeds of its own demise. Specifically, he anticipated that large organizations, because of their bloated bureaucracies, would destroy the climate for innovation, and he also predicted that the intellectual classes would turn against the system, removing its cultural and ideological legitimacy. Thus, after beginning his speech to his economics colleagues saying "I do not advocate socialism," he went on to suggest that he was not hopeful about the future of capitalism: "Capitalism does not merely mean that the housewife may influence production by her choice between peas and beans; or that the youngster may choose whether he wants to work in a factory or on a farm; . . . it means a scheme of values, an attitude toward life, a civilization—the civilization of inequality and of the family fortune. This civilization is rapidly passing away."

Unlike so much of what Schumpeter wrote, this assessment has not been borne out by history—or at least not yet. The decades following Schumpeter's warning were in many ways a golden age for the capitalist economy in America, Europe, and elsewhere.

Sources: Robert Loring Allen, *Opening Doors: The Life and Work of Joseph Schumpeter,* 2 vols. (New Brunswick, N.J.: Transaction Publishers, 1991); Joseph Schumpeter, *Capitalism, Socialism, and Democracy* (New York: Harper & Row, 1942), pp. 83, 416, 419.

famous book, *Capitalism, Socialism, and Democracy,* indicates the range of his intellect and interests. He added to our understanding of capitalism in three ways.

First, he deepened Marx's argument that capitalism creates change, once saying that "Capitalism is by nature a form or method of economic change and not only never is, but never can be stationary."[1] For Schumpeter, change—our time dimension—had to be central to any economic theory. Among his many novel ideas, the most powerful are his theories regarding innovation, on the one hand, and disruptive change, on the other. He called the connection between the two "creative destruction" and applied the term not only to technological innovation but to organizational and social change as well. Capitalism, he wrote, constantly revolutionizes economic institutions and creates new ones. For progress to occur, old methods of doing business must be disrupted in a creative burst. The idea of creative destruction is that old ways must be destroyed to create the basis for new leaps forward.

In Schumpeter's view the important thing about competition is not what is presented in conventional economics textbooks: price competition taking place among small firms under unchanging circumstances. Rather, for him the significance of competition lies in the incentives it provides for firms to achieve monopolies and breakthroughs based on continuous profit seeking and innovation. For Schumpeter, then, it seemed appropriate to explain competition not with mechanical analogies but rather with references to military strategy and counterstrategy.

Second, Schumpeter argued that innovations combined with the competitive edge conferred by advantages of large-scale production result in a tendency for large businesses to dominate small businesses in a capitalist economy. His views on innovation and creative destruction brought Schumpeter to see large-scale enterprises in a novel way. Whereas conventional economics textbooks usually present big businesses as impediments to competition and hence as a source of inefficiency and misallocation of resources, Schumpeter argued that such companies make possible the concentration of resources required for making big innovative jumps. Whereas the conventional textbooks focus on the negative effects of a monopoly at a particular moment in time, Schumpeter envisioned the dynamic potential inherent in concentrations of economic power. We consider this point further in a later chapter.

Third, Schumpeter looked at the broad history of capitalism and wrote about what have come to be called "long waves," or "long swings," in economic activity. A long swing, also known as a "Kondratieff cycle" in memory of the early 20th-century Russian economist who first noticed it, is an extended period of prosperity, or boom, that lasts perhaps for 20 or 30 years and is followed by a lengthy period of stagnation, or economic hard times.

JOHN MAYNARD KEYNES

Considered by many to be the greatest economist of the 20th century, the Englishman John Maynard Keynes was another very important contributor to political economy. Combining theory with practice, he gave advice to the British government before and during World War II and also played a major role at the 1944 Bretton Woods (New Hampshire)

---

[1] Joseph Schumpeter, *Capitalism, Socialism, and Democracy* (New York: Harper & Row, 1942), p. 82.

conference that established the institutional framework, including the International Monetary Fund and the World Bank, for the postwar global economy.

Keynes greatly influenced both neoclassical economics and political economy. However, the version of Keynesian theory that appears in conventional economics textbooks today—Keynes's collaborator Joan Robinson termed it "bastard Keynesianism"—does not accurately convey the ideas of this great economist.

Keynes's main contribution to political economy was to provide a model of the capitalist economy as a whole. Pioneering what is now called "macroeconomics," Keynes observed that in a modern capitalist economy there are often unemployed people looking for work while at the same time there are underutilized factories. He concluded that government intervention is needed to overcome chronic unemployment.

In neoclassical economic theory, unemployment exists only as a temporary problem as people move between jobs. Before Keynes many economists reasoned as follows: in a competitive labor market the wage will settle at the level at which the supply of labor by workers will be exactly equal to the demand for labor by employers—hence the presence of unemployment is only a sign that some workers are asking for a wage that is too high. In the neoclassical model, then, unemployment is either *temporary* or *voluntary unemployment,* brought on by workers themselves asking for a higher wage than the one that would equalize the supply of and demand for their labor. Accordingly, all but temporary unemployment could be eliminated if workers would only agree to work for a lower wage. (We explain in Chapter 8 how "supply" and "demand" interact in markets.)

Some economists today analyze employment and unemployment in the same way that they explain why lowering the prices of automobiles will clear a car dealer's lot of unsold inventory. They believe that in every market there is an *equilibrium price* that equates supply to demand. The proposition is applied to the labor market by treating the wage as the "price" of labor. Thus, if the supply of labor is equal to the demand for labor, everyone who wants to work (that is, to supply labor) should be able to find a job. If there is unemployment, it can be eliminated in the same way the car dealer would move his unsold supply of cars out of the lot, that is by lowering the "price" of labor until the supply of it is equal to the demand for it.

Keynes rejected this reasoning. He argued that unemployment results not from wages being too high but from the demand for the goods that labor produces being too low. And if the problem is insufficient demand for output, said Keynes, the cure might be to raise rather than cut wages. His reasoning was that since wages pay for the goods people consume and thus make possible a large part of the demand for the output of the economy, higher wages might lead to an increase in demand that, in turn, would lead to an expansion of output, increased employment, and less unemployment.

Keynes's theory demonstrated (a) that capitalism has no automatic mechanism for eliminating unemployment and (b) that unemployment in a capitalist economy may well be *involuntary unemployment,* that is, unemployment that would not go away even if wages were lowered. Published in 1936, shortly after the Great Depression had driven the rate of unemployment in the U.S. up to 25 percent, Keynes's most important book, *The General Theory of Employment, Interest, and Money,* took the economics profession by storm. In his book Keynes challenged Adam Smith's view of the economy as a self-adjusting mechanism and advocated a type of government intervention in the economy that would regulate total demand for output in order to reduce unemployment.

JOHN MAYNARD KEYNES: SAVIOR OF CAPITALISM (1883–1946)

John Maynard Keynes was born in the same year in which Karl Marx died. Keynes was no revolutionary, but his ideas revolutionized 20th-century economics.

Keynes spent much of his career at Cambridge University, first as a student and then as a teacher, as an editor of a professional journal, and as a writer of numerous articles and books on economics. He was also a leading member of the elite English literary circle known as the Bloomsbury Group, and the story of his personal life includes a number of serious romantic and sexual relationships with men as well as a long-lasting and passionate marriage to the famous Diaghilev ballerina Lydia Lopokova.

Keynes served both as a director of the Bank of England and as the financial adviser to Cambridge University's King's College, where he had been a student and subsequently became a highly regarded member of the faculty. His speculations in financial markets increased the assets of King's College 10-fold. In reward for his important service to the British government, Keynes was appointed to the House of Lords by the king of England.

Because some think that Keynesian policies prevented a second Great Depression, Keynes is often credited with having saved capitalism. If so, it was not out of love for the capitalist system. In 1933 he wrote: "The decadent international but individualistic capitalism, in the hands of which we found ourselves after the [First World] War, is not a success. It is not intelligent, it is not beautiful, it is not just, it is not virtuous—and it doesn't deliver the goods. In short, we dislike it and we are beginning to despise it. But when we wonder what to put in its place, we are extremely perplexed."

Though he favored a larger role for government and advocated policies to reduce unemployment, he did not think of himself as a socialist or as an ally of the working class: "When it comes to the class struggle as such," he wrote, "my [own] personal patriotisms . . . are attached to my own surroundings . . . [and] the class war will find me on the side of the educated bourgeoisie."

Sources: Robert Skidelsky, *John Maynard Keynes,* 3 vols. (New York: Viking Penguin, 1986, 1994, 2001); J. M. Keynes, "National Self-Sufficiency," *The Yale Review,* vol. 22, summer 1933, pp. 755–769; J. M. Keynes, "Am I a Liberal?" (1925), in *Essays in Persuasion* (New York: Norton, 1963), pp. 323–338.

Keynes explained that the process of investment and growth in a capitalist economy depends on a precarious balance between what are now called the cost conditions affecting investment and the demand conditions affecting investment. Left to its own devices, he argued, a capitalist economy is not likely to achieve this balance in such a way as to provide jobs all the time for all who seek them. For this reason Keynes urged the adoption of policies that, when necessary, would increase the government's demand for goods and services. Such policies, he argued, could help to maintain a level of total demand (including also that of consumers and businesses) sufficient to ensure both full employment and adequate profits.

Because he supported the idea of more government involvement in the economy, Keynes's theories were initially regarded as "dangerously radical" by some business groups. But what came to be known as Keynesian economics gradually became the accepted basis of government policy. John F. Kennedy, a Democrat elected in 1960, is considered to have been the first Keynesian president, but it was a Republican president, Richard Nixon, who proclaimed a decade later: "We are all Keynesians now." Partly as a result of the spread of Keynes's ideas in the advanced capitalist countries, major depressions have been avoided in the post–World War II era, and unemployment rates have been generally lower than they had been before the war.

RECENT DEVELOPMENTS

During the last half of the 20th century, economics, which had long since ceased to be called political economy, became a unified but increasingly narrow field of study strongly influenced by Adam Smith's "invisible hand" metaphor and, to a lesser extent, by the work of John Maynard Keynes. In economics courses students rarely encountered the ideas of Joseph Schumpeter, and those of Karl Marx were hardly taught at all. Thus, the workings of markets became the main focus of economics. The "creative destruction" occasioned by technical change and economic progress and the class conflicts arising from economic inequalities were thought to be of little interest. Of the three dimensions of what we term three-dimensional economics—competition, command, and change—only the first was seriously studied. Command and change were relegated to political science, history, or other disciplines. The "one-dimensional" approach, described in the previous chapter as *neoclassical economics*, eclipsed its rivals, except in the Communist countries, where a crude version of Marxian economics ("bastard Marxism") dominated the curriculum.

However, as the mainstream of 20th-century academic economics moved further and further away from the ideas of Schumpeter and Marx, the real-world problems that had stimulated their thinking stayed around in one form or another. As described in Chapter 1, the global economy continued on its lurching course, buffeted by rapid technological developments, climate change, and a widening gulf between the world's haves and have-nots. Conflicts within and between nations continued unabated, and the role of hierarchy—command—in economic life was at least as prominent at the end of the 20th century as it had been a century earlier.

It is not surprising, then, that a series of innovations occurred in the discipline of economics in the final quarter of the 20th century, some of which are now widely accepted and commonly taught in economics courses. A few of the new ideas were set forth earlier in the century but came to be fully appreciated only in recent decades. For example, game theory, the study of how individuals interact strategically (buying, selling, bargaining, threatening, commanding, and submitting), was developed just after World War II by several scholars, including John Nash (played by Russell Crowe in the film *A Beautiful Mind*). Only recently, however, has game theory become widely studied and practiced in economics. It is introduced in Chapter 9 of this book with accounts of "the prisoner's dilemma" and "the tragedy of the commons."

Some of the late 20th-century innovators in economics won Nobel Prizes. Recent honorees include Douglass North and Robert Fogel, who focused mainly on economic institutions and their history; Gary Becker, who expanded the scope of economics to include analyses of the family, schooling, addiction, and crime; Kenneth Arrow, who is at once one of the greatest contributors to neoclassical economics and one of its most trenchant critics; Joseph Stiglitz and George Akerlof, who challenged the neoclassical economists' theory of how markets work; and Daniel Kahneman and Herbert Simon, whose contributions were in the psychology of individual behavior (they were not even economists by training). Also among the Nobel Laureates who have made major contributions to contemporary economics are Ronald Coase and Amartya Sen, both of whom advocate taking an interdisciplinary approach to the study of economic problems. It is an irony as well as a tribute to his intellect that Coase is considered to be a conservative even though one of his most important ideas is an extension of some of Karl Marx's thinking. It is equally ironic that Amartya Sen, usually considered a progressive economist, derived much of his inspiration from some long-ignored ideas of Adam Smith.

RONALD COASE

This great 20th-century thinker made two important contributions to political economy. First, he showed that, with its exclusive focus on market interactions, neoclassical economics cannot explain some very important aspects of a modern economy unless its approach is broadened. Second, he found a way to specify precisely the conditions under which a completely unregulated market economy would achieve efficient (if possibly unfair) solutions to problems.

At the age of 27 (in 1937), Coase posed a question that shocked many economists: if market competition is as good as Adam Smith and his successors claim it is, why do we have anything *other than* markets? In particular, why do we have entities called "firms," ranging in size from dozens to hundreds of thousands of people, that are organized not by exchange relations but by command relations, with some people (supervisors, executives) giving orders to other people (workers)? In his pioneering and now classic article "The Nature of the Firm," Coase made the following statement: "It is important to note the character of the contract into which a [worker] enters [when he or she] is employed within a firm." With regard to the "character" of such an employment contract, Coase went on to say that the worker "for certain remuneration . . . agrees to obey the directions of an entrepreneur [employer]."

Having introduced the concept of obedience to authority, Coase proceeded to define the firm with reference to its *political,* not its market, structure: "If a workman moves from department Y to department X, he does not go because of a change in prices but because he is ordered to do so . . . [T]he distinguishing mark of the firm is the suppression of the price mechanism." Coase then observed, quoting one of his contemporaries, that firms are to the market like "islands of conscious power in this ocean of unconscious cooperation[,] like lumps of butter coagulating in a pail of buttermilk."[2] Writers after Coase have referred to the authority structure of the firm as a "visible hand" that works in combination with Smith's invisible hand. The everyday fact that employers exercise power over their employees—not news to most employees—had been a central theme in Marx's economics, but it was (and generally continues to be) overlooked by most neoclassical economists.

Early in his studies Coase noted the similarity between the hierarchical organization of capitalist firms, with their reliance on command relations, and the then-existing system of centralized economic planning in the Communist countries, where production was carried out in accordance with orders from higher authorities and where market competition played little role. This similarity intrigued Coase because most economists, then as now, believed that economies based on command relations do not work very well.

Coase stated the issue as follows: "How [does] one reconcile the views expressed by economists on the role of the pricing system [markets] and the impossibility of successful central economic planning with the existence . . . of these apparently planned societies, firms, operating within our own society?" Answering his own question, he first noted that there are costs of carrying out exchanges—for example, finding someone to exchange with, haggling over prices, and making sure that a contract is fulfilled—and he called such costs *transactions costs.* Using this novel concept, he then went on to argue that for some kinds of activities, at least, the cost of running things from the top down is less than the cost of getting them done with reliance only on market exchanges. His conclusion was that firms exist because the transactions costs of organizing what they do by command are less than the transactions costs would be of organizing the same activities by market exchanges.

Coase's idea had the ring of truth about it. Imagine how much time and effort would be wasted if, instead of being organized in a team with a boss, workers on a production line were all independent contractors, each contributing to the completion of a product, pausing to sell it to the next person on the line, and then turning to the person "upstream" to buy another less complete product. Alternatively, imagine the cooks at a fast food restaurant selling cooked burgers to the wait staff, who then sell them to the customers.

The idea of transactions costs has become central to our understanding of how markets work, why they do not work well in certain situations, and when nonmarket organizations such as families, firms, and governments may do a better job of organizing production. Where transactions costs are substantial—and Coase believed that this is just about everywhere—neoclassical economics falls short. He summarized his critique as follows: "In an economic theory which assumes that transactions costs are non-existent, markets have no function to perform and it seems perfectly reasonable to develop the theory of exchange by an elaborate analysis of individuals exchanging nuts for apples in the edge of the forest or some similar fanciful example."

In the real world, economic activities take place not only in markets but also in institutions such as firms and families. And nonmarket transactions differ in important ways from market exchanges. As we explain in later chapters, the employment of labor, the

---

[2] The quotations from Ronald Coase here and in the preceding paragraph are from Ronald Coase, "The Nature of the Firm," *Economica,* vol. 4, 1937, pp. 386–405, as reprinted in Louis Putterman and Randall Krozner, eds., *The Economic Nature of the Firm: A Reader,* 2nd ed. (New York: Cambridge University Press, 1996), pp. 89–104.

taking out of loans, and even purchases of new computer systems are hardly the same as buying and selling nuts and apples. The varieties of capitalism in the world today are distinguished from one another by how they govern transactions in firms, markets, governments, and other institutions.

Coase's other big idea was to point out that one does not necessarily need the invisible hand of the market to make a completely decentralized laissez-faire economy work; unimpeded private bargaining might do the trick.

A classic argument against the invisible hand and in favor of government regulation focuses on situations in which the activities of one person (or firm) impose costs on another (or others). In these situations, such as environmental pollution, for instance, there are what economists call *spillover* effects (or externalities). (These were defined in Chapter 3 and are discussed at length in Chapter 9.)

Taking the now-quaint example that Coase himself used, suppose that a railroad passes through farming country and that the grass in fields adjacent to the tracks is occasionally set on fire by sparks from passing engines (the trains he was referring to were still pulled by coal-fired steam engines). Before Coase it was taken for granted that railroads should be held liable in a court of law for any such damages done to farmers' fields. Alternatively, it was held that the government should simply require the railroad to install "spark-free" engines.

Coase's response to the problem was both surprising and ingenious: the engines should be redesigned only if the damage they imposed on farmers was greater than the cost to the railroad of redesigning the engines. But if this were really the situation, the farmers would presumably offer the railroad a sufficient sum to motivate it to retire the offending engines. In this case, both parties might come out ahead: the farmers would end up with more value in their fully-grown crops than it cost them to pay the railroad, and the railroad would be better off with whatever amount of cash the two parties had agreed on than it would have been if it had been sued in court for the entire amount of the damages or if its incendiary engines had been banned by the government.

In this case there seems to be no need for government regulation: a satisfactory solution to the problem is available privately by means of bargaining between the farmers and the railroad over the appropriate payment in return for the redesign of the engines. However, such a solution is possible under only two conditions. The first is that both parties have clearly established property rights to whatever is involved in the conflict. (This condition does not exist in many spillover situations, such as environmental pollution, when the air or water affected belongs to nobody in particular.) The second condition is that there be no impediments hindering either party's ability to bargain with the other party. This would be the case only in situations in which there are no transactions costs.

Coase did not argue that the farmers (not the railroad) should actually pay for the redesign of the coal-fired engines: the question of who pays is an entirely different issue. He simply pointed out that *in the absence of transactions costs,* the spillover problem can (theoretically) be solved in many situations without government regulation. The extent to which transactions costs hinder the bargaining is something that must be factually determined on a case-by-case basis. If there were just a single farmer, for example, bargaining would be a lot less costly than if there were a thousand, and the situation would be more complicated if there were some farmers with fields near the rail line and some whose fields were more distant from it.

RONALD COASE: THE INVISIBLE HAND AND THE VISIBLE HAND (1910–)

When Ronald Coase received the Nobel Prize at the age of 81, he recalled that while growing up in England at the time of World War I, he was "often alone [but] never lonely." "When I learnt chess, I was happy to play the role of each player in turn." A taste for solitude would serve him well, for he was to be a maverick: his first published article, "The Nature of the Firm," written in his mid-20s, was ignored for decades.

Both of his parents had left school at the age of 12, and both worked at the Post Office. Coase's own education was somewhat haphazard, with a false start in chemistry ("the mathematics was not to my taste"). That he won the Nobel Prize in Economics, he explained at his award ceremony, "was the result of a series of accidents." One such "accident" had to do with the origin of his most famous article, "The Problem of Social Cost." A group of professors at the University of Chicago—among them some of the leading exponents of conservative laissez-faire economics—had read a paper by Coase and considered it to be mistaken. They invited him to dinner to correct his error, but it was Coase who prevailed, and they then persuaded him to repeat his reasoning in print. It was this paper that made the so-called Coase Theorem famous and, more than anything else, won him the Nobel Prize. There is actually no theorem—there is not a single equation in the article (remember his math aversion)—but one of his dinner partners that night thought it would be catchy to call the idea a theorem, and the term caught on. Shortly thereafter he was offered a professorship at the University of Chicago Law School, where he taught until his retirement in 1979.

Because the so-called theorem appeared to advocate a limited economic role for government, Coase became a hero of many conservative economists and business groups. But, in fact, he was a critic of the then-dominant neoclassical approach to economics. Eschewing the highly abstract and mathematical approach of most economists, he urged others "to write about the way in which actual markets operate and about how governments actually perform." He chided his fellow economists for knowing little about the institutions of a capitalist economy and for giving bad advice to other countries, especially those that had rejected communism in the early 1990s: "Without the appropriate institutions no market economy of any significance is possible. If we knew more about our own economy, we would be in a better position to advise them."

Sources: Ronald Coase, autobiography, published on the Nobel Prize website: http://www.nobel.se/economics/laureates/1991/coase-autobio.html; Ronald H. Coase, "The Nature of the Firm," *Economica,* vol. 4, 1937, pp. 386–405; Ronald H. Coase, "The Problem of Social Cost," *Journal of Law and Economics,* vol. 3, no. 1, 1960, pp. 1–44; Ronald H. Coase, "The Institutional Structure of Production," *American Economic Review,* vol. 82, no. 4, 1992, pp. 713–719; Ronald H. Coase, *The Firm, the Market and the Law* (Chicago and London: University of Chicago Press, 1988).

Art Source: From Mark Blaug, *Great Economists since Keynes: An Introduction to the Lives and Works of One Hundred Modern Economists* (Cambridge University Press, 1985).

The key assumption—the absence of transactions costs—is crucial, and it is often ignored by advocates who use Coase's work to support their arguments against government regulation of business activities, such as those that degrade the environment or result in other spillovers. Coase himself made the implications of his work clear: "Of course it does not imply, when transactions costs are positive, that government actions . . . could not produce a better result than relying on negotiations between individuals in the market. Whether this would be so could be discovered not by studying imaginary governments but what real governments actually do. My conclusion: let us study the world of positive transactions costs."

AMARTYA SEN

Like Ronald Coase, Amartya Sen is also motivated by concerns about the world as it really is, but Sen's contributions are of an entirely different nature. Addressing deep philosophical issues and often using advanced mathematical techniques, Sen has taken up precisely the questions of fairness that Coase set aside in his famous "theorem."

What does it mean to say that someone is "well off" or " better off" than another person? How can we measure these things? And how can policies help to establish conditions that allow most people to be well off? Sen begins his paper "The Economics of Life and Death" with the following statements: "Economics is not solely concerned with income and wealth but also with using these resources as means to significant ends, including the promotion and enjoyment of long and worthwhile lives. If, however, the economic success of a nation is judged only by income . . . the important goal of well-being is missed." Well-being, to Sen, requires more than *having* things; it requires *being able to do* things, or what he terms *capabilities*. Of course, the goods and services that income can buy are crucial to well-being in Sen's sense, but they are a *means* to well-being, not ends in their own right. More than income is required.

Sen points out that some very poor people—for example, the populations of China, Sri Lanka, and the Indian state of Kerala—are much healthier on average than are poor people in countries five times richer (by the standard of average income) such as Brazil and South Africa. The difference is due to two things. First, income is very unequally distributed in Brazil and South Africa, so the poor in those countries suffer severe deprivation of nutrition and other necessities. Second, Kerala, China, and Sri Lanka have adopted public health policies that address many of the needs of the most vulnerable members of their populations.

Rather than measuring the economic development of nations by such indexes as average income and then devising policies to raise income levels, Sen proposes that we make our concept of well-being explicit. He begins his book *Development as Freedom* with these words: "Development can be seen . . . as a process of expanding the real freedoms that people enjoy. . . . If freedom is what development advances, then there is a major argument for concentrating on that overarching objective rather than some particular means." Sen goes on to say that "Development requires the removal of major sources of unfreedom," including poverty, poor economic opportunities, systematic social deprivation, intolerance, neglect of public facilities, tyranny, and repressive states.[3]

---

[3] Amartya Sen, *Development as Freedom* (New York: Random House, Anchor Books, 2000), p. 3.

AMARTYA KUMAR SEN: FREEDOM AND FAMINE (1933–)

Amartya Sen was born on a university campus in Santiniketan, near Calcutta, and wrote in his autobiography: "I . . . seem to have lived all my life in one campus or another." He has taught at Harvard, Oxford, and Cambridge Universities, the Delhi School of Economics, and the London School of Economics, and he has also served as president of the American Economic Association. Yet his contributions to economics extend from the highly abstract to the very practical. There are few economists about whom one can say with confidence "this person's research has saved lives." In the case of Sen one could say "millions of lives." Two childhood experiences shaped his career.

In his childhood home of Dhaka (now in Bangladesh), religious intolerance was rampant, and tensions ran high between Hindus and Muslims. One afternoon a man came to Sen's parents' home screaming in pain. He was a poverty stricken Muslim who had been seeking work in the mostly Hindu neighborhood. He had been stabbed in the back by a mob of Hindus. His wife had warned him not to seek work in a Hindu neighborhood, even though their family was in dire straights. Sen's father rushed the man to the hospital, but he died there of his wounds. "The experience devastated me," Sen later wrote in accepting the Nobel Prize; "it alerted me to the . . . fact that economic unfreedom, in the form of extreme poverty, can make a person a helpless prey in the violation of other kinds of freedom."

The second formative experience for Sen, also occurring before he was a teenager, was the Bengal famine of 1943. Though 2 to 3 million people perished, he later wrote: "I had been struck by its thoroughly class-dependent character. I knew of no one in my school or among my friends and relations whose family had experienced the slightest problem during the entire famine; it was not a famine that afflicted even the lower middle classes—only people much further down the economic ladder, such as landless rural laborers."

Not surprisingly, Sen's life work has addressed questions of poverty, inequality, freedom, and intolerance, reaching far beyond the usual confines of economics. In an article in *Scientific American* he showed that life expectancy is not only lower for African Americans than for European Americans, it is lower for African Americans even than for the people of China or the state of Kerala, one of India's poorest. He also documented the fact that in much of the world including India, Bangladesh, China, Pakistan, and the Middle East, female children do not have equal access to health care and nutrition. The result, he calculated, is that there are more than 100 million "missing women"—girls who did not survive their relative deprivation.

Continued . . .

In India Sen is a powerful voice for religious tolerance and for addressing the health and educational needs of the poor. Regarding antiglobalization protests, he has said: "Insofar as [the] protesters focus on the huge inequities of the world, they deserve a careful hearing, not a roughing up by [the police]." But he is for the most part a scholar, not an advocate: "I am used to thinking of the word 'academic' as meaning 'sound' rather than . . . 'unpractical,'" he remarked when accepting the Nobel Prize.

Sources: Amartya Sen, autobiography, published on the Nobel Prize website: http://www.nobel.se/economics/laureates/1998/sen-autobio.html; Amartya Sen, "The Economics of Life and Death," *Scientific American,* May 1993, pp. 40–47; Amartya Sen, "Addressing Global Poverty" in Dudley Fishburn, ed., *The World in 2002* (London: *The Economist Publications,* 2002), p. 50.

Art Source: Amartya Sen, *Development as Freedom* (New York: Alfred A. Knopf, 1999).

Given his concern for such values as freedom and tolerance, it is hardly surprising that Sen has explored the role of ethical norms in our individual behaviors. In contrast to the self-interested and amoral economic man that is the behavioral foundation of much of conventional economics, Sen observes that while selfish behavior is common, people also regularly act out of a concern (sympathy) for others, even for strangers. We also honor commitments to uphold moral norms even in circumstances in which we could benefit from violating them. (In Chapter 2 we presented evidence in support of this position.) In a paper titled "Rational Fools," Sen declares: "The purely economic man is indeed close to being a social moron."

In one of his most influential works Sen asked the very practical question: why do famines occur? The conventional answer was simple: too little food and too many mouths. But Sen showed that lack of food is rarely the cause of famine. For example, the 1974 famine in Bangladesh occurred despite the fact that per capita food availability was higher that year than it had been in the previous two years or was in the next year. The cause of the famine was massive unemployment caused by a weather-related disruption of planting activities that usually provided employment for vast numbers of poor landless workers. Without wages, the unemployed could not buy the available food, and as a result thousands starved. Moreover, as starvation spread, more affluent people began buying and hoarding large amounts of food, driving up its price and making it even further out of reach for the poor.

Thus, Sen showed that the famine resulted not from a lack of food but from an extremely uneven distribution of food caused by a very unequal distribution of income. The famine could easily have been averted had government policies been used to support the buying power of the poor. A contributing factor was that U.S. food shipments were held up during the famine (due to a dispute about Bangladeshi exports to Cuba), but the main failures were those of the government of Bangladesh. The fundamental problem, Sen argued, was governmental indifference to the plight of the very poor: "Famine is entirely avoidable if the government has the incentive to act in time. . . . No democratic country with a relatively free press has ever experienced a major famine."

The following table summarizes the contributions of these six great economists to the development of political economy.

TABLE 4.1 The Key Ideas of Six Great Economists	
Adam Smith (1723–1790)	Labor is the basis of wealth; satisfaction of human needs is the measure of the wealth of a nation. The division of labor implies economic interdependence. Markets are self-regulating systems for the orderly coordination of the division of labor. The individual pursuit of self-interest in competitive market interactions has socially beneficial effects (that are brought about by "the invisible hand").
Karl Marx (1818–1883)	All known economic systems have divided societies into "haves" and "have-nots"—or "dominant" and "subordinate" classes. Members of classes work together in the pursuit of their common interests. Technical progress, the growth of knowledge, and conflict among classes all foster perpetual change. Capitalism as an economic system is irrational in the sense that it does not allow full use of modern science and technology to meet human needs.
J. Schumpeter (1883–1950)	The key to progress is innovation, and capitalism above all other economic systems fosters innovation. The operation of a modern economy is determined by a relatively small number of large-scale organizations—businesses, unions, and governments—rather than by a large number of small businesses and individuals. The growth of the capitalist economy is uneven: periods of prosperity and stability alternate with periods of stagnation and instability.
J. M. Keynes (1883–1946)	The market system is not self-regulating: left to its own devices the market system fails to make sensible use of our productive potential. Unemployment is a chronic problem in a capitalist economy. Government intervention in the economy can reduce unemployment and instability.
Ronald Coase (1910–)	Bargaining among private individuals can often solve problems that governments or market exchanges cannot solve. Government policies should facilitate these private bargains. Firms are mini-command economies based on the giving and following of orders rather than on market exchange. Capitalism is a mixture of competition and command.
Amartya Sen (1933–)	Economic policy should seek to promote freedom, tolerance, and well-being. Famines are not the result of shortages of food. Rather, they result from shortsighted government policies and unequal distributions of income. Democratically elected governments are more likely to pursue policies that address problems of poverty.

Smith, Marx, Schumpeter, Keynes, Coase, and Sen (and many others) have all contributed to the development of political economy, or what we call the three-dimensional approach to economics. In the chapters ahead we do not always label a particular idea Smithian, Marxian, Schumpeterian, Keynesian, Coaseian, or Senian, in part because modern-day political economy builds on, integrates, and changes many of the ideas of these great economists in light of current realities. But you will no doubt recognize the general themes that these thinkers first introduced.

SUGGESTED READINGS

Ronald H. Coase, "The Nature of the Firm" (1937), reprinted in Louis Putterman and Randall Krozner, eds., *The Economic Nature of the Firm: A Reader,* 2nd ed. (New York: Cambridge University Press, 1996), pp. 89–104.

Ronald H. Coase, "The Problem of Social Cost," *Journal of Law and Economics,* vol. 3, no. 1, 1960, pp. 1–44.

Robert Heilbroner, *The Worldly Philosophers: The Lives, Times, and Ideas of the Great Economic Thinkers,* 7th ed. (New York: Simon & Schuster, 1999).

Eugene Kamenka, ed., *The Portable Karl Marx* (New York: Penguin Books, 1983).

John Maynard Keynes, *Essays in Persuasion* (New York: Norton, 1963), especially "A Short View of Russia" (pp. 297–311), "The End of Laissez-Faire" (pp. 312–322), "Am I a Liberal?" (pp. 323–338), and "Economic Possibilities for our Grandchildren" (pp. 358–373).

Karl Marx, *Wage-Labor and Capital* (New York: International Publishers, 1976).

Karl Polanyi, *The Great Transformation* (Boston: Beacon Press, 1944).

Amartya Sen, *On Ethics and Economics* (Oxford: Basil Blackwell, 1987).

Amartya Sen, *Poverty and Famines: An Essay on Entitlement and Deprivation* (Oxford: Oxford University Press, 1981).

Amartya Sen, "Rational Fools: A Critique of the Behavioral Foundations of Economic Theory," *Philosophy & Public Affairs,* vol. 6, no. 4, 1977, pp. 317–344.

Joseph Schumpeter, *Capitalism, Socialism, and Democracy* (New York: Harper & Row, 1942).

Adam Smith, *An Inquiry into the Nature and Causes of the Wealth of Nations* (New York: Modern Library, Random House, 1937).

CHAPTER 5

The Surplus Product: Conflict and Change

Walk into almost any travel agency and you will see posters that tell a very interesting economic story. You may see a poster of India showing the Taj Mahal. Beside it may be a picture of the Egyptian pyramids. Another poster invites you to visit Rome and see the ancient Coliseum or the fabulous treasures of St. Peter's. Then on to France to view the delicate opulence of the chateaux and the sheer splendor of the palace of the Sun King (Louis XIV to his close friends) at Versailles. Far-off China beckons with the attraction of the Great Wall. One may also take a tour of the southern United States, visiting the great plantation houses of the former slaveholders.

What story do these posters tell us? What do the Taj Mahal, the pyramids, the Great Wall, and the slaveholders' mansions have in common? Simply this: even today, these great edifices inspire awe (and attract tourists) not only because of their great beauty but also because of the almost inconceivable amount of labor that was required to build them. How was it possible in poor societies such as ancient Egypt and medieval France for so many resources to be devoted to such construction projects? Where did the rulers of these societies—kings, bishops, emperors, or slaveholders—obtain the means to realize such magnificent plans?

The answers to these questions may be found in the concept of *surplus product,* another of Adam Smith's important ideas. The surplus product is *that part of the total output of an economy that is in excess of what is needed for reproducing and replenishing the labor, tools, materials, and other inputs used or used up in production.* There is no reason why a surplus *must* exist, but it *does* exist and *has existed* in all but a few human societies. The surplus product may be used in a variety of ways. It can take the form of cathedrals, palaces, luxury goods, military spending, more or better productive equipment, higher levels of education, improved health, and many other things.

93

The surplus product concept is a powerful lens that can help us understand how a society works. Why, for example, did the economy of China grow rapidly over the last two decades of the 20th century, greatly improving the living standards of most Chinese, while at the same time the economy of the Philippines stagnated, leaving most Filipinos desperately poor? The simple answer is that in China the surplus was invested in new factories, new equipment, and increased education, while in the Philippines the rich used much of the surplus in luxury consumption.

How the surplus comes to exist is also a key to understanding how a society works. As in other economic systems, the existence of a surplus in a capitalist economy depends on the power exercised by the dominant class over the producers. In a capitalist economy, however, the surplus results not only from the direct exercise of power by an employer over his or her employees; it also arises indirectly from the way markets work, particularly from the prices at which goods and services, including labor, are exchanged.

In the Soviet Union under communism, a large surplus came about due to the central administration of the economy. In yet other societies, for example the bands of hunting and gathering ancestors of modern humans who made their living before the dawn of agriculture, there was no surplus at all. The absence of a surplus in such societies helps to explain why they left behind no monuments for archaeologists to study—or for travel agencies to put on posters.

A focus on the surplus product is of primary importance in political economy. This focus is one of the main ways in which political economy differs from neoclassical economics. Looking at society through the lens of surplus product enables the political economist to see economic systems as having historically specific qualities, with one economic system being differentiated from others by the ways in which the surplus product is generated and controlled. How do we know what "capitalism" is? The answer offered in this book is that it is an economic system with a distinctive way of generating and disposing of its surplus product.

Understanding the surplus product requires the use of all three dimensions of the three-dimensional approach to economics. First, the command (or vertical) dimension must be called upon to understand how a society's producers are induced to settle for less than the whole of what they have produced, for only then can there be a surplus product. The horizontal dimension helps us understand how the surplus is affected by relationships among people at the same level in society. Are relationships among the producers competitive or solidaristic? Do members of the ruling group just compete with one another? When individuals act in concert with others at the same level of society, how do they suppress their competition? Finally, the historical, or change, dimension comes into play because the disposition of the surplus—be it luxuriously consumed, used to build monuments, or invested to create new productive capacity—will determine whether a particular society is stationary or experiencing change.

The main idea of this chapter is that *how the surplus arises, the size of the surplus, who controls it, and how it is used are the most important issues to be considered when analyzing the structure of any society, tracing a society's evolution over time, or determining the extent to which its economy allows for and supports a flourishing life for all of its people.* In this chapter the general concepts needed for understanding the surplus in any type of society are introduced; in the next chapter these concepts are applied specifically to the analysis of capitalism as an economic system.

This chapter's central idea is expressed in three main points:

---

1. An economy is a collection of *labor processes*. Each labor process is made up of a *technology* (a relation between inputs and outputs) and a *social organization of production* (the relations of people to the production process and to one another in the workplace). Each labor process produces one or more outputs.

2. A *surplus* is produced whenever the labor processes in an economy produce more than is needed to maintain the producers at the standard of living to which they are accustomed and to replace the materials and restore the machines used or used up in production.

3. The size of the surplus in any economy depends on relationships both within the country involved and among people in different national economies. Both the "domestic" and the "international" relationships that determine the size of the surplus are often highly conflictual.

ECONOMIC INTERDEPENDENCE, PRODUCTION, AND REPRODUCTION

> **Economic interdependence** exists when the livelihood of a person depends on the activities of another person. See also *vertical economic interdependence* and *horizontal economic interdependence*.

> The **division of labor** (or **economic specialization**) exists when people are not economically self-sufficient but instead produce things used by others and use things produced by others.

> **Horizontal economic interdependence** is based on specialization and is not necessarily based on unequal advantage or command.

In all societies people are *economically interdependent*. The story of Robinson Crusoe is of such great interest because, among other things, it is a story about someone who is entirely self-sufficient: he grows his own food and makes all the things he needs to sustain himself. This provokes fantasies exactly because it is so different from our own experience. In all real societies everyone depends on the products of other people's labor, and when we work together we generally do better than we would if we just subsisted independently. This point is illustrated in Daniel Defoe's novel itself: Crusoe does better when he happens to acquire a slave (Friday).

If people worked only in isolation, we would not need economics; Daniel Defoe would be good enough. The most important thing that requires us to engage in economic inquiry is the fact that people generally do depend on other people and are thus interdependent with them. Economic interdependence is virtually universal because it allows for greater productivity. The superiority of working in interdependent ways can also be derived from the observation that many of us work in firms with thousands of coworkers, thereby producing particular goods or services more cheaply than they could be produced in small enterprises (recall the point about increasing returns to scale in Chapter 3).

Every society, no matter how it is organized, must solve two economic problems: first, how to organize the interdependent economic activities of people and, second, how to distribute the resulting products. Addressing the first of these issues—how to organize our interdependence—we find that economic interdependence itself occurs in two ways. The first involves *horizontal* relationships that may be explored with reference to *economic specialization,* or *division of labor.* The people who make up an economic system produce different things: some make shoes, others generate electricity, others cook meals. No one produces all the things that he or she needs, and, at the same time, people usually produce (or help to produce) more of something than they can consume. The excess of each person's output beyond what he or she needs is then distributed through some kind of process to others in return for the others' excess output.

The second form of economic interdependence involves *vertical* relationships. A vertical relationship occurs when one person *controls* the labor and the products produced by another. The slave owner, for example, was economically dependent on the slaves' labor, for it was this labor that kept the plantation going and enriched its owner. The slave, in turn, was dependent on the owner for a livelihood, however meager it was. The modern day employer in a capitalist economy is likewise dependent on his or her employees: without their labor there can be no production or profit. And the employee, in turn, is dependent on the employer for a job and a wage.

> **Vertical economic interdependence** exists when one person controls the labor and the products of another; it is based on a relationship of unequal advantage and command.

With a relationship of vertical interdependence there is a top and a bottom, and the relationship is one of *command*, for example between the slave owner and the slave or between the employer and the employee. Although both parties in these relationships are mutually dependent, the slave owner and the employer are bosses: they command the work activities of the slave or the employee and benefit from the fruits of their subordinates' labor. Vertical interdependence thus differs from horizontal interdependence since the horizontal kind does not involve a ranking of superiority and inferiority between, say, the buyer and the seller of something.

As we saw in the previous chapter, Adam Smith was the first major economist to illuminate horizontal economic interdependence, while Karl Marx subsequently advanced our understanding of vertical interdependence. It is worth noting, however, that Smith was not oblivious to vertical interdependence. Indeed, in his analysis of medieval European agrarian life in *The Wealth of Nations,* he used the term *surplus produce,* defining it with reference to "a great proprietor" who lives off "[that part of] the produce of his lands which is over and above the maintenance of the cultivators."[1]

> A **labor process** is any activity performed with the intention of producing something.

In order to analyze vertical economic interdependence we must look at production. All human production must involve at least one *labor process,* defined as any activity of people performing purposeful work with the intention of producing something. Thus, any labor process will require *inputs* (such as human work and means of production such as machines and raw materials), and it will also produce *outputs* (such as a ton of steel, a computer program, or a haircut).

Think about making something, say, pancakes. If you made a list of all the ingredients needed (stating how much of each) and you included all the various activities required to mix the batter, turn on the stove, flip the pancakes, and so on, you would have a very complete recipe for pancakes. This recipe would describe the labor process for making pancakes. Similar lists of inputs and activities could describe the labor processes for

---

[1] Adam Smith, *The Wealth of Nations* (New York: Random House, Modern Library, 1937 [1776]), Book 3, Ch. 4, fifth paragraph.

> **Technology** is the relationship between inputs and outputs in a labor process.

> **Technical progress** is a change in the relationship between inputs and outputs that permits the same output to be produced with less of one or more of the inputs.

> An **economy** is a collection of labor processes.

> **Production** is a labor process whose output is a good or a service.

> **Reproduction** is a labor process whose output is people; it includes not only biological reproduction but also such activities as child rearing, training, feeding, and caregiving.

making the flour used in the pancakes, for producing the gas that is burned in the stove, for making the stove itself, and for supplying the other inputs as well.

A recipe such as the one for making pancakes—or any other set of relationships between inputs and outputs in a labor process—is called a *technology,* and *technical change* refers to a change in any of these input-output relations. An example of a technical change would be a way to make pancakes with a different kind of flour, say, one that does not need to be sifted. *Technical progress* is a technical change that allows the same amount of some output to be produced with less labor or less of another input.

In its most fundamental sense, an *economy* is *a collection of labor processes.* Of course, countless numbers of different things are produced in an economy—it has many types of outputs—and an economy also uses a great variety of inputs, including many different kinds of labor. In order to discuss these inputs and outputs and their corresponding labor processes, we have to group them in some way, and how we group them depends on what we want to find out.

For our purposes here we divide the economy into two sectors, each producing a certain kind of output. The first sector produces as its output all the goods and services that we consume or that businesses use as inputs. We are quite familiar with outputs of this kind, for they correspond to the normal everyday meaning of the term *production.* The second sector is not usually thought of as being part of the economy at all: it produces people. (Recall "The Economy Produces People" section of Chapter 2.)

The fact that people are produced by labor is suggested by the expression that a mother giving birth is "in labor." But these people-producing labor processes involve not just biological reproduction but also feeding, caring for others, training, imparting skills, and all the other tasks of caring for and rearing children that are associated with family life. Not only children but adults as well need to be fed and cared for. When we prepare a meal, eat, and relax after a day's work we are, among other things, replenishing our energy and maintaining our ability to continue functioning in the economy.

To distinguish the two sectors (with reference to the types of outputs that define them) we call the first one *production* (because it produces goods and services) and the second *reproduction* (because it reproduces people). This book focuses primarily on the production sector, especially within capitalism, but we will also take into account the vitally important reproduction sector since production and reproduction are clearly and indispensably interwoven with each other.

Figure 5.1 is a picture of the economy that shows the ways that the production and reproduction sectors are linked together through their inputs and outputs. Labor processes producing goods and services (production) are at the top; labor processes producing people (reproduction) are at the bottom.

We first consider the links between the production and reproduction sectors by looking at the *outputs* of each sector. The outputs of labor processes in the production sector may

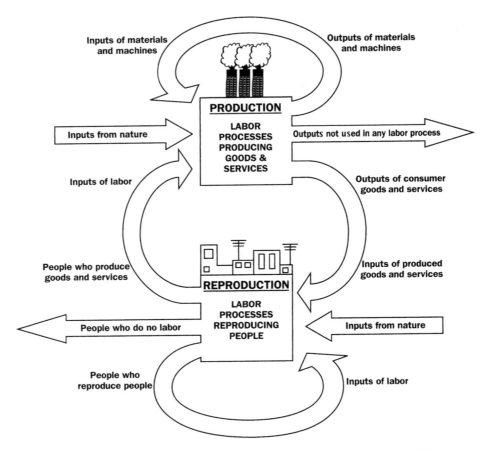

FIGURE 5.1   The production–reproduction cloverleaf.   The economy is composed of two interdependent sectors, one producing goods and services and the other reproducing people. The arrows represent the movement of goods or people from one sector to the other or back into the same sector. Each sector uses three types of inputs: inputs produced elsewhere in the economy, inputs produced in the same sector, and inputs from nature. Each sector also produces three different types of outputs: outputs used in the same sector, outputs used as inputs in another sector, and outputs not used as inputs anywhere in the economy.

circle back into this sector as materials, machines, or services for use in another production process. Alternatively, they may be consumer goods or services to be used by people in the reproduction sector. Finally, they may be outputs, such as cathedrals and weapons systems, that are not used again in any labor process.

Looking at the outputs—people—of the reproduction sector, we can see that some of them find employment in the production sector (producing shoes, steel, haircuts, etc.), whereas others (such as parents who care for children) will continue to work in the reproduction sector. Still others will not be engaged in productive labor at all (we will return to them in a moment).

Of course, many people work in both sectors, contributing both to production and to reproduction. For example, it is often the case that those who are employed outside the home have two "jobs," one at "work" and the other consisting of the housework, child care, and other tasks that throughout much of history have been performed mainly by women in the home.

The other way of identifying links connecting the production and reproduction sectors is to look at the *inputs* to each type of labor process. Starting with the production sector, we can see that some of its inputs (for example, materials or machines) come from this sector itself, while others (the people who set its labor processes in motion) come from the reproduction sector, and still others (such as inputs from nature) come from outside the economy altogether.

> **Capital goods** are goods used in production—machines, buildings, and the like—that are durable and will be used up only over the course of years.

If an output of the production sector is a physical object that circles back and becomes an input into a labor process in the same sector, it is classified either as a *material* or as a *capital good*. The term *capital good* refers to durable production equipment and structures, including machines, tools, buildings, and other long-lasting things needed in production.

Materials, on the other hand, are different from capital goods in that they are entirely *used up* in the course of a production cycle, whereas capital goods are merely *used*. While they are being used, capital goods are subject to a certain amount of wear and tear—called "depreciation"— but they are only used up over a period of several years. The cotton that ends up in a shirt or the fuel that is burned in the process of making it are examples of materials, whereas the sewing machine that is used to sew together a large number of shirts is a capital good.

> **Materials** are goods used in production that are used up during the process of production.

With regard to the *people* going from the reproduction sector to the production sector, they are put to work as the labor that sets labor processes in motion. We define *labor* as any activity performed by a person that contributes to production or reproduction.

> **Labor** is any activity performed by people that contributes to production or reproduction.

We can illustrate the concepts just introduced by going back to our example of pancake making, this time looking at a labor process producing pancakes at a fast-food restaurant. (See box "The House of Pancakes.")

This is an example of a labor process in the production sector that is turning out a consumer good directly consumed by people. The pancakes might well have been produced at home, in which case the process of making them would be considered part of the reproduction process. In this example, however, they are an output of the production sector.

Returning to Figure 5.1, we can now summarize how the economy's labor processes are interconnected. First, some outputs of the production sector are used as inputs into labor processes in the same sector. For example, coal is used to make steel, and machinery used in coal mining is itself made out of steel. Another type of output of the production sector, consumer goods of all kinds, goes to the reproduction sector and is used in the "production" and maintenance of people.

The output of materials and machines may be sufficient not only to *replace* but also to *expand* the supply of machinery, raw materials, buildings, and the other things used or used

THE "HOUSE OF PANCAKES"
PANCAKE TECHNOLOGY

Inputs:

Labor	Mixing the batter
	Pouring the batter into the frying pan, turning the pancakes over, and so on
	Waiting on customers
Materials used up	Flour
	Eggs, etc.
	Gas or electricity
Capital goods used	Wear and tear on the stove
	Wear and tear on the frying pans, bowls, mixing spoons, and other utensils
	Depreciation of the building (physical facilities)

Output:

Consumer good	Pancakes

up in production processes. Similarly, the supply of consumer goods and the reproduction of people may support an increasing number of producers. As we saw in Chapter 1, one of the defining characteristics of capitalism is its tendency to expand both production and reproduction.

There are two kinds of outputs in Figure 5.1 that are special in that they do not end up being used in any labor process. First, there are physical objects produced, such as luxury goods, monuments, cathedrals, and military equipment, that do not reenter as inputs into labor processes in either the production or the reproduction sectors. However important they may be to the culture or even to the survival of the society in question, they are not used in the production of anything. Second, there are people who are created and maintained in the reproduction sector—from panhandlers to playboys—who do not end up participating in any labor process.

Just as there are outputs not used in any labor process, there are also inputs not produced by a labor process. We call these "inputs from nature," using "nature" to refer to our physical environment—air, water, arable land, the minerals in the earth's substratum, the sun, and so on. These inputs are presented in Figure 5.1 as arrows entering the two types of labor processes from outside the system. Saying that they are provided by the environment does not mean they cannot be used up. Although there are a few inputs from nature (such as the sun) that can be used indefinitely (to grow crops, to warm houses) without being exhausted—these are "renewable resources"—many natural inputs are nonrenewable in the sense that they can be used up. Indeed, we now know that human production and consumption are using up so many things in our environment—such as clean air and water and the protective quality of the earth's ozone layer—that the future viability of the ecosystem itself is in doubt.

Summing up what we have said thus far, an economy is a collection of labor processes that are specialized in the production of distinct outputs and that are connected by relationships of both horizontal and vertical economic interdependence. To pursue our investigation of the vertical dimension we now turn to the surplus product.

THE SURPLUS PRODUCT

What did the great kings and queens of the past live on? And the legendary warriors and otherworldly saints? Who produced what they ate, and why? What made possible the glittering Versailles Palace, the Great Wall of China, the imposing Jefferson Memorial, and the war machine of Adolf Hitler? And how was metalworking transformed from the humble blacksmith's shop to the great mills of Pittsburgh, Kobe, and Dortmund? These questions all refer to the tangible, physical manifestations—impressive in their sheer magnitude—of the surplus product.

No less impressive, however, are the intangible forms of the surplus product, such as the accumulated knowledge of untold years of work by scholars to be found in a modern encyclopedia (now available on a single CD); the awesome beauty of the ceiling of the Sistine Chapel in Rome, the result of many hours of creative work by Michelangelo; and the wisdom in the sacred texts of the Muslim, Hindu, Jewish, and Christian religions, the Koran,

> The **total product** is the total amount of goods and services produced in an economy during a given period of time.

the Bhagavad Gita, the Talmud, and the Bible. To understand both the tangible and the intangible phenomena just described, we need to define the concept of the surplus product.

In defining the surplus product, the first step is to note that a society produces a certain quantity of goods and services during a year. This is the *total product*. The total product is in turn divisible into two parts: the necessary product and the surplus product. Thus:

$$\text{total product} = \text{necessary product} + \text{surplus product}$$

> The **surplus product** is what remains out of the total product after the necessary product has been deleted.

The *surplus product,* then, is what is left of the total product after the necessary product has been deducted. But what is the necessary product? It consists of three parts.

The first is the *consumption of the producers,* which is that part of the total output—food, clothing, and other items—that must be distributed, through some mechanism, to those who produce the total product so that they may maintain themselves at their "customary" standard of living (this is defined in the caption under Figure 5.2).

> **Depreciation** is the cost (due to wear and tear) of restoring the capital goods used up in producing last year's output.

Second, all wear and tear on the capital goods used in production must be repaired. Since this may be postponed until particular machines or tools are ready to be replaced, the annual reduction in the value of the capital goods is called *depreciation*.

Third, the materials used up during production have to be replaced. Putting together the three parts of the necessary product, it can be defined it as follows:

necessary product = consumption of + depreciation of + replacement of the producers at capital goods used materials used up their customary standard of living

The **necessary product** is the portion of the total product that is needed to maintain the inputs in the labor process—workers, materials, and tools—at their current level or in their current condition for the next round of the production process.

One can see, then, that the word *necessary* in the term *necessary product* refers to what is required to maintain the inputs into the labor process—producers, tools, and materials—at some particular level in order that production may be carried on in the same way in the next period. The continuance of an economy at a specific level is the basic idea of the necessary product. It does not refer to the adequacy of a society's living standards, the level of its technology, or the diligence of its workers.

Although we began this discussion referring to the total product of a society, total product is, in fact, not a very useful measure of economic output. This is because it includes that part of the total output that must be set aside to replace the machinery and materials used or used up in the production process. A more useful measure of output is *net product,* defined as the total product minus ("net of") the amount of goods and services that must be used for replacement of materials and depreciation of capital goods. Net product is sometimes called "value added." Figure 5.2 summarizes the relationships among the concepts introduced here.

Net product is the total product minus materials and capital goods used up in the course of producing the total product.

How, then, does the concept of the surplus product help us understand who produces what, and why? Will it help us ascertain why there is a surplus product? And will it help us answer a fundamental question about a capitalist economy, namely, *how is the rate of profit determined?*

If an economy produced only enough to support its producers and replace the machines and materials used up in production, it would not produce any surplus at all. In this case, the total product would be just equal to the necessary product, and there would be no surplus product. People lived this way a long time ago and, in fact, did so for most of the 100,000 or so years of human existence before the domestication of plants and animals. This ancient but long-lasting way of life preceded the emergence of hierarchies, the division of societies into classes, and the appearance of distinctions between political elites and those they govern.

Although many early human societies were far from affluent, a society without a surplus is not inevitably a poor one, nor must it be a "subsistence" society. As long as the "necessary product" is being produced, a society can maintain its members at their "customary standard of living." Every society's customary standard of living is defined by its particular culture: it may be high or it may be low, as long as it allows the producers to meet their culturally defined needs. Moreover, the normal workday in any given society might be longer or shorter than eight hours; many hunters and gatherers work for shorter days than office and factory workers in the U.S., for example. Whatever the length of the normal workday, the producers in a no-surplus economy are not supporting anyone but themselves.

Historically, the appearance of a surplus can be attributed to the emergence of some kind of power relationship. Depending on the type of economic system, the surplus product

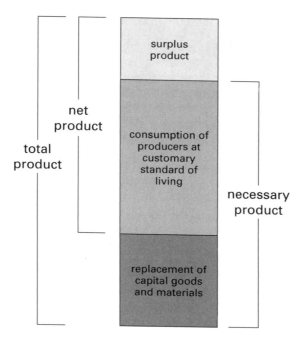

FIGURE 5.2   Total, net, necessary, and surplus products.   This figure shows how the total product of an economy (whatever its specific form) is allocated among various uses. The bottom segment of the bar represents the part of the total product that must be devoted to replacing the materials and capital goods used in producing the total product. The amount of replacement shown is exactly the amount that is needed to allow the next production cycle to begin with the same conditions that existed at the beginning of the present cycle; it does not provide for any expansion of productive capacity. The middle segment of the bar represents the amount of the total product that must be allocated for the "customary" level of consumption of those who produce the total product. Conflicts between workers and those who own the capital goods and control the work process often play a part in determining the level of the customary standard of consumption of the workers. Then, what is left of the total product after the first two requirements have been taken care of is the *surplus product* (represented by the top segment of the bar). It is owned and controlled by those who own the capital goods used in production and control the work process. They can dispose of the surplus as they choose, for example, spending it on luxury goods for themselves or reinvesting it to expand productive capacity. This figure provides the basis for many of the concepts presented in Chapter 10, "Capitalist Production and Profits."

may take the form of the rents and feudal dues paid by serfs to feudal lords, it may constitute the income of slave plantation owners, it may be that portion of the harvest that is turned over by sharecroppers to their landlords, or it may appear as profits for the owners and top executives of today's business corporations.

The surplus product is important because it allows for economic growth and change. All or part of the surplus may be used to improve or expand the stock of capital goods, making possible either increased output or shorter working hours or both in the future. Devoting

MEGAYACHTS AND BULL MARKET BOATS

If you stand on the bridge of *Dream,* you might imagine that you are the captain of a tanker or a supply ship. With its global positioning system equipment and its four engine-room video monitors, the 184-foot yacht is capable of circumnavigating the globe on a single tank of fuel. *Dream* has smokestacks like a real ship and two cranes, similar to those on a small freighter. The original owner used the cranes to offload two tenders, a 36-foot fishing boat and a submarine.

Dream is an expedition yacht, a private boat with a hull and superstructure like those on a commercial ship but with all the amenities of a luxurious pleasure yacht. Among other things, *Dream* carries a grand piano and a hot tub.

Some expedition yachts are new, modeled after commercial ships, while others are conversions of tug boats, fishing trawlers, and even icebreakers. The biggest, at 355 feet, is *Le Grand Bleu,* owned by John McCaw, the cofounder of McCaw Cellular. It looks like a research vessel or work boat and is said to have its own dry-cleaning plant. One of its tenders is a 73-foot sailboat with its own captain and crew.

Another expedition yacht, *Turmoil,* is owned by Gary C. Comer, the founder of Lands' End. Recently, Mr. Comer has been cruising in the Arctic with *Turmoil.* It is said that the term *expedition yacht* was first used in 1996 to describe this boat.

But an expedition yacht is not the only kind of very expensive boat that has appeared since the 1990s. The term *megayacht* is sometimes used to refer to anything more than 80 feet long, and the total number of such boats went from several hundred in the mid-1980s to more than 5,000 at the end of the 1990s. This escalation in the population of huge privately owned vessels, whether gleaming white fiberglass motor yachts, high-tech sailboats, or classic wooden boats, is associated with the long boom in the stock market (a "bull," as opposed to a "bear," market) that occurred during the same period.

The high-end boat business has been fueled not only by recent increases in the wealth of the richest 1 percent of the population but also by the 1993 repeal of a 10 percent tax on new boats costing more than $100,000. Now, it is easier for wealthy boaters to play the game of one-upmanship, trading in their giant yachts for even bigger ones.

As reported recently in the *Wall Street Journal,* James Stever of Mercer Island, Washington, has already bought and sold three big boats in the past several years and is waiting on a fourth to arrive from Hong Kong. It is a 65-foot-long motor yacht with three bedrooms, four bathrooms, and a list price of about $1.7 million. But it may not be enough: the retired executive is already talking to his broker about a bigger model. "We'll try the 65-foot boat for a full season," he says, then "think about moving up."

Sources: Doug Sease, "Bull-Market Boats: Size Does Matter," *Wall Street Journal,* April 23, 1999, p. W1; Penelope Green, "Go-Anywhere Luxury Yachts Bull Out to Sea," *New York Times,* July 22, 2001.

> **Investment** means spending money to repair, replace, improve, or add to a firm's productive equipment, software, facilities, or workforce skills in order to increase productive capacity and productivity.

the surplus to research activities may expand the stock of knowledge relevant to production. When the surplus is used in these ways to increase productivity, it is called *investment*. When the surplus is invested, it can make it possible for people to work less hard or for fewer hours without experiencing a reduction in their living standards. Indeed, such productivity-enhancing investment can even support increases in the living standards of the producers without reducing those of the class in power. An enlargement of the surplus may also allow for population growth: instead of the system simply reproducing the current number of producers, it could support a larger number of people at the same standard of living.

Of course, it is also possible that the surplus will be used in ways that do not increase productivity. For example, all or part of it may be used by those who control it to engage in displays of opulence. In the world today, an important example of the use of the surplus in a way that does not increase productivity is *capitalist consumption*. (See box, "Megayachts and Bull Market Boats.")

A MODEL OF PRODUCTION AND REPRODUCTION

The idea of the surplus product is so important that we need to make it more precise. We will do this by means of a simple example—a model—designed to bring out the most significant points while ignoring what is not essential to our present inquiry.

ECONOMIC MODELS

E conomic models, like all scientific models, are attempts to simplify a problem so that we can understand it better. The purpose of a model is to represent what is important for the task at hand, not to represent every detail of the problem. For example, an airplane model used in a wind tunnel does not have seats in it, but great care is taken with every detail concerning the shape of its fuselage, wings, and tail. Similarly, an architectural model focuses on the visual and spatial aspects of a proposed building; the fact that the model is made of wood and plastic, not the concrete and steel that will go into the building itself, is unimportant.

Models allow us to think about complex problems in simple ways. Economic models that successfully highlight what is important without ignoring essential aspects of a problem are tools as necessary to economic reasoning as the telescope is to astronomy. However, models can be very misleading when they are based on unrealistic assumptions or when they oversimplify things to such an extent that essential aspects are left out. Economists would do well to heed Albert Einstein's advice: "Make things as simple as possible, but no simpler."

The point of our model is to clarify the relationships among the concepts introduced in this chapter: specialization, technology, technical change, replacement of inputs (materials and capital goods), reproduction of producers, and the total, net, and surplus products.

To simplify things we will focus on the labor processes of a single family that is part of a society that includes many similar families. Our representative family engages in two kinds of labor processes, child rearing and farming, but produces only one good, grain. Another simplifying assumption in our model is that grain is the only input used, other than labor and nature, in the labor processes. These assumptions will allow us to highlight various economic relationships without introducing more complicated elements, such as money.

In our model farm work produces grain, and once it is produced the grain serves three different functions. First, it is a *consumer good* used in the reproduction of people: people eat the grain (as bread) and they drink the grain (as beer). Second, it is a *capital good* used to feed the draft animals employed in the fields so they will be able not only to aid in the current production of grain but also to reproduce themselves, ensuring that there will be draft animals to help with future crops. Third, grain is a *material* input because grain itself must be used as seed for the next crop. Summarizing the different roles that grain plays in the production sector of our simple model, we can represent the various inputs and outputs as constituting a technology.

The way the grain technology is presented here makes it easy to distinguish between total product and net product: *total product* is all the grain that is produced, while *net product* is all the grain produced minus the amount of it that must be put aside to replace whatever is used or used up in production (in this case the feed for the draft animals and the seed for next year's crop).

Is our model family producing a surplus? In order to answer this we will have to determine how productive the technology is, how hard and how long the family members work at grain growing, and what their customary standard of living is.

THE GRAIN TECHNOLOGY

Inputs:

Labor	Planting, harvesting
Materials used up	Grain used as seed
Capital goods used	Grain for maintaining and reproducing draft animals
Inputs from nature	Land, rainfall, sunshine

Outputs:

Consumer good	Grain to be consumed
Materials	Grain to be used as seed the following year
Capital goods	Grain to be used as food for draft animals

Suppose the family comprises two adults who together spend a total of 1,000 hours of labor on child rearing and 1,000 hours of labor growing grain each year. Also suppose that it takes 10 hours of labor to produce a bushel of grain. (This is unrealistically high for a modern economy as a glance at Figure 1.1 will show.) Under these assumptions, the family will harvest 100 bushels of grain each year.

Now imagine that the harvest is in, and the 100 bushels make up a huge pile of grain. The family divides this large pile into three smaller piles: the first pile will have to be large enough to replace the materials and capital goods used up in production (seeds and draft animal feed); the second pile is the amount set aside for the family's own consumption (at the customary level) until the next harvest; and the third pile, whatever is left over, is the surplus. The first and second piles together are the necessary product, while the second and third piles together are the net product. (The different piles in this example correspond to the three segments of the bar in Figure 5.2.)

One possibility is that the family model owns its farm and is therefore in control of the surplus it has produced. In this case the family may choose to do whatever it wants with the surplus, which may be anything from improving the quality of the technology it uses to building a swimming pool in the backyard. In Chapter 7 we examine a time in American history when independent or self-employed producers of commodities—farmers, craftsmen, self-employed artisans, and other independent producers—accounted for approximately 60 percent of all people participating in the production sector.

But the other possibility, the one that corresponds more to realities in the world today, is that the family is working someone else's land and has to get by with the portion of the total output that is allocated for consumption by the producers. In this case, who gets the surplus? This is one of the most important questions addressed by political economy.

Much of human history has been about battles over the surplus. In some economies the surplus product is claimed as rent by a landlord, and so in many farming communities the third pile is literally trucked off to the landowner's warehouse. Or perhaps the family in our model is employed by a large agribusiness corporation. In this case the family gets only the second pile, its wages; the corporation sets aside the first pile for replacement and claims the third pile, the surplus, as its profits. Alternatively, the family in our model may have taken out a loan from a bank, perhaps in the form of a mortgage, to purchase its land and draft animals. In this case the surplus may go entirely to the bank. The important point in each of these cases is that the producers themselves do not get the surplus. We will return to this point in greater detail when we discuss classes and economic systems in the next chapter.

To see how big the surplus pile will be, imagine, in the first instance, that 30 bushels must be set aside for replacement of materials and capital goods, specifically to provide seed for the next year and to feed the draft animals used in tilling the fields. (The allocation here is 10 bushels for the seed and 20 bushels for the animals.) Subtracting the 30 bushels needed for replacement from the total product of 100 bushels, the net product is 70 bushels. If the customary consumption level for the family is 50 bushels per year, the surplus product will be 20 bushels.

How might those who control the surplus make it larger? There are a number of possible answers to this question. First, the standard of living of the farming family might be cut, say, from 50 to 40 bushels per year. In this case the surplus would rise from 20 to

THE SURPLUS PRODUCT: AN EXAMPLE

(1) Total hours of labor devoted to grain growing per year:	1,000 hours
(2) Bushels of grain produced per hour worked:	1/10 bushel/hr.
(3) Total product of grain per year [(1) × (2) = (3)]:	100 bushels
(4) Replacement of materials and capital goods used up in producing the total product (seed and draft animal feed) = (Pile #1):	30 bushels
(5) Net product per year [(5) = (3) − (4)]:	70 bushels
(6) Customary consumption level of the family = (Pile #2):	50 bushels
(7) Necessary product [(7) = (4) + (6)]:	80 bushels
(8) Surplus product [(8) = (5) − (6)] = (Pile #3):	20 bushels

30 bushels. This illustrates why, in any society in which some people control and benefit from the labor of others, there will be an incentive for the former to try to reduce the standard of living of the latter, setting up a situation that is inherently conflictual.

The consumption of the farming family in our model can be reduced from 50 to 40 bushels without changing the total amount of grain produced if a *labor-saving technical change* is introduced. A labor-saving technical change is defined as a change in the technology that increases the amount of output that can be produced with a given amount of labor. But the benefits of a labor-saving technical change can be taken either as an increase in total product using the same amount of labor or as production of the same total output with less labor. Here we assume that a labor-saving technical change increases the productivity of labor by 25 percent and that those who control the labor process choose to maintain total output at its current level (100 bushels) while at the same time reducing the amount of labor employed from 1,000 hours to 800 hours. This makes possible a reduction in the amount of grain allocated for producer consumption from 50 to 40 bushels, for only 80 percent as much labor is now required to produce the total output of 100 bushels.

> A **labor-saving technical change** is a new technology that increases the total output produced with a given amount of labor.

A second way of enlarging the surplus would involve changing the technology in such a way that fewer seeds or less animal feed would have to be set aside for the next year. This technical change could take the form of better seeds, or it might be a new way of storing the animal feed so that less is lost to spoilage. In our example, if only 20 bushels of grain (instead of 30) had to be set aside to replace the capital goods and materials used up in production, the surplus product would increase from 20 to 30 bushels (assuming no increase in the standard of living of the producers). What we have in this case is a *capital goods–saving technical change,* defined as one that reduces the amount of capital goods or the quantity of materials required to produce the total product.

> A **capital goods–saving technical change** is a new technology that reduces the capital goods and materials necessary to produce a given amount of total output.

The two ways of enlarging the surplus product by means of technical change are shown, along with our example's original allocation, in

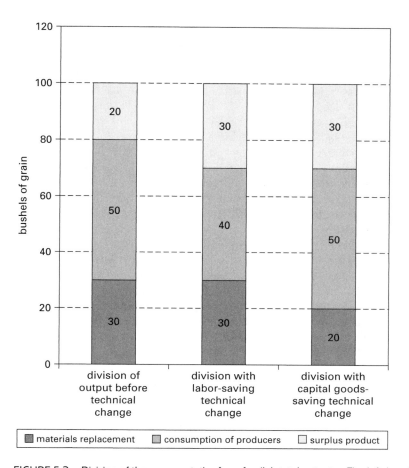

FIGURE 5.3   Division of the representative farm family's total output.   The left-hand bar in this figure represents the division of total output as set forth in the original example in the text: total output is 100 bushels, with 30 used for replacing the material inputs to the production process (capital goods depreciation as well as materials used up), 50 allocated for the consumption of the producers, and 20 remaining as the surplus product. The middle bar shows the division of total output after there has been a *labor-saving technical change*. Since there has been an increase in labor productivity, the same total output (100 bushels) can now be produced with less labor (800 rather than 1,000 hours) so only 40 bushels (rather than 50) need be allocated for the consumption of the producers. Since 30 continue to be used for replacing the material inputs (as before), the surplus product is increased to 30 bushels. The right-hand bar shows what happens when there is a *capital goods–saving technical change*. In this case, both the total output (100 bushels) and the consumption of the producers (50 bushels) are unchanged from the original example, but the reduction in replacement costs from 30 to 20 bushels allows the surplus to be enlarged to 30 bushels.

Figure 5.3. This figure uses bars divided in the same way as the bar in Figure 5.2. The left-hand bar represents the division of the total product in our original example. The middle bar shows how, with a labor-saving technical change, the surplus product can be enlarged to 30 bushels while the consumption of the producers is reduced to 40 bushels. The right-hand bar shows the surplus product expanded by means of a capital goods–saving technical change. An important point here is that the surplus can be increased with *either* a labor-saving technical change *or* a capital goods–saving technical change.

Just as a labor-saving technical change does, a capital goods–saving technical change results in more net product produced for any given amount of labor performed. Accordingly, these two types of innovations make it possible for both the surplus product and the standard of living of the producers to be increased. Many technical changes are both capital saving and labor saving, meaning that they reduce the amounts of all of the inputs needed to produce a given quantity of total product.

Still another way of increasing the surplus product is to (somehow) induce the producers to work harder without increasing the total number of hours that they work or the portion of the total product allocated for their consumption. (If we assume that the producers are paid according to the number of hours they work, keeping their hours constant will mean that they will continue to receive the same amount of grain for their consumption, even if they are working harder.) This way of enlarging the surplus product is called an increase in the *intensity of labor*.

> The **intensity of labor** is how much work effort producers must expend per hour of work, or more simply, how hard they work.

Referring to our grain model once again, if the intensity of labor were to be increased so that the 1,000 hours of grain-growing labor produced 130 rather than the previous 100 bushels, the surplus would increase from 20 to 50 bushels (assuming that the proportions of the total product allocated to producer consumption and replacement of nonhuman inputs remains the same).

A final—and perhaps the most obvious—way in which the surplus might be increased is one that is not based on any increase in the productivity or living standards of the producers. They can simply be induced to spend more hours growing grain. This could be achieved in two ways. First, the length of the working day (or the total number of hours worked in a year) could be increased, in which case the amount of free time (time available for leisure activities, eating, sleeping, etc.) would be reduced. The second possibility, which might well happen as a result of the first, is that the number of hours spent by the family on child-rearing activities (or reproduction in general) could be reduced, with the hours saved being reallocated to grain growing activity.

Much of the analysis we have applied to the production sector may be used just as effectively to analyze the 1,000 hours spent on child rearing and other reproduction activities by the family in our model. For example, we have noted that a reduction in the number of hours worked in the reproduction sector allows for an increase in the surplus product because those who are in control of production may then get the producers, who are the same people as those involved in the reproduction activities, to work longer hours producing grain.

Child rearing and other reproduction activities are obviously necessary to enable families to continue supplying labor to the production sector. By using analyses like the ones we have applied to activities in the production sector we can speculate about the consequences of introducing an innovation such as a labor-saving technical change in child rearing and other reproduction processes. For example, a TV set might allow parents to spend fewer hours with their children, a vacuum cleaner might enable the family to keep the house clean with fewer hours of labor, the acquisition of frozen foods or an automatic dishwasher might reduce the amount of time that has to be spent in the kitchen, and so on.

We can also imagine several families getting together to share day care responsibilities, thereby reducing the number of hours each individual family needs to devote to child-rearing activities. All of these examples illustrate the point that production and reproduction activities are interconnected in many ways. Accordingly, changes in the reproduction sector may affect—or be required for—changes in the size of the surplus product.

INTERNATIONAL EXCHANGE AND THE SURPLUS PRODUCT

By simplifying reality, our grain model has made it easier to explain a number of important determinants of the surplus product. However, there is one important shortcoming of the model as presented thus far: the people in it seem to have no relationships with people in other countries. This is clearly not the way the world is in the 21st century. More important, a model that leaves out the rest of the world does not permit an understanding of all the factors that determine the surplus product of any one country. To remedy this defect we will now complicate the model by introducing international exchange.

We will continue to focus on the same representative family, but with these changes: the family now uses plows to till their soil, and the plows are made in a neighboring country. The use of the imported plows has two significant consequences. First, the introduction of the plows is a *labor-saving technical change* because the number of hours required to produce a bushel of grain is reduced from 10 hours without the plows to 5 hours with the plows. Hence, 1,000 hours of grain-growing labor now produces 200 bushels of total product (rather than the 100 bushels produced before). Also, in modification of our original assumption that 10 bushels of the total grain output were required to provide seed for the next year's crop, we now assume that the doubling of the total grain output will require twice as much seed—20 rather than 10 bushels of grain—to be used as an input for growing each year's crop.

The second consequence flows from the fact that the plows are not produced domestically and thus have to be acquired from the other country. To acquire the plows our grain-growing family must pay for them in grain, and the prevailing exchange rate in the world market is 10 bushels of grain for one plow. Thus, 10 bushels is the "price" (measured in grain) of one plow. (We will come back to the question of how this exchange rate is determined.) Because the plow is imported and the grain is exported, this price can be thought of as the *real price of imported inputs*. It is the price of imported goods measured by how many of the domestically produced goods must be exchanged to buy one unit of the imported good. In other contexts the prices that countries must pay in order to exchange goods with each other are referred to as the *terms of trade*.

The **real price of an imported input** is the amount of domestically produced goods required to purchase one unit of the imported good. It is thus the price of the imported good divided by the price of the domestically produced goods, when both are measured in the same currency.

Suppose each family uses two plows in the course of a year and, to keep things simple, let us say that a plow wears out in one year. In this case both plows must be replaced at the end of the year. When we calculate the surplus product we have to deduct from the total product the cost of replacing the capital goods and materials used up in production, and this will now include not only the seed and draft animal feed but also the cost of replacing the plows. This cost can be thought of either as two

THE SURPLUS PRODUCT WITH INTERNATIONAL EXCHANGE

(1) Total hours of labor devoted to grain growing per year:	1,000 hours
(2) Bushels of grain produced per hour worked:	1/5 bushel/hr.
(3) Total product of grain per year [(1) × (2) = (3)]:	200 bushels
(4) Replacement of materials and capital goods used up producing the total product (20 bushels each for seed, animal feed, and replacement of the two plows) = (Pile #1):	60 bushels
(5) Net product per year [(5) = (3) − (4)]:	140 bushels
(6) Customary consumption level of the family = (Pile #2):	50 bushels
(7) Necessary product [(7) = (4) + (6)]:	110 bushels
(8) Surplus product [(8) = (5) − (6)] = (Pile #3):	90 bushels

plows or as the 20 bushels of grain needed to buy the replacement plows from the other country.

The surplus product can now be recalculated as follows. Total output is increased to 200 bushels, up from 100 because of the labor-saving technical change (the introduction of the plows). Replacement of materials and capital goods is now 60 bushels: 20 bushels to replace the worn-out plows (obtained by exchanging grain for the plows produced in another country) and 40 bushels for seed and animal feed, assuming, as noted earlier, that an extra 10 bushels of seed is required to produce the additional 100 bushels of total output. If the level of consumption of the producers remains at the customary 50 bushels, the surplus product will be increased from 20 to 90 bushels. Thus, the introduction of international exchange—and the labor-saving technical change made possible by it—led to a substantial increase in the surplus product. Once again, a bar chart like Figure 5.2 can be used to compare the situations of our model farm family before and after the introduction of international trade in grain and plows (see Figure 5.4).

What would happen if the terms of trade changed in a way that required the grain-growing family to spend twice as much grain to import the same two plows? In this case the real price of the imported inputs (plows) would increase from 20 to 40 bushels, the amount of grain required for replacement purposes would rise to 80 bushels (40 for the plows and 40 for seed and animal feed), and the surplus would be reduced to 70 bushels.

But what if those who control the surplus were not willing to see their share of the total output cut to 70 bushels? One possibility would be that they could somehow force the producers to reduce their level of consumption (or standard of living) from 50 to 40 bushels, thereby leaving 80 bushels for the surplus product. This example brings out, once again, the inherently conflictual nature of production and exchange whenever a society is divided between the producers of the total output and those who control the production and distribution of it.

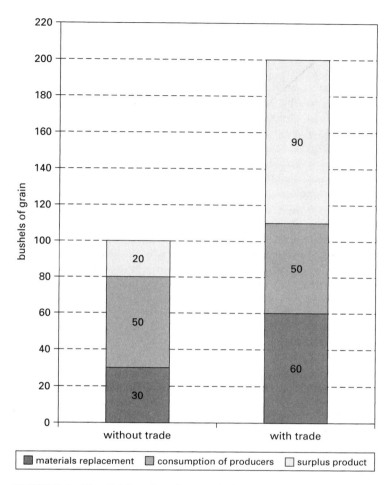

FIGURE 5.4   The division of total output before and after the introduction of international trade.   This figure shows that engaging in international trade may benefit those who control the surplus. In this case the importation of two plows (and the labor-saving technical change made possible with them) allows for a doubling of total output from 100 to 200 bushels of grain. Even after the customary (unchanged) 50 bushels have been allocated to the producers for their consumption, the farm animals have been fed, the necessary amount of seed for next year's crop has been set aside, and the imported plows have been paid for—see adjacent text for the details—the surplus product increases from 20 to 90 bushels.

THE SURPLUS PRODUCT AND CONFLICT

In a society that produces a surplus product, two things are very likely: conflict and change. Conflict arises in two ways, one having to do with relationships within nations and the other occurring between groups in different nations.

Conflict within nations arises when the producers are not allowed to keep the surplus that they have produced. Under such circumstances the producers' interests are opposed to the interests of those who own and control the surplus. The latter—whether they be slave owners, feudal landlords, the owners of capitalist corporations, or dictatorial governing elites—will probably seek to enlarge the surplus. To do this they will need to get the producers to work harder, work longer, or consume less. The producers, however, would like to enjoy less arduous work, have more free time, and benefit from a higher standard of living. Thus, what they want is in direct opposition to what those who control the surplus want. The producers and those who control the surplus constitute different social classes, and the conflict between them can be understood as a class conflict. (We discuss classes and class conflict in subsequent chapters.)

The conflict between the interests of the owners of a surplus and the interests of the producers of that surplus can be better understood if we list the determinants of the size of the surplus product and contrast these with the determinants of the economic well-being of the producers. (See box "The Surplus Product and the Producers' Well-being.")

As we can see from the accompanying box, the producers will be better off if their customary consumption level is higher, if their work is less intense, and if they have more hours for leisure and for child rearing. These are the determinants most relevant to the economic well-being of the producers. However, just the opposite movements in these same determinants are required if the surplus product is to be increased. Here, the conflicts of interest between those who produce and those who control the surplus product are evident.

THE SURPLUS PRODUCT AND THE PRODUCERS' WELL-BEING: A RECIPE FOR CONFLICT

How to Increase the Surplus Product	How to Increase the Producers' Well-Being
Reduce the level of consumption of the producers.	*Raise* the level of consumption of the producers.
Implement a *labor-saving* technical change.	*Share* the resulting increase in the surplus product with the producers.
Implement a *capital goods-saving* technical change.	*Share* the resulting increase in the surplus product with the producers.
Increase the intensity of labor.	*Reduce* the intensity of labor.
Lengthen the labor time of the producers (without changing their customary consumption level).	*Shorten* the labor time of the producers (without changing their customary consumption level).
Reduce the real price of an imported input (by assertion of power over the exporter).	*Share* the resulting increase in the surplus product with the producers.

The box also shows that there are some determinants that, if increased, would benefit the surplus owners without necessarily hurting the producers (possibly even allowing an improvement in the standard of living of the producers while at the same time expanding the surplus product). Labor- or capital-saving technical changes would fall into this category, as would a reduction in the real price of an import (oil or computers, for example), which would reduce the portion of the total product that must be allocated to replacing the capital goods or materials used in production. In this case, however, the benefits available (potentially) to both surplus owners and producers in the "home" country might be offset by reductions in the standards of living of both producers and owners in the exporting nation or nations.

If the customary consumption level of the producers is very low, of course, the workers may be so poorly nourished, weak, or unhealthy that they cannot produce very much. Likewise, if they are working so many hours in grain growing that they have little time to take care of themselves and raise their children, they may not be very productive, and the next generation may be even less so. In these situations those who control the surplus may see that it is not in their interest to impoverish or overwork the producers, for poverty and overwork can serve no group's interests. If consumption is barely above, or actually below, the subsistence level, it is likely that an increase in consumption would *both* improve the living standards of the producers *and* enlarge the surplus product. From the point of view of the surplus owners in this set of circumstances, then, an increase in the producers' consumption would more than pay for itself, and for this reason an increase in their consumption is likely to occur.

Using the numbers from our first grain model (when the net product was 70 bushels), Figure 5.5 illustrates the conflict that exists between the producers and those who control the surplus. Reading the graph from right to left, the point at 70 on the horizontal axis shows what would happen if the entire net product were to be distributed to the producers for their consumption. In this case the surplus product would be zero. The part of the line that slopes upward to the left from this point shows that as the consumption of the producers is reduced from 70 to 25 bushels, taking them well below their customary consumption level of 50 bushels, the surplus rises from zero to a maximum of 45 bushels. (The net product remains at 70 bushels; each bushel cut from the producers' consumption is simply transferred to the surplus product.) Beyond this point, however, any further reduction in the producers' consumption level will diminish their ability to produce grain, and the surplus product will fall, eventually reaching zero when the producers' consumption is down to 15 bushels. At this point the net product itself is only 15 bushels, and in order for the society to continue to exist, all of it has to be devoted to sustaining, however inadequately, the producers.

If Figure 5.5 is read in the other direction (from left to right), it illustrates how, at very low levels of consumption, the interests of the surplus owners and the producers may coincide. The part of the curve that slopes upward to the right shows that any increase in the consumption of the producers between 15 and 25 bushels will benefit both groups. At 15 bushels of consumption there is zero surplus product, whereas at 25 the maximum of 45 bushels of surplus is produced. Beyond this point, of course, further increases in the producers' consumption will reduce the surplus product. This is because once the producers are able to consume 25 bushels of grain they are fully productive, the net product is at

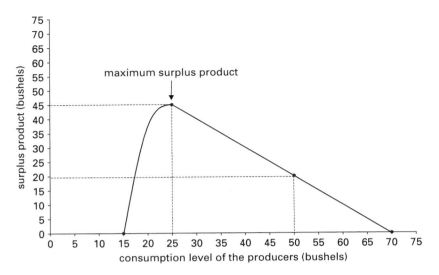

FIGURE 5.5 Conflict over the consumption level of the producers. This figure shows a hypothetical relationship between the level of consumption of the producers and the size of the surplus product. Each point on the line in the graph is an answer to the hypothetical question: for each level of consumption by the producers, how large will the surplus product be? If the producers' consumption level is 50 bushels, for example, the surplus product will be 20 bushels (as it was in our first presentation of the grain model—see Figure 5.4, left bar). If the producers' consumption level increased to a level of 70 bushels, the surplus product would be zero. Reducing the level of consumption will increase the surplus, but only to a point. The surplus reaches a maximum of 45 bushels when the consumption level is 25 bushels. Consumption levels below 25 bushels actually reduce the surplus product. If the consumption level were to fall to 15 bushels, the workers would be so impoverished that they would not be able to produce more than 15 bushels of net product a year, leaving no surplus product.

its maximum of 70 bushels, and each bushel added to the producers' consumption beyond this level means that there is one less bushel left for the surplus product.

A second type of economic conflict is one that occurs between groups in different nations. This can be seen in our grain-growing example after international exchange—and the possibility of importing plows—is introduced. In this example those who control the surplus in the "home" country would benefit from a lower real price of imported plows (an improvement in the terms of trade for them). If the price of importing a plow fell, say, from 10 bushels to 5 bushels and the cost of importing the two plows was thus reduced from 20 to 10 bushels, the surplus product would rise to 100 bushels (assuming that the consumption of the producers remains at 50 bushels). These calculations may be confirmed by referring back to Figure 5.4 and rereading the paragraph in the text that introduces this figure.

But what of the plow producers in the neighboring country? They will now be receiving just half as much grain per plow as they had received before the terms of trade changed. This illustrates how international conflict can affect the size of the surplus product in a particular nation. The dominant group in a powerful country may use force, threats of force, or other more subtle forms of bargaining power to induce people in other nations to agree to exchanges on terms more favorable to the group in the more powerful country. As illustrated in the example presented in the previous paragraph, such actions will lead to increases in the surplus product in the more powerful country because they will lower the real price of imported inputs. The benefits of the cheaper inputs may be shared with the local producers, but they need not be. In our example the reduction in the price of imported plows did not benefit the grain producers since their level of consumption remained the same. This may have been because they did not own or control the plows.

Using the numbers from our model of the surplus product with international exchange (see Figure 5.4), Figure 5.6 illustrates the conflict that arises between nations once trade is introduced. It shows that as the real price of an imported input (represented on the vertical

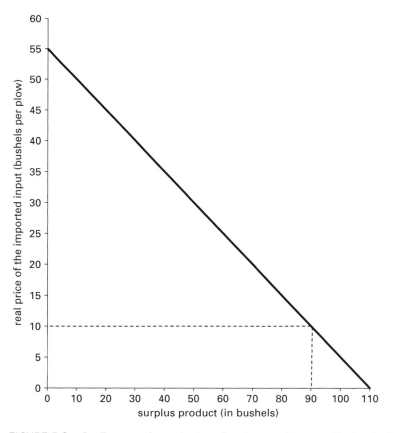

FIGURE 5.6   Conflict over the real price of an imported input.   The line in this figure shows the relationship between the real price of an imported input and the potential size of the surplus in the importing country. At higher prices of imported plows the surplus product will be lower, and at lower prices of imported plows the surplus product will be higher.

axis) rises, the surplus product in the importing country (shown on the horizontal axis) falls. This illustrates the conflict between the interests of the people supplying the import (they would like to be paid a higher price) and the interests of those who control the surplus product in the importing country (they would like to pay less for the imported input).

For example, if the price of an imported plow is 10 bushels (as in our earlier example), the surplus product will be 90 bushels (see Figure 5.4). However, the surplus product (in the importing country) would be reduced to zero if the international price of a plow were to rise to 55 bushels. In this case the total product (200 bushels) would be entirely spent on the consumption of the producers (unchanged at 50 bushels), the replacement costs (20 bushels for feeding the draft animals and 20 bushels to be set aside as seed for next year's crop), and paying the cost of the two imported plows (110 bushels).

On the other hand, if an army from the plow-importing country ("Grainland") were to invade and take over the plow-producing country ("Plowland"), the price of the imported plows might be reduced to zero, allowing the surplus product in Grainland to be maximized at 110 bushels. (Even at the zero price, the plow producers in Plowland would naturally be provided with their customary level of consumption by their Grainland invaders so they could turn out the plows that would be appropriated and shipped home by the Grainland soldiers.)

Conflicts over the real price of an imported input, such as the one just described between Grainland and Plowland, differ from consumption-surplus-product conflicts such as the one depicted in Figure 5.5. In the consumption-surplus-product type of conflict there is a lower limit to the consumption level (if the producers are to continue producing), whereas in a conflict over the real price of an imported input the price of the imported input can (at least conceptually) fall to zero.

Conflict over the real price of imported inputs is obviously international by its very nature. However, the divergence between the interests of two countries is often not just a simple conflict between nations. Although some conflicts pit whole nations against each other, with virtually all of the people in the "winning" nation benefiting to some degree from the clash and most everyone in the losing nation being worse off as a result, not all international conflicts are of this sort. In our example, it may seem as though the contention over the terms of trade is simply between Grainland and Plowland, but this is not the whole story. The producers of grain may not benefit at all from a lower price of imported plows, while those who control the surplus certainly do.

We might have designed a model in which the benefits of a lower price of imported plows were shared between the owners and the producers of the surplus. The point we want to make, however, is that distinct classes often have differing interests when it comes to international conflicts. Nationalistic sentiment may obscure this fact, and it often happens that what appears to be a conflict between nations is in reality a conflict between some group in one nation and a different group in another nation, while bystanders (such as the farmers in Grainland) have interests that do not coincide with the interests of the combatants from their own country.

As we will discuss in later chapters, much of what we see around us in politics, in economic policy, and even in culture and religion is shaped directly or indirectly by the international and class conflicts that arise from the production and control of the surplus. The surplus is also the key to understanding the process of change in societies.

THE SURPLUS PRODUCT AND CHANGE

The necessary product (as defined above) is dedicated to uses that are conservative in the literal sense of the word: it is used to reproduce existing conditions. The surplus product, on the other hand, may be used to alter the status quo. Such change can take various forms. In capitalist societies a significant portion of the surplus is *invested*. This means that the surplus is used to increase the productive capacity of the economy—by paying for education and training, by acquiring more and better capital goods, or by supporting the invention of new technologies. When it is used in any of these ways, the surplus benefits not only those who control it but others as well, and conflicts over its production are therefore diminished.

Other uses of the surplus are conservative in a different sense. Not only do they not produce change, they work against it and may even involve using force to maintain the power of the dominant class. When, for example, the surplus is used merely to support extravagant consumption by the wealthy, it is not promoting change; it is benefiting only the elite. When the surplus does not go into supporting the private consumption of the wealthy but is used to build monuments, temples, or churches, it may enrich the culture or serve the spiritual needs of the population, but it also may have the effect of reinforcing the status quo.

In a capitalist economy the way the surplus is typically used produces rapid change. The reason is that those who control the surplus (mostly the owners of large corporations and the people they hire to manage their affairs) are engaged in a relentless competition for survival as capitalists, and the key to survival is innovation—the introduction of new products, new technologies, new information, or new ways of organizing businesses. The elites of other economic systems—slavery, feudalism, or communism, for example—had it easier: competition was less intense and more easily controlled, and what these elites needed to do in order to win was not to innovate but rather to maintain their position in society.

Those who control the surplus product usually have a considerable amount of political power. Because they have money to spend, they wield a lot of influence over the actions and policies of the government. They also use the surplus to maintain the upper hand in the international and class conflicts that arise from the process of producing and claiming the surplus. Thus, to preserve the existing structure of society—and the corresponding distribution of wealth and income—part of the surplus is used to pay for the services of police, armed forces, security personnel, work supervisors, and even teachers and religious leaders who enforce and maintain the prevailing power relationships or propagate the ideology that explains and supports these relationships. This use of the surplus product is discussed further in Chapter 19.

Our model of the surplus product, technology, labor, and consumption illustrates the relationships among these concepts almost as an architect's drawing illustrates the spatial relationships among the parts of a building, but it does not do much more than that. It does not tell us why the technology is what it is, why the members of the family work a total of 2,000 hours annually, why they work as hard as they do, or how the "customary" level of consumption is established. The model does not even determine who gets the surplus (if there is one) or what is done with it. The job of the model is to help us *ask* these questions in a precise way, not to answer them. To answer these questions we need to take up the idea of class and ask how class relationships define economic systems. We do this in the next chapter.

SUGGESTED READINGS

Perry Anderson, *Lineages of the Absolutist State* (London: Verso Books, 1976).

Christopher Boehm, *Hierarchy in the Forest: The Evolution of Egalitarian Behavior* (Cambridge, Mass.: Harvard University Press, 2000).

Nancy Folbre, *Who Pays for the Kids? Gender and the Structures of Constraint* (New York: Routledge, 1994).

E. J. Hobsbawm, *Industry and Empire: The Making of Modern English Society* (London: Penguin Books, 1968).

Margaret Levi, *Of Rule and Revenue* (Berkeley: University of California Press, 1988).

Karl Polanyi, Conrad Arensberg, and Harry Pearson, eds., *Trade and Market in the Early Empires* (New York: Free Press, 1957).

Marshall Sahlins, *Stone Age Economics* (Chicago: Aldine Publishing, 1972).

Paul Sweezy, *The Theory of Capitalist Development* (New York: Monthly Review Press, 1942).

Charles Tilly, *Coercion, Capital, and European States, AD 990–1990* (Cambridge, Mass.: B. Blackwell, 1990).

CHAPTER 6

Capitalism as an Economic System

C ambridge, England—home to one of the world's great universities—sits at the edge of a low plain stretching north and east to the sea. Here the earth itself reveals how capitalism has transformed society. Before the advent of capitalism this marshy, swampy ground (called the "fens") had poor drainage, and in the rainy season much of it lay flooded and unusable. A town called Ely grew up on a small hill—the "isle of Ely"— that usually escaped the flooding.

In the Middle Ages a part of the surplus product of feudal England was used at Ely to build the first of several churches. In the ninth century an abbey was established, burned down, and then was rebuilt. Soon after the Normans conquered England in the 11th century, workers under their command began building the great cathedral that stands on the site today. Massive and elegant, the cathedral consumed the labors of thousands of artisans and required 110 years to build. But it was never really finished: new chapels were built, more elaborate furnishings were added, and the tower was heightened. Its west tower now soars 200 feet above the surrounding floodplain (and so would its east tower if it had not collapsed in the 14th century). For centuries it stood as a dry monument to the religious use of the surplus, while all about it the waterlogged fens frustrated cultivation.

Then, in the 17th century the fens themselves were transformed. The Duke of Bedford, owner of some 20,000 acres in the area, sensed the possibility for profits and organized an investment company to drain the fens. Engineers were hired, and workers dug two huge ditches, 100 feet wide and 30 miles long, to carry the excess water to the sea. Many additional miles of feeder ditches and channels carried water to the main ditches. This colossal construction project transformed the marsh into well-drained and fertile agricultural land and, as a result, made the duke a very rich man.

The modern visitor to Ely can see both marvels, the cathedral and the ditches. The cathedral, magnificent and dominating, represents feudalism, absorbing the region's surplus product but leaving the economy unchanged and stagnant. The less glamorous ditches represent the capitalist enterprise that invested the surplus product and drained the fens, repaying the investors many times over and supplying food to the region. The important point is that the fen ditches, humble and easy to overlook, revolutionized the entire system of production in the area. They are an example of the productive use of the surplus product characteristic of the capitalist system.

The story of the fens has a distinctly 21st-century (and noncapitalist) twist: in 2003 the Royal Society for the Protection of Birds announced plans to acquire most of the area from the "barley barons" who now farm it and to restore the fens' rivers, pools, and marshland, making it a homeland to the marsh harriers, black tailed godwits, and other bird species that disappeared when the Duke of Bedford drained the area four centuries earlier.

In this chapter we investigate how different societies determine the uses of their surplus products and who benefits from the ways they are used. Often people who do not produce the surplus product nonetheless control it. This was the case, for instance, in ancient Athens as well as in the U.S. South before the Civil War, when slaveholders lived off the products of their slaves' labor. The relationship between those who produce the product, including the surplus product, and those who control the use of the surplus product is called a *class relationship*. Class relationships exist between different *classes,* defined as groups of people who share a common position in the economy. The producers, excluded from control, are one class; the controllers of the surplus product are another class.

Of course, the distinction between producers and controllers is not always as clear-cut as it is on a slave plantation. The owners of a large capitalist corporation, for example, may participate in the production of the surplus in so far as they perform socially necessary tasks such as coordinating the work of many producers. At the same time, because of their position of power in the economy, they also have control over the disposition of the surplus product. Complications such as these mean that it is not always easy to draw clear lines between one class and another.

In any case, a society that is based on an economic system in which most producers exercise little or no control over the use of the surplus product is a *class society*. Capitalism is a class society. Though very different from U.S. capitalism, the economic system of China today makes it a class society, too. In both China and the United States the surplus product is produced by the work of millions of workers of all descriptions. But in both countries, even though their economic systems are very different, the disposition of the surplus product is controlled by a relatively small group of people.

The main idea of this chapter is that *economic classes are defined by how the surplus is controlled and used, and classes and the surplus product are the keys to understanding how different economic systems work and how they change.*

This main idea is expressed in four primary points.

---

1. A *class society* is one divided into two groups of people: those who *produce* the product but do not control the use of the surplus product, and those who *control* the use of the surplus product. In such a society class is the principal aspect of the vertical, or command, dimension of the economy. (Other vertical relationships, such as racial or sexual domination, are also important, and we will discuss them in later chapters.)

2. *Economic systems* represent different ways of organizing and controlling labor processes based on various systems of ownership, and these property systems in turn determine how the surplus product is used. The way in which the surplus product is controlled and by whom are what distinguish one economic system from another. Thus, each economic system will have a distinct set of classes—and a dominant *class relationship*—associated with it.

3. *Capitalism* is a particular economic system in which the private owners of *capital goods,* employers, hire *wage labor* to produce *commodities* for the purpose of making a *profit.* In this system there are two main classes, workers and capitalists, although other classes (the "middle" classes) are also important.

4. In capitalism the surplus appears as *profits.* Profits may be either retained within a firm and reinvested to expand production or paid out as rent, interest, dividends, or other payments to the owners of the capital goods used in production. Both those who receive such payments and those who control any retained profits may either save their money or spend it to buy the commodities, including capital goods, that make up the surplus product.

At Ely the various uses of the surplus product left visible reminders for us to see of the differences between feudalism and capitalism. The cathedral is hard to miss; the ditches, by contrast, are not so obvious unless we know where to look and what we are looking for. Similarly, while it is reasonably easy to see how the feudal economic system worked, understanding capitalism is more difficult unless we know where to look and what to look for—in this case classes and the surplus product.

CLASS AND CLASS RELATIONSHIPS

The word *class* is used in many different ways. If a ball player has class it means that he plays with a certain flair. If people are middle class it may mean that they have a certain lifestyle, perhaps owning a house and two cars. If a person is said to be a member of the upper class it means that she is rich, and so on. In political economy, however, the word has a different and very precise meaning.

> A **class** is a group of people who share a common position in the economy with respect to the production and control of the surplus product.

As noted already, a *class* is a group of people who share a common position in the economy with respect to the production and control of the surplus product. Thus, a *class relationship* exists when one group of people—one class—produces the total product, including the surplus product, while another group—another class—controls the use of the surplus product. Both groups, the *producers* of the surplus product and those who *control* its use, are classes. Slaves were one class, slaveholders another; the serfs who worked the land in medieval Europe constituted a class, their feudal lords a different one.

> A **class relationship** exists between the producers of the total product, including the surplus product, and those who command the use of the surplus product.

Four aspects of the concept of class are important. First, every class is defined in terms of a relationship. It is like the word *cousin,* which refers to someone, but which is meaningless unless there is another person who is also a cousin. You cannot be your own cousin; you cannot be a cousin by yourself; you can be only your cousin's cousin. A class cannot exist by itself, it can exist only in relationship to some other class.

Second, a class relationship refers to a labor process. Classes are defined by the particular positions that they occupy with respect to the labor process. A class is not defined either by its status or by the social esteem that others may attribute to its members nor is a class defined by the income of its members: the rich and the poor are not classes, though it is generally the case that most of the rich are in one class and most of the poor in another. A status group such as "the well educated" or an income group—say, those receiving more than $50,000 a year—is a collection of people defined by some characteristic. However, they are not defined by their relationship to another group in the labor process. For this reason they are not classes.

Members of a class may be very different from one another. They may live in different parts of the country or even in different areas of the world, they may be more or less well off, they may have different lifestyles, and if they are workers they may have very different jobs. They may even be in competition with one another—to find jobs, to sell products, or in other ways. Thus, it is possible that the only thing two members of a class will have in common with each other is their relationship to the labor process and to the other class (or classes).

A number of social groups very important to economic analysis are not classes. Nations are not classes, races are not classes, and sexes (genders) are not classes: the inclusion (or exclusion) of people in (or from) such groups is not based on their particular position in relation to a labor process. Females and males, for example, are defined biologically and culturally, and though men and women often do different kinds of work, it is not their position in a labor process that identifies them as men or women.

Third, class relationships are hierarchical, or vertical: they refer to a group on top and a group below. What is vertical about the relationship? Why do we call it hierarchical? The group on top is not necessarily happier, nor are they better people or more productive. Consider the slaveholders, for example. A group is said to be on top because it controls the labor and the products of those below. This is why class relationships are central to what we call the "command," or vertical, dimension of an economy.

The slaveholder employed the overseer who controlled the work of the slaves. What the slaves produced, in turn, belonged to the slaveholder. In the medieval era serfs worked about half of each week in the lord's fields, where the lord's bailiff directed their work. What the serfs grew on the lord's land belonged to the lord. Today, the owner (or owners) of a company, usually working through a board of directors, selects the management that hires and directs the work of the company's employees. The commodities produced by the employees are then owned by the company's owner (or owners).

In each economic system, of course, the producers must consume some of the output. This may be either a part of what they themselves have produced or goods and services produced by other workers. Slaves and serfs were allowed to till small plots of land on the plantations or estates on which they lived. In this way they were able to produce for themselves most of what they ate and wore. In contrast, workers today must buy most of what they consume in markets using the wages or salaries they are paid in return for their work. Note that in each case the producers—slaves, serfs, or workers—produce more than they consume. Correspondingly, the class on top receives something that it did not produce.

Those on top may also participate in production. Capitalist employers, for example, may put in some hours on the shop floor. As noted earlier, top executives perform work when they function as coordinators of the production process. But the income of employers does not flow primarily from productive work. Rather, it derives mainly from their ownership of the capital goods used in production and their control over the labor of others.

Fourth, the interests of producing and controlling classes are usually, but not always, in conflict. In most cases a gain for workers will show up as a loss for employers, but there are exceptions to this general rule. In certain situations both classes will have a common interest in relation to classes in other countries. Also, as we have seen in the previous chapter, both classes may benefit from some forms of technical change. Finally, almost everyone will be better off if a country's government is honest and efficient.

There are often more than two classes in a society, so usually the class relationships are more complex and involve more than just the relationship between the producers and those who control production. For instance, in the 19th century in the United States, an important relationship existed between the (northern) working class and the (southern) slaves. The relationship between these two classes was not vertical—the slaves did not live on the surplus product of the workers, or vice versa. Their relationship was partly one of class interdependence, since slaves grew the cotton needed in the mills where workers were employed. Also, the mills' demand for cotton provided the revenues that kept the slave plantations going, and the textiles produced in the mills became the slaves' clothing. Political relations also existed between these two classes, as when workers volunteered in the northern armies to fight for the emancipation of the slaves. However complex the relationship between slaves and workers may have been, both of these classes were defined with respect to a particular vertical relationship: slaves to slaveholders and workers to employers.

CLASSES AND ECONOMIC SYSTEMS

What is an economic system? We have already named several different economic systems: slavery, feudalism, self-sufficient households, and capitalism. We also know that what they have in *common*—what makes them economic systems—is that they organize labor processes. But what makes them *different* from one another?

Each economic system has a distinct set of class relationships, and each set of class relationships is identified with a specific way of organizing and controlling the system's labor processes. This combination of class relationships and associated methods for controlling labor processes is usually expressed legally in a set of *property rights*. Property rights, in turn, are what establish an owner's right to control property, to decide who can and cannot use it, to determine the purpose for which it is used, and to benefit from its use, improvement, or sale.

> **Property rights** establish the owner's right to control the property, to decide who uses it for what purpose, and to benefit from its use or sale.

For instance, *slavery* is an economic system defined by the class relationship between slaves and slaveholders. Inherent in the very definitions

Slavery was the dominant economic system in the U.S. South before the Civil War; slaveholders obtained the surplus product by owning all of the inputs (including slaves) and the output of slave production.

of *slaves* and *slaveholders* is a particular method for organizing labor processes based on the fact that the human input to production is itself owned as a piece of property. Thus, the slaveholder was a slaveholder because of his or her ownership of a particular piece of property (a slave), and this ownership conferred certain rights on the owner: the right to direct the slave's labor, the right to own the product of the slave's labor, the right to own any children the slave might bear, and the right to sell the slave.

In slavery as it existed in the American South before the Civil War, there were not only the two principal classes, slaves and slaveholders. There were also other classes such as non–slave-owning white farmers, overseers, urban craftspeople, free blacks, and merchants. However, the slaveholders were the dominant class, and, as noted, they owned all of the inputs to the slave labor process—including the laborers themselves. The slaves produced the total product, all of which was also owned by the slaveholders, and this consisted mainly of tobacco, rice, and raw cotton. Food was also grown on the plantations, and some of this food, together with other supplies purchased with revenues derived from the sale of the crops, was used to feed, clothe, and house the slaves. This portion of the total product, then, provided for the customary level of consumption for the slaves. Another part of the output had to be set aside to feed mules, replace worn out tools, or otherwise replace capital goods that had been used up in producing the output. What remained—the surplus product—was left for the slaveholder to use for personal consumption, for the purchase of more slaves, for the construction of beautiful mansions, for education of the slaveholder's children, for foreign travel, and so on.

Another type of economic system, *feudalism,* was how most economic activities were organized in Europe during the Middle Ages. As in slavery, there were two principal classes in feudalism, the lords (either church officials or members of the "noble" class) and the serfs (or peasants). Other classes in feudal Europe included artisans, bailiffs and other people in a lord's retinue, and merchants. The serfs produced the total product (except for goods made by artisans), some part of which, the customary amount of consumption, they retained for their own use. But the lords garnered a significant part of the total output, the surplus product, to support themselves, to build castles and cathedrals, to finance their Crusades, and, more generally, to maintain their noble lifestyles.

Feudalism was the dominant economic system in Europe in the Middle Ages; lords obtained the surplus product through rents and other customary obligations owed by the serfs.

How did the lords obtain the surplus product? Why did the serfs turn over part of the total output to them? To answer the question of *how* first: serfs usually owed rents to their lords, rents that were to be paid *in kind* (for example, two sheep and eight chickens) rather than in money. In addition, the serfs on an estate generally owed labor services to their lord: they were obligated to work on the lord's land for a certain number of days per week, and the lord owned what was produced on this land. (This system made it easy for anyone to see that during part of the week the producers were working on their own land to support themselves while during the other part of the week they were producing a surplus product for the lord on the lord's land.) Sometimes serfs were obligated to pay other fees, such as the common one for milling grain at the lord's gristmill or, in a less common instance, to support the lord's dancing bear. In this case the serfs had to continue paying the fee even after the bear died!

In feudalism, then, the surplus product was paid by the serfs in rents, labor duties, and fees owed to the lords. However, the lords did not own the serfs in the same way that slaveholders owned slaves. For example, a lord could not sell a serf nor even, in most instances, displace a serf family from its customary hut and plot. So why did the serfs pay? The answer is that they were legally obligated under feudal law to make these payments, and local feudal courts (usually controlled by the lords) enforced the lords' property rights. As a last resort the lords also had the military power—in the form of knights on horses—to punish any serf who refused to pay. In these ways, then, the lords controlled the production and use of the surplus product in the feudal system. (It should be noted here that sometimes a serf, when driven to desperation, would manage to escape to a nearby town, to move to open land, or to transfer to the service of another lord.)

These examples illustrate the underlying point that whether one is considering slavery, feudalism, capitalism, or something else, each economic system is characterized by a distinct class relationship. As we have said, each system also has corresponding ways of organizing labor processes and establishing property rights that, together with the class relationships, establish who controls labor processes and disposes of the surplus product. In Table 6.1 we summarize the main features of a wide variety of economic systems, offering suggestions for further reading about each type of system (see the suggested readings at the end of this chapter for full citations).

TABLE 6.1 Varieties of Economic Systems

Economic System	Characteristic Social Relationships	Examples	Suggested Readings
Hunting and gathering (foraging bands)	Cooperative acquisition and sharing of food and information; consensus decision making; no government; little private property; little inequality; no surplus product.	Most of the 100,000 years of human history before the development of agriculture 11,000 years ago; a few tribal societies in the world today.	Sahlins (1974) Diamond (1997) Boehm (2000)
Slavery	Slaves do most of the productive work; their owners own what the slaves produce (including the capital goods used in production) and also control the government; the surplus product takes the form of profit for the slave owners.	Ancient Rome; U.S. prior to the Emancipation Act of 1863.	Finley (1973) Genovese (1965) Fogel and Engerman (1974)
Feudalism	Serfs work both for themselves and for hereditary lords; the lords own the land and exercise most governmental functions; the surplus product takes the form of rents and forced labor on the lords' land (a required number of days per year) imposed on serfs.	Much of Europe from 1000 to 1500.	Bloch (1961) Anderson (1974) Aston and Philpin (1985)

(Continued)

TABLE 6.1 (continued)

Economic System	Characteristic Social Relationships	Examples	Suggested Readings
Independent production	Families do most of the work; they own the land, capital goods, and the products of their labor; they make decisions independently; government is minimal.	Much of England prior to the development of capitalism; nonslave states of the U.S. during the 19th century.	Allen (1992)
Agrarian despotism	A political elite governs the population, claiming the surplus product by imposing taxes on farmers—both those who own their land and tenants.	China prior to the 20th century; the Mughul Empire in India (1200–1700); much of Europe from 1500 to 1800.	Spence (1990) Richards (1993) Anderson (1972)
Central planning	Most economic decisions are made according to a plan drawn up and implemented by a powerful government; capital goods are state owned; political power is centralized; economic inequality is limited; the government controls the surplus product.	Soviet Union, 1921–1990; China and other Communist-ruled countries during second half of 20th century.	Dobb (1966) Allen (2003)
Capitalism	Owners of capital goods hire wage labor to produce commodities with the intention of making a profit; the employers make most economic decisions; there is substantial economic inequality; employers and others receive the surplus product as capitalist profit and other property income.	Parts of Europe since 1600 and most of the world today. Exceptions are China and the few other nations that continue to be Communist-ruled.	Dobb (1964) Wallerstein (1974) Gray (1998) Schumpeter (1942) Gordon, Edwards, and Reich (1982)

In different times and places the production and distribution of goods and services have been organized in a great variety of ways. Particular economic systems are distinguished not by *what* is produced but by *how decisions are made* concerning such things as who does what kind of work; what is to be produced, how, and when; and who will own or control the resulting goods and services. Listed in this table are seven major kinds of economic systems. Over the course of human history we have seen many variants not only of these seven systems but also of others not listed. In the future it is likely that completely new kinds of economic systems will appear. See the suggested readings at the end of the chapter for complete references to the works listed in the right-hand column of this table.

Economic systems are distinguished by *how decisions are made* concerning such things as who does what kind of work; who determines what is to be produced, how, and when; and who controls the resulting goods and services. There are seven major kinds of economic systems represented in the accompanying table. Over the course of human history there have been thousands of variants of these seven systems, and it is likely that in the future there will appear economic systems not yet even imagined.

Taking the analysis a step further, we can think of an economic system as a set of *rules of the game* governing economic life. From this point of view, economic systems may be understood using an analogy to games. What defines any game is the rules by which it is played. For example, what makes baseball different from basketball is not who plays it, or where it is played, or when, or anything else other than the rules by which each game is played.

The same is true of economic systems. Each economic system can be thought of as having a distinct set of rules of the game, that is, a particular set of rules governing the way in which classes interact with respect to the production and use of the surplus product. Economic systems are not defined according to *what* is produced (grain, steel, haircuts, or computer programs); *where* it is produced (in urban areas or in the countryside, in the United States or in Botswana); or *who* makes up the economic system. As in sports, it is the rules of the game that distinguish one economic system from another.

Class relationships, along with their particular rules of the game, were easy to see in precapitalist societies. In slave and feudal societies, for example, the slaveholder-slave and lord-serf relationships were quite visible. In contrast, the class relationship central to a capitalist economy is not so easy to see, especially when the capitalist economy in question is coupled with a democratic political system. In such a society everyone is said to be "equal under the law," and the rules of the game *do* involve a certain kind of parity among individuals that was not present in either slave or feudal societies. But legal equality is not social or economic equality. As Anatole France quipped, "the law, in its majestic equality, forbids the rich as well as the poor to sleep under bridges, to beg in the streets, and to steal bread."[1]

Regardless of the fact that people have equal legal rights in most capitalist societies, there is nevertheless a distinct—and defining—class relationship at the core of every capitalist economy. We turn now to an examination of the specific qualities that set capitalism apart from other economic systems.

CAPITALISM

> **Capitalism** is an economic system in which employers, using privately owned capital goods, hire wage labor to produce commodities for the purpose of making a profit.

Capitalism is a particular economic system in which employers, using *privately owned capital goods,* hire *wage labor* to produce *commodities* for the purpose of making a *profit.* Thus, the primary class relationship of capitalism is the one between employers (capitalists) and workers—*the capital-labor relationship.* Other classes—the "middle" classes—are also important, and they are discussed in the next chapter.

Capitalism is defined by three characteristics of its labor processes. First, most labor processes in the production sector produce commodities. Second, the capital goods used in production are privately owned. And third, the labor time devoted to producing commodities is purchased in labor markets. With each labor market transaction, a person agrees to provide his or her labor services to an employer for a certain period of time in return for a wage (or salary). Accordingly, the capitalist form of work is referred to as "wage labor."

We now discuss, in turn, each of the three aspects of a capitalist labor process: commodity production, private ownership of the capital goods used in production, and wage labor.

---

[1] Anatole France, *Le Lys Rouge* (Paris, 1894), Ch. 7.

Commodities

A *commodity* is any good or service that is produced, whether for a person to consume or for a business to use as an input, *with the intention of selling it* to make money. *Commodity production* therefore requires the presence of *markets* in which things are bought and sold.

> A **commodity** is any good or service that is produced with the intention of selling it in order to make a profit.

To clarify the idea of a commodity, think about pancake making. In the previous chapter we focused on the recipe—or technology—for making pancakes. Now we turn to the social organization of pancake making. To do this we will have to say where the pancakes are being made and why they are made. The labor process for making pancakes at home on a Sunday morning is organized in a very different way from the labor process for making pancakes at the House of Pancakes or some other restaurant.

Let us start with the House of Pancakes case. What explains who is doing what tasks in the restaurant? What explains how the pancake eater gets the pancake? The answer to both these questions is markets. The labor market determines the answer to the first question, and the pancake market, along with other markets that allow the pancake consumer to earn an income, determines the second.

The pancake eater gets the pancake by paying for it. He or she gives up something—some money—to acquire ownership of the pancake. In Chapter 8 we note that a market exchange is the (legal) way in which the ownership of things is transferred in a capitalist society. How much money is required? The price is determined by the competitive interaction of buyers and sellers, a process that we analyze in Chapter 8 with the help of supply and demand curves.

How the pancake eater gets the pancake also explains why the pancake is made. It is made to be sold in exchange for money. (This is what is meant by "commodity production.") The pancakes are not made at the House of Pancakes because the workers particularly like making pancakes or because they want the customers to be well fed. They make the pancakes because they are paid to do it. If they did not get paid they would quit. If they could make more money making hamburgers, they would probably be seeking employment at McDonald's.

Also, the pancake is probably not made because the owner of the House of Pancakes enjoys presiding over pancake making. He or she may live in another town or even another country. He or she may never have seen this particular House of Pancakes. In any case, if the owner could make more money by investing in steel making or sheep raising, he or she probably would not be the owner of the House of Pancakes.

The goal is making money, not making pancakes, and that is why a pancake produced at the House of Pancakes is called a commodity. The purpose of producing a commodity is, as we have said, to sell it. The likes and dislikes of producers or owners—their concern (or lack of it) for the nutrition or enjoyment of buyers—may be very real, but these factors (in most cases) will not determine what commodities are produced or who will get them. The outcomes regarding the *what* and the *for whom* questions will be determined by the *prices* at which the goods can be sold and the *costs* of producing them. Moreover, in a capitalist society commodity exchanges are generally anonymous: anyone who comes into the House of Pancakes and offers to pay the listed price for them will be provided with a stack of pancakes. It does not matter who the buyer is; only the price matters. In this respect capitalism undermines attitudes such as racial and other forms of discrimination.

Around the Sunday morning breakfast table at home, however, the situation is very different. If a stranger walked in, he might be asked to come back later—or never. It is also conceivable that he might be invited to sit down and have some pancakes. But it is not likely that he would be given some pancakes for no other reason than because he offered to pay for them.

Pancakes made in the kitchen of an army base are not commodities, either. They are made because someone in authority ordered them to be made, and those making them do so because they are following orders. No price is charged for the pancakes; to get a pancake one must simply belong to one of the units at the base.

Although the spread of capitalism in the modern world has brought with it the commodification of more and more aspects of social life—turning more and more things, previously not for sale, into commodities—there are still many products that are not produced as commodities. Take, for example, elementary and secondary education. Although there are more than 3,000 private schools in the United States, the vast majority of American children go to public schools that are financed not by tuition payments (which buy education as if it were a commodity) but rather by communitywide tax dollars distributed through local governments. Activities financed through the government are not thought of as producing commodities because they are not producing things that are *for sale* in a market. In our example, children have the right to go to a public school in their community because they live in the community, not because they can buy the right to go to a particular school.

With few exceptions, *people* are not produced as commodities. Although the work that a mature person does will almost certainly be influenced by market forces, the birth, care, nurturance, and upbringing of that person—all involving labor processes in the reproduction sector—will not usually be undertaken with the aim of producing an object for sale. Exceptions would include the incubation of an embryo by a surrogate mother for a fee (a service that might be advertised as "womb for rent") and the breeding of slave children on American plantations in the antebellum South for the purpose of selling the children in slave markets for profit.

In any case, Figure 6.1 shows that commodity-producing labor amounts to less than half of all labor performed in the U.S. today. Recent surveys of "time use" (surveys that collect data on how people divide their time among various activities) have shown that about half of all work in industrialized countries (including the U.S.) takes place outside the market. This work is not paid for, most of it is household labor, and much of it involves caring for family members, especially young children. The surveys also found that of men's total work time in the industrialized countries, roughly two-thirds is spent in paid activities and one-third in unpaid activities. For women, however, the proportions are exactly reversed, with one-third devoted to paid activities and two-thirds to unpaid activities.[2]

Among Americans who sold their working capacities in labor markets in 2001, 84 percent were engaged in the production of commodities while the other 16 percent were non–commodity-producing government employees. Thus, the relative percentages of non-market, commodity-producing, and government labor—shown in Figure 6.1 as percentages of the total number of hours worked in the U.S. in an average week in 2001—were 50 percent, 42 percent, and 8 percent, respectively.

Much household work is devoted to tasks such as child care, grocery shopping, cooking, cleaning, folding laundry, gardening, and mowing the lawn, most of which require large

---

[2] United Nations, *Human Development Report 1995* (New York: United Nations, 1995), pp. 88–89.

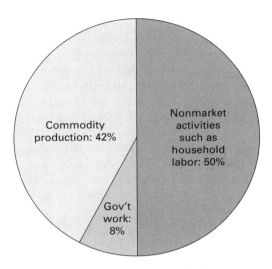

FIGURE 6.1 Household labor and other nonmarket work, commodity-producing labor, and government work. Here we consider three types of labor processes: household labor and other nonmarket activities, labor in the private sector dedicated to the production of commodities, and work in the public sector that involves the paid (but not commodity-producing) labor of government workers (federal, state, and local). Approximately 10.8 billion hours of labor were performed in a typical week in the U.S. in 2001, and the percentages in this figure represent shares of this total number of hours. The data are presented in terms of hours of labor rather than numbers of workers because most people participate in more than one kind of labor process, for example, performing household labor while also holding a job in the outside world. The figure is based on an estimate that half the work performed in the U.S. is nonmarket (unpaid) labor. All such estimates are, of course, subject to error, particularly since the government does not collect data on nonmarket labor.

Sources: United Nations, *Human Development Report 1995* (New York: United Nations, 1995), pp. 88–89; U.S. Census Bureau, *Statistical Abstract of the United States: 2001* (Washington, D.C.: U.S. Government Printing Office, 2001), Tables 10 and 580; U.S. Census Bureau, www.census.gov/statab/www, *USA Statistics in Brief,* "Employment" table.

amounts of time. In a society such as the U.S., however, where two-earner couples have become the norm, parents of young children (particularly mothers) enjoy very little leisure time. Many such parents, if they have sufficient income, purchase substitutes for goods and services they once provided for themselves, paying for child care and buying more restaurant and take-out meals. There are few paid family leaves from work in the U.S., and there is considerably less public support for child care than there is in other rich countries.

Another important form of nonmarket work is the volunteer labor that people provide to community organizations, schools, and other institutions in their neighborhoods. Such activities sustain our civic life, but people now seem to have less and less time for them as more and more of the typical family's time has to be spent working in the paid labor force.[3]

---

[3] Robert Putnam, *Bowling Alone: The Collapse and Revival of American Community* (New York: Simon & Schuster, 2000).

Although commodity production accounts for less than half of the labor performed in a modern capitalist society such as the U.S., it was even less important in precapitalist societies in the past, and it is also less important in noncapitalist societies today. For example, market exchanges in food were forbidden in some societies because their people regarded nourishment as too important a function to be left to the buying and selling activities of individuals. Even today in the United States as well as in many other countries, government price supports and other kinds of state intervention prevent the price of food from being determined entirely by unregulated commodity exchange. In the global economy today, however, food *is* a commodity—and this has a lot to do with the persistence of hunger around the world. (See box "Money Talks (And Eats.)")

MONEY TALKS (AND EATS)

On any given day between 1997 and 1999, 815 million people—nearly one-eighth of the world's total population—were undernourished in the sense that they did not get enough food to meet their daily energy needs, even for moderate activity. Although it is difficult to determine exactly how many people die of hunger in any particular year—the exact cause of death is uncertain in many cases—authorities on the subject believe that the number is between 30 and 50 million.

The facts regarding the world's children under five years of age are better known: one-third of them were undernourished during the 1990s, and toward the end of that decade more than 10 million of them were dying of hunger each year.

The overwhelming majority of the world's hungry people, 777 of those 815 million in 1997 to 1999, reside in the poor countries of Africa, Asia, and Latin America. Although the proportion of hungry people in the poor countries, relative to their total populations, fell from 37 percent at the beginning of the 1970s to 17 percent at the end of the 1990s, the absolute number of such people remains stubbornly high. It fell less than 5 percent during the decade of the 1990s.

While most of the world's hungry people live in poor countries, the phenomenon of undernourishment is also to be found in more affluent regions. For example, a survey done by the U.S. Department of Agriculture found that in 1998 there were 10.5 million American households (36 million people, 14 million of them children) without enough food to meet their daily nutritional needs.

Why are there so many hungry people in the world, many of them children who die before they reach five years of age? The main reason is that land and income, both within and among nations, are very unequally distributed—and those who do not have much land or income cannot produce or buy enough food to nourish themselves adequately. Paradoxically, many of the world's hungry people are farm workers or farmers who depend on part-time employment in

Continued . . .

nonagricultural jobs to make ends meet. Unemployment is a far more common cause of hunger than crop failure.

Food is a commodity, and this means, first, that it is distributed though markets and, second, that market prices determine how much is produced, and for whom. Since we live in a highly integrated global economy, food will be purchased and consumed by those, wherever they may live, who can afford to pay the highest prices for it.

In recent years small agricultural producers (peasant farmers, for example), once able to provide for their own subsistence, have been displaced by large commercial farms that are more likely to produce "cash crops" for the export market. Thus, food is exported to more prosperous countries where already-well-fed consumers are willing and able to pay relatively high prices for it. The sad consequence is that in a world of persistent hunger, food flows through global markets from areas of need to areas of wealth. We live in a world in which money not only talks but also determines whether or not a person can eat.

Sources: Frances Moore Lappé, Joseph Collins, and Peter Rosset, *World Hunger: 12 Myths* (New York: Grove Press, 1998); U.S. Department of Agriculture, *Advance Report on Household Food Security, 1995–1998* (Washington, D.C.: U.S. Department of Agriculture, 1999); Food and Agriculture Organization of the United Nations (FAO), *The State of Food and Agriculture 2001* (Rome: FAO, 2001); FAO, *The State of Food Insecurity in the World 2000* and *The State of Food Insecurity in the World 2001* (Rome: FAO, 2000 and 2001); FAO, *Agriculture: Towards 2015/30, Technical Interim Report,* April 2000, Chapters 1 and 2 (available at http://www.fao.org/es/ESD/ at2015/toc-e.htm); UNICEF, *The State of the World's Children 2001,* Table 1 (available at http://www.unicef.org/sowc01), and *The State of the World's Children 2002,* Introduction (available at http://www.unicef.org/sowc02).

Commodity production, then, is very different from other ways of organizing production and distributing its results. Other ways of coordinating economic activities include relations within a family, military commands at an army base, and the democratic processes of deliberating and voting. However, understanding commodity production is one of the keys to understanding the economy of the United States—and that of the world—today.

By itself, commodity production does not define capitalism, nor is capitalism synonymous with commodity production (or "market economy"). Historically, there have been economic systems that were oriented to commodity production but in which there were no capitalists. One such example, already discussed, is the slave economy of the pre–Civil War American South, in which slaves produced tobacco, rice, and cotton on plantations and the owners sold the slaves' products as commodities in the world market.

At roughly the same time, another way of organizing economic life coexisted with slavery in the U.S. This economic system—to be discussed at greater length in the next chapter—consisted of home production of items for direct use and the production of commodities by independent self-employed producers such as farmers, craftsmen, and artisans. This economic system, in which production was carried on by households that owned their own capital goods and frequently exchanged their products—but not their labor—in markets accounted for approximately 60 percent of all production in the U.S. at that time. It was something like this, a property-owning democracy, that was advocated by Thomas Jefferson.

During the 20th century, proponents of *market socialism* argued that markets might be used to coordinate an economy that would form the basis of a socialist rather than a capitalist society. What they envisioned is a system in which worker-owned firms would sell their products competitively in markets (thus avoiding the need for central planning) but in which there would be neither capitalists (since capital goods would be owned by worker-controlled firms) nor wage labor (since workers would have access to their own capital goods and would, in effect, be hiring themselves). Whatever one may think of such proposals, the fact is that commodity production has occurred historically in various noncapitalist economic systems and could occur in future noncapitalist systems.

For commodity production to be termed capitalist production, there must also be employers and workers. The relationship between employers and workers (the capital-labor relationship) is, in turn, defined by two other characteristics of the labor process: private ownership of the capital goods—the tools, factories, offices, and other (durable) goods used in production—and labor employed as wage labor.

Privately Owned Capital Goods

The second defining feature of capitalism (after commodity production) is that the capital goods used in production are the *private property* of capitalists. Private property means, first, that what is owned may be used or sold at the discretion of the owner or people he or she selects; second, that the owner has a claim on any income or other benefits that may result from the use of the object owned; and third, that the owner is entitled to exclude others from using whatever it is that is owned, for example, land or factories. A sign that reads "Private Property, No Trespassing" conveys the third meaning of private property.

> **Private property** is a social institution (or rule) that gives individuals or firms the right to use, lend, or sell things such as land, buildings, and artistic or intellectual creations of any kind; it means that one can have or use such things only if one has made, rented, purchased, or been given them.

Private ownership of capital goods, while not unique to capitalism, is nonetheless far from universal. For instance, many Native American peoples did not have a concept of private property in land, and this led to misunderstandings between them and the European settlers who thought they were buying things from the Native Americans in accordance with Western notions of private property. The derogatory expression "Indian giver," referring to someone who gives something and then wants it back, illustrates this point: the phrase arises from the Europeans' (and, later, some Americans') inability to understand that among Native Americans some things such as land were neither mine nor yours but ours or no one's. Other societies have also had very complex notions of property, as the description of property rights among the Arapesh of New Guinea illustrates. (See box "Property Rights among the Arapesh of New Guinea.")

> **Privately owned capital goods** are machines, buildings, offices, tools, and other durable things needed in production and whose owner, because of a property right, determines how the property will be used.

How could capital goods *not* be privately owned? In some cases a government body, such as a municipal electric company, may own them. Even in the private sector it is possible for the capital goods in a particular company to be owned by its workers. Indeed, it occasionally happens that when a company is on the verge of bankruptcy and needs to be "bailed out" to prevent it from "going under," its managers and workers will get together, raise the capital necessary to buy a majority of the

PROPERTY RIGHTS AMONG THE ARAPESH OF NEW GUINEA

A typical Arapesh man [lives] *for at least part of the time . . . on land which does not belong to him. Around the house door are pigs which his wife is feeding but which belong either to one of her relatives or to one of his. Beside the house are coconut and betel palms which belong to still other people and the fruit of which he will never touch without the permission of the owner. . . . He hunts on bush land belonging to a brother-in-law or a cousin at least part of* [his] *hunting time, and the rest of the time he is joined by others on his bush, if he has some. He works his sago in others' sago clumps as well as in his own.*

Of the personal property in his house, that which is of any permanent value, like large pots, well carved plates, [and] *good spears, has already been assigned to his sons, even though they are only toddling children. His own pig or pigs are far away in other hamlets; his palm trees are scattered three miles in one direction, two in another; his sago palms are still further scattered; and his garden patches lie here and there, mostly on the lands of others.*

If there is meat on his smoking rack over the fire, it is either meat which was killed by another—a brother, a brother-in-law, a sister's son, etc.—and has been given to him, in which case he and his family may eat it; or it is meat which he himself killed and which he is smoking to give away to someone else, for to eat one's own kill, even though it be only a small bird, is a crime to which only the morally—which usually means in Arapesh mentally—deficient would stoop.

If the house in which he is living is nominally his, it will have been constructed in part at least from the posts and planks of other people's houses, which have been dismantled or temporarily deserted, and from which he has borrowed timber. He will not cut his rafters to fit his house, if they are too long, because they may be needed later for someone else's house which is of a different shape or size.

This then is the picture of a man's ordinary economic affiliations, crosscutting every defined line of geography and blood kinship, [and these affiliations are] *based on personal ties between individuals which serve to tangle the members of each group into many other groups and to blur every possible distinction between groups.*

Source: Margaret Mead, *Cooperation and Competition Among Primitive Peoples* (Boston: Beacon Press, 1961), pp. 31–32. Reprinted with permission from the Institute for Intercultural Studies, Inc., New York, N.Y.

company's shares in the stock market, and—often with wage reductions and other measures—put the company back on a firm financial footing.

There is a large number of enterprises in the U.S. that are owned and controlled by their workers, the most well known of these being a group of plywood manufacturing companies in the Pacific Northwest (see box, "Own Your Job. Elect Your Boss"). In the Mondragon region in Spain more than 100 workers' cooperatives manufacture and sell everything from home appliances to machine tools. Similarly, Germany has a system—called "codetermination"—that requires that boards of directors of companies include (as directors) a certain number of labor representatives and that democratically elected workers' councils be allowed to participate in the decision-making processes of German corporations. In Italy there are almost 40,000 worker cooperatives.

As noted, private ownership of capital goods not only grants their owners the right to use or sell them; it also gives employers the right to exclude others from using them. The right to exclude others implies the right to fire workers, since that is just a way of excluding workers from the workplace. The related right, the right to determine who is included, is the right to hire. So the power to hire and fire is an aspect of the property rights of capitalist employers.

OWN YOUR JOB. ELECT YOUR BOSS

In 1921 a group of loggers, carpenters, and mechanics in Olympia, Washington, formed the Olympia Veneer Plywood Cooperative. In return for an investment of $1,000, a member gained the right to work in the plant and to share equally in any profit. Members who wished to leave were to sell their shares, and prospective members, if approved by the membership, were required to purchase shares, which by 1923 were selling for $2,550 per share. In 1939, 250 workers in nearby Anacortes each invested $2,000 to set up a second cooperative plywood mill. Strong wartime demand for plywood boosted the value of each of their shares to $28,000 in 1951, and members paid themselves wages at rates double the union wage in nearby conventionally organized plywood mills.

Stimulated by the success of Olympia Veneer and Anacortes, between 1949 and 1956, 21 more coops entered the plywood industry in the states of Washington and Oregon, 9 of them by buying out existing conventional firms. Some coops had either transformed themselves into de facto conventional firms or sold out to conventional firms. Until the entire industry moved from the Northwest to the Southeast in the 1980s and 1990s, about half the plywood firms were coops, the rest being conventional firms, some with unionized labor forces and some with nonunion ones. Though the coops and conventional firms used virtually identical machinery, the coops specialized in the more labor-intensive "sanded" plywood because, as one analyst of the coops commented, it "puts a premium on worker effort."

With few exceptions the worker-owners of the plywood cooperatives in the Northwest received equal pay, and their jobs were often rotated. The body of worker members elected management. Some nonmembers were hired under conventional wage contracts, their numbers making up an average of a quarter of the total workforce. High levels of productivity were maintained through a strong work ethic among members, enforced by peer pressure. The resulting saving in supervision costs was substantial: when one conventional firm converted to a coop, the number of supervisors was reduced to a quarter of its previous level. Shares that were relinquished by retiring or departing members were advertised

Continued . . .

in local newspapers. Average share prices ranged from the equivalent of one year's annual earnings to three times that amount.

Conventional firms and cooperatives alike were able to attract both labor and capital over their 75 years of coexistence in the Northwest, but the firms differed in a number of ways. The productivity (output per unit of all inputs) of the coops was substantially higher than the conventional firms. The reason why the coops did not take over the whole industry is that their potential members had difficulty raising the funds needed to buy a share. Another difference: rather than laying off members when demand for plywood was slack, the coops reduced the pay of all their workers, thereby spreading the pain but also insuring members against the calamity of job loss.

Today in the U.S. more than one-fifth of employees own stock in the companies where they work, though few own substantial amounts, and, unlike the members of the plywood cooperatives, almost none can elect their boss. While there have been some well-publicized failures of worker ownership, such as United Airlines, firms with a significant amount of ownership by employees generally achieve higher labor productivity than conventional firms, particularly when employees also participate in decision making about the work process.

Sources: Adapted from Samuel Bowles, *Microeconomics: Behavior, Institutions, and Evolution* (Princeton: Princeton University Press, 2004). See also: Douglas Kruse, "Research Evidence on the Prevalence and Effects of Employee Ownership," *Journal of Employee Ownership Law and Finance* vol. 14, no. 4, 2003, pp. 65–90; John Pencavel, *Worker Participation: Lessons from the Worker Co-ops of the Pacific North-West* (New York: Russell Sage Foundation, 2002).

The right to use one's property at one's own discretion is considerably limited by zoning laws, union contracts, public health codes, occupational health and safety regulations, pollution controls, and the like. Even with such limitations, however, private ownership of capital goods is one of the legal conditions that makes capitalist production possible.

When discussing ownership of capital goods it is useful to distinguish between *wealth, property income,* and *earned income* (or earnings). Wealth refers to what a person or a corporation owns at any particular moment in time, and for that reason economists think of it as a "stock." On the other hand, income—whether from property or from labor—is regarded as a "flow," and it is measured over a certain period of time: an hour, a week, a month, or a year.

> **Wealth** is the ownership of a stock of durable things or intangibles that yield income or other benefits over an extended period of time.

Wealth involves the ownership of durable things that may yield income or other benefits to their owner over time. Thus, a person's wealth at any given moment may consist of such tangible items as houses, cars, factories, and land; it may also include intangible sources of income such as securities, copyrights, and patents. Things owned by individuals or corporations are commonly called *assets,* and the terms *net assets* and *net worth* refer to everything owned minus liabilities or debt owed to other people or institutions (such as banks and credit card companies). When a person is described as being "wealthy" it means that he or she owns a significant quantity of assets over and above any liabilities or debts. Bill Gates is an example of a wealthy individual: his net worth in 2003 (according to *Forbes* magazine) was $46 billion. (See box "Brother, Can You Spare a Billion?")

BROTHER, CAN YOU SPARE A BILLION?

E very year since 1982, *Forbes* magazine has published a list of the 400 richest people in America, called the Forbes 400. More recently *Forbes* has begun publishing a list of "the world's billionaires," of whom in 2003 there were 476 spread among some 40 countries. As it happens, Bill Gates, the Microsoft founder, is currently at the top of both lists, with a net worth of $46 billion. Gates began his ascent to the pinnacle of wealth using his skills as a computer software designer, but nearly a third of the 400 richest Americans are on the Forbes list because they inherited a substantial amount of wealth from their parents or grandparents.

To qualify in 2003 for the *Forbes* list of the 400 wealthiest Americans—more than half of whom were billionaires—one needed to have a net worth of at least $600 million. Taken together, these 400 richest Americans had a total of $955 billion of net assets, or as *Forbes* put it, "just one Bill Gates away from $1 trillion." The wealth of these 400 was approximately equal to the combined net financial assets of the 83 million poorest households in the U.S.

Top Ten of the World's Billionaires

Name	Net Worth	Country	Source of Wealth
William H. Gates III	$46.0 billion	U.S.	Microsoft
Warren Edward Buffett	$36.0 billion	U.S.	Investments
Theo & Karl Albrecht and family	$25.6 billion	Germany	Aldi Stores
Paul Gardner Allen	$22.0 billion	U.S.	Microsoft
Sam Walton's widow and four children	$20.5 billion each	U.S.	Wal-Mart Stores
Lawrence Joseph Ellison	$18.0 billion	U.S.	Oracle
Prince Alwaleed Bin Talal Alsaud	$17.7 billion	Saudi Arabia	Investments
Liliane Bettencourt	$14.5 billion	France	L'Oreal cosmetics
Kenneth Thompson and family	$14.0 billion	Canada	Publishing
Ingvar Kamprad	$13.0 billion	Sweden	IKEA
Michael Dell	$13.0 billion	U.S.	Dell Computer

Sources: Forbes Magazine, March 17, 2003, and October 6, 2003; Edward N. Wolff, "Recent Trends in Wealth Ownership, from 1983 to 1998," in Thomas M. Shapiro and Edward N. Wolff, eds., *Assets for the Poor* (New York: Russell Sage Foundation, 2001).

Income, on the other hand, is a different matter, though not entirely different. We can calculate from the information presented in the box "Brother, Can You Spare a Billion?" that each member of the "Forbes 400" had, on average, a net worth of $2.39 billion (that's 2,390 million dollars!) in 2003. If these 400 individuals invested—or hired someone to

Property income is income that is received in the form of profit, rent, interest, or dividends as a result of owning an asset such as a business, a piece of land, an existing structure, a bond, or a share of corporate stock.

invest for them—their assets in such a way as to produce even a 5 percent return each year (not an unreasonable assumption to make for the "Forbes 400"), each of them would enjoy, on average, an annual income of nearly $120 million. Moreover, such an income would consist entirely of property income: generating it would require only as much effort as it takes to select a skilled investment manager to handle one's account. To confirm this: Imagine what would happen if a person in such a situation were to pass away. Roughly the same amount of income would flow into his or her "estate" until the net assets in it were passed on in accordance with the person's will.

High net worth is usually based on ownership of a significant amount of corporate stock (private ownership of the capital goods used in production). Figure 6.2 shows that if the 108.2 million households in the U.S. in 2001 are ranked by the amount of corporate stock they owned in that year (the latest year for which data are available), the top 1 percent owned 33.5 percent of the corporate stock, the top 10 percent owned 76. 9 percent of such stock, and the bottom 90 percent of American households owned 23.1 percent. (See sources cited below Figure 6.2.) This uneven distribution of the ownership of corporate assets helps to explain why some people are employers while others (the majority of the population) are workers.

The last two decades of the 20th century witnessed a dramatic increase in stock ownership among American households. If *indirect* ownership—through mutual funds, trusts, IRAs, Keogh plans, 401(k) plans, and other retirement accounts—is included, the percentage of households owning at least some stock went from 24.4 percent in 1983 to 48.2 percent in 1998. These numbers also show, of course, that in 1998 more than half of all American households owned no stock at all. In that same year families with more than $100,000 of income owned 91 percent of all corporate stock.[4]

The significance of privately owned wealth is that the more of it one has, the less one is required to work. Table 6.2, "Sources of Income for U.S. Taxpayers, 2001," presents IRS data for 2001 (the latest year for which data are available). It shows that the higher a taxpayer's income, the less of it comes in the form of wages or salaries. The logic of it is as follows: Wages and salaries are earned income, while unearned income comes in the form of interest, dividends, rent, royalties, and realized capital gains, all of which are but different kinds of property income. Hence, from the columns on the left and right sides of the table we can draw the following conclusion: the higher a taxpayer's income, the lower is his or her earned income (wage or salary) as a percent of total income (both earned and unearned). As we follow the income brackets (in the left-most column of the table) from less than $20,000 to more than $1 million, we can see (in the right-most column) that the corresponding percent of total income that is earned falls from 92.8 to 35.8 percent.

Although many very-high-income taxpayers—for example, chief executive officers (CEOs) of large corporations, as well as others—work very hard, the magnitude of their property income means that they generally do not *have* to work. We present more complex definitions of the capitalist and working classes—and also the "middle" classes—in the next chapter. However, one important conclusion that can be drawn from the preceding set

---

[4] U.S. Department of Commerce, Census Bureau (www.census.gov/statab/www), *Statistical Abstract of the United States, 2000* (Table no. 837); Edward N. Wolff, "The Rich Get Richer . . . And Why the Poor Don't," *The American Prospect,* Feb. 12. 2001, pp. 15–17.

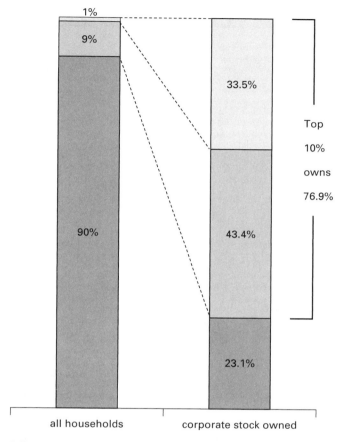

FIGURE 6.2   The concentration of ownership of capital goods.   The bar on the left represents the 108.2 million households (families and individuals) that made up the U.S. population in 2001. The bar on the right represents the value of all the publicly traded stocks of corporations in the same year (the latest year for which data is available), and it shows the proportions of stocks that were owned—whether directly or indirectly through mutual funds, trusts, and retirement accounts—by the various segments of the U.S. population. The figure shows that the wealthiest 1 percent of households owned 33.5 percent of the corporate stock, that the top 10 percent (which includes the top 1 percent) owned 76.9 percent of such wealth, and that the bottom 90 percent of American households (ranked according to their ownership of corporate stock) owned 23.1 percent.

Sources: U.S. Census Bureau, *Statistical Abstract of the United States: 2003*, Table No. 66; Edward N. Wolff, "Changes in Household Wealth in the 1980s and 1990s in the U.S.," in Edward N. Wolff, ed., *International Perspectives on Household Wealth* (Northampton, Mass.: Edward Elgar, forthcoming).

of facts is that if a person's property income is substantial, he or she *can* choose not to work while still maintaining a decent standard of living, whereas a person without much property income *cannot* make such a choice. It is this distinction (among others) that separates the capitalist class from the working class.

TABLE 6.2 Sources of Income for U.S. Taxpayers, 2001

Income Level*	% of Taxpayers	% of Total Income	% of Total Wages and Salaries	Wages and Salaries as % of Total Income***
Zero to $20,000	38.2%	6.6%	8.2%	92.8%
$20,000 to $100,000	53.3%	52.7%	57.7%	81.0%
$100,000 to $1 million	8.3%	31.3%	29.5%	69.6%
$1 million or more	0.15%	9.4%	4.5%	35.8%
Total:	100.0%	100.0%	100.0%	
	Total no. of taxpayers** (millions)	Total income (millions)	Total wages and salaries (millions)	
	130.3	$6,171	$4,565	

* "Income level" refers to the "adjusted gross income" reported on the tax returns filed with the IRS in 2001.

** No. of "taxpayers" refers to the number of *tax returns* filed with the IRS in 2001. Since many multiple-earner families file "joint" tax returns, the number of returns will be less than the number of income-earners. The data in this table is based on tax returns.

*** Total income includes, in addition to wage and salary income: interest, dividends, rent, royalties, and capital gains, all of which are forms of property income. Other sources of nonwage income (generally smaller amounts than those derived from property) include: business and professional income, social security benefits, alimony, and unemployment insurance.

Source: U.S. Treasury Department, Internal Revenue Service, SOI-2001, Individual Income Tax Returns, March 2004, Table 1.4. Available at http://www.irs.gov/taxstats/article/0,,id=96981,00.html.

> The **capitalist class**, or **capitalists**, are those who own capital goods used in production and exercise control over the labor of others; they receive their income in the form of profits or other payments (such as interest and rent) for the use of their capital goods.

Thus, we can say that the *capitalist class* consists of that group of people—a minority of the population—who own the capital goods used in the production of commodities. They control not only their own work (if they work) but also (and more importantly) the labor of others, and most of their income is property income. The *working class,* on the other hand, consists of people—the majority of the population—who do not own sufficient capital goods to live on and must therefore work under the control of others. Workers receive their income in the form of wages or salaries. People in the working class typically do own cars, homes, and other personal property, and some even own corporate stocks or shares in mutual funds, but such possessions do not give workers control of the capital goods used in production.

> The **working class**, or **workers**, are those who perform wage labor; they neither own the capital goods used in their labor processes nor command control over the labor of others.

Wage Labor

The third defining characteristic of a capitalist economic system (after commodity production and privately owned capital goods) is *wage labor.* Wage workers are people who must live on the wages or salaries they

Wage labor is work performed under the direction of an employer in return for a wage or salary.

receive in return for working for an employer; hence, their work is called wage labor. Everyone who earns a living as an employee is a worker.

What other kind of work is there? As we explain in the next chapter, most people in the United States 200 years ago did not work as wage workers. They were independent farmers or other self-employed persons, or they were slaves. Some producers in the United States today are still not wage workers. These are the people who work for themselves, or in partnerships, or in cooperatively owned establishments. Some work at their own family farms or shops.

People who work for themselves make their livings either by producing what they themselves consume or by selling a commodity they have produced. Wage labor is fundamentally different. People who work for wages or salaries make their living by renting themselves out, or more precisely, by selling their time. In exchange for the wage, they work under someone else's direction, producing things that they will not own.

Concentration of ownership of capital goods in one part of the population implies the need for wage work among most of the rest. Only people who own a substantial amount of property can live on their property income, while those who own few or no capital goods usually must have jobs to survive. Thus, the concentration of ownership of capital goods in the hands of relatively few people and the existence of wage labor are closely related.

An example will make this point clear. At the dawn of the 21st century, workers in the United States worked with, on average, more than $90,000 worth of capital goods (including software as well as equipment and buildings).[5] Most U.S. workers, of course, do not own the capital goods with which they work. American workers usually own cars, and most own their own homes but little else. Thus, a typical worker is not wealthy enough to acquire the capital goods he or she would need in order to be an independent producer. If workers each had an extra $90,000 of wealth, they might be able go into business for themselves, perhaps by pooling their wealth with friends or family members. Since most workers cannot raise enough money to start their own businesses, the tools they work with and the place they work in are generally owned by somebody else. That "somebody" is their employer, on whom they depend for their livelihoods.

CAPITALISM, THE SURPLUS PRODUCT, AND PROFITS

We can now see the link between the basic class relationship of capitalism and the surplus product. Employers (capitalists) hire workers to produce commodities (the total product), which the employers then own. The employers then sell the commodities that the workers have produced. Assume that, out of their sales revenues, the employers pay wages sufficient to provide each worker with the customary amount of consumption. Assume also that the employers set aside from their revenues whatever is needed to replace the materials used up and to provide in advance for the depreciation (wearing out) of the tools, machines, and other capital goods used in producing the total product. As explained in the previous

---

[5]*Business Week,* April 1, 2002, citing data from the U.S. Bureau of Labor Statistics and the U.S. Department of Commerce, Bureau of Economic Analysis.

chapter, the remaining revenue represents the surplus product. In a capitalist economic system the surplus product takes the form of profit.

In the simple grain model of the last chapter the surplus product was a quantity of grain representing a certain amount of labor time. In capitalist economies, however, the surplus is not only a quantity of goods (or labor time); it is also a quantity of money, called *profit*. Profit provides the basis for the capitalist's income—whether such income comes in the form of interest, dividends, rent, or capital gains—and it flows from, as we have explained, ownership of capital goods and control over labor processes.

> **Profit** is the form of the surplus product in a capitalist economic system; it is what is left over, out of sales revenues, after wages, the costs of materials used up, and wear and tear on machines have been paid.

An employer may not be able to keep all the profit resulting from a capitalist labor process. For one thing, the government takes part of the surplus product in taxes to pay for public services, public goods, and amenities of various kinds. (It is also true that to finance its activities, the government also imposes taxes on income that is not part of the surplus product, for example, the income of wage earners.) We discuss the government's role in the economy in Chapter 19.

Another part of the surplus may be used to pay *interest* to a bank or to an individual who has lent money to a firm. Interest payments are often regarded as costs, and they *are* costs to a business. However, they are also just a different form of profit, since they are paid to those who *indirectly* own the capital goods used in production. If a bank has lent money to a firm, it will have received in return a commitment on the part of the firm to pay interest and ultimately to repay the money that was loaned. Although the bank does not directly own any of the capital goods, it has acquired a claim on part of the profit, or surplus product, generated by the use of the capital goods.

> **Interest** is a contractual payment made by the government to owners of U.S. Treasury bonds, bills, or notes. Alternatively, it is a contractual payment made by a corporation to owners of its bonds or to banks that have provided loans to the corporation.

Similarly, a firm may pay out part of its profit in the form of *dividends* to holders of stock in the company. A share of stock signifies that its holder is a part-owner of the company and is therefore entitled to a dividend if the company decides to pay dividends. Although they are not contractually obligated to do so, companies usually do pay dividends every quarter in order to maintain the attractiveness of their stock to current or potential investors, thereby helping to keep up the price of the stock in any stock market in which it is traded. Any profits that are not paid out either as interest or as dividends are called "retained earnings." These are part of the profits that companies set aside to be used to pay for new investments.

> A **dividend** is a payment made by a corporation to an owner of a share of its stock.

Although dividends are different from interest (companies are not obliged to pay them), they are similar to interest in that they are one of the forms that the surplus product takes in a capitalist society. Accordingly, they are counted as part of total profits.

Most of the profits received by capitalists (including such property income as interest, rent, and dividend payments as well as the "retained earnings" of corporations) are spent to buy commodities of one kind or another. When capitalists' profits are spent on buying new machinery for a factory (above and beyond what is needed to replace the capital goods worn out during production), on research and development activities, or on other goods and services intended to raise productivity in the future, such spending is called *net investment*. Profits may also be used to pay for *consumption* of necessities and of such items as mansions, yachts, luxury cars, private jets, and so on. (Recall the box on "Megayachts and Bull Market

Boats" in Chapter 5.) The surplus product may be thought of as all the things on which profits are spent, and accordingly it consists of a bewildering variety of goods and services. What all these goods and services have in common—what makes them part of the surplus product—is that none of them goes toward maintaining the producers at their customary standard of living or toward replacing the materials and machines used or used up in production.

As we have said, it is ownership of capital goods that gives control over the disposition of the surplus product to the capitalist class. This control may, in turn, be seen in two ways. On the one hand it may be seen as granting *income rights* to capitalists. These are the rights that establish claims on the interest, rent, dividends, and other payments resulting from ownership of the capital goods used in production. On the other hand, ownership of capital goods gives employers *control rights* that establish their right to control what goes on in the workplace, including the way in which it is organized. The significance of this dimension of capitalist rights is that it gives the owners of capital goods *power* over their employees, giving the owners the right to make the decisions (or select the managers who will make the decisions) that affect the jobs, incomes, and safety of their workers. We discuss at some length in Chapters 12 and 13 the various ways in which this control may be exercised.

An additional dimension of the power of capitalists has to do with their participation in politics. Owners of substantial wealth are not only rich; they are also highly influential. Their high incomes give them the ability to hire lawyers and lobbyists, to make major political campaign contributions—sometimes even financing their own campaigns—and to engage in other activities that may enable them to influence the way in which legislation is written or policies selected. Such legislation or policies will sometimes make it easier for employers to maintain the control that they have over the labor process and over their employees, thus ensuring that they will be able to continue making profits in the future. This is discussed in Chapter 19. Our point here, however, is that even if they have nothing to do with the government, substantial owners of capital goods have a lot of power—over those they employ and others affected by their decisions about the technologies used, the products to produce, and where to locate production.

CONCLUSION

To conclude this chapter, we return to our basic characterization of capitalism as a way of organizing labor processes involving commodity production, private ownership of capital goods, and wage labor. Our definition of capitalism stresses the social organization of the labor process; nothing is said about its technology or about what is produced. A capitalist economy may turn out factory goods or farm products, tanks or teletubbies. What is capitalist about it is how it is organized.

This definition of capitalism also says nothing about the form of government. Capitalism may coexist with democratic governmental institutions, as it does in the United States, with fascism as it did in Hitler's Germany, or with other forms of dictatorship. Moreover, democratic government may exist alongside other economic systems besides capitalism. For instance, as we explain in the next chapter, during the early days of American democracy capitalist organization hardly existed at all.

Capitalism operates in accordance with one set of "rules of the game," one set of procedures and class relationships that determine how social decisions are made. Slavery and feudalism went by other sets of rules and other methods for making social decisions. In families the authority of adults, particularly male household heads, as well as custom and tradition, provide still a different way of determining how things are done. This book is mainly about the capitalist rules of the game.

SUGGESTED READINGS

Robert Allen, *Enclosure and the Yeoman* (Oxford: Clarendon Press, 1992).

Robert Allen, *From Farm to Factory* (Princeton: Princeton University Press, 2003).

Perry Anderson, *Lineages of the Absolutist State* (London: Verso, 1972).

Perry Anderson, *Passages from Antiquity to Feudalism* (London: NLB, 1974).

T. H. Aston and C. H. E. Philpin, eds., *The Brenner Debate: Agrarian Class Structure and Economic Development in Pre-Industrial Europe* (Cambridge: Cambridge University Press, 1985).

Marc Bloch, *Feudal Society, Volume I: The Growth of Ties of Dependence* (London: Routledge, 1961).

Christopher Boehm, *Hierarchy in the Forest* (Cambridge, Mass.: Harvard University Press, 2000).

Jared Diamond, *Guns, Germs, and Steel* (New York: Norton, 1997).

Maurice Dobb, *Studies in the Development of Capitalism* (New York: International Publishers, 1964).

Maurice Dobb, *Soviet Economic Development Since 1917* (New York: International Publishers, 1966).

M. I. Finley, *The Ancient Economy* (Berkeley: University of California Press, 1973).

Robert Fogel and S. Engerman, *Time on the Cross; The Economics of American Negro Slavery* (Boston: Little, Brown, 1974).

Eugene Genovese, *The Political Economy of Slavery; Studies in the Economy & Society of the Slave South* (New York: Pantheon, 1965).

David M. Gordon, Richard Edwards, and Michael Reich, *Segmented Work, Divided Workers: The Historical Transformation of Labor in the United States* (Cambridge: Cambridge University Press, 1982).

John Gray, *False Dawn: The Delusions of Global Capitalism* (London: Granta, 1998).

Eileen Power, *Medieval People* (New York: Barnes & Noble, 1963), especially Chapter 2, "The Peasant Bodo: Life on a Country Estate in the Time of Charlemagne."

John F. Richards, *The Mughal Empire* (Cambridge: Cambridge University Press, 1993).

Frank Roosevelt and David Belkin, eds., *Why Market Socialism?* (Armonk, N.Y.: M. E. Sharpe, 1994), especially Chapter 2, "Thinking about Socialism: Achievements, Failures, and Possibilities" by Irving Howe (pp. 51–82).

Marshall Sahlins, *Stone Age Economics* (Chicago: Aldine Publishing Company, 1974).

Joseph Schumpeter, *Capitalism, Socialism, and Democracy* (New York: Harper & Row, 1942).

Jonathan D. Spence, *The Search for Modern China* (New York: Norton, 1990).

Immanuel Wallerstein, *The Modern World-System: Capitalist Agriculture and the Origins of the European World-Economy in the Sixteenth Century* (New York: Academic Press, 1974).

Erik Olin Wright, *Class Counts, Student Edition: Studies in Marxism and Social Theory* (Cambridge: Cambridge University Press, 2000).

CHAPTER 7

American Capitalism: Accumulation and Change

In 1774 Joseph Hubbard invited his few neighbors to a meeting in his recently built barn, where they founded the town of Leverett, Massachusetts. Like his neighbors, Hubbard and his family grew crops, made tools, processed food, slaughtered livestock, wove cloth, made clothing, tanned leather, made shoes, and pressed apples for cider. The Hubbards also tended their own sick, educated the young Hubbards, and entertained themselves with stories and song. Of the things they needed, there was little that they did not produce.

When Joseph passed away his will listed (in beautiful script) his entire belongings, mostly tools for types of production that today would be carried on not under a single roof but in dozens of sectors of the economy. The Hubbards bought only a few things from their neighbors or others outside their household: salt, some iron goods, Joseph's gun, and not much else. The Hubbard family was a minieconomy in its own right. Though items of personal clothing were virtually absent from Hubbard's will—only "the coat" was mentioned, suggesting that he did not have a closet full of them—they were far from poor, and in the years following Joseph's death, the next generation of Hubbards added larger rooms with plastered walls. We know all of this because one of the authors of this book lives in the house that Joseph Hubbard and his family built.

The Hubbard family was typical of most families of European descent then living in North America: they were what we now call independent producers. The Hubbards probably never even considered *hiring* someone to operate their cider press or harvest their fields. They certainly never hired themselves out to anyone else. *Slaves* worked for someone else, but not by choice, and while there were a few slaves in Boston and the other seaports, they were unknown in the rural western hinterland of the Massachusetts Bay Colony. In the homes of the rich, *servants* worked under the direction of the madam of the house, but no one in Leverett or anyplace nearby was that rich. The single word best to describe the Hubbard family economy is *independence*: they neither worked for anyone else, nor did they depend on others for their livelihood.

In the U.S. today independent family economies like that of the 18th-century Hubbards are a rarity, sustained in myth and by a few oddball "mountain men" (and women) trying (mostly in vain) to live according to its antiquated precepts. Families today make their livings by working for someone else, employing others to work for them, or both. The home continues to be an important work site, but gaining a livelihood generally involves working outside the home. In most cases employment takes place in a business whose objective is to make profits (something the Hubbards never even would have considered) or for a government (the town of Leverett that Hubbard founded hired its first employee only a century later).

An essential part of employment, whether in a business or in government, is taking orders or giving orders. Whether subtly or harshly, employment in the modern economy involves what we term *command*. (Command was not absent in Joseph Hubbard's world, but he exercised it over his wife and children, at least until his failing years, not over his neighbors.)

A second essential aspect of employment is *dependence* on others: one needs a job in order to live, and it is generally the case that someone else ultimately controls whether one has a job. The Hubbard family was buffeted by the occasional dry summer, cold winter, or other vagary of nature, but unlike employees today, their livelihood did not depend on the decisions of other people. With the changing social structure of economic life has come a vast increase in material abundance, improvements in health, and an ability to communicate with and experience the rest of the world that would have dazzled Joseph Hubbard and his family. This chapter is about how fundamental *change* in economic life comes about. Here we bring the time dimension of our "three-dimensional" approach to the fore, focusing specifically on the way in which change is brought about by the capitalist organization of production. In this chapter we examine American capitalism and its historical development as a case study of the process by which the forces inherent in a capitalist economy can bring about wide-ranging social change. We have already seen, in Chapter 1, some of the enormous social, political, and economic changes that have occurred in the world during the capitalist period of history. Now we ask: How and why does capitalism cause change? And how has American capitalism been changed by the process of its own historical development?

Our answers to these questions form the main idea of this chapter: *The competition that is built into a capitalist economy compels business owners to produce better products cheaper, and this requires them to invest—rather than consume—a large portion of the surplus product. This investment, in turn, not only raises productivity and living standards, it also generates continuous technological, economic, social, and political change, thereby transforming both the class structure and the institutional framework of the economy.*

This main idea is expressed in seven primary points:

1. *Competition for profits* arises because the only way a firm can stay in business is to make profits. Each business owner has no choice but to engage in a never-ending race to avoid falling behind. The surest way to stay ahead is to produce better goods or services at lower cost. To keep up each firm must not only replace the capital goods and

materials that are used up in the production process, it must also expand and improve its own product line, break into new markets, introduce new technology, and find lower-cost ways of getting the necessary work done.

2. Competition thus compels the owners of each business to *invest* (rather than consume) most of the profits they make. Investment may take the form of installing better equipment, building production units in new locations, conducting research to develop new product lines or methods of production, purchasing the patents and trademarks necessary to do the above things, and more. The process of investment as part of competition for profits is called *accumulation.*

3. As a result, the capitalist class is the first economic elite in world history whose members are compelled, as a requirement of remaining in the elite, to revolutionize the way goods and services are produced and distributed. The fact that no business owner can escape the race to produce better goods more cheaply is what makes capitalism so productive and dynamic.

4. Propelled by the competition for profits during the 18th and 19th centuries, *capitalism became the dominant economic system* in the United States. As it has in many other countries, capitalism has replaced independent production, slavery, and other economic systems that were more important in the past.

5. American capitalism has, over time, been characterized by a number of distinct institutional settings that have facilitated the accumulation process. We call these institutional settings *social structures of accumulation.*

6. The following social structures of accumulation have defined successive *stages of American capitalism* since the mid-19th century: *competitive* capitalism, *corporate* capitalism, *regulated* capitalism, and contemporary *transnational* capitalism.

7. Modern American capitalism is a part of the global capitalist economy; many Americans have more economic interactions with their counterparts in the rest of the world than they do with their neighbors down the street. While in some respects the U.S. economy is integrated with the rest of the world, it is not itself homogeneous. Parts of the U.S. economy are as different, one from another, as are different nations.

ACCUMULATION AS A SOURCE OF CHANGE

Accumulation is profit-driven investment, including the process of mobilizing, transforming, and exploiting the inputs required in capitalist production and then selling the output.

Accumulation.   Profit-driven investment is the motor of change in a capitalist economy. Both investment and profit-making are shaped by competition as owners of businesses vie with one another for profit opportunities. In turn, the activities of profit seeking and investment inevitably transform labor processes, draw in new supplies of labor, increase the stock of capital goods, create new knowledge, and mobilize or transform other resources to make them available for use in commodity production. The word *accumulation* refers to this whole interrelated set of activities.

Thus, in the accumulation process, profit is both a lure and a lever for change. It is a lure because the possibility of making a profit is what motivates business owners to reinvest their profits; it is a lever because profits, when invested, create change.

Karl Marx believed this process to be the central feature of capitalism: "Accumulate, accumulate!" he said. "That is Moses and the prophets!"[1] Just as Moses and the biblical prophets have inspired people in the Judeo-Christian tradition, so does accumulation drive the capitalist economic system.

The idea here is that given the dynamism of capitalism, *the present is different from the past,* and *what has happened in the past affects both the present and the future.* Because of accumulation, day 2 is generally not identical with day 1 because day 2 does not begin with the conditions that prevailed at the beginning of day 1. Rather, the conditions that day 2 begins with are affected by whatever changes or development occurred during day 1. Similarly, the latter part of a historical period is different from the earlier part because the change or development that occurred in the earlier part influences the latter part.

Thus, the introduction of political economy's third dimension, change, can shed light on how the process of profit making evolves. To see the link between accumulation and change in a capitalist economic system, consider the following example.

Suppose an entrepreneur decides to spend a sum of money to start up a T-shirt manufacturing business. At the beginning of a period of time—say, period 1—she uses this money to purchase the necessary inputs (machines, materials, and labor) and then during the period itself supervises the production of T-shirts. At the end of the period, the T-shirts are sold for more than the cost of the inputs, thus generating a profit. Even after repairing the wear and tear on the machinery and paying for the materials used and the labor employed, the revenue brought in from the sale of the T-shirts allows the entrepreneur not only to get back the original sum of money but also to make a profit—an amount of money over and above that which was originally spent. What will be done with this profit?

The entrepreneur may choose to use most of the profit to buy goods for her own consumption, allocating just the same amount of money as before to continue in the T-shirt business. Since the T-shirt–making machinery would in this case have been restored to its original condition, its productive potential is the same as it was at the beginning of period 1.

But factors outside the manufacturing process will almost certainly have changed. As a result, the T-shirt business owner will not be able to do in period 2 what she did in period 1 and expect to achieve the same results. For example, if the price of one or another input has increased, an expenditure of the same amount of money will purchase less of this input in period 2 than it did in period 1. Or perhaps T-shirt customers' preferences will have changed, and they no longer want to buy as many as they previously did of this particular producer's kind of T-shirt. It is also possible that some other businessperson, noticing the amount of profit made by the original T-shirt manufacturer, will decide to start up a competing T-shirt business. If any of these things happen, our T-shirt producer will not be able to do in period 2 just what she did in period 1—and make the same amount of profit.

Note that the story presented here is not applicable to a noncapitalist economic system. In the self-sufficient household or on the medieval manor there was little uncertainty about

---

[1] Karl Marx, *Capital,* vol. 1 (Harmondsworth, U.K.: Penguin Books, 1976), Chapter 24, Section 3, p. 742.

social factors such as input prices or the preferences of customers. The household or the manor provided most of its own inputs, and most of its output was not a commodity, being consumed directly by its members. If the head of the family or the feudal lord insisted that production be carried on in the same way year after year, the cycle of production and consumption could probably be repeated without difficulty.

But businesses producing commodities for profit cannot operate in the same way: they cannot stand still without falling behind. Not only do they face uncertainty with regard to unpredictable events, they also face the certainty of having to deal with competition in the market. They know that other businesses, also fearing uncertainty and seeking higher profits, will attempt to increase their profits. To do so these competitors will make changes in their production processes and introduce new products in order to raise their profit rates. Thus, any individual business owner must know that others are actively making changes to increase their profitability, and he or she will need to act with similar intentions. This will lead to constant change.

Competition for profits.   What drives all businesses in a capitalist economy constantly to change their operations and seek improvements is the competition for profits. Those who do not engage in this competition will find themselves left with higher-priced inputs, more costly methods of production, or obsolete and unsold output. Only those who constantly revolutionize their operations have a chance of surviving, and of those, only the ones who make the right changes will succeed.

> **Competition for profits** is the struggle for survival and expansion among firms seeking new ways of doing business, new markets, new products, and other possibilities for profitable investment.

Those who succeed in one period are like runners who are ahead halfway through a race: the leaders maintain their lead only by continuing to run fast, and those who slow down or stop will see the other runners go by. There are, however, two peculiar features of this capitalist "race." The first is that new competitors keep jumping into the contest from the sidelines as the race progresses. Thus, even as some firms fall behind or drop out of the race, new firms will enter afresh, and even the leaders will have to worry about the new competition.

The second peculiar feature is that there is no end to the capitalist race: it just keeps going. Those who fall behind do not have a chance to start again at a common starting line in a new race. Recalling our discussion of the "rules of the game" in the previous chapter, capitalist competition works like this: if you finish at the end of one game 15 points behind, you start the next game with a score of minus 15.

The imperative of competing for profits applies even to owners and managers who do not personally care about making profits. The survival of a firm—and the ability of its owners and managers to remain owners and managers—depends on profits. In competing for profits, business owners are not simply trying to maximize their personal income; they are trying to hang on to the way of life associated with their class position.

A firm grows by investing, that is, by using its profits to increase the quantity and/or the productivity of its capital goods and other inputs. Employers can do this by purchasing more and better machinery, building new factories and offices, acquiring ones that already exist, supporting research activities within the firm, or enabling their workers to develop additional skills. If business owners invest all their profits, the increase in the value of the productive assets of their firms will be exactly equal to the amount of their profits.

Thus, if a firm is not making a profit, it cannot grow: zero profit means zero growth. And if a firm does not grow, it will soon be outpaced by others that do grow. In a capitalist economy, survival requires growth, and growth requires profits. This is capitalism's law of the survival of the fittest, analogous to Charles Darwin's notion of the evolution of species through natural selection. In the capitalist version, Darwin's idea of fitness—success in producing offspring—becomes success in making profits.

Capitalism is differentiated from other economic systems by its drive to accumulate, its predisposition toward change, and its built-in tendency to expand. These qualities, taken together with the characteristics discussed in the last chapter, are its distinctive features. In earlier economic systems—feudalism and slavery, for instance—the surplus product was mostly *consumed* by social elites in economically unproductive ways such as consuming luxuries, buying armaments, and constructing monuments. The presence of a capitalist elite with even more lavish consumption habits than those of feudal lords or slaveholders is a highly visible aspect of our economic system. But it is not the megayachts that make capitalism distinct; the difference is that this economy requires the *investment* of a major portion of its surplus product.

In feudal society there was relatively little market activity, hardly any economic competition, and even less long-distance trade. For these reasons the lords had little incentive and few opportunities to invest the surplus to increase productivity. Indeed, their positions as lords or church officials were strengthened by their consumption of the surplus product. Secular nobles spent their portion of the surplus product on things that demonstrated and enhanced their power and prestige. Thus, they used the surplus to build castles, go on crusades, and maintain a large retinue of subordinate knights and other retainers. The high clergy, including those at Ely, spent their portion of the surplus product in similar ways, erecting cathedrals and supporting the large number of cardinals, bishops, priests, and other functionaries in the church hierarchy. Whatever other consequences these uses of the surplus may have had—especially in reinforcing the ideology, class structure, and institutions of feudal society—they left the productive system for the most part unchanged. Old ways of producing things were held on to or modified only gradually; few resources were made available for introducing new production processes or expanding old ones.

Capitalism is the first system to have an elite whose members *must* invest the surplus—and thereby revolutionize production—in order to survive and maintain their positions as members of the elite. A feudal lord whose fields were unproductive was just a shabby noble. In contrast, the capitalist whose factories turn out high-cost or low-quality products may soon be an ex-capitalist.

In sum, capitalism's normal functioning produces tremendous pressures for change. It creates not only the incentive (competition for profits) for individual capitalists to introduce change but also the means (the profits themselves) for implementing change.

CAPITALISM COMES TO THE UNITED STATES

The American economy did not begin as a capitalist economy (neither has any other economy). Rather, over the past two centuries capitalism has grown from being a relatively small part of the U.S. economy to being its dominant economic system.

TABLE 7.1	Percent of the Population Engaged in Different Economic Systems in the U.S. in 1780

| Question: | Are the capital goods used in production privately owned? | |
	Yes	No
Is wage labor the main form of productive work? — Yes	Capitalism (6%)	Government activities (less than 1%)
Is wage labor the main form of productive work? — No	Slavery (32%) Home production and commodity production by independent producers (60%)	Native American communal/kinship production (2%)

Economic systems can be sorted into categories based on the answers—yes or no—to two questions: (1) Is wage labor the main form of productive work, and (2) are the capital goods used in production privately owned? Each of the boxes in the table represents one of the four possible combinations of answers to the two questions, with the answers to the first question given in the *rows* and the answers to the second question given in the *columns*. The percentages in each box indicate, for all of the persons engaged in production, the approximate percentage involved in each economic system in 1780. Because of the absence of available data on them, people who were engaged in reproduction—child rearing and related tasks—are not included in this table, and the percentages do not add up exactly to 100 percent because of rounding of the particular percentages.

Sources: Jackson T. Main, *The Social Structure of Revolutionary America* (Princeton: Princeton University Press, 1965); and Gary B. Nash, *Class and Society in Early America* (Englewood Cliffs, N.J.: Prentice-Hall, 1970).

If we look at how labor processes were organized in 1780—around the time when the Declaration of Independence (1776) and the U.S. Constitution (1787) were written—we can clearly see that capitalist production was only a small part of the economy. Table 7.1 shows that in 1780 a number of different economic systems coexisted, with people involved in capitalist class relationships (capitalists and workers) being no more than 6 percent of the economy.

As indicated in Table 7.1, two other economic systems accounted for more than 90 percent of the economic activity in the early American economy. One of these systems was slavery. Considering slaves and slaveowners together, the slave system encompassed about a third of the population of early American society.

The other important economic system in the early American economy consisted of people like the Hubbard family engaged in *independent production of commodities.*

Independent production of commodities is an economic system in which the producers own the capital goods needed in production and use (primarily) their own labor.

Independent, or self-employed, producers of commodities—farmers, craftsmen, self-employed artisans, and other independent producers—constituted approximately 60 percent of the people participating in production. Independent producers of commodities owned the capital goods needed for their own particular labor processes. For instance, small farmers owned the land they farmed as well as the tools, livestock, barns, and other capital goods needed in farming. They used mainly their own labor (together with that of other family members) and only rarely—or to a small degree—depended on the labor of slaves or wage workers.

Independent producers of commodities often produced some items for their own consumption (food and clothing, for instance) as well as output for sale through the market. Who did what work in independent commodity production was determined partly by markets and partly by the assignment of tasks within the family, decisions often dominated by the father. The hallmark of independent producers of commodities was that they were self-employed: they were their own bosses.

Early capitalism emerged in the U.S., then, within an economy that consisted mainly of independent commodity production and slavery. Soon, however, competition intensified and expanded, especially between independent producers of commodities and capitalists. (Slave-based production was concentrated mainly in tobacco, rice, and cotton in the South, and it was not displaced by capitalist production until after the Civil War.)

Independent shoemakers, for example, found themselves increasingly competing in the market for shoes against shoemaking wage laborers working under the direction of capitalists. The capitalist producers had the advantage because they could organize production on a larger scale and benefit from the resulting gains in productivity—gains that, as Adam Smith observed in 1776, came as production was reorganized to achieve more division of labor within the workplace. The capitalist firms could thus afford to sell their shoes at a lower price while still covering their costs and making a profit, and this is what enabled them to drive the independent shoemakers out of business. In similar ways and with similar results, self-employed blacksmiths, weavers, spinners, harness makers, and other independent producers found themselves increasingly drawn into competitive struggles against the new capitalist firms that invaded their markets with cheaper products.

HOW THE ACCUMULATION PROCESS TRANSFORMED WORKERS' LIVES: A 19TH-CENTURY VIEW

The village blacksmith shop was abandoned, the roadside shoe shop was deserted, the tailor left his bench, and all together these mechanics [workers] turned away from their country homes and wended their way to the cities wherein the large factories had been erected. The gates were unlocked in the morning to allow them to enter, and after their daily task was done the gates were closed after them in the evening.

Silently and thoughtfully, these men went to their homes. They no longer carried the keys of the workshop, for the workshop, tools, and keys belonged not to them, but to their master. Thrown together in this way, in these large hives of industry, men became acquainted with each other, and frequently discussed the question of labor's rights and wrongs.

—Terrance Powderly, Grand Master Workman, Knights of Labor (1889)

Source: Thirty Years of Labor 1859–1889 (Columbus, Ohio: Excelsior Publishing House, 1889).

Soon the independent producers had to choose between surviving or falling behind. To survive, they had to reinvest their profits, expand their operations, and seek cheaper methods of production; in the process, those who succeeded found that they had become capitalists themselves. If they fell behind they would see their incomes decline. Eventually they would have to abandon their independent status and become employees of one of the new capitalist firms.

A large number of people resisted becoming wage laborers, enduring all kinds of hardships to avoid this fate. They ran away to sea, became prospectors in the gold fields, or took up homesteading in the West. Although such decisions sometimes delayed individuals' capitulation to wage employment, in the long run they could not alter the course of history.

At the same time, a significant influx of immigrants contributed to the growing supply of wage workers. Many of the immigrants possessed little wealth, and so, without alternative ways of earning a living, most of them entered directly into wage employment.

Comparing Tables 7.2 and 7.3, one can see the effects of all the processes through which most people became either capitalists or wage laborers. Table 7.2 shows the U.S. class structure in 1780, and Table 7.3 depicts the class structure in 1990.

Box (1) in both Table 7.2 and Table 7.3 lists the classes—capitalists or slaveowners— that *both* owned the capital goods *and* controlled the labor of others in the production process. In 1780 these classes together constituted about 4 percent of everyone who was

TABLE 7.2   The U.S. Class Structure in 1780

Question:		Owns the capital goods used in production?	
		Yes	No
Controls the labor of others?	Yes	(1) Capitalist class (1%) Slave owning class (3%)	(3) New middle class (1%)
	No	(2) Old middle class (60%)	(4) Working class (5%) Slave class (30%)

Classes can be categorized based on answers to two questions: (a) Do the members of the class control the labor of others and (b) do the members of the class own the capital goods used in production? (To be consistent with the available data, we say that the answer to the first question is negative for entrepreneurs who employ fewer than 10 workers.) Each of the boxes represents one of the four possible combinations of answers to the two questions. The two most important class relationships in 1780 were between box (1) and box (4)—between the capitalist class (answers yes and yes) and the working class (answers no and no) and between the slave–owning class (yes/yes) and the slave class (no/no). The numbers in parentheses indicate, for each class, what percentage of the labor force its members were. The labor of those involved in child rearing and other aspects of reproduction does not appear in this table or in Table 7.3 because such labor is not directly part of the class structure.

Sources: Estimates based on data in Jackson T. Main, *The Social Structure of Revolutionary America* (Princeton: Princeton University Press, 1965); and Gary B. Nash, *Class and Society in Early America* (Englewood Cliffs, N.J.: Prentice-Hall, 1970).

TABLE 7.3 The U.S. Class Structure Today

Question:		Owns the capital goods used in production?	
		Yes	No
Controls the labor of others?	Yes	(1) Capitalist class (5%)	(3) New middle class (29%)
	No	(2) Old middle class (12%)	(4) Working class (54%)

This table presents today's answers to the same two questions that were posed in Table 7.2 for Americans in 1780. As in that table, each of the boxes presents the numbers (as percentages of the labor force) for one of the four possible combinations of answers to the two questions. Between 1780 and the present, the slave-owning class has disappeared from box (1), while the capitalist class has grown from 1 percent to 5 percent of the labor force. The old middle class declined from 60 to 12 percent, while the new middle class grew from 1 to 29 percent. Perhaps most significantly, slaves were freed and the working class grew from 5 percent of the labor force in 1780 to 54 percent today. Thus, the working class today, having grown by a factor of 10, is not only a majority of the working population but is a larger percentage of it than were the slave and working classes combined in 1780.

Source: Estimates based on data in Erik Olin Wright, *Class Counts: Comparative Studies in Class Analysis* (Cambridge: Cambridge University Press, 1997), p. 99, Table 3.2.

involved in labor processes in the production sector. By 1990 the slaveowning class had, of course, long since disappeared, but, as Table 7.3 shows, the dominant class in production—by now just capitalists—was approximately the same percentage of the labor force (5 as opposed to 4 percent) as the slaveowning and capitalist classes together were in 1780.

Box (4) in Tables 7.2 and 7.3 lists the classes consisting of people who neither owned capital goods nor controlled the labor of others, namely, slaves and wage workers. In 1780 slaves represented about 30 percent of those participating in production, and, of course, there are no slaves today. *Wage workers, however, have grown from only 5 percent to more than half the labor force today.*

Here we see the transformation of American society. Wage work under the direction of a boss—once an abhorrent status thought to be destructive of one's independence and therefore to be avoided—has now become the most common condition for a majority of the population employed outside the home.

> **Middle classes** in capitalist society possess one but not both of the attributes of capitalists; they therefore stand between capitalists and workers.

And what of boxes (2) and (3) in the two tables? Recall that the capitalist class and the working class are defined with reference to two features of capitalist production, ownership of capital goods and control of the labor of others, capitalists being those who both own capital goods and control the labor of others, whereas workers neither own capital goods nor control the labor of others. We define the *middle classes* as composed of those groups, represented in boxes (2) and (3), that possess either *one* but *not both* of the defining characteristics of the capitalist class. The term *middle classes* is plural because there are two quite distinct middle classes, each of which has its own defining relationships to other classes and labor processes.

The *old middle class,* shown in box (2) in the tables, is composed of people who, while they *may* employ a few (say, less than 10) workers (see the caption under Table 7.2), *do not* regularly employ or control the labor of others. Significantly, however, they *do* own the tools of their trade or whatever capital goods they need in order to carry on their work. The difference between the capitalist class and the old middle class is that capitalists are involved in a power relationship with their employees, while members of the old middle class generally are not.

> The **old middle class** consists of those who do own the capital goods used in their own labor processes but who do not regularly control the labor of others; they are self-employed or are small business employers.

The old middle class includes self-employed persons and independent commodity producers such as self-employed doctors, carpenters, artists, family farmers, mom and pop storekeepers, and other small business owners who employ few or no workers. (As noted in the caption under Table 7.2, we set the limit at 10 workers to be consistent with the available data.) Members of the old middle class do not sell their time as wage workers. Rather, they sell a commodity, whether it be their crops or services such as medical treatment. These independent producers are not involved in capitalist labor processes, but they will most likely have to relate to capitalist enterprises through buying and selling. The old middle class is called "old" because it existed before capitalism developed.

The *new middle class,* on the other hand, is composed of those who *do* control the labor of others but who generally *do not* own the capital goods used in production; they are shown in box (3) in the tables. The new middle class is composed of managers, supervisors, and people who are now called "expert-managers." The people in this new middle class usually receive a salary (rather than a wage), are paid for their labor time and expertise (rather than for their services or products), and can always be fired (because they are under the authority of others). Although controlling other people's labor is a large part of what they do, their own work is controlled by others such as owners, top executives, or other supervisors in the

> The **new middle class** consists of those who do not own the capital goods used in their own labor processes but who do regularly control the labor of others; it includes managers and supervisors.

organizations in which they are employed. The reason they are said to be in the middle class is not that they have middle-level incomes; in fact, their incomes range widely—from that of a top manager to that of a supervisor of a maintenance crew, for example. They are "middle class" because they are *in the middle* between capitalists and workers.

Let us now return to Table 7.2. Here we can see that the old middle class was the largest category in 1780, but as capitalism has grown the old middle class has withered. Independent commodity production, the economic activity of the old middle class, is much less prevalent today than it was in 1780. As shown in Table 7.3, the old middle class now amounts to less than a third of the entire middle class and makes up only 12 percent of the labor force as a whole. What is remarkable, however, is how ways of life of the early American economy live on in people's memories and hopes. Indeed, most Americans are very likely, at some point in their lives, to dream of working for themselves, perhaps as the owner of a small business, rather than for a boss.

SOCIAL STRUCTURES OF ACCUMULATION

The accumulation process has not only destroyed earlier economic systems—feudalism, slavery, independent production—transforming the class structure of these economic systems and unleashing a whole series of social changes, it has also restructured capitalism itself. Thus has American capitalism undergone its own historical transformations.

The basic "rules of the game" of capitalism in the U.S. (and elsewhere) remain unchanged, however. Private owners of capital goods continue to employ wage labor with the intention of making a profit. Thus, the American economy continues to be a capitalist economy.

Yet the capitalist economy itself changes. The types of products made, the technologies used, the geographical location of production, and the kinds of work that people do are constantly in flux. The most important changes are the changes in the institutional setting within which accumulation takes place.

We refer to this institutional setting as a *social structure of accumulation* (SSA), meaning the laws, institutions, and social customs that provide the basic rules of the game governing accumulation. Accumulation, the making and reinvesting of profits by individual capitalists or firms, occurs within this "social structure." The rules of the game, of course, influence how the game is played.

> A **social structure of accumulation (SSA)** is the institutional setting within which accumulation occurs; it structures relations among capitalists, between capitalists and workers, among workers, and between government and the economy. Two phases of an SSA can be distinguished: first, its "consolidation" and, second, its "decay."

While the goal—profit—remains the same, the conditions under which employers try to make profits change. Thus, *the strategies for profit making that are open to the firm change as the social structure of accumulation changes, and the profits that can be made with each strategy also vary.*

For example, in the 19th century there were few large firms, whereas today there are many. A firm today, no less than its 19th-century predecessor, seeks to make profits, but the strategy it adopts will be different because it must consider how to compete with large corporations. A hundred years ago relocating some of the firm's operations to another country was not an option; today it is. Around the middle of the past century most large private employers had to negotiate with a labor union in the hiring and management of labor; this is much less common today. Before 1970 a firm faced few if any restrictions concerning the effect of its operations on the natural environment; today, firms must comply with environmental regulations or calculate the likelihood of paying penalties if they do not. All of these developments reflect changes in the social structure of accumulation.

Think of the capitalist economy as a game. In most games the rules say what the members of each team may do with the members of their own team, with (or to) the members of the other team, and so on. The social structure of accumulation is no different. Each social structure of accumulation can be described by the way its rules influence, and are influenced by, several important relationships, namely,

- relationships among employers,
- relationships between employers and workers,
- relationships among workers, and
- relationships between the government and the main private economic actors.

While all capitalist economies have fundamental similarities, particular countries have distinctive social structures of accumulation: American capitalism, Swedish capitalism,

Japanese capitalism, and Brazilian capitalism are distinctive in important ways. And each of these, American capitalism included, of course, changes as time passes.

Each social structure of accumulation is long-lived, but no particular SSA is a permanent feature of capitalism. Typically, each SSA lasts for several decades or more. As explained below, the U.S. economy has seen four social structures of accumulation in the past century and a half (before that the U.S was not a capitalist economy). Each SSA lasts a long time because it consists of highly interrelated social relationships: sets of laws, institutions, class relationships, organization of political parties, beliefs, expectations, and customary ways of producing and consuming. It is difficult to change such a structure piecemeal, for it is only interactively that the parts work at all. Moreover, each of these arrangements, once established, works to the advantage of some individuals or groups in the society, and the latter become the existing SSA's natural defenders. Until these defenders lose their influence—or until their interests change—the SSA will persist.

Though long-lived, an SSA is not immortal, and like other "mortals," there are different phases in its life. If the existing structure is successful, the relationships among the key players will be such that profit rates are high and owners of firms and other wealthy individuals will have confident expectations for the future. As a result, they will invest substantial sums in expanding the productive capacity of the economy, and the economy will work well not only for investors but for most people in the society. This type of situation is called the *consolidation* phase of the SSA.

Eventually the social structure becomes less and less capable of providing a favorable environment for accumulation. The consolidation phase is thus followed by a period of *decay* of the SSA. At this point economic problems multiply and people's expectations—especially investors' expectations—for the future become more modest or even pessimistic. As a result investment lags, and the growth of productive capacity stagnates.

A **long swing** occurs over a period of 30 to 50 years. The first part generally coincides with the "consolidation" phase of a particular social structure of accumulation (SSA) and is characterized by relatively high rates of investment and economic growth and relatively little unemployment. The remainder of a long swing is associated with the "decay" phase of an SSA; it is a period of stagnation of economic growth with relatively little investment and high unemployment.

The alternation between consolidation and decay can be seen in what are called *long swings* in economic performance. Long swings are different from the short-term ups and downs of the economy (sometimes called expansions and recessions) that are discussed in Chapter 16. The latter, usually referred to as *business cycles,* generally last 3 to 10 years from peak to peak. A number of these shorter cycles may occur during a long swing, but long swings commonly run 30 to 50 years between the end of one period of decay and the end of the next. Consolidation is reflected in a lengthy period of good economic times, or boom, whereas decay is indicated by a long period of hard times. (Near the beginning of Chapter 16 we present data on the long swings that have occurred in the U.S. economy between the Civil War and the beginning of the 21st century.)

Why does a boom not last forever? What tips an SSA from consolidation into decay? The answer is that the (successful) accumulation process itself may erode the favorable conditions associated with the consolidation phase of an SSA; this seems to have been the case in the 1920s and 1960s. The requirements for continued accumulation may become more inconsistent or self-contradictory as accumulation proceeds; this, too, occurred in the 1920s and 1960s. And there may be other causes as well.

But the question—why does decay set in?—cannot be answered in general terms. The most that can be said is that whereas an SSA changes slowly because of its interlocking relationships and the defense of it by particular interest groups, the accumulation process organized within it changes rapidly as new technologies are developed and new kinds of opportunities for making profits emerge. When a tension develops between the (slowly changing, or "sticky") institutions and the (rapidly changing) profit-driven investment process, the old social structure no longer provides a favorable climate for accumulation. The particular causes that force consolidation to give way to decay are the result of specific historical forces; they are likely to be different for each SSA.

The period of decay may create a "crisis," during which large numbers of people become disaffected and social conflict is heightened. This occurred, for example, in the U.S. during the Great Depression, when more than a quarter of those wanting work were jobless and many turned against capitalism as a system. When this happens, new ways of organizing the economy are proposed, employers are forced to speed up their efforts at innovation, especially organizational innovation, and workers are likely to demand a "new deal." At the same time some of the erstwhile defenders of the old SSA find that they are getting less and less out of it. In the U.S. many Depression-era businessmen also came around to supporting the idea of a "New Deal" as a way of "saving capitalism."

As the consolidation phase of an SSA turns into decay, the old alignments may change, and new electoral coalitions may emerge, sometimes reforming the dominant political party from within, sometimes establishing a new dominant party. Electoral realignments brought on by the decay of an SSA often produce what political scientists call "critical elections." Examples include the 1896 defeat of the agrarian populism of William Jennings Bryan, the 1932 election of Franklin Delano Roosevelt that led to the adoption of "New Deal" programs, and the 1980 Reagan revolution that ushered in conservative populism and made the South Republican for the first time since before the New Deal.

Out of a period of crisis, decay, conflict, and change may come the construction of a new set of social relationships—a new SSA. Such a reconstruction is by no means inevitable, since it depends on the outcome of many specific conflicts and negotiations. Nonetheless, the crisis creates a situation in which the inadequacies of the old SSA become apparent, the economic problems become more serious, and the demands for action become increasingly urgent. It may then be possible to overcome the inertia of the old institutions and develop a new SSA.

THE STAGES OF AMERICAN CAPITALISM

The **stages of American capitalism** are distinct phases in the development of U.S. capitalism, with each being defined by a particular social structure of accumulation.

Each social structure of accumulation defines a stage of American capitalism. Table 7.4 illustrates these stages and the distinctive aspects of the key social structure relationships discussed above. In what follows we elaborate briefly on each successive stage.

Competitive capitalism (1860s–1898).   The first stage, competitive capitalism, saw the growth of what was initially a small capitalist enclave overshadowed by both slavery and independent commodity production.

TABLE 7.4	The Stages of American Capitalism: Four Social Structures of Accumulation			
Key Relationship	Competitive Capitalism (1860s–1898)	Corporate Capitalism (1898–1939)	Regulated Capitalism (1939–1991)	Transnational Capitalism (1991–)
Capital-capital	Small-business; competition in local and regional markets	National-level competition among large corporations (trusts)	Large U.S. corporations extend their reach and are dominant in global competition; SEC regulates financial markets	U.S-based and other transnational corporations compete in all major markets of the world; global outsourcing; winner-take-all competition in the information economy
Capital-labor	Strong craft-based unions in some industries; extensive workplace control by skilled workers	Employers are dominant, labor unions weak and/or illegal; corporate paternalism and company towns in some sectors, open conflict in others	Labor unions are legalized, increase their membership, and become important players in wage setting and politics; NLRB established; "labor accord"—real wages rise with productivity	Labor accord ended; global mobility of capital increases its bargaining power over labor; union membership falls; inequality between workers and employers grows; political and economic polarization of the nation
Labor-labor	Craft-based distinctions between skilled and unskilled workers; immigration increases labor supply	Homogenized labor; non-unionized semiskilled factory workers become relatively more numerous; immigration ends	"Primary" and "secondary" labor markets; unions strong in "primary" markets and among mass production workers	Inequality among workers increases; "good" industrial jobs decline, "'high-end" and "bad" jobs grow; U.S. workers now compete with workers throughout the world; immigration rising
Government-economy	Limited government: military and police functions; land policy; tariffs; canal building; subsidies to railroads	Federal Reserve System is established to regulate money supply and banking system	Macroeconomic stabilization through deficit spending, expansion of social security, medical, unemployment, and other insurance; U.S. military defends U.S. corporate interests worldwide	Weakening of environmental regulations; slowing of the growth of government spending; creation and enforcement of intellectual property rights; steps toward global governance through autonomous institutions (IMF, World Trade Organization)

American capitalism has passed through three stages and is now in its fourth. Historically, there have been the stages of *competitive* capitalism, *corporate* capitalism, and *regulated* capitalism. The current stage is *transnational* capitalism. Each stage is defined by a distinct social structure of accumulation. The key aspects of the social structures of accumulation are listed in the first column. They include relationships (a) among the owners of the capital goods used in production, (b) between the owners and the workers, (c) among workers, and (d) between all the economic actors and the government. The other four columns summarize the particular characteristics of the U.S. economy in each of its four stages.

Capitalism was established as the economic system that would clearly become dominant in the future. Slavery, a competing economic system, was destroyed, and the competition between capitalism and independent producers of commodities turned decisively in favor of the former.

American capitalism during this stage was characterized by small businesses that employed fewer than 20 people and competed with one another in the widening markets mainly by price cutting. The prices of most goods fell over the latter part of the 19th century. Workers, many of whom retained the skills they had acquired in independent commodity production, now found themselves working for a wage under capitalist supervision. In many cases they also retained their associations ("brotherhoods" or trade unions) to bargain over wages and working conditions. The government played a crucial role in enforcing the rules of the game (for example, in enforcing contracts and in breaking strikes), but otherwise it played a minor part in the economy.

Corporate capitalism (1898–1939).   The second stage of American capitalism was inaugurated by the rise of many large corporations (then called "trusts") around the turn of the 20th century. This stage lasted until the end of the 1930s.

Corporate capitalism was characterized, in the leading industries, by large firms engaging in competition with one another but with substantial market power. Employers opposed labor unions, and workers who had attempted to organize and defend unions suffered such serious defeats that unions enjoyed little influence until the very end of the period. Workers had few rights, and there was no unemployment insurance, so the loss of a job meant the loss of a livelihood. The government, although slightly more involved in the economy than it had been during competitive capitalism, continued to play only a limited role in the economy. The decay of this SSA was provoked by the onset of the Great Depression and the resulting mass unemployment of workers and low profits for employers.

Regulated capitalism (1939–1991).   The next stage of American capitalism was one characterized by an increase in both direct regulation of economic relationships and indirect regulation of the economy, especially its rate of employment and growth. The increase in the regulation of economic relationships came about as a result of institutional innovations that occurred during the New Deal and World War II. During the New Deal, for example, the Securities and Exchange Commission (SEC) was set up (in 1934) to regulate financial markets as well as the financial practices of corporations, while the Wagner Act (1935) created the National Labor Relations Board (NLRB) to regulate the relationships between corporations and labor unions. Indirect regulation of the economy increased especially following World War II as the ideas of John Maynard Keynes (see Chapter 4) affected our understanding of how macroeconomic policies could be used to influence the rate of job creation and economic growth.

The size of the government grew in relation to the total economy as more payments were made to individuals in the form of Social Security, medical insurance, and income support (unemployment insurance). New policies were adopted to protect workers' health and safety on the job and to address environmental problems. After World War II workers in labor unions were powerful enough to force employers to recognize and bargain with them, producing a compromise arrangement called the *labor accord*.

In addition to regulating the overall level of employment and economic growth and providing the social programs mentioned above, the government maintained a military force that extended over much of the globe. The inability of that force to win the Vietnam War signaled a weakening of U.S. global power, an important factor that contributed to the decay of this SSA. Other contributors to its decay included the sharp reduction in the rate of profit during the late 1960s associated with the increased bargaining power of workers and the costs of worker-friendly and proenvironment policies adopted during the 1960s and 1970s.

Transnational capitalism (1991–). We call this SSA transnational because its most distinctive feature, compared to what came before, is the integration of the U.S. economy into a world system of trade in goods, migration of people, exchange of knowledge, and footloose investors seeking profit wherever conditions are most favorable. The U.S. military presence around the world has greatly increased and, since the breakup of the Soviet Union in the 1990s, has been unquestionably stronger than that of any other nation.

Global economic integration has altered the way firms compete. U.S. firms in many industries must now compete not only with a relatively small number of (mostly large) U.S. firms; they must also compete with a much larger number of similar firms from all the countries of the world. Competition has taken other novel forms. In many sectors—information, telecommunications, entertainment, and pharmaceuticals, for example—success in competition depends less on older strategies such as price cutting and more on newer tactics such as gaining exclusive control of intellectual property rights (patents, copyrights, and the like) and preventing others from producing and distributing things, such as drugs and CDs, that are governed (or supposed to be governed) by such rights.

While facing stiffer competition from one another, the global mobility of capital has given employers the upper hand over union members and other employees in many situations. U.S. workers are now in competition not only with one another but also with workers throughout the world. The weakening of unions has led to the demise of the labor accord: in most parts of the economy unions are no longer partners with businesses, not even the "junior partners" that they were under regulated capitalism. As a result, real wages for most workers actually fell in the last quarter of the 20th century, and workers who were already working for low wages saw their real wages decline even further.

The result is growing inequality among wage and salary earners, with the well-paid pulling away in both opportunities and lifestyle from the poorly paid. Well-paid workers now fear losing their jobs not primarily because the alternative is unemployment, but because the alternative may be a lower-wage job with few benefits.

Under the transnational capitalist SSA there have been numerous attempts to eliminate or roll back the environmental protection laws and other governmental regulations of the economy that were adopted during the period of regulated capitalism. Most of these attempts have failed. Despite the "smaller government" rhetoric of both Republican and Democratic leaders in the period since 1980, the government has grown larger, not smaller, as measured by total taxes collected as a fraction of total income (from 27 percent of GDP at the time of Ronald Reagan's 1980 election to 30 percent two decades later). The same has occurred in most other advanced capitalist countries.

The fact that the government's role in the economy is larger under transnational capitalism than it was under regulated capitalism may be traced to two sources. The first is that the causes of the growth of government under regulated capitalism (see Chapter 19) have not disappeared: popular support is undiminished for insurance against medical calamities and other risks, for smoothing out the peaks and troughs of the business cycle, and for protecting the environment from the consequences of unrestrained profit seeking. The second is that after the sea change in American politics signaled by Ronald Reagan's election, many of the erstwhile advocates of smaller government found that their ability to influence how government revenues are spent was greater than anticipated, so they were more able to benefit from a larger, not a smaller, government.

Two features of the transnational SSA, dualism and globalism, are especially important. We now consider these.

American Capitalism Today: Economic Dualism

Focusing on changes in the class structure is one way to look at the U.S. economy. It dramatizes differences among people, it illuminates the kinds of social relationships that are involved in making a living, and it traces how these have changed over time. One can imagine being a boss, an employee, an independent producer, or someone who is able to live well even without working at all. But the accumulation process has done more than change the class structure of the American economy.

Perhaps more fundamentally, the accumulation process has changed the quality of jobs and the nature of work itself. To understand the process we need to examine how relationships between employers and employees have been reshaped over time. One recent development in the American economy is that business investment and competition for profit have widened differences *within classes* with regard to the ways people secure their livelihoods.

Among those wealthy and powerful enough to be classified as capitalists, for example, some are substantial owners of the giant firms that constitute the core of the U.S. economy, while others are owners of small firms, shops, or farms. Among wage workers, on the other hand, some enjoy job security, high pay, and good prospects for regular promotion, while others are in low-wage, dead-end jobs.

Relating the differences among firms to those concerning the quality of jobs, we can see that the good jobs tend to be in large-scale core firms, while many poorly paid, dead-end jobs are in smaller, more peripheral firms. The industrial structure of *core* and *periphery*—core firms, peripheral firms, and the associated differences between good jobs and bad jobs—is referred to as *economic dualism.* To gain perspective on economic dualism, we begin with a look at the history of the trade union movement.

The rise and fall of labor unions.   During the late 19th century, as many in the old middle class had to give up independent production and become wage workers subject to the command of a boss, employees often sought the protection of a union. Workers in a particular trade or craft would form their own union and, in that way, could become quite powerful. Then, stitching together their specialized unions at the national level, they established the American Federation of Labor (AFL).

Most production in the late 19th- and early 20th-century U.S. was carried on by well-defined crafts, and unions reflected the craft nature of production: most of them enrolled only skilled workers in the particular occupations they were organized to represent. Furriers, railway engineers, iron molders, carpenters, and plumbers each belonged to a separate *craft union.* In the same industry or even the same workplace, each type of skilled worker would belong to a different union.

Eventually many workers recognized that craft unions, although they unified workers within a craft, perpetuated division and disunity among the workers of different crafts. Moreover, most unskilled workers were not permitted to join these unions. African American and women workers were also usually excluded. Despite these limitations of the narrow craft unions, attempts to form broader unions open to all workers failed. From the late 1890s through the 1930s, workers had great difficulty in establishing or maintaining unions. The power of employers was buoyed by the ample supply of labor resulting from the rapid displacement of workers by labor-saving technical change, the decline of employment in agriculture, and immigration from Europe.

The next major effort to build unions occurred in the late 1930s. The Great Depression had begun in 1929. At its worst it had thrown a quarter of the labor force out of work. By 1934 and 1935, after five or so years of this social disaster, few workers believed that capitalism was functioning well, and having a union to defend their interests seemed more important than ever. Despite continuing high unemployment (which weakened the bargaining position of employees), American workers successfully launched the modern U.S. union movement.

In the mass-production industries—steel, autos, textiles, electrical products, rubber tires, and others—employers had thoroughly reorganized labor processes in ways that blurred the lines between one craft and another. As a result the old system of craft unions was no longer appropriate. So now workers began to form *industrial unions.* All workers employed in an industry, whether skilled or unskilled and without regard to craft, were offered the opportunity to join the same industrywide union.

Union organizers developed new tactics to force employers to accept their unions. In San Francisco, for instance, workers organized a *general strike:* instead of workers in just one plant or one industry going on strike, workers in nearly all industries joined to support the longshoremen's strike. In the tire and auto industries workers developed the *sit-down strike:* instead of walking off the job (and out of the factory) to go on strike, the workers simply sat down inside the factory.

An important victory for workers was the passage of the Wagner Act in 1935. Under the pressure of a rising number of (sometimes violent) strikes, Congress passed and President Roosevelt signed a bill designed explicitly to protect workers' efforts to form unions. The Wagner Act established the National Labor Relations Board (NLRB) to mediate disputes between business and labor, to block unfair labor practices by employers (such as harrassment of prounion employees), to oversee elections in plants to determine if workers wanted a union, and to obligate employers to bargain in good faith with the leaders of unions so chosen. Although the NLRB was intended to be a neutral body, favoring neither business nor labor in any disputes, appointments to the board since the presidency of Ronald Reagan have given it a decidedly probusiness bias.

Although public sector unions (those representing federal, state, and local government workers) have grown rapidly in recent years, since the 1960s there has been a significant decline in the overall percentage of the labor force belonging to unions. As the lower half of Figure 7.1 shows, union membership peaked at a bit more than a third of the workforce in 1950 and has been declining since then. In 2003 only 12.9 percent of all wage and salary

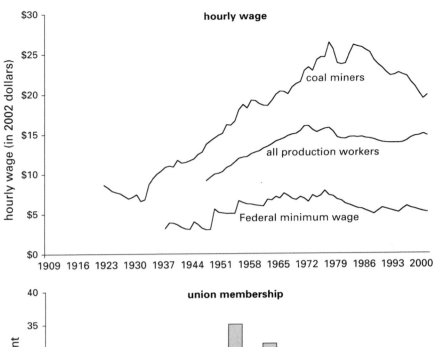

FIGURE 7.1   American wages and union membership in the 20th century.   The lower part of this figure shows that membership in U.S. unions grew in the first half of the 20th century but declined in the second half. The top part of the figure shows that real wages rose along with union power during the first half of the century but stagnated or declined since the 1970s. The wages of coal miners are charted because they are the only type of workers for whom we have continuous wage data since World War I. "Real" means corrected for inflation; nominal wage data have been adjusted using the Consumer Price Index of the Bureau of Labor Statistics.

Sources: U.S. Bureau of Labor Statistics, *Union Membership Summary: 2000* (Washington, D.C.: U.S. Department of Labor, 2001); U.S. Bureau of Labor Statistics, *Historical Data Series*, available at http://data.bls.gov/; the minimum wage data is available at http://usgovinfo.about.com/library/blminwage.htm.

workers belonged to a union—and the number was just 8.2 percent for private-sector employees.

The top half of Figure 7.1 shows changes (corrected for inflation) in various categories of wages over the course of the 20th century. The data for coal miners (the only type of workers for which we have continuous wage data going back to the pre–World War I period) are indicative of how workers have benefited or been set back as the power of unions has grown and receded. Similarly, the data for all production workers (that is, workers who are not supervisors) have tracked the rise and fall of unions.

Although most U.S. workers do not belong to a union, the very existence of unions, as well as their strength, of course, affects how well nonunion workers fare with *their* employers. If a nonunion employer generally resists wage increases, for example, such resistance may motivate that employer's workers to attempt to join a union (if there is one) or to form one (if there is not one). Hence, it is the case that some employers—Delta Airlines is one—have paid relatively high wages in order to dissuade their employees from joining unions.

Figure 7.1 also shows the real value (that is, the value corrected for inflation) of the legislated federal minimum wage from its inception in the late 1930s to the present. The real value of the minimum wage increased steadily until the 1970s and then declined. The post-1950 fall-off in union membership and the subsequent erosion in the real value of the minimum wage and, indeed, of all production workers' wages, reflect the increased political influence of business owners relative to that of labor during the final quarter of the 20th century.

It is worth noting that in many other countries workers' organizations have fared considerably better. In 1960 union membership as a fraction of the labor force ("union density" is the term used) was about the same in Finland as it was in the U.S. (about 30 percent), but in Finland it rose to more than 80 percent by the turn of the present century. Over the same period, union density in Sweden rose from about 50 to more than 90 percent.

In the 1930s and 1940s almost all American union members were blue-collar, private-sector workers. Although unions have continued to gain some new private-sector members, especially where low wages and stringent employer controls have been imposed on white-collar and service workers, on balance these gains have not offset losses among other workers. Indeed, if it were not for the 37.2 percent union membership among public-sector workers, reflecting the high unionization rates of police officers, firefighters, teachers, sanitation workers, clerical staff, hospital aides, and other state and municipal employees, the 12.9 percent overall union membership rate (2003) would be even lower. The gains of public-sector unions represent the only significant advance for the union movement since the 1940s.

Figure 7.2 shows how people in various groups and occupations differ with regard to their rates of union affiliation. Note that African Americans, older workers, and people employed in construction, transportation, and government are more likely than are others to be union members.

After the intense class conflict of the 1930s and 1940s, core corporations and unions developed an uneasy but nonetheless enduring working relationship. This "accord," or truce, was never an explicit, formal agreement. Rather, it consisted of a set of understandings and expectations that unions and corporations shared. The most important of these

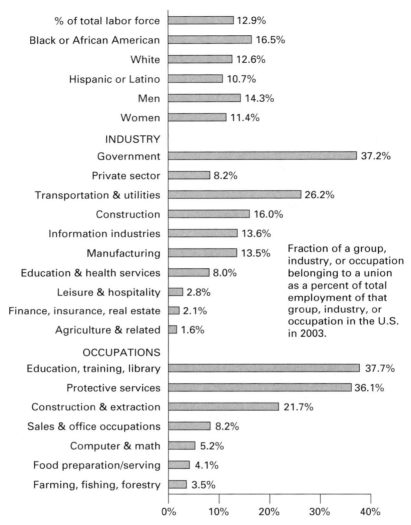

FIGURE 7.2 Who belongs to unions in the U.S.? This figure shows the unionization rates for various categories of American workers in 2003. The bars represent the number of union members as a percent of the total number of workers employed in each group, industry, or occupation.

Source: U.S. Bureau of Labor Statistics, *Union Membership Summary: 2003* (Washington, D.C.: U.S. Department of Labor, 2004). Available annually at http://www.bls.gov/news.release/union2.nr0.htm.

shared understandings was that through "collective bargaining" unions would obtain for their members relative job security and steadily rising real wages, sharing with employers the gains resulting from increases in productivity. In exchange, the corporations would retain the freedom to introduce new technology, to reorganize production as they saw fit, and to invest their profits (the surplus product) wherever they pleased. The accord was intended to give workers a fair deal and employers a free hand.

Neither side would have chosen voluntarily to make the concessions embodied in the post–World War II accord. Corporations were forced to compromise because the unions were too strong to be destroyed. As a huge wave of strikes in 1946 showed, if employers were to have any sort of labor peace they would need to come to some kind of an agreement with the unions. The unions were also forced to compromise because, while they had grown larger and become more powerful in the 1930s and 1940s, they still could not match the economic and political clout of the business community. And for all the workers (a majority of the labor force) who remained unaffiliated with unions, there was no labor accord. Although a few nonunion corporations—IBM and Polaroid, for example—introduced employee protections similar to the ones achieved by unions through collective bargaining, these were the exceptions, not the rule. Indeed, it is clear that such corporations did these things to discourage their workers from joining unions.

For various reasons the postwar labor-management accord began to break down in the 1970s. Growing hostility to unions on the part of employers, declining union membership, and intensifying international competition altered the balance that had made the accord possible. Increasingly, employers sought to do business without unions instead of with them.

Segmented labor markets. The limited coverage of the labor accord reflects another important institutional feature of contemporary American capitalism—*segmented labor markets*. Labor markets are *segmented,* that is, divided into separate, or distinct, markets, when the demanders and suppliers of labor in one market do not compete with demanders and suppliers in other markets. Instead of having one large market for all jobs and all workers, there are, in effect, different markets—called "market segments"—each with its own demand for labor (by employers) and supply of labor (by workers). Labor markets may be segmented either because workers in some jobs are *shielded* from competition with other workers or because workers are excluded from competing for certain jobs.

The development of unions and the postwar labor accord tended to create segmentation by shielding some workers from wider competition. Unionized workers, through strikes and collective bargaining, won increased job security for themselves. Union contracts obligated employers to limit arbitrary firings, to grant workers increased job security as their seniority increased, and to abide by grievance procedures. Although there remained substantial competition for entry-level jobs (the jobs people get when they are first hired), unionized workers in higher-level jobs (usually with more seniority) were shielded to a considerable extent from outside competition. Union contracts prevented employers from simply firing more experienced workers in order to replace them with people standing in the unemployment line.

Unionized workers had won important protections from labor market competition, but since only a portion of the labor force was unionized, these protections were enjoyed by only a part of the labor force. A segmentation, or division, was created between the jobs in which the workers were covered by union protections and those in which they were not.

Even in sectors of the economy in which workers did benefit from union protections, core firms came to rely more and more on *bureaucratic control,* organizing their labor processes by stratifying their work forces, establishing job ladders, and awarding seniority-based pay and promotions according to explicit rules. Although these changes were often improvements over the arbitrary and sometimes capricious practices of some employers, they contributed to a widening gulf in work experiences and pay levels between workers in the larger core firms and employees of firms in the rest of the economy.

Adding to the effects of bureaucratic control and the uneven spread of the labor accord, *job discrimination* prevented some workers from competing for certain jobs, and this also tended to segment labor markets. An example of discrimination in hiring is that female job applicants have been in certain situations considered for clerical work but not for production or managerial jobs. Similarly, racial discrimination sometimes channels black or Hispanic workers into certain jobs while barring them from others. The effect of job discrimination, then, was to increase labor market segmentation by *exclusion.* To this day women as well as black and Latino males have difficulty getting top-level corporate positions usually held by white males.

Discrimination, the emergence of a labor accord, and the spread of bureaucratic control eventually produced three relatively distinct labor markets. Two of these markets, the *independent and subordinate primary markets,* incorporate the jobs of workers who are covered by the labor accord or are organized bureaucratically in some way. The remaining segment, the *secondary market,* encompasses the jobs of all the workers who are neither covered by the accord nor organized bureaucratically and who are therefore not shielded at all from labor market competition.

> The **independent primary labor market** includes those jobs with highly elaborate bureaucratic or professional career patterns; it contains mainly the jobs of craft, technical, professional, and lower-level supervisory workers.

The *independent primary labor market* includes those bureaucratically organized jobs that offer stable employment with considerable job security, clearly defined career paths, and relatively high pay. It includes bookkeepers, technicians, scientists, engineers, lower-level supervisors and managers, commercial artists, and craftworkers such as electricians, telephone linemen, machinists, hair stylists, and skilled ironworkers.

Independent primary jobs typically require skills learned in apprenticeships or acquired in schooling that is high-level or specialized in some way. Workers may need graduate school degrees, special licenses, or other credentials to qualify for these jobs, and formal credentials are highly rewarded. Some independent primary workers are organized in craft unions. In any case, success in their jobs is often judged according to occupational or professional standards (not just the employer's approval) that establish what constitutes good work. The reason such jobs are labeled "independent" is that they frequently permit and sometimes require independent initiative or self-pacing of work.

> The **subordinate primary labor market** includes those jobs in workplaces organized according to the collective bargaining agreements of the labor accord; it contains mainly the jobs of the traditional, unionized, industrial working class.

The *subordinate primary labor market* includes the jobs of the traditional unionized, industrial working class: autoworkers, truckers and railroad workers, underground coal miners, steelworkers, dockworkers, and so on. These jobs are distinguished from jobs in the secondary labor market mainly because the people who hold them, or at least substantial portions of their industries, are unionized. Because some industries, steelmaking, for instance, contain both unionized and nonunionized firms, it is the particular quality of a job (especially whether its wages and working conditions are negotiated by a union), not its industry, that places it in the subordinate primary market.

Subordinate primary labor market jobs are generally better paid than are jobs in the secondary market and typically include some medical and retirement benefits. When the firms in which they are located are growing, they generally involve long-term, stable work with prospects for pay raises and some job security. Indeed, seniority is usually highly rewarded. On the other hand, these jobs are distinguished from independent primary jobs in that they require work that is repetitive, routinized, and often subject to machine pacing. The required skills can be learned rather quickly and are often acquired on the job, but the jobs themselves provide little autonomy and offer few opportunities for the exercise of independent initiative.

> A **layoff** refers to a firm's temporary or permanent dismissal of workers when the firm must reduce its workforce because of a shortage of customers.

Despite their protection by union-negotiated grievance procedures from being fired arbitrarily, workers in subordinate primary jobs remain highly vulnerable to layoffs. The term *layoff* refers to a firm's temporary or permanent dismissal of workers when the firm must reduce its workforce because of a shortage of customers. Millions of unionized workers employed in the old "rustbelt" manufacturing industries (steel, autos, and the like) have been laid off in recent years, and many will never return to their old, well-paying jobs.[2]

The decline of private-sector unions, especially during the 1980s and 1990s, led to a significant shrinkage of the subordinate primary labor market. For example, in such industries as automobiles, steel, and other heavy manufacturing, some production remains unionized, but newer plants have been set up without unions, and a substantial portion of manufacturing has been moved overseas. Many U.S. workers have been laid off in the subordinate primary market and reemployed in the secondary market.

> The **secondary labor market** includes jobs in workplaces that lack the formal organization (such as collective bargaining agreements, bureaucratic control, or professional or craft patterns) of primary markets; it contains jobs such as those of service and retail workers, clerks, seasonal workers, and nonunionized employees of small businesses.

The secondary labor market includes most of the remaining workers. It is highly diverse, unified only in that it is the preserve of workers in dead-end jobs who have few protections from economywide labor market competition. These workers lack both union-achieved employee rights and the benefits of elaborate employer-imposed ways of organizing work (those that have the advantages as well as the disadvantages of bureaucratic control). Here the relation between boss and worker is simple and direct, and workers must continually face the threat of being replaced.

The secondary market includes the jobs of blue-collar workers in nonunion factories; nonunion janitors, waitresses, hospital orderlies, messengers, guards, retail sales clerks, data entry personnel, file clerks, and recordkeepers; seasonal or migrant farm workers; and many other employees of small businesses. What marks these as secondary labor market jobs is that they lack the features that shield workers in primary labor markets from economywide competition. Secondary jobs are usually less secure. They also are less well paid and typically lack a designated career path. Secondary market workers do not progress up a job ladder or acquire more skill, pay, job security, and responsibility as they gain seniority. Instead, they are more likely to find themselves, sooner or later, at a dead end. Neither schooling nor seniority is highly rewarded in these jobs.

---

[2] Clare Ansberry, "Laid-Off Factory Workers Find Jobs Are Drying Up For Good: It's Not Just the Slowdown—Structural Changes Strand Many With Basic Skills," *Wall Street Journal,* July 21, 2003, p. A1.

GOOD JOBS, BAD JOBS, AND NO JOBS: THE COST OF JOB LOSS IN A SEGMENTED LABOR MARKET

Good jobs are getting harder to find, and low-paying jobs are increasingly the only jobs available. These changes affect the cost of job loss: the threat of being bumped into a worse job may be as effective a means for controlling workers as the threat of being unemployed.

In the segmented labor markets of the U.S. the cost of losing your job may be much higher than the cost of a bout of unemployment: the real cost may be that you end up in a far worse job when you eventually get rehired. And you may get stuck there. Workers in the primary labor market enjoy higher wages, better health and other benefits, and greater job security than do those in the secondary labor market. So losing a primary labor market job can inflict a major loss on a worker even if he or she can easily find another job in the secondary labor market.

To see how this works out in practice, imagine that as a machine operator in the manufacturing sector of the economy you are part of the primary labor market, making $350 a week after taxes. If you lose your job you will be unemployed for some time (perhaps half a year) and finally land a new job. While unemployed you will most likely receive weekly unemployment insurance benefits of something like $180 until your benefits run out (normally 26 weeks). Your new job might be equivalent to your old job in pay and conditions, or it might be a job in the secondary labor market, working, say, as a sales person for about $200 a week after taxes.

The cost of losing your job is thus comprised of two parts: the part you lose while unemployed, and the part you lose after getting a new job. If there are not new jobs in the primary sector (quite likely as manufacturing employment is not increasing), the cost of job loss would look like this:

cost during unemployment: ($350 − $180) × 26 weeks = $4,420

subsequent cost due to worse job: ($350 − $200) per week = $7,800 per year

If you remain stuck in the secondary labor market job for five years (not at all unrealistic), you would lose a total of $39,000 over those five years (leaving aside the cost to you of the unemployment period itself). And this does not even take account of the probable loss of adequate medical benefits and other differences in benefits between the primary and secondary labor markets. When labor markets are segmented the cost of job loss to those in the primary sector can be very high, *even when the rate of unemployment is low.*

AMERICAN CAPITALISM TODAY: GLOBALISM

Even while dividing the labor market into distinct segments, the accumulation process has created an economy that is more integrated with the rest of the world. Increasingly, America has been brought into the world economy, and the rest of the world's products and even its peoples have been brought into America.

For most of its history the sheer size of the U.S. and its distance from the large population centers in Asia and Europe isolated the American economy from the rest of the world. No more. Over the past 100 years, the cost of transporting goods over long distances has dramatically fallen. The nature of goods has changed, too: many products can be "shipped" electronically at virtually zero cost. The cover of this book is a reminder of both trends.

Increasingly, firms based in the U.S. operate on a world scale, with some of the major companies operating on every continent. Thus, the accumulation process is now a global phenomenon. Figure 7.3 shows that the fraction of all U.S. profits that are made abroad has been increasing. Half a century ago, for every $20 of American profit, just 1 was made outside the U.S.; now 1 in 3 is made abroad. (We return to the globalization of the accumulation process in Chapter 15, where we address the question: when U.S. firms seek greener pastures abroad, where do they go and why?)

While U.S. businesses benefit from profit-making opportunities around the globe, they and their American employees face stiffer competition from goods produced abroad (including goods produced by U.S. companies operating abroad). Although both consumers and businesses may benefit from the lower prices of imported goods, U.S. firms and workers are often hard hit when they have to compete with low-cost producers in other nations. Figure 7.4 shows the fractions of particular goods sold in the U.S. that are produced in another country. Such a fraction is termed an *import penetration ratio*: it measures the degree to which imports have "penetrated" a particular market. While food products are still for the most part domestically produced (the U.S. is among the world's lowest-cost producers of grains and other foods), more than a third of the cars and trucks (including SUVs) sold in America are produced elsewhere. (Cars and trucks produced by foreign-owned companies in the U.S. are counted as being domestically produced.)

A significant trend, shown in Figure 7.4, is that import penetration increased for many products between 1990 and 2000. However, the figure also shows that even in the highly competitive markets for vehicles and household electronic equipment, the great majority of goods that are consumed in America are produced domestically.

While the internationalization of the U.S. accumulation process is new, the fact that America is a global nation in its ancestry is as old as the Pilgrims, conquistadores, and slavery. As high school history textbooks explain, many immigrants came to America fleeing from religious intolerance and oppression, and these "huddled masses, yearning to breath free" are celebrated by the Statue of Liberty in New York Harbor. However, as Figure 7.5 shows, the fraction of U.S. residents born in another country has varied considerably over the past 150 years.

The big upsurge in immigration in the latter half of the 19th century was not simply the result of people fleeing from intolerance and oppression, however. It was also driven by an early episode of globalization—but one quite different from the globalization we see

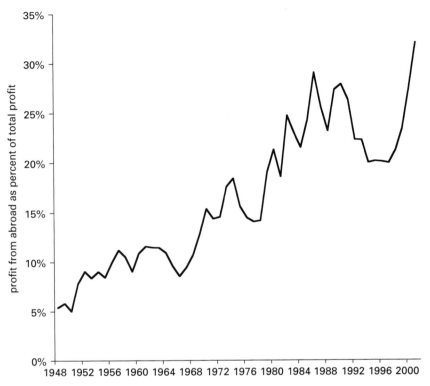

FIGURE 7.3 The growing importance of international profits, 1948–2002. This figure charts the profits received by U.S. residents from economic activity in other countries as a percentage of all profits between 1948 and 2002. (Corporations as well as individuals are considered residents.) U.S. profits coming from abroad include: (a) dividends received by American individuals or corporations from incorporated foreign affiliates of U.S. companies; (b) American companies' share of any reinvested profits of their incorporated foreign affiliates; and (c) profits of unincorporated foreign affiliates net of related tax payments. By this measure, corporations and individuals in the United States have been receiving more and more of their profits from abroad.

Source: U.S. Department of Commerce, Bureau of Economic Analysis, *National Income and Product Accounts of the United States: 2002* (Washington, D.C.: U.S. Department of Commerce, 2003), Table 4.1.

around us today. In the latter part of the 19th century, what happened was virtually the reverse of the process as we now know it: U.S.-produced goods were putting people in other countries out of business.

With the construction of the railroads across the American and Canadian Midwest, and with the sudden decline in ocean freight rates following the replacement of sail by steam power, cheap North American grain flooded into Europe. The effect was not unlike the import penetration illustrated in Figure 7.4—but this time it was happening the other way around. Just as the growing availability of inexpensive foreign cars and electronic devices has eliminated the jobs of those Americans who were unlucky enough to be producing

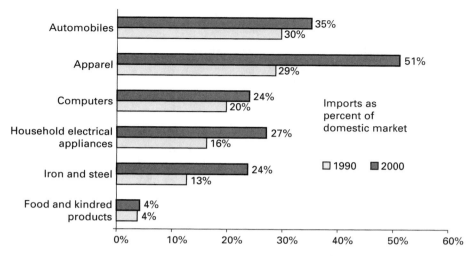

FIGURE 7.4   Import penetration, 1990 and 2000: U.S. firms and workers face increasing competition from abroad.   The bars in this figure show ratios of imports to overall domestic consumption of various products in 1990 (lower bars) and 2000 (upper bars). They show that consumption of imported goods relative to domestically produced goods rose between 1990 and 2000, but the percentage numbers located at the end of each of the upper bars show that domestic firms still accounted, in 2000, for most of the sales in most of the industries listed here. The information presented in this figure was derived using the U.S. Commerce Department's SIC and NAICS industrial categorization codes. The SIC categories were replaced by comparable NAICS categories in 1996.

Source: U.S. Department of Commerce, International Trade Administration, *U.S. Industry Trade Data 2001* (Washington D.C.: U.S. Department of Commerce, 2002), Trends Table, available at http://www.ita.doc.gov/td/industry/otea/industry_sector/tables.htm.

similar products, imports of cheap North American grain devastated European farmers in the second half of the 19th century. Some of these farmers were able to switch to other ways of making a living where they were, but many migrated to the U.S. (or to Argentina or Canada).

The decline in the fraction of the American population born outside the U.S. following World War I was the result of a deliberate policy to restrict immigration. This tightening of U.S. immigration laws has been relaxed somewhat during the past few decades, but as Figure 7.6 shows, the latest wave of immigrants has come primarily from Latin America and Asia, not from Europe. One result is that America is becoming truly a global nation.

The never-ending competition for profits has changed the structure of the U.S. economy in other ways, too. When people think about the economy, they often visualize smokestacks, mine shafts, and fields of waving grain. Think again. Visualize point-of-sale terminals, restaurants, keyboards, call centers, classrooms, and hospital beds. Driving through an unfamiliar town, you may have wondered: what do people *do* here to make a living? What do they *produce?* They may in fact *produce* nothing, at least not in the usual sense of

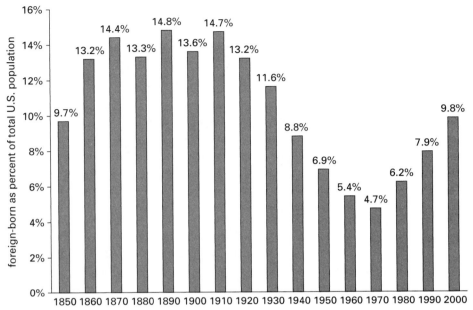

FIGURE 7.5   Percent of U.S population born in other countries, 1850–2000.   This figure
shows that the number of foreign-born individuals as a percentage of the U.S. population as a whole
has varied significantly over the past 150 years. From 1860 to 1920, the portion of the American
population that was foreign-born hovered between 13 and 15 percent, reflecting primarily the large
flow of immigrants from Europe during that period. After 1920, however, immigration into the U.S.
was restricted, and the percent of foreign-born Americans declined. U.S. immigration laws started to
become less restrictive again in the 1960s, and immigration has increased since then. As a result, the
percentage of Americans born in other countries rose from 4.7 percent in 1970 to 9.8 percent in
2000. During this period, most immigrants have come from Latin America and Asia.

Sources: Campbell J. Gibson and Emily Lennon, "Historical Census Statistics on the Foreign-born Population
of the United States: 1850–1990" (Washington, D.C.: U.S. Bureau of the Census, 1999); U.S. Bureau of the
Census, *Profile of the Foreign-Born Population in the United States: 2000* (Washington, D.C.: U.S. Bureau of
the Census, 2000).

producing a material object, a good. Nowadays, there are far more people in America *selling* things than making them. Moreover, most Americans neither sell nor make goods: they
provide *services* by educating, healing, waiting on tables, transporting goods, and doing
many other useful things.

As Figure 7.7 shows, the number of Americans producing goods—in agriculture,
mining, construction, or manufacturing—has not grown since the mid-1970s. Rather, it has
remained flat at around 25 million. Meanwhile, the number of people employed in selling
things and providing services has been rapidly growing. By the mid-1980s *both* sales *and*
services accounted for more jobs than goods production. Half of all American workers produced goods of one sort or another 50 years ago; today the number is less than one in four.

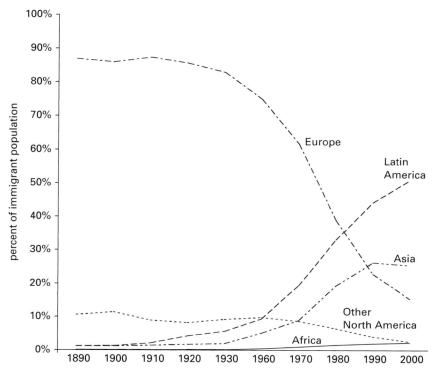

FIGURE 7.6   Where do American immigrants come from? Region of origin of U.S population
born in other countries.   Focusing on the region of origin of the immigrant population in the U.S.,
this figure shows trends in the place of origin of people coming from five different areas of the world
between 1850 and 2000. The percentages have changed significantly over the past 150 years. In
1850 more than 90 percent of the American immigrant population was European-born, and
European immigrants remained the largest fraction of the foreign-born population in the U.S. for more
than a century. Now, however, European-born immigrants are only about 15 percent. Since 1930 there
has been a rapid growth in the number of immigrants coming from Latin America and Asia, so the
Europeans are now in third place behind people from these two areas.

Sources: Campbell J. Gibson and Emily Lennon, "Historical Census Statistics on the Foreign-born Population
of the United States: 1850–1990" (Washington, D.C.: U.S. Bureau of the Census, 1999); U.S. Bureau of the
Census, *Profile of the Foreign-Born Population in the United States: 2000* (Washington, D.C.: U.S. Bureau of
the Census, 2000).

Why has goods-producing employment remained flat in the U.S. for the past 30 years?
One reason is that productivity growth in the production of goods has enabled the same
number of people to produce increasing quantities of grain, steel, cars, and most other
things, allowing more people to move into—or take their first jobs in—sales and service
occupations. But there have been other factors as well, such as the fact that American companies have increasingly shifted their manufacturing operations to countries where the

FIGURE 7.7 The changing composition of employment in the U.S., 1919–2002. This figure shows that the composition of employment in the United States, much like that in other rich countries, has changed over time. In the early part of the 20th century, more people were employed in the production of goods than in the production of services or in sales. By the end of the century, however, both service sector employment and the number of people in sales had surpassed the number of people employed in the production of goods. The employment figures for "sales" include people selling real estate.

Source: U.S. Bureau of Labor Statistics, *Historical Data Series* (Washington, D.C.: U.S. Department of Labor, Bureau of Labor Statistics), available at http://data.bls.gov/.

wages are lower and the regulations less stringent. (See box "Globalization: American Winners and Losers," and accompanying figure.) By one estimate, 1.3 million manufacturing jobs have been moved from the U.S. to Mexico and other low-wage countries (primarily in East Asia) since 1992.[3]

The sales and service sectors of the U.S. economy differ in many ways from the goods-producing ones. Of course, there are large differences between "good" manufacturing jobs—unionized jobs in the automobile and steel industries, for example—and "bad"

---

[3] Clare Ansberry, "Laid-Off Factory Workers Find Jobs Are Drying Up For Good: It's Not Just the Slowdown—Structural Changes Strand Many With Basic Skills," *Wall Street Journal,* July 21, 2003, p. A1.

GLOBALIZATION: AMERICAN WINNERS AND LOSERS

G lobalization is controversial in most countries, and the U.S. is no exception. Many U.S. workers attribute job losses or the difficulty in finding a good job to the fact that U.S. firms are building new plants outside the U.S. or to the competition from imports suffered by U.S.-based firms. Others resent competition for jobs (and admission to professional training) from newly arrived immigrants or overseas applicants. Some of these claims are exaggerated, but many are not. We know, for example, that U.S. unions bargaining with firms that have plants outside the U.S. have less success in raising wages (see box "Hardball: Owners, Workers, and Taxpayers in the Global Economy" in Chapter 13, pp. 317–318).

Many U.S manufacturing workers have found that when their firm relocates operations to another country, they remain jobless for long periods and eventually find work at lower pay. In 1992, for example, the Smith-Corona plant in Cortland, New York, was moved to Tijuana, Mexico. A sample of 159 laid-off workers was interviewed three years later. Men lost an average of a quarter of their previous

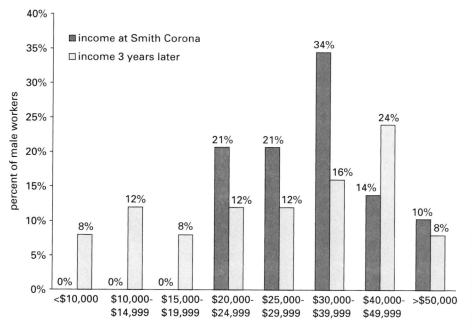

**Male Workers' 1995 Incomes After Being Laid Off
from a Smith-Corona Plant in New York in 1992**

Continued . . .

income; women lost 36 percent. The before and after earnings of the men are shown in the chart on the previous page. Note that the "after" earnings are not only lower on average, they are also much more unequal, with almost a third of the workers earning somewhat more after the plant closing, but many earning much less.

But Americans gain, too, from globalization. The U.S. is enriched by the cultures and talents brought by recent immigrants, and there are also more mundane gains. The reason why Smith Corona moved to Mexico is that it can produce there at lower cost. And (excepting those producing competing products) Americans benefit when these lower-cost goods are imported to the U.S. As import penetration in clothing and footwear has increased over the past 30 years, for example, the prices of these goods have fallen to half their original prices (adjusting these prices to take general price inflation into account).

Whether you think the freer movement of goods, people, and investment is a good thing may depend on whether you benefit from the lower-cost goods or suffer from the competition with producers from the rest of the world (including new immigrants to the U.S.). But many people also care about the impact of globalization on others, not only in the U.S. but also around the world. The workers in the new Smith Corona plant in Tijuana needed the jobs, too.

Sources: Lourdes Beneria and Luis E. Santiago, "The Impact of Industrial Relocation on Displaced Workers: A Case Study of Cortland, New York," *Economic Development Quarterly,* vol. 15, no. 1, 2001, pp. 78–89; James Heintz, "The New Face of Unequal Exchange: Low Wage Manufacturing, Commodity Chains, and Global Inequality" (Amherst: Political Economy Research Institute, University of Massachusetts, 2003).

manufacturing jobs—certain jobs in food-processing plants and clothing sweatshops (yes, sweatshops still exist in America). But the differences between "good" and "bad" jobs in the service and sales sectors are far greater. For example, many jobs in the financial services industry are among the best paid in the world, while in the U.S. people who perform "domestic" and janitorial services are paid very little. Sales workers tend also to be very poorly paid, and, because few of them are represented by a trade union, they have little bargaining power and minimal on-the-job rights. Selling real estate, on the other hand, is quite lucrative, and many government and transportation workers (both classified as being in the service sector) belong to unions and have secure jobs and relatively high pay.

SUGGESTED READINGS

Joyce Appleby, *Capitalism and a New Social Order: The Republican Vision of the 1790s* (New York: New York University Press, 1984).

Samuel Bowles and Herbert Gintis, *Schooling in Capitalist America: Educational Reform and the Contradictions of Economic Life* (New York: Basic Books, 1976).

Alan Dawley, *Class and Community: The Industrial Revolution in Lynn* (Cambridge, Mass.: Harvard University Press, 1976).

Eric Foner, *Thomas Paine and Revolutionary America* (New York: Oxford University Press, 1976).

David M. Gordon, Richard Edwards, and Michael Reich, *Segmented Work, Divided Workers: The*

Historical Transformation of Labor in the United States (Cambridge: Cambridge University Press, 1982).

Morton J. Horwitz, *The Transformation of American Law, 1780–1860* (Cambridge, Mass.: Harvard University Press, 1977).

Grant McConnell, *The Decline of Agrarian Democracy* (Berkeley: University of California Press, 1953).

Samuel Rosenberg, *American Economic Development Since 1945* (New York: Palgrave Macmillan, 2003).

C. Vann Woodward, *The Strange Career of Jim Crow* (New York: Oxford University Press, 1957).

Erik Olin Wright, *Class Counts: Comparative Studies in Class Analysis* (Cambridge: Cambridge University Press, 1997)

Howard Zinn, *A People's History of the United States* (New York: Harper & Row, 1990).

Michael Zweig, *The Working Class Majority: America's Best Kept Secret* (Ithaca, N.Y.: Cornell University Press, 2000).

PART 2

Microeconomics

CHAPTER 8

Supply and Demand: How Markets Work

bn Battuta, the great 14th-century Arab geographer, reported that long-distance trade occurred as follows along the Volga River in what is modern-day Russia:

> Each traveler . . . leaves the goods he has brought . . . and [the travelers] retire to their camping ground. Next day they go back to . . . their goods and find opposite them skins of sable, miniver, and ermine. If the merchant is satisfied with the exchange he takes them, but if not he leaves them. The inhabitants then add more skins, but sometimes they take away their goods and leave the merchant's. This is their method of commerce. Those who go there do not know whom they are trading with or whether they be *jinn* [phantoms] or men, for they never see anyone.[1]

Herodotus, the ancient Greek historian, describes similar exchanges—called *silent trade*—between the Carthaginians and the people of Libya in the fifth century BC. After having left their goods, Herodotus reports, the Carthaginians withdrew, and the Libyans "put some gold on the ground for the goods, and then pull back away from the goods. At that point the Carthaginians . . . have a look, and if they think there is enough gold to pay for the cargo they take it and leave." Herodotus describes how the process continued until an acceptable price was hit upon, remarking with surprise that "neither side cheats the other . . . [The Carthaginians] do not touch the gold until it is equal in value to the cargo, and the natives do not touch the goods until the Carthaginians have taken the gold."[2]

---

[1] Ibn Battuta, *Travels in Asia and Africa: 1325–1354* (London: Routledge and Kegan Paul, 1929), p. 151.

[2] Herodotus, *The Histories* (New York: Oxford University Press, 1998), pp. 300–301.

Silent trade is but one of the many ways that people have devised to engage in the process of exchange. Transfers of goods among strangers can range from gifts at one extreme, through mutually advantageous exchanges, to what might be called plunder at the other extreme. The potential gains from trade are often greater the more distant geographically or socially the parties to the exchange are. The fact that the parties to a silent trade did not meet face to face helped to reduce the chances of outbreaks of violence among the often heavily armed traders.

Other kinds of trade are anything but silent. The trading floor of one of the world's stock markets is a din of offers and bids, and a fruit market in modern Nigeria resounds with the almost musical call of market women advertising their wares and the hum of haggling over prices. Other modern markets are as silent and anonymous as the silent trade. When you buy a shirt or a book online, the only sound you hear is the mouse click when you hit the shopping cart icon on your screen. Similarly, you can buy an entire basket of groceries at a supermarket without saying a word, and, in contrast to the Nigerian fruit market, the only need for verbal communication occurs when the checker asks if you want plastic or paper bags for your goods! If you buy an item online through an auction market (such as e-Bay), you will experience an entirely different kind of market: there you will compete with others in posting a price for a good, the sale going to the highest bidder.

Goods and services are exchanged in many different ways. Families exchange gifts at holiday times, individuals work at jobs in return for money, and one member of a couple cares for the kids while the other works for the wages that pay the rent. In each case, who gets what in return for what is determined in a particular way, sometimes by custom, sometimes by law, and sometimes by the competitive forces of supply and demand. The main idea of this chapter is that *competitive markets—an important form of exchange—can be analyzed using the concepts of supply and demand.* This idea is expressed in two key points:

1. *Competitive markets* consist of many potential buyers and sellers, each acting independently, with no one participant having enough power to dictate terms to any other.

2. The key concepts in understanding how competitive markets work are *supply curves, demand curves,* and *market-clearing.*

THE NATURE OF MARKETS

A *market exchange* occurs when the owner of a good or service sells it to someone else. Selling it usually means that it is exchanged for money: the seller transfers ownership of the item to the buyer and receives money in return. The other side of the transaction is that the buyer pays money to acquire ownership of the good or service. If money is not involved in a transaction—if one product is traded directly for another—this is called *barter.*

> A **market exchange** is a transfer of title to a piece of property (a good or a service) to another party in return for some form of payment at mutually acceptable terms.

A market exchange is thus a transfer of title to a piece of property (a good or a service) to another party in return for some form of payment on mutually accepted terms. To say that the terms of a market exchange are mutually accepted means that under the circumstances, both parties would rather make the exchange on the terms that are being offered than make no exchange at all.

People always have the right to refuse a market exchange. Therefore, by definition, all market exchanges that take place can be said to be *voluntary* in nature. But sometimes the right to walk away from an exchange does not mean much. For example, a severe illness in your family may force you to sell your home to pay the medical bills. It is not that someone is holding a gun to your head and telling you to sell your home, but sometimes circumstances can force people into exchanges they would otherwise avoid. (Recall Marlon Brando in "The Godfather" saying to one of his henchmen: "Make him an offer he can't refuse.")

The term *market* refers to the buying and selling activities of all those who want to trade (buy or sell) a particular good or service. Market activities are sometimes but not always concentrated in one location. Examples of markets with specific locations are the New York Stock Exchange and the Tokyo fish market. In these cases you can see the buying and selling of stocks or fish in one location. For other markets, however, there is no single specific place where you can "see" the market. For example, the Chicago labor market includes all the potential buyers and sellers of labor time who are meeting and coming to terms (or not coming to terms) anywhere in the Chicago area. A market, then, is not a place but rather a set of buying and selling activities.

> A **market** refers to all the buying and selling activities of those persons wishing to trade a good or service; a market consists of suppliers wanting to sell and demanders wanting to buy.

Markets work to determine two basic economic outcomes: the *price* at which a good or service is exchanged and the *quantity* of it that will be bought and sold. These two outcomes affect many other aspects of society. The labor market, for example, determines not only wages (and hence living standards) but also the amount of employment (and hence also the number unemployed).

Each market has two types of participants: *demanders,* or those wishing to buy the good or service, and *suppliers,* or those wishing to sell the good or service. A market may comprise, say, two potential demanders facing three potential suppliers. This might occur in a local real estate market. Or the market might have a small number of suppliers and millions of demanders, as in the computer industry. Some markets have thousands of suppliers and just a few demanders, as in the labor market of a town with just a few large employers.

In this chapter we focus on markets with large numbers of potential demanders and suppliers. Following in the tradition of Adam Smith, such markets are termed *competitive markets* since the rivalry of the different participants—each one competing to make an advantageous purchase or sale—greatly affects the actions of all the others. Many markets in the United States and throughout the world are not competitive in this sense. We explain the workings of markets with smaller numbers of competitors in Chapter 11.

> **Competitive markets** are those with many actual or potential demanders and suppliers.

The most important consequence of having large numbers of participants in competitive markets is that no one of them is powerful enough to influence the price at which goods will sell. If there were just one seller, for example, a large corporation, it could gain a higher price for its product by making less of it available. But this strategy is ruled out in competitive markets.

SUPPLY AND DEMAND

We can understand how markets work by looking at the interaction of demanders and suppliers. We do this with the help of demand curves and supply curves.

A *demand curve* is a graphical representation of the buyers' side of the market. It shows how much of a particular commodity the demanders of this product will want to purchase at each possible price, given their taste for the product and the amount of money they have at their disposal. Each point on the curve represents a particular combination of a price (represented on the vertical axis) and the corresponding quantity demanded (measured on the horizontal axis).

> A **demand curve** indicates, for each possible price, how much of the good or service demanders are willing and able to buy.

Consider, as an example, the market for a certain item, say, beer in Iowa City, Iowa. (In the remainder of this chapter we assume that the beer referred to is all of the same type and quality; in the jargon of economics, we are assuming that beer is a *homogeneous* commodity.) Imagine that we asked every person in Iowa City (and all those who might travel to Iowa City to buy beer), "How many bottles of beer would you buy today if the price were $2 per bottle?" We would then add up all the answers. If the total came to 1,040 bottles, we would have one point on the demand curve: at a price of $2, buyers will demand 1,040 bottles on this day.

We might then repeat the survey, asking buyers how many bottles they would buy, first, if the price were $1 and, second, if it were $0.50 per bottle. Suppose we obtained answers of 2,000 bottles at a price of $1 and 3,760 at $0.50. We would then have two more points on the demand curve for beer in Iowa City on this day.

In Figure 8.1 the demand curve DD shows the various quantities of beer that buyers in Iowa City will demand on a certain day at all the possible prices, including the prices of $2, $1, and $0.50 for which we obtained answers in our survey. It is important to remember that both the demand curve and the supply curve present answers to *hypothetical* questions. In the case of the demand curve, the question is, "If the price were to be _____, what quantity would you buy today?" As we will explain shortly, most of the combinations of price and quantity on the demand curve and the supply curve will not actually be chosen.

Demand curves are almost always thought of as sloping downward to the right, or having a negative slope, as does DD in Figure 8.1. The economic reason for this is that, in general, the lower the price, the more of the good buyers will want to buy. In our beer example (Figure 8.1), if the price is high, say, $2 per bottle, then consumers will want to buy relatively few bottles per day. If the price is low, say, $0.50 per bottle, they will buy a much larger quantity each day.

Note that the demand curve does not represent what buyers *need.* It reflects only what they *want* and are *able to purchase,* given the *price* and their *incomes.* Adam Smith defined what is reflected in a market as "effectual demand" (saying that a poor man's wish for a carriage drawn by six horses would not be an effectual demand), and modern economists have followed in his footsteps, defining "demand" simply as a want backed up by money.[3] We cannot tell from DD whether the buyers of beer are desperately thirsty after performing

---

[3] Adam Smith, *Wealth of Nations,* Book I, Chapter VII, eighth paragraph.

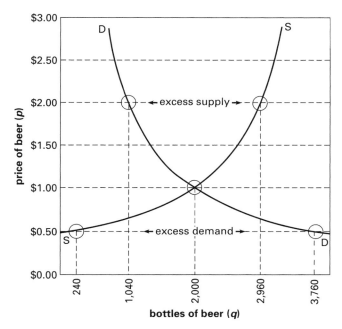

FIGURE 8.1 The demand curve and the supply curve. The demand curve DD provides the following information. If the price of beer per bottle is *p* dollars, the amount demanded by consumers will be *q* bottles a day. For example, if the price is $2 a bottle, consumers will buy 1,040 bottles a day. The supply curve SS provides similar information about what producers will offer on the market. If the price is *p* dollars per bottle, suppliers will offer *q* bottles per day on the market. For example, if the price is $2 a bottle, beer suppliers will want to sell 2,960 bottles a day. Normally, demand curves slope downward (to the right) and supply curves slope upward.

arduous labor or whether they have already had more beers than they should have had. Indeed, if there are some people in Iowa City who desperately want beer but have no money to buy it, their wants will not be expressed in DD at all, since the demand curve expresses only what people are willing and able to buy. All the demand curve tells us is how much beer consumers will buy at any given price.

How much beer people want to buy will depend on many considerations besides the price. As we have noted, it will depend on the buyers' incomes. If everybody suddenly got a pay raise, people might want to buy more of many things, including beer. Another factor is the number of potential buyers. If new people came to town, that would tend to increase the demand for beer. More importantly, demand will change with the strength of people's desire—or, as economists put it, their "preference"—for a product. Thus, a consumer in Iowa City may want to buy more beer if she recently watched an effective beer ad on TV. A final variable is the price of a competing product. For example, people might buy less beer if the price of wine suddenly dropped. Such products are termed *substitutes*.

A demand curve, then, expresses how much the buyers are willing and able to buy at the various possible prices, *assuming* that nothing else affecting their demand changes. If nothing else changes, the demand curve allows us to say how a change in the price will affect the quantity demanded. For instance, in Figure 8.1 we can see that if the price drops from $2 to $1 per bottle, *and if nothing else changes,* the quantity demanded will rise from 1,040 to 2,000 bottles a day.

> A **supply curve** indicates, for each possible price, how much of the good or service suppliers wish to sell.

The *supply curve,* by contrast, represents the sellers' side of the market. It depicts the suppliers' willingness to sell beer at different prices, and this willingness to supply beer will depend to a large extent on the costs incurred by beer-producing firms. In Figure 8.1 the supply curve SS shows, for a particular day, what quantity of beer sellers will supply to the market at various prices. For instance, if the price were to be $2 on some day, suppliers would try to sell 2,960 bottles that day; at a price of $0.50, suppliers would try to sell 240 bottles; and so on.

Supply curves are almost always thought of as sloping upward to the right (having a positive slope), as does the supply curve SS in Figure 8.1. When prices are high, suppliers will want to sell a lot of beer compared to when prices are low. At higher prices it will pay to put on extra shifts of workers at the brewery. The high price may also attract new suppliers from nearby cities where sellers are not able to get such a high price. When the price is low, on the other hand, some suppliers in Iowa City may try to find other cities in which to sell their product; some of them might even stop producing beer.

Other factors besides price influence how much of a product suppliers will want to sell at each price. The cost of producing beer compared with the rewards available from producing and selling other items will affect how much beer the suppliers will want to sell at each price. For example, if a labor-saving technical change occurs in the brewery industry, the cost of producing beer will fall, and the profits to be made in brewing and selling beer will rise. As a result more firms will be attracted into the industry and the amount supplied will increase. Similarly, if the grain used in making beer becomes more abundant, its price will drop, the costs of brewing will fall, and the quantity of beer supplied at each price will increase.

A supply curve, then, represents the quantities of a commodity that sellers will supply to the market at various possible prices, assuming that everything else affecting its supply remains unchanged. If nothing but the price changes, the supply curve tells us how the quantity of the good supplied will change when the price changes. In Figure 8.1, for example, if the price of beer rises from $1 to $2 per bottle on a certain day, suppliers will want to increase the amount they offer in the market that day from 2,000 to 2,960 bottles.

A complete list of factors determining the position of the supply curve would include

- the technologies available for producing the good;
- the costs of the various inputs and how these may vary with the amounts of the inputs used;
- the cost of obtaining the necessary permission to reproduce something from a copyright or patent holder (if the firm's activity requires it), which means the right to use someone's idea, invention, or other creative product (such as a musical composition or work of art) that is patented or copyrighted; and
- the number of firms producing the good, including those that may enter or leave the industry if the price rises or falls enough to attract new firms or cause existing firms to cease producing the good.

You may want to test your understanding of the supply curve by asking yourself how changes in any one of the above factors will shift the supply curve in Figure 8.1 either to the right or to the left. For example, what would happen to the supply curve if a new technology for producing beer were to be invented, one that would allow the same quantity of output to be produced with less labor?

All the influences that affect the position of the supply curve combine also to determine the *marginal cost* of a commodity's production. "Marginal cost" is defined as the *increase in the total cost incurred by a firm when it increases its total output of a commodity by one unit.*

> **Marginal cost** is the increase in the total cost incurred by a firm when it increases its total output of a commodity by one unit.

To grasp the significance of the concept of marginal cost consider the following step-by-step reasoning: Small movements up a supply curve show, at each point along the curve, how much the price of a good must be increased to induce some supplier of that good to produce and offer for sale in the market one additional unit of the good. Even when the market price of something goes up, however, we know that no firm will produce an additional unit of the good in question unless the higher price covers the cost of producing an additional unit of it. Since the cost to a firm of producing an additional unit of a good is, in fact, its marginal cost, we can say that a supply curve shows not only the amount of a good that will be supplied at each price but also what the marginal cost of the good is for at least one firm in the market.

Of course, what happens in a market is not based on the decisions of a single firm. Indeed, the amount supplied in a market on any particular day will be the amount that results when the outputs of all the firms in the market are added together. The point here is simply to establish the idea that there is a marginal cost of producing and offering for sale one additional unit of a good. Since the production of an additonal unit of a good requires allocating more of a society's resources for its production, under certain circumstances we can think of its marginal cost as the cost *to society* of producing an additional unit of it.

The marginal cost of producing a product differs from the *average cost* of its production, which is defined as *the total cost of producing a certain number of units of a good or service divided by the total number of units produced.* While the marginal cost is the addition to the total cost of producing just *one* additional unit at a particular level of output, average cost is a measure of the cost of producing *all* of the units being produced at any given time.

> **Average cost** is the total cost of producing a certain number of units of a good or service divided by the total number of units produced.

In many cases both the marginal and the average costs of producing a commodity *rise* as more units of it are produced (beyond some minimum level of output). This is because as production expands more of at least one input becomes more costly to obtain, and this makes it more expensive to produce additional units of the commodity. For this reason the marginal cost curves for many commodities will be upward sloping to the right on a graph that has the number of units of output (per time period) on the horizontal axis and the corresponding marginal cost for each level of output on the vertical axis.

The reason average and marginal costs may rise with increasing output is easiest to see in agriculture or other natural resource–based industries. In these cases there is a limited amount of good land (or easily exploited natural resources), so production will be more costly at higher levels of output. This is because poorer quality land—or deeper mines or more remote forests—must be used.

However, there are situations in which average cost *falls* as more is produced. Such a fall in average cost will result whenever there are *increasing returns to scale*. Increasing returns to scale exist when an increase in inputs—an increase in the *scale* of production—brings about a more than proportional increase in output. For example, we could say that increasing returns are present when doubling all of the inputs has the effect of producing more than twice as much output. Thus, as explained in Chapter 3, increasing returns produce *decreasing average costs,* and the two terms, since they refer to the same phenomenon, can be used interchangeably. To avoid confusion, however, we will generally use the term *increasing returns to scale,* and hereafter we will often just refer to *increasing returns*.

Increasing returns to scale exist when an increase in inputs—an increase in the *scale* of production—brings about a more than proportional increase in output.

Situations in which firms experience falling average costs (because of increasing returns) are common and important throughout the economy. Surprisingly, however, this familiar situation—in which average costs are falling—is rarely discussed in conventional economics textbooks, and we will see why in the next chapter. But first we must carry the discussion of supply and demand a bit further.

SUPPLY AND DEMAND INTERACTING

We can now join the two strands of the story by explaining how supply and demand together will determine both the price of a good and the amount of it that will be traded (the *price* and the *quantity*). It will be useful here to refer once again to the hypothetical beer market in Iowa City and in the process to consult Figure 8.1 one more time (since it combines in a single graph both the supply curve and the demand curve for beer in Iowa City).

Of course, neither the buyers nor the sellers see the supply and demand curves. These are just analytical tools that *we* use to understand what *they* do. In most markets the sellers, not the buyers, set prices. Each seller sets a price assuming that a higher price will mean more profits per unit sold and that a lower price will mean more units sold. Depending on the demand curve, a move in either direction (that is, moving the price higher or lower) might increase the total amount of profits.

The price that maximizes profits will depend on what the other sellers are doing and how strong the demand is, two pieces of information about which a seller can guess but cannot know in advance. The one thing that sellers do know and may act on is what happened in the recent past. If goods have piled up on their shelves, they may wish that they had been charging a lower price, and they will most likely consider reducing the price. Conversely, if they sold out before the end of the day (or the month), or if they have accumulated a waiting list of eager customers, they probably will be considering a price hike. Other sellers are engaged in the same trial and error method to get the price right.

Excess supply exists when at a particular price more of some good or service is supplied than is demanded.

To see how this process works, suppose, looking at Figure 8.1 again, that the average price of beer in Iowa City is $2 per bottle. What will happen? As pointed out earlier, suppliers will wish to sell 2,960 bottles at this price, but demanders will want to buy only 1,040 bottles. The difference of 1,920 bottles is referred to as *excess supply*. Those suppliers who can find buyers at $2 a bottle will be happy, while those who cannot find buyers at this price will be dissatisfied, and the second group will then offer slightly lower prices, say, $1.75 or $1.50 per bottle, in an effort to attract customers.

As long as excess supply persists, some suppliers will cut their prices in order to try to gain customers, and this will exert a downward pressure on the market price. When the prevailing price has fallen to $1 per bottle, the quantity that suppliers wish to sell (2,000 bottles) will be just equal to the quantity demanders wish to buy (also 2,000 bottles), hence there will be no more excess supply. Price cutting by suppliers will therefore stop at this price.

> **Excess demand** exists when at a particular price more of some good or service is demanded than is supplied.

Consider the opposite situation. If the initial price in the market had been $0.50 per bottle, there would have been *excess demand.* As noted earlier, the demand for beer at this price would be 3,760 bottles, but the supply would be only 240 bottles, leaving an unmet (or "excess") demand of 3,520 bottles. The supply of beer would fall short of the demand by this amount, and those unable to buy would tend to bid up the price. Excess demand would be eliminated only when the market price reached $1, which, of course, is the same figure we arrived at in the analysis of excess supply.

> The **market clearing price** is the price at which buyers want to purchase exactly the quantity that sellers want to sell.

Summing up, we can say that competition in the market for beer pushes the whole market toward a *market-clearing price*—the price at which sellers want to sell exactly the quantity that demanders want to buy. At such a price neither excess supply nor excess demand will exist, and the market is said to "clear." As can be seen in Figure 8.1, the market-clearing price in the Iowa City beer market is $1, for at this price the quantity of beer supplied is precisely equal to the quantity demanded (2,000 bottles).

Figure 8.1 also shows that the market-clearing price and quantity are located at the *intersection* of the supply and demand curves. For this reason—and, as we shall see, only in markets similar to the one for beer in this example—it can be said that supply and demand *determine* the price and the quantity, meaning, more precisely, that the particular positions of the supply and demand curves (and, of course, the factors that themselves determine the positions of these curves) determine the market-clearing price and quantity.

> **Equilibrium** refers to a situation—a price and quantity exchanged—in which there are no forces internal to the situation pushing it to change.

In a market such as the beer market, market clearing is often described as an *equilibrium* situation, and the concept of equilibrium is important in economic reasoning. It is used to describe *a situation in which there are no forces internal to the situation pushing it to change.* This concept is borrowed from physics, and it can be illustrated with a physical example: if one drops a marble into a bowl that is sitting on a table, the marble will roll around for a while, eventually stopping at the bottom of the bowl. The result is an equilibrium, for nothing internal to the situation (the location of the marble in the bowl and the shape of the bowl) will cause it to change. If one were to tilt the bowl or push on the marble, of course the marble would move, but these would be forces external to the situation.

Economists reason the same way. In the beer market the price and the quantity sold will remain at the market-clearing price and quantity until something from the outside changes them. A change coming from the outside would be something like a change in people's taste—or, as economists like to say, their "preference"—for beer relative to other things, and such a change would bring about a movement of the demand curve DD. Similarly, the adoption of a new technology for producing beer would change the position of the supply curve SS. The resulting movements in these curves would change the market-clearing price and the amount of beer sold. But as long as the demand and supply curves remain in their present positions, the equilibrium price and quantity will not change.

As we will see, the equilibrium price in some very important markets is not the market-clearing price. Nevertheless, the stability of an equilibrium situation (barring the appearance of any external, or *exogenous,* source of change) means that nothing an individual buyer or seller may try to do can change the equilibrium price or quantity. Thus, none of the buyers or sellers of beer in Iowa City can benefit from any possible change in their behavior, given what all the other market participants are doing.

For example, a buyer might like to pay less than the going price for a bottle of beer. But if such a buyer tried offering a lower price, no supplier would sell her or him any beer. Similarly, a supplier might like to sell beer at a price higher than the market-clearing price. But if any company raised its price, its sales would fall drastically since similar beer would be for sale in the market at a lower price and this particular company's customers would switch to other suppliers, especially if the company persisted in charging a higher price for a long period of time. (Recall that throughout this chapter we are assuming that any bottle of beer in the Iowa City market is exactly the same as any other bottle; although this assumption is somewhat unrealistic in this case, there are other commodities, such as wheat, corn, and milk, that are more like the *homogeneous* product in our example.) Thus, the prevailing market price (since it is available to anyone in the market) limits what any individual buyer or seller can do. This is the way a competitive market works.

In reality, of course, individual sellers will try changing their prices to see if they can do better. Even when there is no excess supply or demand, therefore, not all prices of a good will be the same. This may be confirmed by pricing beers at a few local stores or by checking the price of a book both at Amazon.com and on the Barnes and Noble Web site. But it is not likely that prices of the same good will differ very much if there is a high degree of competition in the market for that particular good.

An important result of the analysis of the interaction of supply and demand in competitive markets is that *when a competitive market is in equilibrium, the price of the good will be equal to its marginal cost.* Another way of putting this is to say that in equilibrium $P = MC$ (where P stands for the price and MC represents the marginal cost). We will have more to say about this idea later, but the logic of it is as follows: If P is *not* equal to MC the amount supplied will change, so the market cannot be in equilibrium. To see this, imagine that P is greater than MC for some firm. A firm in this situation can gain by producing one additional unit, increasing its revenue by P at a cost of only MC. Similarly if P is less than MC for some firm, that firm can gain by producing one unit less (reducing its costs by MC but reducing revenues by only P). So the amount supplied by a firm will not change only if $P = MC$. Moreover, for the market as a whole to be in equilibrium (recall the definition of an equilibrium) P will have to be equal to MC for every firm in the market.

SHIFTS IN DEMAND OR SUPPLY

So far we have been considering how price and quantity are determined when the supply and demand curves are in a particular position. We have looked at each curve and asked how the quantity demanded or the quantity supplied would change in response to a certain

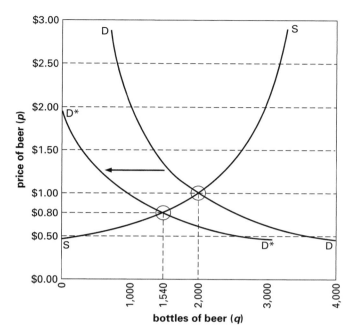

FIGURE 8.2   A shift of the demand curve.   When something other than the price changes, there will be a *shift* of the demand curve, either to the right or to the left. A shift of the demand curve is different from a *movement along* the curve, which is what happens when only the price changes. In this figure, D*D* shows the position of the demand curve after it has shifted to the left, indicating that there is now less demand for beer at every price. It is also possible that, with a different change in one of the influences on the demand curve, it would shift to the right.

change in the price. We will now consider what happens if something else besides the price changes.

For example, suppose that the demand curve DD in Figure 8.2 represents the demand for beer in the middle of a certain semester at the University of Iowa. As the semester comes to an end and students leave campus for home, the situation will change, and smaller quantities of beer will be demanded in Iowa City at every possible price. This change is represented by a leftward *shift* of the whole demand curve from DD to D*D* (see Figure 8.2). On the other hand, an effective advertising campaign during the semester would have the opposite effect: it would shift the demand curve rightward by bringing about an increase in the consumers' preferences for beer.

The difference between the effect of a change in price and the effect of something that changes the position of a demand curve can be understood as follows: a change in the price alone produces a *movement along* the demand curve, whereas a change in one or more of the conditions underlying the demand for the product produces a *shift* of the demand curve. As can be seen in Figure 8.2, the shift of the demand curve from DD to D*D* changes the market-clearing price from $1 to $0.80 per bottle and the quantity sold from 2,000 to 1,540.

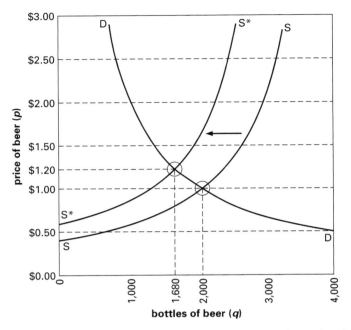

FIGURE 8.3   A shift of the supply curve.   When something other than the price changes, there will be a *shift* of the supply curve, either to the right or to the left. A shift of the supply curve is different from a *movement along* the curve, which is what happens when only the price changes. In this figure, S*S* shows the position of the supply curve after it has shifted to the left, indicating that there will now be a smaller amount of beer supplied at every price. It is also possible that, with other changes in one of the influences on the supply curve, it would shift to the right.

Similarly, the supply curve for beer will shift if there is a change in something affecting supply other than the price. Suppose, for instance, that the price of the grain used in making beer rises. What will happen? The additional cost will reduce profits in the beer industry, and this will lead some suppliers to withdraw from the beer market, perhaps to utilize their resources in a more profitable industry. The higher costs will also cause other beer producers to scale back their operations in the hope that this will restore their previous level of profits. These two developments will shift the whole supply curve from SS to S*S* (see Figure 8.3). As can be seen in Figure 8.3, this shift in the supply curve, with DD unchanged, will cause the market-clearing price to rise from $1 to $1.20 per bottle and the quantity sold to fall from 2,000 to 1,680.

As with the demand curve, a change in the price of the good creates a movement along the supply curve, whereas a change in something else affecting supply causes a shift of the entire curve. Shifts of a supply or a demand curve occur whenever one of the determinants of these curves' positions changes—whether it is, in the case of our beer market example, a

TABLE 8.1	Determinants of the Positions of Supply and Demand Curves

The Supply Curve	The Demand Curve
Technology	Consumers' tastes or "preferences"
Costs of inputs, including the costs of obtaining the necessary permissions to use patented ideas, copyrighted material, etc.	Consumers' incomes and their distribution: more income at the high end will mean more demand for luxury goods; more at the low end will mean more demand for basics
Alternative opportunities for profit available to suppliers	Number of alternative products, and their prices, available to consumers
Number of potential producers	Number of potential buyers

new brewing technology, cheaper grain, a successful advertising campaign, or a change in the size of the relevant population. The determinants of the positions of supply and demand curves are summarized in Table 8.1.

CONCLUSION

Markets, then, provide a way of coordinating economies by means of buying and selling, or exchange, relationships. Competition, both among buyers and among sellers, tends to produce a market-clearing price, at which the quantity demanded is equal to the quantity supplied. The result is that market interactions determine both the prices of goods and the quantities of them that will be bought and sold.

But what does it mean to say that the equilibrium price of beer and the quantity of it that is sold are "determined by supply and demand"? This is a little like saying that a murder was committed by the gun. What actually determined the price and the quantity was whatever determined the positions of the supply and demand curves, because these determinants are what made a particular combination of price and quantity necessary to clear the market.

Supply and demand curves themselves do not do anything: they are even less involved than the gun. Rather, they are ingenious devices that help us understand and explain the many and complex influences on prices and quantities. The invention of supply and demand curves did not change the way markets work. However, it did lead to a better understanding of how markets function.

To summarize: Price and quantity are determined by all the factors that determine the positions of both the supply curve and the demand curve. The process of competition, in turn, works to make actual prices and quantities move toward equilibrium prices and quantities.

As we will see in later chapters, competition does not always cause markets to clear. In the labor market, for example, excess supply (unemployment) can persist for long periods of time or even indefinitely. In Chapter 12 we explain why wage reductions do not have the effect of clearing the labor market—as price reductions in a beer market do—when there is excess supply. A similar situation exists in many credit markets: at the going interest rate for a given type of loan, some prospective borrowers are refused a loan, indicating that although the credit market may be in equilibrium, there is excess demand for such loans.

When markets do not clear, supply and demand will influence the price and the quantity but can hardly be said to determine them, for there is obviously some other important influence at work if the market is not clearing. Our next chapter extends the analysis of supply and demand, explaining how markets may, under certain curcumstances, coordinate the economy in beneficial ways, while, under other circumstances, they may fail to do so.

SUGGESTED READING

Alfred Marshall, *Principles of Economics,* 8th ed. (London: Macmillan, 1920).

CHAPTER 9

Competition and Coordination: The Invisible Hand

In the late 1980s and early 1990s the governments of Poland, the Soviet Union, Czechoslovakia, and other once Communist countries took a dramatic turn. Not only did they begin the process of granting voting rights and democratic freedoms to their citizenry, they also began to place more emphasis on markets rather than centralized economic planning as a way of coordinating their economies.

For more than 70 years in the Soviet Union and for 40 years in the other countries, the government made most important economic decisions. A system of economic planning collected information and then implemented decisions on such issues as how much steel and other investment goods to produce, what technologies to use, how many schools to construct, how many and what type of consumer goods to produce, and how much workers, managers, doctors, and others should be paid.

These centrally planned economies initially achieved major improvements in education, health, and other aspects of living standards, particularly for the less well-off members of their societies. But during the 1980s their governments began to implement major economic and political reforms in response to popular dissatisfaction not only with the lack of democratic rights but also with the slowing down or even reversal of economic growth. The most important economic reform was to allow private companies and individuals to make more economic decisions, and this meant relying on markets to coordinate millions of decisions. Certainly Adam Smith would have been pleased with these reforms. His idea of the invisible hand (coordination by markets) was spreading to populations whose rulers had seemed to be influenced by the single line in all of Karl Marx's writings in which he asserted that the purpose of communism was to do away with markets.

It will be decades before we can tell whether the economic reforms of the past two decades in these countries have been successful. Even then, the debate will probably continue, for the meaning of *success* will not be easy to agree upon. But the changes in economic approach in eastern Europe and the former Soviet Union dramatize the main idea of this chapter: *markets provide a way for individuals and firms to organize some aspects of their interdependence; as they do this, markets coordinate the many and complex activities that make up the economy, with no one in particular directing the process.* This idea is expressed in two main points:

1. By rewarding success and punishing failure, competitive markets provide a decentralized system of *motivation;* through market prices they also transmit *information* about the relative scarcity of various goods and services.

2. Under certain circumstances markets *coordinate* the economy in ways that are generally beneficial, but when the right circumstances are not present, markets fail to perform this function well.

COORDINATION

The "production-reproduction cloverleaf" presented in Figure 5.1 is like an aerial photograph of the economy. It represents the horizontal dimension of the economy as a complex circulation of goods and services—and people. Things produced in one location end up being used in another. People born and raised in the home leave and take up employment in factories, offices, or their own businesses; sometimes they work in their own or other people's homes. The circulation of goods, services, and people is called the horizontal dimension because from this perspective things and people do not move "up" or "down" in the economy. Rather, they move "across," that is, from place to place.

Understanding the horizontal dimension of the economy means explaining the movements of things and people from one place to another, answering questions such as: Why do some people work at certain jobs and some at others? What determines who and how many will raise children, pour concrete, or make shoes? Why do the resulting products move from one labor process to another? How do the shoes get from the shoe worker to the shoe wearer? Why and where do the children go to work when they grow up?

In various societies over the course of human history and around the world today, these questions have been answered in very different ways. Consider, for example, a self-sufficient family farm on the American frontier in the early 19th century. Here most of the labor processes and movements of products shown in Figure 5.1 took place *within* a single household. The production of necessary inputs as well as the reproduction of people all took place (more or less) under one roof. Tools were made and repaired, draft animals were tended, a new fence was put up, food was prepared, firewood was collected, children were born and raised, and clothing was made—all of which meant that the farm was largely *self-sufficient*. What products were produced and how they were used was coordinated by a combination of custom, necessity, and patriarchal authority. Tasks were assigned according to age and sex. Though not common today, this is one distinct way of determining who will do what labor and how the resulting output will be used.

If each family does not produce everything its members use (if the family unit is not self-sufficient)—as is the case in almost all of the modern world—the situation is much more complicated. *Specialization* will exist among, as well as within, family units, and families will have to engage in some form of *exchange* with other families. Various social arrangements will determine how labor will be specialized and how outputs will be distributed.

In some parts of India, for example, people are born into occupational groups (castes), so what one does is determined by birth. This is not as exotic as it sounds: in many parts of the world the job one does is determined by one's sex. And, as noted on the first page of this chapter, the distribution of output as well as the allocation of jobs in countries such as the Soviet Union were determined by central planners until the collapse of the Soviet-type system. Historically, there have also been some societies in which theft or tribute has played a significant role. In still other societies production and distribution have been organized almost entirely by an elaborate process of gift giving. Caste, custom, plan, gift, theft, and tribute are all ways of determining what will be produced, for whom, and by whom. They are all different methods of *economic coordination*. While many of them play a part in most economies that we know of, by far the most important methods of economic coordination in the modern world are markets and planning. We refer to these as "coordination by rules" and "coordination by command."

COORDINATION BY RULES AND BY COMMAND

Seldom in history has anyone proposed so startling a notion as Adam Smith's concept of the invisible hand. As we saw in Chapter 4, Smith held that the economy, even if it is quite complex, does not need to be run by anyone at all. Another way of putting this is to say that the economy will run itself—if it is simply subjected to the right rules.

Imagine someone telling you that an invisible hand will coordinate the landings and takeoffs of planes at O'Hare Airport in Chicago (where there are, on an average day, more than 100 landings and takeoffs per hour). The advocate of the invisible air traffic controller might say, "We don't need the control tower. Pilots should just keep right and yield to traffic on their left or below them." Given this method for coordinating air traffic at O'Hare, we suspect that most people would decide to avoid air travel to Chicago.

Even though the amount of activity at O'Hare is awe-inspiring, the interactions that occur in a whole economy, such as that of the U.S., are infinitely more complex. In the U.S., for example, the economy involves the interactions of approximately 25 million businesses, 100 million households, and 200 million adults, each of which are making decisions every day that affect at least some of the others. When the additional complexity of global economic interdependence is brought into the picture, one can easily see how daunting the task of coordination is—and how radical it was of Adam Smith to suggest that the economy need not actually be coordinated by anyone at all.

But Smith's notion of the invisible hand is not as preposterous as it sounds. Many of our interactions are, in fact, coordinated without a coordinator. Consider another traffic problem, this time for automobiles. In the United States we follow a simple rule—drive on the right—and it does a pretty good job of coordinating the interactions of millions of drivers passing each other every day.

> **Coordination by rules** takes place when interactions are governed by general principles of behavior.

> **Coordination by command** takes place when interactions are governed by orders specifying precise behavior.

The point is that coordination can be achieved by either of two means: (1) with no one dictating anyone else's precise behavior, but everyone observing a set of rules, or (2) with someone (or perhaps more than one) directing the behavior of others. We refer to the first of the two means as *coordination by rules* and the second as *coordination by command*. The basic difference comes down to obeying rules versus obeying orders. A rule specifies a range of behaviors appropriate in a given situation (drive on the right) without specifying particular behaviors (where and when to drive). An order specifies a particular behavior (United flight 407 is to make a 90-degree left turn and land on runway 14A).

Which works better? Obviously, we need both types of coordination in our economy, by rules and by command, and the most appropriate method will vary with the situation. Adam Smith advocated the invisible hand because of his dissatisfaction with the particular kind of coordination by command that prevailed in 18th-century Britain. This involved, among other things, wage and price setting by the government and governmental creation of large monopolies such as the famous British East India Company. But even though he was generally in favor of less state intervention in the economy, Smith did specify several functions that he thought needed to be performed by the government (see Chapter 4).

We can understand how markets work if we first review two problems with coordination by command (planning), one having to do with *information* and the other with *motivation*. The individuals giving the commands (the planners) may not have enough information to do the job well, and those who are supposed to carry out their commands may have little motivation to do so. Moreover, the planners themselves may have little incentive to do the job well.

Air traffic coordination by command works well because all relevant information is available to the controllers (visually, on radar screens and on computer monitors), and the pilots have a powerful motivation to obey the controllers' orders: both their own and their passengers' lives depend on the accuracy with which they follow the commands. And, certainly, the controller has every reason to want to do his or her job well: a mistake might result in a loss of many lives as well as the loss of his job.

But in other situations neither the motivation nor the information is adequate. The central planners in the Soviet Union could not possibly have known the consumer tastes of the 300 million citizens of the country, so they could not make adequate decisions about what consumer goods to produce. Nor could they accurately determine the output capacity of each factory, mine, and office, so they could not assign production targets efficiently.

The problem in a large centrally planned economy is not exactly a *lack* of information: the consumers know more or less what they want, and the plant managers know more or less how much they can produce. So the information exists. The problem is that it is not in the right place: the relevant information is not readily available to the planners (the decision makers). Those who have the information may have an interest in keeping it from the

HUNGER VS. COMPULSION: COORDINATION BY RULES AND COORDINATION BY COMMAND

In England in Adam Smith's time, local governments were responsible for feeding the poor. In return for their food, poor people were required to work at particular jobs. This system, regulated by what were known as the Poor Laws, is an example of coordination by command.

Joseph Townsend (1739–1816), a geologist, collector of fossils, sometime physician, longtime Anglican parish priest, and prolific 18th-century writer, was one of the most severe critics of the Poor Laws. He thought it would be better to let hunger do the job of getting people to work. In 1786, a decade after the publication of Smith's *The Wealth of Nations*, Townsend wrote the following words in his essay *A Dissertation on the Poor Laws:*

Hope and fear are the springs of industry.... [But] *what encouragement have the poor to be industrious and frugal ... when they are assured that if, by their indolence and extravagance* [and] *by their drunkenness and vices, they should be reduced to want, they shall* [then] *be abundantly supplied not only with food and raiment but with their accustomed luxuries, at the expense of others...In general it is only hunger which can spur and goad them on to labour. Yet our laws have said* [that] *they shall never hunger. The laws ... have likewise said* [that] *they shall be compelled to work. But then legal constraint is attended with too much trouble, violence, and noise* [and it also] *creates ill will and never can be productive of good and acceptable service. Whereas hunger is not only a peaceable, silent* [and] *unremitt*[ing] *pressure but* [is also] *the most natural motive to industry and labor, it* [therefore] *calls forth the most powerful exertions...The slave must be compelled to work, but the freeman should be left to his own judgment and discretion, should be protected in the full enjoyment of his own* [wealth], *be it much or little, and* [should be] *punished when he invades his neighbor's property. By recurring to those base motives which influence the slave, and trusting only to compulsion, all the benefits of free service, both to the servant and to the master, must be lost.*

Anticipating by three centuries the arguments of some of today's advocates of "welfare reform," what Townsend was actually proposing in his *Dissertation* was a system of coordination by rules. The rules he was putting forward for consideration were: (1) you can eat only what you grow or buy and (2) you have no right to take anyone else's property, no matter how little you have or how hungry you are. The subtitle of Townsend's book was *By a Well-Wisher to Mankind.*

Source: Joseph Townsend, *A Dissertation on the Poor Laws* (Berkeley: University of California Press, 1971 [1786]), pp. 23–24. Some punctuation in the quoted passage has been slightly altered—and the words in brackets have been added—to assist the reader in following Townsend's train of thought.

THE KEY ROLE OF INFORMATION

The late philosopher-economist Friedrich A. Hayek posed the age-old challenge of how best to organize an economy—dating to before Adam Smith—as a problem of how to make the best use of information:

Which of these systems [central planning or competition] *is likely to be more efficient depends on the question under which of them can we expect that fuller use will be made of the existing knowledge. And this, in turn, depends on whether we are more likely to succeed in putting at the disposal of a single central authority all the knowledge which ought to be used but which is initially dispersed among many different individuals, or in conveying to the individuals such additional information as they need in order to enable them to fit their plans in with those of others.*

—F. A. Hayek, "The Use of Knowledge in Society," *American Economic Review,* September, 1945.

planners or in lying to them. Consumers may wish to exaggerate their needs in hopes of getting more, and plant managers may want to understate their production capacities so that they will not have to produce so much.

The difficulties with coordination by command do not end with problems of information. The *motivations* of the planners and the other economic actors may also be a problem. Unless the planners happen to be saints—and especially if they are not working within an effective form of democratic control—they may have little incentive to make decisions that benefit most of the people most of the time. Even if the planners had both the desire and the information to come up with a perfect plan, it would not be implemented unless both the plant managers and the workers had sufficient incentives to carry out the planners' orders.

Given the problems associated with coordination by command, we need to examine the other main method of coordination in the modern world, coordination by rules. Adam Smith's idea was that markets can take the place of planning as long as two rules govern the economy: competition and private property.

The way in which competition works to establish market prices (and quantities) was explained in the previous chapter. And in Chapter 6 we explained that the rule of private property means that the only ways by which one can rightfully acquire something are by labor, by purchase, or by gift (and the purchase or the gift must be from someone who rightfully acquired the object in the first place). Hence, if you want something and nobody will give it to you, your only options are to make it yourself or to buy it. You cannot simply take it. Thus, if private property prevails, if gifts meet few of our needs, and if most people are not self-sufficient, then market activities—buying and selling—will have to play a major role in the economy.

THE INVISIBLE HAND

Adam Smith was not interested in the price of beer in Iowa City. He was interested in how the British economy should be organized: should it be run by royal decree or should most economic outcomes be determined by the interactions of millions of buyers and sellers in competitive markets, with nobody in particular making the key decisions? He advocated the latter, a system of coordination by the rules of the competitive market. Since Smith's time his argument has been considerably refined, and some of its shortcomings have been clarified. The gist of it is quite simple, but to understand it at a deeper level we have to see what markets really do.

We are, however, not interested in what *particular* markets do: fish markets make fish available to consumers; housing markets make apartments and houses available. Rather, we want to know what markets do in general, especially when they are part of a system in which not only fish and apartments are marketed, but also those things that went into catching the fish and building the apartments—labor, materials, and capital goods.

As noted earlier, markets perform two important functions: they transmit economically important information and they provide the motivation to act on the information. Under ideal circumstances, then, markets address the two main shortcomings of coordination by command: they overcome the difficulties involving information and motivation.

> **Scarcity** is a relationship between a desire for something and how difficult it is to obtain. A highly desirable good that is difficult to obtain is said to be scarce.

The information markets provide is about the degree of *scarcity* of each good or service. In a competitive market the price of a good is a measure of its scarcity. If the price of a good rises (relative to the prices of other goods), we conclude that it has become more scarce; if it falls it has become less scarce. By *scarcity* we mean *both* how desirable the good or service is *and* how difficult it is to acquire. Something very desirable and even necessary, such as air, may not be scarce if it is in abundant supply. And something both costly and rare—say, the ballet *Swan Lake*

THE INVISIBLE HAND

[E]*very individual . . . employs his capital* [and] *endeavours . . . to direct* [it in such a way] *that its produce may be of the greatest possible value. . . .* [Thus] *every individual necessarily labours to render the annual revenue of the society as great as he can. He generally, indeed, neither intends to promote the public interest, nor knows how much he is promoting it . . .* [H]*e intends only his own gain, and he is in this . . . led by an invisible hand to promote an end which was no part of his intention. Nor is it always the worse for the society that it was no part of it. By pursuing his own interest he frequently promotes that of the society more effectually than when he really intends to promote it.*

—Adam Smith, *The Wealth of Nations* (New York: Random House, 1937), Book IV, Ch. II, p. 421.

performed by elephants—will not be scarce unless it is in great demand. Under some conditions (as we will see shortly), market-clearing prices provide a measure of both the desirability of a good to consumers and the difficulty of acquiring the good.

The motivation the market provides is of two kinds. First, markets encourage consumers to try to meet their needs with goods that are less scarce than other goods. This happens, perhaps without their knowing it, when people shop around for the best buy, seeking the good that will satisfy a particular need at the lowest available price. If, for example, certain people would be just as happy with a hamburger as with a tenderloin steak, the relative prices of the two dishes will induce them to satisfy their hunger in the way that takes the smaller toll on society's resources.

Second, the market encourages producers, either companies or individuals, to produce things that are scarce using inputs that are not so scarce. This happens because things that are scarce tend to fetch a high price, and profit-seeking firms will try to produce them with the least costly (least scarce) inputs they can find.

Thus, both consumers and producers will seek to do something very sensible, namely, to conserve what is scarce and use what is abundant. Nobody will require them to do this. They will do it simply because it is in their personal interest to do it. As Adam Smith implied, the market achieves its results behind the backs of the participants. This is the basic argument that supports his notion of the "invisible hand."

The key idea here is that the *price* of a good measures its scarcity. According to a widely held notion of scarcity, fish are scarce when there are none or only a few to be bought; apartments are scarce when the vacancy rate is low. Thus, most people think of scarcity as an issue of quantity. Nevertheless, economists insist that scarcity is best measured by price. Why is this the case?

The quantity notion of scarcity is essentially misleading. Consider the example of gasoline. When the Organization of Petroleum Exporting Countries (OPEC) decided in 1973 to limit production of oil in order to drive up prices, what happened? At first there were long lines of cars at gas pumps. There was a shortage of gas. Everyone knew that gas was scarce, and the price rose (from $0.39 a gallon for unleaded gasoline in 1973 to $1.31 eight years later). But over time the lines at the gas pumps disappeared. Though gas was still scarce in 1981, there was enough to go around because by then the higher prices had changed people's driving habits and tastes in cars, so people were buying less gasoline than before.

The quantity notion of scarcity says that something is scarce if there is excess demand for it. But what happens when excess demand exists? The price rises, and the excess demand tends to disappear. Thus, rather than focusing on excess demand, the economist takes a higher equilibrium price as a better measure of increased scarcity.

THE INVISIBLE HAND IN ACTION

The case for competitive markets—the invisible hand—rests ultimately on the claim that even if all of the economic actors behave only with regard to their own self-interest, markets can allocate scarce economic resources in a desirable way. Advocates of laissez-faire (limited government) argue that competitive markets not only address the problems of information and motivation but in so doing offer a method of coordination that is superior to central planning (coordination by command).

The beer market in Iowa City offers an example of how a competitive market can induce producers and consumers both to respond to a change in tastes and to economize on society's scarce resources. First, imagine that the beer market is in equilibrium and that the market-clearing price is $1 a bottle. Then, suddenly, the U.S. Surgeon General comes out with a report saying that drinking wine causes baldness. What will happen in the beer market?

As people switch from wine to beer, the demand curve for beer will shift to the right, indicating that there is now a greater demand for beer at each price. The result, shown in Figure 9.1, is an excess demand for beer. At the price of $1, producers are willing to supply 2,000 bottles. This means that, as before, they can make as much profit producing and

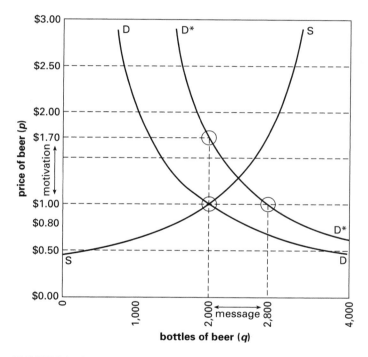

FIGURE 9.1   Market messages and market motivation.   The shift of the demand curve to the right (from DD to D*D*) creates excess demand in the hypothetical Iowa City beer market. An excess demand of 800 bottles will exist if the price per bottle remains at $1.00 because at that price the supply is only 2,000 bottles while the demand is for 2,800. Although the first 2,000 buyers will get their beer at the going price of $1.00 per bottle, there will be a line of 800 disappointed customers, none of whom will get any beer—even though some would have paid up to $1.70 for a bottle—because the supply will have run out. Thus the market is sending the *message:* "More beer!" Since consumers are willing to pay more than $1.00 per bottle, suppliers will find it profitable to provide an additional bottle of beer at any price above $1.00. Thus, at any price between $1.00 and $1.70, additional supplies (and sales), up to 2,800 bottles, will be pleasing both to suppliers and to consumers. Because suppliers can increase their profits by selling more while also raising the price, they will be motivated to increase the supply of beer. Thus, the price differential of $0.70 is the *motivation* provided by the market. It says: "Producers who pay attention to the market message will make more money."

selling 2,000 bottles of beer at that price as they could doing anything else with the resources available to them. But if, at that price, they were to produce only that quantity, there would be an excess demand of 800 bottles (since the demand for beer at a price of $1 is now 2,800 bottles). $1 is obviously no longer the market-clearing price, and the market (in the form of excess demand) is sending the beer producers the *message* that more beer could be sold without lowering the price.

Now look at the excess demand another way, not as a quantity, but as a price. Notice that in the situation in which only 2,000 bottles are available (that is all the producers are willing to supply at a price of $1), some consumers are willing to pay $1.70 a bottle (this is the price the new demand curve shows that consumers would pay for that quantity). The difference of $0.70 between the two prices provides crucial information: the price consumers are willing to pay for another bottle of beer is greater than the cost producers would have to pay to supply another bottle. It is obvious that there is some price between $1.00 and $1.70 at which an increase in the amount of beer supplied would please both consumers and producers. From this economists would conclude that more beer in the market would benefit all concerned.

How, then, does the market provide the *motivation* to produce more beer? If the producers notice the presence of excess demand—how could they miss it?—they will also realize that they can raise their price and still sell at least the 2,000 bottles they are now producing. But once they have raised their price, they will be making more profit brewing beer than they could make in any other activity. (Among the assumptions about competitive markets made in this chapter is the notion that in equilibrium the level of profit in each industry will be the same as the level in every other industry, otherwise the economy would not be in equilibrium since there would be a tendency for some entrepreneurs to shift their resources from a low-profit to a higher-profit industry. Hence, when the beer industry was in equilibrium, the market-clearing price of $1 per bottle would allow beer producers to make just the level of profit that was being made in every other industry.)

Accordingly, the motivation to expand the production of beer comes from the opportunity now available to beer producers to make more profit by selling beer at a higher price. The higher rate of profit per bottle of beer will induce the beer suppliers to produce more beer. This is, of course, just another way of describing the process through which the market-clearing price and quantity are arrived at. However, this analysis leads to an important conclusion: the profit seeking of the beer suppliers will not only lead them to do what is in their own interest, it will at the same time lead them to do what is in the interest of consumers. Moreover, insofar as this process leads to the best possible use of the economy's resources, it may also be said to promote the interests of society as a whole.

To summarize: If excess supply exists, the market provides producers with motivation in the form of a *stick:* firms must either adapt to the information the market is providing—by producing less—or go out of business. When excess demand exists, the market offers producers a *carrot:* higher profits await those who grasp the meaning of the market's information and expand production. In this way the market directs self-interested producers and consumers to do what is in the interests of both, even if neither cares about the well-being of the other. This is the invisible hand in action.

How did the invisible hand overcome the two main shortcomings of coordination by command, namely, the planners' lack of relevant information and the absence of incentives either to plan well or to carry out good plans should they happen to occur? The answer is

TABLE 9.1	Prices Are a Decentralized System of Information and Motivation

Prices as *information*

- to *consumers:* the price measures how much it costs to produce an additional unit of a commodity.
- to *producers:* prices measure how much demand there is for an additional unit of the commodity and how much it costs to acquire the necessary inputs.

Prices as *motivation*

- to *consumers:* prices, in conjunction with the need to stay within one's budget, motivate consumers to satisfy their wants as cheaply as possible.
- to *producers:* prices, in conjunction with the need to make money in order to stay in business, motivate the lowest-cost production of goods and services that consumers want.

TABLE 9.2	The Invisible Hand: Assumptions and Conclusions

If the prices of goods, as they are sold to consumers, measure the ability of the goods to satisfy human needs, and

If the costs of producing goods, as measured by firms, take into account the social costs of acquiring and using the goods,

Then the profit made on each unit of a good (the price minus the cost per unit) will measure the social contribution made by producing each good, and

Hence the pursuit of self-interest (firms seeking greater profits and consumers trying to maximize their satisfactions) will result in a socially desirable allocation of our human and natural resources.

decentralization. Prices provide information about consumers' wants and producers' capacities and costs, and this information is communicated directly among all the market participants without first having to go through a central planning office. Also, the incentives to "do the right thing"—with regard to the efficient allocation of resources—are based simply on the self-interest of all the participants. When all the players in the market seek the best possible deal for themselves, everyone benefits.

If all this sounds a little too good to believe, it is because we have not yet asked how the invisible hand argument might work (or not work) if the ideal circumstances we have been assuming are not, in fact, present.

Coordination failure occurs when markets or other types of coordination by rules fail to coordinate an economy in such a way as to produce outcomes that are desirable.

PROBLEMS WITH THE INVISIBLE HAND

There are many situations in which markets do not perform so well. When markets fail to coordinate an economy in such a way as to produce outcomes that are desirable, economists call this a *coordination failure.* Two parables can be used to introduce the concept of a coordination failure. The first is "the prisoner's dilemma," and the second, "the tragedy of the commons."

The Prisoner's Dilemma and the Benefits of Cooperation

This widely circulated story makes the following point: individuals who *cooperate* may come closer to achieving their personal objectives than do those who pursue their self-interest without regard to the well-being of others. The theory of how markets coordinate an economy—conveyed in Adam Smith's metaphor of "the invisible hand"—shows that *under certain conditions* competition based on self-interest but coordinated by markets will bring about a desirable allocation of economic resources. The story of the prisoner's dilemma, however, dramatizes the fact that *under other conditions* lack of cooperation results in a coordination failure.

The story goes as follows. Two individuals suspected of committing a crime are picked up by the police and placed in separate cells. The police have not been able to gather sufficient evidence to convict either of the prisoners (who we will refer to as prisoners "A" and "B"), so the local prosecutor must attempt to get at least one of the prisoners to confess to the crime and implicate the other one. The prosecutor offers each of the prisoners the choice of confessing to or denying involvement in the crime, and the consequences of all the possible choices are explained. Each prisoner, in turn, must decide independently on the best strategy to pursue.

The possible outcomes are as follows:

1. If A denies involvement in the crime and B does the same, they will both be convicted of a lesser offense (regarding which the prosecutor has ample evidence), and they will each receive sentences of two years in jail.
2. If A denies involvement in the crime but B confesses, implicating A, A will be sentenced (on the basis of the evidence provided by B) to four years, and B will go to jail for only one year.
3. If A confesses, implicating B, but B denies involvement in the crime, B will be sentenced (on the basis of the evidence provided by A) to four years, and A will go to jail for only one year.
4. If both prisoners confess to the crime, they will each be sentenced to three-year terms.

These four options are summarized in Table 9.3. The shaded cells in it are numbered in accordance with the four options presented above.

TABLE 9.3 Prisoner's Dilemma

		Prisoner B	
		Confesses	Denies
Prisoner A	Confesses	4 A and B both get 3 years	3 A gets 1 year B gets 4 years
	Denies	2 A gets 4 years B gets 1 year	1 A and B both get 2 years

First, assume that both prisoners make their choices with regard only to their own interests. What choices will they make? It will become apparent that under this assumption each prisoner can do better—*whether the other prisoner confesses or denies*—by confessing to the crime and implicating his or her partner.

Imagine that you are prisoner A. If you deny involvement in the crime while your partner is confessing (implicating you), you will be put away for four years (shaded cell 2). If, however, you confess while your partner is confessing, you will get only three years (shaded cell 4). So in the case that B has confessed you (A) would be better off if you confessed. If, on the other hand, you deny involvement while your partner is denying, you will get two years (shaded cell 1), but you will get only one year if you confess while your partner is denying (shaded cell 3). In this case, too, you are better off confessing. It is evident that confessing to the crime will leave you better off whatever your partner does—hence self-interest will lead you to confess. And if your partner is self-interested, too, he or she will come to the same conclusion. In this situation, then, you will both confess to the crime, and you will both be put away for three years (shaded cell 4).

Now imagine (a) that both you and your partner care enough about each other to want to keep the other from being put away for four years, and (b) that you are both willing to adhere to this objective even though it might not seem to serve your own interest. These assumptions mean that *cooperative* behavior will prevail. In this case neither of you will confess, and both of you will serve two years in jail (shaded cell 1). This outcome is clearly better for each of you than the one resulting when you both act with regard only to your own interest (shaded cell 4). The preferred outcome would also occur if both you and your partner are people who keep promises (whether or not keeping them seems to be in your own interest) and if, before committing the crime, you each promise to deny involvement if arrested.

The moral of the prisoner's dilemma story is not that it is a good thing for criminals to serve as little time as possible in prison (whether or not they have actually committed a crime). The moral is that in some situations the pursuit of self-interest by all parties leads to outcomes in which none of the participants benefit. These situations are just the opposite of the situation described by the invisible hand.

The prisoner's dilemma can help us find answers to such questions as: why is it so difficult to prevent destruction of the environment or to establish minimum standards of workplace health and safety among nations? In these cases the choices are not to confess or deny, but to "adhere to environmental (or workplace) standards" or "violate the standards."

The prisoner's dilemma and global warming.   There is a major obstacle to the progress of efforts to slow the pace of global warming: the government of any particular country would probably like to see all *other* nations limit *their* emissions of greenhouse gases (primarily carbon dioxide) while avoiding the politically unpopular task of limiting its own citizens' freedom to pollute. Many people in the rich countries resist any restraint on activities, such as driving a car, that pollute the environment; at the same time, many people in the poor countries of the world believe that limiting greenhouse gas emissions in their countries would hamper their attempts to industrialize and raise their living standards to those now common in rich nations.

The countries of the world thus face a coordination problem: if each nation's government acts independently and seeks to serve only the perceived interests of its own citizens

TABLE 9.4   North's Action/South's Action

		North's Action	
		Nothing	Protect
South's Action	Nothing	Third best for both	Best for S Worst for N
	Protect	Best for N Worst for S	Second best for both

(or its most powerful ones), no nation will adopt the measures necessary to avert major climatic change. To see why this is so, imagine that there are just two countries, called North and South, and just two options, called Nothing (meaning do nothing to prevent global warming) and Protect (meaning adopt protective measures to slow or halt global warming). Each country would like the other one to reduce its greenhouse gas emissions while avoiding the costs of doing so itself. Thus, for each the best alternative is to do Nothing while the other does Protect. The worst alternative for each is to Protect while the other does Nothing. The second-best alternative for both is that both Protect, and the third-best alternative for each is that both do Nothing.

The options available to the players in this simple game are represented in Table 9.4. This is a prisoner's dilemma situation, and as we have seen earlier, what is best for each is worst for all. If each country makes its decision independently and they both do what their own people see as being in their own self-interest, both countries will do Nothing. (As noted earlier, what is best for each does not depend on what the other does.) They would both be better off, however, if they both chose to Protect.

The best outcome can be achieved, however, only if the two countries agree to Protect, perhaps accomplishing such an agreement by signing an international treaty committing themselves to the implementation of protective measures. But two problems immediately arise. First, who will enforce the agreement? There is no world government or any other body that could force each nation to abide by its agreements. The second problem is that different ways of protecting the global environment result in differing costs and benefits for each country. Why, for example, would the poor countries of the world agree to pay an equal share of the costs of reducing greenhouse gas emissions, most of which are now caused by the high-income countries?

The poor countries might argue that each nation should have the right to pollute in proportion to its population. In this case any solution to the problem would require drastic reductions in carbon dioxide emissions in the rich countries (where pollution per capita is high), while leaving the poor countries relatively free to industrialize in a way that increases pollution. While this solution may seem fair to many people, it is likely to be politically unpopular in the rich countries.

Extending the lesson of the prisoner's dilemma more generally to economic systems, we can say that reliance on competitive markets may fail to coordinate an economy in a desirable way: the pursuit of self-interest by individuals may result in outcomes that are not optimal from the point of view of any member of the society. This is what is meant by the term *coordination failure*.

The Tragedy of the Commons

Another illustration of a coordination failure is referred to as "the tragedy of the commons," a parable set forth in 1968 by Garrett Hardin in a now-classic article in *Science* magazine.[1] This parable is about the possibility that environmental destruction will result from the uncoordinated pursuit of individual self-interest.

Imagine a large lake, its shores dotted by the houses of people who fish in the lake to earn their livings. No one owns the lake: it is the common property of all the members of the surrounding community. The situation described here, one that involves communal ownership of an important shared resource, is similar to arrangements that were widespread in many of the early settlements in New England (it has, of course, also existed in other parts of the world at various times in history), and it takes its name from the shared grazing land for cattle and other livestock that was referred to as the town "common."

In the parable of the lake, each person decides independently the number of hours to fish each day (or, alternatively, how many fish to catch) before heading back to shore. As self-interested people, they fish as long as the additional benefit of another hour (or another fish) is greater than the inconvenience or discomfort of the additional time and effort spent fishing.

However, as in the case of the prisoner's dilemma, what is rational for one is not beneficial for all. The more each person fishes, the more difficult it is for the others to catch fish. The reason for this is simple: there are a limited number of fish to be caught, and as each person catches more of them, fewer are left to be caught by the other lakeside residents. Each person would like to see limits put on the fishing of the others while remaining free, herself, to fish without limit. As long as there are no limits placed on anyone's fishing, there will be overfishing. The end result is predictable: there will soon be hardly any fish left in the lake, and, eventually, the lake will be entirely "fished out." That is the tragedy.

This story is about fishing in a lake, but it might just as well be about overgrazing open pastureland, dumping sewage into a river, or polluting the air. The moral of the story is that the pursuit of individual self-interest can be highly irrational because it can have very negative, possibly irreversible, consequences.

A real-life example of the tragedy of the commons is the case of what happened with a particular effort to harness geothermal energy for the generation of electricity. A potentially cheap and environmentally clean way of generating electricity involves tapping the steam that shoots in geysers out of the earth. In the years since this method of producing electric power became practical, a huge field of geysers 70 miles north of San Francisco has been regarded as a promising place to try it out. When energy prices suddenly rose in the mid-1970s, the geysers north of San Francisco became the focus of intense but largely uncoordinated energy development. However, as more and more electricity-generating plants were built there, the amount of steam available for earlier-installed plants fell. (In

---

[1] Garrett Hardin, "The Tragedy of the Commons," *Science*, no. 162, Dec. 13, 1968.

such a field of geysers there is a common but limited amount of steam deep beneath the earth's surface.) Eventually, so much steam was being tapped that none of the electricity-generating plants could operate at full capacity. By the early 1990s it became clear that because the number of plants had not been limited, the geysers were no longer an efficient source of energy.[2]

How can tragedies like this be avoided? There are many answers to this question, but all involve finding some way to take others' interests into account when making decisions. The most obvious solution to the problem would be simply to regulate access to the common resource. In the fictitious case described above, the fishing people around the lake could have met, ascertained how many fish might reasonably be taken from the lake each week, and decided collectively on a fishing limit for each member of the community that would have allowed the weekly target to be met. In fact, there are fishing villages in Japan, Turkey, and elsewhere that engage in this practice.[3]

If, on the other hand, the problem was overgrazing, those with the animals could figure out how much grazing the common land could support and then decide on the number of animals each herder would be allowed to graze. Solutions to the problem such as the ones mentioned so far all involve what is termed *social regulation of the commons.*

An alternative, which might be termed the *private property solution,* would be for the commons to be owned by a private individual or company. Such an owner would, say (in the cases mentioned above), not only employ the lake residents to fish or the animal herders to graze their livestock, but also would, in self-interest, limit the use of the common resource in order to prevent its deterioration. Obviously, the owner would not want to see the lake overfished or the pasture overgrazed. A problem with this "private property solution" to the tragedy is that the common resource is often too large to be owned by a single individual or company. Something like the tragedy of the commons is currently being played out in the ozone layer high in the atmosphere above the earth, and the world's oceans are a similarly threatened common resource. For such large commons, private ownership is obviously not possible, so the social regulation approach is all there is. However, as noted earlier (see "The Prisoner's Dilemma and Global Warming" above), social regulation is not easy to work out in practice.

Market Failure

> A **market failure** is said to take place when the spontaneous interactions of buyers and sellers on markets each pursuing their own objectives results in outcomes that are generally undesirable.

The term *coordination failure* refers to *any* situation in which the self-interested behavior of individuals results in an outcome that is less beneficial to them than one that might have been achieved by better-coordinated, or cooperative, behavior. The term *market failure,* on the other hand, refers to the specific type of coordination failure that happens because of how *markets* work. Neither the prisoner's dilemma nor the tragedy of the commons, much as they may shed light on the problems

---

[2] Richard Kerr, "Geothermal Tragedy of the Commons," *Science,* no. 253, July 12, 1991, pp. 134–135.

[3] F. Berkes, D. Feeny, B. J. McCay, and J. M. Acheson, "The Benefits of the Commons," *Nature,* no. 340, July 13, 1987, pp. 91–94.

associated with (self-interested) market behavior, are in themselves examples of market failure (since they do not involve *exchange* relationships).

Why, then, does the invisible hand of the market fail, in many situations, to coordinate economic activities in ways that produce desirable results? The general answer is that people affect one another's well-being in countless ways, and market prices often fail to take into account all the effects of our actions on others. In small groups, such as families and friendships, we typically consider the costs and benefits of our actions not only with regard to ourselves but also as they might affect the others we care about. Such consciousness, also known as altruism, is an essential part of social life, but it obviously does not prevail when we are interacting with large groups of strangers, about whom we may know little and care less.

The underlying assumption of the invisible hand is that *if prices are right* (in the sense that they measure the true scarcity of all aspects of human interactions), all the effects of people's actions on one another will be taken into account in the prices of goods and services. Thus, Adam Smith's theory (including its modern version) holds that—if we assume (as Smith did) that the existing distribution of wealth is acceptable—coordinating an economy with markets will bring about an optimal allocation of society's resources.

Proponents of the invisible hand theory offer examples such as the following to support the theory: When a certain consumption choice, say, ordering a tenderloin steak, uses up a lot of society's resources, that consumption choice will be appropriately paid for in the price of the steak. This is because the price will be equal to the marginal cost—hence the consumer will be paying exactly the amount it cost to produce that tenderloin steak. Proponents of the invisible hand theory would also argue that the marginal cost is a good measure of the amount of other goods—vegetables for vegetarians, for instance—that might have been produced with the same resources that went into producing the steak.

Another example of optimal pricing would be if a person's uniquely skillful work went into producing a product that brought great joy to others, such a product would fetch a high price (reflecting its marginal cost as well as the demand for it), and its producer would be handsomely rewarded when the product was sold.

The problem is that *prices are often not right* (in the sense just described). There are many examples. If the technology used by a particular company helps it to produce a valuable product at low cost but also gives off a high level of airborne toxins, the company may be rewarded with high profits, but it does not pay for the pollution it imposes on others. In this case the company does not pay for the clean air it uses up, it pays only for the inputs it has to buy in the market. As a result, the price of the product, although it may be equal to the marginal cost *to the company* of producing the product, does not take into account the additional costs that production of this product imposes on others.

Another example: If an individual develops a new computer software application that proves exceptionally valuable to its users but is costless to copy, the "right price" (the price that is equal to the marginal cost of producing additional copies of the application) is zero. This price will obviously not allow the developer to be appropriately rewarded, and it will certainly not provide an incentive for others to develop valuable software. One might think that patent protection would solve this problem—and indeed it might from the point of view of the individual developer—but the enforcement of this legal right (assuming it could be enforced) would not result in an optimal allocation of resources. This is because if others are prevented from using the application without paying its developer a substantial price, the price charged would be much higher than its marginal cost of production.

A final example: If you spend many hours of your time at local school board meetings or doing volunteer work to improve the quality of life in your neighborhood, you will undoubtedly reap personal benefits from these activities. However, there will not be a market price—or payment—that compensates you for any of the benefits received by your neighbors. Moreover, if you are a renter of your house or apartment, there will be no payment rewarding you for the resulting increase in the value of your residence, since it belongs to your landlord. Indeed, your landlord might raise the rent she is charging you, arguing that the market values (and rental prices) of houses and apartments in your neighborhood have gone up as a result of the improvements in the neighborhood and its schools.

Why do markets fail in these cases? One reason is that in these cases prices do not adequately measure the scarcity of the goods in question. The product of a polluting factory is more scarce than its low price seems to indicate because the cost to society of the factory's pollution is not included in the price of the good. The computer application, once produced, is not scarce at all: it can be copied over and over again at zero marginal cost. Hence, if its developer somehow manages to sell it at a profit, its price will overstate its scarcity. But if it were to be sold it at its true scarcity price (zero), it would have to be given away, in which case there would be no incentive to produce it in the first place. Finally, the volunteer activities of citizens are, by definition, not paid for, so it is impossible to put market prices on such activities even though the supply of community-oriented labor is a scarce as well as a valuable resource from the standpoint of other citizens and society as a whole.

Private costs are the costs borne by the user of a good or service (a person or a company), while the total costs borne by all members of a society are termed **social costs.** At best, prices only measure private costs.

In all these cases there is a discrepancy between (a) the costs and benefits borne or received by the decision maker and (b) the costs and benefits experienced by all the members of society (including the decision maker). The costs and benefits accruing to the decision maker are referred to as the *private costs* and benefits of the activity in question, whereas when added together all the costs and benefits experienced by everyone (again including the decision maker) are termed the *social costs* and benefits.

When private and social costs diverge, economists say (as we explained in Chapter 3) that there is an *externality* because individuals or groups "external" to a transaction experience some of its effects. Another way of putting this is to say that there are *spillover* effects if some of the effects of a transaction "spill over" and confer benefits or impose costs on individuals or groups not directly involved in a transaction. We favor the use of the term *externality* because it explicitly distinguishes people who are "internal" to—or directly involved as decision makers in—a transaction from those who are "external" to—or not direct participants in—the transaction.

When there is an externality it can be either positive or negative, positive if the external effects (or spillovers) of a transaction are beneficial to others, negative if they impose costs on others. Thus, there are positive externalities and negative externalities. In addition, however, positive externalities are sometimes referred to as *external economies,* while negative externalities are termed *external diseconomies.* How confusing! We continue to favor the use of the simpler term *externality*—as in positive externality and negative externality.

An important consequence of externalities is that when they exist, private marginal costs are not equal to social marginal costs. In this case even if prices are equal to private

TABLE 9.5 Positive and Negative Externalities

Action	Externality	Price Not Equal to Social Costs/Benefits
Drinking too many beers	The costs of alcohol abuse on families, friends, and medical providers	The price of the beer does not reflect such negative externalities
Driving a car	This can contribute to traffic congestion, and it also causes environmental degradation from both the production and the use of fossil fuels	The price of the gas used does not reflect these negative externalities
Research	The benefits of any good ideas produced will most likely be enjoyed by other people or companies	Any increase in the profits of the firm that supported the research—or rise in the salary of the individual who conducted it—may not take into account all the benefits of the resulting knowledge enjoyed by others
Education	The benefits of one person's education are enjoyed by neighbors and workmates	The individual benefits (higher earnings) do not capture the positive externalities enjoyed by others
Training employees	Some employees will move to other firms, the owners of which will benefit from the training paid for by the firm that did the training	The training firm's profits do not reflect the benefits flowing to other firms with the workers who move
Wearing a $500 watch (luxury consumption)	This may have the effect of lowering the (relative) status of others, creating envy	The $500 price of the watch does not include the status and envy costs imposed on others

marginal costs, they will not be equal to social marginal costs. Hence, they will not measure the cost to society of producing an additional unit of a good.

Important sources of positive externalities are education, the production of knowledge, and the introduction of new technologies. Important examples of negative externalities are pollution, other kinds of environmental degradation, and automobile traffic congestion in metropolitan areas. Some examples of positive and negative externalities are presented in Table 9.5.

Another reason why externalities exist in competitive markets is that while some costs and benefits are covered in contracts, others are not. As noted in Chapter 3, this is the problem of *incomplete contracts*. When someone sells a commodity to another person, the buyer pays the seller the contracted price. But when there are social costs involved—such as the costs of dealing with the consequences of pollution or enforcing the provisions in a contract—the contracted price does not cover the costs of health care, cleaning up toxic wastes, or paying other expenses involuntarily imposed on the buyer, the seller, or other members of society.

The problem of incomplete contracts can be illustrated using the examples already mentioned. In the case of software, even if there is a contract saying that copies of it cannot be made by—or distributed to—persons other than the purchaser (think of the printed seal that is affixed to the envelope enclosing a CD containing a just-purchased piece of software), such a contract is virtually (no pun intended) impossible to enforce.

If someone's volunteer efforts have the effect of improving the quality of a neighborhood or its schools, there is no contract enabling that person to collect from the local landlords or homeowners any portion of the resulting increase in property values. And neither is there any way for the volunteer to be directly compensated by his or her neighbors for the improved quality of the neighborhood or its schools.

Another example of an incomplete contract is the wage bargain negotiated between employer and employee. The employer contracts (at least implicitly) to pay the employee a certain wage rate per hour on the job, and the employee, in return for the wage, agrees to come to work for a specified number of hours per day and for a certain number of days each week. But the amount of work actually to be done by the worker is not—and cannot be—covered in the contract. Ensuring that the employee does enough work to make the enterprise profitable is the basic problem of *management* that faces every employer. How hard the employee works, the "intensity" of his or her labor, will depend to some degree on his or her "work ethic," but it can also be affected by the type of incentives offered by the employer in return for hard work (the carrot) or the degree to which the employer can coerce the worker (by threat of firing, use of tough supervisors, etc.) into working hard (the stick). The condition of the worker at the end of the day, another variable not covered in the contract, will depend on the quality of the work environment provided by the employer and the way in which the employer exercises his or her managerial powers to get the worker to work. The challenge to employers of getting workers to work hard is discussed at length in Chapters 12 and 13.

In addition to the problem of incomplete contracts, markets may also fail for the more obvious reason that there are too few competitors, or even potential competitors, in the market. The invisible hand argument assumes that markets are competitive, with many actual or potential buyers and sellers in every market. Given this assumption, no producer can charge more than the marginal cost of producing a particular commodity.

In the real world, however, many markets are not competitive. In the case of a *monopoly,* a single producer with no actual or potential competitors can raise the price buyers must pay for its product without fear that its customers will switch their patronage to another supplier. A monopoly has *market power* since it can raise the price of its product merely by producing (and selling) less of it. This will create an artificial scarcity in the market for the product and drive up its price. In this situation the price charged will be higher than the marginal cost and hence will not be consistent with an optimal allocation of society's resources.

Of course, if there were other firms that could produce the same product, they would enter the market, would compete for customers by charging lower prices, and would continue doing this until the price of the product fell to its marginal cost. It is this process that leads to the result that in a competitive market, the market-clearing price will be equal to the marginal cost ($P = MC$) in every firm. But with barriers to the entry of new firms, which is what makes a monopoly a monopoly, a monopolist does not have to fear competition from new firms. The workings of imperfectly competitive markets are discussed at length in Chapter 11.

Prices often exceed marginal cost for yet another reason, one that has nothing to do with monopoly. To see this, ask yourself what the marginal cost was of the last CD you purchased. If the album was relatively popular and the CD you purchased was, say, the 423,589th one produced, its marginal cost was probably not much more than a dollar. This is considerably less than its average cost of production because, as explained in Chapter 8, marginal cost is just the increase in the total cost resulting from the production of one *additional* CD, whereas average cost takes into account not only the cost of producing the additional CD but also what the CD-producing company had to pay for such things as advertising, permission to use copyrighted material, rent for the use of the production facilities, interest paid to the bank for loans, and any other expenses that do not vary as a result of producing one more CD. Economists refer to such costs as *fixed costs*. They are included in the total cost but are spread out over the total number of units produced, which is one reason why average cost (total cost divided by the number of units produced) declines as more units are produced. In the music industry and other parts of the economy such as book publishing, fixed costs are called *first copy costs*.

Of course, there are also costs associated just with the production of the one CD you purchased. The company that produced it had to acquire a blank CD, burn the music onto it, purchase its jewel case, print and install the tray card, and wrap the final product in cellophane. But when the production run is large the costs of all these steps will be very low for each individual CD because things such as blank CDs and jewel cases can be purchased in large quantities for only a few cents each. And the process of burning music onto a CD, if it is repeated thousands of times, is also very cheap. Even if the costs of paying royalties to artists and distributing the CDs to retail outlets are taken into account, the marginal cost per CD will still be very low.

Since the marginal cost of your CD was probably in the neighborhood of $1 while the price you paid for it was most likely $14 or more, the CD market is obviously not working well: it is not setting a scarcity price ($P = MC$) on the CD. There are almost certainly quite a few people out there who felt they could not afford to buy the CD at $14 but who would have purchased it—and enjoyed listening to it—had the price been $1 or $2. The existence of a number of frustrated buyers who would have been willing to pay the cost of the resources required to make available an additional copy of the CD means that *the invisible hand is not working* in this case. Why is this?

CDs are manufactured and sold by hundreds of companies, so the gap between their prices and their marginal costs of production is not due to monopoly power. Rather, the gap is probably the result of a phenomenon (discussed in Chapter 3) that prevails in many parts of the economy: *increasing returns to scale.*

As noted earlier, the presence of increasing returns means that the *average cost* of producing a product will *fall* as the quantity produced rises. And if this is the case, *the marginal cost of production will be below the average cost.* We know that this is true because of the mathematics of the situation: if average cost is rising, the marginal cost must be above the average cost (in order to be pulling it up), while, for the same reason, marginal cost must lie below average cost if the latter is falling (in order to be pulling it down).

To illustrate this point with a concrete example, assume that the total cost of producing 100 CDs is $1,005, which means that the average cost of producing the 100 CDs is $10.05. (Recall that the average cost is equal to the total cost divided by the number of units produced.) If the CD-producing company now decides to produce 101 CDs and finds that the total cost of producing that many CDs is $1,010, the average cost of producing the

101 CDs will have dropped from $10.05 to $10.00. To calculate the marginal cost in this example, we compare the total cost of producing 100 CDs ($1,005) with the total cost of producing 101 CDs ($1,010), finding that the marginal cost of producing the 101st CD is $5. Since $5 is less than $10, it is clear that when average cost is falling (as it is in this case), the marginal cost will be less than the average cost.

Returning to our example of a CD that is being produced in very large quantities: if the retail price of the CD (say, $14) exceeds the marginal cost by a large amount (say, by $13 per CD), why are new firms not entering the industry, expanding the production of CDs, and driving the retail price of them down (as the invisible hand theory of competitive markets would predict)? The answer is that the market price may be above the *average cost* only by something like $3, thereby allowing the CD-producing company to make a profit of only $3 on each CD produced. If this provides the company with a rate of profit that is not out of line with the rate of profit being made in other industries—in other words, if it is roughly equal to the average rate of profit in the economy as a whole—other firms will not have an incentive, say, to stop making frisbies in order to enter the CD-producing industry. (We provide a precise definition of the rate of profit and an analysis of how it is determined in Chapter 10.)

Although there is, as we have demonstrated, a market failure in this case, it is important to note that the CD-producing company can hardly be expected to sell its CDs at their marginal cost: to do so would mean making losses rather than profits. Rather, the problem arises because of the *system* of profit making and pricing, not because the company is breaking the rules. The company is simply charging a price that allows it to make something like the average rate of profit in the economy.

The phenomenon of increasing returns provides but one more way of explaining why markets fail. If we put all of the explanations of market failure together—inadequate pricing, externalities (spillovers), incomplete contracts, market power, and increasing returns—we arrive at a more complete understanding of the concept of market failure. As noted above, the term refers to any situation in which the market interactions of buyers and sellers result in outcomes that are undesirable either to individuals or to society as a whole. The accompanying box ("The Invisible Foot . . .") provides a list of some of the more common types of market failure.

The type of market failure that stems from increasing returns leads at least some countries to avoid relying on privately owned companies for the supply of such things as electric power generation, transportation networks, and phone systems, all of which are usually characterized by increasing returns. Such countries choose, instead, to have either their governments or regulated enterprises carry on these types of economic activities. Whether these solutions work better in practice than private production without regulation depends on the nature of the governments in question.

The fourth category of market failure listed in the "Invisible Foot" box raises, again, the issue of efficiency and income distribution discussed in Chapter 3. The question is whether one can say that an economy is efficiently allocating a society's resources if some people have huge incomes while others do not have enough income to provide for their most basic needs (see the box "Efficiency, Profitability, and 'Pareto Optimality'" in Chapter 3, p. 63). The general problem is brought out here in the box "Voting With Dollars," and the box on "Sleeping Sickness" provides a concrete illustration of it.

THE INVISIBLE FOOT: WHEN MARKETS FAIL

M arket failures occur when the market interactions of buyers and sellers result in outcomes that are undesirable either to individuals or to society as a whole. Thus, market failures result

- *when markets are controlled by a small number of buyers or sellers.* (For example, when there is a single monopoly seller, the price charged for a good will exceed the cost to the firm of producing another unit of the good.)
- *when environmental degradation or other negative externalities resulting from production occur.* (In this case, the cost to the firm of producing another unit of the good will not be the same as the cost to society—the social cost will be greater than the private cost—and the price charged by the firm will not reflect the true scarcity of the product.)
- *when externalities in consumption are present.* (Here, the benefit or cost to the individual consumer will not accurately measure the benefit or cost to society as a whole. An example of a positive consumption externality would be another person's—or a whole neighborhood's—enjoyment of one family's beautiful garden; an example of a negative consumption externality would be the imposition of unwanted smoke by a smoker on nonsmokers.)
- *when people's needs are not reflected in market demands.* (This may happen when individuals, such as homeless people, do not have enough money to purchase necessities, such as housing, for themselves in the market, or it may result from a person's mistaken belief about the ability of a certain good—say, one more gadget—to satisfy his or her needs.)

More recently, some economists have argued that success stories such as London's congestion fee system (see box "Private Incentives, Public Benefits") are the exception, not the rule. They point out that governments generally cannot be trusted—any more than markets can—to perform in accordance with some ideal. Such skeptics have warned that granting a government the right to interfere with the workings of markets may do more harm than good. They have coined the term *government failure* to suggest that the government might not be any more successful than an unfettered market would be in accomplishing a task or solving a problem. According to this view, moreover, giving government more of a role might increase the chances for favoritism, bribery, or other forms of corruption, all of which would result in less-than-optimal allocations of a society's resources.

Still other economists, following the lead of Ronald Coase (see Chapter 4), have favored improving the nature of contracts—basing them on more precisely defined property rights—so that more of the relevant social interactions among economic actors will be

VOTING WITH DOLLARS

It is sometimes said that markets are like elections, in which consumers "vote" with their dollars for the commodities they want. If a large number of dollar "votes" are cast for yellow shirts, a large number of yellow shirts will be produced. In a capitalist economy competition for profits will see to it that resources are allocated in such a way as to produce commodities in the proportions determined by dollar votes.

Voting for commodities in markets is an unusual kind of election, however, because some people vote more times than others. If every dollar of household income had been cast as a vote in 2002, the average household in the richest fifth of the U.S. population would have had more than 14 times as many votes (143,559) as the average household in the poorest fifth (9,931). Rather than the one-person, one-vote principle of democracy, this is more like an economic version of ballot-box stuffing.

Source: U.S. Census Bureau, "Household Income (2002)" available at: http://www.census.gov/hhes/www/income.html.

SLEEPING SICKNESS: "IT REALLY IS A FAILURE OF CAPITALISM."

Sleeping sickness is a horrible disease common in Africa; it attacks the brain, driving the afflicted insane before killing them. Spread by the tsetse fly, it strikes more than a quarter of a million people each year. A cure for the disease has been discovered, "efornithine," and it is so effective that even comatose sleeping sickness patients have been revived. Grateful Africans have dubbed it the "resurrection drug."

Wonderful news. A triumph of modern medicine? Not exactly. Although researchers have known since the early 1990s that efornithine is effective in the treatment of sleeping sickness, it was not put into production because early hopes that the drug would also cure cancer were not borne out. There are no markets (or profits to be made) for something that saves only poor people: they cannot afford to buy it. Now, however, the Bristol Myers Squibb Company is producing efornithine because, as an ingredient in something called Vaniqa, it can be marketed as a cream that removes women's facial hair. Bristol Myers recently promoted

Vaniqa with a six-page advertising supplement in *Cosmopolitan* magazine that contained the following text: "If the mustache that prevents you from getting close is yours (not his), it may be time for a beauty about face." The price of a two-month supply of Vaniqa, enough to make a woman's moustache disappear, greatly exceeds the cost of producing enough eformithine to rescue a person from sleeping sickness, madness, and death in Africa.

Bristol Myers is now working with the World Health Organization and such groups as Doctors Without Borders to find a way to make eformithine available in a form that can be used to combat sleeping sickness (rubbing on Vaniqa does not help). But Robert Laverty, a Bristol Myers spokesman, expressed concern about the bottom line: "The question is how this will be funded indefinitely."

The possibility of eradicating sleeping sickness in Africa is a happy accident of the market for facial hair treatments in rich countries. About 3 million people in low- and middle-income countries die of malaria, measles, tetanus, and diarrheal diseases every year, but such deaths will probably not be prevented anytime soon. Only 1 percent of the global market for medicines is in Africa, and the people of the state of Connecticut spend more on health care than do the entire populations of the 38 lowest-income nations of Africa. The profitable markets for pharmaceuticals lie elsewhere: three-quarters of the world's drug sales are in the U.S., Europe, and Japan, where less than one-fifth of the world's people reside and where the incidence of disease is relatively low. Private firms carry on about half of global medical research, but less than 5 percent of that is focused on diseases that are common in poor countries. Of the 1,233 drugs licensed worldwide between 1975 and 1997, only 13 were for tropical diseases.

On his Friday evening PBS show *Now*, Bill Moyers asked Microsoft's Bill Gates, "What does it say to you that 11 million children, roughly, die every year from preventable diseases? What does it say to you that of the 4 million babies who die within their first month, 98 percent are from poor countries? What do those statistics tell you about the world?" Gates replied, "It really is a failure of capitalism. You know, capitalism is this wonderful thing . . . But in this area of diseases of the world at large, it's really let us down." Moyers then countered: "But markets are supposed to deliver goods and services to people," and Gates responded, "and when people have money it does . . . Here what we have is . . . not only don't the people with money have the disease, but they don't *see* the people who have the disease. If we took the world and we just reassorted each neighborhood to be randomly mixed up, then this whole thing could get solved. Because you'd look out your window and you'd say, you know, there's [a] mother over there whose child is dying. You know, let's go help that person." The Bill and Melinda Gates foundation is funding efforts to reduce the incidence of disease in Africa.

Sources: Michael Kremer, "Pharmaceuticals and the Developing World," *Journal of Economic Perspectives,* fall 2002, pp. 67–90; Donald McNeil, "Cosmetic Saves a Cure for Sleeping Sickness," *New York Times,* February 9, 2001, p. A1; *NOW with Bill Moyers,* PBS, May 9, 2003.

PRIVATE INCENTIVES, PUBLIC BENEFITS

Until recently the congested traffic in central London crept along at a snail's pace. Confronted with approaching gridlock, Mayor Ken Livingstone tried a radical solution: charge those operating private cars for the congestion costs they impose on others. In February 2003 the city imposed a fee of $8 a day to operate a car in the central part of London. This fee had to be paid by everyone except central London residents. A high-tech computer system kept track daily of who had paid (among the ways to pay, one could use the text message option on a cell phone). License plate number-recognition devices installed throughout the central part of the city nabbed scofflaws.

The traffic congestion costs (like the costs of pollution) that one imposes on others are examples of external diseconomies, or negative externalities. Livingstone's plan forced drivers to take these costs into account. Economists call this "internalizing the externality." The scheme had the effect of increasing the private marginal cost of driving in the center of London by an amount equal to the fee, thus making the private marginal costs more nearly equal to the social marginal costs. Livingstone's plan could have been lifted straight from the pages of an economics textbook: virtually all economics textbooks, including this one, say that people will change their behavior when the potential costs or benefits of their choices are altered. (See our discussion of *shifts* of supply and demand curves in Chapter 8.)

Livingstone's critics thought that his plan would worsen the traffic problem and hurt businesses in the affected area. To the surprise of many, however, it worked. Traffic flowing into central London was reduced by 20 percent, and delays were cut by almost 30 percent. Average traffic speeds in this previously congested area jumped from 9.5 mph to 20 mph. On an average day in March 2003, about 100,000 motorists were paying the congestion fees. The fees they paid—plus the hefty fines imposed on the dwindling number of people who thought, erroneously, that they could beat the system—generated more than $1 million of revenues each day for the city government. A third of the companies in the affected area said that Livingstone's new policy was helping them; only 5 percent said it was hurting their business. After six weeks of operation, half of all Londoners liked the policy, while only a third of them disliked it. Livingstone's popularity ratings hit an all time high, and London's red double-decker buses are no doubt enjoying a popularity surge, too.

Source: "Ken's Coup," *The Economist,* March 22, 2003, p. 39.

taken into account. They focus specifically on the question of how to narrow the gap between the private and the social costs or benefits borne or received by the decision makers in any given situation.

An example of the Coasian approach is the system under which the government sells or otherwise distributes pollution rights, or "emissions permits," that allow companies to emit a certain quantity of pollutants into the atmosphere, soil, or water during a particular time period. Once such rights have been acquired, they can be exchanged among companies in what is, in effect, a market for pollution rights. In such a market pollution rights can be traded for anything from cash to pollution-absorbing forests. What generally happens, however, is that a company builds a state-of-the-art environment-friendly plant and therefore has a surplus of pollution rights—rights it does not need to use because its new plant emits less pollution than most older plants. This company can then sell its unused pollution rights to another company whose plant exceeds the pollution standard set by the government. Under this system the more a company pollutes the more it will have to pay. Moreover, if the price of a pollution right is set correctly, a company will have to take into account in a precise way the harm it does to others when it decides what technology to use when it is planning, say, the construction of a new plant. With this system, its proponents argue, profit and loss calculations will bring about a desired amount of pollution reduction in the most efficient possible way.

Because millions or billions of dollars as well as life and death matters of public health are affected by policies to correct market failures, the special-interest groups that stand to benefit or lose from their adoption often dominate debates about these policies. An as yet unanswered question is: how can ordinary people build up enough influence in policy-making centers such as Washington, D.C., to equal or outweigh the influence that lobbyists, representing a small number of individuals or corporations, exert on the legislators and others who determine which policies will be adopted—or not adopted—to correct for the various types of market failures discussed in this chapter?

SUGGESTED READINGS

Allen E. Buchanan, *Ethics, Efficiency, and the Market* (Totowa, N.J.: Rowman & Allanheld, 1985).

John Eatwell, Murray Milgate, and Peter Newman, eds., *The New Palgrave: The Invisible Hand* (New York: Norton, 1989).

Milton Friedman, *Capitalism and Freedom* (Chicago: University of Chicago Press, 1962).

F. A. Hayek, *The Fatal Conceit: The Errors of Socialism* (Chicago: University of Chicago Press, 1988).

David Jenkins, *Market Whys and Human Wherefores: Thinking About Markets, Politics and People* (London and New York: Cassell, 2000).

Robert Kuttner, *Everything for Sale: The Virtues and Limits of Markets* (New York: Knopf, 1997).

Marie Lavigne, *The Economics of Transition: From Socialist Economy to Market Economy,* 2nd ed. (New York: Palgrave, 1999).

Charles E. Lindblom, *The Market System: What It Is, How It Works, and What To Make of It* (New Haven, Conn.: Yale University Press, 2001).

Amartya Sen, *Poverty and Famines: An Essay on Entitlement and Deprivation* (Oxford: Oxford University Press, 1981).

Cass R. Sunstein, *After the Rights Revolution: Reconceiving the Regulatory State* (Cambridge, Mass.: Harvard University Press, 1990).

CHAPTER 10

Capitalist Production and Profits

apitalism is often said to be a system of profit and loss. And so it is—when viewed from the standpoint of a firm. Yet capitalists as a group generally see profits every year, not losses. This was true in the U.S. for all of the 20th century—except 1932 and 1933, the two worst years of the Great Depression—and it continues to be the case today. Even in 1932 and 1933, owners of capital goods who received their income in the form of interest or rent did not suffer losses. Despite the misfortunes of particular companies, the capitalist class as a whole makes a profit every year.

Moreover, the magnitude of profit is usually substantial. In the U.S. in 2001, for instance, profit and other property income amounted to $1,855 billion, more than one-fifth of the nation's total income in that year. (See box "Calculating Total Property Income" on p. 230 to find out how this calculation is done.) Such income was not wage or salary income, but it was real money received by investors, banks, stockholders, bondholders, landlords, pension funds, and retirees, among others.

Why, in a system of profits and losses, does the capitalist class as a whole usually make profits, not losses? And what determines the amount of its profits? These are the questions we address in this chapter. Analysis of the profit rate illuminates the control of the surplus product and the perpetuation of the class system. Later in the book we show how the profit rate is the concept that best brings together the horizontal, vertical, and time dimensions of economic life—competition, command, and change.

The profit rate is affected by conflicts among employers as well as by conflicts between employers and workers. In Chapter 11 the profit rate is central to our examination of how employers compete and collaborate with other employers in their attempts to increase profits. In Chapters 12 and 13, we focus on how the profit rate is involved in conflicts between employers and workers. In Chapter 19 we look at how the actions and policies of governments may affect the profit rate.

BUSINESS AND PROFIT

Business functions around one predominant organizing principle, profitability.

—Robert E. Rubin, former U.S. treasury secretary, in a speech to the
Economic Club of Chicago, February 22, 2001

The main idea of this chapter is that *the profit rate is the basic tool for analyzing how capitalism works, and understanding the profit rate requires understanding how the capitalist class prevails in its conflicts with other claimants on the national product.* This main idea is expressed in four main points:

1. *Profit* is the remainder, or surplus, left for employers after their output has been sold and the inputs—materials used, wear and tear on machines, and labor employed—have been paid for. Profit would not exist if the payments for materials, machine use, and wages and salaries added up to the value of the entire output of the economy.

2. The *profit rate* is defined as the amount of profit divided by the value of the capital goods owned.

3. How high the profit rate is for the capitalist class as a whole depends on how successful that class is in waging a three-front war: to extract high levels of effort from *workers* at a low wage cost, to gain necessary services from *the government* at a low tax cost, and to acquire *raw materials and other inputs* at a low cost.

4. The *determinants of the profit rate* constitute a list of the various ways in which outcomes of the conflicts between the capitalist class and other groups influence the profit rate.

WHAT ARE PROFITS?

The search for profit and the rate of profit are the keys to understanding how capitalism works. But what exactly are profits?

The answer to this question is not readily available in the financial and business press, where profits are often referred to, incorrectly, as "earnings." "Earnings per share" (of stock) is one of the measures used by investors to track the performance of a corporation. Here, however, we will speak of profits as "made" rather than "earned."

> **Commercial profits** result from selling something for more than it cost to purchase ("buying cheap and selling dear"); no labor process is involved.

There are two basic ways to make a profit, and they are quite different. One way to make a profit, as Adam Smith observed, is to "buy cheap and sell dear"—in other words to sell something for a higher price than you paid for it.[1] The profits that result from buying cheap and selling dear are called *commercial profits.*

Buying cheap and selling dear results in a profit even if you have not improved or in any other way changed the item in question. Ticket scalping for World Series games or rock concerts is one example. Buying gold in the hope that the price will go up—this is called speculation—is another.

The distinguishing characteristic of commercial profits is that these profits do not result from a labor process: they come about because the price of something differs depending on the time or place. Profits made from buying and selling real estate, stocks, and national currencies account for some of the world's largest fortunes, but aside from the sums involved, they are not very different from the profits made from scalping, since trading in real estate, stocks, and currencies does not *produce* anything.

Capitalist profits, on the other hand, are profits that result (directly or indirectly) from a labor process. Unlike commercial profits, they do not depend on the existence of different prices for the same item. Something is produced, and profit results because the price of what is produced is greater than the cost of the labor time and other inputs used to produce it. Our focus in this chapter is on capitalist profits.

> **Capitalist profits** are profits that result from a labor process.

Figure 10.1 depicts the process by which a firm attempts to make capitalist profits. It shows the various transactions and activities of the firm from the time it purchases its productive inputs to the time it sells its products to other firms or individuals. This figure illuminates the distinction between "commercial profits" and "capitalist profits." As explained above, the former result from selling an item for more than was paid for it, while the latter are achieved after inputs have been purchased, production has been carried out, and the output sold (if possible) for more money than was paid for the inputs.

A diagram showing how commercial profits are made could be much simpler than Figure 10.1. It would have to consist of only three boxes, the first showing a merchant (or firm) with a certain amount of money (M), the second picturing the same individual (or firm) possessing the commodities (C) purchased with the money, and the third representing the merchant (or firm) with the amount of money (M′) that has been received from the sale of the commodities. As in Figure 10.1, there would be two exchanges, the first involving an exchange of money for commodities and the second being an exchange of commodities for money. Also, the profit (or loss) would be the difference between M′ and M.

In the commercial profits diagram, however, there would be no triangle in the middle representing production, with its hierarchical (command) relationships. The process of commercial profit making occurs entirely within the (horizontal) relations of the market: it does not involve (vertical) class relationships. (Of course, firms engaged in the business of making commercial profits might well have vertical relationships within them.) Moreover, commercial profit making is not a process that is found only in capitalism. It occurred in various societies long before—as well as since—the advent of capitalism.

---

[1] Adam Smith, *The Wealth of Nations* (New York: Random House, The Modern Library), 1937 [1776], Book 4, Chapter 2.

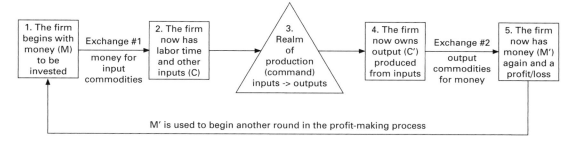

FIGURE 10.1   Exchange and command in the profit-making process.   This figure shows that profit making is a process involving five stages. In stage 1, a firm has a certain amount of money (M) to be invested. To get to stage 2, it must enter markets for inputs and purchase appropriate amounts of labor time, materials, and machines (capital goods); these are the commodities (C) required for production. The next move is from stage 2 (where the firm has the necessary inputs) to stage 3, the process of production itself (P). Note that everything so far has taken place in the horizontal realm of the market: people and firms buying and selling on an equal footing. But the social relationships now become vertical: interactions take place among superiors and subordinates, the former issuing commands, the latter carrying them out.

After production has taken place, the firm owns the commodities (C') that have been produced (stage 4). To get from stage 4 to stage 5, the output must be sold. When it is sold (assuming that it is), the firm ends up with an amount of money (M') that is either larger or smaller than the original amount of money (M). If it is larger the firm will have made a profit—if smaller, a loss. Whichever it is, at least a part of the proceeds from the sale of C' is likely to be reinvested, and the entire process will begin again.

In the two buying and selling parts of the process (between stages 1 and 2 and between stages 4 and 5), the economic actors come together in markets, and their activities are regulated by supply, demand, competition, and other market conditions. In the production part (stage 3), the economic actors (employers and workers) come together in workplaces, and their interactions involve command relations.

It is important to note, however, that Figure 10.1 does not *explain* the existence of profits in a capitalist firm or economy; it merely depicts the various stages in a capitalist profit-making process. Explaining the existence of profits—or, more precisely, explaining why there is a positive rate of profit—requires explaining why various prices are at certain levels, including the "price" of labor time (the wage rate), the prices of materials and capital goods, and the price of the output commodities. There will not be a positive rate of profit—profits will not "exist"—unless the total revenues generated by the sale of the output commodities are greater than the total costs of production, including wages, materials costs, depreciation, and so on. And total revenues cannot exceed total costs unless the average cost of producing a unit of the output commodity is less than the price of it.

When looked at from the standpoint of the economy as a whole, capitalist profits appear in a different light. From this standpoint, total profit can be seen as the monetary value of the economy's surplus product. This is because profit is what remains of total sales revenues after all costs of production have been paid, including the depreciation of capital goods as well as the costs of the materials and labor used in production.

TWO CHEERS FOR PROFITS

. . . let us recognize an unassailable fact of economic life. All Americans will benefit from more profits. More profits fuel the expansion that generates more jobs. More profits mean more investment, which will make our goods more competitive in America and in the world. And more profits means that there will be more tax revenues to pay for the programs that help people in need. That's why higher profits in the American economy would be good for every person in America.

—Richard Nixon, October 7, 1971

Texas Instruments exists to create, make, and market useful products and services to satisfy the needs of our customers throughout the world. Our ability to meet those demands is determined by our innovative skills and measured by our profits. But that profit is not an inherent right. We are permitted to operate by the societies we serve and any profit we do make is our incentive as well as our reward for doing our job well. Society will pass judgment on our value. If we do not meet genuine demands we will not make a profit and will cease to exist.

—Mark Shepherd, Jr., CEO, Texas Instruments, testimony to Congress, 1980

CALCULATING TOTAL PROPERTY INCOME

How much of the U.S. national income takes the form of profit or other property income? That is, how much is income other than wages and salaries? The answer to this question can be arrived at in various ways. Here is how we calculated it for 2001:

Type of Income	$Billions
Corporate profits	580.9
Proprietors' income*	364.0
Rental income	137.9
Net interest	772.5
Total property income	1,855.3
National income	8,122.0
Property income/NI	22.8%

* Proprietors' income is actually reported as $727.9 billion. We divided this number in half on the assumption that one-half of total proprietors' income should be counted as wages paid to proprietors in return for the labor they perform in the businesses (proprietorships) that they own.

Source: U.S. Dept. of Commerce, Bureau of Economic Analysis (http://www.bea.doc.gov), *National Income and Product Accounts* (NIPA), table 1.15 (lines 1 and 54–57).

From the standpoint of the national income accounts that are published by governments such as that of the United States, the total profit received by the capitalist class includes not only what is reported by businesses as "profit" but also such expenses as rent and interest. Although rent and interest payments are seen as costs from the standpoint of the firm, for the economy as a whole they are forms of income received by other members of the capitalist class, such as landlords and bankers who receive rent and interest as a result of their ownership, direct or indirect, of the capital goods used in production. Such incomes are thus only different forms of property income.

Profit does not, of course, include wages, salaries, or other income received as a result of labor. It is sometimes difficult to draw the line between different forms of income, especially when the same person is receiving both a salary and a return from ownership and control of productive assets, but income from labor is certainly different from property income and is therefore not a part of profit. There are a number of other forms of personal income, such as gifts, winnings from gambling, and thefts, but they are not considered as part of capitalist profit, either. A few other types of income, such as welfare payments, subsidies to business, and other transfers from the government, will be discussed when we introduce taxes and government spending in Chapter 19.

CALCULATING THE RATE OF PROFIT

When we discussed the concept of the surplus product in Chapter 5, we introduced a "grain model" with grain-growers producing a grain surplus. But we presented this model without connecting it to any particular economic system or class structure. We now bring back the grain model, this time specifying that it represents a capitalist society with all the land owned by capitalists. Grain is the only commodity. Thus, in order to survive, the representative family must sell its grain-growing labor time for wages to a capitalist. In this case the total output of grain will belong to a capitalist. (See box "Capitalism Comes to Grain Growing.")

Because profits are simply the surplus product measured in monetary terms (rather than bushels of grain), the amount of profit is determined by the same factors that determine the size of the surplus product. However, profit in a capitalist economy differs from the surplus product in our simplified grain example in the following ways: The capitalist economy, like most economies, produces a variety of different outputs, not simply grain, and workers are, obviously, not paid in grain. This means that we will not be able to measure all the outputs and inputs in bushels or any other physical measure. We will have to measure them in terms of their monetary, or market, values. Thus, profits are necessarily calculated in *monetary* terms.

The most important thing we are interested in is the *ratio* of the amount of profit *to* the value of the capital goods owned by a capitalist or group of capitalists. This ratio, which is the amount of profit divided by the value of the capital goods, is the *rate of profit*. It is important to distinguish this ratio from the *amount* of profit. A big firm will typically make a large amount of profit, while a small firm will make a smaller amount. The rate of profit indicates how well each firm is doing *per dollar of capital goods owned*. In mathematical terms, the rate of profit can be represented

> The **rate of profit** is the total amount of profit divided by the value of the capital goods owned by a firm.

CAPITALISM COMES TO GRAIN GROWING

S uppose that a farm produces only grain and that the average producer on this farm works 1,000 hours a year to produce 100 bushels of grain. Of this, 30 bushels are used to replace the seed, feed the draft animals, and take care of other maintenance activities, leaving a net output of 70 bushels a year per producer. (This is similar to the situation depicted in the "grain model" in Chapter 5).

Now suppose that this farm is part of a capitalist society and that its producers are workers hired by a capitalist. Assume that they are paid a wage of $5 per hour, that the market price of grain is $100 per bushel, and that a typical worker spends his or her annual income of $5,000 purchasing 50 bushels of grain from the capitalist. These 50 bushels represent the customary level of consumption for workers.

The net output of 70 bushels per worker is owned by the capitalist. As stated, 50 bushels of this are sold to the workers. The other 20 bushels are exported, also at a price of $100 per bushel, and the $2,000 received is spent on imported consumption goods for the capitalist. Total sales revenue for the year is $7,000, of which $5,000 is paid to the workers, leaving the capitalist with a profit of $2,000 per worker.

These relationships can be summarized as follows:

In Bushels		In Dollars	
Total output	100 bu.	Total revenues (assuming that all of the output is sold)	$10,000
Grain to be set aside for materials and capital goods for next year	30 bu.	Depreciation (feed and seed)	$3,000
Net output	70 bu.	Net revenues (from sale of net output)	$7,000
Consumption of producers	50 bu.	Wages paid	$5,000
Surplus product	20 bu.	Profit	$2,000

as follows:

$$r = \frac{R}{K} \tag{10.1}$$

where r = rate of profit

R = amount of total profit (dollars per year)

K = value of capital goods owned (dollars)

In short, the profit rate is an indicator of the degree of success in the profit-making process. It indicates how much profit was made *in relation to* how much money was invested in capital goods to make the profit.

As indicated earlier, the total amount of profit made in the economy as a whole includes a number of different types of payments that are made to the owners of the capital goods used in production. The first type of payment consists of *dividends.* As explained in Chapter 6, a dividend is a payment made by a corporation to owners of shares of its *stock.* The second type of payment is the *interest* that is paid to owners of corporate *bonds* and to bankers who have provided direct loans to firms (see Chapter 6). A third type of payment is *rent,* paid to owners of land, office space, buildings, or other facilities used by firms to carry out their operations. Finally, there are *retained earnings,* the part of total profit that is set aside by corporations for future investment or other purposes. Thus, the total amount of profit in an economy (R) is the sum of all the payments made to people or institutions that own, directly or indirectly, any private property used in production processes.

Equation 10.1 can be used to calculate the rate of profit of a particular company. For example, Philip Morris stated in its annual report for 2000 that it owned assets of various types worth $79.1 billion, and in the same report it noted that it had made a profit, before taxes, of just under $14 billion. Thus, its rate of profit, before taxes, was 17.7 percent. Subtracting the $5.45 billion in taxes it paid that year, Philip Morris ended up with an "after-tax" profit of $8.5 billion in 2000, providing it with an after-tax rate of profit of 10.7 percent.

Similarly, Equation 10.1 can be used to calculate the profit rate (r) for an entire economy, such as that of the U.S. In this case R is the total amount of profits and K, the economy's total capital stock. Most economic activity in the U.S. is conducted by *corporations*—they account for more than two-thirds of the nation's total employee compensation—so here we calculate the profit rate for the American corporate business sector.

In 2002 total corporate profits (R) in the U.S. amounted to $751 billion. In that same year American companies had "fixed assets" (K)—including equipment and software as well as structures—valued at $8.7 trillion. Thus, the overall profit rate of U.S. corporations in 2002 (calculated using Equation 10.1) was 8.6 percent.

Figure 10.2 shows how the U.S. corporate profit rate, both before and after taxes, varied in the second half of the 20th century. The trend was generally downward, with corporate profits before taxes hovering at around 16 percent in the two decades following World War II and then declining to roughly half that rate, on average, in the last two decades of the century.

What is shown in Figure 10.2 is the rate of profit (r) of the *average* company in the U.S. corporate business sector. This rate of profit is calculated by dividing the profit (R) made by all American companies each year by the total value of their capital stock (K) in the corresponding year. Thus, the

A share of **stock** represents a share of ownership of a corporation and entitles its holder to receive a dividend—a specific amount of money per share—whenever a corporation decides to pay out a portion of its total profits in the form of dividends to its stockholders.

A **bond** is an "IOU" that contractually commits the issuer of the bond (the government or a corporation) not only to "paying back" the value of the bond but also to making regular payments, at a specified rate of interest, to the owner of the bond.

Rent refers to payments that firms are required to make to the owners of land, office space, buildings, or other facilities in return for the right to use or occupy them.

Retained earnings are the part of total profit that is set aside by corporations for future investment or other purposes.

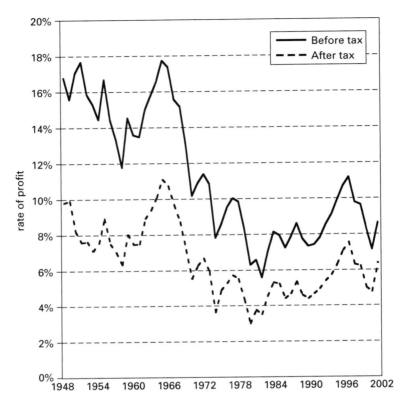

FIGURE 10.2   The U.S. corporate profit rate, 1948–2002.   This figure traces the rate of profit for U.S. business corporations, before and after taxes, between 1948 and 2002. (The box "What is a Corporation?" on p. 235 explains how corporations are differentiated from other forms of business enterprise.) Profits received by U.S. corporations on their foreign operations are excluded from the calculations here, and so is the part of their capital stock that is located outside the U.S. To determine the rates of profit shown in this figure, the total amount of profit in current dollars is divided by the current value of the capital stock in each year.

Source: U.S. Department of Commerce, Bureau of Economic Analysis, National Income and Product Accounts (NIPA) Table 1.14, "Gross Value Added of Domestic Corporate Business in Current Dollars" (Washington, D.C.: U.S. Department of Commerce, 2004), available at http://www.bea.gov/bea/dn/nipaweb; U.S. Department of Commerce, Bureau of Economic Analysis, Fixed Assets (FA) Table 4.1, "Current-Cost Net Stock of Private Nonresidential Fixed Assets by Industry Group and Legal Form of Organization" (Washington, D.C.: U.S. Department of Commerce, 2004), available at http://www.bea.gov/bea/dn/FA2004.

profit rates shown in Figure 10.2 are averages, from year to year, for the whole corporate business sector. In any given year, of course, some companies will do better than the average and others will do worse. Notice in Figure 10.2 that the distance between the before-tax profit rate and the after-tax profit rate shrank between the 1950s and the 1980s, showing that the tax rate on corporate profits declined during this period.

WHAT IS A CORPORATION?

A corporation is one of three ways in which a business can be organized. Firms owned by single individuals are called *proprietorships,* and more than 70 percent of the 25 million firms in the U.S. are proprietorships. Although relatively easy to set up, proprietorships usually have difficulty raising money to finance their operations. Once established, however, this type of business benefits from a direct connection between ownership and control: every dollar made above costs is a dollar earned by the proprietor, so there is a strong incentive for him or her to work hard and diligently. Moreover, a proprietor has total control over every aspect of his or her enterprise.

When two or more people go into business together they usually form a *partnership.* Partnerships are less numerous and more complicated than proprietorships. Less than 10 percent of U.S. firms are partnerships, and they must operate on the basis of a legal document (a "partnership agreement") that specifies what each partner's contribution to and reward from the business will be. Thus, each partner's share of the profits is agreed upon in advance. Partnerships are commonly used by professionals—from lawyers to singing groups—to organize their business activities.

One thing that proprietorships and partnerships have in common is that in both cases the firm's owners bear *unlimited personal liability* for paying back all of its debts. If worse comes to worse, a creditor—for example, a bank—has the right to seize and sell the assets of the firm *and the personal property of the proprietor or partners* to recoup the value of an unpaid debt.

A *corporation* differs from the other two forms of business organization in that its investors have only *limited liability* for its debts or other obligations. At most, the owners of a corporation—people who have purchased or otherwise come to own shares of its stock—can lose only the value of their stock; their other assets, business and personal, cannot be appropriated by the firm's creditors.

The "limited liability" aspect of a corporation gives it a distinct advantage over proprietorships and partnerships. Whereas the capital assets of these types of businesses are generally limited by what the proprietors and partners (and their friends) can bring to the enterprise, a corporation is in a position to raise money for its operations by selling its "stock" to outside investors. As a result, corporations tend to be larger than proprietorships and partnerships; though they comprise only 20 percent of American businesses, they account for 85 percent of U.S. business revenues. On a global scale the largest 1,000 corporations produce about four-fifths of the world's output.

Corporations that sell stock to outside investors are said to be selling shares to "the public." Hence, the terms *public* and *publicly-owned* are used to describe

Continued . . .

such enterprises. In fact, however, "public" corporations are in no way account-able to the public. Unlike proprietorships and partnerships, they are not even lim-ited by the bounds of personal ownership and liability. As a result, corporations have historically been required to obtain a *charter* from some political authority, and the political authority granting the charter has had the right to supervise and regulate the practices of the chartered corporation. Recall that the first European settlers in America were sponsored by the Massachusetts Bay Company, a corpo-ration chartered by the king of England.

In the U.S. today a corporation must obtain its charter from a state govern-ment. It used to be difficult to get such charters—and state governments generally kept a close eye on the practices of the corporations they chartered. These days, however, a business can obtain a charter without much trouble, and state govern-ments rarely look into or regulate the affairs of corporations.

Investors usually do not have a personal interest in a corporation in which they invest. They hold its stock in order to make money, either from the dividends the corporation may pay to its stockholders (the amounts being based on the num-ber of shares owned) or from appreciation in the value of the stock. Though ob-ligated to pay interest to their bondholders, corporations do not have to pay divi-dends to their stockholders. When they decide to do so, they pay the dividends out of their after-tax profits.

The most important difference between a corporation and the other two forms of business organization is the separation of its management from its own-ership. In this context the term *management* refers to the directors of a corpora-tion as well as the managers they hire; ownership lies with the stockholders. Although ownership of a share of stock confers a legal right to participate in the governance of a corporation, the diffusion of share ownership among a large number of people generally makes this right meaningless. And although a stock-holder has the right under certain conditions to submit a proposal for considera-tion at the annual meeting of a corporation, the management's collection of "proxies" normally gives it the power to defeat all proposals other than its own. Thus, unless one holds a substantial fraction of a company's stock, the only ef-fective way to express displeasure with the management of a corporation is to sell one's shares in a stock market.

The separation of management and ownership in early corporations led Adam Smith to warn: "The directors of such companies . . . being the managers rather of other people's money than their own, it cannot well be expected that they should watch over it with the same anxious vigilance with which the partners in a private co-partnery frequently watch over their own. . . . Negligence . . . must al-ways prevail, more or less, in the management of the affairs of such a company." Smith's words still have the ring of truth today.

The directors of a corporation are supposed to represent the interests of its stockholders—they are, in fact, elected, at least formally, by the stockholders—and the directors and the managers they hire are together responsible for maxi-mizing the profits of their companies. The term *corporate governance* refers to the system used to run a corporation. It involves, in particular, the relationships among directors, top managers, and stockholders. In recent years corporate governance has become a hot topic as the accounting and governing practices of disreputable companies such as Enron and WorldCom have come under scrutiny. Questions have been raised about the "independence" of directors from their managers and of accounting firms from the corporations they audit.

In many corporations the C.E.O. (chief executive officer) is also the chairman of the board of directors. In addition, ties of friendship or business interests often connect a majority of the directors with the C.E.O. In such situations the directors might not exercise independent judgment of the practices of the top managers of their companies, and they might have a hard time firing the C.E.O. even if the company is being poorly run. Similarly, if the accounting firm hired by a corporation to audit its financial statements has lucrative consulting contracts with it in other areas such as legal services, the accounting firm will not want to risk its other business with the corporation by pressing it to issue accurate financial statements.

When the Enron Corporation went bankrupt in 2001 after numerous "irregularities" in its accounting practices had been revealed, there was a widespread loss of trust in the governance and financial reporting of U.S. corporations. The ensuing decline in stock prices was at least partly due to a rising skepticism among investors regarding their ability to estimate the profitability of corporations.

In 2002 the U.S. Congress passed the Sarbanes-Oxley Act to institute reforms such as one that requires corporate boards to have a majority of "outside" directors. Whether the Sarbanes-Oxley reforms substantially change corporate governance is as yet unclear, but the corporation, in one form or another, will continue to be the dominant form of business organization.

Sources: John Micklethwait and Adrian Wooldridge, *The Company: A Short History of a Revolutionary Idea* (New York: Random House, The Modern Library, 2003); Ted Nace, *The Gangs of America: The Rise of Corporate Power and the Disabling of Democracy* (San Francisco: Berrett-Koehler Publishers, 2003).

THE DETERMINANTS OF THE PROFIT RATE

> The **determinants of the profit rate** are the things upon which the profit rate depends; they determine how high the profit rate will be.

The profit rate depends on (is determined by) the *determinants of the profit rate*. Knowing the value of each of these determinants—or, in some cases, the direction in which they are moving—will allow us to understand why the profit rate is high or low or moving upward or downward.

We already know some of the determinants of the profit rate from our analysis of the surplus product in Chapter 5. To see exactly how these determinants affect the profit rate and to discover what other determinants might exist as well, we need to derive the precise relationships between the profit rate and its determinants. We begin with the definition of the profit rate as before:

$$r = \frac{R}{K} \tag{10.1}$$

where r = the profit rate

R = total profits (dollars per year)

K = value of capital goods owned (dollars)

For reasons that will be explained shortly, we need to rewrite this equation using the concept of *net product* that was introduced in Chapter 5. In that chapter we defined the net product as the value of what is left of the total product after subtracting—this is what makes it the "net" product—the materials and capital goods replacement costs. (We strongly advise the reader at this point to look again at Figure 5.2 on p. 103 to see how the algebra here relates to the concepts depicted graphically in that figure.) Since the terms *total product, total output,* and *total sales revenue* all refer to the same thing in our analysis, we will use these terms interchangeably in what follows, and, similarly, we will often use the term *net output* in place of the term *net product.* (Another term for *net product* is *value added.*) Using Y as its symbol, then, we can represent net output as follows:

$$Y = S - M \tag{10.2}$$

where Y = value of net output (dollars per year)

S = value of total sales (dollars per year)

M = cost of materials and capital goods used (dollars per year)

In this equation, and in the rest of the book, we use M (or, as we explain shortly, m) inclusively to refer to the costs of both (a) materials and (b) capital goods replacement (depreciation), since, in economic terms, these are both *intermediate goods.* These are considered to be "intermediate" because they are inputs into a labor process (like cotton used in the production of shirts and the wear and tear on the sewing machines used to produce the shirts) as opposed to "final" goods (like the shirts themselves) that are produced for people's consumption. We also assume, for the time being, that all of the output of the economy is sold, an assumption that allows us to use total sales (S) to represent total output.

Since net output is divided between profits and wages ($Y = R + W$), and since we can rearrange this equation to state that total profits (R) are equal to net output minus wages ($R = Y - W$)—the economic meaning of this algebra can easily be seen in Figure 5.2—we can now rewrite the simple profit rate equation (10.1) as follows:

$$r = \frac{Y - W}{K} \tag{10.3}$$

where r = the profit rate

Y = net output (dollars per year)

W = total wages and salaries (dollars per year)

K = value of capital goods owned (dollars)

This equation simply tells us that the rate of profit is calculated by taking the net output of the economy, subtracting total wages and salaries from it, and dividing the resulting amount by the value of capital goods owned by capitalists.

To illustrate the concepts introduced here, imagine a fishing company, the Good Cod company, that owns 10 nets and employs 10 workers, with each worker using one net. The workers catch fish by throwing the nets out from the shore, and each worker, on average, brings in 25 pounds of fish per hour. To simplify things we assume that there are no other capital goods and no other materials used. The workers are paid $10 an hour, and they each work 100 hours a year for Good Cod. (We assume here that the fish come close to the shore only 100 hours each year and that the workers have some other job during the rest of the time.) Each net costs Good Cod $1,250, and it wears out after 100 hours of use; it therefore has to be replaced every year. Finally, the price of fish in the market is $1 per pound.

What is Good Cod's rate of profit? To answer this question (using Equations 10.1, 10.2, and 10.3), we first determine total sales revenues (S) by multiplying the price of fish ($1 per pound) by 25,000 pounds of fish (the amount of fish that 10 men, each working 100 hours a year, will bring in during the year), finding that $S = \$25,000$. Next, we note that it will cost Good Cod $12,500 to replace the 10 nets that are worn out during the year (10 × $1,250 per net), hence $M = \$12,500$. We then calculate the value of net (sorry!) output ($Y = S - M$) by subtracting $12,500 from $25,000 to get $Y = \$12,500$. Good Cod is paying $10 an hour in wages to each of 10 men for 100 hours per man, so $W = \$10,000$. This allows us to calculate the total amount of profit ($R = Y - W$) by subtracting $10,000 from $12,500 to get $R = \$2,500$. Finally, since the value of capital goods owned (K) is $12,500 (10 nets at $1250 per net), we can calculate Good Cod's rate of profit:

$$r = \frac{R}{K} = \frac{\$2,500}{\$12,500} = 20\%$$

THE RATE OF PROFIT PER WORKER HOUR

In this book we analyze the workings of capitalist economies with a focus on the relations of workers to employers. We want to be able to refer directly to the wage per hour of labor (the hourly wage) and to the net output per hour of labor (labor productivity). These two concepts will allow us to calculate the amount of profit made per hour of labor. Accordingly, we now rewrite Equation 10.3, dividing each term on the right side by the number of hours of labor (N) performed each year:

$$r = \frac{\dfrac{Y}{N} - \dfrac{W}{N}}{\dfrac{K}{N}}$$

The denominator of this equation (K/N) depends in part on the amount of capital used by each worker. It tends to be larger the more developed an economy is, and it also varies from one industry to another. For example, it is quite high in the petrochemicals industry (in which a few workers work with a large amount of capital, such as an oil refinery), while it is quite low in the garment manufacturing industry (in which many workers work with relatively small amounts of capital, such as sewing machines).

To make clear the difference between this equation and Equation 10.3, we use lower-case letters for the variables to indicate that they are now in *per-labor-hour* terms. Using the definitions $y = Y/N$, $w = W/N$, and $k = K/N$, then, we can rewrite Equation 10.3 as follows:

$$r = \frac{y - w}{k} \qquad (10.4)$$

where $r =$ the profit rate

$y =$ value of net output per hour of labor

$w =$ wage rate per hour of labor

$k =$ value of capital goods owned per hour of labor

Equation 10.4 is important to much of the analysis in this book. It enables us to see mathematically what we already know intuitively, namely, that raising y or lowering w or k will raise the profit rate. Likewise, it shows that any movements of these variables in the other direction will lower the profit rate. The numerator of this equation ($y - w$) measures the amount of money left over for the employer: it shows the amount of profit that employers make for each hour that workers work.

To illustrate the concepts presented here, we again calculate Good Cod's rate of profit, this time using the per-labor-hour form of the profit rate equation (10.4). Dividing the figures for net output, total wages, and value of capital goods owned by the total number of hours worked (1,000 hours per year), we get:

$$y = \frac{\$12,500}{1000} = \$12.50$$

$$w = \frac{\$10,000}{1000} = \$10.00$$

$$k = \frac{\$12,500}{1000} = \$12.50$$

The employer's profit for each hour that a worker works is $y - w$ ($\$12.50 - \$10$), or $2.50, and the rate of profit is:

$$r = \frac{\$2.50}{\$12.50} = 20\% \qquad \text{(as before)}$$

It is worth noting that in a capitalist economy, workers generally receive less than the value of the net output they produce each hour. When workers are paid less than the value of their net output, some say (as Marx did) that they are "exploited." But would eliminating this exploitation be a good thing? If workers were (somehow) paid the full value of their net output, wages (w) would consume all the net revenues ($y = w$), the rate of profit would be zero ($r = 0$), and capitalists would receive nothing. If this were to happen, any capitalist economic system would grind to a halt. This is because in this type of economic system profits are what motivate capitalists to make investments and organize labor processes.

What we have established so far is only the *short form* of the profit rate equation. For reasons that will become clear, we now need to examine the terms y, w, and k in Equation 10.4 in greater detail to arrive at the *complete* profit rate equation.

THE LABOR DETERMINANTS OF THE PROFIT RATE

By far the easiest term to understand in the basic profit rate equation (10.4) is w, the *wage rate:* it is simply the payment for a worker's time. We treat it here as a per-hour payment, but it could just as well be a monthly or a yearly salary. However we think of it, w is the one term in Equation 10.4 that does not require further elaboration.

> The **wage rate** is the amount paid to a worker for each hour worked.

The other term in the numerator of the profit rate equation is y, the *value of net output per hour of labor.* On what does y depend? Recall that before we converted all the variables in the profit rate equation to per-labor-hour terms, we found that net output was equal to total sales minus the cost of the materials used and the wear and tear on machines ($Y = S - M$). Now, to determine S and M (and remembering that these variables are measured in amounts of *money*), we need to know the price of the output commodity (P_z) and the price of the material inputs to the production process (P_m). Knowing these prices is important because, for one thing, total sales (S) is equal to the total number of units produced (Z) multiplied by the price per unit (P_z). Thus, in our Good Cod example we calculated total sales revenues by multiplying 25,000 pounds of fish by the price of fish ($1 per pound), finding that $S = $25,000$.

> The **value of net output per hour of labor** is the dollar value of the total output minus materials and machine costs divided by the total number of hours worked.

However, the net output per hour of labor is affected not only by movements of output and input prices; it also depends on (a) how much output workers produce in an hour (labor productivity) and (b) the value of materials required per hour and the wear and tear occurring on the machinery and other capital goods each hour. We use the letter z to refer to the first of these variables (labor productivity) and the letter m to refer to the second one (materials used per hour and hourly capital goods depreciation combined).

The output produced per hour of labor (z) is itself the product of two other variables: the level of work effort, e, and the efficiency of labor, f. It is not difficult to understand the concept of *work effort.* Anyone who has held a job knows that the intensity of work can usually be varied, at least to some extent. Thus, "work effort" refers to how hard a person works. Although hard to measure, work effort, defined as the amount of effort put out by a worker during an hour at work, is an important variable in the determination of the profit rate. An hour of labor time during which an employee works hard will result in a higher rate of profit (all other things being equal) than an hour of labor time during which the employee "slacks off."

> **Work effort** refers to a worker's level of exertion (intensity of work) on the job during a certain period of time, say, an hour.

> The **efficiency of labor** refers to how much output can be produced as a result of a certain level of work effort.

The *efficiency of labor* (f) refers to how effective a person's work is in producing a product, *given his or her level of work effort*. It will depend on the technology—the type, quantity, and quality of capital goods and materials—used in the production process. These factors will determine how much output (z) is produced with any given amount of work effort (e) put forth during an hour of labor.

Another way of looking at the meaning of e and f is to say that a labor process begins with a certain amount of labor time (as well as other inputs), is driven by work effort, and results in a particular amount of output of one kind or another. In this process,

e = the transformation of *labor time* purchased by the employer into
work effort per hour of labor

f = the transformation of *work effort per hour* of labor into
output per hour (z)

The first of these transformations is the basic challenge facing an employer in the workplace: how to get workers to put out as much work effort as possible during all the hours they have been hired for. The second transformation also depends on decisions made by the employer, namely, those that determine—by means of *investment*—the quantity and quality of the capital goods provided for workers to work with. Together, these two transformations summarize the process that starts with an employer purchasing labor time in a labor market (and also other inputs in other markets) and ends with the employer having output that he or she can sell in a product market (in hopes of making a profit).

Many economists do not distinguish between e and f, preferring instead to assume that there is a fixed relationship (a "production function") between the number of hours of labor time purchased and the amount of output that will be forthcoming (for any given quantity and quality of capital goods). In making this assumption they ignore the fact that how hard an employee works (e) is a variable that depends on such things as the way in which work is organized (see Chapters 12 and 13).

To add to your understanding of the concepts e and f, imagine that you are a worker in your college's post office and that your job is to put stamps on all the outgoing mail from the college's offices. If the post office does not have an automatic postage-metering machine and you have to put the stamps on by hand (and by tongue), the efficiency of your labor (f) will be quite low. Even if you work very hard (your e is high), it will take you a long time to get the job done, and your output per hour (z) will be relatively low. Now imagine that the college spends the money to acquire an automatic postage-metering machine. Immediately, the efficiency of your labor (f) will rise dramatically. Even if you put out less work effort (your e is lower) now, the job will get done rapidly and your output per hour (z) will be higher.

Since $z = e \times f$ (output per hour is equal to work effort per hour multiplied by the amount of output that results from any given amount of work effort), we can sum up the preceding discussion as follows:

$$\text{Total revenues (per hour of labor)} = P_z z = P_z e f$$

where P_z = the price of the product

z = the number of units produced per hour

e = the intensity of work

f = the efficiency of labor

Then, looking at the situation of a private profit-making corporation, we can ask: what is the relationship between the corporation's rate of profit (r) and the variables we have just introduced, P_z, z, e, and f? It turns out that the relationship is "positive" in each case: a movement (up or down) of one of these variables will cause the profit rate to move in the *same* direction as the variable.

For example, if the corporation manages to achieve a greater degree of monopoly power in the market for its product and is therefore able to raise the price of its product (P_z), this will enable it to earn a higher rate of profit. The same is true for e and f, and hence z. Any increase in work intensity or the efficiency of labor will increase output per hour, thus enabling the corporation to sell more units and earn more profit per hour of labor (assuming, of course, that there is sufficient demand for the product to allow more units to be sold).

MATERIALS AND CAPITAL GOODS AS PROFIT RATE DETERMINANTS

We can complete the expansion of the profit rate equation's numerator by introducing terms referring to the materials and machines (capital goods) used in the process of production. As mentioned earlier, both materials and machines are intermediate goods, so we lump them together and use M to refer to their total amount and m to represent the amount of them used per labor hour. We use P_m as the symbol for their (average) *price*. Thus, the total amount of money required to pay for the cost of materials and machines used per labor hour is $P_m m$ (the price multiplied by the quantity of the materials and machines per hour of labor).

Again looking at the situation of a profit-making corporation, we can ask: what is the relationship of the variables P_m and m to the corporation's rate of profit? As one would expect, in both cases it is "negative" (i.e., they move in the opposite direction from the profit rate). If a corporation has to use more materials or machines or pay more for them (m increases or P_m rises), its profit rate will fall. An example of the first of these developments would be the passage of a law requiring the corporation to install "scrubbers" in its smokestacks to protect the environment from harmful emissions. This would require the corporation to use more capital goods per hour of labor (increasing m), thereby reducing its rate of profit. Similarly, if there is a rise in the price of the oil that the corporation needs to use as an input (increasing P_m), its profit rate will also fall. Conversely, if it can find a cheaper source of the materials or machines that it uses—or find a new technology that uses smaller amounts of them to produce the same amount of output per hour of labor—its profit rate will rise.

Summarizing all this, we can write the profit rate equation with its newly expanded numerator as follows:

$$r = \frac{(P_z ef) - (P_m m) - w}{k} \tag{10.5}$$

where $r =$ the profit rate

$P_z =$ the price of the product or output

$e =$ the intensity of work

$f =$ the efficiency of labor

$P_m =$ the price of materials and machines

$m =$ materials and machines used per hour

$w =$ wage rate per hour of labor

$k =$ value of capital goods owned per hour of labor

This equation simply tells us that we can determine the profit rate by starting with total revenues ($P_z\, ef$), subtracting the cost of materials and machines ($P_m\, m$) and the wages of labor (w), and then dividing the resulting amount by the value of capital goods owned per hour of labor (k). As we have seen, these are not just abstractions, they are concepts that refer to real aspects of a capitalist economy (aspects that we will explore further in the chapters ahead).

To illustrate the concepts we have just introduced we return to the Good Cod story, adding just one more piece of information. The new information is that each of the workers throws his or her net into the water five times each hour and, on average, brings in five pounds of fish with each throw of the net. (This is consistent with our earlier statement that each worker, on average, brings in 25 pounds of fish per hour.) The advantage of this example is that unlike many situations in the real world it, allows us clearly to separate the work effort (e) from the efficiency of labor (f). In this case e is the number of times the typical worker throws a net into the water each hour, while the efficiency of labor (f) is the quantity of fish (in pounds) the net brings in (on average) each time it is thrown (assuming that this quantity is determined by the quality of the net, not the density of fish in the water).

To show why it is important to break down output per hour, z, into its components, e and f, we ask what happens to Good Cod's rate of profit if the workers decide to throw their nets into the water four times instead of five times an hour ($e = 4$ rather than 5), with f remaining at 5 pounds of fish coming in with each throw of the net. Now, each worker brings in 20 pounds of fish per hour, which adds up to $2,000 worth of fish per worker per year (assuming that each worker continues to work 100 hours a year). Since there are still 10 workers, Good Cod's total revenues are now $20,000, and net revenues are $7,500 (since the cost of the nonhuman inputs, M, remains at $12,500). Using Equation 10.3 we can easily calculate the new rate of profit:

$$ r = \frac{Y - W}{K} = \frac{\$7,500 - \$10,000}{\$12,000} = \frac{-\$2,500}{\$12,500} = -20\% $$

This simple calculation shows that as a result of the workers' more relaxed pace of net throwing, Good Cod's rate of profit goes from *plus* 20 percent to *minus* 20 percent (i.e., to a 20 percent *loss*), without anything having changed other than the intensity of labor. No wonder corporations place a high priority on getting their workers to work hard!

THE ROLE OF CAPITAL GOODS (AGAIN)

All that remains to be done here is to expand the term k (*value of capital goods owned per hour of labor*), which is the denominator of the profit rate equation. Because k is a value (measured in monetary terms), it is directly affected by the price of capital goods (P_c). If we leave aside for a moment the number of labor hours performed and just look at K (the total value of capital goods owned), we can say that K is equal to the price of capital goods multiplied by the total stock of capital goods: $K = P_c \times CG$ (using CG to refer to all the capital goods owned).

> The **value of capital goods owned per hour of labor** is the value of the firm's total investment in capital goods divided by the total number of hours worked by employees.

How, then, do we get from K to k? The key consideration here is the fact that the number of machines, nets, or other capital goods *in use* will generally not be the same as the total number of machines, nets, or other capital goods *owned* by a firm. As long as the price of the capital goods (P_c) does not change, K will not vary with the number of machines in use. But k—the capital stock owned *per hour of labor employed*—*will* most likely vary with the number of machines in use because $k = K/N$, and N (hours of labor employed) will usually vary with the number of machines in use: fewer workers are needed to run fewer machines, and vice versa.

As a first step, then, we can represent k as follows:

$$k = \frac{K}{N} = \frac{P_c(CG)}{N} = P_c\left(\frac{CG}{N}\right) \tag{10.6}$$

where k = value of capital goods owned per hour of labor

K = value of capital goods owned

N = number of labor hours employed

P_c = price of capital goods (per "machine")

CG = total capital goods owned

To fully determine k, however, we need to introduce two new concepts: u, the capacity utilization rate, and g, the quantity of capital goods in use per labor hour. These two concepts both involve the idea that at any given time there are a certain number of capital goods—machines, nets, or computers, for example—*in use*, a number we can refer to as *CG in use*. The difference between u and g lies in what *CG in use* is related to.

On the one hand, the *capacity utilization rate* (u) is defined as *CG in use/CG*, the fraction of owned capital goods (CG) that are in use at any given time. On the other hand, we define g (capital goods in use per labor hour) as *CG in use/N*, with N (labor hours employed) replacing CG (capital goods owned) as the denominator of the fraction that has *CG in use* as its numerator.

> The **capacity utilization rate** is the percentage of all owned capital goods currently being used.

Going further, we can establish how u, g, CG, and N are all related. If we multiply g by $1/u$ (the inverse of the capacity utilization rate)—thus dividing g by the capacity utilization rate—we get the total number of capital goods *owned* per hour of labor. That is, $(1/u)g = CG/N$. But why do we go through this process? We go through it because having separated out the concepts of g (*CG in use/N*) and u (*CG in use/CG*), for reasons to be set forth below, we need to divide g by u in order to keep the denominator of the profit rate equation as the total number of capital goods owned by the firm per hour of labor (*CG/N*).

To illustrate this point, recall our earlier example of the "Good Cod" fishing company that owned 10 nets and employed 10 workers, each of whom worked 100 hours per year. What would happen if the demand for the company's fish fell by 20 percent? In that situation the company would use only 8 of its 10 nets, employing 8 workers, each of whom would continue to throw out a net for 100 hours a year. In this case, N would fall to 800, and g would be the number of nets in use (8) divided by the total number of hours worked (800), or 0.01. Since the company would now be using only 8 of its 10 nets, its capacity utilization rate (u) would be 0.8, $1/u$ would be 1.25, and $(1/u)$ g would be 1.25×0.01, or 0.0125. That this is indeed the number of nets (capital goods) now owned by the company *per hour of labor employed* can be confirmed simply by dividing the number of nets owned by the company (10) by the number of labor hours employed (800). Thus, $(1/u)$ $g = CG/N = 0.0125$.

Having established that $(1/u)g = CG/N$, we can substitute $(1/u)g$ for CG/N in Equation 10.6 to produce a more useful equation for k:

$$k = P_c(1/u)g \qquad (10.7)$$

where k = value of capital goods owned per hour of labor

P_c = price of capital goods (per "machine")

u = the capacity utilization rate

g = capital goods in use per labor hour

The economic meaning of this equation is as follows: To calculate the value of capital goods owned per hour of labor (k), we multiply the number of machines actually *in use* per hour of labor (g) by the inverse of the capacity utilization rate ($1/u$)—thus dividing g by the capacity utilization rate—to get the total number of capital goods *owned* per hour of labor. We then multiply $(1/u)g$ by the price of each capital good (P_c) to get the total *value* of the capital goods owned per hour of labor (k). P_c differs from P_m in that the latter refers to the price of *all* the material inputs to the production process, including materials as well as capital goods, while the former (P_c) refers only to the price of capital goods ("machines").

These last steps enable us to see how changes in *either* the capacity utilization rate (u) *or* the amount of capital goods in use per labor hour (g) will affect the profit rate (r). But why did we need to further complicate the profit rate equation by introducing u and g? While it may seem that they are just different sides of the same coin, these two variables are, in fact, influenced by different forces in the economy. On the one hand, the capacity utilization rate (u) will depend on the level of demand for the product of a particular company (or for the output of the economy as a whole). On the other hand, the quantity of capital goods in use per hour of labor (g) will vary—even if u remains constant—with different technologies (changing, say, if a firm switches to a more labor-saving technology).

The end result is that with the two additional variables, u and g, we are able to expand the denominator of the profit rate equation from k to $P_c(1/u)g$. Substituting this expanded denominator for k in Equation 10.5, we can now write the *complete* profit rate equation:

$$r = \frac{(P_z ef) - (P_m m) - w}{P_c(1/u)g} \qquad (10.8)$$

where $r =$ the profit rate

   $P_z =$ the price of the product

   $e =$ the intensity of work

   $f =$ the efficiency of labor

   $P_m =$ the price of materials and machines

   $m =$ materials and machines used per hour

   $w =$ wage rate per hour of labor

   $P_c =$ price of capital goods (per "machine")

   $u =$ the capacity utilization rate

   $g =$ capital goods in use per labor hour

Of course, what really matters to a capitalist firm is the profit that remains *after* taxes have been paid. (Recall that Figure 10.2 shows how the after-tax profit rate in the non-financial corporate business sector has varied in the period since World War II.) Its after-tax profit is what gives the firm its incentive to invest, and after-tax profits are the major source of funds from which new investments can be made. If corporate taxes take the form of a specified tax rate applied to total profits, and if we use the symbol t to stand for this rate, then the amount of money remaining in the hands of the firm after taxes have been paid can be calculated as $(1 - t) \times$ the total amount of before-tax profits. For example, if the tax rate on corporate profits is 25 percent, t will be 0.25, $(1 - t)$ will be 0.75, and the firm will have 0.75, or 75 percent, of its before-tax profits left over after its taxes have been paid. Accordingly, we can say that after-tax profits will be equal to $(1 - t) R$, where R stands for total profits received before taxes. Taking this logic one step further and relating all this to the profit *rate* (r) rather than to the total *amount* of profit (R), we can see that the after-tax rate of profit (*atr*) will be $(1 - t) \times$ the before-tax rate of profit (r). Thus, $atr = (1 - t)r$. These concepts are discussed at greater length in Chapter 19.

Conclusion: Understanding the Profit Rate

Despite the impression the preceding passage may have left, the profit rate is not determined by mathematics. The math just allows us to see *what the profit rate depends on*. Understanding the profit rate means understanding the things that it depends on. The math allows us to break the profit rate into parts, enabling us in the chapters ahead to look at each of the profit rate determinants one by one. But the basic idea in all of what follows is simple. Whether profits are higher or lower will be determined to a large degree by the outcomes of conflicts over how our national product is to be divided. Behind each of the profit rate determinants are people—employers, workers, consumers, retired people, people in the rest of the world, government officials, and so on—trying, often in conflictual ways, to get the things they want in life.

We end this chapter with a review of the conflictual *relationships* that determine the profit rate. Our strategy for understanding the profit rate has been straightforward: after having developed Equation 10.4, the basic equation for the profit rate, we examined each of its three main terms, y, w, and k, in greater depth and learned that there are ultimately *nine* determinants of the profit rate. Figure 10.3 shows how all these determinants affect the profit rate. In this figure the determinants of the profit rate are situated on the left side of the diagram and the causal relationships between the nine determinants and the profit rate are represented by arrows moving from left to right. After going through various intermediate steps, shown by the boxes in the middle of the diagram, the determinants eventually lead to the profit rate (r) on the right side of the diagram.

In Figure 10.4 we illustrate the same causal relationships with the numbers previously used in our example of the Good Cod fishing company.

At various points in our discussion we have noted the *direction of influence* between particular determinants and the profit rate. In Table 10.1 each of the determinants of the profit rate is listed (with its symbol) in the first column, and it is also accompanied by a + sign or a − sign showing the direction of influence between the determinant and the profit rate. A + sign indicates that the profit rate will tend to move in the *same* direction as the direction of change in the determinant. Conversely, a − sign means that the profit rate will tend to move in the *opposite* direction of the direction of change in the determinant. Thus, if a particular determinant has a + beside it, a movement upward in it will, if there are no changes in any of the other determinants, result in an increase in the profit rate.

The middle column of Table 10.1 lists some of the ways in which capitalists, either as owners of a single company or as members of a class, may attempt to change the determinants in such a way as to bring about increases in their rates of profit. Similarly, the column on the right lists ways in which consumers, workers, suppliers, or other groups may resist efforts by capitalists to raise their profit rates. The reader is encouraged to think of strategies for raising the profit rate—or ways to resist such strategies—other than the ones we list here in Table 10.1.

Notice that some of the strategies listed in Table 10.1 may be inconsistent with other strategies, even for an individual employer. For example, one way of increasing the market for a product, putting idle factories to use—strategy number 9—would be to lower the price of the product, but this would be contrary to strategy number 1. Similarly, a technical change that would raise the amount of output for any given level of work effort—strategy number 3—might require an increase in the amount of machinery in use per labor hour employed, but this would be contrary to strategy number 8.

Moreover, the efforts by some employers to increase *their* rates of profit may have the effect of reducing the profits of *other* employers. For instance, suppose one employer is in the business of selling a material—say, oil—that is needed in the production processes of other employers. If the first employer raises his or her output price (strategy number 1), his or her profit rate will increase, other things remaining constant. But the profit rates of the other employers will fall because for them the rise in the price of oil is an increase in P_m, contradicting strategy number 5.

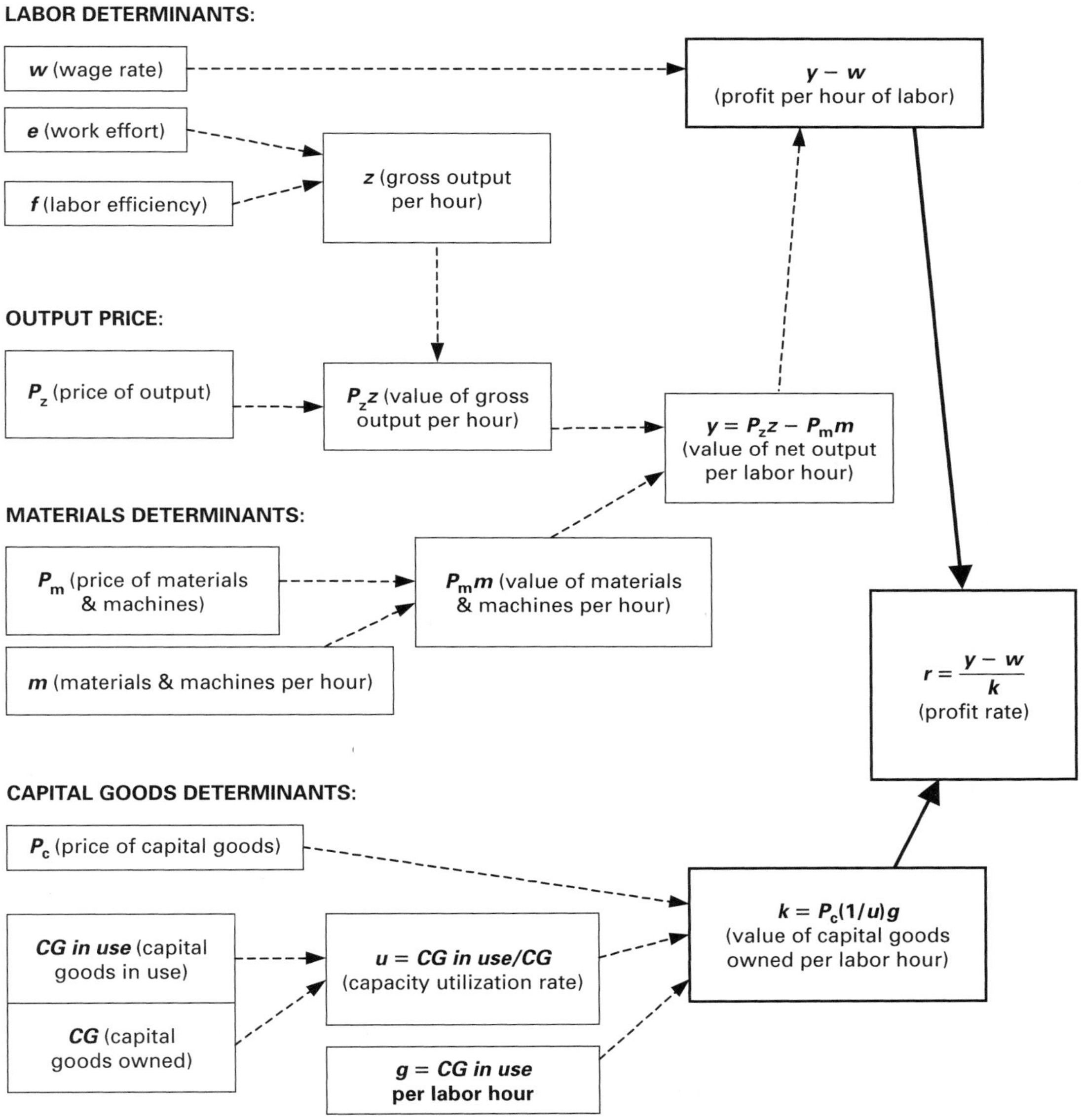

LABOR DETERMINANTS:

w (wage rate)

e (work effort)

f (labor efficiency)

z (gross output per hour)

$y - w$
(profit per hour of labor)

OUTPUT PRICE:

P_z (price of output)

$P_z z$ (value of gross output per hour)

$y = P_z z - P_m m$
(value of net output per labor hour)

MATERIALS DETERMINANTS:

P_m (price of materials & machines)

m (materials & machines per hour)

$P_m m$ (value of materials & machines per hour)

$r = \dfrac{y - w}{k}$
(profit rate)

CAPITAL GOODS DETERMINANTS:

P_c (price of capital goods)

CG in use (capital goods in use)

CG (capital goods owned)

$u = CG\ in\ use/CG$
(capacity utilization rate)

$g = CG\ in\ use$
per labor hour

$k = P_c(1/u)g$
(value of capital goods owned per labor hour)

FIGURE 10.3   Determining the profit rate.   This figure traces the steps in the process of determining the profit rate. The profit rate determinants are arrayed down the left side of the diagram, and the arrows show how the process moves along from the basic determinants to the more complex intermediate steps and finally to the profit rate itself (in the heavy box on the right side of the diagram). This figure provides a checklist of all the important determinants of the profit rate, and it also traces out the routes by which they determine it. But, of course, we cannot know what the profit rate will be or understand *why* it hovers at this or that level until we know the values of each of its determinants and the forces pushing them in one direction or another.

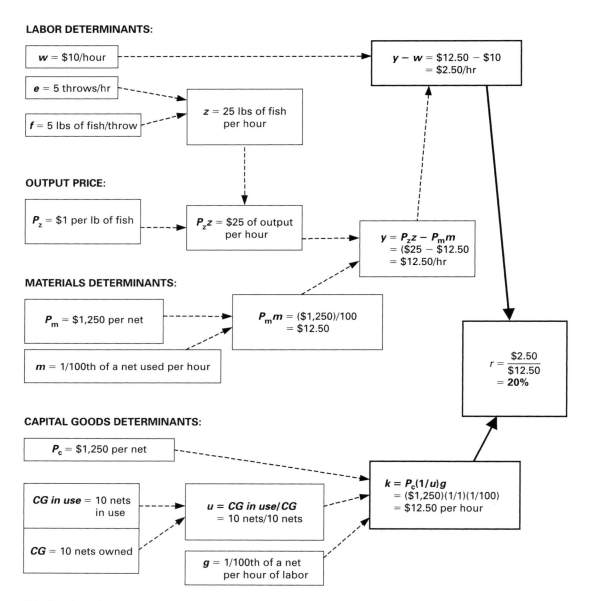

FIGURE 10.4   Determining "Good Cod's" rate of profit.   This diagram fills in specific numbers for each of the determinants listed in Figure 10.3. The numbers come from the example of the "Good Cod" company that was set forth earlier in this chapter. As one might expect, the profit rate determined by this method—20 percent—is the same as the one arrived at using Equation 10.8.

TABLE 10.1 Conflicts over the Profit Rate

The Determinants of the Rate of Profit and the Direction of Their Influence on It	Ways in Which Individual Firms, or the Capitalist Class as a Whole, May Seek to Raise Profit Rates	Ways in Which Workers, Consumers, Suppliers, or Citizens May Counter Efforts to Raise the Profit Rate
1. Price of output (P_z) (+)	Gain monopoly power so that prices can be raised	Consumers buy cheaper (substitute) products
2. Work effort per hour of labor (e) (+)	Speed up production line; hire more supervisors to control the pace of work	Workers work at only a tolerable pace; bring in a union; bargain for rest breaks
3. Efficiency of labor; output from any given level of work effort (f) (+)	Introduce more efficient, labor-saving technology	Workers bargain to save jobs
4. Amount of materials and machines used per hour of labor (m) (−)	Develop new methods of production, reducing wastage of materials and cutting the rate at which tools are broken	
5. Price of materials and machines (P_m) (−)	Using the internet or going abroad, find suppliers offering lower prices; support military intervention abroad to gain control of lower-cost raw materials	Domestic suppliers push for tariffs on imported inputs; citizens oppose military intervention abroad
6. Hourly wage (w) (−)	Use cheaper labor, e.g., recent immigrants or third world workers; decertify unions; roll back workers' rights to organize unions	Workers organize or join unions; bargain for higher wages; extend organizing efforts to third world; aid prolabor politicians
7. Price of capital goods used in production (P_c) (−)	Use capital goods supplied at lower prices such as imported machines	Domestic suppliers push for tariffs on imported machines
8. Capital goods in use per hour of labor employed (g) (−)	Use production methods requiring fewer capital goods, for example ones that are more efficient but which may pollute or be less safe for lack of safety gear or waste-treatment equipment (such as "scrubbers")	Bring public attention to social costs of environmental spillovers or health effects of unsafe working conditions; join environmental, labor, or other groups pushing for more government regulation
9. Capacity utilization rate, or percentage of owned capital goods actually in use (u) (+)	Find new markets for output so that idle factories or machines can be put to use; support government policies to increase total demand	

Similarly, suppose all employers are able to cut their wage rates (strategy number 6). Would this increase their rates of profit? Possibly it would, but much of the market demand for employers' output comes from consumers who earn their incomes as workers. Thus, if wages were cut across the board, many employers would find that, contrary to strategy number 9, they could no longer find customers for as much of their output as before. Capacity utilization (u) would fall, and their profit rates would decline.

We now have a foundation for understanding how the rate of profit is determined since we know something about all the determinants listed in Table 10.1. In subsequent chapters we ask how each of these determinants is itself determined. In Chapters 12 and 13 we look at the vertical dimension of the capitalist economy (command) and examine how e, the amount of work effort per hour, is influenced in various ways. Meanwhile, in the next chapter we focus on the horizontal dimension of the economy and analyze the ways in which capitalist firms compete with one another, attempting to maximize their rates of profit.

SUGGESTED READINGS

Gérard Duménil and Dominique Lévy, *The Economics of the Profit Rate: Competition, Crises and Historical Tendencies in Capitalism* (Brookfield, Vt.: Edward Elgar, 1993).

Duncan Foley, *Understanding Capital: Marx's Economic Theory* (Cambridge, Mass.: Harvard University Press, 1986).

David M. Gordon, *Fat and Mean: The Corporate Squeeze of Working Americans and the Myth of Managerial "Downsizing"* (New York: Free Press, 1996).

Francis Green and Robert Sutcliffe, *The Profit System* (Middlesex, U.K.: Penguin, 1987).

CHAPTER 11

Competition and Concentration

A pple Computer introduced its first Macintosh product in 1984. Combining in one very small plastic box a central processing unit, a display (screen), and a strikingly original, user-friendly interface that relied on "icons" rather than complicated commands, the Macintosh was a bold innovation. Because its new product was so different from anything else on the market, Apple was able to achieve, in setting the price of the Macintosh, a much higher "mark-up" over costs than could other computer companies. As a result, this small, young new company was able to reap enough profit to finance a large research and development operation, and this enabled it to continue to bring out innovative products.

Apple's mistake was that it failed to target its products toward business users. This failure allowed IBM and other PC manufacturers to maintain their dominance in the corporate sector. In the end Apple secured only a small share of the total computer market, and, predictably, the larger computer manufacturing firms, supported by their software-producing partner, Microsoft, were soon imitating Apple's user-friendly interface, icons and all, thus ensuring that their customers would not be tempted to switch to a Macintosh.

Microsoft itself, having achieved dominance in the computer software market, was found guilty in 1999 of violating the antitrust laws of the United States. In one of the most publicized court trials of its kind in the 20th century, the federal district court judge in charge of the case found that the company "enjoys monopoly power in the relevant market." The court noted that it had so few competitors that it could raise the price of its Windows operating system without having to fear a reduction of the demand for it. The verdict was that to achieve its monopoly power Microsoft had stifled innovation, used heavy-handed and illegal tactics against its competitors, erected significant barriers to entry into its market, and, in the process, had acted against the interests of consumers. The judge concluded: "Microsoft has demonstrated that it will use its prodigious market power and immense profits to harm any firm that insists on pursuing initiatives that could intensify competition against one of Microsoft's core products."

Competition is often depicted in economics textbooks as a game played by countless numbers of small, powerless, anonymous firms—all ultimately serving the expressed wishes of consumers. For some markets this characterization is quite accurate. There are, for instance, hundreds of thousands of American farmers who sell their output in international grain markets, and there are millions of Americans who buy or sell stock through their stockbrokers.

As noted in Chapter 1, however, the largest 1,000 companies in the world produce about four-fifths of its industrial output. The concentration of economic power is also evident in the U.S., where 1,200 corporations, the leaders of which could fit comfortably into a large university lecture hall, produce about half the nation's output. These 1,200 large companies produce roughly as much as the other 25 million American businesses combined.

That so much of the U.S. economy is run by so few people should not be taken to mean, however, that the most potent American corporate leaders can do whatever they want, that they all agree, or even that they have the same interests. The most powerful corporations in the U.S. have to compete with the large enterprises of other countries in the global marketplace. With the lowering of barriers to trade and the increasingly rapid movements of capital and people from one country to another (discussed in Chapters 1 and 7), corporations based in Japan and western Europe are challenging the market dominance and profits of large American firms. Thus, competition, even for the patronage of U.S. consumers, is becoming more and more global, and the increasingly global character of competition makes it necessary for us to develop further the idea of *competition for profits* introduced in Chapter 7.

Business owners invest money in order to make more money. The prospect of profits spurs them to action, but competition channels their activity. Competition limits what any one can do but shapes what all of them (considered as a group) are driven to do. And competition for profits generates constant change in the economy.

Neoclassical economists depict competition as producing "equilibrium" rather than change. They ask the student to imagine a marketplace—say, an open-air fruit market—where there are many sellers and many buyers. As explained in Chapter 8, there will be a tendency in this type of (competitive) market situation for the market to move toward equilibrium. Equilibrium will occur if competition can drive the price of fruit to a level at which suppliers want to sell exactly the quantity that demanders wish to buy. In this case supply and demand will have determined the price and quantities of fruit exchanged, and the market will clear. The next day will dawn, the sellers will return with a new supply of fruit to be sold, the buyers will bring a new demand for fruit, and the competitive market process will be repeated. In the conventional view, then, equilibrium is achieved every day, and competition itself provides little impetus for change.

The conventional view of market relations is not wrong, but it is limited and therefore misleading. Once equilibrium is achieved in the conventional model, nothing changes until something from the outside—an "exogenous" force—intervenes.

In Chapter 8 we explained the idea of equilibrium using the example of a marble coming to rest at the bottom of a bowl. Here we add the time dimension and offer a different example: a bicycle can stay upright only if it is moving forward. The process of competition for profits is more like the bicycle than like the marble in the bowl. With competition for profits, the economy is in perpetual motion (like the bike), not at rest (like the marble). The metaphor of the bicycle captures what economists and others refer to as *dynamic equilibrium*—a durable process of change—while the marble, when it has settled at the bottom of the bowl, portrays *static equilibrium*—a given way that things are. Both are useful ideas, but one cannot understand capitalism without the bicycle.

The conventional approach is one-dimensional in that it focuses on the horizontal (competition) dimension of the economy but considers neither the vertical (command) nor the time (change) dimensions. In this chapter we present a three-dimensional view of competition. Such an approach supplements the conventional analysis by showing how power (command) relations affect competition and how something internal to the economy—the process of competition itself—brings about change and development.

The main idea of this chapter is that *as business owners search for profits, competition drives them to change their operations. The competitive scramble limits what any one firm can do, shapes what they all are driven to do, and produces an enormous pressure for continual change in the economy as a whole.*

This main idea is expressed in six key points:

---

1. Business owners compete for profits by seeking to *manipulate the determinants* of their own profit rates. They are severely limited in what they can do, however, by the forces of competition.

2. Business competition takes three principal forms: (a) efforts to achieve a price advantage (*price competition*), (b) efforts to create new situations in which potential competitors are at least temporarily left behind (*breakthroughs*), and (c) efforts to eliminate competition (*monopoly power*).

3. For all three types of competition, firms must *invest to compete*. Investment is the primary way that firms achieve price advantages, breakthroughs, and monopoly power.

4. Because firms must invest to compete, competition is inherently *dynamic*: the process of business competition contains within itself powerful forces for change. This internal dynamic (the pressure for change) inexorably changes every market situation even as competition occurs, and it imparts a powerful dynamic tendency to the economy as a whole.

5. The competitive scramble produces different profit rates among firms, but, conversely, it also tends to equalize profit rates. Whether there is an overall tendency toward *equalization of profit rates* will depend on the balance between the opposing forces.

6. The dynamics of competition produce both economic *concentration* (which results when large firms displace or acquire smaller firms) and *less concentration* (resulting from new firms entering the market or smaller firms increasing their market share). Whether there is or is not a *trend toward economic concentration* will depend on the balance between these opposing tendencies.

COMPETITION FOR PROFITS

Entrepreneurs seek profits, and for this purpose they invest. But how can they tell which projects will be most profitable? And, having invested, what can they do to ensure high profits?

Most investments entail *risk* because they involve long-term commitments and there is no way for the investors to be sure what future profit rates resulting from them will be. Still, they can know what to look for. In Chapter 10 we learned that a firm's rate of profit depends on nine determinants (see Table 10.1).

As businesses search for ways to influence and improve (from their point of view) the determinants of their profit rates, they will run up against competition from other businesses, and this will limit their range of options. For instance, a business may not be able to increase its profits simply by raising its output price. Why? Because if one seller tries to set a price higher than the prices being charged by other suppliers of the same product, some or all of the customers of the price-raising business will buy the product from the other firms. The result will be a decrease in sales for the price-raising firm, and at least some of its output will remain unsold.

Similarly, a business usually cannot reduce the price it pays for materials, capital goods, or labor. Again, the reason is competition: suppliers of these inputs will sell them to firms offering higher prices.

And there are other factors besides competition that limit profit making. For some of the profit determinants, a business is limited by the present state of knowledge or technology. For example, it may be impossible to raise the efficiency of labor (f), cut down on the quantity of materials used (m), or reduce the amount of wear and tear on machines per labor hour (also in m) until new technologies are developed.

The social interactions that occur within firms must also be taken into consideration. For example, the intensity of labor—the amount of work effort per hour (e)—can be increased only if employees can be induced or compelled to work harder. But if a firm attempts to speed up production by coercion, such actions are likely to be met with opposition from its employees, and the firm may have difficulty attracting the best-qualified people to work for it. Moreover, if the employees of a particular firm are pressed to work harder than workers normally work, those employees can quit their jobs at that firm and seek employment in other, more conventional firms.

In all these ways, then, businesses are limited by competition. Moreover, one business's profits are often another's loss. For instance, the quadrupling of oil prices after the formation of OPEC (the Organization of Petroleum Exporting Countries) in 1973 increased the profits of multinational oil companies by billions of dollars, but it also reduced the profits of firms in energy-using sectors of the economy, such as the automobile and steel industries, by a comparable amount.

Just as competition limits what any one business can do to change its profit determinants, changing those determinants may erode the conditions that sustain its current rate of profit. Every time an investment raises the rate of profit for a particular firm, other firms may be enticed to enter that firm's market. Thus, current success can lead to greater competition—from more competitors—in the future.

Profit making is a never-ending struggle by each firm to break out of the limits set by competition. The ensuing warfare among the combatants will sort out the winners from the losers.

Because competition produces incessant change, a capitalist economy is ever changing. If a static equilibrium happens to occur—like the marble in the bowl—competitive investments by profit-seeking firms will soon throw out of balance the underlying conditions of that equilibrium. A lasting equilibrium is as unimaginable as the bicycle remaining upright even when brought to a stop. Accordingly, the idea that an equilibrium might continue until some external force disrupts it is misleading: competition itself will immediately put it out of existence.

Moreover, the dynamic of competition continues *without end or limit.* After all, the end of one period of competition is but the beginning of the next period. Firms that do not take advantage of every opportunity for growth will be left behind by firms that do. There is no rest for the weary, and there is none even for the victors in a capitalist economy.

THE FORMS OF COMPETITION

There are three principal forms of, or strategies for, competition. Each offers a way to stay even with, or get ahead of, one's competitors.

Price competition is a form of or strategy for competition in which firms attempt to attract customers primarily by offering lower prices.

Price competition occurs when firms attempt to attract customers by offering them products equivalent to those offered by other firms but at a lower price. A firm following a price-competitive strategy will continue to pursue its current activities while making small improvements here and there as opportunities arise. Price competition may lead an employer to try to cut wages, speed up the pace of work, eliminate waste in production, or otherwise cut costs in order to be able to reduce the price of the output and still make a profit. Many other firms may also be engaging in price competition; success will go to those firms that are able to offer the lowest prices to their customers.

A **breakthrough** occurs when a firm discovers or develops a new method of doing business, such as a new way of organizing work, a new product, or a new market.

Breakthroughs occur when firms discover or develop something totally new—a new source of inputs, a new method of organizing production, a new product, or a new market. In this case a firm can earn greater profits, often big profits, not because it is the best at the old game but rather because it is the first player in an entirely new game.

If a firm with a breakthrough has developed a new product, it may have little competition at all. If, on the other hand, its breakthrough creates a large cost advantage in producing a product that is already being made by other firms, the breakthrough firm may be able to cut the price of its product and still make more profit than it was making before.

Monopoly power is the ability of one or a few firms in an industry to exercise substantial control over the market price and other aspects of competition, usually by excluding other firms.

A firm that consistently achieves breakthroughs is more likely to attract skilled personnel, develop superior production know-how, reduce costs, and obtain credit more easily and thus have a better chance to grow. Being first gives a firm relief from competition, and this lasts until other firms catch up or new firms enter the market with similar products or production processes. Big profits are sooner or later likely to attract competitors who want to capture some of these profits for themselves.

Monopoly power exists when firms are able to exercise significant power in a market by excluding some or most potential competitors. A

Oligopoly, or **shared monopoly,** is a market situation in which several firms together, but no one firm by itself, can exercise substantial monopoly power.

firm can rarely exclude all other firms (this would be "pure monopoly"), but it can often, together with two, three, or four other firms, control a major portion of a particular market and thus achieve what is called "monopoly power." When there are only a few firms in a market, the situation is referred to as *oligopoly,* or *shared monopoly.*

For monopoly power to last for a significant period of time, it must be supported either by some enduring economic advantage or by barriers that prevent other firms from entering and competing in the market. In either case firms are able to charge higher prices for their output, pay lower prices for their inputs, or have sole access to superior technologies or methods of organization.

Price Competition

Price competition confronts each firm with a dilemma: the firm can attract more customers with a *lower* price, but, other things being equal, its profits will be higher the *higher* is its price. Obviously, it cannot cut its price and raise its price at the same time.

The dilemma confronting the firm arises because a change in its price will affect the determinants of its profit rate in different ways. To understand this we need to separate out two fundamental profit rate determinants—one that is familiar, the capacity utilization rate (u), and one that is new, the rate of profit on capital goods in use (r_u), which we now define.

Recall that the rate of profit (r) is the total amount of profit divided by the value of capital goods owned (see Equation 10.1 on p. 232). Thus, if a firm owns 10 machines, each of which costs $1,000, it will own $10,000 worth of capital goods ($K = \$10,000$). If it can bring in a profit (R) of $1,000, its rate of profit (r) will be $1,000 divided by $10,000, or 10 percent.

Now imagine a different situation in which the firm can sell only enough of its output to justify using 8 of its 10 machines (leaving 2 of them idle) while still being able to make the same total amount of profit ($1,000). In this situation the firm's capacity utilization rate (u) will be .8, or 80 percent. Although it is making the same amount of profit as before, it will now be in a less advantageous competitive situation vis-à-vis its rivals. Why is this?

New firms may enter the market, building plants with only eight machines. Assume that each of the new firms is also able to bring in $1,000 of profit. Since *their* rates of profit (r) will be calculated on a base of *owned capital goods* (K) of only $8,000 (the cost of eight machines), their profit rates will be 12.5 percent (significantly higher than the older firm's 10 percent), and this will put each of them in a more competitive position vis-à-vis the original firm (which, say, is stuck with paying off a bank loan—a *fixed cost*—large enough to have allowed it to buy its original 10 machines).

To understand the type of competitive situation illustrated in the above example, we need to introduce a new concept, the *rate of profit on capital goods in use,* which we will refer to as r_u. This is, in fact, only an imaginary rate of profit because a firm's real rate of profit continues to be r.

As explained previously, a firm's actual rate of profit (r) is not calculated on the basis of its capital goods *in use*. Rather, it is calculated as a proportion of the value of *all* the capital goods it owns. Hence, if we want to relate a firm's profit rate (r) to its capital-goods-in-use profit rate (r_u), we will have to take into consideration its capacity utilization rate (u).

We can do this using the following equation:

$$r = (r_u)(u) \tag{11.1}$$

where r = the profit rate

r_u = the profit rate on capital goods in use

u = the capacity utilization rate

Where does Equation 11.1 come from? It is derived algebraically, first by multiplying both the numerator and the denominator of Equation 10.8 in Chapter 10 by u to get:

$$r = \frac{(P_z ef) - (P_m m) - w}{P_c(g)}(u) \tag{11.2}$$

where r = the profit rate

P_z = the price of the product

e = the intensity of work

f = the efficiency of labor

P_m = the price of materials and machines

m = materials and machines used per hour

w = wage rate per hour of labor

P_c = price of capital goods (per "machine")

u = the capacity utilization rate

g = capital goods in use per labor hour

But the rate of profit on capital goods in use (r_u) is the total amount of profit (per labor hour) divided by the value of the capital goods in use (per labor hour):

$$r_u = \frac{(P_z ef) - (P_m m) - w}{P_c(g)}$$

Hence, we can substitute r_u for the term

$$\left(\frac{(P_z ef) - (P_m m) - w}{P_c(g)} \right)$$

on the right side of Equation 11.2 to arrive (back) at Equation 11.1:

$$r = (r_u)(u) \tag{11.1}$$

Thus, Equation 11.1 can be derived from Equation 11.2—with Equation 11.2 itself being merely a slightly different form of the complete profit rate equation, Equation 10.8 (developed in the previous chapter).

To illustrate the economic logic of all this, we return to the example of the firm that can only sell enough of its product to justify using 8 of its 10 machines. If this firm is making a profit of $1,000 (as in the earlier example) and each of its 10 machines cost $1,000, its rate of profit (as before) is 10 percent. But we can now calculate its rate of profit on the number of machines it has in use—its r_u—by rearranging Equation 11.1 to read

$$r_u = \frac{r}{u}$$

and plugging in the relevant numbers:

$$r_u = \frac{10\%}{80\%} = 12.5\%$$

If this firm could put its unused capacity to use, raising its capacity utilization rate (u) from 80 to 100 percent, while at the same time maintaining its r_u at 12.5 percent, it would be able (assuming that nothing else in the economy changed) to increase its rate of profit (r) from 10 to 12.5 percent, an increase of 25 percent. This can be shown by using Equation 11.1 and comparing the numbers for (a) the situation in which u is 80 percent with those for (b) the situation in which u is 100 percent:

$$r = (r_u)(u) \tag{11.1}$$

(a) $10\% = (12.5\%)(80\%)$

(b) $12.5\% = (12.5\%)(100\%)$

How does all this relate to the idea of price competition? It does so as follows: One way a firm can increase its sales, and increase its capacity utilization rate (u), is to lower the price of its product (hoping that its competitors will not immediately reduce their prices by the same amount). But because profit is the difference between the price of a product and the cost of producing it, lowering the price will also reduce the rate of profit (r_u) on the proportion of the firm's capital goods that are in use (because each unit of output will now be selling at a lower price). Thus, lowering the price will have both positive and negative effects on the firm's actual rate of profit (r). And the same is true for a firm that decides to raise the price of its product, the only difference being that in this case the effect of the price change on u will be negative, while the effect on r_u will be positive.

We can see from Figure 11.1, a demand curve, how a change in price will affect both u and r_u. If the firm lowers its price (P_z) from P_1 to P_2 (and everything else affecting the market remains unchanged), the quantity that can be sold (Z) will rise from Z_1 to Z_2. This increase in sales will be made possible by an increase in the firm's output, raising its capacity utilization rate (u), say, from 70 to 90 percent—and this, in turn, will *tend* to raise its profit rate (r), as we can see from Equation 11.1. However, the price reduction will simultaneously lower the rate of profit (r_u) that the firm had previously been making on its capital goods in use, and this will counteract the positive effect of the rise in u and tend to push down the firm's profit rate.

On the other hand, if the firm were to raise its price (P_z) from from P_1 to P_3 (and everything else affecting the market remained unchanged), the quantity that could be sold (Z) would fall from Z_1 to Z_3. The price rise itself would increase r_u, but if the firm did not want

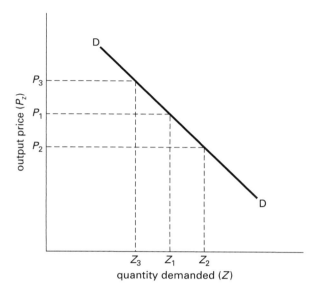

FIGURE 11.1   The demand curve limits a firm's choice of price and output.   The demand for a firm's product is represented by the line DD. Reducing the price from P_1 to P_2 will bring about an expansion (from Z_1 to Z_2) of the demand for the firm's output, increasing its sales but (if average cost does not change) reducing its profit per unit. Conversely, raising the price from P_2 to P_1 will result in a shrinkage (from Z_2 to Z_1) of the demand for the firm's output, reducing its sales but (again assuming constant average cost) raising its profit per unit. Thus, the demand curve shows how a firm's profit-raising strategies are constrained by competition with other firms in the market.

to see unsold goods piling up on its shelves, it would have to adjust to the smaller quantity being sold by cutting back on production, thereby lowering its capacity utilization rate (u) —and this would tend to push the firm's profit rate down.

The overall effect of a price change on a firm's profit rate (r) will depend on how much r_u and u change as a result of the price change. This analysis shows why firms are faced with a dilemma whenever they consider raising or lowering their price as a way of competing with other firms in the market: cutting a price will probably raise u while lowering r_u, whereas increasing a price is likely to raise r_u while lowering u. Competitive markets tend to limit a firm's profits, allowing it to make about the economywide average rate of profit on the value of the capital goods it owns.

In order for profits to be made, the price of a good must include a *markup* over its cost of production. This "markup" can be explained in two steps. First, the price of a good is broken down into its various components (including profit as well as costs), showing how the money received from the sale of a unit of output is allocated:

$$\begin{array}{l} \text{price of} \\ \text{a unit of} \\ \text{output} \end{array} = \begin{array}{l} \text{materials cost} \\ \text{plus wear and} \\ \text{tear on machines} \\ \text{per unit of output} \end{array} + \begin{array}{l} \text{labor costs per} \\ \text{unit of output} \end{array} + \begin{array}{l} \text{profit per} \\ \text{unit of output} \end{array}$$

Then, combining the two types of costs (materials costs and labor costs), we rewrite the equation to show, for each unit of output sold, how much of the sales revenue is used to cover costs and how much of it becomes profit resulting from the markup over costs:

sales revenue per unit = costs of production per unit + *markup* **per unit**

A markup is different from r (the rate of profit). A markup is intended to give rise to a profit that is calculated on the basis of the *material and labor costs* incurred per unit of output ($P_m m$ and w multiplied by the number of hours it takes to produce a unit of the product), whereas r is the rate of profit calculated on the basis of the *value of the capital goods owned by the firm* (k). (See box "Markup Pricing" for further explanation.)

Market competition tends to establish prices that reflect current levels of supply and demand. If such prices allow a lower profit rate to be realized than could be made producing other products, at least some firms will leave the industry they are in, and some may be induced to switch to another industry in which they can make at least the average rate of profit. If the price of the product in a particular industry is so high that its profit rate is above the economywide average rate, new producers will be attracted to that industry. Thus, the movement of firms—or "capital"—among industries will tend to push the rate of profit in each industry toward the average rate for the economy as a whole.

Breakthroughs

Firms want to break out of the limits set by price competition. For that purpose they search for breakthroughs and monopoly power, both of which introduce elements of command (or power) in the relations among owners of firms and between them and other groups such as consumers and labor.

A *breakthrough* is something new—a new product, a new way of recruiting labor, a new technology, or anything innovative that gives one firm an advantage over its rivals. Breakthroughs change the terrain on which the competitive struggle is fought. If price competition is like trench warfare, breakthroughs are like tank warfare.

A breakthrough creates a competitive advantage because it enables a firm to be first in a market. Other firms may attempt to follow it, but until they can catch up, the firm with the breakthrough will achieve a higher profit rate.

Breakthroughs may involve any of the determinants of the profit rate. For instance, a firm may discover or create a new product that is superior in some way to other products in the same market. This may allow it to charge a higher price for its product (P_z) or use more labor with its capital goods, thereby reducing its g, which, as explained in Chapter 10, is the ratio of its capital goods in use to the number of labor hours employed. If a firm is already using all the capital goods it owns, one way for it to reduce g would be to hire more labor and run its factories at the rate of two or three shifts per day rather than one. Since P_z is in the numerator and g in the denominator of the profit rate equation (Equation 10.8), either a rise in P_z or a reduction of g—or both—will allow the firm to increase its rate of profit.

There are also breakthroughs that affect other profit rate determinants. Take w (the wage rate), for example. The front page of the *Wall Street Journal* carried an article in July 2002 that reported on how some corporations are moving plants to, or opening new plants in, poor countries to achieve breakthroughs involving w. The article, titled "Auto Makers

MARKUP PRICING

We can use Equation 10.5 (see previous chapter) to show how the price of a product (P_z) may be set to include a "markup" over costs. Substituting z for ef in equation 10.5, we have:

$$r = \frac{(P_z z) - (P_m m) - w}{k}$$

If we then multiply by k, divide by z, and rearrange the resulting terms, we have:

$$P_z = \frac{P_m m}{z} + \frac{w}{z} + \frac{rk}{z}$$

In this equation the first term to the right of the equal sign, $P_m m/z$, represents the materials costs, including both the cost of the materials used and the cost of the wear and tear on machinery (depreciation) per unit of output. The second term, w/z, is the cost of labor (the wage) per unit of output. The final term, rk/z, is profit per unit of output. Thus,

price of output = unit materials cost + unit labor cost + unit profit.

When the components of price are separated out in this way, "unit profit"—the profit made on each unit of output sold—can be seen as a markup over the (combined) costs of producing a unit of output. The firm, in setting the price, first calculates its unit costs and then adds a markup on these costs to yield the desired amount of profit per unit. Suppose, for example, that the materials and labor needed to produce an IBM personal computer cost \$2,000. If IBM seeks to achieve a markup of 50 percent, it will set the price at \$3,000. In this case,

the price of an IBM computer = \$2,000 + 50% of \$2,000

= \$2,000 + \$1,000 = \$3,000

In setting the price of its computer at \$3,000, IBM may find that it has either too few or too many customers. If it has too few customers (and it wants to maintain its 50 percent markup), the company will have to cut back production, reducing its capacity utilization (u). If it has more customers than it has computers to sell, it can charge a higher price and increase its markup. Supply and demand, then, may affect either capacity utilization or the markup—or both.

Look for Another Edge Farther from Home," described how several large automobile companies in the rich countries are now finding that their cars can be produced in poor countries just as well as—or even better than—they can be produced "at home." The article's main point was summed up as follows using a quote from a Japanese auto executive: "Wages in Africa, Thailand, and Latin America often are less than a tenth of what workers earn in developed [country] markets. That more than offsets the added costs of shipping key parts to the remote factories and bringing them back. Adding plants in developing countries to its global production network 'will dramatically increase our competitiveness,' says Honda Chief Executive Hiroyuki Yoshino."[1]

The ease with which companies can shift production to developing countries means that they can often gain the upper hand in labor negotiations just by threatening to move their plants to a low-wage country. Thus, the increasingly integrated character of the global economy offers employers many new possibilities for achieving breakthroughs involving the wages they must pay to their employees. (See box "Hardball: Owners, Workers, and Taxpayers in the Global Economy" in Chapter 13, pp. 317–318.) Moreover, if a firm can bring about the "decertification" of a labor union that currently represents its workers in collective bargaining, it will most likely be able to pay lower wages and become more competitive without moving its production facilities abroad.

There is one large American company that has had what is, in effect, a breakthrough involving wages from the very beginning of its existence. Delta Air Lines, the third-largest airline in the world, was founded in Atlanta, Georgia, a city with a strong antilabor tradition. As a result, Delta was able to begin its operations with only nonunion employees, and to this day it has been largely successful in campaigns to keep its workers from joining unions. At the present time only Delta's pilots, one-sixth of its employees, have a union to represent them in negotiations regarding wages and working conditions.

Breakthroughs, then, raise a firm's sales revenues or reduce its costs sufficiently to produce a higher-than-average profit rate. This competitive advantage lasts only until other firms catch up. In the meantime, however, the temporary relief from competition may produce substantial profits. And while the other firms are catching up, the firm with the breakthrough not only makes more profit than its competitors but, as a result, can spend more money searching for a new breakthrough. This is the attraction of breakthroughs.

Capitalist competition can also create a fear of being left behind, and this, too, may spur a firm to search for breakthroughs. Even an employer content with his or her firm's current rate of profit must fear other firms' potential breakthroughs, for any subsequent competitive disadvantage could well wipe out current profits. So here, as always, competition provides both the carrot and the stick. Firms must keep running, as if on a treadmill, just to stay in the same place.

Monopoly Power

Capitalists can also make higher profits by achieving monopoly power. Much like a breakthrough, monopoly power enables a firm to escape competition or at least to insulate itself from the effects of competition. If a firm can use monopoly power to erode or eliminate

---

[1] Todd Zaun, Gregory L. White, Norihiko Shirouzu, and Scott Miller, "Auto Makers Look for Another Edge Farther from Home," *Wall Street Journal*, July 31, 2002, p. A1.

competition, it will be able unilaterally to influence its profit rate determinants in ways that raise its rate of profit.

The term *monopoly power* can be used to refer either to the situation of a single firm (perfect monopoly) or to the power of a small group of firms that are able to dominate a particular market (oligopoly, or shared monopoly); in either case, if some firm or firms can exclude others from a market, monopoly power exists.

> **Barriers to entry** are obstacles that make it more difficult or costly for new firms to enter a market; examples include technical secrets, initial investments that are very large, and exclusive marketing arrangements.

Breakthroughs and monopoly power are quite similar: both generate a higher profit rate for the breakthrough or monopoly firm by giving it an advantage over other firms. Indeed, the economist Joseph Schumpeter (see Chapter 4) understood breakthroughs as creating "temporary monopolies," and his insight points to the main difference between the two concepts: breakthroughs are temporary, lasting only until other firms catch up; monopoly power is longer lasting and is usually based on some economic, legal, or institutional obstacle that excludes other firms. Such obstacles are called *barriers to entry*.

Just as with breakthroughs, monopoly power may be used to change any of the determinants of the profit rate. But although there are examples of monopolists affecting each of them, monopoly power is most often brought to bear on the price of a product (P_z), setting it above the price that would prevail in a competitive market.

Firms can achieve monopoly power—whether perfect (total) or shared—in three ways: first, they can be or become the only seller of a particular product; second, they can collude (conspire) with other producers of the same product to eliminate competition; or, third—and this is the most common way in which monopoly power is exercised—they can establish informal or tacit relations with other companies in their market to limit competition.

One example of the only-seller case is the local electric power company. If you want electricity service in your home, in many areas you have little choice but to buy it from your regional power company. Since electric power is frequently provided by a monopoly, the government often regulates the price of electricity.

The second way of exercising monopoly power is referred to as "collusion." Although outright collusion is against the law, the impulse to collude is common among large corporations. When the U.S. Department of Justice was prosecuting the large agricultural products company Archer Daniels Midland (ADM) for price fixing, one of the top executives of ADM admitted that the company's view was that "our competitors are our friends; our customers are our enemies."

A classic instance of collusion involved General Electric (GE) and Westinghouse in the decades before 1960. GE, Westinghouse, and some other companies in the industry were convicted of fixing the prices of electrical equipment, the market for which adds up to billions of dollars in sales each year.

More recently, in December 2001 the world's two largest "auction houses" for valuable art, jewelry, and furniture, Christie's and Sotheby's, were found guilty of colluding to fix the commissions they charged their sellers, a practice they engaged in for six years and that resulted in overcharges of hundreds of millions of dollars. The two companies agreed to pay $537 million to settle price-fixing lawsuits brought against them by their customers, and the former chairman of Sotheby's was sentenced to pay a $7.5 million fine and spend a year in prison even though he was 78 years old. Since the defendant showed no remorse for his actions, he was ordered to pay the cost of his incarceration, a judgment that cost him $21,601.

Monopoly power also exists when a few large firms dominate a particular market. As explained earlier, such a situation is referred to as oligopoly, or shared monopoly. This is not only the most common method for asserting monopoly power, it is also the most complicated. In the breakfast cereal, steel, and tobacco industries, for example, a few firms have dominated their markets for many years. The firms in these industries "share" monopoly power in the following sense: without engaging in direct conspiracies or acts of collusion, they have developed ways of behaving that permit them to avoid price competition and thus to share in the higher profits associated with monopoly power. In other words, each shared-monopoly firm has learned to live by certain rules, or ways of doing business, that all similar firms accept, and their competition is governed by these rules.

> A **cartel** is a combination of states or business firms operating in concert to regulate the production, pricing, and marketing of goods by its members.

In some parts of the world, shared monopoly power can be achieved by direct cooperation. When this happens the cooperating firms or countries are referred to as a *cartel*. The Organization of Petroleum Exporting Countries (OPEC) is one of the best-known examples of a cartel. By jointly regulating its members' supply of oil, OPEC has achieved the ability to determine, or strongly influence, the price of oil on the world market. (See box "Cartels.")

Shared monopoly is like an uneasy coalition among potential enemies. It holds together as long as each partner perceives the agreement not only as working to advance the interests of the entire group of large firms but also as functioning in a way that serves the interest of each firm individually. The higher profits to be gained from cooperation are indeed beneficial, and these provide an incentive for individual firms to continue their adherence to the shared monopoly arrangement. But it is also true that a failure to cooperate—breaking the rules—can be very costly for the rule-breaking firm because the most powerful oligopolistic firm or firms may retaliate, say, by price cutting in such a way that the misbehaving firm is severely damaged.

> **Nonprice competition** involves sales efforts, style changes, or other marketing strategies to increase the appeal of a product without lowering its price.

If shared monopoly operates on the basis of a set of tacit or informal rules to which all the large firms in an industry subscribe, what are these rules? The two most important are that shared monopoly firms have to develop ways of avoiding price competition and that such firms may find it necessary to engage in *nonprice competition,* for example, in sales promotion.

Price competition is avoided when shared monopolists can develop informal, tacit, or indirect ways of establishing more or less fixed or steadily rising prices. The particular method of avoiding price competition varies from one industry to another, with each industry's system being shaped by historical circumstances and each firm's technique reflecting the long experience it has had dealing with other firms in its industry.

> A **market share** is one firm's sales as a percentage of the total sales in an industry.

But if price competition is avoided, other forms of competition attain a new intensity. The demand curve for a particular product still limits the total quantity that the producers of it can sell at each price. Hence, if the price does not change, an individual seller's gain can come only at the expense of the sales of another firm. This means that the main action in the market will involve battles for *market share,* with each shared-monopoly firm trying to maximize its market share. Moreover, if the average cost of

CARTELS

Despite legal and organizational obstacles, cartels continue to be a feature of the modern economy in many industries. More than 50 firms were indicted by the U.S. Department of Justice in the last decade of the 20th century for colluding to fix prices, and there undoubtedly are many more that were not indicted. The table below lists some of the industries, time periods, and countries in which a few of the indicted firms operated; the market share controlled is listed in the last column.

Industry	Period	Countries Where Firms Operated	Market Share
Beer	1993–1998	Belgium	Two companies controlled 70% of the Belgian market.
Cement	1983–1994	Europe: 33 firms	The cartel controlled 80% of the European market.
Fine arts	1993–1999	U.S., U.K.	Two companies controlled 95% of the world market.
Plastic tubes	1986–1995	Switzerland, U.S.	Three companies controlled 95% of the U.S market.
Nucleotides	1992–1996	Japan, South Korea	One company controlled 45% of the world market.
Plastic dinnerware	1990–1992	Canada, U.S.	Two companies controlled more than 90% of the U.S. market.
Sugar	1986–1990	Ireland, Denmark, U.K.	Two companies controlled more than 90% of the U.K. market.
Vitamins	1990–1999	Canada, Germany, Japan, Switzerland, U.S.	Three companies controlled more than 75% of the world market.

Source: Margaret Levenstein, Valerie Suslow, and Lynda Oswald, "Contemporary International Cartels and Developing Countries: Economic Effects and Implications for Competition Policy" (forthcoming in *Antitrust Law Journal*).

producing a product falls as output increases, and if the price of it remains steady (by mutual agreement of the shared monopolists), the profits of any firm in the industry will rise if it can increase its market share and thereby increase its output. Thus, a corporation's profits will increase directly with its sales, and this will drive each company in an oligopolistic industry to go all out to sell more of its product.

> The **sales effort** consists of all those activities by a firm that relate to the selling of the firm's product.

All of the activities of a firm that are undertaken in order to increase sales of its product are referred to as its *sales effort*. The sales effort includes anything that firms do to persuade customers to buy their products. Corporations recruit armies of sales agents. They hire public relations firms and spend billions on advertising. They continually repackage their products (recall the number of times you have heard about the "all-new" whatever). They spend enormous sums of money obtaining celebrity endorsements. They sometimes bribe—and are convicted of bribing—foreign governments. They sponsor sports events. They contribute to charities and sponsor programs on public television to burnish their image, and so on. All such efforts are aimed at increasing a firm's market share.

Monopoly power, like a breakthrough, makes possible a higher-than-average rate of profit. It relaxes (but does not abolish) the limitations set by competition by eliminating some of the competition. Firms compete to see who can first or most effectively escape competition.

INVESTING TO COMPETE

One aspect common to all three forms of competition is *investment*. Price competition, breakthroughs, and monopoly power all require that firms invest to achieve the benefits of any of these strategies.

To compete at all in the marketplace, firms must invest. A firm must reinvest its profits from one year if it wants to remain competitive in the next year. Moreover, profits previously earned may provide a firm with the resources it needs if it is to try to get ahead and/or stay ahead of its rivals.

All of the profit determinants listed in Table 10.1 become potential targets for reinvestment. If the firm can discover a way to reinvest its profits so as to change one or more of these determinants in its favor, then it will have achieved a higher profit rate.

Conventional economics textbooks portray competition as leading to a static equilibrium in which all firms achieve an average rate of profit and all resources are allocated in an optimal fashion to satisfy existing consumer preferences. Political economy, in contrast, sees firms as engaging in dynamic competition, always seeking to move past the present state of competition and put themselves in a position to capture higher profits. In dynamic competition no state is permanent because at least some firms will always be altering the requisite conditions for it. Thus, the real world of competition is a never-ending process in which firms attempt, not always with success, to break out of the limits set by competition itself. Some firms will succeed and achieve high enough profits to compete in the future; others will fail and be driven out of business.

A firm will reinvest profits only if it expects to earn more profits. So every firm, when considering what to do with its profits, must compare the *cost* of investments with the *expected return* from those investments.

For example, consider a firm that is thinking about making a certain investment, say, buying a new machine. Suppose the firm must pay I dollars to the machine maker to buy the machine. How might the firm estimate whether this investment will be profitable? To do so it will have to go through three steps.

First, the firm will have to calculate what the return might be on its investment. Suppose the machine costing I dollars will last just one year. (After producing the goods it was designed to manufacture the machine crashes and has no value at the end of the year.) At the end of the year, then, the owner has the goods produced but no machine, and she sells the goods. The revenues from this sale minus the wage and materials costs are called the *total return on the investment*. This can be expressed as follows (with I representing the value of the investment and r being the anticipated rate of profit on it):

$$\text{total return on the investment} = I + rI \qquad (11.3)$$

> The **interest rate** is the cost of renting money; for a firm that borrows money, it is the percentage of the amount borrowed that must be repaid in addition to the amount borrowed.

Of course, the investor hopes that r will be positive so that the investment more than pays for itself. But it might not be, in which case the investor would not even get back the amount of money that the machine cost.

The second step a firm must take in order to evaluate the potential profitability of an investment is to determine the *cost* of an investment. There is, of course, the cost of buying whatever it is that constitutes the investment—in this case, the machine—which is I dollars. In addition, however, there is the cost of the money used to make the investment. What is this cost? It can be looked at in two ways.

> A **bond** is an "IOU" that contractually commits the issuer of the bond (the government or a corporation) not only to paying back the value of the bond but also to making regular payments, at a specified rate of interest, to the owner of the bond.

On the one hand, a firm may borrow the necessary funds at the prevailing *interest rate* (i) from a bank (or other lending agency) or from people who are willing to buy *bonds* from the firm. A "bond" is like an IOU that commits the issuer of it not only to paying back to the purchaser of the bond the amount of money exchanged for it but also to paying a fixed rate of interest on it to the owner of the bond over a certain number of years—the life span of the bond.

On the other hand, a firm may finance an investment using funds available (internally) from previous profits. In this case it must forgo the opportunity of lending these funds to other firms at the prevailing rate of interest (i). This forgone opportunity is termed the *opportunity cost* to the firm of using its own previously generated funds to make an investment. It is equal to the cost the firm would have had to pay if it had borrowed the funds (externally) from a bank. What *opportunity cost* refers to, therefore, is the cost of the opportunity lost when the firm, instead of lending out its money, uses it to make an investment (in the current example, to buy a machine).

> An **opportunity cost** is the value of the best opportunity given up (forgone) in order that whatever was chosen could be undertaken.

Whichever way the firm chooses to finance its investment, the *total cost of investment* is the amount of money (I) used to make the investment (in our example, to buy the machine) *plus* the explicit cost—or opportunity cost—of obtaining the money so used. This cost is equal to iI—the cost per dollar (i) times the number of dollars required for the investment (I). Thus,

> The **total cost of investment** consists of two parts, the cost of the capital goods purchased and the opportunity cost of the money used to purchase them.

$$\text{the total cost of an investment} = I + iI \qquad (11.4)$$

The last step in the analysis of investment profitability is to estimate the potential *profit from an investment* (net of the cost). The latter can be determined from the first two steps: it is the anticipated total return (determined in the first step) *minus* the cost of making the investment (as determined in the second step). This can be expressed as follows:

profit from an investment = return on the investment − cost of the investment

Put in terms of Equations 11.3 and 11.4, the expected profit from an investment is

$$R = (I + rI) - (I + iI) \qquad (11.5)$$

where R = the anticipated amount of profit

   I = the amount invested

   r = the expected rate of profit

   i = the rate of interest

With simple algebra we can transform Equation 11.4 as follows:

$$R = I + rI - I - iI = rI - iI$$

ending up with:

$$R = (r - i)I \qquad (11.6)$$

Equation 11.6 allows us to focus on r and i—the rate of profit and the rate of interest—as the key determinants of the total amount of profit (R) resulting from the investment. In Equation 11.6, the amount invested, I, is always a positive number. But what about $(r - i)$? This term can be either positive or negative, depending on which is larger, r or i.

If r is greater than i, the term $(r - i)$ will be positive, and the firm will receive sufficient profits on an investment to be able to more than cover its interest payments to a bank (or to bondholders), if, in fact, it had to borrow the money to make the investment. Even after paying them, though, the investing firm would have money left over, making the investment a profitable one. The same logic would also have to be applied to the case in which a firm finances an investment from internally held funds. In this case the investment can be considered "profitable" only if the firm ends up with more money than it would have ended up with had it loaned out its money instead of investing it.

If r is less than i, the term $(r - i)$ will be negative, and the investment will result in a loss to the firm. This will be the case even if the profit rate (r) is positive because the firm will have had to pay more in interest to the bank (or to its bondholders) than it received in profit. If the firm financed the investment from its own retained earnings, it would still, in effect, suffer a loss because it could have made more money by lending the equivalent of its investment to another firm at the prevailing rate of interest (i). The point is that no matter what the rate of profit (r), a firm must compare r and i to see if a particular investment is worth making.

Unfortunately for the firm, it cannot compare r and i directly. When a firm undertakes an investment, it cannot know how the investment will work out. The payoff to any investment is uncertain, and, therefore, making it necessarily involves *taking a risk*. A firm usually will know how much an investment will cost (I), and it will also know what the prevailing interest rate (i) is. As noted, however, it cannot know with certainty what the (future) profit rate (r) will be.

> The **expected profit rate on investment** is a firm's estimate of the future profit rate that it thinks will be earned on its investment.

In the *absence of certainty* about the future, whenever a firm is evaluating an investment—deciding whether to make it—it must compare the *expected profit rate on the investment,* which may be called *expected r*, with the prevailing interest rate, *i*. The expected profit rate is the rate that the firm thinks or expects it will achieve; of course, this expected rate of profit may or may not turn out, in the end, to be the one that is actually achieved.

Based on its expectations, then, a firm will choose to invest only when the expected profit rate on an investment is greater than the prevailing rate of interest:

$$expected\ r > i$$

In general, decisions for or against investing depend in large part on investors' optimism or pessimism about the future. If they are optimistic and are confident of good or better conditions in the future, they will tend to evaluate investment projects more favorably, seeing the positive possibilities and downplaying the dangers; in this case, *expected r* will tend to be high throughout the economy. If, on the other hand, investors are pessimistic, expecting difficult times ahead, they will be more wary, worrying that investments will not pay off; *expected r* will in this case tend to be low. Investors' optimism or pessimism will lead, therefore, to larger or smaller amounts of investment. Of course, each investor will view the future somewhat differently, and some will have expectations that turn out to be more correct than others.

There is another conclusion that can be drawn from our analysis of the factors that influence a firm's investment decision. Considering how the relationship between *r* and *i* (the profit rate and the interest rate) affects the profitability of, and hence the desirability of making, an investment, one can see that the level of investment in the economy as a whole will be influenced by the rate of interest. A low interest rate will tend to stimulate investment, whereas a high interest rate will tend to choke off investment. This places a significant amount of responsibility with a nation's central bank (for instance, the Federal Reserve System, or "Fed", in the U.S.) because it has the power to move interest rates up or down and thus to discourage or stimulate investment.

Finally, the amount of investment a firm undertakes will depend on its rate of capacity utilization, *u*. If $u < 1$ (meaning that the firm is not using all the machines, or capital goods, that it currently owns), any new machines available for purchase will have to be significantly better than the currently owned machines before the firm will decide to invest in them. It obviously does not make sense to buy new machines when a firm is not using all the ones it already owns.

THE DYNAMICS OF COMPETITION

We can now see the close connection between investment and competition. *Investment is the firm's way of carrying on competition in the future.* And competition, because it forces firms to invest, is inherently dynamic.

Consider our earlier example (see Chapter 8) of a beer market consisting of a large number of relatively small firms all producing the same kind of beer. Each firm will attempt

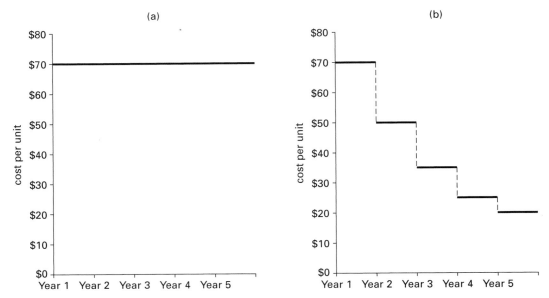

FIGURE 11.2   Dynamic cost advantage.   Panel (a) of this figure shows what happens when firms do not reinvest their profits. Assuming that the prices of inputs (including the wage) remain unchanged, such firms will see their unit costs remain constant from one period to the next. Panel (b) of the figure shows what happens when firms successfully reinvest their profits (in better equipment, for example). These firms will see their unit costs falling from one period to the next—again assuming that changes in input prices do not counteract the effects of their investments. Lower unit costs will allow firms to achieve higher unit profits or reduce their prices. Higher unit profits or lower prices (or both) will give the reinvesting firms competitive advantage over firms that do not reinvest.

to make as much profit as possible, but price competition will limit most firms to making just the average rate of profit.

What will be done with the profits of a firm in our hypothetical beer industry? The owner (or owners) of the firm could decide to spend their profits on unproductive activities, such as consumption of luxuries. Alternatively, he or she (or they) could reinvest some or all of the firm's profits to improve its competitive position in the future. Owners who decide to reinvest profits will spend their money on things that may reduce the firm's costs of production—things such as research, new machinery, and more effective supervision of workers.

Figure 11.2 shows how future costs of production will differ between (a) firms that do not reinvest their profits and (b) those that do reinvest their profits. We can see that both kinds of firms start out in year 1 with costs of $70 per barrel of beer. But whereas the firms that do not reinvest (shown in the diagram on the left) continue to have costs of $70, those firms that do reinvest (shown in the diagram on the right) see their costs fall as time goes on—to $50 in the second period, $35 in the third period, and so on. The firms with the ever lower costs will have higher profit rates than the higher-cost firms. They will be able to charge lower prices for their product, sell more beer, and increase their rate of capacity utilization (u). Alternatively, they may use their cost advantage to enjoy a higher markup over costs. In any case they will have a competitive advantage over their rivals, and this will put them in a position to expand their share of the (beer) market.

Firms that reinvest may also choose to expand their scale of output. While it is theoretically possible for reinvesting firms to undertake cost-reducing investments without trying to expand their output, this is an unlikely scenario. It is more likely that profit reinvesting firms will use their resulting cost advantage to undercut their higher-cost rivals, capture a larger share of the market, and increase their output as well as their sales. (Otherwise, why would the owners of such firms have sacrificed their consumption in order to reinvest their firms' profits?) The lower-cost firms will have investment opportunities that the higher-cost firms will not have: they can profitably invest in expansion of output, and it will be profitable for them to grow larger.

> **Decreasing costs** refers to a situation in which the average cost of producing something declines as the volume (scale) of production increases.

Notice that it will be profitable for a dynamic, profit-reinvesting, and lower-cost firm to grow even if it is not able to continue to reduce its costs beyond a certain point. Such a firm may choose to expand by building an additional factory that just replicates its existing (already lower-cost) facilities. In this case doubling output may not lead to further reductions in unit costs, but it will reproduce the advantages (and higher profit rate) of current operations. Of course, if *decreasing costs* are also present, then it will be even more advantageous for such a firm to grow.

Dynamic competition will tend to produce uneven results: there will be winners and losers. Some firms will be highly effective or lucky, investing in things that pay off, while others will be unsuccessful or unlucky and never see their higher expected profits materialize. Moreover, not all firms will be equally well situated. Some firms may have better access to needed raw materials (for example, mountain water), be closer to big markets, or simply have better management or luckier owners. The well-situated firms will have higher profit rates than the poorly situated ones. Firms that achieve high profits in one period will have more to reinvest in the next period. The higher the profit rate, the more there will be to reinvest; unsuccessful firms have low profit rates and, hence, little to reinvest.

What are the consequences of the constantly changing, dynamic, disruptive pursuit of profits? On the grandest level, the process drives the constant transformation that is characteristic of capitalist society (see Chapters 1 and 7). More immediately, the process has consequences for firms. It may tend to bring about more equal profit rates among firms, and then again it may not. It may lead to greater economic concentration, and then again it may not.

TOWARD EQUAL PROFIT RATES?

At any particular time many different profit rates exist in the economy. Some firms will have low profit rates, others high profit rates. Competition produces the divergence of profit rates, and it also tends, over time, to bring them closer together.

Equalization of profit rates refers to the process by which competitive pressures on firms in different industries, different geographical regions, or different markets push their profit rates toward a common, or average, level.

The profit rate (r) achieved by a firm during a given year depends on the profit rate determinants affecting that particular firm (see Chapter 10). How effectively a firm manages its inputs of materials and capital goods (m), how much work effort per hour (e) it gets from its workers, and many other factors will determine the firm's profit rate. Some firms will be able to manage at least some of their profit rate determinants well (or they may just happen to be lucky). Other firms will not be able to do so (or they may just have bad luck). The result is that there will exist a diversity of profit rates, some low, some slightly higher, some much higher, and so on.

The dynamics of competition, by forcing firms to invest in new and risky projects, continually generates new sets of diverse profit rates. Breakthroughs and monopoly power, for instance, make possible exceptionally good profit opportunities. Relative to other firms, firms with breakthroughs and monopoly power will have high profit rates. Firms that must compete with the breakthrough or monopoly-power firms, however, will likely have lower profit rates. The advantage enjoyed by firms with breakthroughs or monopoly power is, correspondingly, a *disadvantage* for the firms they compete with.

In contrast to these ways in which it produces divergent profit rates, competition also involves processes that tend to equalize profit rates. Price competition tends to equalize profit rates. As many firms try to squeeze out small cost or marketing advantages, their profit rates will be limited by competition from other firms, and as a result all firms' profit rates will tend to move toward an average rate. In addition, when firms invest or reinvest, they will often pull out of markets, industries, or sectors where the rates of return are low and move their operations to markets, industries, or sectors where the rates of return are high. This process will also tend to bring about more equal profit rates.

Consider the opportunities facing a firm that wants to undertake an investment. It must compare the cost of each dollar invested (i) with the projected returns (*expected r*) from each potential investment project. Investments in areas of the economy—in markets, industries, sectors, geographical regions, or even other countries—currently experiencing high profit rates will be likely to have higher projected returns than areas with lower profit rates, so the high-profit areas will attract more new investments than the low-profit areas.

The movement of firms and investments out of low-profit areas to high-profit areas will have two effects, both of which will tend to make profit rates more equal between the two types of areas. First, the exit of firms from low-profit areas will shift to the left the industry supply curves for such areas. In Figure 11.3 this is shown (in the left diagram) as a shift in a particular industry supply curve from S_1 to S_2. This shift in the supply curve will raise the market-clearing price (P_z) for that industry or area from P_1 to P_2. However, since some firms will have left the industry (thereby reducing its overall production capacity), the higher price will not reduce the capacity utilization rates (u) of the remaining firms as much as it would have done if there had been no change in the number of firms and each one had been faced with a diminished demand for its output. As a result the higher price (P_2) will have the effect of raising the profit rates of the firms remaining in the low-profit areas.

Second, as new firms enter the high-profit areas, the industry supply curves for these areas will shift outward to the right, as illustrated by the movement in a particular industry of S_1 to S_2 in the right diagram in Figure 11.3. The expanded supply (at every price) will cause the market to establish a lower market-clearing price, a movement illustrated in the

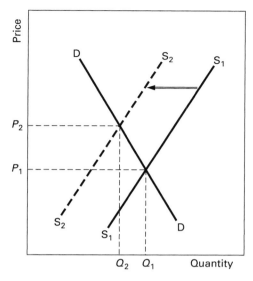

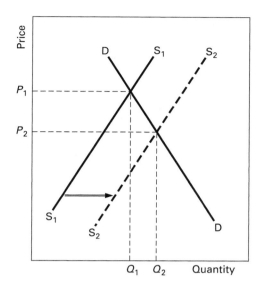

Exit of firms from low-profit industry
raises prices

Entry of firms into high-profit industry
lowers prices

FIGURE 11.3 **Exit and entry of firms from and into markets tend to equalize profits.**   Low profits will drive
some firms out of an initially low–profit industry. Such exits will cause the supply of output in that industry to contract,
as indicated in the diagram on the left by the leftward shift of the supply curve from S_1 to S_2. This shift will allow the
remaining firms to raise their price from P_1 to P_2, thus increasing their profits. Exactly the opposite happens in an
initially high–profit industry (represented in the diagram on the right). The high profits will induce new firms to enter this
industry, and as the output of the new firms increases total output, the industry supply curve will shift to the right,
showing that there is an expanded supply at each price. The entry of new firms forces all the firms in the industry to
sell their output at a lower price (P_2), and this will drive their profit rates down. Thus, the profit rates in the two
industries will tend to converge.

right diagram in Figure 11.3 by the price change from P_1 to P_2. And though the lower price
(P_2) will attract new customers to the particular industry (or area), these new customers
must be shared with the additional firms that have recently entered this market, thus bringing about reduced profit rates in high-profit areas.

The movement of firms (as they invest and reinvest their profits) therefore tends to
make profit rates more equal between areas or industries that initially had widely divergent
rates of return. Exits raise the profit rates in low-profit industries; entries reduce the profit
rates in high-profit industries. If this process were to continue long enough and if it were
not offset by the creation of new profit rate differences, the average profit rate would eventually be the same in each industry and area.

Whether competition tends to equalize profit rates or make them more unequal depends on which set of opposing forces is stronger: those forces (such as breakthroughs and
monopoly power) that create divergent profit rates, or those pressures (such as price competition and exit and entry) that tend to equalize profit rates.

TOWARD ECONOMIC CONCENTRATION?

> **Economic concentration** is the extent to which the economic activity of an industry or the whole economy is conducted by the largest firms.

Economic concentration refers to how much of an industry or of the whole economy is controlled by very large firms. Consider, for instance, two industries of equal size in terms of the value of sales. In one industry there are 100 firms, all about the same size, whereas in the other industry there are only four firms. The second industry is said to be more concentrated than the first. Similarly, for the economy as a whole, the greater the role of big firms, the more concentrated is the economy. Dynamic competition produces either more or less economic concentration because, just as it affects the equalization of profit rates, competition both generates and erodes economic concentration.

Competition generates concentration because greater size will almost always enhance a firm's ability to increase its profit rate, and therefore bigger firms usually can out-compete smaller firms. As a result, big firms often grow at the expense of smaller firms.

Why does greater size almost always enhance a firm's ability to make a profit? Three factors are at work: (a) greater size permits a firm to reap the benefits of the decreasing costs that occur when there are increasing returns to scale; (b) greater size increases a firm's ability to achieve breakthroughs and monopoly power; and (c) greater size expands the firm's bargaining and political power with respect to labor, finance, suppliers, and the government.

As explained in Chapter 8, the term *decreasing costs* (which are the result of *increasing returns to scale*) refers to a situation in which the average cost of production falls as the volume of production increases. For instance, in the first decade of the 20th century, there were more than 200 companies producing cars in the U.S.; small "backyard" shops competed with larger plants that increasingly resembled today's assembly-line factories. The bigger firms not only produced more cars, but, because they were able to spread out the sizable "fixed costs" of producing cars—the costs required just to "set up shop"—over a larger number of cars, they had lower average costs.

Wherever decreasing costs (increasing returns) are available, bigger firms will have lower average costs than smaller firms. Moreover, the larger firms can reduce their costs even further by (a) increasing f, the output derived from each unit of work effort (this would be the expected consequence of installing more and/or better machines for each worker); (b) reducing m, the amount of the materials used and the wear and tear on machines per hour of labor input; and (c) reducing k, the value of capital goods invested per worker hour, or altering any of the other profit rate determinants, such as w, in directions favorable to the company. And, obviously, increasing f or reducing m or k will at least make it possible for a big firm to raise its rate of profit (r); the only situation in which its profit rate would not rise would be if the firm decided to lower the price of its product in proportion to each reduction in its average cost of production.

There are also other ways in which greater size can enable firms to raise their profit rates: it puts them in better positions to achieve breakthroughs and monopoly power. With monopoly power the cause-and-effect relationship is obvious. If a firm is large enough to control the whole market for a product, it is a *monopoly,* and it can charge whatever price brings it the most profit. High rates of profit can also be achieved in the more common situation in which monopoly power is shared by a few firms who, perhaps tacitly, make decisions about pricing their products together.

Shared monopoly is more easily established and maintained if there are only a few (large) firms in a particular industry. If there are many firms in an industry, the task of establishing cooperation is very difficult: it is like trying to get a large number of people to agree on a decision. Hence, the presence of only a few large firms in an industry makes it easier to establish and maintain monopoly power and thereby to achieve increased rates of profit.

Size also enhances a firm's ability to achieve breakthroughs and, more importantly, to profit from them. Consider technological innovations, for example. The first possibility is that since larger firms have higher profit rates, they can spend more on research—not just more dollars, but a proportionately larger share of their revenues—to discover new opportunities for innovations. Studies of corporate research budgets suggest, however, that big firms do not spend (proportionately) more on research. If anything, they spend less (as a fraction of their total revenues).

A second possibility is that big firms may be more efficient in their research activities because of increasing returns to scale (or decreasing average costs of discovery) in research. But the evidence seems to discount this possibility as well: small and mid-sized companies seem to produce at least their share of innovations.

Things are different, however, when it comes to exploiting the profit potential of a breakthrough: here, the big firms dominate. To profit from a breakthrough (say, in personal computers), the new product must be produced in quantity, advertised extensively, distributed widely, and defended against would-be competitors. For instance, Apple, Osborne, and other small companies pioneered the small desktop computer, but giant firms actually captured most of the market—and reaped most of the profit—for such computers.

A small firm, even one with an important innovation and big marketing ideas, generally cannot carry out all its desired marketing activities successfully. As a small company, it has limited profits and will not have access to the large amounts of credit needed to bring the innovation to fruition. Indeed, sufficient credit may be granted only on the condition that the bank or other lender be given control of the project. The small firm typically has no existing distribution network, its name is not widely recognized, and it has no funds for large-scale advertising.

In this situation many small firms choose to sell their innovations to big firms. In other cases a small company will be sold in its entirety to a large firm. Although the selling price may provide the small firm with a large profit (relative to its modest size), the remaining profit to be made from exploiting a breakthrough will be captured by the large firm.

Yet another way in which greater size may raise the profit rate of a firm is by increasing the bargaining and political power of the firm. Big corporations have more clout than small businesses. More bargaining power may mean easier entry into foreign markets, or lower interest rates and easier access to credit when a firm borrows money from banks. Political power may be translated into more access to government contracts, better treatment in tariff or export policy (such as subsidies through the Export-Import Bank), and favorable government loans or loan guarantees.

Thus, large firms may very well be able to translate political power into higher profits. Perhaps the best examples of this are in the military-industrial complex, the relationship between giant corporations and the Pentagon. This relationship keeps lucrative contracts flowing to such firms as Halliburton, General Dynamics, and Boeing.

Notice that only when decreasing costs are present is it true that a larger scale of operations will *directly* translate into higher profits. In all other cases, greater size will increase a firm's ability to do something else (such as gain monopoly power) that will, in turn, raise its profit rate. In real life firms may grow because all these factors are mixed together: growth based partly on decreasing costs may lead to the creation of monopoly power, breakthrough profits may finance a firm's growth and enable it to capture the benefits of decreasing costs, and so on.

Increasing costs refers to a situation in which the average cost of producing something increases as the volume (scale) of production increases.

If firms encounter substantial *increasing costs*—unit costs *rising* as production expands—then such costs will limit growth. With increasing costs, the larger a firm gets, the greater is its cost disadvantage. However, increasing costs are almost always experienced at the plant (not the firm) level, so increasing costs limit the size of individual plants, not firms. Since increasing costs occur at the plant level but do not limit a firm's size, large firms can—and do—operate many plants. For example, a very large firm such as General Motors operates hundreds of plants rather than concentrating production in one enormous plant. Increasing costs appear to be a minor factor limiting the growth of firms.

Competition does, however, sometimes work against economic concentration. The high profit rates attained by big firms, like high profit rates anywhere in the economy, attract competitors. New firms, or old firms seeking new profit opportunities, will attempt to enter industries in which profit rates are high, even if the industry is dominated by a few large firms. For instance, Dell, the largest manufacturer of computers, is a relatively new firm. As competition intensifies in industries with a small number of long-successful firms, their high profits will tend to be competed away. For example, there are now firms in the computer manufacturing industry that are beginning to use Linux as their operating system, thereby undercutting Microsoft's monopoly in this market.

Aggregate economic concentration is the ratio of large companies' sales, profit, or number of employees to the economy's total sales, profit, or employees. If large firms are able to increase their share of particular markets while other large firms are not losing their share of other markets, concentration in the economy will increase. The extent of concentration in each industry and in the economy as a whole depends, then, on which set of opposing forces is stronger—those forces (such as the advantages of size) that tend to increase concentration or those forces (such as the formation of new firms) that tend to erode concentration.

Have large, highly publicized mergers among U.S. firms in recent years brought about increased concentration in the U.S. economy? In the late 1980s and early 1990s there were $200 billion worth of mergers every year for several years in a row. Then in the late 1990s there was an even larger merger wave in which the total value of mergers exceeded $1 trillion per year. There is no doubt that in certain industries, for instance, the media industry, huge mergers (such as the one involving AOL and Time Warner) between firms (such as those engaged in publishing books and newspapers, producing movies, and providing internet services) have increased the influence of large firms and jeopardized the continued existence of many smaller firms that do these things. This, of course, means that readers,

THE TIME WARNER EMPIRE

TELEVISION

- HBO
- CNN and subsidiaries
- Court TV (with Liberty Media)
- Time Warner Cable
- Road Runner
- New York 1 News
- TBS Superstation
- Turner Network Television (TNT)
- Turner South
- Cartoon Network
- Turner Classic Movies
- The WB Television Network

FILM AND MUSIC

- **Film:** New Line Cinema, Fine Line Features, Turner Original Productions, Warner Bros., Hanna-Barbera Cartoons, Telepictures Production, Witt-Thomas Productions, Castle Rock Entertainment, Warner Home Video
- **Music:** Atlantic, Big Beat, Blackground, Breaking, Igloo, Lava, Mesa/ Bluemoon, Modern, Rhino Records, Elektra Entertainment Group, Elektra, East West, Asylum, Elektra/Sire, Warner Brothers Records Group, Reprise Group, American Recordings, Giant, Maverick, Revolution, Qwest, Warner Music International, WEA Telegram, East West ZTT, Coalition, CGD East West, China, Continental, East West; *Joint Ventures:* Columbia House, Music Sound Exchange, Music Choice, Music Choice Europe, Viva, Channel V, Heartland Music, MusicNet; 10 others

PRINT

- **Magazines:** Time, Fortune, Business 2.0, Life, Sports Illustrated, Inside Stuff, Money, People, Who, Weekly (Australian edition), Teen People, Entertainment Weekly, The Ticket, In Style, Southern Living, Progressive Farmer, Southern Accents, Cooking Light, Parenting, The Health Publishing Group, Weight Watchers, Real Simple, Asiaweek, Wallpaper (U.K.), Field & Stream, Freeze, Golf Magazine, Outdoor Life, Popular Science, Salt Water Sportsman, Ski, SNAP, Verge, Yachting Magazine, Warp, Travel & Leisure, Food & Wine, Your Company, Departures, DC Comics, Vertigo, Paradox, Milestone, Mad Magazine

Continued . . .

- **Publishers:** Time–Life Series, Book-of-the-Month Club, Paperback Book Club, Children's Book-of-the-Month Club, History Book Club Money Book Club, Home Style Books, Crafter's Choice, One Spirit, International, Little, Brown and Company, Bulfinch, Press, Back Bay Books, Brown and Company (U.K.), 15 others

OTHER

- **Professional sports teams:** Atlanta Braves, Atlanta Hawks, Atlanta Thrashers, Turner Sports, Good Will Games, Phillips Arena
- **Other entertainment:** Netscape Communications, Netscape Netcenter portal, AOL, MovieFone, iAmaze, Amazon.com (partial), Quack.com, Streetmail (partial), Switchboard (6 percent)

Time Warner controlling ownership (6 percent): Janus Capital. 2002 Revenue: $41 billion.

Source: The Nation, January 7/14, 2002. available at http://www.thenation.com/special/bigten.html

moviegoers, internet users, and citizens in general may now have access to a much more limited range of artistic expressions, perspectives, and opinions. A possible consequence of such mergers, then, is that citizens will not have the variety of information and opinion they need in order to participate in a well-informed way in the political process.

However, even with the highly publicized mergers of recent years, and even as the average firm has gotten larger, the degree of concentrated economic power in the U.S. economy has not increased. Figure 11.4 shows that the market power of the top 500 firms in the U.S. economy, whether measured by profitability or by employment, actually declined between 1980 and 2000. In 1980 the profits of the 500 most profitable U.S.-based corporations were equal to 71.3 percent of total U.S. corporate profits in that year; in 2000 the share was 57 percent (see the caption to Figure 11.4 for details regarding the calculations of these percentages). Similarly, the largest U.S. corporations in 1980 accounted for 21.2 percent of American private sector employment; in 2000 the comparable figure was 16.3 percent.[2]

The data cited in the previous paragraph suggest that the trend, in the U.S. at least, is in the direction of reduced economic concentration. And when the increasing integration of the world economy—globalization—is taken into account, one can hardly escape the conclusion that we are living in an economy that is becoming more competitive. One indication of this trend is that although there once was a time when the U.S. car market could be described with reference to "the big three" (GM, Ford, and Chrysler), American consumers can now choose to buy a car from any one of at least a dozen companies with headquarters in Japan, Korea, and western Europe as well as the U.S.

As companies get larger and larger, however, their influence in the political process becomes greater in relation to that of individuals. Thus, even if the U.S. and other economies continue to become more competitive, the issue of economic concentration will continue to merit our attention.

---

[2] Lawrence J. White, "Trends in Aggregate Concentration in the United States," *Journal of Economic Perspectives,* vol. 16, no. 4, fall 2002, Table 8, p. 156.

FIGURE 11.4   Declining concentration in the U.S. economy, 1980–2000.   This figure shows that the relative importance of the top 500 U.S. corporations, whether measured in profitability or in employment, declined between 1980 and 2000. The data on the profit share is taken from *Forbes* magazine's annual list of the 500 most profitable U.S. companies, with the total profits made by these companies (not necessarily the same firms every year) expressed as a fraction of the total amount of profits made by all corporations in the same years. The fractions for each year are shown in the figure as percentages. These percentages are substantial because the *Forbes* profit data come (by definition) only from companies that are making huge amounts of profit, whereas the data on the profits of all corporations take into account the losses incurred by some corporations. Thus, in the recession year 1982 the total profit made by *Forbes*'s 500 most profitable firms actually *exceeded* the total profit of *all* corporations, many of which did not do well in that year; this explains the 103 percent data point for the 500 most profitable firms' share of corporate profits in 1982. The data on the employment share of the largest corporations are also taken from the *Forbes* annual lists and are similarly calculated as a percent of the total employment of all U.S. corporations (see the dotted line in the figure). Over the two decades represented in this figure there was some movement up and down in both sets of data (especially the one pertaining to the profit share), but both the profit share and the employment share of the top 500 companies were lower in 2000 than they had been in 1980.

Source: Lawrence J. White, "Trends in Aggregate Concentration in the United States," *Journal of Economic Perspectives,* vol. 16, no. 4, fall 2002, pp. 137–160.

SUGGESTED READINGS

Richard J. Barnet and John Cavanaugh, *Global Dreams: Imperial Corporations and the New World Order* (New York: Simon & Schuster/Touchstone, 1995).

Michael Best, *The New Competition: Institutions of Industrial Restructuring* (Oxford: Polity, 1990).

Alfred Chandler, *The Visible Hand: The Managerial Revolution in American Business* (Cambridge, Mass.: Harvard University Press, 1977).

John Kenneth Galbraith, *American Capitalism: The Concept of Countervailing Power* (Piscataway, N.J.: Transaction Publishers, 1997).

David Kotz, *Bank Control of Large Corporations in the United States* (Berkeley: University of California Press, 1978).

Joseph Schumpeter, *The Theory of Capitalist Development* (Cambridge, Mass.: Harvard University Press, 1934).

Carl Shapiro and Hal R. Varian, *Information Rules: A Strategic Guide to the Network Economy* (Boston: Harvard Business School Press, 1999).

William G. Shepherd and Joanna M. Shepherd, *The Economics of Industrial Organization,* 5th ed. (Long Grove, Ill.: Waveland Press, 2003).

CHAPTER 12

Wages and Work

O ur society is often described as a consumer society, one in which people express their creativity and enjoy a sense of freedom by consuming. Thus, we go window-shopping, make our choice of just the right blouse or shirt, and expect that wearing it will say something about who we are. Some of us even go on shopping sprees to fight off boredom or depression.

If consumption is the bright side of the capitalist economy, however, production is often thought of as its dark side. People do not say, "I'm feeling a little down, I think I'll go down to the office and put in a little work." Indeed, in our society work has a bad reputation. The great American novelist William Faulkner expressed our generally dim view of labor in this way: "You can't eat for eight hours a day nor drink for eight hours a day nor make love for eight hours a day. All you can do for eight hours a day is work. Which is the reason why man makes himself and everybody else so miserable and unhappy."[1]

Perhaps Faulkner had a point. Although it is generally a good thing to be employed, a job may be little more than a way of making the money one needs to be able to consume later. Work may be necessary or preferable to doing nothing, but in many cases it does not make an individual feel creative or fulfilled. Instead, it frequently engages people in repetitive tasks and subjects them to the unwelcome authority of supervisors.

Despite its deficiencies, however, work is a very important aspect of people's lives. Of course, we depend on our jobs for income. But work is also, for many of us, a central aspect of our identities: it allows us to say who we are. We spend a major portion of our waking hours working, so whether work is a happy or an anxious experience, whether it fosters boredom, resentment, fear, or pride, it will affect our overall mental state. Where we work may be where we find our "place" in the world, it may provide us with an experience of

---

[1] Quoted in Studs Terkel, *Working* (New York: Pantheon Books, 1972), p. ix.

283

community, it will certainly be among the places where we get to know other people, and quite possibly it will be a place where we have friends. Moreover, our job may offer us the chance, however limited, to exercise responsibility, show creativity, or rise to the challenge of hard work. For all these reasons access to work and the conditions of work are enormously important for most of us.

Nevertheless, many people object to the fact that they have very little choice about what they do at work or how they do it. Why is production organized from the top down, with nearly every work process overseen by executives, managers, supervisors, "team leaders," or other authorities? Is the top-down control of work and its fragmentation into repetitive tasks an inevitable result of modern technology? Or is it just "natural" that work is unpleasant, perhaps because it requires exertion?

If one's job is often a problem, not having one can be even worse. Joan Robinson, a 20th-century British economist, once quipped that the only thing worse than being exploited by a capitalist is not being exploited by one. Moreover, the loss of one's job can be not only a financial disaster but a personal calamity as well. Suicide rates, marital breakups, and mental illnesses are all quite closely correlated with the number of people who are looking for work but cannot find it.

This chapter investigates the organization and remuneration of work. As noted in Chapter 7, the majority of people in the United States work for an employer—an individual, a group of individuals, or a corporation. We also explained in Chapter 6 that the relationship between employers and workers is a class relationship, with employers and workers constituting different classes. The relationship between employers and workers is different from the relationships examined in the last chapter—capitalist-capitalist relationships— and it is also different from the relationships workers have with other workers. Whereas capitalist-capitalist and worker-worker relationships are horizontal in nature, the employer-worker relationship is a vertical one.

All economic relationships contain elements of both competition and command, but competition is more important in some relationships while command prevails in others. When capitalists compete with other capitalists—or workers compete with other workers— the relationships involved are "within-class" relationships; as noted, they are horizontal, and they are (most often) competitive. In contrast, the capital-labor relation is a "between-class" relationship, and it involves what we call the command dimension of an economy. Between-class relationships are vertical in the sense that, within them, people relate to each other as supervisors and subordinates, with some being higher up and others lower down in a hierarchy. Of course, most people in a hierarchy are *both* supervisors *and* subordinates, holding power over those below them while at the same time having to obey (or please) those above them.

Many economists do not take account of the ways that employer-worker relationships differ from other economic relationships, for example those that consumers enter into when they buy groceries. They assume, first, that workers and employers agree ahead of time on the amount of work effort (e) to be performed each hour and, second, that workers, after they have agreed to work for a certain wage, willingly put out the expected amount of work effort. Labor can therefore be treated as just another input to the production process, comparable to such nonhuman inputs as land, capital goods, and materials. Indeed, Paul Samuelson, one of the most highly regarded economists of the 20th century, once said:

"In the competitive model, it makes no difference whether capital hires labor or the other way around."[2] He obviously could not have been referring to a capitalist economy, because in such an economy the fact that capitalists hire workers does make a difference.

This chapter focuses on the relationship between workers and their employers. The main ideas of the chapter are that (a) *employers and their employees have fundamentally conflicting interests in the workplace,* and (b) *employers organize work hierarchically, in a top-down way, in order to extract work from their employees so as to make profits.* These central ideas are expressed in six main points:

1. The activity of producing things—*work*—is not naturally boring, oppressive, or limiting. Neither is it naturally exciting and liberating. It is not "naturally" anything. What work is like—our experience of it and our reaction to it—depends in important ways on how the labor process is organized, how the rest of society is organized, and where we fit into the labor process.

2. A capitalist enterprise—a "firm"—is a *system of command,* in which power is exercised from the top down. In the marketplace people and firms interact primarily through voluntary offers and agreements; within firms the main form of interaction involves the exercise of authority by supervisors over workers.

3. There is a conflict between what *employers* and *employees* want to get out of the labor process. This conflict is over wages and the pace of work, two of the most important determinants of the profit rate. The conflict between employers and employees arises from their opposing positions in the labor process and is inherent in a system geared toward profit making.

4. Capitalist firms are organized hierarchically, with control exercised from the top, in order to enhance the ability of employers to *extract work* from their employees. Work must be extracted because it cannot be secured by contract.

5. Employers are able to exercise power over their employees because good jobs are scarce and because there is almost always an excess supply of labor—*unemployment*—in the labor market. The labor market does not operate like other markets, which tend to "clear," thereby eliminating excess supply. Rather, excess supply is a chronic feature of labor markets.

6. Excess supply occurs in labor markets because employers wish to exercise power over workers. To achieve this power they pay wages that are above the minimum that their employees would accept, thus putting the workers in situations in which they have "something to lose" if fired. Similar workers without jobs would be happy to take the employed workers' jobs at lower wages, but the employers are not interested in offering the jobs at lower wages. Hence the workers without the jobs are *involuntarily unemployed.*

---

[2] Paul A. Samuelson, "Wages and Interest," *American Economic Review,* vol. 62, no. 6, Dec. 1957, p. 894.

In this chapter we investigate the organization of labor processes and examine conflict in the workplace. Why is work organized hierarchically? What exactly is the conflict about, and why does it exist? In the next chapter we explore how employers and employees respond to the conflict.

WORK, SLOTH, AND SOCIAL ORGANIZATION

Though some people enjoy their work, others start living when they get off work in the afternoon and spend their time looking forward to the weekend. Many think of their days as divided between "work" and "leisure"—the first being a "bad" that must be endured in order to be able to acquire "goods" for consumption.

Conventional economists say that people derive "utility" from consumption and get "disutility" from work. This view undoubtedly expresses what many people feel about work. But it is incomplete in two ways. First, it implies that work is *naturally* a "bad," something that by its very nature is unpleasant. Second, it ignores many aspects of work that make working an important and positive experience for people.

It is true, of course, that work takes time, and there are only 24 hours in the day. Because of this there is always an *opportunity cost* to work. If you are working, you cannot also be at the beach (unless you are a lifeguard). In this respect, of course, work is not different from any other activity (including going to the beach): whenever we spend time doing something, we are spending time doing it that we could have spent doing something else.

Why, then, should work be singled out for disparagement? One reason often given is that humans have a natural tendency toward sloth and therefore dislike doing things that require effort. Another view is that people do not like work because they do not like accepting the authority of others. A third opinion is that people hate work because it requires the repetition of limited tasks. But, in fact, none of these problems are actually rooted in human nature or intrinsic to work itself.

The view of people as naturally slothful is contradicted by the fact that many people get pleasure from exerting themselves in sports or other recreational activities. Most people can think of occasions when they have worked very hard, even at extremely demanding tasks, and greatly enjoyed it. People building a new room on their house, for example, may put in long hours on weekends, working at a pace that would provoke resentment if it were required in the office or at the plant. To cite another example, parents engage in one of the most physically, intellectually, and emotionally challenging types of work, raising children, but they often find the process rewarding.

With regard to the dislike of having to accept authority, it happens that people who resent supervision on the job may enjoy performing under the direction of a talented orchestra conductor or being told what to do by an experienced football coach. Thus, the aversion to accepting authority is hardly universal.

Finally, it is entirely understandable that people do not enjoy work when it involves performing the same task over and over again. But, again, such conditions are not intrinsic to work itself.

The problem, it seems, is not that work is naturally unpleasant or boring but, rather, that some types of work are objectionable. The examples mentioned above suggest that work may be repugnant because of the way it is organized or for whom it is done. Physical exertion, discipline, and responsibility—whether in sports, homebuilding, music, or child rearing—are often gladly accepted, even welcomed, if the activity is one that a person has chosen, believes in, benefits from, or performs for someone he or she cares about.

The idea of work as a "bad"—or as generating "disutility"—is wrong for another reason. People often derive satisfaction from producing useful things, from developing their skills, or from associating with others at their workplaces. Respect, friendship, pride of accomplishment, and a sense of doing something useful are all, at least potentially, by-products of human labor.

If many people see work as an undesirable activity, it is because of how production is organized, who controls it, and how the benefits from it are distributed. In the United States today—indeed, in all capitalist economies—most work other than raising children at home or performing other household tasks is done in firms. Understanding work thus requires an understanding of the organization of firms.

ON HUMAN WORK: EXCERPTS FROM A PAPAL ENCYCLICAL

. . . through work man not only transforms nature, adapting it to his own needs, but he also achieves fulfillment as a human being and indeed in a sense becomes "more of a human being." . . . [But] it is well known that it is possible to use work in various ways against man, . . . that work can be made into a means for oppressing man, and that in various ways it is possible to exploit human labor, that is to say, workers.

It is obvious that when we speak of opposition between labor and capital we are not dealing only with abstract concepts or "impersonal forces." . . . Behind both concepts are people, living, actual people. On the one side are those who do the work without being the owners of the means of production, and on the other side are those who . . . own these means or represent the owners.

Since the concept of capital includes not only the natural resources placed at man's disposal, but also the whole collection of means by which man appropriates natural resources and transforms them . . . it must immediately be noted that all these means are the result of the historical heritage of human labor.

Furthermore, in the church's teaching, . . . [the means of production] cannot be possessed against labor, they cannot even be possessed for possession's sake, because the only legitimate title to their possession—whether in the form of private ownership or in the form of public or collective ownership—is that they should serve labor and thus by serving labor that they should make possible the achievement of . . . the universal destination of goods and the right to common use of them.

—From the papal encyclical *On Human Work*
Pope John Paul II
September 14, 1981

THE CAPITALIST FIRM AS A COMMAND ECONOMY

A capitalist economy is composed of both firms and markets. Markets, as we have seen, involve *exchanges* of commodities for money and of money for commodities, and these exchanges are mostly voluntary (see Chapter 8).

> **Command relations** are relationships between superiors and subordinates in which the superior exercises substantial power over the subordinate.

The firm, however, is different. Inside the firm—behind the office door or inside the factory gates—people are generally not engaged in exchanging one activity for another; rather, their interactions are governed by *command relations*: they give and take orders. Accordingly, the capitalist firm can be described as a "command economy" (a term usually used in reference to centralized economic systems such as that of the former Soviet Union).

Picture a capitalist economy as a sea dotted with many islands, some large, some small. The sea is the market and each island is a firm producing a particular product. The islands exchange their products with other islands, and they also sell products to individuals in the sea. The trades *among* islands and individuals involve (horizontal) market exchanges; but, *within* islands, production is organized by means of (vertical) command relations.

A shorthand way of describing one important aspect of a capitalist firm is to say that it is a social organization of production in which some people attempt to get other people to do the work. What distinguishes the political economy approach from the view of the economy presented in conventional textbooks is the inclusion of the social relations of production—treating the firm as a command economy—in the overall picture of the profit-making process.

Just as in political economy (see Chapter 11) conventional economists view profits as being made because some entrepreneurs are able to anticipate better than others where demand will be growing faster than supply, where a new product or production process (a breakthrough or a technical innovation) might provide an advantage over competitors, or where a degree of monopoly power might be achieved. And of course conventional economists also see profit as a reward for risk-taking on the part of investors and business owners. But in the conventional approach one does not encounter such things as the power of employers to limit their employees' demands for higher wages and to get them to work hard. Nor does one hear about the power of corporations in one country to hold down the prices of the inputs they may get from (or in) other countries. Indeed, command relationships are ignored altogether.

It is important to reiterate that, as shown in Figure 10.1 (p. 229), a capitalist economy involves both exchange relations—competition—and command relations. The previous chapter focused on product market competition among firms (exchange 2 in Figure 10.1) seeking to maximize their sales and profits. Here we examine exchange transactions in the labor market (included within exchange 1 in the figure) and command relations in the workplace (the "realm of production" in the figure).

Of course, saying that the firm is a command economy does not mean that all the commands given in a particular firm will be willingly obeyed. Employers generally have the upper hand, but they do not always get what they want.

THE CONFLICT BETWEEN WORKERS AND EMPLOYERS

Workers and employers occupy different positions in the production process. Their interests differ, and they are often in conflict. Workers perform the work required to produce something and are paid a wage for their labor time. Employers hire workers, direct their activities in the workplace, and have the right to sell the firm's output.

What do employees want from their jobs? They want their jobs to be not excessively tiring; they want their wages to be as high as possible; they want to have interesting work; they want to work in safe and healthy workplaces; they want to have flexible hours, a say in how the workplace is run, long vacations, the right to stay home when a child is sick or another one is born, and so on. In order to keep things simple and to explain the main points, our discussion here will focus on two issues: (a) how tiring a job is, and (b) how much it pays. Employees want e (work effort per hour) to be not excessively high and w (the hourly wage) to be as high as possible.

And what do employers want? Employers seek to maximize their firms' profit rates. Focusing only on those variables in the profit rate equation (10.8, p. 247) that directly involve employees and their working conditions, we can see that profit rates will be higher

the *higher* are
   (1) employees' work effort per hour (e)
   (2) output produced per unit of effort (f)
and the *lower* is
   (3) the hourly wage (w)

This point can be illustrated using the concept of *markup pricing* introduced in Chapter 11:

| price of a unit of output | = | materials cost plus wear and tear on machines per unit of output | + | labor costs per unit of output | + | profit per unit of output |

This equation, with the "profit per unit of output" being the markup, can be translated into algebra as follows (recall that all variables in lower case are in per-labor-hour terms, as explained in Chapter 10):

$$P_z = \frac{P_m m}{z} + \frac{w}{z} + \frac{rk}{z} \qquad (12.1)$$

where P_z = the price of the product (per unit)

   P_m = the price of materials and machines

   m = materials and machines used per hour

   w = wage rate per hour of labor

   r = the profit rate

   k = value of owned capital goods per hour of labor

   z = dollar value of output per hour

> **Unit labor cost** is the labor portion of the average cost of producing each unit of output.

As can be seen from the preceding statement of Equation 12.1 in words, the second term on the right side of this equation (w/z) is the firm's *unit labor cost,* a concept we will henceforth represent with the letters *ulc.* It is the amount of money that employees must be paid for each unit of output produced. Thus, unit labor cost is defined as *the wage cost per unit of output.* It can be represented as follows:

$$ulc = \frac{wage/hour}{output/hour} = \frac{w}{z} = \frac{w}{ef} \qquad (12.2)$$

where ulc = unit labor cost

w = hourly wage rate

z = dollar value of output per hour of labor

e = intensity of work (work effort)

f = efficiency of labor

This equation clearly shows that unit labor costs are equal to the wages paid per hour divided by the number of units of output produced in that hour. Recall our earlier story about the Good Cod fishing company (see Chapter 10): if the company pays wages of $10 per hour and each employee, on average, brings in 25 pounds of fish per hour, then Good Cod's unit labor costs can be calculated as follows:

$ulc = \$10/25 = \$0.40$ in labor costs to produce each unit (pound) of the product

A company can raise its rate of profit (assuming no changes in its other profit rate determinants) by finding ways to reduce its unit labor costs (ulc). As Equation 12.2 shows, this can be done by lowering w, raising e, raising f, or achieving some combination of all three. Thus, employers seeking to increase their rates of profit will try to reduce w and increase e and/or f.

For two of the elements in unit labor costs, employers and their employees want exactly opposite things: employers want lower w and higher e, whereas employees want higher w and lower e. With regard to f, the third variable determining ulc, the interests of employees may coincide with those of their employers; we discuss this point in the next chapter.

With w and e, then, the conflict between an employee and his or her employer is direct and obvious. A company can raise e only by getting its employees to work harder (more rapidly), and it can reduce w only by paying lower wages.

> **Collective bargaining** occurs when, in negotiating wages and other employment conditions, all workers in a firm or occupation are represented collectively by a union; employers may also be collectively represented by an employers' association.

What determines the levels of e and w? Both are determined in important measure by the relative bargaining strengths of employees—individually or collectively—and their employers.

Consider wages first. For 11 out of 12 private sector employees (nongovernmental employees, that is), wage bargaining is mostly a matter between individual employees and their employers, since only 1 of 12 private sector workers belongs to a union. When employees are represented by a union, the bargaining takes place between union negotiators and

UNIT LABOR COSTS

I n 2001 it took a worker in the U.S. an average of 7.4 minutes to make a man's shirt. Thus, 8.1 men's shirts could be produced with an hour of labor. The average hourly wage of a production worker in the U.S. "cut and sew apparel" industry in 2001 was $8.60. Thus, the *unit labor cost* for producing men's shirts can be calculated as follows:

$$ulc = \frac{\$8.60 \text{ per hour}}{8.1 \text{ shirts per hour}} = \$1.06 \text{ per shirt}$$

The total cost of producing a man's shirt in the U.S. would, of course, include the costs of materials and machine wear and tear. And the production of the required materials (yards of cloth) and machines (stitching machines) would itself involve labor costs (wage dollars per hour), and these labor costs are, in fact, part of the cost of producing the shirt. But such indirect labor costs are not regarded as labor costs by the company making the shirts: the company sees only the cost of a yard of cloth and the cost of a machine that will wear out after being used to produce a certain number of shirts. For this reason the unit labor cost calculated above understates the actual unit labor cost of producing men's shirts in the U.S.

Sources: U.S. Census Bureau, *Statistical Abstract of the United States: 2003* (Washington, D.C.: U.S. Government Printing Office, 2003, Tables 631 and 632); Imre Bernolak, *Productivity Analysis . . . in Selected Asian Countries* (Asian Productivity Organization, 1987).

representatives of the employer, and this is called *collective bargaining*. In the coalfields of the eastern United States, for example, the United Mine Workers (UMW) union represents the unionized coal miners in this area, while a mine owners' council bargains for the coal mining companies.

What can be "won" in collective bargaining depends on a number of things that are largely beyond the control of both employees and employers. Employers cannot choose to set just any wage. If the employer's wage offer is too low, the firm will have difficulty attracting and keeping employees. Thus, labor market conditions—the level of wages in similar jobs and, particularly, the rate of unemployment—will set boundaries on the employers' wage offer.

Similarly, a union, no matter how strong it may be, cannot demand or expect to receive just any wage. To take an extreme case, if the wage demanded would make the unit labor cost (*ulc*) higher than the price of the product, the employer could not make a profit by hiring labor, even if there were no other costs. In this case the profit-maximizing employer would hire no one at all.

A wage bargain will be struck within a range of possible wages limited by conditions in the labor market, the productivity of labor (z), and output prices (P_z). The wage will be

THE BARGAINING POWER OF OWNERS AND WORKERS

It sometimes happens . . . that a single independent workman has stock [capital] sufficient both to purchase the materials of his work, and to maintain himself till it be completed. He is both master and workman, and enjoys the whole produce of his own labour. . . . Such cases, however, are not very frequent, and in every part of Europe, twenty workmen serve under a master for one that is independent. . . .

What are the common wages of labour depends everywhere upon the contract made between these two parties, whose interests are by no means the same. The workmen desire to get as much, the masters to give as little as possible. . . .

It is not, however, difficult to foresee which of the two parties must, upon all ordinary occasions, have the advantage in the dispute, and force the other into a compliance with their terms. . . . In all such disputes the masters can hold out much longer. A landlord, a farmer, a master manufacturer, or [a] merchant, though they did not employ a single workman, could generally live a year or two upon the stocks which they have already acquired. Many workmen could not subsist a week, few could subsist a month, and scarce any a year without employment. In the long run the worker is as necessary to his master as the master is to him; but the necessity is not so immediate.

—Adam Smith, *The Wealth of Nations* (1776)

The proprietors of . . . establishments and their operatives do not stand upon an equality; their interests are, to a certain extent, conflicting. The former naturally desire to obtain as much labor as possible from their employees, while the latter are often induced by the fear of discharge to conform to regulations which their judgment, fairly exercised, would pronounce to be detrimental. . . . In other words, the proprietors lay down the rules and the laborers are practically constrained to obey them.

—U.S. Supreme Court (1898)

Sources: Adam Smith, *An Inquiry into the Nature and Causes of the Wealth of Nations* (New York: The Modern Library, Random House, 1937), Book I, Chapter VIII; U.S. Supreme Court, *Holden vs. Hardy,* 169 U.S. 366 (1898).

toward the lower end of the range if the employer has the upper hand, and it will be toward the higher end if the employees (usually if they have a union) are stronger. Wage bargains are then formalized in contracts that set the hourly rate of pay (w) and some of the conditions of work (such as the time set aside for lunch).

LABOR DISCIPLINE: CARROTS AND STICKS

Just as with the wage, the amount of effort to be put out by employees each hour (e) is subject to a bargaining process. This bargaining process, however, is one that goes on every day and is never settled by a contractual agreement. Why is this?

An employment contract usually specifies three conditions: (1) the wage rate, (2) the hours of work, and (3) the right of the employer to direct the employee's efforts during work hours. The first two conditions can be stated in advance with precision. Wage rates, for instance, are often specified down to the penny for each hour worked. Also, the hours of work can be stated to the minute, stipulating the amount of time allowed for coffee breaks, lunch, and even, in some cases, trips to the bathroom.

The third aspect of the employment contract, however, the one that gives the employer the right to boss the employee around, cannot usually define in advance precisely how much work effort will be forthcoming from the employee. How hard must an employee work? With what precision must the employee obey the boss's commands? Only the broadest limits can be settled when a worker is hired. At one extreme, employees can put all their energy into doing everything their boss asks them to do. At the other extreme, they may do only as much as they need to do to keep from being fired. The actual outcome within this range cannot be specified in advance of the work itself.

What the employer purchases in the labor market is the right to *potential* labor services. Yet a moment's reflection will reveal that this is not at all what an employer needs. What is required is actual human productive activity—real *work*—not just the right to direct employees during the time they are in the workplace. Only human effort itself will produce the commodities that the firm must be able to sell in order to make a profit.

> **Labor time** measures the number of hours worked; it does not measure how much work gets done, since there are many different levels of work effort (intensities of work) possible.

To put it another way, what the employer purchases in the labor market is *labor time*. This is, as we have noted, not the same as the actual *labor* that has to be performed in order for production to occur. To make a profit the employer must somehow ensure that a certain amount of labor is forthcoming during the labor time that has been purchased. Thus, the employer must be able to *extract work* from his or her employees.

The worker may see the situation from a different perspective. The wage specified in the employment contract will be paid. But the amount of work actually performed by the employee is variable. The amount actually performed depends on such factors as how much the employee likes the work, how resentful he or she may be about having to do the work, and how easy it is for the employer to observe how much work the employee is doing. Depending on such factors as these, the employee may choose to do more than, as much as, or less than the amount of work the employer wants. There are, of course, methods available to the employer for ensuring that employees work hard, and we will examine some of these in the next chapter. The point here is that unless employees want to do as much work as employers expect from them, there will be a conflict between employees and employers over the level of work effort (*e*).

One reason for the conflict is that employees do the work and employers end up owning what is produced. What would happen if workers owned the materials, machines, and other capital goods used in production? Instead of having to work for someone else, the producers would then have the option of working for themselves. They might do this as independent commodity producers—for example, just as people in the "old middle class" in the U.S. did, and to some extent still do, before the capitalist way of organizing production became dominant (see Chapter 7).

Alternatively, people wishing to work for themselves could organize a worker owned and controlled enterprise (see box "Own Your Job. Elect Your Boss" in Chapter 6, pp. 137–138). Whether as independent producers or as worker-owners, self-employed workers would own not only the capital goods used in production but also the product produced. For this reason they would have an interest in working hard or at least making sure that their workmates did not shirk. Many observers have found that people who work for themselves—and enjoy the fruits of their own labor—work harder than do people who are paid an hourly wage by an employer.

However, as we saw in Chapter 7 (see Table 7.3), the great majority of people who work outside the home in countries such as the United States are not independent producers or owners of their own enterprises. Rather, they work for employers other than themselves in order to earn a wage or salary. As a result, conflicts between employees and employers are widespread in most highly developed economies today.

The process by which an employer transforms labor time into productive work is referred to as *extraction* rather than *exchange* because it occurs under different circumstances from those that prevail in a market. In order to control labor processes and extract work from their employees, employers organize work hierarchically, with CEOs at the top, vice presidents under them, and a chain of command extending all the way down to the actual production workers. The various layers of bosses, foremen, and supervisors constitute the *management* of a firm, and the management structure is what enables employers to extract work from the workers. Because of the central role played by management in the labor extraction process, the relationships between employers and their employees are sometimes referred to as "labor-management relations."

> The **extraction of work from workers** is the process of transforming the labor time that an employer has purchased into work done.

Of course, management does more than just extract work from employees. Managers and executives must organize the hiring of workers, coordinate the firm's operations, make decisions about investment, and arrange for the output to be sold. Even with respect to labor processes, managers do more than organize the extraction of work. In labor processes involving highly specialized tasks and a complex division of labor there is a need for coordination of the employees. In a shoe factory, for example, the leather cutters might need to be told how much and what shapes of leather the stitchers need. On the other hand, many labor processes do not require bosses for coordination. It is possible, to take the same example, that the stitchers in a shoe factory might be able to communicate their leather requirements directly to the leather cutters.

It is interesting to note that the need for a hierarchical power relationship to ensure the transformation of an input into output exists for only one input commodity, labor. When a ton of steel or a new machine is purchased, one can predict exactly how these inputs may be transformed into output. A ton of coal of a given type and quality will yield a certain number of BTUs of heat in a particular furnace. Steel and machines have no wills of their own; when the boss commands, they do not resist. There certainly does not have to be a line of unemployed machines standing outside the factory gate to get the machines inside to work hard!

In the old slogan "a fair day's work for a fair day's pay," both parts of the equation are subject to bargaining and conflict. The wage (the "fair day's pay"), of course, is bargained

An **incomplete labor contract** is a contract (explicit or implicit) between an employer and a worker that is incomplete in the sense that it specifies the wage rate but does not specify the exact tasks to be performed or the amount of effort to be provided by the worker.

A **contract specifying work to be done** is an agreement between an employer and a worker that specifies payment for actual work activities instead of for work time.

A **piece rate** is a form of wage payment in which a worker is paid for each unit of output produced instead of for work time.

over and contracted for when the worker is hired (or when the union-negotiated contract comes up for renewal). What constitutes a "fair day's work," however, cannot be written into a contract and is determined only in the subsequent work process. We say that the labor contract is incomplete to stress that while it covers the wage (which as a result can be enforced by the courts), it does not cover the amount of effort to be provided by the worker (which must therefore be determined by a daily clash of wills between the two parties).

To avoid the management problem, why do employers not offer to pay only for actual work rather than for potential work? Why would they not pay for labor rather than for labor time? One way to do this would be for the employer to specify carefully in the employment contract all the tasks to be performed. The employee's pay could then be withheld until the tasks were completed. This approach can be used for simple tasks such as having one's lawn mowed and the grass raked up; in such a situation, the pay can be withheld until the tasks are completed. Another method is the *piece rate* system in which an employee is paid a certain amount of money (say, $0.50) for each piece of work completed (sewing a collar on a shirt, for example). In both methods (and there are others), the employer would be paying for actual work, not potential work, and there would be no need for command-type relations.

Although the detailed contract and the piece rate methods of labor compensation are sometimes used, there are real problems with each of them. For one thing, the contract method is inflexible and costly. Imagine trying to write a contract specifying every activity required to do a job. It might take a lengthy document just to list all the tasks. And even a lengthy contract cannot list all the things an employee must do to contribute to profits. Indeed, an effective form of employee protest is to "work to the book," that is, to follow work rules and regulations exactly, with the result that production is significantly slowed down.

An additional problem with the contract method is deciding whether the stipulated amount of work has been done. It is easy enough to see whether or not a lawn has been mowed. In many situations, however, determining exactly how much work (and of what type and quality) each employee has done can be a costly process. And who is to decide? Both employees and employers would have their own reasons to argue about it. Moreover, every time a new task needed doing or the employee needed to be reassigned, a new contract would have to be written.

The piece rate system is flawed for some of the same reasons. One problem is that it cannot be applied in many labor processes. If an employee is to be paid a piece rate, it must be possible to separate his or her productive contribution from that of each of the other employees; where many employees cooperate in a complex production process (say, in an automobile factory), it is not possible to separate one employee's contribution from another's, so the piece rate system cannot be applied. Another difficulty is that a given piece rate can be paid only when an employee performs a certain task over and over again. In more complicated jobs there would have to be a different piece rate for every task. Finally, there remains the issue of the pace of work. It may seem that an employer should not care whether a piece rate employee works fast or slow (since the employer is paying for output, not time). In fact, however, this is not the case. To the extent that employees use capital goods such as buildings that their employer must pay fixed amounts for, the speed of the employees' work will affect the profit rate of the enterprise. (This is because higher rates of output will allow fixed costs per hour of labor to be reduced.) In all such situations, employers will have an interest in making sure that their employees work rapidly—and, accordingly, the labor extraction problem will remain.

For these reasons and others, neither the contract method nor the piece rate pay system is widely used today. The contract system (in the form of subcontracting) is sometimes used to hire electricians, plumbers, and other highly skilled workers, but otherwise its application is very limited. Piece rates have been more extensively employed, especially in manufacturing and also in some agricultural jobs. Use of the piece rate system is, however, still quite limited. In general employers have found that other ways of organizing the labor process are more profitable since they make it easier to transform labor time into work.

Workers, however, typically resist efforts to make them work faster than they consider to be a normal pace. In response to unreasonable demands, they may develop individual strategies of resistance, join together in informal work groups, or openly resist through their unions. We will explore workplace conflicts in more detail in the next chapter.

The Labor Market, the Wage, and the Intensity of Labor

A **labor market** is a market in which workers sell their labor time (not work itself) in return for a wage; employers are the demanders, and workers are the suppliers of labor time.

Employers hire workers, and workers find jobs through the *labor market.* In this market employers are the demanders of labor time, workers the suppliers of it. As in all markets, *voluntary exchange* exists; no one is obligated or forced to sign a contract. But in the workplace, employers must exercise some power over employees in order to be able to extract work from them. Their ability to do this is rooted in the distinct character of the labor market. The labor market does not work like other markets. It shares some features with other markets but differs from them in fundamental ways.

The labor market shares with other markets the features of competition and conflict. As we saw in the previous chapter, commodity markets involve greater or lesser degrees of competition. Labor markets are generally very competitive: there are usually many demanders for labor time and, in most cases, many suppliers of it.

Whereas commodity markets are battlegrounds in which corporate giants fight for competitive advantage vis-à-vis consumers or other firms, the labor market is a different kind of battleground. Here the conflict is between employers and workers, and the issues are wages, the intensity of work, workplace safety, and often other things such as health and retirement benefits.

A key weapon in the employer's arsenal is the capacity to provide—or take away—the job that the worker needs. Although employers and workers both need each other, employers can often last longer without workers than workers can get by without employers. As Adam Smith said, "In the long run, the workman may be as necessary to his master as his master is to him, but the necessity is not so immediate" (see box "The Bargaining Power of

Owners and Workers" on p. 292). If a worker happens to be in that small fraction of the labor force that is organized in unions, he or she may be supported for a short time by a union strike fund, but such funds run out fairly quickly. Thus, workers have to depend primarily on their jobs for income (out of which they may pay union dues), but employers often have other means of support (such as property income from other investments).

It is the ownership of capital goods by employers—and the lack of such ownership by workers—that gives the former a degree of control over the livelihoods of the latter. There are two reasons for this. First, one of the prerogatives flowing from their ownership of capital goods is that employers have the right to grant access to or exclude others from entering the property they own. This prerogative is what gives employers the right to hire and fire workers. Second, because workers generally do not own the tools and materials they would need to go into business for themselves, they do not have this option. Hence, they must work for an employer in order to make a living.

> The **cost of job loss** is the loss of income a worker experiences as a result of quitting or being laid off from a job.

Since the owners of capital goods have the right to hire and fire workers, employers have control of the income of employees. The loss of income that may result from the loss of a job is termed the *cost of job loss* (or *cjl*). How much control an employer will have over an employee depends in important measure on the magnitude of the cost of job loss facing an employee. The higher the cost of job loss the more power an employer will have over an employee. If an employee has access to another source of livelihood, such as an alternative job possibility or a generous unemployment insurance benefit, the cost of job loss will be lower, and the employer's power will be reduced. Employers and employees thus have a direct conflict of interest over the things that determine how high the cost of job loss will be—for example, the availability of jobs and the availability and level of unemployment insurance.

Other factors may also influence the conflict between employees and their employers. If employees belong to a labor union, for example, employers may have to deal with strikes or work slowdowns. Of course, employers cannot convincingly threaten to fire employees who have skills that are essential to the firm's operation and that can be taught to other employees only with considerable cost. It is also the case that variations in the wage rate and the pace of work will often be limited by widely shared values concerning what is fair to expect employees to do and employers to pay. Such values are termed *work and pay norms*.

Another important influence on the pace of work and the rate of pay is the government. Government policies can set minimum wages, establish standards for health and safety conditions in workplaces, and put in place other rules such as those affecting the rights of employees to organize and join unions. There is hardly a market that is not affected in some way by government policies, and the labor market is no exception. (The relationship between government and the economy is considered at length in Chapter 19.)

In most situations, however, it is the cost of job loss (*cjl*) that is the most important factor in determining the intensity of work (*e*) and the wage rate (*w*)—and the magnitude of this cost can be estimated with at least a degree of certitude. If an employee is laid off, she will face a period of unemployment and, if the necessary requirements can be met, will receive unemployment insurance payments from the government amounting to some fraction of her previous wage. While unemployed she will naturally search for a new job and, presumably, will find one at some point. Suppose, for the moment, that she eventually gets a job at the same wage as before. Given this sequence of events, we can express the cost of job loss as follows:

$$cjl = (ww - ui)(ud) \tag{12.3}$$

where cjl = the cost of job loss

ww = the previous weekly wage (after taxes)

ui = the available weekly unemployment insurance benefit

ud = the expected number of weeks (duration) of unemployment

The meaning of Equation 12.3 is that the cost of job loss (cjl) will be equal to the amount by which the previous weekly wage (ww) exceeds the current weekly unemployment insurance benefit (ui) multiplied by the expected number of weeks (duration) of unemployment (ud). When the worker finds another job, assuming that he or she is able to find another job, the cost of losing the previous job will actually be known.

Consider, for example, a laid-off worker who had been earning a wage of $400 a week, after taxes. If this worker is able to qualify for unemployment insurance—eligibility requirements vary from state to state but generally one must have worked for the same employer and earned a certain amount in the previous year in order to qualify—he or she will be entitled to receive, say, a $200 unemployment insurance check every week. (The amount of the benefit is always considerably less than the previous wage had been, and in the U.S., for example, the government normally pays such benefits for only 26 weeks.) If the worker is able to find another job in 20 weeks (five months), the cost of job loss in this case may be calculated as follows:

$$cjl = (\$400 - \$200)(20) = \$4,000$$

If the worker had not been laid off, he or she would have had an annual income (after taxes) of $20,000. With the 20-week spell of unemployment, however, the same worker's annual after-tax income would be $16,000.

Recall that in the preceding example we assumed that the laid-off worker was able to find another job at the same wage level. One problem with this assumption is that in the U.S., for instance, the manufacturing sector has been shrinking (see Chapter 7). Hence, workers who have lost manufacturing jobs have often had to take lower-paying jobs in the expanding service sector. (See box "Globalization: Winners and Losers," pp. 179–180.) For these workers—and, indeed, for all workers who cannot find new jobs at comparable or better wages—the cost of job loss is much greater than Equation 12.3 would suggest. The total cost of job loss would have to include not only the income lost during the period of unemployment but also the ongoing difference between the workers' old and new wage levels.

Our simple example underestimates the cost of job loss in other ways, too. The first is that because of stringent eligibility standards and a 26-week maximum duration of unemployment benefits, a majority of the people who are unemployed at any given time in the U.S. do not actually receive unemployment insurance payments. Thus, for most unemployed people the net weekly loss of income ($ww - ui$) will be exactly equal to whatever their previous weekly wage (ww) had been. Second, many workers will have lost more than the wage itself: any health insurance benefits that may have been provided by their previous employer will also have been lost. Finally, there are the noneconomic costs of being unemployed, including inconvenience, anxiety, and personal trauma. A person's self-esteem is closely tied to the holding of a job. Thus, even after the trauma of being fired has worn off, an unemployed person may feel that he or she is not retaining the respect of others. (See box "Unemployment Hurts" in Chapter 16, p. 442.)

How much is it worth to an employee to avoid the cost of job loss—even if we consider only the economic cost? One way to determine this is to ask how low the current job's wage would have to go before the employee would not care if he or she lost the job. At such a wage level the employee might well decide to quit. Before deciding to quit, however, the employee would have to estimate the cost of job loss, taking into consideration such things as the length of time it might take to find another job, the potential cost of being unemployed for that period of time, and the possibility that the new job might pay less,

> The **fallback wage** is the wage at which an employee has no preference for keeping his or her current job as opposed to being fired or quitting; it varies with the employee's income prospects in the absence of the current job.

have less generous health benefits, or be less satisfying than the current job. Hypothetically, at least, the employee would be willing to take a pay cut of a certain amount at the present job in order to avoid the estimated cost of job loss. For example, an employee currently earning $8 an hour might be willing to continue working until his or her wage had been cut to $5 an hour, at which point keeping the job would no longer be better than being fired or quitting. The lower wage, $5 an hour, is called the employee's *fallback wage.* The fallback wage reflects, from the standpoint of the employee, his or her prospects (including the cost of job loss) in the absence of the current job. Thus, the fallback wage is a measure of the opportunity cost to the employee of keeping his or her present job.

If the employer offers only the fallback wage, the employee will not care whether he or she is kept on or fired. At this point the cost of job loss (*cjl*), as seen by the employee, is zero. And since employees being paid the fallback wage will not mind being fired, they can be as lax or as diligent on the job as they please. (When offered any wage lower than the fallback wage the employee will not bother coming to work and nothing will be produced.) If an employer is paying just the fallback wage and attempts to elicit more work effort (*e*) by threatening to fire the employee, it would have no effect. At $5 an hour the employee would be likely to respond to any threat of dismissal by saying to the employer "Make my day!"

If an employer wants to get more than the minimum amount of work out of an employee, he or she will have to pay more than the fallback wage. Only with a higher wage will the employee have a stake in keeping his or her job. The higher the wage, the more the employee will have to lose, and the more likely it will be that he or she will work as hard as asked to by the employer. Responding to both the stick (of possible unemployment) and the carrot (of the higher wage), the employee will work hard. Indeed, it is possible that the employee will work harder and produce more output with each successive increase in the wage.

This presents the employer with the following dilemma: In the situation described, the wage paid must be higher than the fallback wage to motivate the employee to work hard—and getting the employee to work hard is, of course, essential to making profits. But the payment of a higher wage will increase one of the main costs that must be subtracted from sales revenues in calculating profits. What wage should the employer offer? He or she must balance the (positive) effect of the higher wage on the intensity of work (*e*) against the (negative) cost of paying a higher wage rate (*w*).

An employer can resolve the dilemma of what wage rate to pay by focusing on the objective of minimizing unit labor cost (*ulc*). Minimizing unit labor cost will have the effect of maximizing the profit rate (see the explanation of this relationship in the paragraphs following Equation 12.1 earlier in this chapter). By focusing on this variable, then, the employer can determine exactly the wage that will maximize the firm's rate of profit.

Recall, from Equation 12.2, that unit labor cost (*ulc*) is equal to the wage rate (*w*) divided by *z*, the output per hour of work. Recall also that output per hour (*z*) is equal to the intensity of labor (*e*) multiplied by the efficiency of labor (*f*). Therefore we know that $ulc = w/z = w/ef$.

How, then, can the employer achieve the objective of minimizing unit labor cost? In seeking the answer to this question we can assume that the efficiency of labor (*f*) will not change when the wage rate changes. This is a reasonable assumption to make because *f* depends on the quantity and quality of the equipment with which the employee is expected to work, and this will not change in the period of time under consideration here. Hence, the direction of change in unit labor costs (*ulc*) will depend entirely on the relationship between the wage rate (*w*) and the level of work effort (*e*).

Imagine a situation in which an employer is paying just the fallback wage, represented by w̲. In this situation the employer may be able to gain by raising the wage rate. Why? As the wage is increased there may be a more than proportional increase in work effort (*e*) and hence a fall in *ulc* and a rise in the profit rate. Moreover, in this type of situation the employer might continue to gain by offering a higher and higher wage rate. This would continue as long as each increase in the wage caused the intensity of labor (*e*) to go up more than proportionally with the wage rate (*w*). As long as this is the case, the increases in *w* will cause the denominator of w/ef to rise faster than the numerator (because *e* is increasing faster than *w*), and this will drive down unit labor cost (*ulc*). The result, of course, will be a rise in the firm's rate of profit.

There is a catch, however. Because there is a limit to how hard a person can work—and because the harder one works, the closer one comes to this limit—the additional amount of effort put out by a worker in response to increases in his or her wage will eventually tend to become smaller and smaller as this "effort limit" is approached. At some point it will no longer be in the interest of the employer to continue raising the wage. When raising the wage does not bring about an increase in work effort large enough to reduce unit labor cost, the profit-seeking employer will stop raising the wage: at this point raising *w* will not increase the profit rate. Exactly at this point the employer will be paying the wage that maximizes the firm's rate of profit. (Some economists call this the "efficiency wage.")

To illustrate the analysis presented here we offer the following (hypothetical) case study. Imagine that a firm has, through years of observation, found that its employees produce more output per hour as their wage rate goes up. Output rises because employees work harder at higher wage rates, responding to both the "carrot" of being paid more for each hour of work and the "stick" of having, at higher wage rates, more to lose (the potential cost of job loss). The observed relationship between the wage rate and the workers' output per hour in our hypothetical firm is presented in Table 12.1.

It is assumed here that nothing will be produced unless the wage is at least $5 an hour. This is the fallback wage. But as the wage rate goes up, employees will put more effort into what they are doing, and output per hour (*z*) will rise. As predicted, however, the *increases*

TABLE 12.1 The Wage-Output Relationship	
Wage Rate	**Output per Hour**
$5	20 units
$6	34 units
$7	46 units
$8	56 units
$9	64 units
$10	70 units
$11	74 units
$12	76 units

in output per hour obtained for each additional dollar of wage paid, while quite substantial at low wage levels, are likely to become smaller and smaller as the wage goes up. We can think of such increases in output as *marginal* changes in the output per dollar of wage paid.

> The **labor extraction curve** describes for each wage rate the intensity of work that the worker chooses to perform.

A curve showing how much output per hour (z) will be produced at each possible wage rate (w) is termed a *labor extraction curve*. Such a curve can be drawn on a graph with output per hour (z) on the vertical axis and the wage rate (w) on the horizontal axis. This is done in Figure 12.1. The most important aspect of a curve like this is the *slope* at each point along it. The slope is not z divided by w. Rather, it is the rate of increase of z at each point on the curve. This can be thought of as the *marginal increase* in *output per dollar of wage paid*.

Consider the situation when our hypothetical firm is paying just the fallback wage of $5 an hour (represented by $\underline{w}$ on the horizontal axis of the figure). If the firm raises the wage to $6 an hour, output per hour will rise by 14 units, a marginal increase in output per dollar of wage paid of 14 units per dollar. But if the firm happens already to be paying $11 an hour and raises the wage to $12, output per hour will rise by only 2 units, a marginal increase in output per dollar of wage paid of only 2 units per dollar. This is because, for the reason mentioned earlier, wage increases gradually become less effective in calling forth additional output per hour.

In the process described here there are two separate decisions being made. The first, made by the employer, is the choice of the wage (w) to offer. The second, made by the worker, is the choice of a particular intensity of labor (e), or, in other words, how hard to work if paid the wage the employer is offering. Employers reason that paying higher wages will enable them to extract more work from their workers, and this knowledge can be represented by a labor extraction curve such as the one in Figure 12.1.

The declining power of wage increases to bring about additional output from workers (declining marginal increases in output per dollar of wage paid) is also reflected in the labor extraction curve. As noted earlier, the declining slope of this curve reflects the fact that workers can increase their output more easily when they are not working too hard but less easily when they are already working hard. So given the fact that f (the output that can be produced with any given amount of work effort) is constant, the shape of the labor

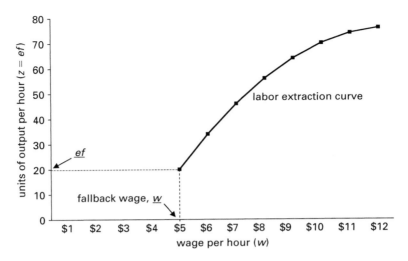

FIGURE 12.1   The wage and the intensity of labor.   The *labor extraction curve* in this figure shows the amount of output per hour (z) that will be forthcoming at each wage rate (w) offered. Output per hour is measured on the vertical axis. Since $z = ef$, the vertical axis also measures *ef*. And since f (the efficiency of labor) is constant (no changes in the technology of production are possible in the short time frame of this analysis), any movements up or down the vertical axis are due entirely to changes in the intensity of labor (e).

The horizontal axis indicates the hourly wage rate (w). The *fallback wage* is $\underline{w}$ and, at this wage rate, the worker's work effort (e) is at its minimum. This is how hard the worker will choose to work if the wage rate sinks to a level ($\underline{w}$) at which he or she is indifferent between keeping the job and losing it. When the wage is at its fallback rate and work effort is at its minimum, the corresponding rate of output per hour (z), shown on the diagram as $\underline{ef}$, will also be at a minimum. Thus, if the employer offers a wage equal to $\underline{w}$, the worker's work effort will be $\underline{e}$ and the rate of output will be $\underline{ef}$.

Increases in the wage rate above its fallback point call forth more output per hour: the levels of output per hour represented by points on the labor extraction curve become higher and higher as the wage rises. But beyond a certain point (the point at which the labor extraction curve becomes horizontal), wage increases do not result in additional output per hour because the worker is already putting out as much effort as possible.

extraction curve will be determined by the amount of work effort (e) that is forthcoming at each wage rate (w).

As one can see in Figure 12.1, the labor extraction curve rises steeply at first and then becomes flatter and flatter with each increase in the wage rate. Since the curve in this figure is based on the numbers presented in Table 12.1, it is again showing—this time graphically—a declining marginal rate of increase in output per dollar of wage paid.

If a profit-maximizing firm has the labor extraction data given in Table 12.1 and represented in Figure 12.1, what wage rate will it offer to pay? We can begin to answer this question by referring to Equation 12.2, the equation showing that unit labor cost (*ulc*) is equal to w/z. But in addition we need to keep in mind the fact that the rate of profit will be

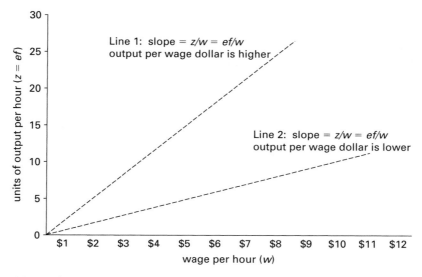

FIGURE 12.2   Output per dollar of wage paid.   This figure shows rays drawn from the origin (at 0 on the vertical axis and $0 on the horizontal one) at various slopes. A ray has the same slope at all points along it, and in this case the slope of the ray indicates how much output per hour can be achieved for each dollar of wage paid. Mathematically, the slope of a ray in this figure is z/w (output per hour divided by the wage rate). The greater the slope of the ray, the higher will be the hourly output per wage dollar paid.

maximized when unit labor cost is minimized. Putting these two ideas together, we can see that *maximizing the rate of profit* (minimizing *ulc* and w/z) requires *maximizing z/w* (output per hour divided by the hourly wage), or ef/w (because $z = ef$). In other words, the firm will be maximizing its rate of profit when this ratio, z/w (or ef/w), is as large as possible. This makes sense intuitively because for any given level of f, the firm's profit will be maximized when the wage being paid is such that each employee is putting out the maximum possible amount of effort (e) for each wage dollar being received. When this is the case the firm will be getting as much output per hour (z) as it can get for a dollar of wage.

The logic of this analysis can be illustrated by referring once again to the labor extraction curve portrayed in Figure 12.1. Now, however, we need to add something to the wage-output graph in this figure. First, we need to draw a new graph, Figure 12.2, with the same two variables, output per hour and the wage rate, on its axes (z or ef on the vertical axis and w on the horizontal axis). On this graph we draw a straight line—any straight line—starting from the origin (the point where the vertical axis meets the horizontal axis) and going out into the graph. In the language of mathematics, such a line is called a "ray." The slope of such a ray will be z/w or ef/w, and because it is a straight line it will have the same slope at any point on it. The economic meaning of this is that the slope of the line—however we draw it—will indicate the average output per dollar of wage paid (z/w): it will show how much output per hour (z) the firm can get for a dollar of wage at any particular wage rate (w) on the horizontal axis.

In Figure 12.2 a *steep* ray (such as line 1) indicates that for each dollar of wage paid there will be a *large* amount of effort exerted (*e*) and output produced per hour (*z*). Thus, a profit-maximizing employer will prefer to be on a steeper ray than on a less steep one. Line 1 in Figure 12.2 shows that the employer can get 15 units of output for a wage rate of $5, whereas on line 2, the employer would get only 5 units of output for the same wage. But the employer cannot choose just any point in the graph. He can only choose one that is *on the labor extraction curve*.

There is another reason why a profit-maximizing employer will prefer to be on a steeper ray than on a less steep one. We saw in Equation 12.2 that unit labor cost (*ulc*) is defined as the wage cost per unit of output, *w/z*, and this happens to be the *inverse* of the slope (*z/w*) of any ray in Figure 12.2. This means that the steeper the ray (the higher its slope), the *lower* will be unit labor cost, which makes sense because we know that any effort on the part of an employer to *maximize profit* will at the same time be an effort to *minimize unit labor cost*.

Figure 12.3 allows us to see that a profit-maximizing employer will choose to pay the wage *w** because this is the wage where the labor extraction curve touches—is tangent to—the steepest possible ray. The slope of this ray will be greater than that of any other ray drawn to a point on the curve. Recall that the labor extraction curve tells us how much output is produced at each wage rate. By contrast, the slope of the straight line from the origin (the ray) tells us the amount of output per wage dollar paid. At any point on the labor extraction curve other than the one where it is tangent to the steepest possible ray, the corresponding wage rate (*w*) will not be one at which *ulc* is minimized and profit maximized. Profit will be maximized only at *w**.

Consider point A on the labor extraction curve in Figure 12.3, where 34 units of output are produced at the wage of $6 an hour. What is the output per wage dollar at this point? We can answer this question by drawing a straight line (line 1) from the origin to the 34 unit/$6 wage point on the labor extraction curve and examining the *slope* of the line from the origin. If we do this, we will find that the slope of the line is not as steep as it could be. The numerical value of the slope is approximately 5.7 (34 divided by 6), meaning that 5.7 units of output are being produced for each dollar of wage paid. But what is important is the relative flatness of the line. It is significant that this line is flatter than other lines that can be drawn to other points on the labor extraction curve. This means that the profit rate of the firm could be raised (*ulc* could be reduced) if the employer would decide to move further up the labor extraction curve by paying higher wages (moving to the right on the horizontal axis). In this case the slope of a ray to the curve would be greater (steeper), *ulc* would fall, and the rate of profit would rise.

Observe what happens if the employer decides to increase the wage rate to $7 an hour. With this increase in the wage, the output of the firm rises to 46 units (see Table 12.1), and the slope of the line drawn to the corresponding point on the labor extraction curve becomes steeper. Its numerical value increases to approximately 6.7, meaning that 6.7 units of output are being produced for each dollar of wage paid. The employer has clearly gained by paying his or her employees more, but the rate of profit has not yet been maximized.

If the employer continues to raise the wage rate, extracting more output per hour with each increase in the wage, he or she will find that the firm's rate of profit will be maximized at point B in Figure 12.3, when the wage rate is $9 and the output per hour 64 units. Here,

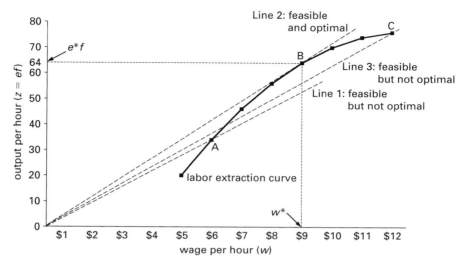

FIGURE 12.3   The labor extraction curve and profit maximization.   This figure brings together the concepts illustrated in Figures 12.1 and 12.2. As noted, the labor extraction curve tells us how much output there is at each level of the wage rate (above the fallback wage), and rays indicate how much output per hour a dollar of wage buys. A profit-maximizing firm will prefer to be on a steep ray because the steeper the ray the more output there is per wage dollar paid. Also, unit labor cost will be lower with a steeper ray since *ulc* is defined as w/z, the *inverse* of the slope of a ray (z/w). But no firm can be on a ray that lies *above* the labor extraction curve. This is because the labor extraction curve indicates the range of *possible* outputs that can be achieved by paying wages above the fallback wage. The objective of the profit-maximizing firm, then, is to find the ray that has the steepest slope (highest output per hour for a dollar of wage paid) while still touching the labor extraction curve. The optimal ray from the standpoint of the firm is the one that is tangent to the labor extraction curve at point B in the figure. Since the wage corresponding to point B is the one toward which the profit maximizing will gravitate, it is labeled w^*, and e^*f will be the output per hour when w^* is the wage. Thus, w^* is the wage rate at which unit labor cost will be minimized and profit maximized, with e^*f as the corresponding rate of output per hour.

To check that the ray passing through point B does represent the maximum profit rate and the minimum possible unit labor cost, note that line 1 in the figure (drawn to point A on the labor extraction curve) has a lower slope (z/w) than line 2. It therefore represents a higher *ulc* (w/z) and a lower rate of profit than line 2. Similarly, line 3 (drawn to point C on the labor extraction curve) also has a lower slope than line 2, so it, too, is associated with a higher *ulc*. In fact, then, line 2 (passing through point B on the labor extraction curve) represents a lower *ulc* and a higher rate of profit than any other such line drawn from the origin to a point on the labor extraction curve. Hence, the particular combination of w^* and e^*f represented by point B offers the employer the lowest possible unit labor cost and the maximum rate of profit.

the line drawn from the origin to the labor extraction curve (line 2) is as steep as it can possibly be, and this ray will be tangent to the labor extraction curve. The wage rate here is w^* because it is the wage toward which a profit-maximizing employer will tend to move.

What will happen, though, if the employer is not well informed and continues to raise the wage? Point C on the labor extraction curve represents the situation in which the wage rate is $12 an hour and the rate of output is 76 units per hour. The slope of the line drawn to this point (line 3 in Figure 12.3) is less steep than the line to point B (line 2). Accordingly, the rate of profit at this wage rate is lower than the one corresponding to the wage of $9 an hour. This shows (again) that if the employer pays any wage that is lower or higher than $9 an hour, the firm's rate of profit will not be maximized. Clearly, then, the profit-maximizing employer will offer a wage of $9 an hour.

Notice an important fact about w^*: it is higher than $\underline{w}$ (the fallback wage). In other words, at a wage rate of w^* an employee would rather keep his or her job than lose it. This is fairly obvious, but there is another implication of this fact: there may be other workers outside the factory gate, on the other side of the office door, or even within the same firm who would also like to have—but cannot get—the job that is paying w^*. Such workers might be among the unemployed, or they might be people who are currently employed in less desirable jobs who would be happy to take the job paying w^* that would open up should the employee currently holding it quit or be fired.

Our analysis of profit maximization can be confirmed by amplifying the information introduced in Table 12.1. In Table 12.2 the same information is presented, but another column is added to indicate the output per dollar of wage corresponding to each wage rate (w). Table 12.2 shows that output per dollar of wage (and the resulting profit rate) is maximized when the employer pays $9 an hour and the output per dollar of wage paid is 7.1 units. The table also shows that output per dollar of wage rises until this point is reached and declines from then on.

Further insight can be gained by looking at how unit labor cost is higher or lower depending on what wage the firm chooses to pay. Table 12.3 supplements information already presented in Tables 12.1 and 12.2: it has an additional column showing that unit labor cost falls and then rises as the wage rate is increased from the fallback wage to $12 an hour. The minimum unit labor cost (14.1 cents per unit) is achieved, predictably, when the wage rate is $9 an hour. This is, of course, not surprising because, as explained earlier, unit labor cost

TABLE 12.2 The Wage Rate and Output per Dollar of Wage Paid

Wage Rate	Output per Hour	Output per Dollar of Wage
$5	20 units	4.0 units/$
$6	34 units	5.7 units/$
$7	46 units	6.6 units/$
$8	56 units	7.0 units/$
$9	**64 units**	**7.1 units/$**
$10	70 units	7.0 units/$
$11	74 units	6.7 units/$
$12	76 units	6.3 units/$

TABLE 12.3	The Wage Rate and Unit Labor Cost		
Wage Rate	**Output per Hour**	**Output per Dollar Wage**	**Unit Labor Cost**
$5	20 units	4.0 units/$	0.250 $/unit
$6	34 units	5.7 units/$	0.176$/unit
$7	46 units	6.6 units/$	0.152$/unit
$8	56 units	7.0 units/$	0.143$/unit
$9	**64 units**	**7.1 units/$**	**0.141$/unit**
$10	70 units	7.0 units/$	0.143$/unit
$11	74 units	6.7 units/$	0.149$/unit
$12	76 units	6.3 units/$	0.158$/unit

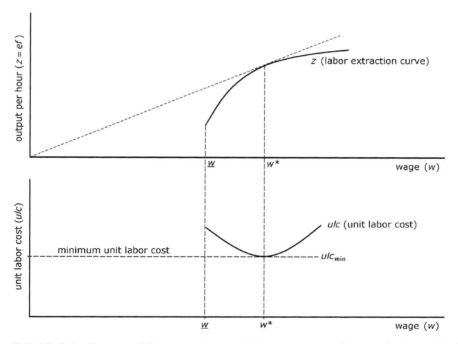

FIGURE 12.4   The wage, labor extraction, unit labor cost, and profit maximization.   This figure illustrates in a different way the idea that the point of tangency between the labor extraction curve and a ray with the slope z/w is indeed where unit labor cost is minimized. The figure makes the same point graphically as was made with numbers in Table 12.3. Both Table 12.3 and this figure show that ulc is minimized when the wage rate is w^* ($9 in the table and the example set forth in the text).

is minimized when the profit rate is maximized, but the additional data presented here will allow us to draw a figure—Figure 12.4—illustrating our analysis of profit maximization in a different way.

The profit-maximizing behavior derived using Tables 12.2 and 12.3 can be confirmed graphically. In Figure 12.4 the curve representing unit labor cost in the lower panel reaches its minimum point at the same wage rate (on the horizontal axis) at which the labor extraction curve in the upper panel touches the line from the origin that has the highest possible slope. So this figure confirms in yet another way what wage rate a firm should offer if it wants to maximize its rate of profit. It shows that the profit-maximizing wage is the one at which two conditions prevail simultaneously: the labor extraction curve (upper panel) is tangent to the ray with the highest possible slope, and the unit labor cost curve is at its minimum point (bottom panel). As before, this wage rate is $9 an hour.

This chapter has focused on the relationship between the wage rate (w) and the intensity of labor (e), assuming that *the wage rate is the only influence on the intensity of labor*. This simplifying assumption will be abandoned in the next chapter. But first there are three additional implications of the labor extraction curve analysis that should be considered.

First, if an employer can find ways to increase the supervision of his or her employees—say, by watching them more closely or by hiring others to do so—unit labor costs may be reduced. Of course, this can occur only if the costs of increased supervision are more than offset by gains resulting from greater effort on the part of the employees. In recent years it has become common for employers to use surveillance cameras or other technology to monitor the performance of their employees on the job (see box "On the Road Again" in Chapter 13, p. 329). An increase in supervision may bring about an *upward shift* of the labor extraction curve. Such a shift would show that employees, being supervised more closely, put out more work effort (and output) at each level of the wage rate. As noted, however, there are many labor processes, especially those requiring intellectual skills or entailing significant quality considerations, for which increased supervision may not raise e and may even lower it.

A second implication of the labor extraction curve analysis can be seen in Figure 12.5. Any increase in the worker's fallback wage will shift the entire labor extraction curve *to the right,* meaning that for any given wage, work effort and therefore output will be lower. This might happen, for example, if it became easier to find a new job at a higher wage or if there were to be an increase in the level or availability of unemployment insurance benefits.

Figure 12.5 shows what happens when there is an increase in unemployment insurance of $1 per hour. An increase in unemployment insurance by this amount shifts the entire labor extraction curve to the right by $1 because the employer has to pay an hourly wage $1 higher than before to extract any given amount of work. The fallback wage rises from $5 an hour ("old $\underline{w}$" in the figure) to $6 an hour ("new $\underline{w}$") because workers are now willing to be fired (or quit) at $6 an hour, the lost dollar being made up for by the extra dollar of unemployment insurance. And now the most profitable wage from the employer's standpoint is higher ($10 rather than $9), as indicated by "new w^*" in the figure. Moreover, the new profit-maximizing wage involves a higher unit labor cost, since the ray to point B has a lower slope than the ray to point A. (In all of the figures in this chapter a ray with a lower slope represents a higher unit labor cost.) This example shows why U.S. employers, working through their lobbyists in Washington (see Chapter 19), usually oppose any increase in unemployment insurance.

The third implication of the analysis has already been briefly mentioned: wages can be too *low* even from the standpoint of the employer. Had the employer offered a wage less than w^*, unit labor costs would have been *higher,* not lower, and this would have meant

FIGURE 12.5   **Effects of more unemployment insurance.**   With an increase in the level or availability of unemployment insurance benefits, the worker's fallback wage rises and the entire labor extraction curve *shifts to the right.* This is because the cost of job loss at every wage rate is reduced. Since the improved unemployment insurance benefits have more of a cushioning effect, employers must offer higher wages to extract the amount of work that they had previously been able to extract at lower wage rates. Note that to get the same rate of output (e^*f) as before, the firm must pay a wage of $10 an hour in place of the $9 an hour that it used to pay. As a result, there will be an increase in the unit labor cost at the new profit-maximizing wage offer (new w^*): the slope of the line drawn to point B is lower than that of the line drawn to point A.

reduced profits. This is because the savings in wages would have been more than offset by the lower level of work effort (e). For this reason unemployed workers cannot succeed in getting jobs by going to employers and offering to work for less than w^*. Such offers will be refused—and the unemployed workers turned away—because employers will see that the lower wage level will mean higher, not lower, unit labor costs. This conclusion is important because it supports Keynes's argument (see Chapter 4) that in a capitalist economy there will generally be a certain amount of *involuntary unemployment*—that is, unemployment that cannot be reduced even if the unemployed workers are willing to lower their wage expectations.

The fact that unemployed workers cannot get jobs by offering to work for less than the going wage rate means that they will remain unemployed. It also means that the wage will not fall even if there is excess supply in the labor market: the unemployed workers will find no takers for their labor. Indeed, neither the worker nor the employer, acting alone, can alter this state of affairs.

Once the wage rate (w^*) and the corresponding level of effort (e^*) have been reached, they will exist in what many economists call a state of equilibrium. Recall that in Chapter 8 an equilibrium was defined as a situation in which there are no forces tending to change the situation other than accidental ones or ones coming from outside the economic system ("exogenous" forces). In Chapter 8 the equilibrium involved the price and quantity of beer; here it is the relationship between a level of work intensity and a wage rate, but the concept is the same in both cases.

On the one hand, the employer controls the wage rate (w), but once w^* has been found, he or she will have no interest in changing it. This, of course, is because w^* is the wage that maximizes the employer's profit rate. The worker, on the other hand, is the one who chooses how hard to work, thereby determining e^*. But here again, once the work effort e^* is being put out, there will be no incentive for the worker to change his or her work pace, for e^* is the level of work effort associated with the wage rate w^*, and this is the equilibrium wage rate. Most likely, the worker would prefer to work less hard and get paid more, but this option is not available. Similarly, the employer would be happy to get more work for less pay, but this is not an option, either. Thus, given a particular labor extraction curve, neither the worker nor the employer will have an incentive to move away from the w^*/e^* equilibrium point. And not even an unemployed person offering to work for a wage lower than w^* can change the situation: as we have seen, such a person will not be offered a job. These, then, are the factors that make the particular situation, in which the wage rate is w^* and the work effort level is e^*, an equilibrium.

There is, however, an important difference between the beer market of Chapter 8 and the labor market analyzed here. In equilibrium the beer market clears: there is neither excess supply nor excess demand. But in the labor market the supply of labor is greater than the demand for it—there is a positive rate of unemployment—even when the market is in equilibrium (there are no forces in the market pushing it to change). Thus, we have equilibrium *without* market clearing.

The two markets are also different, obviously, because people are not beer. But the difference in this regard is more complex than the simple statement of it suggests. When a person pays a dollar for a bottle of beer, he or she gets what is paid for and has the right to use it in any way that is legal. The buyer can send the beer down his or her throat, pour it down a drain, or splash it on someone else's face.

When an employer pays $10 or $15 dollars to purchase an hour of someone else's labor, however, he or she does not end up with something that is totally under his or her control. The reason is that the employment contract by itself will not get the worker to work hard. It is, as we have said, incomplete. Rather, what the employer possesses is authority over the labor time of another human being, and that other human being may or may not want to work as hard or as carefully as the employer desires. An employer pays a wage that is above what an unemployed person would be willing to work for because the higher wage is a way of gaining enough control over the employee to ensure that the expected amount and quality of work will be forthcoming. Nobody pays more for a beer than he or she needs to. The beer is not going to resist being consumed; the labor, however, must be extracted.

While the labor extraction curve illustrates some important aspects of the conflict over work and pay, no simple model can capture the complexity of relationships between employers and employees. To understand the work process more fully, we must look at the firm as a social organization, one made up of flesh-and-blood people whose behavior cannot easily be summarized in a graph. This is the subject of the next chapter.

SUGGESTED READINGS

Harry Braverman, *Labor and Monopoly Capital* (New York: Monthly Review Press, 1974).

Jeremy Brecher, *Strike* (San Francisco: Straight Arrow Books, 1972).

Michael Burawoy, *Manufacturing Consent* (Chicago: University of Chicago Press, 1981).

Richards Edwards, *Contested Terrain: The Transformation of the Workplace in the 20th Century* (New York: Basic Books, 1979).

Louis Putterman, *The Economic Nature of the Firm: A Reader,* 2nd ed. (Cambridge: Cambridge University Press, 1996).

CHAPTER 13

Technology, Control, and Conflict in the Workplace

In 2001 a U.S. coal miner working underground in a "longwall" mine dug 5.2 tons of coal in an average work hour. For this work the miner, if he was fortunate enough to be in the miners' union, was paid about $18 per hour.

Coal miners in the U.S. often work more than 40 hours a week, working additional hours "overtime" to increase their pay and put money in the bank to live on during periods of unemployment. If a miner worked an average of 40 hours a week in a particular year, however, his income for the year, before taxes, would be about $37,500. After taxes (which would vary with such factors as income earned by other members of his family), he might be left with no more than $30,000 to live on. And, as everyone knows, a coal miner's job is dirty, demanding, and dangerous.

Of course, the coal miner would like to be paid higher wages, and he would certainly like his job to be safer. More miners are killed on the job in the U.S. every year than are police officers.

The coal companies, however, have a different viewpoint. They rightly see that making a miner's job safer would require additional investment in safety equipment and, most likely, a slower pace of work. With existing machinery, making coal mining safer would mean slowing the pace of work to allow additional safety procedures to be instituted, and this would result in less output, which, in turn, would mean less revenue coming in and reduced profit. Paying higher wages would also reduce profits by adding directly to costs.

If miners were paid $18 to dig 5.2 tons of coal each hour, the unit labor cost of a ton of coal would be $18/5.2, or $3.46 per ton. The market price of a ton of "longwall" coal in 2001 was about $24. At this price and labor cost per ton, the coal companies, on average, were left with more than $20 per ton for replacement of worn out machinery (depreciation), costs of supervision, new investment, and profit.

As we have seen, however, making the work of a coal miner safer requires either additional investment or a reduction in the pace of work. Either way, if other variables remain unchanged, making the work of a coal miner safer or more remunerative will raise unit labor costs and reduce profit rates. For this reason the interests of the miners and those of the coal companies are often directly opposed.

The fundamental clash of interests between miners and companies has turned the nation's mining regions into centers of intense, bitter, and continuing conflict. Indeed, the conflict has often turned violent. In the 1870s, for instance, the state of Pennsylvania hanged 19 "Molly Maguires"—militant miners seeking to form a then-illegal union. In 1914 the Colorado militia broke up a strike at a Rockefeller-owned coal mine: militiamen killed 21 people, including 11 children and 2 women, in what came to be called the Ludlow Massacre. In Kentucky, "Bloody" Harlan County has witnessed decades-long violence between coal companies and miners. Even today union organizers face frequent harassment, intimidation, and threats of violence.

Violence is the most extreme but not the most common expression of the continuing conflict between employers and their employees. Short of violence, how are the conflicting interests of capitalists and workers resolved? How do employers go about extracting work from employees? What do workers do to defend their interests? This chapter investigates these questions.

The main idea of this chapter is that *every capitalist labor process necessarily combines both a social organization and a technology of production; these two elements shape and are shaped by the conflict between employers and employees over wages and the intensity and conditions of work.*

This idea is expressed in six key points:

---

1. Employers organize workplaces in ways they believe will maximize the profits of their firms. The *social organization of the labor process* derives from the employers' search for profits and, in particular, from their effort to extract work from their employees. Employers establish *systems of control* in the workplace to enhance their ability to extract work.

2. Known and available *technologies of production* impose certain constraints on how employers can organize production. Decisions about which of the available technologies are actually used and what kinds of new technologies are developed are shaped by the conflict between workers and employers.

3. Employers and employees seek to advance their *conflicting interests over wages and over the intensity and conditions of work* within the context of the social organization and technology of the labor process. Workers defend their interests in a variety of ways—for example, by attempting to organize themselves in unions—and employers likewise develop strategies for maintaining or improving their profit rates—occasionally, for instance, by exploiting racial and gender-based tensions among workers.

4. Employers seek to organize labor processes in the most *profitable* way, but this need not be the most *efficient* way. Efficiency is different from profitability, and when there is a

conflict between the two, the ongoing competition among capitalists pushes them to seek out profitability, not efficiency.

5. *Markets and hierarchies* are mutually reinforcing elements in the capitalist profit-making process. Although sometimes thought of as alternate and opposing methods for organizing social relations, they are, in fact, both necessary for the capitalist firm.

6. An alternative to the capitalist firm is the *democratic firm,* owned by its employees and managed by those elected by the employees. Despite many advantages, democratic firms often find it difficult to survive because of the risks involved and the difficulty of raising the necessary capital.

As in previous chapters, the process of profit making is central to understanding the topics discussed here, for it is profit making that gives rise to the conflict between employers and employees. Sometimes this conflict appears to be a conflict between a single employee and his or her boss; sometimes the conflict is evident in the bargaining or struggle between a firm's owner and groups of employees or all the employees of that firm; and in other cases the conflict becomes a more general one between important groups in both the working class and the capitalist class.

THE SOCIAL ORGANIZATION OF THE WORKPLACE

Employers try to organize workplaces in ways that will produce the highest profit rates. Their goal (profits) is no different here than in their other activities, such as the ones discussed in Chapters 10 and 11. How employers organize the workplace and their immediate relations with their employees affects their profit rates most directly with respect to the intensity of work (e), the efficiency of work (f), and the wage rate (w). As we saw in previous chapters, if an employer can raise e or f and/or reduce w, other things remaining unchanged, his or her profit rate will increase.

The most fundamental way that employers and their supervisors, managers, and foremen exercise power in the workplace, as we have seen in the previous chapter, is through their right to hire and fire. The replacement worker standing outside the plant gate keeps the employee inside the factory working hard.

> A **lockout** occurs when an employer locks the workers out of the workplace and closes down production in order to force workers to accept the employer's terms for wages, work pace, or other working conditions.

If all or most of the employees in a workplace do not perform up to the level demanded by the employer—for example, suppose they belong to a union and they resist speedup in their work—then the employer has a bigger problem. Still, several possibilities are open to him or her. For example, an employer can take measures that will provoke a strike and then lock the employees out. In such a situation the employer can close down the plant, lock the gate, wait for the employees to feel the financial pinch, and hope that they will eventually agree to work on the employer's terms. This is referred to as a *lockout.*

Alternatively, a business owner can move his or her plant to a place where employees will be more compliant. For example, the legal and

MAKING STEEL: THREE VIEWS

WORKER

Somebody built the pyramids . . . pyramids, Empire State building—these things just don't happen. There's hard work behind it. I would like to see a building, say the Empire State, I would like to see on one side a foot wide strip from top to bottom with the name of every bricklayer, the name of every electrician, with all the names. So when a guy walked by, he could take his son and say, See, that's me over there on the forty-fifth floor. I put the steel beam in. Picasso can point to a painting. What can I point to? . . . Everybody should have something to point to.

We handle forty to fifty thousand pounds of steel a day. . . . You can't take pride anymore. Its hard to take pride in a bridge you're never gonna cross, in a door you're never gonna open. You're mass producing things and you never see the end result of it.

—Mike Lefevre, steelworker, quoted in Studs Terkel, *Working*
(New York: Pantheon Books, 1972).

PERSONNEL MANAGEMENT CONSULTANT

I can say, without the slightest hesitation, that the science of handling pig iron is so great that the man who is fit to handle pig iron as his daily work cannot possibly understand that science. . . . The man who is fit to work at any particular trade is unable to understand the science of that trade without the help and cooperation of men of a totally different kind of education.

—Frederick Winslow Taylor, founder of "scientific management," 1912 testimony
before a congressional committee as reported in F. W. Taylor,
Scientific Management (New York: Harper, 1947), p. 49.

CAPITALIST

The duty of management is to make money. Our primary objective is not to make steel.

—David Roderick, former chairman of the board, U.S. Steel (now USX),
as interviewed in the film *The Business of America* (1984).

political climate has historically been much more hostile to unions in the U.S. southern states, New Hampshire, and the Rocky Mountain states than it has been in the industrial Midwest and most of the Northeast. Similarly, a company facing a strong union can move—or threaten to move—to a foreign country where wages are lower and unions are weak or even banned. The point is that capitalists can *run away* to a more business-friendly location than the one they happen to be in currently. Because they own the capital goods

A **runaway shop** is a workplace that an employer has moved from an area where workers are strong to an area where workers are weak in order to escape having to meet workers' demands.

Parallel plants are plants owned by the same employer and producing the same product but located in different geographical regions in order to weaken the workers' ability to bargain collectively.

The **social organization of the workplace** refers to the way in which jobs are defined, work tasks assigned, supervisory power delegated, and other social aspects of the workplace organized.

A **hierarchy** is an organization of power in which superiors have command over subordinates.

A **system of control** is an employer's strategy or method for governing the workplace to facilitate the extraction of work from the workers.

they are free to invest (build new plants) or disinvest (let existing plants run down) as they please and where they please. The *runaway shop* leaves its former employees without jobs, and even the threat of relocating may scare employees into accepting the employer's terms.

A third strategy big firms can use in organizing the workplace is *parallel plants,* plants located in different parts of the country or the world making the same product. GE, for instance, makes clock motors in both Massachusetts and Hong Kong. With parallel plants the employer can tell employees in one plant that unless they agree to low wages and/or high work effort, the company will switch production to the other plant. Then it tells the same thing to the employees at the other plant. Unless the employees in these widely separated plants can somehow act jointly (a very difficult task), they will be left in a weak bargaining position.

Employers' methods of maintaining the upper hand all derive from an owner's right to say who works and who does not work in his or her workplace. Private property, as we have seen, includes the right to exclude others from its use, and private ownership of the capital goods used in production brings with it the right to hire and fire. Of course, lockouts, runaway shops, and parallel plants impose costs on business owners as well, so they may choose not to use these means of driving workers. Then, too, each employer must offer job conditions that allow him or her to fill the number of jobs needing to be filled. If other employers offer workers a slower pace of work or better pay, this may limit what the employer can do unless there is a large pool of unemployed workers. Finally, some workplaces, especially those providing services, may not be movable (a Boston hotel owner with striking employees cannot move the hotel to Hong Kong and still service the Boston customers). These considerations constrain an employer's actions.

Employers' powers are further enhanced by the *social organization of the workplace*—the way in which jobs are organized. Generally, a firm's organization is hierarchical. *Hierarchy* in the workplace builds on the right to hire and fire, but it also allows for more finely tuned control. Employers cannot effectively threaten to fire workers every day and every hour for trivial or routine problems as well as important matters. Such threats, if used too often, no longer remain believable, and even if, to make the threats believable, employers do frequently fire employees, the high turnover on the job may well disrupt a firm's operations. Successful employers have developed a series of other incentives—rewards and penalties—to supplement and reinforce their ultimate power of dismissal.

Employers organize the workplace by imposing a whole social organization on the labor process. They define what the different jobs and responsibilities will be, they say what the work rules and workers' rights will be, they establish the powers of supervisors and foremen, and they formulate the rewards for good work and the penalties for the lack of it.

Such a social organization can be thought of as a *system of control.* It is the means by which the employer governs the workplace. A capitalist

HARDBALL: OWNERS, WORKERS, AND TAXPAYERS IN THE GLOBAL ECONOMY

Before deciding to expand its operations in Dublin, Virginia, Volvo Trucks North America (an affiliate of the Swedish multinational firm) asked the Commonwealth of Virginia to share some of the costs. Since Volvo has plants all over the world, Virginia needed Volvo more than Volvo needed Virginia. So the state was anxious to sweeten the deal, and it eventually came up with a package of tax breaks and other incentives for the company that would cost the taxpayers of Virginia $54.2 million. In return, the firm promised to hire 1,277 additional workers over the next six years. (The state was thus paying Volvo more than $42,000 per job created!) However, negotiations with the United Auto Workers (UAW) for hiring the new workers ran into trouble: Volvo wanted the workers to work for wages 30 percent below the former starting wage, and to wait 10 months before getting health insurance. On January 13, 1999, the members of the union local rejected the proposed contract.

Volvo's counter-offer to the workers was not a compromise but an ultimatum: accept the new contract or we will hit the road. Volvo's manager visited two plants in Mexico to look into alternative locations. It was no secret in Dublin that manufacturing workers in Mexico are paid, on average, less than one-fifth of the $12 per hour average wage for production workers at the Dublin Volvo plant. The workers were given two days to vote the ultimatum up or down. On January 29th they swallowed their pride and agreed to Volvo's terms.

The same story, with a different ending, unfolded for the 548 workers in a plant in Dover, Delaware, owned by Dresser Industries, a division of Halliburton, the multinational corporation that provides oil field services. The workers made gas station pumps, and most were represented by the UAW. They went on strike in July 2000, when their contract expired and negotiations over the new contract broke down. At issue were pensions and health insurance. Halliburton and Dresser were already considering relocating (possibly to Mexico), and the strike strengthened their inclination to move. After a round of offers and counter-offers was rejected, Halliburton announced the closing of the Dover plant on October 13, 2000.

In bargaining, the one who can walk away without suffering costs is in the driver's seat. When union members bargain with their employers, it makes a big difference if they are up against a Volvo, a Halliburton, or some other footloose firm on the one hand, or an employer that would find it difficult to relocate, such as a hotel, restaurant, hospital, or public school system.

Firms are becoming footloose, as they build offices and plants around the world. As a result, unions are less effective in raising wages in these industries. A recent study calculated the effect of globalization on labor union bargaining

Continued . . .

power. To measure globalization in a particular industry, the author calculated the number of workers employed in other countries by U.S. firms in that industry compared with the number of workers in the U.S. in that industry. By this measure, the more global industries include drugs, tobacco, cars and trucks, and soaps, cleaners, and toiletries.

The study found that unions are less able to raise wages the more global an industry is, and when an industry becomes more global, union bargaining power—measured by its effect on the wage—declines. For example, in the global industry of soaps, cleaners, and toiletries, wages are lower by about a fifth compared to wages in a hypothetical industry that is otherwise identical but has no global employees.

Sources: Jeffrey P. Carpenter and McAndrew Rudisill, "Fairness, Escalation, Deference and Spite: Strategies Used in Labor-Management Bargaining Experiments with Outside Options," *Labour Economics*, no. 309, 2003, pp. 1–16; Minsik Choi, "The Threat Effect of Capital Mobility on Wage Bargaining," in Pranab Bardhan, Samuel Bowles, and Michael Wallerstein, eds., *Globalization and Egalitarian Redistribution* (Princeton, N.J.: Princeton University Press, 2005); U.S. Department of Labor, Bureau of Labor Statistics, "International Comparisons of Hourly Compensation Costs for Production Workers in Manufacturing, 2002" Release 03-507, September 26, 2003.

workplace is almost never organized democratically; it is run from the top down. And since the reason the employer organizes work is to produce output commodities in order to make a profit, the system of control is designed to enhance the employer's ability to extract work from workers.

Employers have developed several different systems of control within the firm. Each one reflects a distinct strategy within the workplace for extracting work or for reducing unit labor costs. Among the many ways of controlling workers, the following are widely used.

Simple Control

> **Simple control** is a system of control that focuses on the supervisors' personal exercise of workplace rewards and sanctions to maintain the work pace.

One employer strategy for achieving low unit labor costs is to pay wages as low as possible, barely above $\underline{w}$, and to use supervisors and foremen to bully, charm, cajole, motivate, or drive employees to work hard. This strategy, *simple control,* or the *drive system,* aims at keeping wages as low as possible while forcing employees to give high levels of effort. To the degree that such a strategy is successful, it will minimize unit labor cost, *ulc* (see Equation 12.2 in the previous chapter).

A small textile mill or a McDonald's restaurant illustrates simple control. The firm pays wages very near the legal minimum, and the wages by themselves provide little incentive for employees to do more than whatever minimal effort will keep them from being fired.

How do such employers get their employees to work hard? The employer (or the hired manager) personally directs the work, oversees the employees, evaluates their work, and rewards or punishes them accordingly. For instance, the employer may reward a diligent worker by assigning him or her to a better shift or a more pleasant job. Alternatively, the employer may punish an employee deemed to be underperforming by cutting back on his

SIMPLE CONTROL: THE FAST FOOD INDUSTRY

Every year Americans spend more than $100 billion on fast food, which equals a third of the national expenditure on defense. With a work week that is much longer than the average for workers in industrialized countries (see Figure 20.1, p. 534), there is a heavy premium put on time in our society. As a result, fast food, available quickly and cheaply, has become an almost universal feature of the busy American lifestyle.

It is not surprising, then, given the centrality of time to the industry's existence, that the labor process involved has its origins in the assembly line systems adopted by American manufacturers in the early 20th century. In life behind the counter, tasks are broken up into small, repetitive actions that require little or no skill but that can maximize the speed of the output. Typically, fast food restaurants have a target speed that suggests that meals should be delivered in a given number of seconds.

The raw materials arrive precut, packaged, sorted, and frozen so as to minimize the time it takes to gather the materials together for production. The points of production are located so as to maximize the speed at which food products can be processed to the point of consumption. Managers are usually responsible for coaxing, cajoling, and forcing the speed of production to match the demand of consumers arriving.

The fast food industry is the largest minimum-wage employer in the U.S., and those who work in the fast food industry are the lowest paid workers in the U.S. except for migrant farm workers. The owners of the industry are strongly antiunion and have adamantly opposed bills that sought to increase the minimum wage (see box "A Living Wage," p. 373). Many fast food companies have been taken to court in suits that allege that their workers have been made to work overtime for no pay. The typical worker quits or is fired every three to four months and has no benefits and no health insurance. Until recently fast food companies characteristically employed teenagers, but as some teenagers have begun to shun such jobs, firms have begun to hire more poor migrant laborers and the elderly.

The next time you are upset at how long it is taking your burger to arrive, look again behind the counter. Life under the drive system may not be as easy as it seems.

Sources: Eric Schlosser, *Fast Food Nation* (New York: Harper Perennial, 2002); Dirk Johnson, "For Teenagers, Fast Food Is a Snack, Not a Job," *New York Times,* January 8, 2001, p. A1.

or her hours or giving him or her a dirty or unpleasant job to do. Unspoken, the threat of being fired is continually kept in the employees' minds.

Bosses may be petty and tyrannical or they may motivate workers by charm and the force of their personalities. Either way, the result is to reduce unit labor costs by driving employees to put out greater work effort. Fast work and low wages make for a low *ulc.*

Technical Control

An alternative strategy aims at achieving the same result by different means. Given that, as stated in Equation 12.2, $ulc = w/(ef)$, it continues to be the case that paying the lowest possible wages (w) will keep the numerator in this equation down. With *technical control,* however, the work effort (e) part of the denominator is increased not by ever-present supervisors prodding employees but, rather, by the pace of the machinery in the production process. The machinery itself impels the employees to work rapidly. Equally important, with a machine-paced production process it is easier to keep tabs on who is or is not working up to par. Those who consistently fall behind can be singled out and disciplined or fired.

> **Technical control** is a system of control that incorporates a work pace designed into the machinery of production.

For example, on a car manufacturing assembly line it is the speed of the line itself that sets the pace of work. The typical automobile assembly line in the U.S. turns out 60 cars per hour, so in this case each worker must do his or her job in the 60 seconds before the next chassis comes along. Here the boss need not stand over the worker to instruct and exhort since the line itself sets the pace. Similarly, in the call centers described in Chapter 1, the computer software that handles the routing of incoming calls can also be set up to record how much time it takes employees to dispose of their calls. Using this technology supervisors can monitor the speed with which the operators deal with their callers (perhaps reading computer printouts at the end of the day) and then tell the employees to work faster or be fired.

Technical control does not eliminate the need for supervision. What happens if an employee refuses to "obey" the line? In assembly line or other machine-paced factories or offices, bosses are still required for performing the tasks of evaluating employees and disciplining those who fail to meet the expected standards. Still, the pace of work is controlled, in the first instance, by the physical technology of production.

Neither does technical control resolve the issue of who will determine the pace of the assembly line (or any other machine-paced system of production). When employees are weak and not unionized, the boss may determine the line or machine speed without consulting the employees. (This type of situation was humorously but accurately portrayed in the Charlie Chaplin film *Modern Times.*) When employees are highly organized, on the other hand, bargaining between workers and employers often sets the pace of the line. Even with the pace set by bargaining, however, the line imposes the collectively agreed-upon speed of work on each individual employee.

Thus, with technical control the employer's power to design and implement the physical technology of production provides another form of command. The employee is harnessed to a line or machine that runs at a given pace, and he or she must keep up with that pace.

Bureaucratic Control

> **Bureaucratic control** is a system of control that uses job ladders, seniority rewards, and other organizational incentives in order to extract work from workers.

Bureaucratic control is yet another strategy for achieving low unit costs. In a bureaucratic firm the employer pays relatively high wages and, more significantly, pays wages that increase in a predictable way with an employee's seniority. Workers who remain employed by the firm can expect to earn higher wages in the future and perhaps receive other benefits as well.

TECHNICAL CONTROL: THE MEATPACKING INDUSTRY

In 1961 two young executives, Currier Holman and A. D. Anderson, started a firm called Iowa Beef Packers (IBP). Over the course of the next three decades, the company was at the forefront of what became known in the meatpacking industry as the "IBP revolution." The revolution in question consisted of a massive and far-reaching overhaul of the production process in the meatpacking industry.

At the time the meatpacking industry was concentrated in the Midwest and West (with Chicago being its historical center). Meatpacking itself was considered a very good industrial job, involving a high level of skill and a low turnover rate. The industry was unionized and commanded relatively high wages for workers in the industry.

IBP began its revolution by putting its slaughterhouses in rural America, away from the urban centers where labor unions were traditionally stronger and more organized. In the late 1960s, it eliminated its labor union entirely, thereby allowing for the unhindered imposition of its central innovation: a mass production system employing a deskilled and unorganized workforce.

The mass production system was based on the assembly line common to other industries. Livestock were placed on an assembly line on which they were slaughtered and dismembered according to a preset system. Workers' tasks became very simple, regimented, and repetitive. What was once a skilled job involving the conception and carrying out of a complex task (the slaughter, carving, and packing of an animal) was broken down into smaller chores that could be done by relative novices. The jobs have names like knocker, sticker, shackler, rumper, first legger, knuckle dropper, and navel boner, names that attest to both the brutality as well as the partial, deskilled nature of the work. As an IBP executive said of the system: "We've tried to take the skill out of every step."

The combination of an assembly line and deskilled labor mean that the pace of work (*e*) is directly controlled by the firm. In the 1960s a meatpacking plant could pack 50 animals an hour. Today, giant plants in rural areas can pack 400 animals or more an hour. At peak times the assembly line moves so fast that workers slaughter up to one cow every six seconds. The cows zip past the knockers and stickers six times as fast as cars on assembly lines pass their welders.

The meatpacking industry nowadays is heavily concentrated and profitable, with the top four companies controlling 85 percent of the market. The condition of workers, on the other hand, has deteriorated considerably. The turnover rate is 400 percent (i.e., on average, workers quit or are fired after 3 months), and real wages are a third lower now than 40 years ago, adjusting for inflation. Many workers are unskilled immigrants who have few other opportunities in

Continued . . .

the labor market. Given the speed of work, injuries are commonplace. Each year one in three of America's 43,000 meatpacking workers goes to a doctor with an injury or work-related illness, more than three times the national average—one of the reasons why it is sometimes called the most dangerous job in America.

Source: Eric Schlosser, *Fast Food Nation* (New York: Harper Perennial, 2002).

How can high and rising wages *reduce* unit labor costs? They do so if they can bring forth additional work effort (e) at a greater rate than the rate at which wages (w) are increased. In this case the ratio between w and ef that determines ulc will fall (f being constant), driving down unit labor costs and, if nothing else changes, raising the rate of profit. (See Figure 12.2 and the discussion surrounding it in Chapter 12.) Thus, rising wages can lower ulc if there is an even greater increase in work effort. This is the "carrot" approach: with high and rising wages employees will like their jobs enough, will want to keep them enough, or will feel positive enough toward their employers to put out increasing amounts of work effort.

However, there is also an important "stick" in bureaucratic control. The only way an employee can obtain a better job in a firm is by gaining seniority. But as the employee gains seniority, the greater will be his or her "investment" in the particular job. Moreover, along with the additional seniority and the elevated wage comes a higher cost of job loss in the event that the employee is fired. Thus, the longer he or she works in a particular firm, the bigger the stick becomes!

Usually firms that rely on this strategy establish elaborate work rules and procedures to set up sophisticated incentives. Instead of being simply an employee, a worker is hired for a particular job, which has a job title and for which a formal job description exists. The duties and tasks of the job are outlined, and the employee's performance is measured against the prescribed duties.

Job ladders link together a series of related jobs, in which a worker over the years climbs from one job to another and gains access to jobs higher on the ladder only by first succeeding in the lower jobs.

A firm will use *job ladders* to organize a system of bureaucratic control. Job ladders link together a series of jobs, each job being one "rung" on the ladder. For instance, the jobs of file clerk, general clerk typist, secretary, private secretary, and executive secretary may be linked together on one job ladder. The employer hires job applicants from outside the firm for the bottom rung (say, file clerk), and employees are then encouraged to work their way into higher jobs on the ladder by superior performance in the lower jobs. Thus, the way an employee obtains a better job is by working hard in his or her present job. This is another carrot (positive incentive) to bring forth more e.

However, merely setting up job ladders and writing job descriptions does not guarantee that they will be effective. Hence, neither bureaucratic control nor technical control eliminates the need for bosses. Bosses still supervise work, direct workers, and evaluate worker performance. They also determine who gets promoted or fired and who gets rewarded or disciplined. But in firms with bureaucratic control, bosses rule by

TABLE 13.1 Employers' Systems of Control

System of Control	Wages	Supervision
Simple control	Low, with few rewards for long service	Direct observation by bosses
Technical control	Low, with few rewards for long service	Pace of work machine-controlled: laggards machine-detected; less direct supervision
Bureaucratic control	High, rising with longer service	Promotion and firing by a "rule of law" within the firm

Because there is a conflict of interest between employers and employees, a firm's ability to make profits depends on its having an effective system of control over the labor process. The three systems of control represented in this table are used in varying degrees in different industries. Over the years they have been used to a greater or lesser extent in the economy as a whole.

"applying company policy." Since they are merely enforcing company rules, the power relations between them and their underlings are embedded in the organizational structure of the firm and, as a result, are more hidden.

The varieties of control discussed here—simple control, technical control, and bureaucratic control—are but different institutional forms of authority, or command, relations within firms. They are summarized in Table 13.1. Each workplace and firm will have its own blend of forms of control. Yet despite the multitude of control systems—there are many that we have not discussed—they all exist to achieve a single goal for the employer: to reduce unit labor costs.

TECHNOLOGY AND THE LABOR PROCESS

A *technology,* as we defined it in Chapter 5, is a relationship between the inputs and outputs of a labor process. Technical change is a change in the relations between inputs and outputs. Technical change—the introduction of new types of machinery or changes in the method of production, for example—will be brought about by an employer whenever a new technology is available, affordable, and likely to raise the profit rate.

Technical change can raise the profit rate by reducing unit labor costs (ulc). In particular, technical change may raise the efficiency of labor (f) or make possible, as we will see, a greater intensity of work (e) or lower wages (w). Each of these would, other things being equal, reduce unit labor costs and raise the profit rate. Employers, then, are likely to see technical change as a potentially fruitful source of higher profits.

At any particular time known and available technologies impose limits, or constraints, on what employers can do. For instance, existing technology may dictate that at least three tons of iron ore are needed to produce one ton of iron; no matter how much the employer desires to reduce the use of this input, the current technology will not permit it.

Similarly, existing technologies place limits on the social organization of the workplace. For example, some production processes, an assembly line, for example, may require many people to work together, whereas other jobs, such as those of telephone operators, may involve mostly individual tasks. And while some jobs may require few skills and little experience, the current technology may dictate that other jobs require employees with extensive skills and much experience. In these ways current technology limits how an employer can organize work.

The limits set by known and available technologies, however, are usually quite wide. The same product (for example, basic steel) is often produced by different firms using different systems of control, different proportions of skilled and unskilled workers, different relations between bosses and workers, and different wage structures. Most automobile factories involve highly fragmented jobs on assembly lines, whereas other car manufacturers use "teamwork" methods. Telephone operators' jobs may be insecure, dead end, poorly paid, and characterized by heavy-handed supervision (simple control), or they may be entry-level positions on a job ladder leading to more secure and highly paid positions (bureaucratic control).

So while technology places some limits on the organization of work, many different ways of organizing the workplace are often compatible with the existing technologies. And, of course, the existing technologies are constantly changing. Moreover, the constraints imposed by any given technology are likely to become less important as time goes on because the employer's need to impose a system of control shapes the way technology develops.

Employers who seek technical change that will raise their profit rates will naturally be more interested in some types of technical change than others. For instance, suppose a business owner is about to invest in research to develop a new technology. The firm's research staff proposes two projects. The first project would develop a new technology that promises greatly to reduce input materials (m) but would simultaneously reduce the employer's ability to extract work (e) from employees because it would require that workers work on their own, making supervision difficult. The second project promises to reduce m somewhat less but does not reduce the employer's control of the work pace (e) at all. The business owner will be more likely to fund the second project.

Thus, the employer's need to extract work from employees can influence the direction of technical change. Indeed, the process of technical change is "biased": employers, trying to maximize their profits, encourage some types of technical change (those consistent with maximum extraction of work) while discouraging others (those that threaten their power).

The technologies that are known and available at any particular time are the products of a continuing process of technical change. But if this process is biased, the technologies existing at any particular time will reflect, in part, this bias. Not only has existing technology been shaped, but future technical change will also be shaped, by the social organization of production and by employers' need for power in the workplace in order to maximize their profits.

CONFLICT IN THE WORKPLACE

As we have seen, employers and employees bargain over the work pace (e), wages (w), and the conditions of work. The workplace, with its combination of social organization and technology, is the principal arena for their struggle. (They may also contest these matters elsewhere, for instance by attempting to get the government to regulate the safety or other conditions of work.)

MANAGEMENT RIGHTS

It is agreed that the Management of the Employer has the sole and exclusive rights, duties and responsibilities to direct the operations of the Employer and its working forces. Such functions of Management include, but are not limited to, the exclusive rights to determine the products to be manufactured or to be produced, schedules of production, methods and processes, place of manufacture, and acquisition of all materials and parts; to hire, suspend, discharge for just cause, or relieve employees from duty because of lack of work or other legitimate reasons; to introduce new or improved production methods or facilities; to determine the manner and methods by which time studies are made; and [to determine] *the formula used for establishing* [piece] *rates. The above rights are not all inclusive but enumerated by way of illustration the type of rights which belong to the Employer, and all other rights, powers, functions, or authorities which the Employer had prior to the signing of this Agreement, are retained by the Employer except those which have been specifically abridged, delegated, or modified by this Agreement or any supplemental Agreements that may hereafter be made by the Employer and the Union. It is further understood that all matters so reserved shall not be the subject of grievances and shall not be arbitrable.*

—Management rights clause of the 2002 collective bargaining agreement between the Fort Smith Division of the Whirlpool Corporation and P.A.C.E. (Paper, Allied Industrial, Chemical and Energy Workers International Union)

In their conflicts employers and employees use quite different means to defend and promote their interests, or, stated differently, they exercise quite different kinds of power. First, the employers have established the battle's terrain, for it is they who hire the employees for—and organize the production process in—a given workplace. While employees, individually or collectively, may choose to withdraw from this terrain (the workplace) by quitting their jobs or going on strike, they never, or rarely, have the opportunity to organize production themselves.

Because employers, not employees, organize production, employers have the power to initiate action or change circumstances. Workers, on the other hand, are inherently in a defensive position, defending their interests in reaction to the initiatives of employers. This difference in position is evident in such employer strategies as running away or establishing a system of control. It is also evident in the way that technical change affects workplace conflict.

Technical Change and Workplace Conflict

Technical change may affect workers in three principal ways. First, it may raise the productivity of their labor without increasing their workload. In Equation 12.2 in the previous chapter, f is used to signify the "efficiency of labor," in other words, the amount of output produced per unit of work effort. The particular value of f reflects the technology currently in use, because it is this technology that determines how much output can be produced with any given amount of work. As can be seen from Equation 12.2, this first type of technical change lowers unit labor cost by raising f, and it does this even if the amount of work effort (e) being put out remains unchanged.

Consider the following example. A worker in a shoe factory, using a simple electrical stitching machine and working at a comfortable pace, can produce two pairs of shoes in an hour. Hence, z (output per hour) $= 2$. If we assume that the amount of effort being put out by the worker is normal for this type of job, we can say that $e = 1$. Then, since we know that $z = ef$ and $z = 2$, we find that f, the efficiency of the shoe stitcher's labor, is 2. Now suppose that the owner of the shoe factory makes an investment and provides a computer-controlled stitching machine for the employee to work with (in place of the simple electrical machine). This technical change means that the way of making shoes has changed, so that even if the employee works no harder (e is still 1), he or she can now produce 5 pairs of shoes per hour. Accordingly, this technical change—a change in the way of making shoes—raises f from 2 to 5.

Technical change that raises f can reduce unit labor costs without requiring either that employees work harder or that they take pay cuts. Hence, when this type of technical change is a possibility, there is no inherent conflict between workers and their employers.

Nevertheless, even in this situation employer and employee may still fight over f. For example, inadequately paid employees in a particular firm may see that one way of pressing for higher wages is intentionally to obstruct production, thus reducing f. Although this type of action results in no direct benefit for the employees, it does impose costs on their employer. If these costs are greater than the wage increase being sought by the employees, the tactic may induce the employer to agree to the wage increase.

To take a specific example, if the employees in an automobile manufacturing plant feel aggrieved, they may occasionally drop a soda bottle into the door of a car as it passes by them on the assembly line. Since this will create a rattle that must be eliminated before the car can be sent to a dealer, additional employees (more work effort) must be assigned to disassemble the doors and remove the bottles. This kind of "sabotage" reduces the "efficiency of work" (f) because more work is now required to produce the same number of cars. Similarly, when employees "accidentally" spoil materials or break tools during production, this, too, slows down production and reduces f. The Industrial Workers of the World—the "Wobblies"—a militant labor union that organized unskilled workers between 1905 and 1920, captured the idea in a famous slogan: "Good pay or bum work!"

Technical change can affect workplace conflict in a second way. It can provide a means for employers to *speed up* work (raise e), thereby reducing unit labor costs. The most obvious way that employers can use technology to control employees is with technical control and machine pacing of work. When auto companies introduced the assembly line, it immediately gave the employers a new way to control and speed up work. Today, technology enables employers to read employees' e-mail, to listen to their phone conversations, to record the time it takes operators to deal with callers, to keep track of how rapidly typists are typing, and, in the case of drivers (see box "On the Road Again"), to monitor the speed and location of company vehicles. All these capabilities enable employers to get more or better work from their employees.

Speedup is an effort by an employer to increase the pace of work.

BLOWOUT: "GOOD PAY OR BUM WORK!"

Firestone recalled 14.4 million of its tires in August 2000 due to construction flaws resulting in "tread separations" likely to cause blowouts. A month later the National Highway Traffic and Safety Administration announced that Firestone tires were under investigation in cases involving 271 fatalities and more than 800 injuries. As the extent of the public relations debacle became clear, the world's largest tire manufacturer—officially Breakstone/Firestone since its purchase in 1988 by a giant Japanese tire producer—considered dropping the Firestone name. But this was more than an embarrassment to the company. It was a mystery worthy of a modern day Sherlock Holmes: how had Firestone put on the road so many blowouts waiting to happen?

Two economists (associated, ironically, with the industrial relations section of the Firestone Library at Princeton University) have uncovered clues leading them to a single plant during a two-year period in the mid-1990s. The apparent "scene of the crime," a Firestone plant in Decatur, Illinois, was one of three plants making the type of tires that were recalled (the others were in Wilson, North Carolina, and Joliette, Quebec). Tread separations on tires built at the Decatur plant during 1994 to 1996 were much more likely than on tires built at the Decatur plant during other years or at the Joliette or Wilson plants in any years. And lab tests by Firestone engineers showed the same pattern: Decatur had had two bad years, distinguishing it from the other plants and from its own record in other years.

What was special about Decatur during the mid-1990s? The answer, it appears, is *labor strife*.

Early in 1994 the company proposed increasing shifts from 8 to 12 hours and operating the plant 24 hours a day, with workers alternating night and day shifts. Firestone also wanted to pay new workers 30 percent less and to reduce pension and other benefits. In April 1994 the 4,200 employees went on strike. Firestone replaced the striking workers at much lower pay, subsequently announcing that the replacements would be permanent and that the strikers could seek reemployment at reduced pay when the need for additional work arose.

Over the next year many took up the offer, but under highly difficult conditions. According to a union account: "Forced to work alongside scabs who had taken their jobs . . . the strikers were assigned to the hardest jobs on the worst machines, rather than the jobs they had held for 10, 20 and even 30 years. The company supervisors had a field day harassing, intimidating and firing union members for the smallest infractions." Building quality tires may not have been the workers' first priority.

The economists conclude their study: "Unless another factor can be found that explains the sudden rises in defects in tires when Breakstone Firestone

Continued . . .

demanded contract concessions . . . and again when replacement workers and recalled strikers worked side by side, we think the weight of the evidence points to labor strife as being at the root of many of the defective tires." They estimate that faulty tires produced at the Decatur plant during the years of strife accounted for at least 40 deaths, and the number would have been twice that had it not been for the recall.

A century ago the International Workers of the World (IWW), a radical American labor group, demanded, "A fair day's pay for a fair day's work" and pointedly threatened, "good pay or bum work!" Firestone would have saved a lot of money (and lives) had they recognized the force of these demands.

Source: Alan Krueger and Alexandre Mas, "Strikes, Scabs, and Tread Separation: Labor Strife and the Production of Defective Bridgestone/Firestone Tires," *Journal of Political Economy,* vol. 112, no. 2, pp. 253–289.

Whereas it had been the case in manufacturing that the work (the particular object being manufactured) was stationary, with the workers moving around to get tools or parts or to pass on finished work to other workers, the introduction of the assembly line reversed the positions: it made the work mobile and the workers stationary. No longer did employees have much chance to move around and get to know other employees in the plant; they had to spend their entire workday working at one "workstation." As a result, workers became more isolated from one another, and the challenge of organizing collective resistance to any speedup became more difficult. Indeed, from the standpoint of employers the fact that the assembly line enhanced their control over both the pace of work and the movements of their employees was one of its main advantages. Later on employers would find that the assembly line was a mixed blessing because it allowed a fairly small group of workers to bring the entire line to a halt. Indeed, this happened in the late 1930s, and the famous "sit-down strikes" of that time led to the formation and recognition by employers of the United Automobile Workers union.

A third way that technical change may be used to control workers is through *deskilling*. Deskilling means changing production methods so that they require fewer skilled workers and rely more on unskilled workers.

> **Deskilling** means changing a production process in such a way as to make it possible to employ workers with fewer skills.

Employers often favor deskilling because skilled workers are the ones who are generally in the strongest position to resist speedup of work and to bargain successfully for higher wages. Skilled workers are those who have some special training, knowledge, or credential. Skilled workers tend to be in shorter supply than unskilled workers, since skilled workers can usually do unskilled work, whereas unskilled workers typically cannot or are not allowed (by their unions) to do skilled work. Moreover, acquiring a special skill or credential may be difficult, expensive, or time-consuming. And because there are fewer skilled workers than unskilled workers, it is usually more difficult to replace skilled workers. For all these reasons skilled workers are generally in a stronger bargaining position than unskilled workers.

When employers seek to reduce unit labor costs, they naturally focus on their skilled workers. After all, the latter are likely to be the highest paid and most powerful employees

ON THE ROAD AGAIN—WITH A BOX LOOKING OVER MY SHOULDER

American culture—as expressed, for example, in Willy Nelson's country & western song, "On the Road Again"—often celebrates the freedom of the cowboy and his modern incarnation, the long-haul trucker. When U.S. trucking companies installed on-board computers during the 1980s, however, truck drivers experienced a sudden curtailment of their freedoms. This was because the computers served as "trip recorders" that greatly improved the companies' ability to monitor the actions of their drivers. The trip recorders provided the companies with verifiable information on the speed, idle time, and other details of the operation of the trucks, and their sole function was to enable the companies to monitor those aspects of the drivers' behaviors in which there was a conflict of interest between the drivers and the companies.

Before the installation of the trip recorders, drivers liked to take long breaks and then make up for them by driving faster than the speed that would minimize fuel costs and wear and tear on the trucks. Since the trucks were dispersed all over the country, there was no way that the companies could force their drivers to slow down. In contrast, the owner-operators—drivers who owned their own trucks—had to pay for their fuel and repairs, so they drove slower. As a result, they were able to compete successfully with the trucking companies on runs where the conflict of interest between the companies and their drivers was particularly strong.

After the introduction of the trip recorders, the trucking companies were able to write contracts with their drivers that specified the speed at which the trucks were to be driven, and drivers who drove faster were penalized. As a result, speeders now made less money. In the end the trip recorders had two effects. First, they induced the drivers in trucks with trip recorders to drive slower, and second, they reduced the market share of the owner-operators because the latter's cost advantages over the trucking companies disappeared.

Too bad horses went out of style.

Source: George P. Baker and Thomas N. Hubbard, "Contractibility and Asset Ownership: On-Board Computers and Governance in U.S. Trucking," forthcoming in *Quarterly Journal of Economics,* vol. 119, no. 4, November 2004.

in the firm. If the production process can be changed in such a way that it no longer requires skilled workers, employers can then hire unskilled workers, and these unskilled workers will cost less and be less able to resist speedup. With deskilling an employer can easily replace currently employed skilled workers with less expensive unskilled workers because the available supply of unskilled replacement workers is greater than the supply of skilled workers in most labor markets.

Technical change can increase the skills required in production, but it often reduces the need for skills. When it reduces the need for skills, technical change offers an important means by which employers can deskill their labor processes.

One way that employers can deskill work is to break up the whole labor process into many small tasks and then assign each employee only one, or possibly a few, tasks to perform over and over again. Since each employee now needs to know how to do only a few tasks, new workers can be trained quickly for the particular jobs.

One of the most common ways of fragmenting and deskilling jobs is called the *separation of conception from execution* in work. *Conception* means planning out the work,

> The **separation of conception from execution** is one method for deskilling work in which the workers who plan production are different from those who carry it out.

preparing in one's mind or in written plans how the output should be produced. *Execution* is carrying out the planned work according to the conception. In earlier times highly skilled workers such as lathe operators had the ability both to plan their work and to carry it out, and part of the enjoyment that came from their jobs was planning the work and then seeing it materialize in their own hands. Today, small farmers, surgeons, parents, artists, self-employed builders, electricians, and other tradespeople continue to do both parts, integrating conception and execution.

In contrast to traditional processes of production, most modern labor processes increasingly separate conception from execution. Employees in planning, drafting, and engineering departments determine the organization of production, but they rarely produce anything except plans or designs. On the other hand, execution occurs in a factory where the employees who actually make the product do only the physical tasks. They do not participate in planning or improving the product they are making. The result is that planning ("white-collar work") takes place in offices, while execution ("blue-collar work") takes place in factories that are often located in entirely different places or even in different countries.

A recent development is that even white-collar work has been subjected to deskilling. Increasingly, such employees as clerical workers, draftsmen, record keepers, and sales personnel have seen their jobs computerized and deskilled. They, too, have become mainly operators of computers, devices with video displays, or other office machines. They have become more like factory workers, and the need—or opportunity—for exercising mental skills in many of their jobs has declined.

In sum, technical change is a many-sided process. On the one hand, it can be introduced in such a way that it helps employers but does not damage their employees' interests; in these situations it is possible for employers and workers to share the benefits of technological progress. On the other hand, technical change can be used by employers to deskill work or introduce new controls on labor (to raise work-effort levels), with the intention in both cases of weakening workers' bargaining power. When technical changes are likely to work against the interests of workers, employers may try to hide the potential effects of a new technology from current employees since these workers will be more likely to resist the introduction of any new technology if they see that it will enable their employers to speed up their work, eliminate the need for their skills, or otherwise damage their interests.

Not surprisingly, the introduction of new technology frequently leads to contention, conflict, and bargaining between employers and their employees. When employees are weak and not unionized, they may not have the ability to resist changes that harm their interests. When employees are stronger, for instance if they belong to a union, they may be able to bargain and prevent the implementation of technical changes that will not benefit them. As a result of conflicts such as these, the introduction of new technologies that could potentially yield benefits to both workers and employers is often delayed or blocked altogether. Control over technical change is never equal. Whether employees are weak or strong, business owners retain the power to make or not make investments, and this enables them to decide whether, when, and where to invest in new technology. Technical change requires substantial investment, both for the research and development stage and for building and installing new equipment. Only capitalists can invest on a significant scale, so they retain the power to initiate (or withhold) technical change. Workers, even in the best of circumstances, can only hope to shape or block technical change. Only rarely will they be in a position to initiate technical change that would promote their interests.

Unions

Workers organize and join unions to increase their strength in bargaining with employers. The principle of unions is simple. If each worker bargains as an individual with his or her employer, then each worker will be competing with every other worker. The outcome will necessarily be determined by those workers who, for whatever reasons, are willing to accept the lowest wages, the fastest work pace, and the least favorable working conditions. The employer will simply choose to make a deal with them and then replace or not hire anyone who insists on better terms of employment. If, however, all or most employees decide to bargain collectively through a union, the union may be able to achieve better results for all or most of the workers in a given firm or industry than they could obtain otherwise.

A **union** is an organization of workers established with the intention of providing a unified and stronger voice on behalf of the members' interests.

A union, then, is a means for reducing (horizontal) competition among workers. If successful, it gives its members a degree of monopoly power in the labor market. For exactly this reason, many employers (such

WHAT DOES LABOR WANT?

What does labor want? It wants the earth and the fullness thereof. . . . We want more schoolhouses and less jails; more books and less arsenals; more learning and less vice; more constant work and less crime; more leisure and less greed; more justice and less revenge; in fact, more of the opportunities to cultivate our better natures.

—Samuel Gompers, first president of the American Federation of Labor, address to the International Labor League, Chicago World's Fair, August 28, 1893 as Delta Air Lines, among a great many others) have successfully resisted the formation of unions. The existence and the power of unions today are the result of more than a century of hard-fought battles between prounion workers and antiunion employers. The antiunion employers fought first to prevent the formation of unions and later to keep them from threatening profits.

Although unions represented 35 percent of the U.S. nonfarm labor force in the 1950s, only 12.2 percent of all American workers belonged to unions in 2002, and in the private sector of the economy union membership amounted to only 8.5 percent of the workforce. The decline of unions in the U.S. since the mid-1950s has been due primarily to a seismic shift of jobs from the manufacturing sector of the economy, where unions have been strong, to the service sector, where they are weak. In 1955 nearly half the private sector workforce was employed in goods-producing industries (mining, construction, and manufacturing), with the other half being employed in service-producing industries (transportation and public utilities; wholesale and retail trade; finance, insurance and real estate; and "services" in fields such as medicine, law, and education). By 2002, however, more than 75 percent of the U.S. labor force was employed in the service sector, with less than 22 percent being employed in goods-producing industries.

The decline in union membership in the U.S. was especially rapid during the 1980s and 1990s, when increased competition from nonunion workers at home and abroad was added to the disadvantages American unions faced as they struggled to maintain their strength in the manufacturing sector while attempting to recruit new members in the rapidly expanding service sector. In the early years of the 21st century—particularly after the events of 9/11/01 made Americans less likely to want to travel—the decline of unions was accelerated by extensive layoffs in heavily unionized industries such as airlines and hotels. Layoffs have also been widespread in the U.S. steel industry as domestic steel-using manufacturers have increased their imports of lower-cost steel from abroad. The only trend in the other direction has been the ability of public-sector unions such as AFSCME (American Federation of State, County, and Municipal Employees) to expand their membership rapidly as the number of government employees grew from 6.9 million in 1955 to more than 21 million in 2002 and people such as federal government employees, postal workers, teachers, police, firefighters, and other municipal employees decided that they wanted to be represented by unions. In 2002, 37.5 percent of all government workers belonged to a union.

Unions engage in two different types of activities. First, they act as agents for their members in bargaining with employers. For employees in a unionized workplace, the union negotiates a contract that stipulates the wage rates and employment practices to be observed during the period of the contract. Depending on the industry and the strength of the union, the contract may specify the general work effort level (the standard or rate) required for each job, the procedures by which new technology is to be introduced and new (different) jobs created, and the method used to assign employees to different jobs. The contract also usually establishes a grievance procedure to decide cases when employees believe that the employer is not following the contract. In these ways a union contract can protect workers from an employer's otherwise unconstrained commands. Of course, the union's ability to provide effective protection depends on how strong the union is, both at

"YOU COULD BE REPLACED!"

One way a boss can increase his or her strength in bargaining over both *e* (work effort) and *w* (wage rate) is to make it easy to replace each worker with someone else. The ultimate power bosses have over workers is the power to fire them. But is the boss's threat to fire workers believable? That depends on how difficult it is to find a replacement worker. Imagine two situations.

The first is that of a skilled crane operator during a time of relatively low unemployment. The boss may bargain with this worker by threatening to find "somebody else to do the job who really wants to work." However, both the boss and the crane operator may know that there are few unemployed crane operators; that the union will protest the firing and may even get other workers to go out on strike; that it takes a long time for a new crane operator to learn the job routine (thus making the other workers on the job less productive while the new operator is learning); that cranes are expensive and accidents—more likely to happen when someone is new on the job—are costly; and that, in any case, the crane operator can easily find another job at the same or better pay. In this case, the worker is in a strong bargaining position.

In contrast, the second situation is that of an unskilled factory worker during a time of high unemployment. Under these circumstances, when the boss threatens to fire the worker if he or she does not agree to work hard for low wages, the threat is entirely believable. There are many people looking for jobs who could, in fact, do this job. It does not take long to learn the job, and there is no union to protest if the worker gets fired. Here, the boss is in a very strong position.

Both bosses and workers realize that their bargaining strengths depend on how easily replaceable the workers are. The more easily the boss can replace the worker, the stronger the boss will be.

contract renewal time, getting the employer to agree to a decent contract, and during the life of the contract, seeing that the employer lives up to the terms of the contract.

A second activity engaged in by unions involves promoting general social changes that may benefit all workers, including not only their own members but other workers as well, whether or not they belong to a union. For instance, unions have often taken the lead in pressing the federal government to pass minimum wage legislation (raising the minimum wage), workplace safety and environmental protection laws, social security and unemployment benefits, civil rights and antidiscrimination laws, earned income tax credits (for low-wage workers), income support for people unable to work, and various other social service programs.

Discrimination

Unions are a method for overcoming competition among workers. By contrast, discrimination, whether practiced by businesses, unions, or individuals, tends to generate and reinforce divisions among workers.

Discrimination means treating someone differently simply because that person belongs to a particular group. The most widely practiced forms of discrimination today in the U.S. are discrimination against women and discrimination against minorities. People with handicaps, homosexuals, and older workers are also frequent targets of discrimination.

> **Discrimination** means treating someone differently simply because that person belongs to a certain group.

Discrimination stems from a variety of sources—historic, economic, religious, political, social, and psychological—which will not be investigated here. What is relevant to our discussion is that the capitalist profit-making process contains opposing tendencies with regard to discrimination: those that tend to perpetuate and increase it, and those that tend to erode and eliminate it.

Capitalism affects discrimination in two ways. One way weakens it and the other strengthens it. Discrimination is weakened when competing firms attempt to minimize their costs by hiring the best persons for their jobs at the lowest possible wage rates. Racial and sexual discrimination has generally meant that job opportunities, especially those involving high-wage jobs, have been limited for women and minorities who are qualified and able to perform the jobs. But if, facing equally qualified workers, employers hire those who cost the least, they will tend to hire women and minorities and thereby increase the demand for the labor of these groups.

Nondiscriminatory hiring will mean more job opportunities for women and minorities, reductions in their unemployment rates, and, possibly, increases in bargaining strength and pay levels. It will also mean that firms with such nondiscriminatory hiring practices will have a competitive advantage vis-à-vis firms that practice racial and/or sex discrimination because the former will have lower labor costs than the latter and thus be able to make the same or greater profits while charging lower prices for their products. Firms seeking to hire minority or women workers and promote them into positions of authority may encounter resistance from their existing predominantly male and white workforces and from the trade unions representing them. But the firms that succeed in hiring and promoting in an unbiased way will, according to this line of reasoning, drive the biased ones out of business, and discrimination, at least in labor markets, will eventually be eliminated.

On the other hand, discrimination is perpetuated when employers try to take advantage of discriminatory attitudes in conflicts with their employees over wages and the pace of work. Just as workers try to achieve greater bargaining strength for themselves through unions, so employers may try to weaken the bargaining strength of workers by encouraging divisions and promoting disunity among their employees. To do this, they may attempt to foster and magnify any differences and conflicts that already exist among their employees. Given the residual racial, sexual, and other forms of bigotry that have endured historically in Western societies, employers may seize upon these to divide workers. Capitalists did not invent racism, sexism, or other forms of discrimination, but they have sometimes used pre-existing prejudices or biases among workers to divide and weaken them. In this they are no different from white and male workers who have sometimes appealed to the same prejudices to limit competition from women, African Americans, and recent immigrants. Indeed, an individual employer may personally be completely free of prejudice yet be pressured by competition to discriminate in order to stay in business. This might occur if discrimination is profitable. Since firms making higher profits have a competitive advantage, the nondiscriminating firm may, over time, be forced out of business. If, on the other hand, the costs of discrimination outweigh the benefits, employers are likely to stop discriminating.

How can discrimination be profitable? To answer this question, we will compare two imaginary firms. The first firm hires both black and white workers, and it treats all its employees equally—for example, paying wages without regard to race. The workers in this firm, black and white together, form a union, and their union presses for higher wages and safer working conditions.

The second firm also hires both black and white workers, but it discriminates: it assigns blacks to lower paying jobs than whites. The employees of this second firm try to form a union, but they have a more difficult time than the employees of the first firm. Not all employees in the second firm have the same interests. Black workers think the proposed union should try to force the employer to eliminate the company's discrimination in job assignments and pay rates. The white workers, on the other hand, want more pay but also are fearful about the possibility of reductions in their wage rates. At this point white workers may form their own union and exclude blacks in order to concentrate entirely on raising their own wages. (This actually happened for many years in the construction industry in New York City, where unions representing white construction workers managed to exclude blacks both from membership in their unions and from jobs in the industry.) However, when the predominantly white union negotiates with the employer, the employer threatens to hire more blacks to replace the white workers. Because of their inability to act collectively, both white and black workers will have to accept lower wages than they might have negotiated had the employer not engaged in discrimination and thereby fostered divisions among the workers.

Comparing these two firms, we can see that in the first firm employers will face (black and white) workers who share a common interest in raising wages (w) and reducing the strain of work (e). To the extent that these workers are successful, the first firm's profits will decline. The second firm, in contrast, faces workers who are divided by racial conflict. These workers will have difficulty forming a union. Consequently, these workers will have less success in their bargaining for higher wages or less strenuous work.

The second firm will have a higher profit rate than the first firm as a result of its discrimination. Indeed, the first firm may be forced to begin discriminating if it wants to compete successfully in the same market with the second firm.

Neoclassical economists (for example, Milton Friedman in his book *Capitalism and Freedom*) argue that discrimination is costly, and hence competition for profits will eliminate discrimination. But this is just one side of the coin, the only side visible when the horizontal aspect of a capitalist economy, competition, is the focus of one's attention. But when the vertical, or command, relationships of the economy are considered, a different picture emerges. When employers discriminate, it may be because discrimination is profitable. If this is the case, competition may drive even unprejudiced employers to discriminate.

If nondiscriminatory policies are more profitable than discriminatory ones, then the workings of the market will tend to eliminate discrimination. If discrimination results in higher profits, however, a capitalist economy will tend to perpetuate—or even increase—discrimination. The fact that competition among profit-seeking businesses can break down the barriers of discrimination is dramatically affirmed by the rapid integration of most professional sports after

Jackie Robinson broke the color barrier and starred for the Brooklyn Dodgers half a century ago. But it does not always work this way. More direct ways of overcoming discrimination may be more effective, as is shown by the fact that the federal government of the U.S. is a much more racially integrated employer—at all levels—than are the leading private corporations. The U.S. Army beats the Fortune 500 when it comes to integration.

PROFITABILITY VERSUS EFFICIENCY

> **Profitability** refers to how much profit is derived from a labor process.

Profitability refers to how much profit is derived from a labor process. Profit is the excess of sales revenues over the costs of purchased inputs.

Technical efficiency refers to the relationship between the output of a production process and its inputs. (This and other concepts of efficiency are reviewed in a box on this topic in Chapter 3.) A production process is said to be technically efficient if, given the existing technology, the output of it cannot be increased without using more of at least one of the inputs.

> **Technical efficiency:** A production process is said to be **technically efficient** if the output of it cannot be increased without using more of at least one of the inputs.

Technical change can improve technical efficiency by reducing the amount of materials and machines used per labor hour (m), by increasing f—the amount of output that can be produced with any given amount of work effort (e)—or by reducing the capital goods needed per labor hour (c). Any such change would reduce the amount of inputs needed to produce any specific quantity of output.

Increased technical efficiency *may* lead to greater profitability. Other things being constant, an increase in efficiency will reduce the amount (and, presumably, the cost) of the inputs a firm needs to produce its output without affecting its revenues from that output. Under these circumstances an increase in efficiency will increase profits. Many economists, observing this connection, presume that profitability is identical with efficiency.

There are many situations, however, in which a less efficient technology is a more profitable one. What is profitable does not always need to be efficient, and vice versa. In fact, the adoption of a new technology may increase profitability while at the same time requiring more of some input—say, work effort, intermediate goods, or capital goods. Such a technological change might therefore be an inefficient one.

How might a less efficient technology be more profitable? Suppose that a new method of production—say, an assembly line—allows an employer to speed up production, thus increasing output per hour of labor (z) by using technical control to increase work effort per hour (e). Assume, also, that the wage rate (w), the hours of labor, and all other variables in the labor process remain the same. The new technology will be more profitable, but will it also be more efficient? Suppose that work effort per hour increases by 30 percent with the introduction of an assembly line, and output per hour goes up by 20 percent. In this case, the assembly line technology will be more profitable because the firm will be getting 20 percent more output for the same labor cost. It will not be more efficient, however, because the ratio of output per hour (z) to one of the inputs, in this case work effort per hour (e), will have *declined*.

> An **inefficient technical change** is one that can bring about an increase in the output of a production process only by utilizing proportionally more of at least one input.

If the assembly line had increased output per hour without requiring a more intense or faster pace of work, and everything else in the labor process had remained the same, the technical change would have been unambiguously *more*

INEFFICIENT TECHNOLOGIES MAY BE PROFITABLE

We think of modern technologies as ways of solving problems. Indeed, engineers evaluate the effectiveness of various ways of producing products, seeking those that are most efficient in the sense that the greatest amount of useful output can be achieved using given amounts of inputs. But some technologies just do not seem to make sense. The reason is that technologies are often developed to make money, not to make sense, and the two are not the same. The history of technology gives us many examples.

During the 19th century food canning in California was primarily the job of unskilled workers, but the task of putting the tops on the cans—capping, as it was called—required more skill. Cappers were both skilled and scarce. They could easily demand higher wages from their employers by threatening to strike just at harvest time, when the fresh food would rot if it were not quickly canned. Employers were overjoyed when James Cox invented his famous machine, called Cox's capper, which made it possible to replace the skilled workers. But the machine did not work very well, so firms that bought it did not put it into use right away. The firms just kept the machines on hand as a visible threat to the skilled workers: if the workers went on strike, the machines could take their place.

Cox himself understood the appeal of his invention: when it was invented it was not the best way of getting the cans capped, but it did put the skilled cappers in their place. Writing 26 years after the invention, he referred to the once powerful position of the skilled capper and the resulting weak bargaining position of the cannery owner: "[The] helplessness of the canner . . . made him a willing advocate of every mechanical means, and made possible the working out, through frequent failures and heavy losses, the perfected mechanical means now in use."

A modern-day example of the divergence of sensible and profitable technology is the compact disc used to store music. Such discs may be made in such a way that they can be easily copied, thus enabling many people to enjoy the music stored on them. But the companies that produce them spend millions of dollars to develop technologies that can render discs difficult, if not impossible, to copy. Such technologies make it possible for music companies to produce discs that are more profitable but less useful to listeners.

Source: Martin Brown and Peter Philips, "The Historical Origin of Job Ladders in the U.S. Canning Industry," *Cambridge Journal of Economics*, vol. 10, 1986, pp. 129–145.

efficient. But the introduction of the assembly line in our example allows the employer to increase the pace of work, and the new production process requires using *proportionally* more of at least one input, work effort (e), in order to achieve the increase in output (z). Since e goes up more than z and nothing else changes, the introduction of the assembly line is an *inefficient technical change* even though it increases profitability.

What makes it possible for profitability to diverge from efficiency here is that the work effort, or *labor,* that actually goes into the production process is not the same as the amount of purchased *labor time.* If the employer in the assembly line example had to pay 30 percent more for the additional work effort required by the assembly line to achieve an increase of only 20 percent in output, the introduction of the assembly line would not have been profitable. In this case, the inefficient technical change would not have occurred.

For capitalist firms, what counts is profitability, not efficiency. Hence firms will tend to introduce the methods of production that are most profitable, regardless of whether they are the most efficient ones available. When business owners invest, including when they invest in research to develop new technologies, they will invest in what is most profitable, whether or not it is more efficient as well.

Thus, the idea put forward in conventional economics that the technologies currently in use and being developed are simply the "best that modern science has to offer" is not necessarily true. Today's technologies—and current corporate research in new technologies—reflect the fact that to a large extent science has been harnessed to the criterion of profitability. The technologies that might be possible if different criteria were used—for example, to minimize the work effort required to produce necessary goods and services—might be quite different.

MARKETS AND HIERARCHIES

Markets and hierarchies are sometimes thought to be alternative ways of organizing society. Markets are said to establish conditions of (horizontal) equality: voluntary exchange between buyer and seller means that either party can back out of a transaction if he or she chooses, and so a kind of equality exists between them. Hierarchy, on the other hand, depends on the existence of (vertical) inequality: command relations require superiors and subordinates, and bosses have power over their underlings.

Hence, markets have sometimes been counterposed to hierarchies, as though an economic system must be organized with only one or the other. Selling gasoline retail is seen as a market-type transaction, whereas the U.S. Army and the Catholic Church are seen as being organized in hierarchies. Conventional economists define capitalism as a market system, while economic systems that use central planning are regarded as hierarchical, or "command," economies. Yet in this chapter we have seen that profit-making firms, in their efforts to gain a competitive advantage over their market rivals, establish huge and sophisticated hierarchies.

It is true that when markets began to replace slavery and feudal hierarchies they offered some relief from traditional command relations. However, the larger truth is that markets brought along with them a complex system of bosses and workers, of superiors and subordinates. The capitalist system's need for hierarchy has called forth whole new fields of study (with their associated experts): industrial psychology, personnel management, occupational testing, and industrial engineering. Corporations invest substantial portions of the surplus product to develop and refine techniques for maintaining hierarchies. Capitalism did abolish precapitalist hierarchies, freeing individuals to enter into voluntary contracts. But we now find that most people in a capitalist economy spend virtually their entire work lives in hierarchically organized jobs. Finding work is not usually a matter of entering into a contract with an equal. Rather, it is most often a matter of choosing which hierarchy to work in or which boss to work under. It may also evolve into an effort to become a boss rather than a subordinate.

In a capitalist economy, then, markets and hierarchies are not alternative and competing methods of organization, much less different types of economic systems. Its horizontal and vertical dimensions, competition and command, are mutually reinforcing and complementary elements of the system as a whole.

DEMOCRATIC FIRMS

Must firms be run from the top down? Or might firms be run democratically, with the employees together owning the firm, electing the management, and participating in major decisions concerning technology, work safety, product design, hours, wages, and the like? Just about any firm will have a structure of authority, with some people giving orders and others taking them. What distinguishes a firm as democratic, then, is that the employees, through an election in which each worker has an equal vote, have chosen the people with authority. (See box pp. 137–138 "Own Your Job. Elect Your Boss.")

> A **democratic firm** is one that is owned by its employees and run by people who are elected by the employees.

We know that *democratic firms* are possible because thousands of them exist, and many of them are very successful. Such firms may also be reasonably large as well as successful and democratic.

One example of a large, successful, and quite democratic firm is the California-based Fortune 500 company Science Applications International Corporation. SAIC has 41,000 employees in 150 cities worldwide and brings in more than $5 billion in annual revenues. What makes it unusual, though, is that its current and retired employees own 96 percent of the company's stock. (Its stock is not traded on any stock exchange, but each share is assigned a "fair market value" through a complex process involving the company's board of directors and expert consultants; any employee who leaves the firm must sell his or her shares back to the company, receiving their fair market value in cash.) SAIC's founder, a man committed to employee ownership, has retained only 1.3 percent of the company's stock, and its top 30 managers own less than 3 percent of it. The top managers are not directly elected—how could 41,000 people know enough about candidates to decide which ones should occupy the firm's top managerial positions?—but employees from every walk of life serve on the committees that resolve internal issues and set company policies. (See http://www.saic.com/about/history.html.)

Many people favor democratic firms for moral or political reasons, on the grounds that firms, like other powerful institutions, should be democratically run. There are also economic grounds for favoring democratic firms.

The economic advantages of a worker-owned and democratically run firm are clear. Because its workers are its owners, their incomes depend directly on the productivity of the firm. For this reason they have an interest in adopting technologies, work methods, and forms of organization that promote the effective use of the firm's resources, including their own time and energy. Ownership of the firm by workers does not change the facts that hard work is hard or that people might like others to shoulder the more onerous tasks of production. But it does fundamentally alter the incentives of workers: a job done well benefits the owners of the firm, so when the workers are the owners, they have strong incentives to see that work is carried out in the most effective manner.

The disadvantages are equally clear. Most workers do not have sufficient wealth to purchase "their" share of the firm, so it is difficult to achieve complete worker ownership. Banks are often reluctant to lend to worker-owned and worker-run institutions. Perhaps most important, for workers to own their own firm they would have to have most, if not all, of their wealth invested in their own firm. Because they would have all their eggs in one basket, they would tend to be very cautious in their decision making: if their firm were to fail, they would lose not only their jobs but also most of their wealth. As a result, workers who own their own firms tend to be cautious about taking the risks necessary for innovation in product design and production processes. By contrast, the owners of a capitalist firm (the stockholders) typically have their assets invested in many firms. Hence, their fortunes are not solely dependent on the success or failure of any one firm. And unlike the worker-owners of democratic firms, most of them are rich. For these reasons capitalist owners are more likely than are worker-owners to tolerate risk taking and innovation by the managers of the firms they own. In addition, the capitalist firm is more likely than are worker-owners to use the latest technologies (as discussed above) to extract increased work effort from their employees. Thus, capitalist firms will tend to have lower unit costs and be more competitive in product markets than worker-owned firms.

Although many studies indicate that worker ownership and democratic participation in a firm's decision making enhance both productivity and worker satisfaction, worker-owned and worker-run firms are the exception in capitalist economies. The fact is that a democratic firm's lack of access to capital, bias against risk taking, and commitment to decent working conditions put it at a disadvantage in competing against capitalist firms.

SUGGESTED READINGS

Eileen Appelbaum, Annette Bernhardt, and Richard J. Murnane, eds., *Low-Wage America: How Employers Are Reshaping Opportunity in the Workplace* (New York: Russell Sage Foundation, 2003).

William J. Baumol, Alan S. Blinder, and Edward N. Wolff, *Downsizing in America: Reality, Causes, and Consequences* (New York: Russell Sage Foundation, 2003).

Joseph Blasi, Douglas Kruse, and Aaron Bernstein, *In the Company of Owners: The Truth about Stock Options (and Why Every Employee Should Have Them)* (New York: Perseus, 2003).

Alan Blinder, *Paying for Productivity* (Washington, D.C.: The Brookings Institution, 1990).

Harry Braverman, *Labor and Monopoly Capital: The Degradation of Work in the Twentieth Century* (New York: Monthly Review Press, 1998).

Henry Hansmann, *The Ownership of Enterprise* (Cambridge, Mass.: Harvard University Press, 1996).

Simon Head, *The New Ruthless Economy: Work and Power in the Digital Age* (New York: Century Foundation/Oxford University Press, 2003).

David Montgomery, *Workers' Control in America* (Cambridge: Cambridge University Press, 1980).

David Noble, *The Forces of Production* (New York: Knopf, 1984).

Michael Reich, *Racial Inequality* (Princeton, N.J.: Princeton University Press, 1981).

Barbara Reskin and Patricia Roos, *Job Queue, Gender Queue: Exploiting Women's Inroads into Male Occupations* (Philadelphia: Temple University Press, 1990).

William F. Whyte and Kathleen K. Whyte, *Making Mondragon* (Ithaca, N.Y.: ILR Press, 1988).

PART **3**

Macroeconomics

CHAPTER 14

The Mosaic of Inequality

In 1998 the Gallup public opinion research firm asked 5,001 Americans why "some people get ahead and succeed in life and some do not." Respondents were asked to consider 12 possible answers and to rank the answers from "extremely important" to "not at all important." The 12 possible answers were "good luck," "hard work," "inherited money," "connections," "education," "dishonesty," "parents and the family environment," "the talent one is born with," "willingness to take risks," "good looks," "one's race," and "being male or female." There was general agreement among the respondents that education, hard work, one's family environment, connections, and luck were important. But there were also significant differences. Those who themselves had higher incomes thought that hard work was more important, while those with lower incomes thought that luck, connections, inheritances, dishonesty, and one's sex were more important. Far more than white men did, both women and African Americans thought that one's sex and one's race counted as significant factors in getting ahead. Lower income respondents as well as women and African Americans all ranked education higher than better-off respondents, men, and whites did. Clearly, there are different opinions as to why some people get ahead while others do not.

Interest in what it takes to get ahead has been growing because those who *are* ahead have been gaining ground over the rest. Indeed, there is concern about the fact that although the playing field has never been exactly level, it is increasingly tilted against the less well-off. Even the president of the New York Federal Reserve Bank, William McDonough, warned in his commencement address to the 2003 graduating class at Johns Hopkins University School of Advanced International Studies that rampant inequality would tear at the social fabric and was "unsustainable in a democracy."

Is it *fair* that being "good looking" makes it probable that you will have a higher income than the rest of the people who are otherwise similar to you? (It does, by the way, for men as well as for women, and even for those in jobs that do not require a person to be "on display.") If you think this is acceptable, how do you feel about the fact (also true) that obese women earn less and that short men also earn less? Most people think it is a *good* thing that hard work and education pay off. But what about race, sex, or one's parents' wealth? The fact that these things do help one get ahead (this *is* a fact) strikes many people as unfair. And if a high-quality education is a way to move up the economic ladder (it is), many people think it unfair that educational opportunities are more available to those with well-to-do parents.

Some people have the free time and the income that allow them to make real choices about such things as where to live and what interests to pursue. Others lack either the time, the income, or both. Racial insults, sexual harassment, and hurtful indignities are experienced by some, but not by others. Some lawyers are paid $1,000 an hour for their services, while kitchen staff at restaurants (working just as hard under less pleasant conditions) get one-half of one-hundredth of that amount.

Why do we call some differences "inequalities," find them unacceptable, and advocate policies to eliminate them? And why do we, at the same time, regard other differences as innocuous or possibly even good because they make for "diversity"? The simple answer is easy: unacceptable inequalities are those that are unfair. But deciding *what* is unfair is sometimes difficult.

Deciding what is unfair often requires knowing how differences come about. If a lawyer's high pay is the result of his hard work in school, while the kitchen worker is low paid because she is lazy, the pay difference would seem more acceptable than if the pay difference is the result of racial discrimination or has to do with the fact that the lawyer is a man and the kitchen worker a woman. The key to fairness here is *equality of opportunity,* as discussed in Chapter 3.

Further difficulties arise if we turn from the "inequality of what" issue to ask: inequality *between whom?* Is it fair that the minimum wage kitchen worker in the U.S. makes five times more in an hour than does the agricultural worker in some other country who tended the crops to produce the food that she is now preparing in the kitchen? Why do we worry about the high-paid lawyer and not about the much lower-paid picker in Mexico or South Africa?

In the previous two chapters we explained how two classes, the capitalist and working classes, interact in labor markets and firms. The capitalist class is defined by its ownership and control of the capital goods used in production and its power to dispose of the resulting surplus product. The working class is defined by its lack of such ownership and control rights. But when viewed from the standpoint of the economy as a whole, this picture is incomplete. There are large numbers of management personnel who lack substantial wealth but nevertheless have control over the labor of others. As explained in Chapter 7, these managers constitute the new middle class. At the same time there are people who still can be thought of as being in the old middle class because they own the capital goods they need to carry on their work but neither have a boss nor are one.

The class structure, however, is not a set of cubbyholes into which the accumulation process sorts people neatly labeled into four homogeneous types: worker, capitalist, new, and old middle class. Rather, there is a continuum of inequalities of many dimensions: of ownership, of income, and of power, all overlaid with differences between men and women and among races and ethnic groups. Moreover, there is a dependent population of individuals surviving on government transfer payments, residing in institutions (such as hospitals and prisons), living by crime, or existing in other ways outside the class system sketched above.

There are also major differences within the four classes considered in this book. Among employers, there are the owners of the largest firms, employing hundreds of thousands, but there are also farmers, architects, and store owners with just a few employees. The differences among employees are equally great. The people in the 10th of the U.S. labor force who are paid at or below the federal minimum wage eke out livelihoods that place them well below the poverty line. They fall even further below this line if they are not employed full time all year. In contrast, some members of the working class make more in a month than minimum wage workers do in a year.

In this chapter we discuss inequalities of income and wealth, not of health, happiness, or other desired goods. We do this because information on income and wealth is especially detailed and comprehensive and because the wealth and income data help us to see some inequalities that matter. Having less or more income and wealth provides individuals with less or more access to goods and services, less or more personal independence, and less or more of a chance to attain such other desired goods as health and happiness.

This brings us to the title of this chapter. A *mosaic* is an ancient art form in which a picture—commonly a portrait, often of a saint or the Madonna—is constructed by assembling small, differently colored pieces of tile. Viewed from a distance, the face and other features are clearly recognizable, but up close what you see are only the pieces. Similarly, the many facets of inequality—race, wealth, sex, schooling, and so on—constitute a kind of "mosaic." In this chapter we examine not only the more significant pieces but also the larger picture.

The main ideas of the chapter are: (a) *among the determinants of economic success in the U.S., one's race, sex, and parental income are very important,* and (b) *by almost any measure, income inequality rose dramatically between the early 1970s and the early 2000s.*

These main ideas are expressed in the following five points:

1. Living standards are not simply a matter of material goods. People's well-being depends on their health, their material comfort, and their access to social and natural environments that contribute to their whole human development. The economy contributes to people's well-being both by providing (or failing to provide) the goods and services necessary to meet these objectives and by shaping the kinds of social and natural environments essential to people's well-being.

2. Inequality of both income and wealth (how much one owns) increased sharply during the last three decades of the 20th century and into the early years of the 21st century.

3. The children of families with high incomes are much more likely to have high incomes when they grow up, and the children of poor families are much more likely to have low incomes. The higher levels of schooling (and better quality of schooling, year for year) enjoyed by the children of well-off parents account for some of these differences, but only some.

4. African Americans and women continue to earn less than men and people of European descent. The significant income gains made by African Americans relative to European Americans from 1939 to 1979 have not continued to the present.

5. Jobs in the U.S. economy remain highly segmented: "women's work" tends to be less well paid, but even in the same jobs, women earn less than men.

MEASURING WELL-BEING AND INEQUALITY

We often make statements such as "The Hernandez family is better off than the Jones family," "People live better in Sweden than in Mexico," or "My living standard is much higher now than when I was just out of college." What do we mean by *better off, live better,* and *living standard?* These terms refer to all the things that influence a person's well-being.

Well-Being and the Economy

A major influence on well-being is access to food, shelter, clothing, health care, and other necessities of life. Also important is access to the amenities and luxuries that make it possible to feel that we are living well, or at least not worse than other people around us. Moreover, a person's sense of well-being depends not only on having the respect of others but also on having a sense of belonging to a community, whether it be a family, a neighborhood, a work group, a religion, or a nation. Without this sense of belonging, life can become meaningless.

Living standards also depend on having enough free time and enough energy left after finishing one's work to enjoy life. The workaholic who makes $90,000 a year but has no free time may not be better off than a person with plenty of free time who earns $50,000 a year. No less important is the ability to make important choices regarding, say, education and other means to the achievement of one's goals in life. The quality of our work experience is also an important influence on our well-being: few things can bring a person down as much as hating to go to work every morning. An additional influence on our well-being is the quality of our natural environment and the extent to which it allows us to experience good health and to enjoy the many pleasures that depend on our natural surroundings. How each of us regards the many influences on our well-being will, of course, differ according to our values. But, however we rank them, the basic components of well-being have to include not only material goods but also such things as health, freedom, respect, and belonging. Thus, living standards depend both on tangible things and on the intangibles that help to determine the quality of life. In Figure 14.1 we sketch some of the factors that can influence a person's well-being.

Obviously, our well-being depends critically on the economy. It is through the labor processes that make up the economy that we get the food, clothing, shelter, amenities, and luxuries that make life possible and enjoyable. Less obvious, but no less important, is that the way the economy is organized influences the quality-of-life aspects of well-being: health, freedom, respect, and belonging. This is true for a number of reasons.

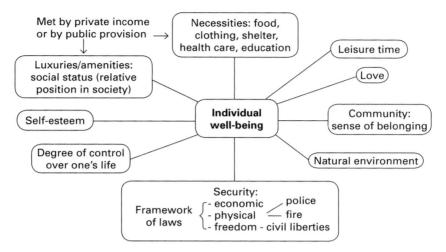

FIGURE 14.1   The determinants of well-being.   Without attempting to be comprehensive or to suggest the relative importance of each determinant, this figure displays in graphic form some of the requirements for well-being in any society.
Source: authors.

First, the organization of the economy affects the health status of the population. Some societies provide adequate health care to all without regard to ability to pay; in other societies adequate health care is available only to those who can pay for it. In any case, there are economies in which workers must work at such a pace that stress is a major health problem; in others the pace of work is more worker-friendly. In a laissez-faire capitalist economy (one allowing the unrestricted pursuit of profits by companies without government regulation) environmental pollution may impair the health of the population.

Second, the structure of the economy also influences how free we are to make or to influence the major decisions affecting our lives. A person's freedom may be curtailed by an economic system—such as that which existed in the former Soviet Union—that determines where a person will work or restricts what a person can do with his or her property. A person's freedom can also be limited by lack of income, denying any real choices other than those focused on making ends meet.

Third, though the respect we feel for one another can be attributable to many different accomplishments and characteristics, if one is much poorer than others, even if one has access to the necessities of life, it can be difficult to gain respect. For example, a woman who has two children might earn $10,000 a year. In the United States she would be regarded as poor, yet the same woman earning the equivalent of the same income in Bangladesh would be considered quite successful (she would be earning 10 times the average family income of the country). The point is not that she could buy more if she were in Bangladesh (in fact, she would find that her dollars would buy more of some things in Bangladesh than in the U.S., but less of others) but that she would *feel* better off, because she would compare herself with others less well off, and others would make the same comparison. One's sense of well-being thus depends at least in part on one's income compared to the income of others.

Fourth, closely related to the sense of respect is the sense of belonging to some group. Some economies are organized around very long-lasting neighborhoods and family units. In other economies people move frequently from one place to another in search of or because of work, with the result that neighborhoods are often made up of people who do not even know one another. Sometimes the workplace itself feels like a large community in which one cares about fellow workers and they reciprocate. In other workplaces people may be simply passing acquaintances or perhaps even hostile competitors.

Measuring Living Standards and Inequality

Measuring living standards and comparing them among people, among national averages, or between different time periods is very difficult. Many of the influences on the quality of life are hard to measure even if we could agree on how important each is. Does a gallon of milk contribute more or less to well-being than, say, a pound of shrimp? The standard economist's answer is that the shrimp is worth more because people are willing to pay $10 for the pound of shrimp but can get a gallon of milk for less than $5.

The most common approach in economics is to measure a person's standard of living by his or her income and to use separate measures to indicate health status, income relative to others, the quality of the natural and social environment, and the like. Similarly, the standard of living in a country is often measured by the total income in the country divided by total population, or per capita income. *Economic growth* is defined as an increase in the per capita income of a country. As an approximation of access to goods and services, measuring by income makes sense. But there are a number of problems with using income as a measure of well-being.

First, by measuring income and not measuring leisure, we fail to take account of one of the main determinants of well-being, free time. By the income standard the workaholic mentioned earlier is better off than someone who works half as hard and makes just a little less money. But by most people's standards the extra sleep, the free time to enjoy one's friends and family, and other such pleasures would make the leisured person with the lower income better off. In Sweden, for example, *income* per employed person increased at about the same rate as in the U. S. over the last four decades of the 20th century (see Figure 15.6 in the next chapter). But the *leisure time* of the average employed Swede grew much more rapidly as work hours in Sweden were cut back by the equivalent of two months work time, while the reduction in work hours in the U.S. was less than half of this (see Figure 20.1 on p. 534). Thus, we can see that the income measure by itself understates the Swedes' improvement in well-being relative to that of Americans during this period.

Second, income measures a person's access to commodities, but many important goods and services are not commodities. Examples are home-cooked meals and all other products of household labor (house cleaning, care for one's children, and the like). Other examples of goods and services that are not commodities are public education, police protection, and other government services. Moving to a town with better schools and better police protection undoubtedly is an improvement in one's living standard, even defining this narrowly to mean simply access to goods and services. Yet this move need not be reflected in any change in measured income.

Third, the prices of goods and services often fail to measure their contributions to well-being. For example, a quarter of a pound of shrimp and a gallon of milk might cost the same, but most people would agree that the milk is in some sense more essential to well-being than the shrimp. The reason is that milk is a necessity, and shrimp is a luxury. To the person who pays $10 a pound for shrimp, doing without it would probably be no hardship. For most people, this is most likely not true of milk. Clearly, then, income is an inadequate measure of well-being because the prices that people pay for different goods—$10 for a pound of shrimp, $2.50 for a gallon of milk, and so on—may not properly value the contribution of each good to well-being.

To see the importance of this point, imagine a society with equal numbers of people in two income groups. The rich eat shrimp (and, of course, other things too), while the poor have a calcium deficiency resulting from an inadequate diet due to their low incomes. If the rich were taxed $2.50 each and gave up eating a quarter of a pound of shrimp, and the poor were each given $2.50 to be spent on milk, we would probably conclude that on average the living standards of the population had risen. Our conclusion is based on the fact that what the rich gave up, a luxury, was less important than what the poor got, a necessity. But the average income of the society did not change.

Because the less well-off tend to spend more of their incomes on necessities and less on luxuries, a given amount of income is likely to contribute more to the average well-being in the society if more of the income goes to the less well-off. For this reason the average *standard of living* (or well-being) depends on *more than* the average amount of *income* at some point in time or in some country. We also want to know whether it is distributed evenly or unequally. Moreover, we are interested in the distribution of income for what it says about the degree to which economic outcomes are *fair* (see our discussion of the criterion of *fairness* in Chapter 3).

Measuring inequality in the distribution of income, like measuring income itself, is difficult. Think of a statement about inequality, such as "Mr. Brown makes 50 times more money than his cook." This phrase gives us some idea of inequality, but it fails to take account of the whole population, including middle-income recipients such as Mr. Brown's business assistant, perhaps. A commonly used approach is to rank all families or individuals by their income from the poorest to the richest and then divide them into fifths—or "quintiles"—of the population. We then take the total amount of income and calculate what percentage of it is received by each fifth of the population. According to the most recent data from the U.S. Census Bureau, in 2001 the bottom fifth of the population received 3.5 percent of the nation's total income. The next fifth got 8.7 percent, so the poorest 40 percent received 12.2 percent of the total income, and so on up to the top fifth, which received more than half of all the income. The richest 5 percent of the population received 22.4 percent of all the income. (See source cited in the caption for Figure 14.4.)

GROWING INEQUALITY

The recent trend toward greater income inequality is especially striking when compared with the longer-term trend toward greater equality. Figure 14.2 shows the fraction of total income received by the richest 1 percent of the U.S. population over a period of almost a

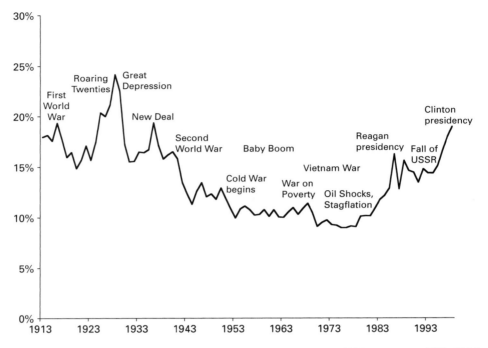

FIGURE 14.2   The lucky few: income share of the top 1 percent of U.S. taxpayers, 1913–1998. This figure shows the share (percentage) of all U.S. income that was received by the top 1 percent of American taxpayers from 1913 to 1998. This share fell from a high of 25 percent in the late 1920s to a low of 9 percent in the late 1970s. It has been rising since Ronald Reagan was elected president in 1980.

Source: Thomas Piketty and Emmanuel Saez, "Income Inequality in the United States, 1913–1998," *Quarterly Journal of Economics,* vol. 118, no. 1, 2003, pp. 1–39.

century. The decline in the income share of the very rich from before World War I continued with only minor reverses until the 1970s. The 1920s were especially "roaring" if you were very rich, but in the subsequent decades—which included the Great Depression, World War II, and President Lyndon Johnson's mid-1960s "war on poverty"—the top income recipients' piece of the pie shrank considerably. The fact that the top 1 percent received about 10 percent of the total income in 1970 means that the typical person in this group had an income 10 times that of the average person's—so the rich person's slice was not all that skimpy. Nevertheless, the share of the top 1 percent had fallen by more than half from its peak in the 1920s.

Among "the lucky few," of course, are CEOs of large corporations. Figure 14.3 shows what the 100 highest-paid CEOs in America made, as a multiple of the average worker's wage, over the three decades between 1970 and 2000. The figure shows an increase in this ratio from 49:1 in 1970 to 373:1 in 1988 to 2,388:1 in 1998.

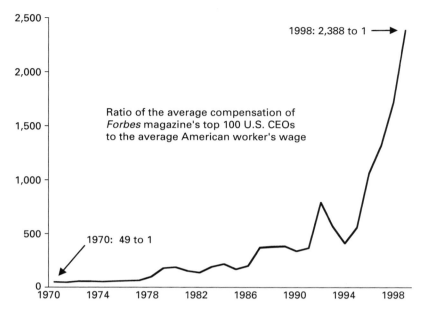

FIGURE 14.3   U.S. CEO pay in relation to the average worker's wage, 1970–1998.   This figure traces the *average* pay of the CEOs selected by *Forbes* magazine between 1970 and 1998 for the magazine's annual list of the 100 highest-paid American CEOs. (The particular CEOs on the list in any given year are not necessarily the same as those who were on the list in other years; the list just shows the CEOs who were paid the most in a particular year.) The line in the figure indicates the *ratio* of the average pay of the 100 best-paid CEOs in each year to the average worker's wage in the same year.

Source: Thomas Piketty and Emmanuel Saez, "Income Inequality in the United States, 1913–1998," *Quarterly Journal of Economics,* vol. 118, no. 1, 2003, pp. 1–39.

Figure 14.4 presents data on the recent upturn in income inequality in a different way. In this figure one can see that in the first year of the last third of the 20th century, 1967, the top 20 percent (or top "quintile") of U.S. households received 43.8 percent of the nation's income, while the bottom quintile received 4 percent. By the beginning of the 21st century—in 2001—the top quintile's share had increased to 50 percent, while the share of the bottom quintile had shrunk to 3.5 percent. Also apparent is the fact that the shares received by all the quintiles other than the very top one fell. If "middle income" is defined as the 2nd, 3rd, and 4th quintiles, the combined share of middle-income households shrank from 52.3 to 46.3 percent of total income between 1967 and 2001. Households in the quintile exactly in the middle, the 3rd quintile, saw their income shrink from 17.3 to 14.6 percent of the total.

The increased inequality shown in Figure 14.4 may be seen not only with reference to the share of total income received but also with reference to the actual amounts of income

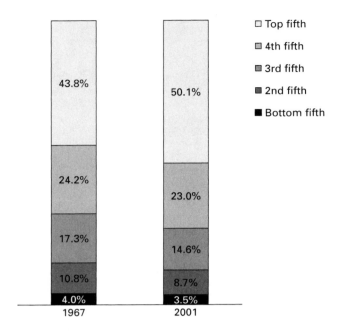

FIGURE 14.4   Income shares by quintile in the U.S., 1967 and 2001.   This figure shows how the nation's income was distributed among American households in 1967 and 2001. The percentages are arrived at by dividing the total number of U.S. households in those years—61 million in 1967 and 109 million in 2001—into five equal groups ("quintiles") organized according to the amount of income they received. The highest-income households are in the top quintile, the next-highest-income households are in the 4th quintile, and so on. The numbers inserted in the individual sections of the bars indicate the percentage of the nation's total income that was received by all the households in the particular quintile in each year.

Source: U.S. Census Bureau, *Historical Income Tables—Households.* Table H-2: Share of Aggregate Income Received by Each Fifth and Top 5 Percent of Households (All Races): 1967 to 2001 (Washington, D.C.: U.S. Census Bureau, September 2002). Available at http://www.census.gov/hhes/income/histinc/h02.html.

received, on average, by households in each quintile of the population. Figure 14.5 shows how much income was received, on average, by households in the five quintiles of the U.S. population over the same span of years covered in Figure 14.4. It shows that average income grew only modestly for households in the lowest four quintiles, while the incomes of those in the top quintile rose by a significant amount. Thus, we arrive at a conclusion similar to—but going beyond—the one we reached on the basis of the information displayed in Figure 14.4: the distribution of income has become more unequal, with people in the top quintile of the income distribution pulling away from those in the other four quintiles—not only in terms of the shares of the pie but also with regard to the sizes of the slices of the pie.

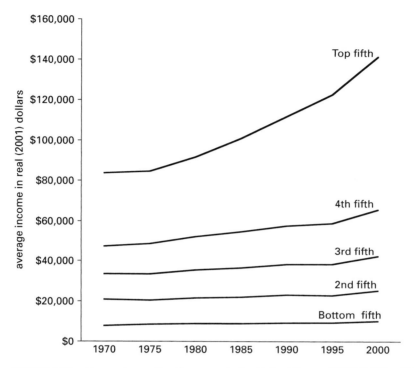

FIGURE 14.5 Unequal growth of incomes in the United States, 1967–2001.   This figure shows how the average household income in each fifth of the U.S. population grew between 1967 and 2001. The income levels are given in "real" dollar amounts, the term *real* meaning that the actual amounts of income received (income in "current" dollars) have been adjusted for inflation; they are presented as if no price inflation occurred before or after the year 2001. Thus, we can say that the amounts of income shown in this chart are in "real 2001 dollars."

Source: Carmen DeNavas-Walt and Robert Cleveland, *Money Income in the United States: 2001* (U.S. Census Bureau, Current Population Reports, P60-218), Table A-3. Available at http://www.census.gov/prod/2002pubs/p60-218.pdf.

WEALTH INEQUALITY

Whereas *income* is what a person, household, or family receives over a certain period of time, *wealth* refers to the assets (such as land, a bank account, rental properties, stocks and bonds, and patents) that a person, household, or family owns. Income is called a *flow* and wealth a *stock*. (If one thinks of a stream and a pond downstream of it, the stream is the flow and the amount of water in the pond is the stock.) Housing is counted as wealth, even if it is the owner's residence, since it is said to provide a flow of "housing services." Cars are also considered wealth: they provide transportation services. One's skills and state of health are also considered to be wealth—they are called "human capital"—because they can contribute to one's income. But when we refer to "wealth" we have in mind the conventional (nonhuman) forms of wealth.

Two different kinds of wealth may be distinguished: (1) ownership of houses, cars, and other personal items and (2) ownership of other types of assets, including corporate stock, direct ownership of companies, and the like. Both kinds of wealth contribute to the living standards and economic security of their owners. Owning such things as a house and a car yields housing and transportation services that, in the absence of them, one would have to purchase. Ownership of other kinds of assets—land, stocks, and rental properties, for example—typically yields income to the owner. Ownership of both types of assets affords economic security, for the owner of a substantial amount of wealth can sell some assets to gain income needed for an emergency or to tide him or her over in bad times.

As Figure 14.6 shows, the *composition* of one's wealth—the allocation of it among different types of assets—varies depending on how much wealth one has. More than three-fourths of the wealth of the wealthiest 1 percent of households in the U.S. is invested in corporate stock or in unincorporated business equity, while less than 10 percent of it is tied up in residence ownership. But households in the middle three-fifths (not the top or the bottom fifth) of the wealth distribution typically hold most of their wealth in the form of ownership

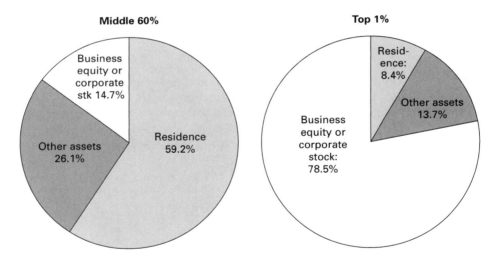

FIGURE 14.6 Composition of wealth holdings at different levels of wealth distribution in the U.S. in 2001.   This figure shows how the typical household in the middle three-fifths of the wealth distribution held its wealth in 2001 (left pie chart) as compared with how wealth was held by the typical household in the top 1 percent of the wealth distribution in the same year (right pie chart). The three categories of wealth used in this figure are (1) ownership of a residence, (2) ownership of equity in an unincorporated business or of stock issued by a corporation, and (3) all other kinds of assets, including such things as the value of pension funds, liquid assets such as funds in savings and bank accounts, automobiles, household furniture, personal items, and so on.

Source: Edward N. Wolff, "Changes in Household Wealth in the 1980s and 1990s in the U.S.," in Edward N. Wolff, ed., *International Perspectives on Household Wealth* (Northampton, Mass.: Edward Elgar, forthcoming), Table 5, Composition of Household Wealth by Wealth Class, 2001.

of their own residences, with corporate stocks and ownership of businesses amounting, on average, to only one-seventh of their total wealth.

The composition of the wealth of the rich and the not-so-rich is of considerable economic and social significance. This is due to the obvious fact that owning a home does not, by itself, enable one to be an employer of others or to work for oneself. To be an employer or to be self-employed, one needs to own assets other than one's home. An employer with a small shop employing, say, 10 people would probably need to own at least a quarter of a million dollars in assets. This might be enough to buy the equipment needed to employ the workers; no less important, it would increase the employer's chances of being able to borrow additional funds from a bank or some other lending source.

Thus, while homeownership can contribute to one's personal autonomy, it is the ownership of other assets, in particular, ownership of capital goods used in production, that allows for true economic autonomy—the freedom to work for oneself, to employ others, or to choose not to work at all. One way in which a person can establish ownership of capital goods is to own stock issued by corporations and traded in stock markets. Such stock can provide not only income but also, if a sufficient amount of stock is owned, control of a corporation. As explained in Chapter 6, income from owning corporate stock takes the form of dividends, and corporations can decide whether to pay dividends. If they are paid, the corporation can determine how much will be paid per share of stock. Figure 6.2 in Chapter 6 shows that the ownership of corporate stock is distributed as follows: the wealthiest 10 percent of U.S. households own more than 75 percent of the total, while the least wealthy 90 percent of households own less than 25 percent.

Net worth, or **net assets,** is the sum of all of a person's assets minus all outstanding debts.

A broad measure of wealth is *net worth,* which is the sum of all of a person's assets minus outstanding debts; the term *net assets* is also used to convey the same idea. The distribution of net assets in the U.S. in 2000, leaving aside home ownership, is shown in Figure 14.7. One can see from this figure that a U.S. household is likely to have more net assets (other than home ownership) the greater the educational attainment of the householder, the higher the income of the household, the more white the household, and the more male the householder.

Some of the facts presented in Figure 14.7 are just as one might expect. For example, as shown in the lower right panel, U.S. households with more income tend to have more wealth. One would expect this to be the case since wealth usually provides income, and income, if saved, adds to wealth. However, what is remarkable about the data here is the size of the difference in asset ownership between the richest fifth of households and other ones: the average nonhome net worth of the richest fifth is *15 times* the average nonhome net worth of the lowest three-fifths of households combined. The same kind of disparity shows up when people are grouped by level of educational attainment: college graduates have four times the nonhome net worth of high school graduates. Also striking are the differences by sex and race. Households headed by men have, on average, five times as much wealth as do those headed by women, and, while the average white household's nonhome net worth exceeds $100,000, the average African-American or Hispanic household's nonhome net worth is negative—meaning that such households, on average, have more debts than assets (home ownership and mortgage debt not included). The differences in wealth in these cases (households categorized by sex and race) are far greater than the corresponding differences in income levels, but these differences in wealth are probably

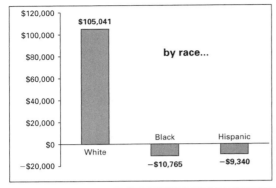

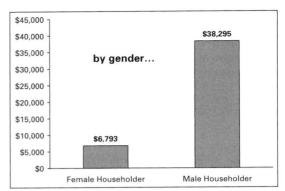

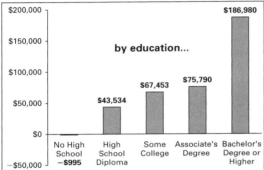

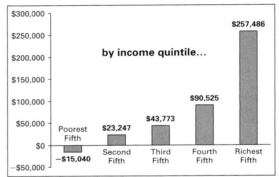

FIGURE 14.7   U.S. nonhome net worth by race, gender, education, and income, 2000.   This figure shows how net assets, other than homes, were distributed among the 104.7 million households in the U.S. in 2000. The word *net* before the word *worth* in the title of the figure means that the households' debts have been subtracted from their total assets, leaving a truer picture of household wealth.

Source: U.S. Census Bureau, *Asset Ownership of Households: 2000* (Washington, D.C.: U.S. Census Bureau, 2003), Table 5: Average (Mean) Value of Assets for Households, by Type of Asset Owned and Selected Characteristics: 2000 (last revised June 4, 2003), available at http://landview.census.gov/hhes/www/wealth/1998_2000/wlth00-5.html.

a better measure of the relative quality of life (including the freedom to make various decisions) enjoyed by people in such households.

A common way of measuring the distribution of wealth is to look at how much of a country's wealth is owned by different segments of its population. As Figure 14.8 shows, the share of the top 10 percent of households in the U.S. increased from 68.4 percent to 71.5 percent between 1983 and 2001. During the same period the fraction of total wealth owned by the poorest 60 percent of U.S. households fell from 6.1 percent to 4.2 percent.

Wealth is not only a possible source of income, it can also provide security. It can be a cushion to fall back on in hard times. But how much of a "cushion" can wealth be? How long could a person survive just by spending his or her wealth? In answering this question, we can look at the inequality of wealth distribution in the U.S. in a slightly different way.

Dividing all households into quintiles (fifths) ranked by the amount of their wealth, Figure 14.9 shows how long (in years) the typical household in each quintile could survive

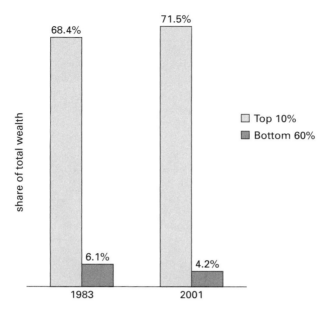

FIGURE 14.8   Increasing concentration of wealth in the U.S. between 1983 and 2001.   This figure shows that the ownership of wealth among households in the U.S. became more concentrated between 1983 and 2001. The pair of bars on the left show that in 1983 the top 10 percent of American households owned 68.4 percent of the wealth in the U.S., while the bottom 60 percent of households owned 6.1 percent of it. The pair of bars on the right show that by 2001 the share owned by the top 10 percent of households had increased to 71.5 percent, while that of the bottom 60 percent of households had fallen to 4.2 percent.

Source: Edward N. Wolff, "Changes in Household Wealth in the 1980s and 1990s in the U.S." in Edward N. Wolff, ed., *International Perspectives on Household Wealth* (Northampton, Mass.: Edward Elgar, forthcoming), Table 2: The Size Distribution of Wealth and Income, 1983–2001.

if the household's *income* stopped coming in and the people in the household could spend *only the household's wealth* at a rate equal to the income of a family defined by the government as being at the borderline of poverty.

Consider, for example, a household with the *average* amount of wealth in the wealthiest fifth of U.S. households. In 2001 a household in this situation (in the top quintile) could have survived for more than 100 years consuming at the poverty rate; a household with the average wealth of the households in the third quintile would have lasted barely five years; and a household with the average wealth of the households in the bottom two quintiles could have survived for only two and a half months. This is similar to the situation Adam Smith was describing when he wrote: "A landlord, a farmer, a master manufacturer, or [a] merchant, though did not employ a single workman, could generally live a year or two upon the stocks which they have already acquired. Many workmen could not subsist a week . . . without employment." (See box in Chapter 12, p. 292, "The Bargaining Power of Owners and Workers.")

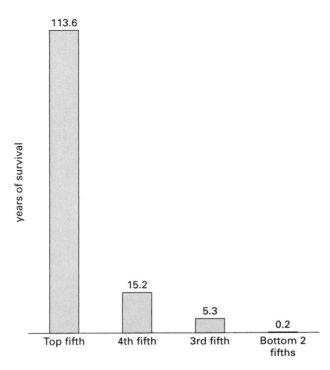

FIGURE 14.9 Years of survival on wealth alone, spending at the poverty rate in the U.S., 2001.
In this figure the living standards of rich, middle-income, and poor people are compared with regard
only to their wealth. This is done by dividing households into quintiles according to the value of their
net assets and then calculating how long people with the *average* amount of wealth in each quintile
could survive living at the *threshold of poverty,* spending accumulated wealth but not spending any
income. (We are assuming, in effect, that there is no income.) The "threshold of poverty" is the
amount of income defined by the government as constituting the borderline of poverty for families
of different sizes; it is increased each year to keep pace with inflation. The wealth data used for the
calculations here pertain to *households,* while the poverty data is defined for *families;* we use the
poverty threshold for a three-person family because the average household in 2001 consisted of
2.6 persons, so the two sets of data are roughly comparable. The numbers at the top of the bars
show how long (in years) households with the average amount of wealth in each quintile could
survive living at the borderline of poverty before using up all of their wealth. For example, in 2001 the
average level of net assets of households in the top quintile of the wealth distribution was $1.6 million,
and the poverty threshold for a three-person family in the same year was $14,128. So if the average
household in the top wealth quintile lived only off of its wealth at a rate of $14,128 a year, its members
could survive for 113.6 years. The heights of the other bars are determined in the same way, using
different amounts of net assets for each quintile but the same poverty threshold. To avoid having
no bar at all for the bottom quintile of the wealth distribution (households in this quintile have
negligible—or negative—amounts of net assets), we have combined the lowest two quintiles.

Source: Calculated by the authors from data in Edward N. Wolff, "Changes in Household Wealth in the
1980s and 1990s in the U.S." in Edward N. Wolff, ed., *International Perspectives on Household Wealth*
(Northampton, Mass.: Edward Elgar, forthcoming), Table 3, Mean Wealth Holdings and Income by Wealth
or Income Class, 1983–2001; and U.S. Bureau of the Census, *Historical Poverty Tables,* Table 1, Weighted
Average Poverty Thresholds for Families of Specified Size, 1959 to 2002, available at
http://www.census.gov/hhes/poverty/histpov/hstpov1.html.

UNEQUAL CHANCES

Those who responded to the Gallup poll that asked what it takes to get ahead in America ranked parents, good education, connections, and inherited money as a good thing to have if you are looking for economic success. They are not mistaken.

One of the enduring cultural ideals for Americans is that the United States is a "land of opportunity" where fortunes are won and lost from one generation to the next through some combination of ambition, sweat, and luck. The ideal originated during the 19th century, when the U.S. welcomed poor immigrants from the class-divided societies of Europe. Many of them found opportunities for land ownership, entrepreneurship, and schooling for their children on a scale that would have been unimaginable in the countries from which they came. The American dream means that how far you get in life is determined not by who your parents are but rather by your own abilities and by how hard you work.

Recent research relating the income of parents to the subsequent incomes of their grown children has shown, however, that having rich parents pays off. Figure 14.10 presents data from a recent study indicating, first, how likely it is that children of rich families in the U.S. will themselves end up being rich and, second, how likely it is that children of poor families will themselves end up being poor. The details of the study are presented in the caption under the figure, but the most striking finding is that children whose parents are in the richest 10 percent of the U.S. income distribution have a better than 40 percent chance of ending up in the richest 20 percent of the population, while children of parents in the poorest 10 percent of the income distribution have a greater than 50 percent chance of ending up among the poorest 40 percent of the population.

Figure 14.10 shows that among children whose parents are in the poorest 10 percent of the income distribution, only 1.3 percent end up as adults in the richest 10 percent of the income distribution. If the playing field were level in the sense that children's incomes were not affected by their parents' income, *10* percent of them would be in the richest 10 percent. Children from the poorest 10 percent have only a 3.7 percent chance of making it into the richest 20 percent of the income distribution. By contrast, among children whose parents are in the richest 10 percent, more than 20 percent (22.9 percent) will have incomes as adults placing them in the top 10 percent, while 40 percent of these offspring of the very rich will be in the top 20 percent of the income distribution. The figure also shows that the children of the rich are very unlikely to wind up poor, while more than half of the children of the poor wind up in the lower 20 percent of the income distribution.

By comparison to Canada, Sweden, and many other nations on which similar research has been done, the U.S. is far from the "land of opportunity" that many have hoped it is. What accounts for the perpetuation of fortune and hardship from generation to generation? Two explanations are widely believed, but neither one is entirely adequate.

According to one explanation, the transmission of economic success across generations occurs because high-income parents pass on their wealth to their children (recall from Figure 14.7 that high-income families have substantially more wealth than do others). Lower-income parents lack wealth (Figure 14.7 again), so their children have to make do without a nest egg. This is true, and it explains why the grown up children of the very rich also tend to be rich. But it does not explain why the children of the somewhat rich are also very likely to be at least somewhat rich, at least by comparison with the children of the

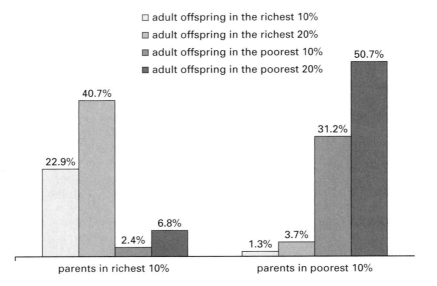

□ adult offspring in the richest 10%
▨ adult offspring in the richest 20%
▨ adult offspring in the poorest 10%
■ adult offspring in the poorest 20%

50.7%

40.7%

31.2%

22.9%

6.8%

2.4%

1.3%

3.7%

parents in richest 10%   parents in poorest 10%

FIGURE 14.10   Unequal chances: Family background and economic success in the U.S.
The four bars grouped on the left side of this figure show what happens to the children of
parents in the richest 10 percent of the population of the U.S. Of these children, 40.7 percent
end up, when they are adults, being in the richest 20 percent of the population, with 22.9 percent
ending up in the richest 10 percent; 6.8 percent end up being in the poorest 20 percent, with
only 2.4 percent ending up in the poorest 10 percent of the population. The four bars grouped
on the right side of the figure show what happens to the children who start off life in families in
the poorest 10 percent of the population. Of these children, 50.7 percent end up in the poorest
20 percent of the population, with fully 31.2 percent ending up in the poorest 10 percent of the
income distribution; only 3.7 percent of the children of poor families end up being in the richest
20 percent of the population, and just 1.3 percent of them end up among the richest 10 percent
of the population.

Thus, children from the richest tenth of the population end up as adults in the top
10 percent of the income distribution 20 times more frequently than do children from the
poorest tenth of the population, while children from the poorest tenth of the population are
15 times more likely than are children from the richest tenth to end up in the bottom 10 percent
of the income distribution. While the cards are stacked heavily against the poor in the scramble
for financial success, children of rich parents seldom experience downward mobility.

The data presented here are from the University of Michigan Panel Study of Income
Dynamics (PSID), a survey that has been regularly conducted among a representative sample
of individuals and families in the U.S. since 1968.

Source: Samuel Bowles and Herbert Gintis, "Intergenerational Inequality," *Journal of Economic
Perspectives,* vol. 16, no. 3, summer 2002, pp. 3–30.

poor. Most people receive no significant inheritance beyond their parents' home. This, too, can be seen from Figure 14.7: it shows that the next-to-the-richest fifth of the population has wealth (other than a home) of only $90,000. Even this amount of wealth could well be used up covering the costs of health care and home care for an aging parent.

According to the second explanation, what counts is the "talent one is born with," in the words of the Gallup poll. It is not a nest egg that high-income parents pass on, but rather their high-income-earning genes. (Poor parents are thought to pass on their "inferior" genes). Of course, there is no such thing as a gene for high income, even though attributes such as intelligence, shrewdness, charisma, stamina, and so on may be, to some extent, passed on genetically, and each of these may have an influence on the income of both the parents and their grown children.

The most commonly suggested candidate for an income-earning trait that is passed on genetically is IQ, meaning how well one scores on an IQ test. Of course, the quality and quantity of schooling, family environment, and a host of other influences affect one's IQ, but nature as well as nurture has an influence. We know this because genetically identical twins are much more similar in IQ than are ordinary siblings (or nonidentical twins). But this explanation is even less valid than the inherited wealth account. The reason is that IQ is not a very important determinant of one's income: things such as the amount and quality of one's schooling and one's wealth are much more important.

What is it, then, that explains intergenerational inequality? The fact that children from higher-income families get more and higher-quality schooling is an important part of the story. It is also likely that successful parents teach their children, either deliberately or by example, the personality traits and behavioral patterns that contributed to their own success. Among these are such things as saving, valuing the future, ways of interacting socially with others, and believing that what one does makes a difference (the opposite of fatalism). Health is another channel: children of lower-income families frequently have health problems that often intensify in their adult years, and these bouts of illness affect incomes. Other important influences derive from the demographic and social groups to which one belongs. People whose parents live in a poor neighborhood or region are themselves likely to remain there, and this perpetuates their low income. If they belong to a group that suffers discrimination, their children are very likely to belong to the same group. This is especially true when it comes to what is commonly called race.

RACE AND INEQUALITY

Many Americans—especially white males—speak of racial discrimination in the past tense. There are indeed some selection processes for jobs, admission to educational institutions, and competitions for other valued resources in which it is a disadvantage to be white or male. But the well-publicized cases in which this is true are a misleading guide to what happens in general.

During 2001 and 2002 an experiment carried out in Chicago and Boston by faculty members at the University of Chicago and the Massachusetts Institute of Technology showed that racial discrimination continues to exist in the labor market. The experiment

"RACE": BIOLOGY OR HISTORY?

"Races" do not exist in the sense that most people mean when they use the word to refer to groups of people differentiated by genetically perpetuated traits. What distinguishes people of African or East Asian or European ancestry when they are classified as "races" are physical markers such as skin color and facial characteristics. These do indeed differ markedly among these groups, and these traits are genetically transmitted.

However, a person who says "whites and blacks are different" usually has in mind something more than the obvious visible traits. They have in mind things such as culture, personality, average incomes, particular talents, and the like. But from a biological standpoint there are very few differences among groups of differing ancestry other than the superficial ones used to define the races. With respect to most of the genetic makeup of people, the members of a "race" are as different one from another as they are from members of a different "race." By a commonly accepted measure, well over 90 percent of genetic differences among people are *within* groups of similar ancestry, while less than 10 percent of the genetic differences are *between* groups.

Some genetic traits thought to be unique to a "race"—sickle cell anaemia among people of African decent, for example—are, in fact, associated with particular climates. People of European ancestry from the island of Sardinia, for example, share high levels of sickle cell anemia with Africans. It has nothing to do with Africanness. It is found among people whose ancestors lived in places where malaria was common in the past, including not only Sardinia and West Africa, but parts of India, too.

What makes races distinctive, other than these physical markers, is history: over long periods of time people of different ancestries have lived under different conditions. In the case of African Americans this includes the experience of many of their ancestors having been brought to America in chains and exploited as slaves.

The conclusion we draw from this is not that race does not matter; unfortunately, it most certainly does. It is that race is not a biological fact. It is, rather, a historical outcome of how people of different ancestries have lived and have treated one another. That is why we do not consider tall people a race. Height, like skin color, has an important genetic component and is highly visible. But while the exploitation of the short by the tall may occur in the dating game and on the basketball court, it is not one of the main story lines of history.

Sources: L. Cavalli-Sforza, *Genes, Peoples and Languages* (Berkeley: University of California Press, 2000); Noah Rosenberg, Jonathan Pritchard, James Weber, Howard Cann, Kenneth Kidd, Lev A. Zhivotovsky, and Marcus Feldman, "Genetic Structure of Human Populations," *Science,* no. 298, 2002, pp. 2381–2385; Marcus Feldman, R.C. Lewontin, and Mary-Claire King, "Race: A Genetic Melting Pot," *Nature,* no. 424, July 24, 2003, p. 374.

proceeded as follows. First, a number of resumes were downloaded from the internet. These resumes were then altered so that some resumes would be seen as being of higher quality than others (i.e., they reflected more experience, more certification, and so on), and anything in the resumes that might have identified the persons who originally prepared them was removed. Following this, "white-sounding" and "black-sounding" names were randomly assigned to the resumes. These names were obtained from historical birth records and were chosen according to the frequency with which they occurred in black and white households. The resumes were then sent out to 1,300 potential employers in the Boston and Chicago areas. Each employer was sent four resumes: one high-quality one with a "white-sounding" name, one high-quality one with a "black-sounding" name, one low-quality one with a "white-sounding" name, and one low-quality one with a "black-sounding" name. It turned out, as shown in Figure 14.11, that one factor alone—whether a resume had a "white-sounding" or a "black-sounding" name on it—accounted for most of the differences in the frequency with which the businesses called back the people who had (supposedly) submitted the resumes, inviting them to come in for interviews. Resumes with "white-sounding" names, whether male or female, were much more likely to result in calls back for interviews than were those with "black-sounding" names. A "Brad" was five times more likely to be called back for an interview than was a "Rasheed," and a "Kristen" was six times more likely to be called back for an interview than was an "Aisha."

We choose to display the study represented in Figure 14.11 because it is one of the most recent and best designed of a number of similar studies. In other investigations otherwise identical white and African-American car buyers, apartment seekers, and loan applicants have been treated differently. A disturbing aspect of the "race-sounding names" experiment is that while qualifications do matter when it comes to opportunities in the labor market, how much they matter is significantly affected by race. Figure 14.12 shows that high-quality resumes with "white-sounding" names are called back 30 percent more frequently than are good resumes with "black-sounding" names. Moreover, high-quality resumes with "black-sounding" names did not elicit many more call-backs than did low-quality resumes with "black-sounding" names. The improvement in the call-back ratio due to the quality of the resume was so small that it could have occurred by chance.

Did the civil rights movement of the 1960s and early 1970s fail? It might be more accurate to say that it ended. Figure 14.13 displays the long-term trends in the incomes of African-American and white men and women since before World War II. The figures show the median annual earnings of people who worked full time throughout the year, so it does not reflect the fact that African Americans are more likely to be out of work than are whites. (*Earnings* refers to income from work, that is wages, salaries, and other compensation for work.) The two left-hand panels make it clear that until 1979 the economy was moving toward racial parity, and at a quite rapid rate. Notice the dramatic progress from the outbreak of World War II through the end of the 1950s, as well as the continuing improvement during the decade of the civil rights movement and the 1970s. The passage (and aggressive enforcement of) legislation making racial discrimination in hiring illegal as well as affirmative action programs seeking to redress racial imbalances in employment contributed to the reduction in the racial earnings gaps during this period. The increase in the fraction of the workforce employed by the government also helped, as the public sector offered relatively more good jobs at more equal pay than did the private

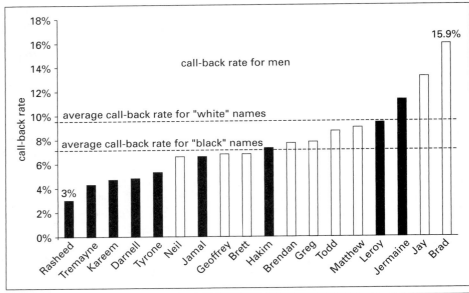

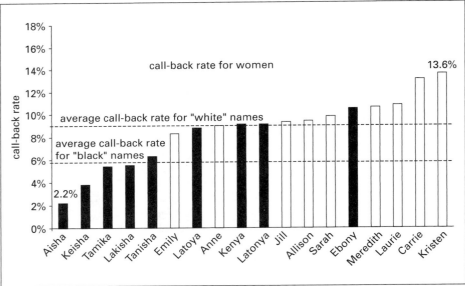

FIGURE 14.11   Racism by any other name: Labor market discrimination in the U.S., 2001–2002.   This figure displays the results of an experiment that was carried out in Chicago and Boston in 2001 and 2002. The two charts here show that for both men and women, a resume with a "white-sounding" name had a much better chance of eliciting a positive response than did a comparable resume with a "black-sounding" name on it. (Please see the text for a fuller description of this experiment.)

Source: Marianne Bertrand and Sendhil Mullainathan, "Are Emily and Brendan More Employable than Lakisha and Jamal? A Field Experiment on Labor Market Discrimination," *American Economic Review,* vol. 94, no. 4, pp. 991–1013.

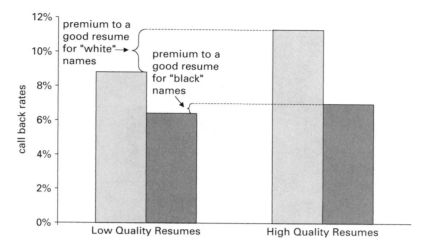

FIGURE 14.12   Good resumes pay off, if your name is OK: Labor market discrimination in the U.S., 2001–2002.   The experiment by Marianne Bertrand of the University of Chicago and Sendhil Mullainathan of the Massachusetts Institute of Technology described earlier (see Figure 14.11) also showed that while qualifications affect one's opportunities in the labor market, such opportunities are significantly influenced by race. Resumes with "white-sounding" names had call-back rates higher by 30% if the resumes were of higher quality. For resumes with a "black-sounding" name, having a good resume rather than a bad one did not result in a statistically significant improvement in call-back rates.

Source: Marianne Bertrand and Sendhil Mullainathan, "Are Emily and Brendan More Employable than Lakisha and Jamal? A Field Experiment on Labor Market Discrimination," *American Economic Review,* vol. 94, no. 4, pp. 991–1013.

sector. African Americans have made few gains in relative earnings since the end of the 1970s.

While racial discrimination in the labor market is part of the explanation for the racial earnings gaps documented in Figure 14.13, it is far from the entire story. Educational differences also matter. While the average number of years of schooling attained by white and African-American people are similar, the quality of schooling—as measured by expenditures and quality of teachers, for example—differs between the races. Finally, we have seen that having high-income parents contributes to having a higher income oneself, and few African Americans have high-income parents.

WOMEN'S WORK, WOMEN'S WAGES

The two panels on the right in Figure 14.13 compare women's and men's median annual earnings for both whites and African Americans. All the data in the figure are for full-time year-round workers, so differences in the typical number of weeks worked between men and women do not account for the gender gap in pay that we see in these data. While

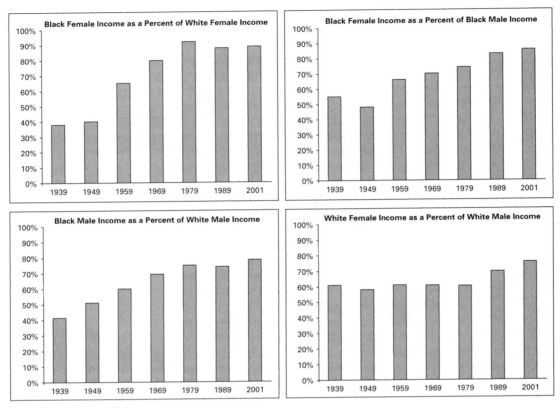

FIGURE 14.13   Halting progress in the U.S. toward a color-blind and gender-neutral economy, 1939–2001.
This figure shows how the incomes of various groups changed in relation to those of other groups during the last six decades of the 20th century. The incomes plotted are the median annual incomes of full-time year-round employees. Thus, any differences in the employment patterns of the different groups are corrected for.

Source: U.S. President's Council of Economic Advisors, *Economic Reports of the President: 1991* and *2003* (Washington, D.C.: U.S. Government Printing Office, 1991 and 2003), available at http://gpoacess.gov/eop/download.html.

African-American women have made very substantial gains compared to African-American men, women of European ancestry have made little progress in catching up with white men, despite some improvement over the last two decades of the 20th century.

The principal reason women earn less than men is *job segregation*. Women tend to work in different kinds of jobs than men do, and women's jobs pay less than men's jobs, on average. Secretaries, elementary school teachers, and nurses, for instance, are usually women, whereas carpenters, mechanical engineers, and airplane pilots are almost always men. Figure 14.14 shows how the sex segregation of jobs results in lower pay for women workers.

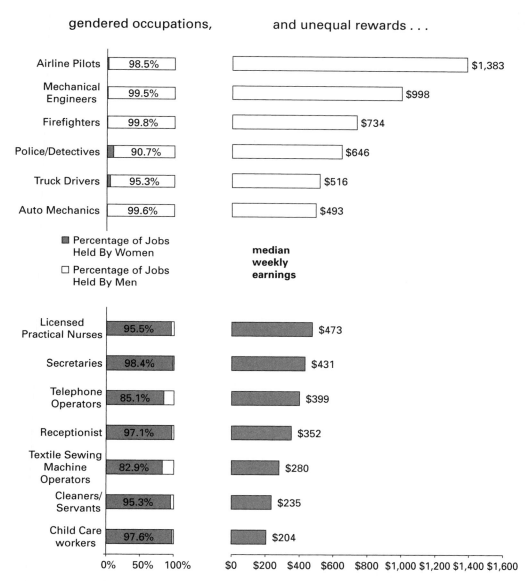

FIGURE 14.14   Women's work, women's wages: Gendered occupations and unequal earnings in the U.S., 1999.   This figure shows that in some occupations almost all the workers are women, while in others almost all are men. The occupations displayed here are some of the most "gendered" occupations. The figure also shows the median weekly earnings for each occupation, demonstrating that "men's jobs" tend to be better paid than "women's jobs."

Source: U.S. Department of Labor, Bureau of Labor Statistics, Report 943: *Highlights of Women's Earnings in 1999* (Washington D.C.: U.S. Department of Labor, 2000), available at http://www.bls.gov/cps/cpswom99.pdf.

IS *SHE* WELL SERVED IF *HE'S* IN CHARGE?

Women are underrepresented in politics around the world. For example, in 2000 less than one-seventh of members of the world's national parliamentary bodies (such as the U.S. Senate and House of Representatives) were women. But does this affect the policies adopted? Does the underrepresentation of women in the legislatures of the world result in men's interests being favored?

Maybe it does *not* matter. *If* elected political leaders simply implement the wishes of the electorate, then the sex of the person elected would not matter. Of course, women might be more likely to be elected in states where the electorate favored policies that women tend to support. So there would be a correlation between the sex of political leaders and the policies they implement. But according to this view, the sex of the leader would not have any *causal* importance; men or women elected from the same electorate would do the same thing.

India, the world's most populous democracy, provides a laboratory for studying whether women's underrepresentation in politics matters for policy. In 1993 the Indian constitution was amended to require that women be the heads of not less than a third of each state's local government councils. In many states the villages that were to be required to elect a woman as *pradhan* (as the council heads are called) were selected randomly: the first village, the fourth, the seventh, and every third village thereafter were selected from a list of all villages in the state.

A detailed study of 261 villages in the states of West Bengal and Rajasthan investigated the ways in which policies have been affected (or not affected) in the villages with newly elected female *pradhans*. All of the villages studied are poor and lack public services. Tap water is available in only 1 in 10 of the Rajasthan villages and 1 in 20 of the West Bengal villages. Public health facilities are available in less than one-tenth of the villages in West Bengal and fewer than half of the villages in Rajasthan.

The researchers studied the kinds of issues raised by men and women in the meetings of the councils. In both states women complained more frequently than men about the lack of tap water. This is not surprising: wherever tap water is lacking, it is the women who have to carry water, often over quite long distances, in pots on their heads. In West Bengal, where women do most of the paid work of road maintenance, women complained more often than men about the condition of the roads. In Rajasthan, where road maintenance is shared between men and women, men often have to travel in search of work. Since men in that state could count on at least half of the road maintenance jobs, they disproportionately favored road improvements.

The councils with newly elected female *pradhans* adopted policies in line with the interests of women. In both West Bengal and Rajasthan they invested more in the provision of water than did the villages that were not selected to have a woman *pradhan*. In West Bengal the councils headed by female *pradhans* invested more in roads, while in Rajasthan less was invested in road improvements.

The effects of India's 1993 constitutional amendment thus present us with some good news about democracy: who gets elected does make a difference. However, since women occupy few top political positions in most countries (including the U.S.), the news from India may not be so good. If the lessons of India's experiment hold for other countries, women's interests in most nations are less well served than are men's.

Source: Raghabendra Chattopadhyay and Esther Duflo, "Women as Policy Makers: Evidence from a Randomized Experiment in India," *Econometrica,* forthcoming.

Job segregation occurs even within occupations and industries. For example, there are industries in which some firms hire mostly men and other firms hire, in those *same* occupations, mostly women. Even the same firm, especially if it has plants located in different regions of the country, may hire mostly men at one plant and mostly women at another. Pay differences, with men earning more than women, usually accompany such segregation. Some of the differences are illustrated in Figure 14.15.

Why women are paid less than men is a matter of dispute. On average, women do not experience many of the economic disadvantages experienced by African Americans: school quality does not differ among men and women, nor (for obvious reasons) do women have poorer parents than men. One reason is that experience on the job is rewarded with higher pay, and in many jobs women have less experience than men. This is in part due to the time women take off of paid work to raise children or for other family responsibilities less likely to fall on men.

Some people attribute pay differences in the same job to women's lesser physical strength or some other skill. Notice, however, that jobs requiring physical strength—farm workers and stock handlers in Figure 14.15, for example—show relatively little difference in pay between men and women, especially by comparison to lawyers, physicians, and insurance adjusters, jobs in which physical strength is not rewarded. For many jobs discrimination increases job segregation by sex and thereby increases the differences in average wages and other disparities between male and female workers.

Social norms about "appropriate" work for women also make a difference. Women who take "male" jobs such as truck driving or auto repair are sometimes seen as sexually unattractive. Another "callback" study by Lee Badgett and Nancy Folbre of the University of Massachusetts confirmed this. They asked survey respondents to rank fictitious personal ads from women and men seeking dates according to the likely number of positive calls they would receive. Ads that portrayed either women or men in atypical occupations, such as a female electrician or a male nurse, were rated lower than others in more typical jobs who had otherwise similar hobbies, relationship preferences, and physical attributes. Women in atypical occupations without much education paid an especially high price in the "dating market."

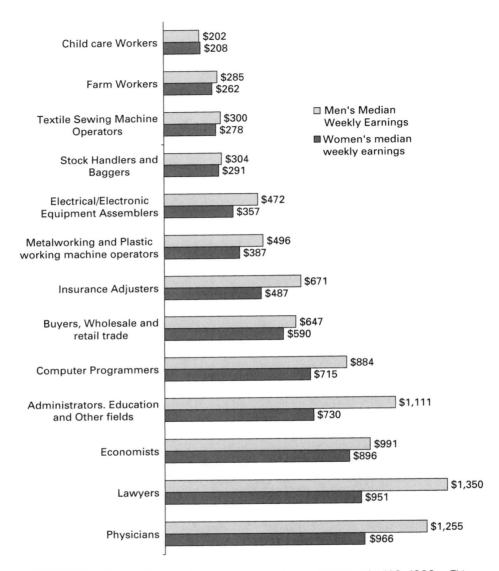

FIGURE 14.15 Men's and women's wages in selected occupations in the U.S., 1999. This figure shows that, except for child care workers (see the first pair of bars at the top of the figure), the median weekly earnings for men exceed those for women in all the represented occupations.

Source: U.S. Department of Labor, Bureau of Labor Statistics, Report 943: *Highlights of Women's Earnings in 1999* (Washington D.C.: U.S. Department of Labor, 2000), available at http://www.bls.gov/cps/cpswom99.pdf.

CONCLUSION: EXPLAINING THE MOSAIC OF INEQUALITY

Why do some families in the U.S. have much more income than others? And why do the income differences among families change over time, increasing as they have been for the last three decades of the 20th century or decreasing as they did for the four decades prior to that?

One way to answer this is to make an analogy between a family and a farmer. The farmer's income will depend on how much of each crop he is able to market and the price he gets for each. The family's income is determined in the same way. Like the farmer and his crops, the family has a set of potentially income-earning assets: the skills and time of its members and perhaps some land or other capital goods either directly owned or through the ownership of stocks. During a given year the family will put some of these assets on the market: renting the land, putting some of their skills and time at the disposition of an employer in return for wages, and so on. Like the farmer, the family's income depends on what they have to put on the market, how much of each they can sell, and the price that each of their income-earning assets fetches.

Take two hypothetical couples, Brad and Carrie and Tyrone and Latoya (yes, the choice of names is deliberate). Brad and Carrie both graduated from college. Brad is a computer programmer working full time, and Carrie works half time as a substitute teacher. Both make $20 an hour. Tyrone and Latoya did not go beyond high school, and both work full time, Tyrone as a machinist at a unionized firm and Latoya as a waitress. Tyrone makes $15 an hour and Latoya $9. Brad and Carie have $200,000 invested in the stock market, while Tyrone and Latoya own their home and car but have no other wealth. You should check the figures in this chapter to see if these hypothetical couples' economic situations are realistic.

Now let us do the numbers. If Tyrone and Latoya both work full time all year (1,750 hours), their income will be $42,000. Brad and Carrie will make $52,500 in wages. Their wealth, if it makes a rate of return of 5 percent per year, will add another $10,000, so their total income is $62,500.

Now consider the two couples in a later year. Brad and Carrie have managed to save, so their wealth is now $250,000 (and the rate of return on their wealth is now 10 percent), and Carrie is now teaching full time. Assume that their wages remained the same. Latoya is still waitressing at $9, but the machine shop where Tyrone worked closed (the firm that owned the shop opened a new plant in Germany). After a year searching for work, he found a full-time job working in a grocery store at $10 an hour. Before he was laid off, Tyrone and Latoya had saved some money toward Latoya going to college at night, but they ran through their savings and went into debt during his unemployment. They owe $10,000 to various creditors.

The numbers look a lot different now. Latoya and Tyrone make $33,250 in wages and pay 20 percent interest on their debt (totaling $2,000), giving them a net income of $31,250. Carrie and Brad now have a wage income of $70,000, and the returns on their wealth add another $25,000, giving them an income of $95,000. Both couples are working hard; neither is rich by American standards. But between the two years, Brad and Carrie went from earning 50 percent more than Tyrone and Latoya to earning three times as much.

The couples are fictitious. But is this a realistic picture of the changes in the distribution of income in the U.S. over the past few decades? Yes. The differences between the two couples and the reasons why their fortunes diverged are realistic in light of the data on the U.S. economy you have seen (and other data you can look up). The keys to the divergence have all been at work in the U.S. economy. Tyrone and Latoya faced job insecurity to a greater extent than Brad and Carrie did. They also lacked ownership of stock, the rate of return of which increased considerably over the period. The cost to Tyrone of losing his job was huge (a year without a job followed by a new job at much less pay). Had Brad or Carrie lost their jobs, their re-employment prospects would have been much better, as their skills are in demand. And Brad and Carrie greatly increased their income when Carrie went to full-time work.

Of course, we have left a lot out of our story. For example, it would have been realistic to add that after Tyrone lost his job at the machine shop, he and Latoya did not have medical insurance, and so they now pay $5,000 per year for private insurance despite the fact that neither of them smoke and both are in excellent health. Brad and Carrie would most likely both be covered by health insurance at work, especially after Carrie went to work full time. Notice that Tyrone's experience is similar to that of a worker described in the box "Globalization: American Winners and Losers" (see Chapter 7, pp. 179–180) whose plant closed. In the later year, all four members of our hypothetical couples worked in the service sector of the economy. Here they were faced with the fact that unlike jobs in manufacturing, service sector jobs tend to be of two types: high-end jobs with job security, health insurance, and good pay and low-end jobs with none of these features.

What lies behind the trend toward greater inequality in the U.S is a much-debated topic. A few contributing factors are widely agreed upon.

- The assets that high-income people have a lot of—education and invested wealth—have become more highly remunerated. The higher pay going to the better educated may be, in part, the result of newer technologies requiring more skills (so-called skill-biased technical change).
- Wealth has become more unequally held.
- More than in the past, high-income men are married to high-income women. This is because today, more than in the past, high-income men tend to be married to highly *educated* women who today are much more likely to work for pay than before. (Less educated women also tend to work for pay, but not more so than in the past.)
- The decline in the strength of trade unions (see Figure 7.1) has reduced the bargaining power of workers.
- Generally accepted norms of fair pay seem to have eroded, allowing extremely high salaries to be paid to CEOs (see Figure 14.3), while very low pay continues to be accepted without effective protest in many sectors of the economy.
- The reduction of income assistance ("welfare") to poor families has pushed more people into the low-wage labor market, while at the same time the real value of the minimum wage has been going down (see Figure 7.1), so it has become all the more difficult for low-wage earners to move up the ladder.
- The shrinkage of the manufacturing sector of the economy (see Figure 7.7) has led to the loss of many well-paying skilled jobs that once supported middle-income families.

A LIVING WAGE?

In the early hours of the morning of February 27, 2003, after weeks of heated debate, the city council of Santa Fe, New Mexico, voted 7 to 1 to pass an ordinance requiring all employers with more than 25 workers to pay a minimum wage of $8.50. At the time, the New Mexico minimum wage, $4.25 per hour, was below the federal minimum wage, the latter therefore being the legally binding effective rate. (San Francisco adopted a similar measure at about the same time.)

Proponents of the measure claimed that the increase would dramatically raise the living standards of the thousands of hotel cleaners and restaurant kitchen and wait staff—many recent immigrants from Mexico and many without health insurance who play a central role in the city's tourist industry. They also pointed out that the value of the federal minimum wage adjusted for inflation had fallen by more than a third in the previous two decades. Opponents argued that hotels and restaurants would lay off staff, that tourists would vacation elsewhere, and that it was unwarranted interference in their right to run their businesses as they chose. (One restaurant owner called it "socialistic.")

Both sides marshaled economic studies. Proponents buttressed their case with findings from a study of an earlier increase in New Jersey's minimum wage, showing that it had had no adverse effect on employment in the fast food industry. Opponents used a study financed by the restaurant industry, attempting to counter these findings. After weeks of public testimony from unions, businesses, affected workers, and other citizens (including one of the authors of this book), the council members concluded that the adverse effects on jobs—if they materialized—would probably be outweighed by the increased pay to Santa Fe's poorest workers. (They also amended the ordinance to include a study of its effects.)

Opponents of the living wage in Santa Fe did not take their loss lying down: they introduced a bill in the state legislature that would deny cities and towns the right to regulate minimum wages. And they challenged the ordinance in court as unconstitutional. On June 24, 2004, Judge Daniel Sanchez, ruling in the case *New Mexicans for Free Enterprise vs. the City of Santa Fe,* upheld the living wage ordinance, implementing it on that date.

For more information about living wages see http://www.umass.edu/peri/. The restaurant lobby and research group can be found at http://www.epionline.org/.

Sources: David Card and Alan B. Krueger, *Myth and Measurement: The New Economics of the Minimum Wage* (Princeton: Princeton University Press, 1995); David Neumark and William Wascher, "Minimum Wages and Employment: A Case Study of the Fast-Food Industry in New Jersey and Pennsylvania: Comment," *American Economic Review,* vol. 90, no. 5, 2000, pp. 1362–1396.

- The growth of the service and sales sectors of the economy has generated a "twin peaks" distribution of jobs, with both "good" and "bad" jobs proliferating while middle-income jobs have been disappearing.
- More than before, workers in the U.S. are competing with workers in the rest of the world (see Figure 7.4). While some of our trade competitors pay higher wages than the U.S. does, many do not. American workers also find themselves competing with a growing population of immigrants willing to work for low wages and not in a position to bargain aggressively with their employers because they are often in the country without legal status or citizenship. All this puts downward pressure on wages, especially in low-wage service sector jobs.

While it seems likely that all of these influences have been at work, there is little agreement about the importance of each.

SUGGESTED READINGS

Lee Badgett and Nancy Folbre, "Job Gendering: Occupational Choice and the Labor Market," *Industrial Relations,* vol. 42, no. 2, 2003, pp. 270–298.

Samuel Bowles and Herbert Gintis, "The Inheritance of Inequality," *Journal of Economic Perspectives,* vol. 16, no. 3, 2002, pp. 3–30.

Samuel Bowles, Herbert Gintis, and Melissa Osborne, "The Determinants of Earnings: A Behavioral Approach," *Journal of Economic Literature*, vol. 39, December 2001, pp. 1137–1176.

Samuel Bowles, Herbert Gintis, and Melissa Osborne, eds., *Unequal Chances: Family Background and Economic Success* (Princeton: Princeton University Press, 2004).

Len Doyal and Ian Gough, *A Theory of Human Need* (New York: Guilford, 1991).

Barbara Ehrenreich, *Nickel and Dimed: On (Not) Getting By in America* (New York: Henry Holt, Metropolitan Books, 2001).

Robert Frank, *Luxury Fever: Why Money Fails to Satisfy in an Era of Excess* (New York: Free Press, 1999).

Arthur F. Jones, Jr., and Daniel H. Weinberg, "The Changing Shape of the Nation's Income Distribution, 1947–1998," U.S. Census Bureau, *Current Population Reports,* P60-204 (Washington, D.C.: U.S. Department of Commerce, June 2000).

Katherine Newman, *No Shame in My Game: The Working Poor in the Inner City* (New York: Vintage, 2000).

Robert Pollin and Stephanie Luce, *The Living Wage: Building a Fair Economy* (New York: New Press, 2000).

Edward N. Wolff, *Top Heavy: The Increasing Inequality of Wealth in America and What Can Be Done About It,* updated ed. (New York: New Press, 2002).

Edward N. Wolff, "Changes in Wealth Inequality in the 1980s and 1990s in the U.S." in Edward N. Wolff, ed., *International Perspectives on Household Wealth* (Northampton, Mass.: Edward Elgar, forthcoming).

CHAPTER 15

Progress and Poverty on a World Scale

S ix centuries ago the Arabic explorer and geographer Ibn Battuta traveled throughout Asia, Africa, the Middle East, Russia, and Spain. He also visited the land now called Bangladesh, where today more than a third of the people are undernourished, and the country is among the world's poorest. He described traveling along its waterways, "passing between villages and garden lands." "It was as if we had been going through a market," he observed. "This is a country in which rice is extremely abundant."[1]

In the 14th century Bangladesh was relatively affluent in relation to the other parts of the world that Ibn Battuta had visited. Europe, by contrast, was reeling under the impact of a deadly bubonic plague that in many areas took the lives of a quarter of its population. Hunger and the desperate struggle for survival were the daylong and lifelong lot of all but a handful of rich and lucky people. The plight of Europe was not unusual: poverty has been the norm for millennia. In the 14th century, the relative affluence of Bangladesh made it the exception, not the rule.

Along with the U.S., Japan, and a few other countries, Europe is now the exception. It has one of the highest standards of living anywhere. The amount of goods and services available surpasses anything imaginable even a few centuries ago. And in some countries people maintain a high standard of living while working fewer hours than before. In Sweden, for example, the work week (for pay) has been reduced to less than 30 hours, and all work—including the work of raising children—typically consumes less than one-sixth of a typical person's waking hours over the span of an entire lifetime. Life, in other words, is mostly about something other than making a living.

---

[1] Quoted in Henry Yule, *Cathay and the Way Thither* (London: Haklyut Society, 1916), pp. 80, 91.

However, in Europe today, and even more so in the United States, some people are still desperately poor. In the U.S. in the early 21st century, one child in six is growing up in poverty. At the same time, a few people in poverty-stricken Bangladesh—a very few—live in a condition of affluence comparable to that of the rich in Europe and the U.S.

Throughout the world today, poverty is not the sole barrier to a decent standard of living. Even those with adequate incomes now find the quality of life and even life itself threatened by HIV-AIDS and other epidemics, the poisonous environmental consequences of rapid economic growth, the failure to regulate new technologies, and a growing frequency of civil war.

THE CHEAP BANANA AND THE RUNAWAY SHOP: ARE *WE* RICH BECAUSE *THEY* ARE POOR?

"**A**re *we* rich because *they* are poor?" This is a haunting question for people in countries where the income levels are many times greater than in poorer countries.

One way to tackle the question is to ask another. If the people of the poor nations of the world were to succeed in raising their incomes by a substantial amount, would this force a reduction in the income of the typical rich-country resident? The answer to this question has at least two sides.

On one hand, the fact that wages are low in poor countries (see Figure 15.8) means that the cost of production in those countries is low, and this translates into lower prices for the goods bought by people in rich countries. Thus, people in Europe, the U.S., and other rich countries get cheap shoes, cheap clothes, and cheap bananas. In this sense, rich-country residents benefit from the poverty in the rest of the world.

The other side of the coin is that when these goods are imported to the rich countries, workers in the U.S. and Europe who produce shoes, clothes, appliances, cars, and many other products often loose their jobs because consumers are buying less expensive goods made elsewhere. And when firms in rich countries such as the U.S. expand operations in low-wage countries while closing plants back home (see box "Globalization: American Winners and Losers" in Chapter 7) or "outsource" things such as software development or medical records processing to low-wage countries (see boxes "'Radiology Sweatshops'?" in Chapter 1 and "Hardball" in Chapter 13, p. 317), the low wages in Africa, Asia, and Latin America are a threat to living standards in the rich countries.

In the U.S. and other rich countries, some benefit from the *cheap banana,* while others' wages are eroded by the threat of the *runaway shop.* Many autoworkers and software engineers would find, if they looked closely at the labels of the clothes they are wearing, that they both benefit and lose. Big questions rarely have simple answers.

How do these massive improvements and striking inequalities in living standards come about? And how do these new threats to our well-being develop? Part of the answer, in a word, is capitalism. We have seen already in Chapter 1 the dramatic changes in output per capita and increases in real wages that have occurred since capitalism took hold in Europe and North America. But wages or per capita output levels, as we have seen in the previous chapter, are just part of what make up our economic well-being. We need to understand the entire process by which some countries and some people get rich while others remain in poverty. We need to comprehend what determines a person's and a nation's living standards. (See box "The Cheap Banana and the Runaway Shop: Are *We* Rich Because *They* Are Poor?")

In this chapter we focus on the world economy and introduce information about the specifically international aspect of economic life. Already we have seen that capitalism is an internationally oriented economic system: firms seeking profits do not let national boundaries get in their way when there is money to be made (Chapters 1 and 7). In Chapter 1 we saw that since the early days of capitalism until very recently, inequalities in the world have grown. We have also seen that the level of the surplus product generally—and the profit rate in the U.S. specifically—depends on the real price of imports; that is, it depends on the price of imported goods compared to the price of goods produced domestically (Chapters 5 and 7). In Chapter 7 we saw that the U.S. economy is increasingly affected by imports from the rest of the world, and that this process has increased the degree of competition among major firms and eroded the power of labor unions. Here we build on these ideas by looking at the experiences of other countries and by studying the processes of investment and exchange that link all countries.

The main idea of this chapter is that *dramatic differences in income levels in the world reflect both the massive productive potential of the capitalist economic system and the uneven distribution of the results of the capitalist economic growth process. Growth and distribution in turn depend on the institutions that regulate the process of production and the pattern of international exchange and investment.*

This central idea is expressed in seven key points:

---

1. Around the world, people have very different living standards.

2. While varying cultures and natural resources are important causes of differences in productivity, the most important differences among nations have to do with the institutions that regulate the economy and govern the way competition occurs.

3. Nations that were able to start the process of modern economic development early often have an advantage over newcomers to the process.

4. Improvements in living standards are made possible when part of the surplus product is used to produce capital goods, new knowledge, and improved technology. In the poor countries major increases in productivity can be achieved simply by adopting newer technology.

5. Capitalism is an economic system that provides strong incentives for rapid increases in the output of goods and services. Nevertheless, many capitalist countries are very poor, and some of them have recently experienced falling per capita income.

6. Generally, the advanced capitalist economies that have been most successful in raising productivity over the last half century have been those in which the government has played an important role in the economy.

7. International investment involves transferring part of the surplus product from one country to another. The transfer of the surplus may go from rich countries to poor countries or vice versa.

POVERTY AND PROGRESS

Today one of the most striking aspects of the world economy is the extent of inequality. In the U.S., the richest fifth of households receives more than 14 times as much income as the bottom fifth does. Even more shocking, though, is the fact that average income in the richest 5 percent of households in the U.S. is roughly *80 times* the average income in Bangladesh, taking into account the differing buying power of the incomes in both countries. And Bangladesh, while very poor, is not the poorest country in the world. This dubious honor goes to Congo, which has an average income about one-half that of Bangladesh and one-fortieth that of the United States.

Look back at Figure 1.5 in Chapter 1. It shows that since 1820 the share of income received by the richest 10 percent of the world's population (almost all of them living in North America or Europe) has risen, and the share of the poorest 60 percent of the world's population (almost all of them in Asia, Africa, and Latin America) has fallen. In recent years this process of income divergence between the haves and the have-nots has slowed and perhaps even reversed. The reason for this is that China, the world's most populous nation, has experienced extraordinarily rapid income growth over the past decade, growing far more rapidly than England did as the leader of the Industrial Revolution in the 19th century. Inequality is also increasing rapidly within China, but the overall effect of China's dramatic catching up is to reduce world inequality. India, the world's second-most-populous nation, is also catching up, though more slowly. As in China, inequality among Indians is growing rapidly.

Income differences, as we have seen, tell only part of the story. In Figure 15.1 we present comparative information on incomes and some other aspects of living standards.

Look first at the upper left panel. This panel shows that the buying power of the average income in the U.S. is much greater than the buying power of the average income in China, India, and Kenya. The panel also shows that the buying power of the average income in the U.S. is greater than the buying power of the average income in Sweden and Japan. (Bangladesh, not shown, lies about midway between Kenya and India on this scale.) The top right panel presents a standard measure of health in a population—how many years, on average, a person will live. Notice two things about this chart. First, Japan and Sweden, though less rich than the U.S., have somewhat better health. Second, differences in health between these relatively high-income countries (as a group) and the others are much greater than the differences in their income levels. Life expectancy in Kenya, for example, is somewhat more than half the U.S. figure, while its average income is barely one-thirtieth that of the U.S. The bottom left panel presents data on another health measure, the fraction of infants who die before the age of five years. Again note that Sweden and Japan are healthier than the

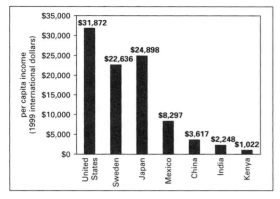
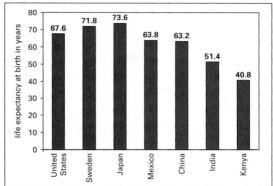
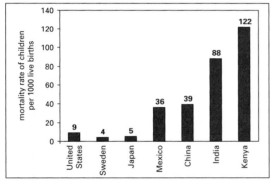
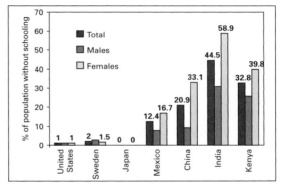

FIGURE 15.1   Income, life expectancy, infant mortality, and schooling in seven countries in 2000.   The four panels in this figure indicate disparities among a representative sample of countries with regard not only to income levels but also to life expectancy, health conditions, and educational opportunities. As one would expect, richer countries, ones with higher per capita incomes adjusted for purchasing power parity (see box "What's a Hamburger Worth?" in this chapter), tend to have lengthier life expectancy (the number of years the average individual can expect to live at birth) and lower infant mortality rates (the number of children per 1,000 live births who die each year before reaching the age of five). Richer countries generally provide more of their people with educational opportunities and, consequently, have smaller percentages of their population without schooling. The lower panel on the right shows the percentage of people in the different countries 25 or more years old who have had no schooling at all. Notice, however, that there is not an exact correspondence between income per capita and the social indicators. For example, Sweden and Japan have lower per capita incomes than the United States but have longer life expectancy and lower infant mortality rates, and in Japan there is hardly anyone without schooling, whereas 1 percent of the U.S. population has not been to school.

Sources: World Bank, "World Development Indicators: 2000," (Washington, D.C.: World Bank, 2001, available on CD-ROM); Alan Heston, Robert Summers, and Bettina Aten, Penn World Tables Version 6.1, Center for International Comparisons at the University of Pennsylvania (CICUP), October 2002, available at: http://webhost.bridgew.edu/baten; Robert J. Barro and Jong-Wha Lee, "International Data on Educational Attainment: Updates and Implications," Center for International Development Working Paper no. 42, (Cambridge, Mass.: Harvard University, 2000) available at: http://www.cid.harvard.edu/ciddata/ciddata.html; World Health Organization, *World Health Report 2001:Mental Health, New Understanding, New Hope* (Geneva, Switzerland: World Health Organization, 2001), Table 4, available at http://www.who.int/whr/en/.

U.S. by this measure. But also note that more than 1 in 10 babies born in Kenya die before they are of school age. The fraction of the population with no schooling is shown in the lower right panel. Note that more than half the women in India have not been to school at all, though most girls today in India do attend primary school at least for a few years.

The living conditions typical of India, China, and Kenya are much more common in the world today than the living conditions of the U.S., Sweden, and Japan. (Well over a third of the world's people live in India and China; Americans make up less than one-twentieth of the world's population.) Figure 15.2 shows how the income of the world is distributed among families at various income levels. Along the horizontal axis are levels of family income measured in units of comparable buying power, translated into dollar amounts. The vertical axis indicates the fraction of the world's population that receives the level of income shown on the horizontal axis. Most of the people represented in the left-hand bars are in China, India, and the other large poor countries such as Bangladesh, Indonesia, Nigeria, and Pakistan. Some of these very poor people are in countries such as Brazil and South Africa that have higher average incomes but huge disparities between rich and poor.

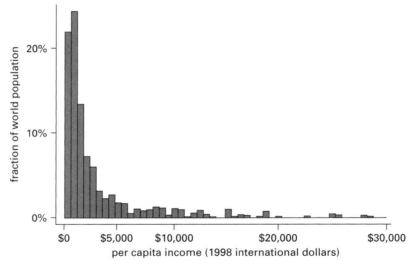

FIGURE 15.2   The income distribution of the world, 1993.   This figure shows how the world's income was distributed among the world's people in 1993. The information displayed here is from 1993 household survey data converted to 1998 dollars using the purchasing power parity method (see box "What's a Hamburger Worth?" in this chapter). The height of each bar shows the percent of the world's population that had the annual income (in 1998 dollars) indicated on the horizontal axis. The *average* annual income of the world in 1993, calculated by adding up the incomes of everyone in the world and then dividing the total by the population of the world, was $3,150. The $3,150 figure is misleading, however, because it fails to take into account the fact that a relatively large share of the total income of the world is received by a relatively small percentage of the world's people. Taking this fact into account, we find that fully 75 percent of the world's population lives on less than $3,150 a year.

Source: Branko Milanovic, *Worlds Apart: International and World Inequality, 1950–2000* (Washington, D.C.: World Bank, 2003).

Most of the income inequality in the world today is *between* countries rather than *within* them. To see what this means, imagine that the world changed in such a way that within every country everyone had the same income, but the total income of each country remained the same. How different would Figure 15.2 look? The answer is, not very different. By most measures, about three-quarters of the income inequality in the world is between nations, not within them. Hence, even if income were to be distributed equally within every country, the world's income would still be distributed very unequally.

Nevertheless, within-country inequality is substantial in many countries—for example, the U.S. and Brazil. Figure 15.3 displays the income levels of each fifth of the populations of India, Brazil, and the U.S. As the figure shows, the average income of the richest fifth in India is less than that of the poorest fifth in the U.S. Since income

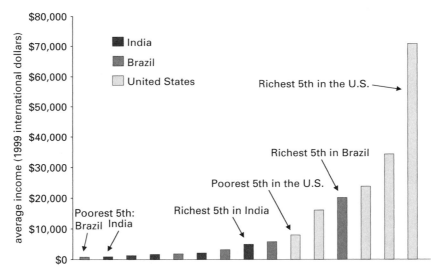

FIGURE 15.3   Comparative inequality: Incomes by quintile in India, Brazil, and the U.S. in 1999. This figure compares the income levels of three countries, showing the income by quintile (fifth) of each country's income distribution and placing the various quintiles—no matter from which country—on the horizontal axis in the order determined by the amount of the quintile's income, with lower-income quintiles to the left and higher-income quintiles to the right. The height of each bar reflects *real* income (corrected for inflation) adjusted additionally (by the PPP method) for the relative *buying power* of a unit of each nation's currency (see box "What's a Hamburger Worth?" in this chapter). As the figure indicates, the poorest fifth of the U.S. population (represented by the shortest white bar) has a higher average income than that of the richest fifth of Indians (represented by the tallest black bar). But the degree of income inequality in Brazil allows the richest fifth of that country's citizens (the tallest dotted bar) to enjoy an average income almost equal to that of the middle quintile of the American income distribution (the tallest dotted bar is only a bit shorter than the third white bar), while the poorest fifth of Brazilians (represented by the shortest dotted bar) has an average level of income lower than that of the poorest fifth in India (the shortest black bar).

Source: World Bank, *World Development Report 2000/2001: Attacking Poverty* (New York: Oxford University Press, 2001).

inequality is very great in Brazil, however, the richest fifth of Brazilians would be almost "middle income" in the U.S., while the poorest fifth of Brazilians are poorer, even, than the poorest Indians.

Are living standards improving throughout the world? It depends on where you look and what you look at. By almost any measure, living standards have been rising *on average*. Access to medical services, basic nutrition, and education have improved in most countries. Figure 15.4 summarizes some of the progress made since 1960. Using the same measures of well-being as in Figure 15.1 but reflecting world averages, the figure shows that income and longevity are both rising, while child mortality and the fraction of people who have not been to school are both falling.

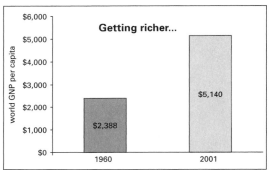
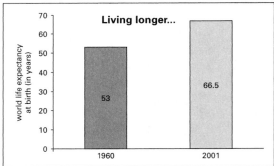
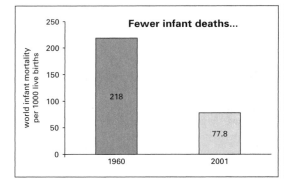
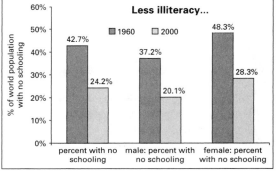

FIGURE 15.4   Progress on a global scale.   The numbers in this figure are averages for all the countries reporting the relevant information. The reporting countries contain the vast majority of the world's people. As the figure shows, dramatic gains in health and education have been made in the last 40 years. The level of GNP per capita is adjusted for inflation and is in 1988 dollars.

Sources: World Bank, "World Development Indicators: 2000," (Washington, D.C.: World Bank, 2001, available on CD-ROM); Alan Heston, Robert Summers, and Bettina Aten, Penn World Tables, Version 6.1, Center for International Comparisons at the University of Pennsylvania (CICUP), October 2002, available at: http://webhost.bridgew.edu/baten; Robert J. Barro and Jong-Wha Lee, "International Data on Educational Attainment: Updates and Implications," Center for International Development Working Paper no. 42 (Cambridge, Mass.: Harvard University, 2000) available at: http://www.cid.harvard.edu/ciddata/ciddata.html; World Health Organization, *World Health Report 2001: Mental Health, New Understanding, New Hope* (Geneva, Switzerland: World Health Organization, 2001), Table 4, available at http://www.who.int/whr/en/.

PRODUCTIVITY AND INCOME

These facts of economic progress and inequality among nations point to an important question: why have some countries made such striking economic progress while others have done so poorly? The answer has to do with differences in economic institutions and the way that international economic competition gives advantages to already successful countries.

Before explaining why economic institutions are important, however, we should consider some familiar explanations of the wealth and poverty of nations. Two come to mind. One is that the rich countries are those with abundant natural resources; the other is that some countries have cultures favorable to economic development. America's riches, for example, are often attributed to our vast resource base and "Yankee ingenuity." But both of these explanations are inadequate.

An abundance of natural resources is a source of income, of course, and lack of access to coal, iron, and sources of power can be a barrier to growth. (See box "Why England Took Off," pp. 10–11.) But an abundant resource base is hardly a guarantee of affluence. The tiny country called the United Arab Emirates is oil-abundant, and its per capita income is among the highest in the world, but mineral-rich Congo has the lowest per capita income in the world. One of the richest countries on a per capita basis—richer than the United Arab Emirates—is resource-poor Denmark. And Japan—over the last century and a half one of the fastest growing of the world's major economies—is practically without natural resources. Japan has no iron ore, no oil, and very little coal, yet it produces more steel than the U.S.

Differences in cultures may also affect economic fortunes. Some cultures are more likely than are others to foster habits of saving, innovation, risk taking, and hard work. But cultural differences by themselves cannot explain differences in national economic performance. Cultures change very slowly over a period of centuries, while the economic performance of a nation can change dramatically in the course of decades. During the 1950s just before China's economic take off, a number of scholars wrote that China would remain impoverished because its culture inhibited individual initiative. In 1990 China and India had the same per capita income, but 10 years later China's was more than 60 percent greater. Cultural differences and cultural changes cannot explain these major differences in economic performance.

PRODUCTIVITY, INCENTIVES, AND THE SURPLUS PRODUCT

The key to increasing income per capita is to increase productivity, that is, to increase the output resulting from an hour's labor (what has been referred to as z in earlier chapters). The reason why incomes in India are, on average, one-fifteenth what they are in the U.S. is that an hour of labor produces much less in India than in the U.S. As has been suggested earlier, some of the factors that contribute to high productivity are:

- the skills and motivation of the workers and managers,
- the technologies used in production,
- adequate systems of communication and transportation among buyers and sellers of goods, as well as adequate supplies of energy and water, and
- the scale of production: it is often more efficient to produce large batches of an item than to produce small batches.

The **infrastructure** of an economy (sometimes called its "social overhead capital") consists of its roads, railways, airports, harbor facilities, bridges and tunnels, water and sewage systems, public utilities and electricity grids, and communications networks such as telephone lines and the internet backbone.

Economies of scale exist when the average cost of producing something falls as more of it is produced.

We refer to the systems of energy and water supply and communication and transportation networks as the *infrastructure* of production. The effect of scale on productivity is commonly referred to as "economies of large-scale production," or simply *economies of scale.*

To summarize: highly skilled and highly motivated workers and managers using the most advanced technologies, producing on a large scale, and using modern systems of communication and transportation are highly productive. How can skills, motivation, technology, the scale of production, and infrastructure be developed to achieve high levels of productivity? All of these depend on a society's institutional structure. The institutional structure sets up the incentives people will have to learn new skills, to save and invest, and to take economically productive risks. Thus, the institutional structure determines the size of the surplus product and how it is used.

The skills of the workforce—both of managers and of workers—depend on the system of education, on opportunities for on-the-job learning, and on the incentives to learn productive skills. Where schooling is of poor quality or available only to a privileged few, and where people have little incentive to develop their skills, productivity will tend to be lower.

The motivation to work hard and well depends, in part, on how work is rewarded. Where work is well rewarded, and especially where the worker benefits directly from a job done well, there will tend to be high levels of productivity. Consider the worker who is self-employed and owns whatever he or she produces: a job done well means more income for the worker. As we saw in Chapters 12 and 13, most workers in a capitalist economy face either the carrot—the reward for a job done well—or the stick—the threat of losing the job.

The technology in use depends on the level of knowledge available, the skills and motivation of the workers, the amount of the surplus devoted to investment in new productive capacity, and the incentives to innovate. New technologies cannot be introduced if workers lack skills, if workers resist new technologies, if the surplus is entirely devoted to uses other than productive investment (such as military spending), or if no one is willing to take the risk of introducing something new. Just as worker motivation increases when workers are paid at least a part of the results of a job done well, good incentives to innovate usually require that risk takers benefit when risks pay off.

The infrastructure of production depends on the level of investment—often investment by the government—in building roads, railroads, air transport, telecommunications facilities, and energy generation and distribution networks. Good infrastructure makes possible communication among the many participants throughout the economy, and this may require such things as computer literacy and the ability to communicate in a common language.

Lastly, the scale of production depends on the size of the population and how much income it has to spend. Large-scale production is easier to achieve in large economies with high incomes, such as Europe and the U.S. Such countries will therefore have higher levels of productivity, and these high levels of productivity will in turn generate high incomes. Another consequence of high productivity is that it will enable a country to be successful in selling its products in world markets.

Notice the importance for productivity of both incentives and the surplus. The surplus product is necessary to provide a well-educated labor force, it is essential to generating the knowledge on which new technologies are based, and it makes possible investment in infrastructure as well as in new capital goods embodying advanced technologies. Incentives are necessary to promote the acquisition of new knowledge, to encourage the learning of productive skills, to motivate workers to work hard, and to inspire managers to innovate.

The structure of incentives and the control over the surplus product are determined by the economic system, that is, by the economic institutions that regulate the way we interact with our environment through labor and with one another through various forms of economic interdependence. The economic system also has a major influence on the amount and types of knowledge available, on the scale of production, and on the size of the surplus. For all these reasons productivity depends on economic institutions. A summary of some of the major lines of influence discussed here is presented in Figure 15.5.

By far the most important economic system in the world is capitalism. We will focus on how it works to promote high incomes in some countries and low incomes in others.

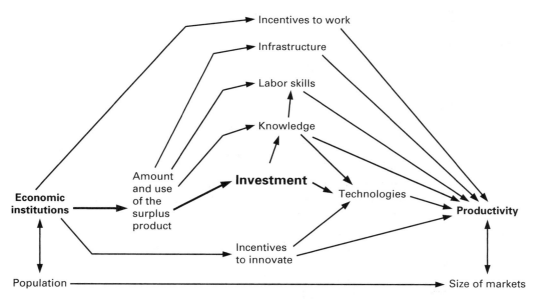

FIGURE 15.5   The determinants of productivity.   This figure portrays various cause-and-effect relationships that affect, in any economy, the level and rate of growth of labor productivity. The arrows indicate the major lines of influence running from economic institutions on the left to productivity (net output per hour of labor) on the right. The link between productivity and market size (shown at the lower right in the diagram) is as follows: increases in productivity lift incomes, and higher incomes, in turn, tend to increase the size of markets. And it works the other way as well: larger markets allow firms to achieve economies of scale—and this makes possible increases in productivity.

CAPITALISM AND UNEVEN DEVELOPMENT

Most countries in the world have capitalist economies. For this reason we cannot explain the vast differences in income and economic growth in the world by differences between capitalism and other economic systems. Inequalities arise because of the way capitalism *itself* works. What needs to be explained, then, is how capitalism promotes rapid economic growth, high levels of productivity, and high incomes in some countries, yet does not promote these outcomes in other countries. This process of rapid growth in some parts of the capitalist world and slow growth or economic decline in others is referred to as *uneven development.*

> **Uneven development** is the process of rapid growth in some parts of the capitalist world and slow growth or even economic decline in others.

WHAT'S A HAMBURGER WORTH?

If one wanted to compare the size of two economies, say those of the U.S. and Japan, how could it be done? First, it would be necessary to face the fact that particular countries measure their outputs (and incomes) in their own currencies. Although a number of European nations now have a common currency (the euro) and are therefore able to measure—and compare directly—their various economies, it remains necessary to solve the multiple currency problem in order make comparative assessments of most of the world's economies.

The GDP of Japan, for example, is expressed in yen, while that of the U.S. is denominated in dollars. To deal with this issue, economists can do one of two things. First, they can use foreign exchange rates—the ratios at which units of different national currencies are traded for dollars in global currency markets—to convert the value of any country's national output in its own currency to an equivalent number of dollars. Using this method, they can then compare the sizes of any two countries' economies in dollars.

However, many economists are skeptical of the foreign exchange rate method of comparing economies. They doubt that the relative sizes of different economies can be accurately assessed in this way. The basis for their skepticism is that the *purchasing power* of one country's currency differs from that of another country's currency, and the exchange ratios of the two countries' currencies in global currency markets may not adequately reflect such differences in purchasing power.

For example, in mid-2004 it was possible to exchange 1 dollar for approximately 113 Japanese yen. It was also possible to buy a Big Mac hamburger in the U.S. for an average price of $2.90 (with tax). But if enough dollars were converted into Japanese yen to buy a Big Mac in Japan (Big Macs are produced in 120 countries), the price in dollars would be only $2.33. As pointed out in a recent issue of *The Economist,* this indicates that the exchange value of Japanese yen in terms of dollars is less than it should be—shouldn't a Big Mac cost the same everywhere?—so any comparison of the size of the Japanese economy and that of the U.S. on the basis of the international exchange rate between dollars and yen will be inaccurate.

Of course, one cannot reach valid conclusions about the difficulty of making international comparisons using only the prices of Big Macs in different countries. And, in fact, serious economists do not do this. It is only the unique sense of humor of *The Economist* that inspires it to assess the relative values of currencies using its "Big Mac Index."

Yet the Big Mac story contains more than a grain of truth. Indeed, major international organizations such as the World Bank and the International Monetary Fund have for many years used what they call the *purchasing power parity* (PPP) method of making international economic comparisons. The way they do this is to construct a particular "basket" of commodities—including, say, a certain number of units of housing, food, transportation, schooling, and other essential goods and services—and then ask how much the same basket of commodities costs in different countries using the countries' own currencies. After this question is answered, PPP exchange ratios between different countries' currencies can be used to make more accurate international economic comparisons. The only difference is that there is more in the "basket" in this case than a Big Mac.

Use of the purchasing power parity approach often greatly affects results. In 2001, for example, Japan's per capita income was higher than that of the U.S. when incomes were compared using the exchange rate between yen and dollars. Using the purchasing power parity approach, however, U.S. per capita income was more than 25 percent higher than Japan's. Since the second measure seems more accurate, we use the PPP approach whenever possible in this book. (See, for example, Figures 15.1, 15.2, 15.3 and 15.7 in this chapter.)

Sources: "The Big Mac Index: Food for Thought," *The Economist*, May 29–June 4, 2004, pp. 71–72; World Bank, *World Development Report 2003: Sustainable Development in a Dynamic World* (Washington, D.C.: A copublication of the World Bank and Oxford University Press, 2003), Table 1.

Let us start with two important facts. First, the richest countries in the world—the United States, Germany, Japan, Norway, Denmark, Sweden, and others—are all capitalist and have been for at least 100 years. Second, the poorest countries in the world—Congo, Haiti, Bangladesh, and others—are all capitalist countries as well.

The rich countries are different from one another in many ways. For example, in the U.S. the role of government in the economy is quite limited, while in most other rich countries it is much greater. Evidence of this is given in Figure 19.4 (in Chapter 19), which shows the relative amounts of government spending in various rich countries. In comparison to all the European countries, government spending as a percentage of GDP is lower in the U.S., and the role of government in the economy is correspondingly smaller. There are other differences among the rich nations. Some countries—the United Kingdom, France, Belgium, Japan, Spain, and Portugal—once commanded substantial empires. Others—Italy and Norway, for example—did not.

REVERSAL OF FORTUNE: THE IMPORTANCE OF INSTITUTIONS FOR ECONOMIC GROWTH

In 1700 Mexico's per capita income was about the same as that of the British colonies that would become the first 13 states of the United States. Cuba and Barbados were significantly richer. At the close of the 18th century, Cuba had a slightly higher per capita income than did the U.S., and Haiti was probably the richest society in the world (on a per capita basis, counting slaves). At the opening of the 21st century, however, the per capita income of Mexico was less than a third of the U.S. level, and Haiti's was even lower. What accounts for this reversal of fortune?

Economic historians Kenneth Sokoloff and Stanley Engerman provide the following explanation. In the parts of the New World in which sugar and other plantation crops could be grown (Cuba, Haiti) or in which minerals and indigenous labor were abundant (Mexico), economic elites relied on slaves or other forms of coerced labor. They consolidated their power and material privileges by excluding others from the opportunities they enjoyed. The institutions they constructed limited access to schooling, public lands, patents, entrepreneurial opportunities, and political participation. Over the ensuing centuries, even after the demise of slavery and other forms of coerced labor, opportunities for saving, innovation, and investment were monopolized by the well-to-do. Literacy remained low, and land holding was highly concentrated.

As the source of wealth shifted from natural resource extraction to manufacturing and services, the highly unequal economies of countries such as Cuba, Haiti, and Mexico stagnated. In the U.S. and Canada, on the other hand, broader access to land, to schooling, and to entrepreneurial opportunities stimulated economic growth. As a result, these far more inclusive economies grew rapidly.

Geography, not culture, seems to have been the source of the initial divergence of institutions among the colonies of the New World. The distinct cultures and policies of the European states that established these colonies does not explain the difference. British Belize and Guyana went the way of Spanish Honduras and Colombia; British Barbados and Jamaica went the way of Cuba and Haiti.

Unlike the Puritans who came to New England, the Puritans who settled Providence Island off the coast of Nicaragua forsook their liberal political ideals and became slave owners. According to its leading historian, "the Puritan settlement . . . with its economy fueled by privateering and slavery looked much like any other West Indian colony." It had more slaves than Puritans when the Spanish overran it in 1641, and it was such a wealthy colony that it attracted two boatloads of Pilgrims who believed they could do better there than in Massachusetts.

Sources: Adapted from Samuel Bowles, *Microeconomics: Behavior, Institutions and Evolution* (Princeton: Princeton University Press, 2004), based on Kenneth Sokoloff and Stanley Engerman, "Institutions, Factor Endowments, and Paths of Development in the New World," *Journal of Economic Perspectives,* vol. 14, no. 3, 2000, pp. 217–232; and Karen Ordahl Kupperman, *Providence Island, 1630–1641: The Other Puritan Colony* (New York: Cambridge University Press, 1993).

Similar differences occur among the poorest countries. Some, such as Congo, were colonies until recently (before 1960 it was the Belgian Congo). Others, such as Haiti, gained their independence from colonial rule in the 19th century.

Why does capitalism promote rapid productivity growth in some circumstances and not in others? We saw in Chapter 1 that circumstances prevailing in Europe, the United States, and Japan from about 1500 on were associated with rapid technological progress and unprecedented growth in per capita income (see Figures 1.1 and 1.3). In Chapters 11 and 13 we explained how the process of competition in both product markets and labor markets forces companies to reinvest and innovate while at the same time driving workers to be productive. So here our explanation of why capitalism enhances productivity growth under certain circumstances can be brief. Capitalism promotes the growth of productivity because it places the surplus in the hands of business owners, who must in turn innovate and invest productively in order not to lose their position in society. Capitalism is the first economic system in history in which the elite is composed of the winners in a competition to produce at low cost the goods that other people want. Capitalism also provides workers with a strong motivation to work hard and well, since the alternative is unemployment.

Two particular circumstances are crucial to the ability of capitalism to promote rapid growth. These are *security of private property* and *insecurity of one's economic position.*

When capitalist property rights are secure, those who own the capital goods used by wage and salary workers will also own the goods that are produced. In this situation the employer who owns the workplace will own the surplus that results when the firm is profitable. However, employers can continue to receive profits only if they keep ahead of the competition, and this requires that they reinvest a substantial portion of the surplus, continually modernizing the production process. The process of competition threatens to eliminate any capitalist who does not reinvest. The security of property rights means that if you win, you win. Nobody can take your prize. But the insecurity of economic position means that if you lose, you lose. If you fail to produce good commodities at low cost, you are not just a poor capitalist, you are an ex-capitalist. Thus, both the property rights that ensure control of the surplus and the insecurity associated with competitive markets promote innovation and investment.

Something similar is true for workers, at least as far as the insecurity part is concerned. Workers' lack of property compels them to work, and the threat of unemployment and the likelihood of ending up with a worse job are constant reminders of the necessity to work hard and well. One of the shortcomings of capitalism as a system of incentives is that workers do not own what they produce. Unlike the rewards of a capitalist, who can count on owning the results of his or her investment, clever management, and risk taking, a worker's pay often does not reflect how hard and well he or she has worked.

The growth of productivity differs greatly even among advanced capitalist nations. From Figure 15.6 we can see that since 1950 the growth of productivity (output per worker) in the United States has lagged behind that of other capitalist nations. Productivity growth in South Korea and Japan was exceptionally rapid because they were able, early in the period, to borrow advanced technology from the leading nations. Most of the European countries have also enjoyed productivity growth higher than that of the U.S.

As we pointed out earlier, however, capitalism does not promote productivity growth equally well under all circumstances. It is puzzling to find that while certain capitalist

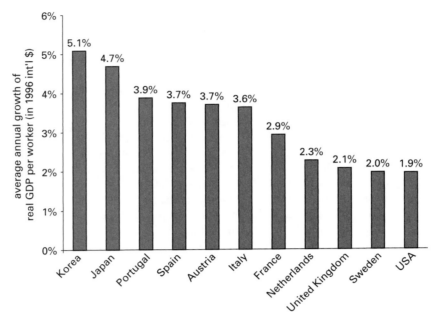

FIGURE 15.6   Average annual growth of real GDP per worker, 1950–2000.   This figure shows how rapidly productivity grew, in *real* terms, in various capitalist economies during the second half of the 20th century. "Real" means that "nominal" values, that is, values in "current" dollars, have been adjusted for inflation, in this case by calculating each country's GDP as if it had been priced each year in "constant" 1996 international dollars. Productivity is usually defined as the amount of output produced per hour of labor, but data on hours of work are not available for all nations. An alternative measure is the total output of an economy (GDP) divided by the number of people employed in a given year. This is the measure used here, so the productivity growth of each country shown in the figure is the percentage change in this variable from year to year, averaged for the years from 1950 to 2000. As can be seen in the figure, productivity growth in South Korea has been, on average, slightly more than 5 percent, while that of the U.S., Sweden, and the U.K. has hovered at around 2 percent. Sweden's relatively low rate of growth of *output per worker* (the measure of productivity used in this chart) was largely due to the fact that Swedish workers, over the period 1950–2000, greatly reduced the number of hours they worked per year, thus trading off faster growth of output for significant increases in leisure time (for example, length of vacations).

Source: Alan Heston, Robert Summers, and Bettina Aten, Penn World Tables, Version 6.1, Center for International Comparisons at the University of Pennsylvania (CICUP), October 2002, available at: http://webhost.bridgew.edu/baten/.

economies and regions have experienced rapid productivity growth and rapidly rising incomes—Europe, North America, Japan, South Korea, Hong Kong, Singapore, Taiwan, and others—this has not been the case throughout the world. Entire regions—Latin America and sub-Saharan Africa, for example—actually experienced declines in per capita income during the 1980s and 1990s. (See box "Does Inequality Grease the Wheels of Progress?")

DOES INEQUALITY GREASE THE WHEELS OF PROGRESS?

For decades economists believed (and taught their students) that rapid growth in productivity and other measures of good economic performance require high levels of income inequality. A "trade-off," they called it: if you want greater equality, you must pay for it with inefficiency and slower economic growth. They reasoned that heightened inequality gives stronger incentives to work hard, to manage well, and to take the risks necessary for innovation. The idea was even enshrined in the title of a famous book, *Equality and Efficiency: The Big Trade-off,* by the Brookings Institution economist Arthur Okun, who wrote, "The conflict between equality and economic efficiency is inescapable." The alleged trade-off became a powerful justification of inequality: a more just society would be nice, but simply too expensive.

Far from being inescapable, however, the trade-off turned out to be hard to find in practice. Suspicion about its existence was prompted by the fact that in

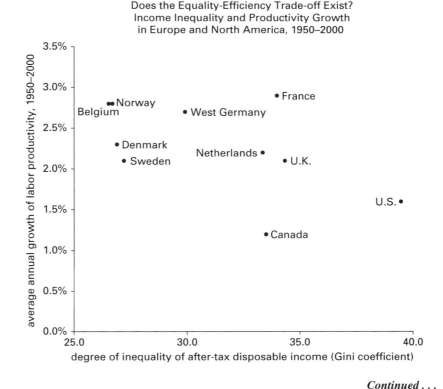

Does the Equality-Efficiency Trade-off Exist?
Income Inequality and Productivity Growth
in Europe and North America, 1950–2000

Continued . . .

recent decades the distributions of income in Japan, Korea, and Taiwan have been among the most equal in the world, yet the growth in productivity in these countries has been much higher than in the most unequal countries such as South Africa and Brazil, not to mention the U.S., the U.K., and other more unequal countries.

Even confining our comparisons to relatively rich countries (which have more accurate statistics), the trade-off does not materialize. In the figure on the previous page we plot the rate of productivity growth (from Figure 15.6) in relation to a measure of family income inequality (called the Gini coefficient), taking account of taxes and payments from the government.

Many economists now think that economic inequality impedes rather than promotes efficiency and the growth of productivity. Inequality often breeds conflicts such as strikes and fosters hostile relationships between employers and employees, wasting output and effort in unproductive ways. In some cases people simply walk away from an opportunity for mutual gain, because no slice of the cake at all seems better than an unfairly small slice (remember the 'ultimatum game' from Chapter 2). Racial and other forms of discrimination, as well as other aspects of unequal opportunity, contribute to the lack of adequate education for many, with a resulting talent loss for the economy as a whole. And when sharp inequalities of wealth mean that most people lack the assets they would need to go into business on their own, the economy loses their capacities for management and innovation as well as the benefit of the incentives that come from owning the fruits of one's own labor. In these cases inequality throws sand in the wheels of progress.

Sources: http://globetrotter.berkeley.edu/macarthur/inequality/; Luxembourg Income Study, available at: http://www.lisproject.org; Alan Heston, Robert Summers, and Bettina Aten, Penn World Table, Version 6.1, Center for International Comparisons at the University of Pennsylvania (CICUP), October 2002, available at: http://webhost.bridgew.edu/baten/; Samuel Bowles and Herbert Gintis, *Recasting Egalitarianism: New Rules for Markets, States, and Communities* (London: Verso, 1999).

The uneven nature of economic development in a world of capitalist economies happens in part because these economies are in competition for markets and for investment. The process of competition tends to reward winners and to punish losers, so the world economy is one of cumulative advantages and disadvantages. While rich countries enjoy the economic benefits of a "virtuous circle," poor countries are caught in a "vicious circle" of poverty. This vicious circle obstructs the growth of productivity and often entraps latecomers to the process of capitalist development. The vicious circle can be seen as having seven major aspects.

First is the problem of market size. Except for the very largest countries, such as China and India, poor economies have small markets, since poor people do not buy much and transportation is often very costly. Even large countries such as India have restricted markets. With a population 30 times that of California, India's total market for goods is half as large as California's. The market of the entire U.S. is larger than all the markets of the poor and middle-income countries of the world combined (more than 100 countries). And the European market is even larger than the U.S. market. This means that in contrast to the U.S. and the other rich countries, the scale of production to meet domestic demand in the poor countries is limited, and the productivity gains made possible through economies of scale require that they export to larger markets. However, when poor countries try to sell their products in the larger markets of rich countries, they often find their way blocked by tariffs and other restrictions on imports.

Second is the problem of the small surplus. Because poor countries generally have low levels of productivity, the surplus product cannot be very large even if wages are near the subsistence level. A small surplus means that there are few resources available for investment in productive new equipment, in infrastructure, or in education and training (human resources). The low rate of investment and the paucity of human resource development perpetuate a low level of productivity. And this low level of productivity means that costs will be high even if wages are low. Just as unprofitable firms have a hard time competing with profitable firms because of the dynamic cost advantages of firms that invest a lot, countries with a small surplus are locked into what may be termed a *dynamic cost disadvantage*. (See Figure 11.2 for an explanation of *dynamic cost advantage*.)

The third problem is the learning barrier. People in poor countries lack experience with modern technology and with high productivity systems of production; many of the skills they need can be acquired only through practice on the job. But until advanced systems of production are in place, there are few opportunities to learn how to use modern technologies.

Fourth is the problem of risk avoidance. People in poor countries are wisely cautious about taking risks, for even a small loss in income may have disastrous consequences for them and their families. For this reason people are often reluctant to introduce new technologies, whether a new type of seed or a new method of manufacturing. Even if these new technologies promise to yield major gains, one can never be sure; the small chance of a loss is often enough to deter the potential innovator.

The fifth problem is self-perpetuating stagnation. Even apart from the low level of income and the problem of risk, a country not already experiencing rapid productivity growth will have a hard time jump-starting the growth process. This is because setting in motion economic growth requires shifting resources from uses that do not promote economic growth—luxury consumption by the rich, maintenance of large religious orders, and staffing and equipping a large military force, for example—to those that do promote growth, such as productive investment, education of the labor force, and building up the infrastructure. In the absence of economic growth, shifting resources to productivity-enhancing uses requires taking resources away from someone. And those who already use resources in unproductive ways are often the most powerful groups in society.

On the other hand, if productivity is already growing, the increase in output can be plowed back into investment, education, and the like without requiring a reduction in anyone's current level of income. Thus, the development process has a chicken and egg aspect to it: it is hard to shift resources to productivity-enhancing uses unless productivity is already growing.

The first five aspects of the vicious circle of uneven development concern a country's own situation; the last two concern its relationships with other countries.

The sixth problem is the cumulative nature of the competitive process. The winners of each round of competition start the next round with an advantage over their competitors. The game of competition in a capitalist economy—as we saw in Chapter 7—is not like tennis, in which each player starts with a score of 0 at the beginning of a new set. It is more like boxing, in which the fighter who has taken some punishing blows in the first round starts the second less able to fight and proves an easy target for a competitor.

Seventh, the governments of the rich countries often adopt policies that impede development in the poor countries. Chief among these are the policies that make it difficult for producers in the rest of the world to sell in the markets of the rich countries. Another is the recent redefinition of intellectual property rights, extending both their scope and duration. Because patents and copyrights are held almost entirely by people and companies in the rich countries, the expansion of intellectual property rights favors the rich nations over the poor. Development in the poor countries is also impeded when rich countries' governments—through financial assistance, military aid, direct military intervention, and other means—protect the political position and economic privileges of the backward-looking traditional elites in the poor countries. Because these elites often resist economic and social change, external support of them effectively blocks the economic development of their countries.

In sum, a country with a high level of income, a large market, decades of experience with modern production techniques, and a large surplus to invest in new equipment, education, research, and infrastructure has a huge competitive advantage over a less well-endowed country. And the advantage may grow over the years as the rich country uses its gains to maintain its productivity growth, while the poor country cannot get productivity off the ground.

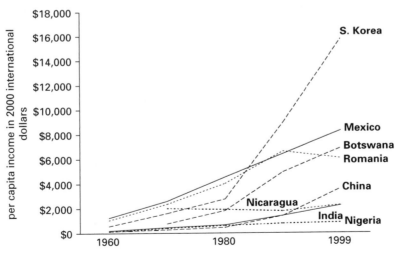

FIGURE 15.7   Uneven development among countries.   The per capita income data shown in this figure are in PPP dollars: they have been adjusted for the buying power of each nation's currency.

Sources: World Bank, "World Development Indicators: 2000" (Washington, D.C.: World Bank, 2001), available on CD-ROM; Alan Heston, Robert Summers, and Bettina Aten, Penn World Tables, Version 6.1, Center for International Comparisons at the University of Pennsylvania (CICUP), October 2002, available at: http://webhost.bridgew.edu/baten.

The fact that development is uneven does not mean, of course, that latecomers can never catch up. Germany and the U.S. were both latecomers—after the United Kingdom—in the 19th century, but they rapidly overcame their disadvantages and now have per capita incomes much higher than the U.K. To cite another example, South Korea was a latecomer that took off during the 1960s and 1970s. And leading nations do not always stay ahead. The U.S. overtook the U.K., and China is now growing much more rapidly than Japan.

Figure 15.7 illustrates the dramatic contrasts of success and failure in the process of uneven development. Over the past two decades per capita incomes in South Korea and the small southern African country of Botswana have quadrupled. During the same period, however, Nigeria's per capita income barely rose. A contrast affecting far more people is China coming from behind and then pulling away from India between 1980 and 1999.

GOVERNMENT AND THE DEVELOPMENT PROCESS

In most countries where the disadvantages of initial poverty have been overcome, the government has played a major role in providing the conditions for rapid productivity growth. The earliest example of governmental participation in the development process was in the U.S. right after the War of Independence. At the time many of the founding fathers, including Alexander Hamilton, reasoned that U.S. manufacturing industries could never compete with their larger and more experienced British counterparts unless the American "infant industries" were sheltered from competition and given some time to get established. Hamilton advocated a heavy tax—a tariff—on imported British manufactured goods, and this policy was then implemented. Tariff protection of industry was also a prominent feature of economic policy in 19th-century Germany, helping it to overtake Britain as an industrial power.

In other countries governments have pursued different strategies. In South Korea beginning in the 1960s, for example, the government used its police and armed forces to help employers in their conflicts with workers. This kept wages low, thus assuring high profits for companies. The government also prevented most companies from investing the profits anywhere but in South Korea. Sending wealth out of the country—a common practice by the rich in most poor countries—was deterred by capital controls designed to curb "capital flight." Under pressure from the government, the major banks in South Korea channeled large sums of money into infant industries. And in sectors in which these strategies failed to bring about sufficient private capitalist investment, the government simply did the investing itself, as it did, for example, in building one of the world's most efficient steel plants under government ownership.

Government programs have also accelerated the borrowing of advanced technologies in order to promote development. Major gains in productivity can sometimes be achieved by adopting the most modern technologies. In fact, this process of technology transfer is one of the few ways in which poor countries can break out of the vicious circle of poverty and catch up with the more advanced countries. But the process of adapting and introducing new technologies, while at the same time developing a labor force able to use them, often requires committing substantial funds over a long period of time, and it entails taking great risks with few immediate opportunities for profit.

As a result, governments often take a leading role in technology transfer. In the late 17th century, when naval architecture and shipbuilding were on the cutting edge of modern technology (akin to computer design today), Czar Peter the Great of Russia, traveling in disguise, took a group of Russian shipbuilders to England and Holland to learn the most advanced methods of ship design and construction. In the late 19th century the Japanese government sent countless missions to Europe to learn about new techniques. More recently, many governments have successfully promoted the introduction of new strains of seeds for crops. In addition, government expenditures for health and education to develop and maintain the productive capacities of the labor force have figured prominently in late-comer strategies for catching up with the rich countries.

As pointed out earlier, however, governmental catch-up policies are not always successful. Indeed, subsidies or tariffs have often been used just to enrich a few well-connected families or to protect the jobs and profits of workers and owners in industries that would never be able to compete on their own. Moreover, government-based catch-up strategies are frequently ineffective because governments—often undemocratic and unresponsive to the needs of the vast majority of the people—do not make sure that improvements in productivity are widely shared. As a result, incentives to increase productivity are weakened.

It is sometimes said that the major advantage—perhaps the *only* advantage—that poor countries have in competing for markets and investment is their poverty itself. With very low wages, these countries may be able to produce goods or services so cheaply that they can sell them to the advanced countries despite all the obstacles. Low wages may lead the multinational companies of the advanced countries to locate new plants in the poor countries. With growing markets and with increased investment from the rich countries, the poor countries—at least some of them—might be able to break out of the vicious circle of poverty. To consider this possible way out of poverty for the poor countries, we need to understand both why companies invest and what they gain from their investments.

INVESTMENT AND PRODUCTION ON A WORLD SCALE

> A **multinational corporation** (MNC) is a firm earning profits throughout the world by locating its facilities wherever the combination of wages, materials costs, markets, government policies, and local markets for the relevant outputs yields the highest profit for the corporation as a whole.

A *multinational corporation* (MNC) is a firm that earns profits throughout the world by locating its facilities where the combination of wages, materials costs, markets, government policies, and local markets for the relevant outputs yield the highest profit for the corporation as a whole. The major U.S. MNCs typically operate in dozens of countries, and some, such as the Ford Motor Company, operate in more than 100 countries. Profits from international operations, as we saw in Figure 7.3, have increased in importance relative to profits made in the U.S.

Multinational Investment

Companies locate their investments where they expect profits to be highest, taking into account both costs and the size of the markets accessible from each location (see box "Sweatshirts").

SWEATSHIRTS

Abigail Martinez used to earn the equivalent of 55 cents an hour at a plant in El Salvador called Charter, sewing cotton tops and khaki pants for GAP, Target, and J.C. Penney. Charter was a sweatshop—an establishment paying wages that are low by U.S. or European standards to workers who are denied the right to organize unions and who often work under unsafe conditions. A few years ago Martinez and a small group of her coworkers organized a series of strikes at Charter to protest working conditions. Target and J.C. Penney canceled their orders, but at the urging of the workers, the Gap stayed. The plant's owners agreed to improve conditions, and Martinez and her friends agreed to call off the protests. Martinez now is paid more, has regular coffee breaks, and benefits from an impartial grievance procedure that allows workers to report continuing abuses.

Rashida Begum, another sweatshop worker, used to work 18-hour days making polo shirts at Chowdhury Knitwears in Bangladesh. Wages for women workers there were the equivalent of 6 to 12 cents an hour. To prevent the workers from leaving or taking breaks, the factory owners routinely locked the doors of the plant during working hours. On November 25, 2000, a fire ripped through the building, taking the lives of 52 of Begum's fellow workers, 10 of them children. Most were crushed to death at the bottom of the stairs trying to break through the locked gates.

In 1911 in New York City, a fire with an uncanny resemblance to the recent Bangladesh fire took the lives of 146 women and girls working at the Triangle Shirtwaist factory. There, too, locked exits barred their escape. The horror of that fire led to the formation of the International Ladies' Garment Workers Union (ILGWU) and the eventual passage of legislation to protect the safety of workers. The response in Bangladesh has been less promising. One factory owner commented sadly: "We suffer from the legacy of the colonial days. We consider the workers to be our slaves, and this belief is made all the easier by a supply of labor that is endlessly abundant."

Most Americans think sweatshop conditions are immoral. In surveys by the Marymount University Center for Ethical Concerns, three quarters or more reported that they would "avoid shopping at a retailer that sold garments made in sweatshops." More than four-fifths said that they were willing to pay $1 more for a $29 garment if they could be sure that it was produced under good conditions. A similar report by the National Bureau of Economic Research (NBER) reported that two-thirds of those surveyed would not knowingly purchase a shirt made under bad sweatshop conditions at *any* price.

Is there any way that the willingness to pay $1 more for a shirt produced under safe conditions at higher wages could be translated into $1 in the pockets of

Continued . . .

the poor workers at the sewing machines? Banning imports of the polo shirts made by Begum or of the tops sewed by Martinez would probably not help them or their coworkers. It would probably cost them their jobs, and working in a sweatshop provides a better livelihood than does most work in El Salvador and Bangladesh. It certainly beats no paid work at all, which is the lot of many.

Exposés of labor abuses at the suppliers of major companies by activists from UNITE (a successor to the ILGWU) and a desire not to benefit from sweatshop labor fueled the meteoric rise of United States Students Against Sweatshops in the early 2000s. When workers organized a union at the BJ&B plant, a hat maker for Nike and Reebok in Villa Altagarcia, Dominican Republic, they were fired. Rumors circulated that the plant would close. But pressure from other Dominican trade unions and from U.S. college campuses gave the story a happier ending. BJ&B stayed, and the union was recognized. The first union contract included not only raises but scholarships as well. Patricia Graterox, a single mother working at BJ&B, looks forward to a better life. She is saving her higher wages to go to nursing school: "Before you could not do that. Now you can. At least I think I can."

Sources: New York Times, April 4, 2003, April 15, 2001, April 24, 2001; Kimberly Elliot and Richard Freeman, "White Hats or Don Quixotes? Human Rights Vigilantes in the Global Economy," National Bureau of Economic Research, August, 2000; James Heintz and Robert Pollin, *The Question of Sweatshops: Globalization and the Struggle for Decent Work* (New York: New Press, 2004); David Von Drehle, *Triangle: The Fire That Changed America* (New York: Atlantic Monthly Press, 2003).

Low wages are a strong attraction if they are accompanied by highly skilled workers, an adequate infrastructure, and low materials costs. Figure 15.8 shows that wage differences around the world are indeed great.

However, the facts of where the U.S.-based multinational corporations locate will surprise many readers. First, these firms make most of their investments, about three-quarters, in the U.S. itself, not abroad. Thus, the amount of investment going to other countries is limited.

Second, contrary to a widely held misconception, the majority of foreign investments made by U.S. multinationals go to the rich countries, not to the poor. The wealthy Netherlands, with a population of 16 million, gets *seven times* as much U.S. direct investment as all the countries of Africa, with a population of more than 800 million. Tiny Switzerland gets more U.S. investment than all of South America. Canada gets more than Latin America (including Mexico). U.S. firms employ more people in Germany and the United Kingdom than they do in Mexico and Brazil, and more in Belgium than in all of Africa. In 1999 U.S. firms employed fewer than 3 million people in all the poor and middle-income countries of the world—less than one-half of 1 percent of the labor available in these countries.[2]

---

[2] U.S. Department of Commerce, Bureau of Economic Analysis, *U.S. Foreign Transactions Position in 2002* (Washington, D.C.: U.S. Department of Commerce, 2003). Available at: http://www.bea.gov/bea/di/usdiacap.xls.

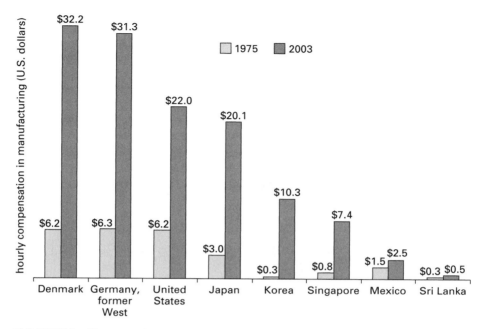

FIGURE 15.8   Wages and benefits in the manufacturing sector in selected countries, 1975 and 2003.   This figure compares the total compensation of manufacturing sector workers in eight countries in 1975 and 2003. The amount of compensation in each country is first measured in units of the country's own currency and then converted into U.S. dollars at the average dollar value of each nation's currency in global currency markets in each of the two years. These measures are appropriate for comparing levels of employer labor costs in the different countries, but since the conversion to dollar values is done using market exchange rates rather than the purchasing power parity method (see box "What's a Hamburger Worth?" in this chapter), they do not indicate the relative purchasing power of the incomes (living standards) of manufacturing workers in the different countries.

Source: U.S. Bureau of Labor Statistics, *International Comparisons of Hourly Compensation Costs for Production Workers in Manufacturing, 2003* (Washington, D.C.: U.S. Department of Labor, 2004), available at: http://www.bls.gov/news.release/ichcc.t02.htm.

The distribution of American corporate investments in foreign countries can be seen in Figure 15.9. In 2002 more than two-thirds of all U.S. direct investment abroad by U.S.-owned multinational corporations was located in Canada, Europe, Japan, and other rich countries. Commenting on the current situation and the past two decades, a U.S. Commerce Department publication notes: "The geographic distribution of MNC activities [has] changed relatively little. Production, sales, and research and development by U.S. MNCs remained concentrated in the U.S. and in other high-income countries" (see source cited in the caption for Figure 15.9).

The information presented in Figure 15.9 may seem particularly surprising if, looking back to Figure 15.8, one notices that wages in manufacturing industries are considerably

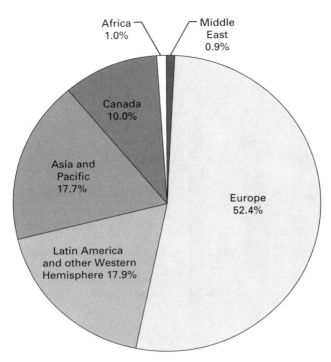

FIGURE 15.9   U.S. direct investment abroad, 2002.   This figure shows how much capital was invested directly by U.S. corporations in various parts of the world in 2002. The term "direct investment" refers to such things as the building of factories, the digging of mines, and the construction of office buildings. Purchases of foreign corporations' stock and "investments" by U.S. citizens in other financial assets abroad are not included. In 2002 the total amount of U.S. direct investment abroad (valued at the cost of investments when they were made) was more than $1.5 trillion. As the figure shows, 52 percent of these investments were in Europe and 10 percent of them were in Canada. Adding to this the U.S. investments in two rich countries that are included in the "Asia and Pacific" category, Japan and Australia (which, taken together, account for nearly 7 percent of American investment abroad), we can see that more than two-thirds of U.S. foreign direct investment goes to other advanced capitalist nations.

Source: U.S. Department of Commerce, Bureau of Economic Analysis, "U.S. Direct Investment Abroad, Balance of Payments, and Direct Investment Position Data," available at http://www.bea.doc.gov/bea/di/di1usdbal.htm.

lower in the poor countries than they are in the U.S. and Europe. The second surprise is that wages in European countries such as Norway and the former West Germany are as high as, or higher than, U.S. wages. The data presented in Figure 15.8 show what U.S. firms had to pay in 1975 and 2001 (in dollar equivalents) to hire an hour of labor in eight countries. Looking ahead to Figure 19.4, one may also be surprised to see that many of the countries that attract large amounts of U.S. investment are also countries in which government spending is greater—and therefore taxes higher—in comparison to the U.S.

There are four main reasons why U.S. firms (and the multinational firms of other rich countries) prefer to invest in rich countries rather than in poor ones.

- First, by investing in rich countries they are building their production facilities close to large and growing markets (and as noted, the European market alone is larger than that of all the 100 or more poor and middle-income countries combined).
- Second, while unit labor costs in shirts favor the low-wage countries, for many products the highly educated, motivated, and skilled labor forces of the rich countries give them enough of a productivity advantage to partially or fully offset the higher wages.
- Third, the rich countries have highly developed transportation and communications infrastructures that serve to increase productivity.
- Fourth, U.S. businesses know that they can expect favorable treatment from most governments in the rich countries. The high levels of conflict and political instability in many poor countries make them an uncertain site for profit making, and hence they are often described as having a poor investment climate. In these countries the insecurity of private property deters investment.

These reasons may be summarized as follows: as magnets for business investment, low wages, low taxes, and lax environmental regulations are no match for a productive workforce, a large market, and security of property rights.

The importance of the globetrotting activities of MNCs may have been overrated both by their advocates and by their critics. In most countries workers employed by U.S.-based MNCs are a tiny fraction of the labor force; in China, India, and Russia the fraction is less than half of 1 percent. In only three of the 200-odd countries in the world is this fraction larger than 10 percent: Ireland, Singapore, and Canada, countries with a combined population much less than that of many of the individual states of India. The fact that China and India are catching up to the rich countries has little to do with international investment; it has everything to do with the very different institutions governing these two economies along with their ability to take advantage of the international exchange of goods, services, and information. The fact that most countries in Africa are falling behind likewise has everything to do with their institutions, that is, the carrots and sticks that affect productive activities in these nations.

CONCLUSION

In this chapter we have posed some of the most difficult questions in economics, those concerning economic growth and world inequalities. The question of long-term economic progress—the wealth of nations—was one of the most important for the founders of political economy. And the question remains an important one today. We have stressed the importance of institutions as a part of the process of development. What governments do—the laws and policies they implement, the constitutions they abide by, and the property rights they protect—greatly affects the performance of economic systems. We will examine the government's role in the economy in Chapter 19. In the next three chapters, we lay the foundation for our discussion of the government's role by looking at how the economy works from a macroeconomic perspective.

SUGGESTED READINGS

James Boyce and Betsy Hartmann, *A Quiet Violence* (London: Zed Press, 1986).

Christopher Chase-Dunn, *Global Formation. Structures of the World Economy* (Oxford: Basil Blackwell, 1989).

Herman Daly and John Cobb, *For the Common Good: Redirecting the Economy toward Community, the Environment, and a Sustainable Future* (Boston: Beacon Press, 1989).

Alexander Gerschenkron, *Economic Backwardness in Historical Perspective* (Cambridge, Mass.: Harvard University Press, 1962).

Fred Hirsch, *Social Limits to Growth* (Cambridge, Mass.: Harvard University Press, 1976).

Kenneth P. Jameson and Charles K. Wilber, eds., *The Political Economy of Development and Underdevelopment,* 6th ed. (New York: McGraw Hill, l995).

Peter Lanjouw and Nicholas Stern, eds., *Economic Development in Palanpur over Five Decades.* (Delhi: Oxford University Press, 1998).

Branko Milanovic, *Worlds Apart: The Twentieth Century Promise that Failed* (Washington, D.C.: World Bank, 2002). Available at http://www.worldbank. org/research/inequality.

The World Bank, *World Development Report* (Washington, D.C., and New York: A copublication of the World Bank and Oxford University Press, annual).

CHAPTER 16

Aggregate Demand, Employment, and Unemployment

One of the hardest things to understand about our economy is the fact that there are often (a) factories lying idle while at the same time (b) a significant number of people are looking for work, and (c) many human needs are not being met. Any two of these could be explained, but why all three are typically true in a capitalist economy is a puzzle. People need the products that the unemployed workers could produce if they were put to work in the idle factories. Yet they are not being put to work.

For example, 2001 was a year in which the American economy did not grow very much, and many manufacturing jobs were transferred to workers in other countries. As a result, 25 percent of the nation's industrial capacity lay idle (the capacity utilization rate averaged 0.75). Even so, approximately $3.6 trillion worth of goods were produced in the U.S. that year. Had the idle 25 percent of manufacturing (goods-producing) capacity been used, however, the total output of goods would have been $4.8 trillion. In this case there would have been an additional $1.2 trillion worth of goods produced, and if these goods had been allocated equally among the 285 million men, women, and children in the U.S. that year, each would have received an additional $4,211 worth of goods. The output lost because of the underutilized manufacturing capacity was not the result of a shortage of workers: on an average day in 2001 there were 6.74 million unemployed people looking for work.

The fact that there can be idle tools, unemployed people, and unsatisfied needs all at the same time is hard to understand because it is inconsistent with our own personal experience. If we need a bookshelf and have the tools, lumber, and time, we can set to work and make ourselves a bookshelf. When we organize our own production—in families, in small groups, or on our own—we do not end up with idle tools, idle hands, and unmet needs. The reason is that when we produce for ourselves, our purpose is to make something that we need (or at least want). If we have unmet needs and the tools and time to produce what we need, we just do it.

The capitalist economy, by contrast, is organized quite differently. A business owner's purpose in producing commodities, as we saw in Chapter 6, is not to meet a need, it is to make a profit. More specifically, if the employers who direct the production process do not believe they will make a profit, they will not engage in production; they will simply leave idle the tools and factories they own and cease hiring workers. The fact that someone may need the goods or services that could potentially be produced is irrelevant. The system of capitalist competition forces business owners to make their decisions solely with regard to profitability.

One of the results of this profit-driven process is that the economy alternates over long periods between good times and hard times. In Chapter 7 we explained the long-term alternation of boom and crisis in the U.S. economy by chronicling its consecutive social structures of accumulation. In Figure 16.1 we present these long swings in concrete terms, showing the rates of growth of total output in the successive periods of consolidation and decay. Of course, during each of the long swings there are the less pronounced ups and downs associated with business cycles (see Chapter 7). While the long term booms and crises occur over several decades, the expansion and recession phases of a particular business cycle are generally completed in a period of less than 10 years. The insert in Figure 16.1 pictures a typical business cycle.

When the economy expands over a considerable length of time, employers tend to hire more workers, so the level of unemployment generally falls during long booms. Conversely, a long period of decay is usually characterized by rising unemployment. The long swings of employment in the U.S. economy between the end of the 19th century and the end of the 20th century are shown in Figure 16.2. As one would expect, the relatively brief business cycles within each long swing are also marked by short-term ups and downs in employment.

The key to understanding unemployment as well as both long and short economic cycles—with their corresponding ups and downs of output and employment—is the total demand in the economy for goods and services. In order to understand changes in overall economic performance, we need to focus on this total demand and examine the reasons for its fluctuation.

One important aspect of the cyclical process is the fact that the amount of money spent by business owners on investment goods varies from year to year, and these changes, in turn, drive accumulation at a faster or slower pace. As explained in Chapter 7, we use the term *social structure of accumulation* precisely because we are interested in whether or not—or to what degree—a particular set of social institutions provides a favorable (or unfavorable) climate for the accumulation process. The successive stages of American capitalism and the corresponding long swings in economic performance are defined with reference to distinct social structures of accumulation and their supportive or dampening effects on investment.

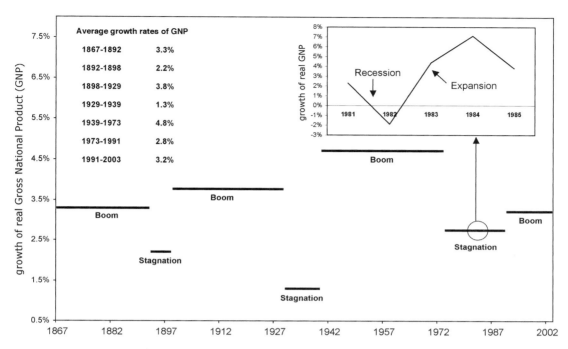

FIGURE 16.1   Long swings and business cycles.   Long swings are long-term fluctuations between booms and hard times; they extend over periods of 30 to 50 years. Business cycles are shorter ups and downs experienced by the economy over a period normally less than 10 years (from peak to peak). This figure shows that the U.S. economy has passed through three long swings during the past century and a half. The first (corresponding to the stage of competitive capitalism) lasted from the 1860s to 1898, with a boom period from 1867 to 1892 and a period of stagnation from 1892 to 1898. The second (corresponding to the stage of corporate capitalism) lasted from 1898 to 1939, with good times until 1929 and then the Great Depression of the 1930s. The third long swing (under regulated capitalism) started around 1939 and lasted until 1991. Since 1991 we seem to have been entering into a fourth long swing (corresponding to the stage of transnational capitalism), but it is too early to say much about this period statistically. Each long swing is characterized first by a long boom, during which the SSA (in its "consolidation" phase) makes possible a relatively rapid rate of growth, and this is then followed by a more or less lengthy period of stagnation (the "decay" phase of the SSA). Business cycles occur within both the booms and the hard times of long swings, with the rate of output fluctuating in the short term without altering the long-term trend. The insert in this figure depicts a typical business cycle, the one that started with a high rate of growth at its peak in 1981, continued with a growth rate that fell and then became negative (with less being produced each year than in the previous year) until a trough was reached in 1982, after which there was a period of accelerating growth in the business cycle expansion of the mid-1980s.

Sources: U.S. President's Council of Economic Advisors, *Economic Report of the President* (Washington, D.C.: U.S. Government Printing Office, various years) available at http://www.whitehouse.gov/cea/pubs.html or http://gpoaccess.gov/eop/download.html); U.S. Bureau of the Census, *Historical Statistics of the United States: Colonial Times to 1970* (Washington, D.C.: U.S. Government Printing Office, 1975).

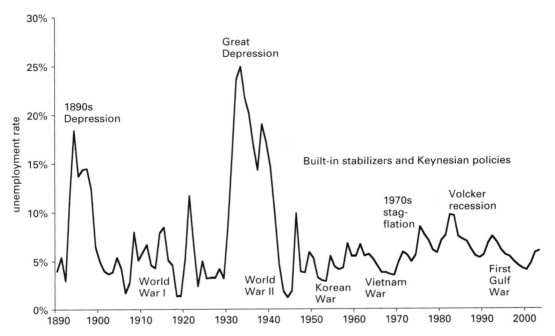

FIGURE 16.2   The U.S. unemployment rate, 1890 to 2003.   This figure traces the ups and downs of the rate of unemployment in the U.S. economy from the last years of the 19th century to the first years of the 21st century. The unemployment rate presented in the figure is the ratio (in percentage terms) of the officially determined number of unemployed people to the officially determined number of people in the civilian labor force (see box "Counting the Unemployed" in this chapter). The unemployment rate went up to about 18 percent in the 1890s and reached a peak of 25 percent during the Great Depression of the 1930s. While the unemployment rate tends to go up in periods of economic stagnation or decline during peacetime, it generally goes down with the onset of a war as workers are employed to produce military goods and as people who would otherwise be in the civilian labor force are drawn into military service. This happened, for example, at the beginning of the 1940s: the unusually high rates of unemployment that had plagued the U.S. throughout the 1930s came down dramatically with the onset of World War II. Of particular interest in this figure is the fact that the rate of unemployment was held to less than 10 percent in the half-century since World War II by means of Keynesian policies and built-in stabilizers such as unemployment insurance and other social insurance programs established as parts of the "New Deal" in the 1930s.

Sources: Council of Economic Advisors, *Economic Report of the President: 2004* (Washington, D.C.: U.S. Government Printing Office, 2004) available at http://www.whitehouse.gov/cea/pubs.html); previous issues of the *Economic Report of the President* (Washington, D.C.: U.S. Government Printing Office, annual) available at http://gpoaccess.gov/eop/ download.html); U.S. Bureau of the Census, *Historical Statistics of the United States: Colonial Times to 1970* (Washington, D.C.: U.S. Government Printing Office, 1975).

Two main ideas are central to this chapter. The first is that *levels of employment and unemployment depend on the total demand for goods and services,* and the second is that *government policies can reduce the level of unemployment and smooth out fluctuations in the level of total demand.* These main ideas are expressed in seven key points:

1. The total amount of goods and services demanded need not equal the total amount produced: total demand may exceed or fall short of supply.

2. When demand for goods and services exceeds supply, firms will hire more workers; when demand falls short of supply, firms will lay off workers; and when demand equals supply, firms will not alter the size of their workforce.

3. When demand for goods and services equals supply (and firms are neither expanding employment nor cutting back), there will generally be some unemployment.

4. One of the main influences on the level of demand for goods and services is the distribution of income between profits and wages. This is because the wage rate influences the demand for consumer goods, and the profit rate influences the demand for investment goods.

5. A government's demand for goods and services, as well as government policies regulating the rate of interest, affect the level of employment; government deficits and low interest rates generally bring about higher levels of demand for goods and services and hence lower levels of unemployment.

6. Raising the wage may result in more jobs, fewer jobs, or no change in the number of jobs, for a wage increase may raise, lower, or leave unchanged the level of total demand for goods and services.

7. The economy typically experiences fluctuations in employment and in output called *business cycles.* During the *expansion* phase of a business cycle, output and employment increase rapidly, and unemployment is low. During the *recession* phase of a cycle, output falls, and the level of unemployment rises. Government policies can dampen the fluctuations of the economy to maintain steadier levels of income and employment.

To simplify the analysis in this chapter, we ignore the fact that a part of total output must be devoted to replacing the materials used up in production and to repairing the wear and tear on capital goods. We focus here on *net output,* and we assume that net output per hour of labor (y) is constant. With this assumption, net output will depend entirely on how many hours of labor are employed. We also assume (in this chapter, but not in later chapters) that the total number of people seeking work is given, that prices are constant, and that wages do not vary with the level of employment.

AGGREGATE SUPPLY AND AGGREGATE DEMAND

Two of the fundamental questions of macroeconomics are these: First, will the total demand for goods and services in the economy tend to equal the total supply? Or will there be excess supply or excess demand in product markets? A situation when no

> A **macroeconomic equilibrium** exists when aggregate demand equals aggregate supply (no excess aggregate demand or excess aggregate supply exists) and there are no forces tending to change the situation other than accidental ones or ones coming from external sources.

> **Full employment** is a situation in which almost everyone seeking work readily finds it.

> The **equilibrium level of employment** is the amount of employment that corresponds to a particular macroeconomic equilibrium (when there is no excess demand or excess supply in product markets).

excess demand or excess supply in product markets exists is termed a *macroeconomic equilibrium.*

Second, if demand and supply for goods and services are equal, will the level of supply be large enough that everyone willing to work at the going wage can find a job? We can ask this same question a different way: if a macroeconomic equilibrium exists, will it be characterized by *full employment*? By *full employment* we mean a situation in which nearly everyone seeking work can find it.

The first question—concerning macroeconomic equilibrium—involves markets for products, while the second question—concerning full employment—focuses on markets for labor. The answer to the first question will likely be yes (the total demand for goods and services in the economy will tend to equal the total supply), but the answer to the second question will generally be no (not everyone willing to work at the going wage will be able to find a job). The result is that while product markets will tend to clear (recall that, as explained in Chapter 8, this means no excess supply or excess demand), labor markets will not tend to clear. Rather, there will generally be an excess supply of labor—also known as *unemployment* (see box "Counting the Unemployed").

The equilibrium of the Iowa City beer market studied in Chapter 8, for example, was one in which the quantity of beer supplied was equal to the quantity of beer demanded. In equilibrium the beer market clears, as do most product markets. By contrast, in Chapter 12 we found that even when the labor market is in equilibrium, it often will not clear. There will generally be workers out of work, with nothing they can do to change the situation, and there will also be nothing that prospective employers would choose to do that would result in more employment.

In this chapter we examine the determinants of how much will be produced, how many jobs there will be, and how many people will be unable to find work. We study the equilibrium levels of output, employment, and unemployment, keeping in mind that product markets clear in equilibrium while labor markets do not. The amount of employment associated with a macroeconomic equilibrium is termed the *equilibrium level of employment.*

Consider the following hypothetical example. A worker produces $25 worth of goods in an hour. If $25 of output is produced, then $25 of income will be generated for somebody as a result. If we ignore the fact that some of the output will go to the government for provision of public goods and services, we can say that in this example $25 worth of goods ends up on the shelf of a retail outlet. Assume now that for each $25 worth of goods produced the worker gets $15 in wages and his or her employer gets $10 in profits. Whether there is enough demand to buy the supply on the shelf depends on whether the worker and the employer spend what they have received in income. If the worker spends all of his or her $15 and the employer spends only half of his or her $10 (saving the rest), there will be $25 worth of supply on the shelf but only $20 worth of demand. The result would be excess supply in the product market.

The opposite could also be true. The employer might want to spend $15, using his or her $10 of profits and an additional $5 borrowed from someone else, while the worker

COUNTING THE UNEMPLOYED

In May 1979 the U.S. Department of Energy, in its "National Energy Plan" for the 1980s, described unemployment as follows: "In the long run, an individual will adjust to this situation either by working, e.g., by acquiring suitable job skills or by taking a lesser job, or by not working, e.g., retiring, living on welfare, etc. In either instance, the worker is no longer unemployed. Unemployment, in short, is a disequilibrium phenomenon [in which] workers are between one of two possible equilibria, namely working or nonworking."

Of course, everyone is "between one of two possible equilibria"—having not yet been born or having died—and, as John Maynard Keynes (see Chapter 4) observed, "In the long run we are all dead." Nevertheless, people live in the short run, and if they are unemployed it makes a difference (see box "Unemployment Hurts" later in this chapter). Unemployment is difficult to measure, however.

On the first Friday of every month the U.S. Bureau of Labor Statistics (BLS) releases its latest findings on employment and unemployment in the American economy. The number that gets the most attention is the *rate of unemployment*. In order to determine the rate of unemployment, the BLS first has to figure out how big the total labor force is, and this means determining who is in the labor force and who is not. Are all people who would like to have a job, whether or not they are currently looking for one, in the labor force? What about all the people who would like to have a full-time job but cannot find one and therefore are employed in part-time jobs? Should they not be considered unemployed? In order to publish its monthly statistics on employment and unemployment the government has to make quite a few judgments about controversial issues.

Around the middle of every month the U.S. Department of Labor (the government department that includes the BLS) hires professional pollsters to visit a carefully designed sample of 60,000 American households. In each household the pollster asks how many household members have jobs and how many do not. For those who say that they have a job, the polltaker asks whether the job is full-time or part-time, and, if part-time, whether the decision to work only part-time is made voluntarily or whether the part-time worker would prefer to have a full-time job. The pollster also asks those without jobs whether they have actively searched for a job during the previous four weeks. If they say they have not, they are not counted as being in the labor force—but if they say that they would, in fact, like to be employed, they are put into the category of *discouraged worker* (i.e., too discouraged about the prospects for finding a job to go out and look for one). Finally, in calculating the total labor force, the BLS excludes everyone who is in the armed services or in some other way in the "institutionalized" part of the population (say, in a prison or a mental hospital). And, of course, only people in the "adult" population, that is, those who are 16 and over, are counted.

Continued . . .

After making judgments on all of the issues, the Labor Department comes up with a measure of the *civilian adult noninstitutionalized employed or unemployed population,* and this is referred to simply as the "civilian labor force." On this basis the unemployment rate is calculated as the ratio of those who are officially unemployed to those who are officially counted as being in the civilian labor force. Using this methodology, the BLS gathered and published, in June 2004, the following estimates of U.S. employment and unemployment for the preceding month:

Civilian labor force:	147.0 million
Employed workers:	138.8 million
Unemployed workers:	8.2 million
Rate of unemployment:	5.6%

Even the government recognizes that numbers such as those presented above do not tell the whole story. The BLS disclosed in its June 2004 report, for example, that about 1.6 million people were "marginally attached" to the labor force. Nearly a third of this number were "discouraged workers" (see above) and the other two-thirds were individuals who wanted and were available to work, had looked for a job sometime in the preceding 12 months, but had not looked for one in the four weeks prior to the survey; like the discouraged workers, then, this last group was, from the government's point of view, neither unemployed nor in the labor force.

If we add the 1.6 million "marginally attached" workers to both the unemployed and the civilian labor force numbers, the unemployment rate becomes 6.6 percent, one percentage point higher than the official unemployment rate:

Civilian labor force (including marginally attached workers):	148.6 million
Employed workers:	138.8 million
Unemployed (including marginally attached workers):	9.8 million
Rate of unemployment:	6.6%

What happens if we continue to regard the total labor force as including the "marginally attached" workers, keep the officially defined employment level at 138.8 million, but add to the unemployed part of the labor force the 4.7 million people who were officially counted as being *employed* but, according to the government, were working part-time in May 2004 "for economic reasons"? When we add these *involuntarily part-time workers*, the unemployment rate jumps to 9.7 percent, more than 4 percentage points above the official rate of unemployment:

Civilian labor force (including marginally attached workers):	148.6 million
Employed workers:	138.8 million
Unemployed (including marginally attached *and* involuntary part-timers):	14.5 million
Rate of unemployment:	9.7%

The long and the short of it is that in May 2004 there were about 14.5 million people, almost 10 percent of the U.S. labor force, who were *underemployed.* Imagine how much the (full-time) productive activity of all these people might have added to the American standard of living.

Sources: U.S. Department of Energy, "National Energy Plan," May 1979; U.S. Department of Labor, Bureau of Labor Statistics, "Employment Situation Summary," June 4, 2004, available at http://www.bls.gov/news.release/empsit.nr0.htm.

continues to spend his or her $15 of wages. As a result there would be $30 worth of demand and only $25 worth of goods. The result would be excess demand in the product market.

Next, consider what happens if excess supply occurs in the product market. Excess supply means that some of the product will go unsold. In this case the seller will respond to the situation in two ways. First, the seller will lower the price, seeking to attract additional customers. Second, if the lower price does not attract many additional customers, the seller will not reorder as much of the good (or maybe not reorder at all) to prevent the goods from piling up on the shelves. With fewer orders coming in, the managers of firms that produce the good will have to lay off workers, so unemployment will increase.

Excess demand produces just the opposite result: the shelves are bare before a new shipment comes in. The seller then places a larger order. As a result, employers hire more workers to produce the larger amounts now demanded.

We thus reach an important conclusion: when excess supply exists in product markets firms will employ fewer workers, and when excess demand exists firms will employ more.

There are two effects of employing fewer workers when excess supply exists. First, there will be less produced and hence a lower level of supply. Second, there will be fewer workers receiving wages, and since those laid off will have less money to purchase consumer goods, there will be a lower level of demand. In the example above, if one worker is hired for one hour less, output will be $25 lower, and demand will also be lower. If we continue to assume that workers receive $15 of the net output they produce and that they spend all of their income, it will be lower by the $15 that the worker would have spent.

These effects raise a troubling question: will the reduction in employment prompted by excess supply in the product market tend to eliminate the excess supply (by reducing supply)? Or will the reduction in employment make the excess supply problem worse (by its effect on demand)?

A similar problem occurs when excess demand exists: firms will hire more people, increasing supply, and this will tend to reduce the excess demand. Yet the additional hiring will give more income to workers, thus increasing demand. Will the result of these opposing effects reduce the excess demand, or will the excess demand problem get worse? These questions will be addressed in the coming pages, and to answer them we will have to look at aggregate demand and aggregate supply in more detail. The central issue is: what effect will changes in aggregate demand and supply have on the output of the economy (see box "Measuring Total Output")?

MEASURING TOTAL OUTPUT

Imagine someone asking you how much stuff you have in your suitcase, and if it is more than he has in his. How would you determine your answer? You could list everything there—a book, two shirts, a pair of shoes, a hair dryer, and on and on. But this would not really answer the question because it would not allow you to figure a specific quantity to compare with the specific quantity of his suitcase contents. If you wanted a single number total, you might weigh the contents, or you could indicate the dollar value of each item and total their worth.

When it is so difficult to quantify what is in a person's suitcase, imagine how hard it is to calculate the total output of a nation. The total output of a country in any particular year is usually considered to be the market value of all the goods and services produced. The good or service need not be sold in order to be counted as output: agricultural products grown and consumed at home are typically counted, even though their value is only estimated.

In measuring output, then, goods and services are valued at their market price (or if they are not sold, roughly at what their price would have been had they been sold). Thus, a pound of shrimp is counted over twice as much as a gallon of milk because the former costs over twice as much to buy (see Chapter 14).

Services that are not offered for sale—such as home cooking or care given to parents or children by family members—are not included at all. Since such work continues to be done mostly by women, the officially measured value of a nation's output fails to take into account much of the labor performed by women. (See Chapter 5 on the importance to the economy of *both* production *and* reproduction.)

Economists use one or another of the following terms to put a value on the total output of an economy:

- The *gross domestic product* of a nation (its GDP) is the total output produced within its territory (including what is produced by noncitizens).
- *Gross national product* (GNP) is another measure of total output, referring to the total output of the citizens of a nation. It is similar to GDP, but it includes income produced by the "nationals" of a country (its citizens)—even when their production takes place in some other country and generates income for them such as profit from abroad. All such income is included in GNP (it is treated as a measure of the output of a nation's citizens); however, no output produced within a nation's borders by noncitizens is included in GNP.
- *Net domestic product* (NDP) and *net national product* (NNP) refer to the above measures *minus depreciation* (the amount of wear and tear on machinery and other capital goods resulting from production during the relevant time period, usually a year). However, the depreciation of

natural resources and the environment that occurs when we erode the soil or use up clean air or water, for example, is generally *not* taken into account in the usual indicators of national output. This means that an increase in *net* output—whether in NDP or in NNP—may not accurately measure a change in our well-being.

When comparing total outputs for a given country at different points in time, we generally make two modifications in our measures of national output, one to correct for inflation and the other to take into account population growth. First, imagine an economy in which inflation (rising prices) occurs but the quantities of goods and services actually produced do not change. In this case the market value of total output will rise even though nothing real changes. Since there is nearly always some inflation occurring in an economy, changes in total output measured on the basis of *current prices* will tend to overstate the amount of growth in output.

Comparisons of total output between one year and another are more meaningful if they are made on the basis of *constant prices*. This means correcting for changes in the general level of prices, and usually this is done by referring to the price level in a "base" year so that comparisons can be made over a number of years using the same benchmark. When total output measures are corrected for inflation in this way, the total output is termed *real,* or *inflation adjusted*. (See box "Money Wages and Real Wages" on pp. 489–490 for an explanation of how this type of inflation adjustment is done for wages.)

Second, we sometimes express total output measures on a per person basis. We do this to indicate roughly how well-off the typical individual is in a particular country and also to take into account any growth (or decline) in its population. To calculate such a figure we simply divide total output by the number of people in the country at any given time. The result is what is called *per capita* output (or income).

Adjusting a country's gross domestic product by correcting it for inflation and dividing it by the population, we arrive at what many economists regard as the best measure of an economy's health: *real per capita GDP*.

> **Aggregate supply** is the total supply of goods and services produced during some period, say, a year.

Aggregate supply (*AS*) is the total supply of goods and services produced during some period, say a year. If we continue to consider only net output, aggregate supply is equal to the number of hours of labor employed in a year (*N*) multiplied by net output per hour (*y*). Thus:

$$AS = \text{(net output per hour)(total hours of employment)} = yN \qquad (16.1)$$

For example, if $y = \$25$ and $N = 2$ million hours, $AS = \$50$ million. Because we have assumed that y does not change, we can graph AS in relation to N as a straight line, the slope of which is y (see Figure 16.3).

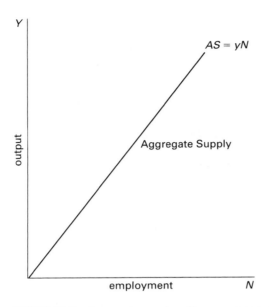

FIGURE 16.3   Aggregate supply.   The aggregate supply curve (AS) shows the total amount of goods and services (at their current market value) that can be produced with any given number of labor hours (N), assuming that net output per labor hour (y) does not change. The value of AS is equal to yN, the total number of labor hours employed multiplied by the net output of goods and services per labor hour employed. It would be more realistic to take into account two important facts relating to y: (1) up to a certain point, *economies of scale* may allow higher rates of net output per hour (y) to be achieved with higher levels of employment (using enlarged production facilities); and (2) beyond some other point, additional hours of employment will result in less additional output per hour (lower y) because of *diminishing marginal returns*. But to introduce such realism here would complicate the picture without adding anything of importance to the analysis in this chapter. For simplicity, then, we assume that y does not change as N changes, and this allows us to represent AS as a straight line. Note: in the remainder of the figures in this chapter, as well as in this one, the rate of increase of this or that variable is represented by a straight line. In the language of economics, however, even straight lines are referred to as "curves" whenever they might conceptually represent nonlinear information, that is, information that would have to be represented by a curved line. Following this practice, we will often refer to straight lines in Figures 16.3 through 16.10 as curves.

For every dollar's worth of AS that is produced, a dollar in income will be received by someone—by workers as wages, by capitalists as profits, or by some combination of the two. Thus, total income (the sum of all persons' incomes) before taxes is always and exactly equal to AS.

Aggregate demand is the total demand for goods and services during some period, say, a year.

Aggregate demand (AD) is the total demand for goods and services during a year. The first component of aggregate demand is C, the total amount of money spent by households buying food, clothing, electricity, and other consumer goods (see box "Born to Shop?"). Consumption spending (C) usually amounts to about two-thirds of aggregate demand.

BORN TO SHOP?

For most of human history—the 100,000 years before the domestication of plants and animals about 10,000 years ago—people owned only what they could carry. Some of our hunter-gatherer ancestors sported beads and other ornaments, but the foraging way of life did not allow the accumulation of much stuff. If contemporary hunters and gatherers are any indication, our ancestors were long on free time and short on closets.

Mahatma Gandhi, the leader of the nonviolent movement that ended British colonial rule of India, was a modern-day exponent of living simply: he typically wore only a homespun *dhoti* (loincloth), sandals, and sometimes a shawl. This is how he was attired when he had tea with King George V at Buckingham Palace in 1931. To reporters' concerns about his dress on such an elevated occasion, Gandhi replied: "The King was wearing enough for both of us."

Americans in the 21st century are not likely to be criticized, as Gandhi was, for underdressing. As the figure below shows, Americans buy, on average, more than 50 new garments each year, with both men and women buying more than 30 outer garments (excluding underwear, infant clothing, and the like) annually.

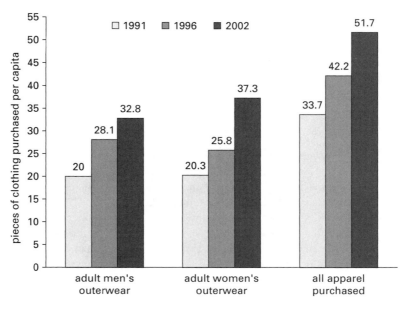

Apparel Consumption in the U.S., 1991–2002

Continued . . .

It is no surprise, then, that Americans complain that they have no room in their closets. What *is* puzzling is that the same people often lament their lack of free time. Why do people not cut back on their work hours and get by on, say, 20 new garments a year? Maybe the problem is that you cannot show off your free time, while the ever-rising standards of "appropriate" consumption are set by the wealthy.

When prodemocracy activists toppled the regime of the Philippine dictator Ferdinand Marcos in 1986, they entered his palace and found to their amazement that his wife, Imelda, possessed 1,220 pairs of shoes (many of them now housed in a museum). Keeping up with Imelda makes keeping up with the Joneses look easy.

Sources: Unpublished estimates by Juliet Schor from U.S. Census Bureau, Census Industrial Reports MQ-315A-Apparel, various years; Juliet Schor, "Cleaning the Closet: Toward a New Ethic of Fashion," in Juliet Schor and Betsy Taylor, eds., *Sustainable Planet: Solutions for the 21st Century* (Boston: Beacon Press, 2002); Juliet Schor, *The Overspent American: Upscaling, Downshifting, and the New Consumer* (New York: Basic Books, 1998); Anthony Read and David Fisher, *The Proudest Day: India's Long Road to Independence* (London: Jonathan Cape, 1997), p. 242.

The second component of aggregate demand consists of investment goods, *I*, and it is equal to the amount of money spent by businesses buying materials and capital goods to maintain or expand the production process. Governments also spend money on things—everything from schools to bombs. Total government demand is labeled *G*. Lastly, foreigners buy products from us (exports), and we buy products from them (imports). When they buy more of our products than we buy of theirs, the result is termed *net exports, X*, with *X* referring to exports minus imports. When we buy more of their products than they buy of ours, we say that net exports are negative. In this chapter we ignore net exports, and we begin by also ignoring government spending. So setting aside *G* and *X*, aggregate demand, *AD*, can be summarized as follows:

> **Net exports** are equal to total exports of goods and services minus total imports of goods and services.

$$AD = C + I \qquad (16.2)$$

What determines *C*, the demand for consumer goods? *C* depends on two things: first, the *total amount* of income and, second, the *distribution* of income between profits and wages. The total amount of income matters because the more income people have, the more they will spend on consumer goods.

The distribution of income matters because people who receive profits tend to save more than wage earners do. Why? There are two reasons. First, people whose income is mostly in the form of wages tend to be less rich than those whose income is mostly in the form of profits. And while the average rich person consumes far more than the average person who is not rich, the rich spend a smaller *fraction* of their income on consumption, saving the rest. Thus, a shift in the distribution of income from profits to wages would raise the overall proportion of the nation's total income that is spent on consumer goods (*C*).

Saving is income minus consumption.

Saving is defined as income minus consumption. From a macroeconomic standpoint there are three components of a nation's total saving. The first is the saving that is done by families and other households. The second is the saving that is done by businesses when they do not spend all their receipts on costs or dividend payments to their stockholders; in such situations the money that is saved is referred to as "retained earnings." The third form of saving occurs when governments take in more money from taxes than they spend on public goods and services; when this happens a government is said to be running a "surplus" (the opposite of which is a "deficit").

For a family saving is the income left after the family has purchased all its consumer goods. What is left after consumption may be nothing, or it may be less than nothing, in which case the family will have acquired a debt (or, if it already was in debt, it will have increased its indebtedness). If a family consumes more than its income, it is said to have engaged in *dissaving*.

The typical family supports itself on wage and salary income and does not have much income from property (see the table "Sources of Income for U.S. Taxpayers" in Chapter 6). The vast majority of such families save very little over the course of a lifetime because they break even in some years, save in some years (typically during middle age), and borrow (dissave) in other years (typically during their 20s and in old age). This pattern is not true of the rich, who usually save a substantial fraction of their income throughout their lives because they generally have more income than they need for consumption.

For the purpose of explaining basic macroeconomic concepts, we will now employ a model with a number of simplifying assumptions. Imagine that everyone in our hypothetical economy either works or is unemployed and that even the owners of firms (employers) receive wages (for the work they perform as managers). To keep things simple, we assume that all employed persons receive the same wage (w), whether or not they also receive a share of profits. The total wage income in the economy, then, is the wage per hour (the wage rate, w) times the hours of employment (N), or wN. The other form of income is profit income, which is simply net output (yN) minus total wages (wN), which can be expressed as $N(y - w)$.

To reflect the fact that the rich save more than the typical family, we make two additional assumptions. The first is that all profits are saved (the rich pay for their consumption entirely out of their wages). The second is that a large fraction of wages—received by both employers and workers—is consumed.

If people spend a large fraction (c), say 95 percent, of their wage income buying consumer goods and save the rest (including all of any profits they receive), then the demand for consumer goods is the fraction c multiplied by total wage income (wN). Thus:

$$C = cwN \tag{16.3}$$

For example, if in our model $c = .95$, $w = \$15$, and $N = 2$ million hours, then $C = \$28.5$ million. As is apparent from this discussion, we are using the letter c to represent the fraction of wage income that is spent on consumer goods, with the rest saved.

We will consider what determines investment shortly, but for now let us say that it is simply a given amount, denoted by $\underline{I}$. Then, aggregate demand is

$$AD = C + \underline{I} = cwN + \underline{I} \tag{16.4}$$

INCOME, CONSUMPTION, AND SAVING

Total income is the sum of the incomes (wages and profits) received by all income earners. Since we are assuming that all output is sold and, hence, that each dollar of aggregate supply generates a dollar of income, we can write total income as the hours of employed labor (N) times the net output per hour (y): Ny. In our simplified analysis all consumption is financed from wage income (Nw), and c is the fraction of wage income spent on consumer goods. Thus,

Total income = aggregate supply = Ny and   Total consumption = Nwc

Total saving is simply total income minus total consumption: $Ny - Nwc$. The same result can be arrived at algebraically by noting that total saving is all profit income $N(y - w)$ plus the fraction of wage income that is not spent on consumption: $Nw(1 - c)$. Thus,

$$\text{Total saving} = \text{wages saved} + \text{all profit income}$$
$$= Nw(1 - c) + N(y - w)$$
$$= Nw - Nwc + Ny - Nw$$
$$= Ny - Nwc$$

For example, if the level of employment (N) is 90 hours and the net output per hour of labor (y) is \$25, then net output (Ny) will be 90 hours times \$25 per hour, or \$2,250. If the wage per hour (w) is \$15 and the fraction of income spent on consumer goods (c) is .95, then total consumption (C) will be equal to 90 hours times \$15 per hour times .95, or \$1,282.50. Total saving can then be calculated by subtracting total consumption (\$1,282.50) from net output (\$2,250), yielding \$967.50 as the amount of total saving.

People whose income is primarily property income consume a smaller fraction of their income than do workers. For example, if $c = .95$, people living wholly on wages will consume 95 percent of their income and save 5 percent of it. By contrast, a person whose income is four-fifths from profit and one-fifth from wages will consume only 19 percent of his or her income. The person will consume 95 percent of his or her wage income, but this wage income will be only one-fifth of total income. Hence, consumption in this case will be .95/5, or 19 percent of total income, leaving 81 percent to be saved.

Aggregate demand (AD) is shown in Figure 16.4 as a relationship between *employment* on the horizontal axis (N in the term cwN) and total demand on the vertical axis ($C + \underline{I}$) or ($cwN + \underline{I}$).

Aggregate demand rises with the level of employment because as more people have jobs, there is more wage income to pay for the purchase of consumer goods (so cwN or C rises). From Equation 16.4 we can see that for every additional hour of labor hired

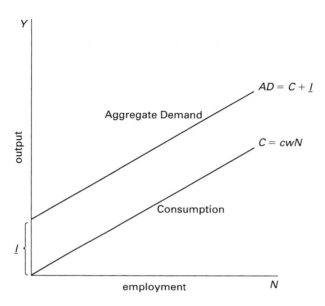

FIGURE 16.4   Aggregate demand with investment constant.   As explained in the text of the chapter here, the total demand for goods and services (aggregate demand, *AD*) is the demand for consumer goods (*C*) plus the demand for investment goods (*I*). Again for the sake of simplicity, we assume that the demand for consumer goods is a constant fraction, *c*, of wage and salary income. If the wage rate (*w*) does not vary, total wage income will be *wN*, and the total demand for consumer goods at any level of employment (*N*) will be equal to *cwN*, the fraction of wage and salary income spent on consumer goods times the wage rate per hour times the total number of hours employed. The total demand for consumer goods at any level of *N* can be represented, then, by a straight line, *C*, the slope of which is *cw*. Finally, since we are assuming a constant amount of investment (*I*) in this figure, aggregate demand (*AD* = *C* + *I*) can be represented as a line parallel to the *C* line and above it by the same amount (the amount of *I*) at all levels of employment (*N*). The slope of the *AD* line is also *cw*.

(which increases *N* by one hour), the demand for consumer goods (*C*)—and hence aggregate demand—rises by *cw* (the fraction of the wage spent on consumer goods times the wage rate). In mathematical terms, then, the slopes of both the *C* and the *AD* curves are equal to *cw*.

In order for product markets to clear (that is, for there to be neither excess supply nor excess demand), aggregate supply must be equal to aggregate demand. We can combine Equations 16.1 and 16.4 to say "aggregate supply equals aggregate demand":

$$AS = yN = cwN + \underline{I} = AD \tag{16.5}$$

Recall that when aggregate supply and aggregate demand are equal, we have a macroeconomic equilibrium. By graphing on the same axes the equations for aggregate supply and aggregate demand, we can find the level of employment, *N*, such that the two are equal.

The equality occurs in Figure 16.5 where the aggregate supply line intersects the aggregate demand line. At this level of employment (labeled N^*) there will be just enough demand to buy the amount that N hours of work produces. The intersection of AS and AD is the level of employment and output that makes yN equal to $cwN + \underline{I}$. At this point on the graph, the equilibrium condition stated in Equation 16.5 is satisfied.

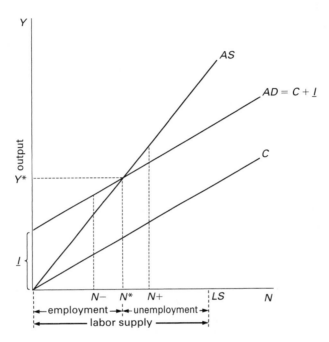

FIGURE 16.5 Macroeconomic equilibrium.   This figure brings together the concepts presented in the previous two figures. It is constructed using exactly the same AS, AD, and C curves (they all have the same slopes in this figure as they did in the previous ones), and it is again based on the assumption of a given amount of I (the same amount as in the previous two figures) at all levels of employment (N). We find that aggregate supply equals aggregate demand—the AS and AD curves intersect—at the N^* level of employment and the corresponding Y^* amount of output. Mathematically, the intersection of AS and AD occurs when $AS = yN = cwN + \underline{I} = AD$ (see Equation 16.5 in the text). The result is that N^* and Y^* are the *equilibrium* levels of employment and output. At $N+$ there will be *excess supply* in the product market (because AS is greater than AD at that level of employment), and at $N-$ there will be *excess demand* in product markets (because AD is greater than AS at that level of employment). As explained in the text, neither of these situations is stable: at both $N+$ and $N-$ the economy will tend to move in the direction of N^*. Also, if the total labor supply is LS, the difference between N^* and LS is *unemployment*. An economy can be at a macroeconomic equilibrium such as the one indicated by N^* and Y^* (total supply equal to total demand in the product market) while at the same time there is an excess supply of labor (unemployment) in the labor market. Note: the distance between N^* and LS on the horizontal axis in the figure is as great as it is only to illustrate the concepts presented here, not to reflect a situation that might actually prevail in an economy (with approximately half the labor force unemployed).

But what of other levels of employment? First consider $N+$, a level of employment greater than N^*. Reading from Figure 16.5, we can see that at this level of employment the *AS* line lies above the *AD* line. Therefore, excess supply exists because aggregate supply exceeds aggregate demand when $N+$ hours of labor are hired. If $N+$ hours of labor are employed, what will happen? The workers will be producing more products than can be sold. When the suppliers notice that excess supply exists, they will reduce employment, laying off workers. And as long as employment is greater than N^*, excess supply will persist, so the layoffs or firings will continue until the employment level is reduced to N^*.

Similarly, if the firms employ $N-$ hours of labor, excess demand will exist, since (as one can see from Figure 16.5) the *AS* line lies below the *AD* line. The workers are not producing enough goods to keep up with incoming orders. In this case more workers will be hired, until the employment level rises to N^*.

We can now answer the "troubling" question posed earlier in this chapter: Will the reduction in employment prompted by excess supply in the product market tend to eliminate the excess supply (by reducing supply)? Or will the reduction in employment make the excess supply level worse (by reducing demand)? The answer is that rather than making the initial excess supply (or excess demand) greater, the effect of employers' decisions to hire fewer workers (or more workers in the case of excess demand) will push the economy toward a point at which no excess supply (or excess demand) exists. The economy will then be operating at the N^* level of employment.

The level of employment N^* is the *equilibrium employment level,* and the corresponding level of output, AS^* (which is equal to yN^*), is termed the *equilibrium level of output.* The fact that AS^* is the equilibrium output level does not mean that AS^* is the amount of output that will actually be produced, or that N^* hours of labor will actually be hired. The actual levels of output and employment may be above or below their equilibrium levels. But, as we have just seen, the economy will tend to gravitate toward the equilibrium levels of output and employment.

The word *equilibrium* has a reassuring ring to it. When things are "in equilibrium" one tends to think of harmony and peace, but this impression is misleading when the equilibrium is a macroeconomic equilibrium. The reason is that, as we will explain, even when there is a macroeconomic equilibrium there will generally be people out of work. For those who are out of work, their lives—and particularly their household finances—will *not* be in equilibrium.

It is important to note here that the N^* equilibrium level of employment is generally not a *full employment* level. We can see that unemployment exists in macroeconomic equilibrium if we compare the equilibrium employment level N^* with the total labor supply level *LS*, indicated on the horizontal axis in Figure 16.5. When there exists a difference between the total labor supply level *LS* and the N^* equilibrium level of employment, there will be unemployment. In this model the level of unemployment, if there is any, is shown as the hours of labor that workers are offering to supply in the labor market but for which there is no demand.

Stepping back from our simplified model, recall the importance of unemployment in a capitalist economy as a basis for the power of employers over workers. As discussed in Chapter 12, the equilibrium level of employment will normally involve some amount of unemployment. Although the unemployed workers would like to get jobs and would even be willing to work for a wage lower than the one currently being paid, they cannot get work. The reason for this is that given any particular level of unemployment, employers

UNEMPLOYMENT HURTS

P eople who are out of work have to deal with a lot more than the loss of a paycheck. For many people, having a job is essential to self-respect, the respect of others, and even the feeling of being a part of a society.

Just how devastating a job loss can be is indicated by surveys that ask people about the quality of their lives. A study of Americans found that people who are widowed, divorced, or separated are much unhappier than those who have not suffered these separations. But the unhappiness associated with being without a job is as great as that associated with having lost a spouse.

Could it be that unhappy people tend to be unemployed rather than the other way around, and that is what the surveys are picking up? Not according to one study that looked at the same persons when employed and when unemployed. People reported being much unhappier when they were interviewed while jobless than in interviews when they had a job. In this study, as in the one referred to above, the psychological costs of joblessness exceeded the effect of the loss of income on one's happiness.

Sources: David G. Blanchflower and Andrew J. Oswald, "Well-Being over Time in Britain and the USA," *Journal of Public Economics*, 2004, no. 887–8, pp. 1359–1386. Liliana Winkelmann and Rainier Winkelmann, "Why Are the Unemployed So Unhappy? Evidence From Panel Data." *Economica*, vol. 65, no. 257, 1998, pp. 1–15.

will be paying a particular wage, and they will not choose to lower the wage just because an unemployed worker shows up at the hiring office offering to work for less. (Remember— from Chapter 12—that even from the employer's standpoint, wages can be too low. Employers have no desire to lower the wage to such a point that the quality and amount of work effort, e, will be reduced so much that unit labor costs will rise.) So, in the real world, unemployment is likely to persist, even when unemployed workers would be willing to work at or below the going wage (see box "Unemployment Hurts").

UNEMPLOYMENT AND GOVERNMENT FISCAL POLICY

Is there anything that can reduce unemployment? Yes, there is. This message of hope was the main lesson offered in the economic theory of John Maynard Keynes, the early 20th-century British economist whose ideas we introduced in Chapter 4.

The basic idea of Keynesian macroeconomic policy is that unemployment is the result of insufficient spending by consumers and firms. In this situation a government can increase aggregate demand (*AD*) and reduce unemployment by spending not only the revenue it receives from taxes but also what can be raised by borrowing from the public, say,

Deficit spending occurs when the government finances its purchases by borrowing from the public.

by selling government bonds. When a government spends more money than it receives from taxes, it is said to be engaging in *deficit spending*. By engaging in greater or smaller levels of deficit spending a government can regulate the level of total output and employment. When a government consciously regulates the rate of taxation and its level of spending we say that it is pursuing a *fiscal policy* (*fiscus* is the Latin word for "treasury").

Government **fiscal policy** uses taxes and spending to regulate the level of total output and employment.

Governments might spend to build schools or to build weapons. What determines the impact of government spending on the level of employment (at least in the short run) is not so much the nature of the spending as how it is financed. To generate more jobs, a government needs to spend more without taxing more. If the government increases spending but at the same time raises taxes to pay for it, taxpaying consumers and firms will have less money at their disposal, and the resulting decrease in their spending will at least partially offset the increased spending by the government.

If, on the other hand, government decides to spend more without raising taxes, it will raise aggregate demand (*AD*) and increase the level of employment. As noted above, the government can spend more without raising taxes by borrowing money from the public. In order to do this, the government will normally offer new treasury bonds for sale in the bond market. People will then use their savings to buy treasury bonds if the rate of interest on them is high enough to attract buyers. (A treasury bond is a government promise to repay, at a later date, the amount of money paid for the bond and to pay interest on that money in the meantime.) Funds that are saved by consumers or firms and used to buy government bonds enable the government to increase its total amount of spending. Such spending directly boosts total demand.

The government can also increase its spending without raising taxes simply by printing money and spending it. When this happens in the U.S., the government—through the Department of the Treasury (the agency that prints the money)—is technically borrowing from the Federal Reserve System, the nation's central bank.

To see how deficit spending will increase the level of employment, return to the equation for aggregate demand (16.4). The demand for goods by the government is typically denoted by the letter G, and the amount of taxes is represented by T, so the level of government borrowing, which we call B, is simply $G - T$. Because we are focusing here on the *net* effect of government taxing and spending on the level of employment, we simply assume that there are no taxes and that all government spending is financed by borrowing. So G and B are the same. We will use the letter B (instead of G) to remind us that we are considering government deficit spending rather than spending financed by taxes.

To see the effects of deficit spending, assume that B is a specified amount, and call it $\underline{B}$. Then, adding $\underline{B}$ to Equation 16.4, aggregate demand becomes:

$$AD = C + \underline{I} + \underline{B} = cwN + \underline{I} + \underline{B} \qquad (16.6)$$

The result, as can be seen from Figure 16.6, is to shift the aggregate demand line upward by the amount $\underline{B}$. Adding $\underline{B}$ generates a higher level of equilibrium employment N^*. The conclusion is that deficit spending can generate higher levels of employment, thereby reducing unemployment.

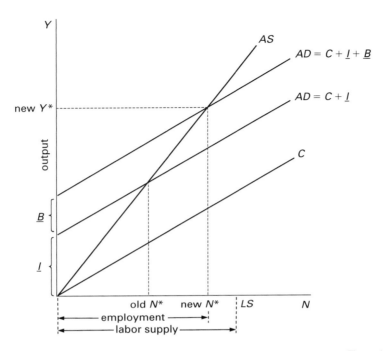

FIGURE 16.6 Macroeconomic equilibrium with deficit spending.   The only difference between this figure and Figure 16.5 is that government deficit spending, denoted by B, has been added to aggregate demand (AD). With this addition, $AD = C + I + B$. If the level of government deficit spending is $\underline{B}$, then the new AD curve will be above the old one by this amount at every level of employment, and the effect will be not only to shift the AD curve upward by the amount $\underline{B}$ but also to increase the equilibrium level of employment from "old N^*" to "new N^*." The figure shows that when employment is below the desired level (say, at "old N^*"), deliberate government fiscal policies involving deficit spending can raise the level of employment (say, to "new N^*"), thereby reducing the amount of unemployment.

The relationship between deficit spending and employment can be clarified by rewriting Equation 16.5 (the equation that defines macroeconomic equilibrium), adding government borrowing (B).

$$AS = yN = cwN + I + B = AD \qquad (16.7)$$

As before (in Equation 16.5), this new equation for macroeconomic equilibrium just states the situation in which aggregate supply (AS) is equal to aggregate demand (AD) in the product market.

To derive the equilibrium level of employment (N^*) that corresponds to the macroeconomic equilibrium just defined, we rearrange Equation 16.7, moving the cwN term to the left-hand side and changing its sign:

$$yN - cwN = I + B$$

This equation can then be rewritten as follows:

$$N(y - cw) = I + B$$

Then, dividing both sides by $(y - cw)$, we get the equation for N^*:

$$N^* = \frac{I + B}{(y - cw)} \qquad (16.8)$$

We add the asterisk to N here, signifying that this equation (16.8) is the equation for the *equilibrium* level of employment (N^*), where aggregate supply and aggregate demand in the product market are equal, and, therefore, the level of employment corresponding to this macroeconomic equilibrium will also be in equilibrium. The denominator of the fraction on the right-hand side of the equation, $(y - cw)$, is the net output per hour of labor (y) minus cw, the fraction of the wage spent on consumer goods (c) times the wage (w). Because the wage must be less than the net output per hour (otherwise there would be no profit!), and the fraction of the wage spent on consumer goods (c) is normally less than 1, cw must be less than y. So $(y - cw)$ is a positive number.

From Equation 16.8 and Figure 16.6, we can see that an increase either in investment or in deficit spending will increase employment. How many new hours of employment will an additional million dollars of government deficit spending generate? $1 million of additional government deficit spending will increase aggregate demand (AD) by that amount, putting the macroeconomy in a state of disequilibrium. As explained earlier in this chapter, the economy will then tend to move toward a new equilibrium. In order for the economy to reach the new equilibrium, aggregate supply (AS) will have to expand by $1 million. (This will be elaborated on in the coming paragraphs.) But supply can only be expanded at a rate of $1 per y hours of labor, since y is the dollar value of net output that results from one hour of labor. Therefore, to determine how many new hours of employment $1 million of additional deficit spending will generate, we have to divide the $1 million by y. Thus, the hours of additional employment will be $1 million/$y$. If y is $25, as in our earlier example, $1 million of additional government deficit spending will directly create 40,000 hours of new employment. (That is the number of hours of labor required to increase aggregate supply by $1 million.) If a full-time job is 2,000 hours of labor in a year, the additional $1 million of spending will result in 20 full-time jobs.

But the effects will not stop there. The newly employed workers will take their wages and spend them on consumer goods, creating more jobs, and the workers in those new jobs will also spend, creating yet more jobs, and so on. Suppose that the $1 million is spent by a local government to build a new gymnasium for the regional high school. The money will be used to employ architects and engineers to draw up the plans and workers to begin the construction. The money will also be used to buy the construction materials needed to build the gym. All in all, the town will spend $1 million buying inputs—labor, engineers' plans, cement, machinery, and so on. The companies that supply the concrete, construction machinery, and engineers' plans will find that the demand for their output has increased. They will hire more people to meet the demand or ask their current employees to work overtime. Jobs will be created not only in building the gym, but also in building or producing the things needed to complete the project.

Furthermore, all the workers who are newly employed or who work overtime building the gym will now have more money to spend. They will head to clothing stores or car dealers to make purchases. Whatever they buy will mean that some company will find that the demand for its product—clothes, cars, or whatever—has risen. That company will then employ more people in order to boost production and meet the demand. The people so employed will, in turn, go out and spend more money.

What is the effect of these many increases of employment and spending—first, the direct effect of the original increase in government deficit spending and then the effects of the successive increases in employment and spending? Like the ever-widening ripples spreading out on the surface of a pond after a stone has been thrown in, the effects of the additional expenditures will spread throughout the economy. Will the effects ever end?

The effects will eventually diminish and come to an end because some of the new money received in each successive round of the process will not be spent; people will choose to save some of it instead. Although an additional hour of employment requires an extra $25 of spending, the worker employed by this spending will receive a wage of less than $25 and will not spend all of it. So the spending on each round will become progressively smaller, with each new round adding a smaller and smaller amount to total employment.

> The **employment effect** is the change in the number of hours of labor employed that results from the direct and indirect effects of a change in business investment or government deficit spending.

Equation 16.8 tells us what the sum of all these effects will be. If, as in our example, government deficit spending is increased by $1 million, we add $1 million to the numerator of Equation 16.8. How much will N^* increase? The answer is ($1 million)/$(y - cw)$, because the change in N^* will be equal to the amount of the change in spending ($1 million) times $1/(y - cw)$. If, as before, y is $25, c is .95, and w is $15, then $(y - cw)$ is $10.75, and a million dollars of deficit spending will create ($1 million)/$10.75, or approximately 93,000 hours of new employment. (See Figure 16.7.) This is the equivalent of about 47 full-time year-round jobs.

> The **employment multiplier** is the hours of new employment directly and indirectly created by an additional dollar of investment or other spending.

Notice that the total *employment effect* of the additional government spending in this case (93,000 hours) is more than double the direct employment effect (40,000 hours). The reason is that additional spending and employment will have resulted from the second, third, fourth, and so on, rounds of the process. Moreover, an increase of $1 million in investment spending (I) would have had exactly the same effect as the increase of $1 million of government deficit spending (B) did in this example (see Equation 16.8).

How can we determine *how large* the employment effect will be? To answer this question we must introduce the concept of the *employment multiplier*, which enables us to know how large the total effect of a change in either I or B will be on N^*. The employment multiplier is defined as the amount of new employment created directly *and* indirectly by one additional dollar of deficit spending or business investment. To see how this works, take Equation 16.8 and make the numerator of it $10. If we then increase this numerator from $10 to $11 we can see how much N^* will change as a result. From Equation 16.8 we can see that the dollar amount of N^* will increase by exactly $\left(\dfrac{1}{(y - cw)}\right)$, since we are increasing the numerator by the difference between $11 and $10. And since the employment multiplier is defined as the change in N^* resulting from a $1 increase in B or I, we can see that the employment multiplier is $\left(\dfrac{1}{(y - cw)}\right)$. In our example, then, the employment multiplier is $1/10.75$, or $.093$.

Figure 16.7 shows graphically how the employment multiplier works: the change in N^* from 200,000 to 293,000 is the effect of an increase in aggregate demand from $2 million ($AD$ original) to $3 million ($AD$ new)—and it does not matter whether this increase in aggregate demand results from an increase in B or from an increase in I or from some combination of the two making up an increase of $1 million. If we had known the value of the employment multiplier in advance (economists often try to estimate its value), we could have predicted that the employment effect of an additional $1 million in aggregate demand would have been 1 million times $.093$, or 93,000 additional hours of employment.

One last question: What makes the employment multiplier larger or smaller? The short answer is that it depends on the relationship between the *slope* of the AD line and the *slope* of the AS line. Recall that the slope of the AS line is y (net output per hour) and that the slope of the AD line is cw (the fraction of the wage spent on consumer goods times the wage rate). But y and cw are the two terms in the denominator of $\left(\dfrac{1}{(y - cw)}\right)$. Since the value of the employment multiplier will be large if the denominator is small (and vice versa), the employment multiplier will be relatively large if the value of cw is close to that of y and smaller when the difference between y and cw is larger.

If we assume that w is less than y (workers are paid less than their net output per hour) and that c is less than 1 (workers, on average, do not spend all of their wages on consumer goods), then cw will be less than y. The question is: *how much less* than y? If cw is significantly less than y, the slope of the AD line will be noticeably less than the slope of the AS line. This is the situation portrayed in Figures 16.5, 16.6, 16.7, and 16.9 in this chapter, and it is also the situation set forth in our previous example.

If y is $25, c is $.95$, and w is $15 (as in our previous example), then $(y - cw)$ is $10.75, and the value of the employment multiplier is $1/10.75$, or $.093$. In this case, as we have seen, an increase of $1 million in aggregate demand results in the creation of 93,000 additional hours of employment. In contrast, imagine the situation in which y is $25 (as before) but w is $23 (workers are paid nearly all of their net output in wages), and c is 1 (workers spend all of their wages on consumer goods). In this case, the slope of the AD line will be quite close to that of the AS line, and the value of the employment multiplier, calculated as $1/(25 - 23)$, will be much larger ($.5$). Under these conditions an increase of $1 million in aggregate demand results in the creation of 500,000 additional hours of employment (1 million $\times$ $.5$), more than five times as much as the 93,000 hours in the previous example. The size of the employment multiplier does make a difference!

Although we have focused here on the effect that an increase (or decrease) in aggregate demand will have on the number of hours of labor employed in the economy—the *employment multiplier*—we can also calculate the effect of an increase (or decrease) in aggregate demand on the *output* of the economy. This is called the *output multiplier* (see box "The Output Multiplier").

We have reached three important conclusions. First, left to its own devices, the private economy will not generally provide jobs for all, because there is no reason to expect that when aggregate demand equals aggregate supply (macroeconomic equilibrium), the

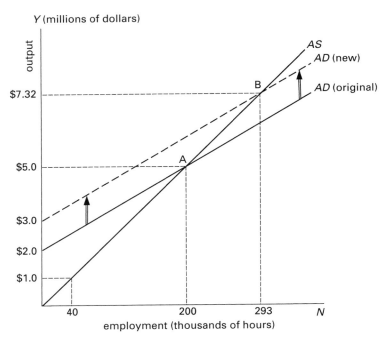

FIGURE 16.7   **The employment multiplier.**   This figure is designed to provide a diagrammatic answer to the question: how much will a given increase in aggregate demand boost employment? In the lower left corner of the diagram we can see from the aggregate supply curve, *AS*, that it takes 40,000 hours of labor to produce $1 million of output. (This ratio of labor hours to output is the same as the one in the example earlier in this chapter in which we assume that an hour of labor produces $25 worth of output.) At the "*AD* (original)" level of aggregate demand in the figure, the economy will be in macroeconomic equilibrium when $5 million of output is being produced by 200,000 hours of labor, as shown by the intersection of the *AS* and *AD* (original) curves at point A. An increase in government deficit spending or in business investment spending will shift the aggregate demand curve upward by the amount of the increase in spending; the vertical arrows in the figure show this effect. If, for example, businesses were to increase their spending on capital goods by $1 million, this would raise the aggregate demand curve from its starting point of $2 million on the vertical axis to a new starting point of $3 million. The upward sloping dotted line beginning at the $3 million point on the vertical axis represents *AD* (new). At the *AD* (new) level of aggregate demand a new macroeconomic equilibrium will occur at point B, where $7.32 million of output is produced by 293,000 hours of labor. Even though the $1 million increase in the demand for investment goods requires only an additional 40,000 hours of labor to meet the immediate increase in demand, the ripple effects of the $1 million increase in spending will have the effect, ultimately, of moving the economy's macroeconomic equilibrium to point B and increasing the demand for labor from 200,000 to 293,000 hours—an increase of 93,000 hours. As explained in the text, the difference between the 40,000 and the 93,000 hours reflects the fact that the employment multiplier in this situation is .093, so an additional $1 million of spending, either by the government or by businesses, will create (.093)(1,000,000), or 93,000, new jobs.

THE OUTPUT MULTIPLIER

W hile the employment multiplier tells us how *employment* will vary with a change in aggregate demand, the *output multiplier* tells us how *output* will vary with a change in aggregate demand. The output multiplier is defined as the amount of additional (or reduced) output that results from a $1 change in aggregate demand. It is equal to the employment multiplier times *net output* per hour (*y*), since *net output* varies with the amount of employment and the employment multiplier tells us how many hours of additional (or reduced) employment results from $1 of extra (or less) spending (aggregate demand). Thus,

$$\text{output multiplier} = (\text{employment multiplier})\ (\text{output per hour})$$

$$= \left(\frac{1}{(y - cw)} \right)(y) = \frac{y}{(y - cw)}$$

Using the same numbers as in our example in the text, the output multiplier can be calculated as follows: $(.093)(25) = 2.32$. Thus, in our example an additional $1 million of spending brings about a little over $2.3 million more net output: each additional dollar spent generates .093 hours of new employment, and each hour of new employment produces an additional $25 worth of net output.

equilibrium level of employment will be such that everyone willing to work—or seeking work—at the going wage rate will be able to have a job.

Second, government spending can generate higher levels of employment. Sometimes people interpret this second conclusion to mean that government fiscal policy can achieve *full employment.* The reasoning is that if deficit spending can increase the amount of employment, and if we know how much employment is generated by each million dollars of deficit spending, the government could simply increase its spending (without raising taxes) until enough jobs were created that everyone seeking work could find it. In the next chapter we explain why a full-employment outcome is generally not possible.

Third, the total employment effect of additional government spending or business investment is considerably greater than the direct effect. This is because of the ripple effects that result from any particular spending decision (by either government or business), these effects being represented in the concept of the employment multiplier.

In the next section we explain why the presence of ripple effects in the economy is a mixed blessing. As in life, so with the economy: there can be too much of a good thing. When the employment multiplier is very large, the economy tends to go up and down like a roller coaster.

THE BUSINESS CYCLE AND THE BUILT-IN STABILIZERS

In the primarily agricultural economies of the precapitalist era, people's incomes fluctuated from year to year, sometimes bringing surprising and welcome affluence or devastating hard times. The main source of this instability was the weather. The right amount of rain at the right time spelled a good harvest and a bountiful year. Too much or too little rain, freezes, hail, or locusts during the growing season spelled belt tightening and a hard winter ahead.

People in capitalist economies experience similar fluctuations in fortune as a result of the *business cycle*. The term *business cycle* refers to the periodic expansion and contraction of output and employment that usually take place every few years. A typical business cycle is shown in the insert in Figure 16.1 near the beginning of this chapter. *Business cycle expansions* are characterized by rapid increases in employment and income. *Business cycle contractions,* or *recessions,* are periods of increasing unemployment, slower growth in total income, and sometimes even reductions in total income. The business cycle generally runs its course, passing from expansion to recession and back to expansion, in anywhere from 3 to 10 years. The top of the expansion is termed the *business cycle peak,* and the bottom is called the *trough.* One can also see the business cycle in the ups and downs in the rate of unemployment (see Figure 16.2).

> The **business cycle** is a periodic expansion and contraction of output and employment usually taking place over a period of 3 to 10 years.

> **Business cycle expansions** are characterized by rapid increases in employment and income.

> **Business cycle contractions** (or **recessions**) are periods of increased unemployment and reduction in output and income.

The good times associated with the business cycle are welcome, and the bad times are hard. But it does not all average out; most people would be happy to do without the business cycle. Its gyrations are unpredictable. For both businesses and families an unexpected downturn in the business cycle can spell financial disaster. For families it means the possibility of being laid off or having work hours reduced and unexpectedly having to meet expenses with less income. For businesses planning for the usual amount of consumer demand, it may mean that goods are produced that will remain on the shelves unsold for months or even years.

Like waves breaking on the shore, each business cycle is a little different from the last: some are mild, some severe, some peak early, others later. Recessions and booms may last only half a year, or they may extend for two or more years. As a result, nobody knows quite what to expect; the business cycle keeps everyone off balance.

In the agricultural economies discussed earlier, weather conditions caused economic uncertainties. In a capitalist economy uncertainties arise because the millions of decisions that together determine total output and employment are *all made independently.* Without any means of coordinating production and spending decisions, the economy we live in often produces too much or too little output in relation to the demand for it. When a prolonged imbalance between aggregate demand and aggregate supply occurs, the economy goes into a recession (if there is too little demand) or expansion (if demand is too great).

To understand how a business cycle works, recall our prior discussion of the size of the employment multiplier. Using the same numbers as in our earlier example (the employment multiplier is .093), imagine what would happen if, for some reason (say, the possibility of an impending war), business owners decide to reduce their annual investment (*I*) by

$1 million. In this case the direct effect of the reduction in investment would be a loss of 40,000 hours of employment, and the direct and indirect effects together would bring about a loss of 93,000 hours of employment. The effect of this much lost employment might lead to a deterioration of the business climate, and this in turn might result in a further reduction in investment, possibly setting off a downward spiral that would cause the economy to go into a recession (see the box later in this chapter "What Determines Investment?").

What would happen, however, if the employment multiplier were .5? In this case (as explained earlier) the direct and indirect effects of a $1 million reduction in investment spending (*I*) would be a loss of 500,000 hours of employment, dramatically increasing the possibility of a recession. Thus, as we have said, a large employment multiplier is a mixed blessing. On the one hand, it means that any given amount of additional business or government spending will have a relatively large employment effect, creating a larger number of new jobs. On the other hand, however, a large employment multiplier will magnify the roller coaster nature of the business cycle.

Countercyclical policies are policies aimed at dampening the business cycle.

One of the objectives of macroeconomic policy is to smooth out business cycle fluctuations. Policies aimed at dampening the fluctuations of the business cycle are called *countercyclical policies*. They are of two types.

First, the government may attempt to offset changes in consumers' or businesses' spending by altering its spending, taxing, or (as we will see in the next section) interest rate decisions. For example, if investors decide to spend $1 million less on capital goods, the government can purchase $1 million more (remember the $1 million gymnasium). If nothing else changes, the result will be that aggregate demand is maintained at the same level, and no contraction in output or employment takes place. If the government could accurately anticipate every change in spending, and if it were free to react instantly by altering its spending level, it could smooth out (or dampen) the business cycle in this way. But these are pretty big "if"s.

It generally takes months, and sometimes a year or more, to figure out how much businesses and consumers are going to spend and how their decisions will affect the economy. If even economists cannot agree on whether the economy is headed for a recession (or whether the business cycle expansion will soon peak)—frequently debated topics—the government cannot know enough to intervene with sufficient accuracy to offset the fluctuations of the business cycle. Nor can the government, in most cases, act quickly enough even when it has accurate information. New taxes and new expenditure programs must be drafted, approved by Congress, and then implemented—a process that may take years.

As an alternative to conscious policy changes intended to offset changes in private spending, a second countercyclical policy is used. Government spending and taxing may be deliberately designed so that as the economy contracts (and unemployment rises), the government will *automatically* spend more and tax less. The idea is to give the economy something like its own thermostat so that it will regulate itself automatically and avoid severe business cycles.

The best example of an automatic economic regulating mechanism is unemployment insurance (UI), which requires the government to make payments to unemployed workers that replace at least a portion of their lost wages. As unemployment rises, the total amount of unemployment benefits paid out also rises, allowing unemployed people to spend even though they are receiving no wages. As a result, the level of demand for consumer goods will fall less than it would have had there been no unemployment insurance. For example, if business demand for investment goods declines and the producers of such goods have to lay off workers, there will be a smaller reduction in output and employment than there would have been otherwise. The effect of unemployment insurance, then, is to reduce business cycle fluctuations.

Similarly, if government spending is financed primarily through income taxes, there will be comparable effects on the business cycle. The reason is that as incomes fall during a recession, so do taxes. Then, if government spending continues at the same level while tax revenues decline, the result will be a government deficit, and this will tend to sustain aggregate demand.

> **Built-in stabilizers** are automatic changes in government spending and taxation that dampen the cycle without conscious policy decisions directed toward this end. Examples are unemployment insurance and income taxation.

Such policies as unemployment insurance and income tax financing of the government help to stabilize the economy. They reduce the severity of both upturns and downturns that take place as a result of shifts in spending by consumers and businesses. These policies are called *built-in stabilizers* because their stabilizing effects do not require particular government decisions to counteract the cycle. Rather, the effects are automatic because they are built into the structure of government spending and taxation.

Both built-in stabilizers and consciously tailored changes in government spending and taxation—the two kinds of countercyclical fiscal policy—are used effectively in the United States. As Figure 16.2 shows, business cycle fluctuations have been much less severe in the U.S. in the period since these policies were adopted after World War II, and the level of unemployment is now at least more predictable. However, in the next chapter we will see that countercyclical policies cannot completely eliminate unemployment.

Many of the fluctuations that make up the business cycle come from changes in investment spending by firms. To understand this source of instability we need to take a closer look at the investment process.

INVESTMENT, AGGREGATE DEMAND, AND MONETARY POLICY

> **Monetary policy** refers to government influences on the rate of interest intended to regulate the level of investment, output, employment, and other macroeconomic outcomes.

At the outset of this chapter we assumed that the level of investment was given and did not vary with wages or the level of employment. This assumption was made for the sake of simplicity, but it was not realistic. Investment not only varies, it can also be influenced by government policies regulating the rate of interest. Government policy that influences the rate of interest in order to regulate the level of investment, output, employment, and other macroeconomic variables is termed *monetary policy*.

The demand for investment goods includes the purchase of such things as machinery and software as well as the building of factories, offices, and the like. To the economist the word *investment* does not mean buying and selling stocks or bonds. It means replacing and adding to productive capacity (see Chapter 5). Firms purchase investment goods both because they wish to repair the wear and tear on their existing capital goods (this is called *depreciation*) and because they want to buy new equipment in order to expand their production (this is called *net investment*). Thus:

Total demand for investment goods = depreciation + net investment

Investment is, as we have seen, an important part of aggregate demand for goods and services, and hence an important source of jobs. It is essential to the economy for other reasons, also. Most important, investment generally increases productivity and thus allows for a higher standard of living. It accomplishes this by acquiring more or better equipment to be used in production, thereby making possible either more output or more leisure, or both. The long-term effects of net investment on net output per hour of labor (y) will be considered later. Here we focus only on the short-term effects of changes in the level of investment (I) on aggregate demand (AD) and employment (N). Thus, in this chapter we treat investments in such things as buildings, computers, and software only as a part of the total demand for goods and services; we do not examine the impact that additional amounts of these capital goods will have on net output once they are put to use.

Investment may be made by governments or by families, but the vast majority of investment in the U.S. is made by businesses. Businesses invest for one reason: to make money. As explained in Chapter 11, investment is essential to enable a business to keep up in the competitive race, for only by renewing and expanding the capital goods used in production can the firm protect and enlarge its share of a market.

However, business owners are not *required* to invest. They can do many things with their money. Building new factories and purchasing equipment are only two possibilities. Rather than investing, they might choose to spend their money on such things as luxury consumption, lobbying the government for better treatment of their company, or advertising. Some of the alternative ways of spending corporate profits (that might otherwise be used for investment) are listed in the box "Investment and Other Uses of Corporate Profits."

A few of the alternative uses of funds that would otherwise be used for investment, such as luxury consumption, contribute to aggregate demand. Lending and paying off debt, however, do not. If business owners are to spend their money on investment, it must be because they expect to benefit more from this activity than from the other possible uses of their funds.

Business owners usually decide how much they want to invest based on the expected profit rate and the rate of interest. As explained in Chapter 11, the expected amount of profit per dollar of investment (expected r) is one of the major determinants of the amount of investment undertaken. Of course, nobody can know in advance what the profit rate will turn out to be on any particular investment project. Much less can anyone know what the profit rate will be over the lifetime of the capital goods such as equipment, buildings, and software that have been purchased (their lifetimes may be very short or may extend for decades into the future). Thus, business owners have to make investment decisions based on estimates, guesses, and hunches. To emphasize the unpredictable quality of the future and the significance of this unpredictability for the investment process, we say that investment is determined in part by the expected profit rate net of the interest cost of funds used for investment.

To determine the expected profit rate, a potential investor has to estimate the values of two main variables: the demand for the product and the cost of its production. The investor must guess whether there will be enough demand to absorb the quantity of the product he

INVESTMENT AND OTHER USES OF CORPORATE PROFITS

W hen a firm makes a profit, investing in the United States is only one of the many things it can do with its surplus funds. Firms can use these funds in various ways, including the following:

Uses of Profit by U.S. Firms	Example
1. Invest in United States	IBM builds a new plant in Kentucky
2. Invest elsewhere	GE builds an assembly plant in Asia
3. Lend (at interest)	ExxonMobil lends money in Eurodollar market
4. Repay existing debt	RJR Nabisco pays off junk bonds
5. Pay dividends to stockholders	GM declares a quarterly dividend of $1.25 per share
6. Hold funds for future investment	Ford adds to its "retained earnings" account
7. Consumption by owners of firm	Donald Trump buys 128-room house in Palm Beach
8. Political expenditures	Lobby to influence political leaders; buy TV commercials

Political expenditures may take the form of election campaign contributions, payment of bribes to public officials, or advertising to influence public opinion; all have the objective of achieving more favorable treatment from the government (for example, getting lower taxes or relief from pollution-control laws). Neither campaign contributions nor advertising to influence public opinion (nor any other kind of expenditures to achieve political objectives) constitute investments, because they do not increase or maintain the economy's productive capacity.

or she is preparing to produce and whether all the projected new productive capacity will be used.

Also, the investor will have to calculate whether wages (w), materials costs ($P_m m$), work intensity (e), and work efficiency (f) will be such that the cost of production per unit (uc) is low enough to make the project profitable, given the product's expected selling price (P_z). An investor may look at the current and the recent past profit rates and then come up with an estimate of the profit rate in the future. Thus, the present profit rate will be a major influence on the expected profit rate and hence on the amount investors decide to invest (I).

Another major determinant of the level of investment, in addition to the expected profit rate, is the rate of interest (i). As we saw in Chapter 11, the interest rate is important for two reasons. First, most investments are made with at least some borrowed money, and a higher interest rate will increase the cost of the investment and reduce the profit available to the investor. Second, any business considering making an investment must determine whether the firm would be better off lending its available funds to other businesses (perhaps through financial intermediaries such as banks) rather than building new productive capacity. If the interest rate is high, the cost of making an investment will be high, and the rate of return on lending out funds will also be high. In this situation the high interest rate, combined with the incentive for lending out funds, will tend to discourage the making of investments.

> The **profit effect on investment** is the amount by which investment will increase for each $1 increase in total profits.

Given the importance of the expected profit rate and the rate of interest as the two main determinants of the level of investment, we can now reconsider the problem of aggregate demand and employment using our more developed understanding of investment. For any given interest rate, the level of demand for investment goods depends on the expected profit rate, which, in turn (as explained above), depends on the current and recent past profit rates. The influence of the profit rate on investment—that is, how much an increase of $1 in profits will increase investment—is called the *profit effect on investment*. We use the letter j as the symbol for this effect. For example, if profits increase by $1 and, as a result, investment increases by 50 cents, then the profit effect on investment is .5, so $j = .5$. The profit effect on investment could also be greater than one: a $1 increase in profits could so excite investors that it stimulates an increase in investment of $1.50 (the investors might finance their purchases of investment goods by borrowing); in this case the profit effect on investment (j) is 1.5.

We can then say that total investment (I) is composed of two parts. The first is influenced by the interest rate and factors other than profits, and it is represented by $\underline{I}$ in Equation 16.9. The second part is influenced by profits. It can be represented as j multiplied by total profit (R).

Then, since $R = N(y - w)$, we can say that total investment is determined as follows:

$$I = \underline{I} + jR = \underline{I} + jN(y - w) \tag{16.9}$$

An increase in the interest rate will lower I (by lowering $\underline{I}$), and a decrease in the interest rate will have the opposite effect. And because higher levels of employment bring about higher rates of capacity utilization (u), they will increase the rate of profit (see Chapter 10), which, in turn, may also stimulate more investment. These relationships are shown in Figure 16.8. Investment is shown as increasing with the level of employment (for the reason just stated), and changes in investment due to changes in the interest rate are shown by the dotted lines in the figure, with higher investment at every level of employment being associated with lower interest rates, and vice versa.

There is another factor that can influence the expected profit rate. If businesspeople become more optimistic about the future—perhaps because a probusiness Congress has been elected and will probably enact legislation favorable to business—the expected profit rate will rise (even if the current profit rate remains unchanged). A heightened optimism will have the same effect as a fall in the interest rate would have, but it works through the second term on the right-hand side of Equation 16.9 (which shows the effect of profit expectations on investment). When increased optimism raises the expected rate of profit, it will shift the investment curve upward. When this happens we can say that the upward shift in

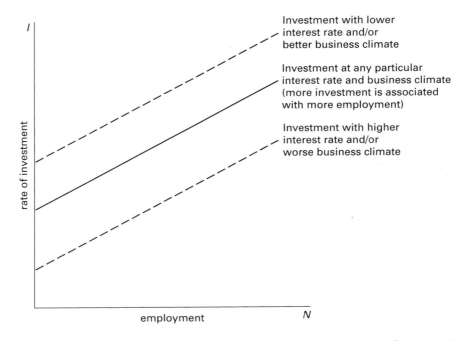

FIGURE 16.8   Investment.   As explained in the text of this chapter, the rate of investment is influenced by a number of factors. Perhaps most important is the expected rate of profit, which is in turn strongly influenced by the current rate of profit (see box "What Determines the Rate of Investment?" in this chapter). Since the current rate of profit will tend to rise as employment and capacity utilization go up (see Chapter 10), the rate of investment is shown in this figure (on the vertical axis) as increasing with rises in the number of labor hours employed (shown on the horizontal axis). While the investment curve slopes upward, the curve itself may shift upward or downward as a result of changes in the interest rate or the "business climate" (see text of this chapter). Decreases in the interest rate and/or improvements in the business climate will tend to shift the investment curve upward (raising the level of investment at any given level of employment), while increases in the interest rate and/or any worsening of the business climate will tend to have the opposite effect. These two effects are represented by the dotted lines above and below the solid line that shows how the rate of investment varies with the level of employment given the current interest rate and business environment.

The **business climate** refers to political, ideological, psychological, and other influences on the expected profit rate. It is sometimes termed the investment climate.

the investment curve is the result of an improvement in the *business climate*. The influences on investment of the expected profit rate, the interest rate, and the business climate are depicted in the accompanying box (see box "What Determines Investment?").

To focus on the ideas introduced here, we assume that the government does not engage in deficit financing, so the B (for borrowing) that appeared when we were analyzing fiscal policy is not included in our analysis at this point. In Figure 16.9 we present a new representation of macroeconomic equilibrium, showing how a change in the business climate or in the interest rate will change the equilibrium level of employment (N^*). As before, a macroeconomic equilibrium—in which aggregate

WHAT DETERMINES INVESTMENT?

One of the hottest debates in economics is about what determines the rate of investment, and this debate influences the choice of policies to promote investment. Most economists agree that the expected profit rate is an important factor and that profit expectations are based in part on the current (or recent past) profit rate. The arrows in the figure below indicate causal effects. Thus, the top arrow indicates that current and recent profit rates influence or determine the expected profit rate.

What determines the rate of investment?

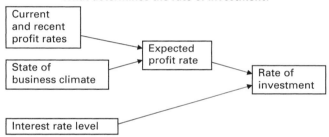

Most economists think that the business climate is important, but there is little agreement about what constitutes a *good* business climate. Some emphasize probusiness policies such as low taxes on profits or less emphasis on environmental regulation; others emphasize the importance of stable market conditions so that businesses can count on an adequate demand for their products in the future.

The importance of the interest rate is also hotly debated. Conservative economists tend to give it a larger role than do liberals because influencing the rate of investment by changing the interest rate can be done without enlarging the size of government or having it engage in deficit spending. The factual evidence about the importance of the interest rate is mixed, but it is certainly true that very high interest rates discourage investment.

supply is equal to aggregate demand in the product market—will determine the equilibrium level of employment in the labor market.

As before, the equilibrium level of employment falls short of the total labor supply (LS), and so unemployment continues to exist. In the previous section we showed how the government could use fiscal policy to generate more jobs. Now we look at how monetary policy (mentioned earlier in this section of the chapter) can be used to boost the equilibrium level of employment.

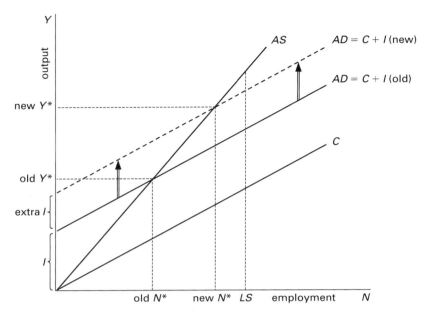

FIGURE 16.9 Effect of a decline in the interest rate or an improvement in the business climate. This figure shows how an upward shift of the investment/employment curve (see Figure 16.8), resulting either from a decline in the interest rate or from an improvement in the business climate (or from both), will motivate an increase in the rate of investment (I), expand aggregate demand (AD), and lead to a rise in the number of labor hours employed (N). Since $AD = C + I$ (for simplicity we ignore deficit spending here), an increase in I will shift the AD curve upward and bring about an increase in the equilibrium level of employment (N^*). In the figure the new AD curve is represented by a dotted line, and the equilibrium level of employment moves from "old N^*" to "new N^*." Thus, a reduction of the interest rate or an improvement in the business climate can have the effect of reducing the rate of unemployment.

All governments exercise some degree of control over the monetary systems of their economies. In the U.S. the Federal Reserve System regulates private banks in various ways, establishing rules and regulations (supplementing those provided explicitly by the legal system). The Federal Reserve System (known as the Fed) also lends money to private banks. Through its activities the Fed can influence interest rates, making it easier or more difficult for private banks to make loans to their customers. The Fed cannot literally dictate what the banks' interest rate (or rates) will be, but it can influence these rates, pushing them up or down. For example, the Fed might purchase some of the treasury bonds that banks or individuals hold. This would have the effect of pumping more money into the economy (increasing the supply of money), and this, in turn, would push interest rates down. Conversely, if the Fed were to sell treasury bonds, it would push interest rates up. The reason is that an interest rate is simply the price of (borrowing) money. Therefore, an increase in the supply of money will have the same effect that an outward shift of a supply curve would have in a product market, lowering (or raising, in the case of a leftward shift) the price of the product (see Figure 17.5 in the next chapter).

Thus, when there is a high rate of unemployment, the Fed could push interest rates down, bring about a higher level of investment, increase aggregate demand (see Figure 16.9), and thereby raise the level of employment. Lower interest rates will also lead to an increase in consumer spending. What is significant for the analysis of how monetary policy can effect employment is that the government—or, more precisely, the Fed, an agency that is independent of the president and the Congress—can influence the rate of interest.

WAGES, AGGREGATE DEMAND, AND UNEMPLOYMENT

Some economists think that if the problem is unemployment, a lower wage is the solution. Economists who think this way make unemployment part of the solution, too, because, they argue, the existence of unemployment will tend to force wages down until the market clears. But this approach to reducing unemployment is wrong on both counts: first, the existence of unemployment does not mean that wages will fall, and, second, if wages did fall, the result might be more, rather than less, unemployment.

The existence of unemployment (excess supply in the labor market) does not mean that wages will fall. Wages can remain unchanged even if there is unemployment. When there is excess supply in the milk market, the price of milk typically falls, supply is reduced, demand increases, and the market eventually clears. But as we saw in Chapter 12, the labor market is different. To the milk *buyer* there cannot be such a thing as too low a price of milk: a price of zero would be fine, thanks. But to an employer there can be too low a price of labor. As we saw in the analysis of the labor extraction curve in Chapter 12, the wage has to be high enough not only to attract workers but also to motivate them to work hard and well. A firm that pays its workers so poorly that they do not mind losing their jobs is unlikely to be a profitable company. As explained in Chapter 12, the profit-maximizing wage will tend to be higher than what an unemployed person would be willing to work for because this higher wage will minimize unit labor cost and thus maximize the rate of profit. But given some particular amount of unemployment, a wage will be chosen by the employer—or be settled upon between employer and employees—and the fact that there is unemployment will not cause the wage to change. So unemployment itself will not cause wages to fall.

The second problem with the conventional approach is that even if wages did fall, the result might be more, not less, unemployment. This point is hard to understand because it is inconsistent with our personal experience. If a person is looking for work and is asking $20 an hour, he or she might have to look for quite a while (or forever) to find a job. But if this person offered his or her services at $5 an hour, he or she would probably find work sooner. For an *individual,* asking for a lower wage generally improves a person's chances of finding employment. From this, one might conclude that if *everyone* were willing to take a pay cut, then fewer people would be unemployed. But this conclusion would, as a general rule, be wrong.

If everyone were to take a wage cut, the result could be (a) lower unemployment, (b) higher unemployment, or (c) no change in unemployment. The reason the outcome is uncertain can be understood using the macroeconomic analysis presented in this chapter.

An employer's demand for labor is a *derived demand*—that is, it is derived from (caused by) the demand for the commodities produced by the particular firm. But the demand for any one firm's output depends on the level of demand in the economy as a whole, or aggregate demand. Higher wages will increase employed workers' incomes, and this will tend to result in an increase in the demand for consumer goods (C). The result may be an increase in aggregate demand (C + I) and, hence, in employment. But if the higher wages reduce profits, the amount of investment (I) may fall. And if investment falls more than consumption rises, the result will be a decline in aggregate demand and less employment (more unemployment).

The question is: how will an increase in the wage (w) affect total employment (N*)? Whether a rise in the wage leads to a growth or a reduction in total employment depends on how firms respond to the rise in w. In a situation in which employees insist on being paid a higher wage, firms may anticipate lower profits and cut back on their rate of investment. If this happens broadly across the economy, the result will be a smaller total amount of investment (I) and, possibly, a reduced level of aggregate demand (C + I). But if firms anticipate that the rise in wages will lead to more aggregate demand and rising sales (through the influence of w on consumption), they may decide to keep I at its present level—or even increase it—and the result will be an increase in employment.

Figure 16.10 shows how an increase in the wage (w) can lead to an increase in employment. It shows what happens when firms do not change their level of investment even when w is rising. An increase in w will increase the amount of demand for consumer goods (C) at each level of employment. This is represented on the graph as a rotation upward of the consumption line from "C (old)" to "C (new)." The slope of the C line rises because its slope is cw, and, assuming that c (the fraction of the wage spent on consumer goods) does not change significantly, an increase in w raises cw. At the same time, if the level of investment (I) remains constant, the AD line will also rotate upwards—from "AD (old)" to "AD (new)"—its slope remaining the same as that of the consumption line. As the aggregate demand line rotates upward, the equilibrium level of employment increases, from "old N*" to "new N*." Under these conditions, then, an increase in the wage (w) leads to a rise in the amount of labor employed.

From the earlier discussion, however, we know that we cannot jump to the conclusion that an increase in the wage (w) will *always* lead to an increase in employment. To determine when a rise in w will have a positive effect on employment and when a rise in w will have a negative effect on employment, we must consider the effect of a change in w on investment (I) as well as on consumption (C). (As we know, aggregate demand is the sum of both consumption and investment.)

Since $C = cwN$, we can deduce that an increase in w of \$1 will raise consumption (C) by the amount cN dollars. Similarly, if w is reduced by \$1, consumption will fall by cN dollars. To determine how a dollar's change in w will affect investment (I), we need to refer to Equation 16.9, where it is established that

$$I = \underline{I} + jN(y - w)$$

$$\text{or}\quad I = \underline{I} + yjN - wjN$$

Given the fact that w is preceded by a minus sign in the term wjN on the right-hand side of this equation (and holding all the other variables constant), we can see that increasing w by \$1 will reduce investment by jN dollars. Similarly, a reduction in w of \$1 will lead to an increase in investment of jN dollars.

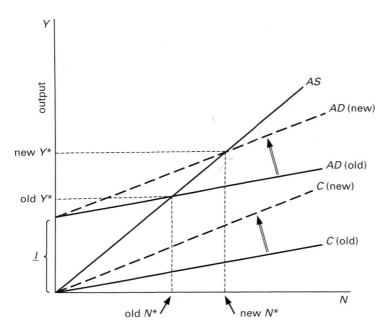

FIGURE 16.10   A wage-led employment situation with investment constant.   The purpose of this figure is to illustrate the point that in a "wage-led" situation, an increase in the wage rate (contrary to what one might think) can lead to an increase in total employment. For this to happen the wage increase must have a positive effect on aggregate demand, through its effect on the demand for consumer goods, that is greater than the negative effect on aggregate demand resulting from the impact of the wage increase on profits and thence, via the profit effect on investment, on the investment component of aggregate demand. To make the point starkly clear in this figure we assume that investment does not change at all as a result of the wage increase, but this assumption is not necessary to the argument: a wage-led situation may exist (see the text of the chapter for the relevant explanation) even when investment is allowed to change.

In this figure C (old) represents a particular relationship—the "old" relationship—between the demand for consumer goods (C) and the amount of employment (N) based on an "old" wage rate. Thus, C (old) = cw (old)N, where w (old) represents the "old" hourly wage rate. Associated with C (old) is an "old" aggregate demand curve, AD (old), understood as: AD (old) = C (old) + I, where I represents the constant level of demand for investment goods. Alternatively, C (new) represents a "new" relationship between C and N such that C (new) = cw (new)N, with w (new) standing for a new hourly wage rate. And associated with C (new) is a "new" aggregate demand curve, AD (new), understood as: AD (new) = C (new) + I.

As explained earlier in this chapter, the slope of any C curve (as well as its corresponding AD curve) is cw, so if w (new) is higher than w (old), cw (new) will be greater than cw (old), the C (new) curve will have a steeper slope than the C (old) curve, and the AD (new) curve will also have a steeper slope than the AD (old) curve. Since both of the C curves start out at the origin (where both employment and consumption are at zero), and since both of the AD curves start from the same point on the vertical axis (a point that is I distance above the origin) the effect of the increase in the wage rate is to cause both the C curve and the AD curve to *rotate* counterclockwise so that they each end up with the slope cw (new) rather than the slope cw (old). (Note that a rotation of a curve is different from a shift of a curve: in the case of a rotation there is a change in the slope of the curve, whereas in the case of a shift the slope remains the same.)

The new, steeper C and AD curves, reflecting the higher wage rate, are shown in the figure as dotted lines. As can be seen in the figure, the new AD curves move the equilibrium rate of employment from old N* to new N*, and they also increase the equilibrium rate of output from old Y* to new Y*. With its simplifying assumptions, this figure illustrates how an increase in w in a "wage-led employment situation" results in higher rates of both employment and output. As pointed out, though, the same result may be achieved even with a variable rate of investment as long as the conditions for a "wage-led employment situation" exist (see text of the chapter for an explanation of these conditions).

We can now see how a change in the wage (w) will affect aggregate demand. Since a rise in w of $1 will lead to an increase in consumption (C) of cN dollars, and since the same $1 increase in w will lead to a decrease in investment (I) of jN dollars, the *net* effect of a $1 wage increase on aggregate demand will be $(c - j)N$ dollars. Whether the wage increase ends up expanding or shrinking aggregate demand will depend on which is larger, the fraction of a dollar in wages that is spent on consumption (c) or the profit effect on investment (j). For example, if $c = .95$ and $j = .5$, a $1 increase in the wage will *expand* aggregate demand by $(c - j)N$, or $(.95 - .5)N$ dollars. Thus, a wage increase expands aggregate demand when c is greater than j, and unemployment falls as a result. Alternatively, if $c = .95$ and $j = 1.5$, a $1 increase in the wage will *shrink* aggregate demand by $(c - j)N$, or $(.95 - 1.5)N$ dollars. In this case the wage increase leads to a reduction of aggregate demand (because j is greater than c), and unemployment rises as a result.

> A **wage-led employment situation** obtains when rising wages increase employment.

> A **profit-led employment situation** obtains when rising wages reduce employment.

A situation in which a wage increase affects employment positively—c is greater than j—is termed a *wage-led employment situation*. A situation in which a wage increase affects employment negatively—j is greater than c—is termed a *profit-led employment situation*.

What types of circumstances determine whether a wage increase will have a positive or a negative effect on employment? The answer, as might be expected, is that "it depends." In some countries and at some times, a wage-led employment situation exists; in other places and at other times, a profit-led employment situation exists. Where most wage or salary recipients are poor, the fraction of wage income consumed (c) is likely to be high, and there will probably be a wage-led employment situation. Where businesses are highly mobile and able to relocate anywhere in the world in response to differing profit rates, the profit effect on investment (j) is likely to be large, so there will probably be a profit-led situation.

Where a nation is in relation to the business cycle may also be important. At low levels of employment and wages—at the trough of a recession, for example—a wage increase is likely to generate jobs (a wage-led situation). And at high levels of wages and employment—toward the end of a business cycle expansion, for example—a wage increase is likely to shrink aggregate demand and reduce employment (a profit-led situation).

Why do circumstances like these make a difference? At low levels of employment and at low wages, the fraction of wages spent on consumption is likely to be high: when most people have a member of their family unemployed or are themselves unemployed, saving is impossible and, as a result, all available income is spent on necessities. In this case c will be high, possibly as high as 1 or even greater than 1 (as families borrow to maintain their living standards).

Also, at low levels of employment and low wages, the profit effect on investment (j) is likely to be relatively low. The reason is that at low employment levels, businesses are likely to have unused productive capacity: they will have machinery and perhaps entire factories idle for lack of demand. Under these conditions they are unlikely to make investments, even if profits are rising, so the profit effect on investment (j) will be low. Thus, depressed economic conditions are likely to be situations in which c exceeds j, a wage-led situation exists, and a wage increase will tend to generate additional employment.

By contrast, at high levels of employment and wages—during a boom, for example—people will be better off and will be making more than they had in recent years, perhaps even more than they had expected to earn. In this case they will find it easier to save, so c will be relatively low. At the same time, businesses will find most or all of their existing productive capacity in use, so they will be ready to invest if the expected profit rate is right. Thus, the profit effect on investment (j) will be high. With c low and j high, there will be a profit-led situation, and a wage increase is likely to lead to more unemployment.

The analysis of wage-led and profit-led situations has important implications for economic policy. For example, when a wage-led situation prevails, there will be greater justification for an increase in the legally mandated minimum wage as an employment-boosting policy. Raising the minimum wage usually brings about rises in wages at every level. With the rise in the average wage (w) there will also be an increase in total employment and hence a reduction in unemployment. In such a situation, then, a policy that improves the living standards of low-wage workers will be beneficial to virtually everyone in the labor force. On the other hand, when a profit-led employment situation exists, there will be a case for cutting taxes on corporate profits on employment-generating grounds. Such a tax cut will, under these circumstances, bring about an increase in after-tax profits, raise the expected profit rate, stimulate investment, increase aggregate demand, and, as in the wage-led employment situation, increase total employment and reduce unemployment.

CONCLUSION

Increasing wages may actually increase the number of jobs. With two options for creating jobs—monetary and fiscal policy—and with the fact that under certain conditions wage increases might help rather than hurt, one might think that the government could make unemployment a thing of the past, as Keynes hoped.

If, to Keynes, the *economics* of full employment seemed promising, the *politics* of full employment must have seemed even more hopeful. Policies to increase the number of jobs are certain to be politically popular. What could be closer to a politician's dream platform than promoting full employment by raising both wages and profits, allowing the government to spend money without raising taxes (deficit spending)?

There can be no doubt that the policies suggested by Keynes have taken some of the roller coaster out of the economy (see Figure 16.2). But the path to full employment turns out to be strewn with thorns, not roses. The main policies we have reviewed—deficit spending, reducing interest rates, and increasing the minimum wage—often work at cross-purposes. Also, as we have seen, not everyone benefits just because (nearly) everyone else has a job. As explained in the next chapter, the government's ability to regulate the level of employment has actually been used on occasion to create *un*employment.

And, as the next chapter also makes clear, Keynes's optimism neglected to take into account some of the realities of the capitalist economy. In particular, he overlooked the fact that sustained full employment had never been achieved, either in his native England or in the U.S. Indeed, few countries have achieved it, and those that have have done so only temporarily during wartime or more permanently by changing some of the basic rules of the game of the capitalist economy.

SUGGESTED READINGS

Jared Bernstein and Dean Baker, *The Benefits of Full Employment: When Markets Work for People* (Washington, D.C.: Economic Policy Institute, 2003).

Robert L. Heilbroner, *Beyond Boom and Crash* (New York: Norton, 1978).

John Maynard Keynes, *The General Theory of Employment, Interest, and Money* (New York: Harcourt Brace Jovanovich, 1972 [1936]).

Paul Krugman, *The Return of Depression Economics* (New York: Norton, 2000).

John Miller, Amy Offner, and the Dollars & Sense collective, eds., *Real World Macro*, 20th ed. (Cambridge, Mass.: Dollars & Sense, 2003).

Thomas I. Palley, *Plenty of Nothing: The Downsizing of the American Dream and the Case for Structural Keynesianism* (Princeton: Princeton University Press, 1998).

Studs Terkel, *Hard Times, an Oral History of the Great Depression* (New York: Pantheon, 1970).

CHAPTER 17

The Dilemmas of Macroeconomic Policy

" A big jump last month in [U.S. workers'] hourly earnings suggests that the wage stagnation [that has been] plaguing so many Americans may be lifting," one newspaper reported in July 1996. On the same day, however, the same newspaper carried a second story with the headline: "Signs of Unexpected Growth Send Markets Tumbling." This article reported that the people on Wall Street who buy and sell stocks and bonds "reacted with alarm to the disclosure that a lot more Americans were working than had been anticipated." Bond traders began selling their clients' bonds as soon as the employment news came out, and in the stock market as well, prices began falling when the market opened (shortly after the jobs report was released), and they "tumbled" 2 percent by the end of the day.[1]

Just the opposite chain of events occurred in February 1995. Newspapers reported then that job growth had been unexpectedly weak in January, and, as a result, the unemployment rate had risen to 5.7 percent—the first such rise in two and a half years. Most people regard a rise in unemployment as bad news. Not Wall Street. On the day newspapers reported that the unemployment rate had gone up, one headline read: "Big Rally for Stocks and Bonds." The article under this headline began as follows: "Wall Street rejoiced yesterday as Main Street showed signs that its economy was slowing and unemployment was rising."[2] People often find such reports hard to understand.

In this chapter we explain why a capitalist economy cannot tolerate too much employment (too little unemployment). In Chapter 18 we go on to discuss an additional obstacle to the achievement of full employment, the fact that many economists and policy makers

---

[1] *New York Times,* July 6, 1996.

[2] *New York Times,* Feb. 4, 1995.

believe high employment will cause inflation. (Expectations about inflation were a factor in both of the historical situations just mentioned.) We begin here with unemployment.

Unemployment imposes two types of cost on society. The first type of cost is the waste that results from it—the loss of goods and services that are needed and could have been produced but were not. The second type of cost is the personal insecurity and hardship that unemployment creates. Workers never know when unemployment will hit, or where; its occurrence is impossible to predict or to plan for.

It is not just those actually unemployed who suffer. Even employed workers who have never been unemployed have to worry that they *might* be laid off at some time in the future. The most vulnerable workers are, of course, those recently hired, those with few skills, and those who are young or old or members of minority groups. But many others—auto workers with seniority, computer programmers in fast-growing companies, salespeople of all kinds, secretaries with seemingly safe jobs, long-term employees, professionals, technicians, and managers—must also worry about being laid off.

Why is unemployment such a big problem? After all, as we saw in Chapter 16, fiscal and monetary policy can generate additional jobs and reduce the amount of unemployment. So, if only 9 out of every 10 workers is employed, why not devise a policy that would result in the 10th worker being employed? Why not shorten the length of the work week so that firms would have to employ the 10th worker if they wanted to produce the same amount of output as they had been producing before? The French government has passed a law limiting the length of the work week to 35 hours. If the hourly wage remains the same with such a policy, of course, all the previously employed workers would have to take a cut in their pay, but the insecurity and hardship experienced by the previously unemployed might be eased.

Alternatively, there could be a system that insured people against unemployment, just as they are insured against other calamities—fires, storms, explosions, accidents, and so on. When your home burns down, your insurance pays to replace it. Why not provide all workers with an insurance program so that if a person is laid off, the insurance would make up for his or her lost wages? In fact, the governments of many countries do provide insurance systems of this kind.

Unemployment compensation consists of regular payments made to some unemployed workers from a government insurance fund to which employers contribute.

In the United States, the states collect small fees from companies in proportion to the size of their workforces and then pay *unemployment compensation* (*unemployment insurance,* or *ui*) to unemployed workers. However, the unemployment compensation that is paid to American workers amounts, on average, to only one-half of their lost wages, and fewer than half of the unemployed receive it. This is because a worker has to qualify for this benefit in order to receive it. For example, to qualify for unemployment compensation in many states in the U.S. a person has to have worked for the same employer for at least one year before he or she was laid off. And even when a person qualifies for it, the benefit is only paid for six months, so a person who is unemployed for more than six months does not receive it. As indicated in the box "Counting the Unemployed" on pages 409–411, at the end of 2003 there were more than 8 million people in the U.S. counted as unemployed. Barely 3 million of these were actually receiving unemployment compensation, however.

Unemployment compensation payments help to stave off acute hardship for as long as they last, but this hardly reduces the fear of unemployment. A person's fear of the consequences of fire would hardly be allayed by fire insurance that was not easily available and that paid to repair only half the damage.

If there are ways of eliminating the insecurity associated with unemployment, why are they not implemented? The answer is simple. A capitalist economy *needs* to have a certain level of unemployment and the insecurity it generates. We explain in this chapter that if there is a sustained period of low unemployment for some reason (war, for instance), and as a result workers lose their fear of being laid off, the economy works in such a way as to restore enough unemployment to bring back the fear of job loss.

In the previous chapter we saw that unemployment does not occur because all of a society's needs have been met. If they were, there might not be enough work to keep everyone employed. But as we saw, unemployment and unused productive capacity can exist side by side with unmet human needs. In this chapter we show that unemployment and its attendant insecurity exist not because we cannot think of ways to employ everyone but because U.S.-style capitalism requires insecurity in order to function, and unemployment is one of the major components of insecurity.

Is unemployment, then, like death and taxes, unavoidable? Not really. Figure 17.1 shows that unemployment rates vary greatly among advanced capitalist nations, with some

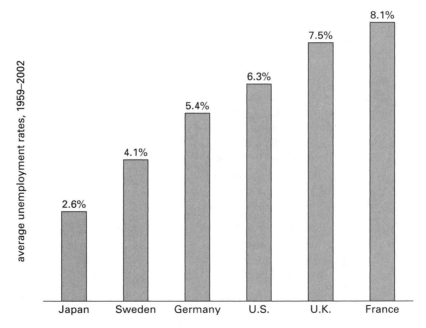

FIGURE 17.1   Average unemployment rates for six countries, 1959–2002.   This figure shows that there are significant differences among the unemployment rates of advanced capitalist nations. Each country defines its labor force, employment, and unemployment statistics in its own way, but the U.S. Bureau of Labor Statistics has recalculated the unemployment rates for a number of countries, including the ones represented in this figure, using the U.S. definitions of the categories.

Source: U.S. Department of Labor, Bureau of Labor Statistics, "Comparative Civilian Labor Force Statistics 1959–2002," available at ftp://ftp.bls.gov/pub/special.requests/ForeignLabor/flslforc.txt.

countries having had higher ones and others lower ones over the past four decades. How do some countries achieve lower unemployment rates? The six countries represented in Figure 17.1 are similar in many ways: they face the challenges of rapid technological change and intense international competition that are often seen as obstacles to the achievement of full employment. Yet some of these nations do provide jobs for most of their workers in most years, while others do not.

The key to achieving low unemployment is replacing the whip of job insecurity with other ways of regulating work and pay. Capitalist nations that have low rates of joblessness often achieve them with mutually beneficial understandings worked out by representatives of business, labor, and government.

In this chapter we explain why unemployment continues to be a major problem in most capitalist countries today even though the theoretical knowledge outlined in the previous chapter, knowledge of how macroeconomic policy can be used to achieve full employment, is widely available. The main idea of this chapter is that *macroeconomic policy cannot achieve full employment in a durable way without fundamental changes in the institutions that coordinate labor processes and regulate labor markets.* This main idea is expressed in four key points:

1. High employment (low unemployment) sustained over a period of years tends to reduce profit, a phenomenon termed the *high-employment profit squeeze.* Profits decline because low unemployment shifts the balance of power toward workers and away from their employers, driving up wages and unit labor costs.

2. The availability of imports and the existence of foreign markets for any country's goods place additional limits on the effectiveness of macroeconomic policies aimed at high employment. Policies designed to stimulate demand for domestically produced goods may lose their effectiveness if consumers and businesses choose to spend their additional income on goods produced in other countries (creating jobs abroad). Similarly, it may not be possible to get foreigners to purchase domestically produced products (generating additional income and jobs at home) without pursuing policies that keep unemployment high and business costs low to enable a nation's firms to sell their products at competitive prices in the global marketplace.

3. Monetary policy and fiscal policy approaches to job creation are both effective, but they may work at cross purposes. Their effectiveness is limited because the government borrowing required by deficit spending often works against the lowering of interest rates that is the goal of full employment monetary policy.

4. Sustained high-employment levels and a further dampening of the business cycle's gyrations are possible, but not without new policies and fundamental changes in institutions.

In the previous chapter we assumed, for the sake of simplicity, that changes in the level of employment do not bring about changes in the level of net output per worker hour, y, or the wage, w. But y and w do, in fact, vary with the level of employment, and in order to identify the difficulties that confront policy makers seeking to promote high employment, we have to understand how they vary. As in Chapter 16, however, we continue to assume that current spending on investment goods, a component of aggregate demand, does not contribute to improvements in productivity (z). Although we close this chapter by listing some institutional changes that might enable a country such as the U.S. to reduce its rate of unemployment, we continue to assume here that the overall institutional framework of the economy—what we call a social structure of accumulation—continues to be that of "transnational capitalism." (The concept of a social structure of accumulation was developed in Chapter 7.)

THE HIGH-EMPLOYMENT PROFIT SQUEEZE

When macroeconomic policies and other influences *do* reduce unemployment, problems develop. The source of the difficulty is this. Just as changes in the distribution of income between wages and profits affect the level of aggregate demand and employment (see Chapter 16), the process also works the other way: changes in aggregate demand and employment affect the distribution of income between wages and profits. Wages tend to rise with high levels of employment (low unemployment), lowering the profit rate, and, conversely, wages tend to fall with high levels of unemployment. One reason for this is that when there is only a small pool of unemployed people, the employed workers will have more bargaining power and will thus be in a better position to push for higher wages. If wages rise, unit labor cost (ulc), the wage cost per unit of output, will also rise, and this will tend to reduce the profit rate (see Chapter 12). A reduction in the profit rate will tend to discourage investment, and the process may then come full circle: if investors hold back, aggregate demand will be diminished, output will decline, and unemployment will rise.

Profits will tend to fall when employment is high (unemployment low) for another reason. High employment occurs when there is strong aggregate demand. But if aggregate demand is strong, the output of the economy will most likely be growing rapidly, and the demand for materials used in production—raw materials, energy, and the like—will be rising. Rising demand for input materials (given limited supplies) tends to push up their prices, so another consequence of high employment is that unit materials cost (umc) rises.

As labor and materials costs rise, profits will fall—unless businesses are able to raise their prices enough to cover the cost increases. But businesses will generally not be able to pass along all cost increases to their customers in the form of higher prices because competition with other businesses in all parts of the world will prevent them from doing so. Any individual business that raises its price too much will find that its share of the market, its sales, and most likely its profits, too, will have fallen. If all businesses raise their prices at the same time, the result will be inflation, a circumstance we discuss in the next chapter. In the following two subsections we discuss the two types of cost increases that can push down the rate of profit.

The High-Employment Wage Push

When employment is low and unemployment high, workers feel fortunate to have their jobs. They may not like their work, but the alternative for them is no work at all—or at least a prolonged spell of unemployment. In this situation workers will be willing to work hard and well for relatively low pay. They will not be inclined to demand improvements in working conditions, nor would their employers be likely to accept such demands. Furthermore, when unemployment is high, labor unions are not likely to resort to strikes as a way of pushing up wages: with high unemployment there will be many people out of work and eager to take the jobs of striking workers.

As unemployment falls, however, the picture changes. Workers begin to feel more confident about finding new jobs. Employers know that it will be harder to replace a worker who quits or goes on strike. The shoe is now on the other foot: workers can demand higher wages, call for safer working conditions, and insist on a pace of work that is less exhausting. In order to hold on to their current employees—especially those considered essential to a company's ability to make a profit—employers must be willing to accept at least some of their workers' demands, even if doing so will result in a lower rate of profit.

Why do workers have more bargaining power when employment rises? As the level of unemployment falls, workers' alternative income-earning opportunities improve, and this lifts what was defined in Chapter 12 as the fallback wage. Recall that the fallback wage is based on the wage available to a worker in some other job and that it is affected by the amount of income the worker can expect to receive while unemployed. If an employer is willing to pay only the fallback wage, the worker will not care whether he or she keeps the job; in this case the worker is unlikely to be responsive to any demand by the employer for hard work.

If we assume that there is a legally defined rate of unemployment compensation (ui) and that a worker can anticipate earning a particular wage in another job, the worker's fallback wage will depend on how long he or she expects to be unemployed (see Chapter 12). The important point here is that the expected duration of unemployment will vary with the rate of unemployment. The more unemployment there is, the longer the worker must expect to remain without work, and, hence, the lower will be the fallback wage. Conversely, as unemployment falls, the expected period of unemployment will be shorter, and the fallback wage will rise.

When the fallback wage rises, a process called the *high-employment wage push* comes into play. Figure 17.2 shows how such a process occurred during the long economic boom of the 1990s in the U.S. The first dot on the left side of the graph refers to the second quarter (April–June) of 1992. This point shows that in that quarter the employment rate was 92.4 percent, the unemployment rate 7.6 percent, and the real wage $7.79. The term *real* means that the wage then being paid would purchase $7.79 worth of goods and services valued in 1982 prices (1982 being the base year for measuring recent inflation). Of course, the actual (or "nominal") wage was higher than this—it was more than $10 an hour—but prices had also risen since 1982, so the purchasing power of $10 in "real" terms was considerably less than $10. (See box "Money Wages," pp. 489–490.)

The U.S. economy expanded steadily between the beginning of 1991 and the end of 2000, and as a result the employment rate rose from 92.4 to 96.1 percent, bringing down the unemployment rate from 7.6 to 3.9 percent. What Figure 17.2 shows is that after a while, unemployment was reduced enough to give workers the power to push up wages. Thus, by the fourth quarter of 2000 the real wage had risen from $7.79 to $8.33. This is indicated by the point on the graph that is higher and farther to the right than all the others.

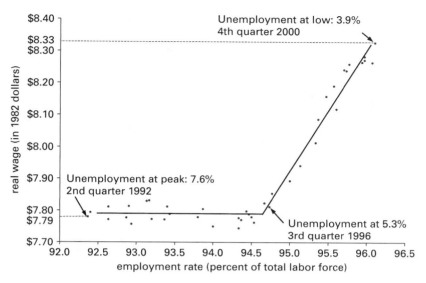

FIGURE 17.2   Employment and real wages during the 1990s boom in the U.S. economy.   This figure shows that the "high-employment wage push" still exists; the data here prove that it was at work in the American economy during the business cycle of the 1990s (see text). What is plotted in the figure is the average real wage of U.S. production workers (in 1982 dollars) in relation to the U.S. rate of employment from the second quarter of 1992, when unemployment was at its cyclical peak of 7.6 percent and the average real wage was $7.79, to the fourth quarter of 2000, when unemployment reached its cyclical low of 3.9 percent and the real wage was $8.33. The percentage rates of unemployment displayed inside the diagram are the difference between 100 percent and the percentage rates of employment shown on the horizontal axis. The real wage is calculated starting from the *nominal* hourly wage (in current dollars) paid to production ("nonsupervisory") workers on the payrolls of private companies, excluding farm workers (who make up less than 1 percent of the workforce). The nominal wage data is then "deflated" by *dividing* it by the Consumer Price Index (CPI) for urban wage earners and clerical workers (the CPI-W), thereby converting it into *real* wage data. The CPI is a measure of how much prices have risen during a specified period, and it is calculated using 1982 as its benchmark (or "base") year, so 1982 = 1 (or 100, since CPI data are provided as three-digit numbers, with 1982 = 100). Without changing anything conceptually one can use the CPI data calibrated with a single digit and three decimal points. While the average *nominal* wage earned by production workers in 1992 was more than $11 an hour, the CPI-W was at 142.5, or 1.425, meaning that prices had increased 42.5 percent since 1982. Hence the average *real* wage of production workers in 1992 (deflated by the increase in prices) was $7.79 an hour (see the left-most data point in the figure). Similarly, we can deflate the $14.50 actually earned by production workers in 2000 to a real wage (in 1982 prices) of $8.33 an hour (see the highest data point on the right side of the figure). The reason for converting nominal wage data to real wage data is to be able to show that while the average nominal wage of production workers in the U.S. increased by more than 23 percent between 1992 and 2000, with the rise in prices taken into account their average real wage increased by just 4 percent in the same period.

Source: U.S. Department of Labor, Bureau of Labor Statistics, detailed statistics on "Employment & Unemployment," "CPI-Urban Wage Earners and Clerical Workers (CPI-W)," and "Compensation & Working Conditions," available at http://www.bls.gov/data/home.htm. Calculations by Arjun Jayadev, University of Massachusetts at Amherst.

Notice in Figure 17.2, however, that the real wage remained virtually unchanged, hovering around $7.80, until the second half of 1996. Only in the third quarter (July–September) of that year did the real wage come unstuck and start to go up. The fact is that U.S. workers, on average, saw no improvement in their living standards during the first five years of the economic boom that began early in 1991. Moreover, if the expansion of the economy and the corresponding fall in the unemployment rate had stopped in 1996, there probably would not have been any improvement in their living standards. It was only when the unemployment rate fell below 5.5 percent in the third quarter of 1996 that workers' wages headed up (see the sharp turn up in the line in Figure 17.2). At this point, the real wage began to rise—it went to $7.81 in the third quarter of 1996—and it continued to rise steadily until it reached its peak (for this business cycle) of $8.33 in the fourth quarter of 2000. The steady rise in the real wage between the third quarter of 1996 and the fourth quarter of 2000 can be attributed to the fact that during this period the unemployment rate fell from 5.5 to 3.9 percent.

Wage increases will drive up unit labor cost unless labor productivity (output per hour) goes up just as fast as (or faster than) the wage. But this generally will not happen because at high rates of employment (low rates of unemployment) workers will be less afraid of losing their jobs. Accordingly, they will hardly be inclined to put out the higher levels of work effort that would be required to offset (with productivity increases) the rise in their wages.

The Materials Cost Push

Just as high employment rates produce higher labor costs, the cost of materials will also go up as employment rises. And the increase in unit materials cost (*umc*) will have the same effect on the profit rate as the high-employment profit squeeze.

When output and employment increase, more materials must be used in the production process in order for output to increase. As firms demand more materials, the sellers of materials will probably be able to raise their prices. Such price increases will in turn tend to push the rate of profit down—hence the high-employment materials cost push.

To understand how the materials cost push works, consider a particular input, for example, the oil that is used in a great number of production and consumption processes. Increases in the output of the economy will not only generate more employment, they will also require the use of additional amounts of other inputs, such as oil, and as a result the demand curves for these inputs will shift to the right. As explained in Chapter 8, the effects of such shifts will be to create excess demand in input markets, and this will tend to push up the prices of input materials. The result is that just as a rise in employment ensuing from an increase in aggregate demand will tend to raise the wage and squeeze profit, an increase in the demand for material inputs will tend to have the same effect by raising unit materials cost.

The High-Employment Profit Squeeze

Would employers, then, like to have the employment rate be as low possible (the unemployment rate as high as possible)? No, of course not. It is true that widespread unemployment strengthens the bargaining power of employers vis-à-vis both workers and materials suppliers. But to make a profit a firm has to do more than produce a product at a low cost, it has to produce and sell a high volume of its product.

Production of a high volume of output cannot be achieved without employing substantial numbers of workers. Moreover, selling large amounts of products is easier to do when people have large amounts of money to buy products, and they will have large amounts of money only if they have jobs that, in the aggregate, generate large amounts of income. At high rates of unemployment the income of many workers will be reduced, and since workers are also consumers, the total demand for the economy's output will be commensurately lower. It is clear that unemployment has a direct effect on the income of unemployed workers; in addition, however, high unemployment weakens the bargaining power and limits the wage increases of employed workers as well. Thus, high rates of unemployment will hold down the income of all workers.

We can conclude, then, that employers will see that some levels of employment are too *low* to allow them to maximize their profits; in this case, consumers will not have enough money to buy their products. Similarly, employers will see that some levels of employment are too *high* to allow them to maximize their profits; in this case, wages and other costs will be too high.

A **high-employment profit squeeze** occurs when the high demand for labor creates both labor and materials cost increases, which in turn reduce profits.

When employment is below a certain level, increases in employment (reducing unemployment) will raise profits. However, as employment increases, a point will be reached at which the profit rate will be at its maximum and further increases in employment will only cause the profit rate to fall. This is because beyond the profit-maximizing rate of employment, rising wage and materials costs will squeeze profits. When increases in employment have a negative effect on the profit rate, we say that there is a *high-employment profit squeeze.*

Here is how the high-employment profit squeeze works. Intuitively one might think that with more labor hours employed more units will be produced, and if these additional units of output can be sold, total profit (R) will increase. Even if the additional units can be sold, however, there is a problem with this line of reasoning: it is based on the assumption that the cost of producing the additional units will not rise as employment and output rise.

Under certain circumstances the assumption of constant costs might be a reasonable one to make, and in this case total profit would certainly increase as employment and output expanded. This might be the situation when, at low rates of employment (high unemployment), increases in demand for labor and materials will not result in significant increases in wages or materials costs. These are circumstances when increases in employment (N) are most likely to have a positive effect on the rate of profit (r).

Under other circumstances, however, assuming labor and materials costs to be constant would not be justifiable because, in fact, these costs will increase as additional labor and materials are used to produce more output. Eventually, the increases in input costs will outweigh the positive effect of increases in employment and output on the rate of profit. In such situations the net effect of increases in employment (N) on the rate of profit (r) will be negative, hence there will be a high-employment profit squeeze.

Figure 17.3 shows how movements in the two important variables, unit cost (uc) and output produced, will have varying effects on the rate of profit (r) at different levels of employment. The top panel of the figure shows that as employment expands (moving from

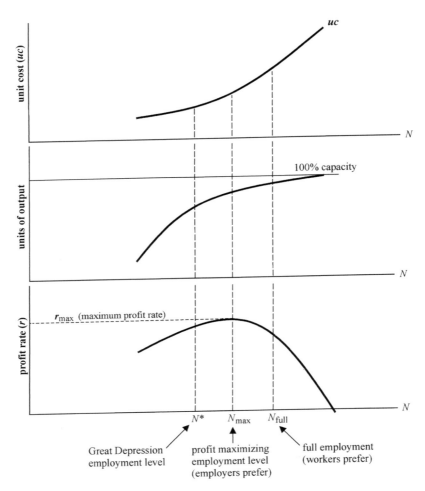

FIGURE 17.3   **Unit cost, output, and the profit rate.**   This figure illustrates the set of complex interacting relationships, described at length in the text, among the number of labor hours employed (N), the number of units of output, the cost per unit, and the profit rate of a firm. Moving from left to right in the figure, the bottom panel shows that the rate of profit rises as long as the positive contribution to profit resulting from producing and selling more output (middle panel) outweighs the negative effect on the rate of profit resulting from rising unit costs of production (top panel). At the point where these positive and negative effects are just in balance, the level of employment will be the one (N_{max}) where the rate of profit is at its maximum—and this is, of course, the level of employment that is optimal from the standpoint of the employer. But this profit-maximizing level of employment will most likely be *below* the *full employment* level (N_{full}) because at full employment the bargaining power of workers would probably be strong enough to enable them to push wages up to a point where unit labor cost—and unit cost as a whole—would be high enough to have already pulled the rate of profit down from its maximum level. Thus, the level of employment desired by workers (N_{full}) will generally be above the level of employment desired by employers (N_{max}). Also shown in the figure

left to right on the horizontal axis), unit cost (*uc*) rises at first slowly and then, at higher levels of employment, goes up more and more rapidly. Thus, the unit cost curve is nearly flat at low levels of employment and then becomes steeper and steeper as employment rises. Rising unit materials cost (*umc*) is a factor driving up unit cost here, but the main contributor to the upsurge in unit cost is the high-employment wage squeeze (increasing *ulc*) discussed earlier and displayed in Figure 17.2.

The middle panel of Figure 17.3 shows that as employment increases, output (as one would expect) also increases. At first the output curve rises somewhat steeply, showing that each additional labor hour hired results in a significant increase in output produced. However, as employment goes to higher levels, the increases in output generated by additional employment become smaller and smaller, and the output curve flattens out as firms approach their maximum rates of output (maximum productive capacity).

Finally, the bottom panel of Figure 17.3 shows how the two counteracting influences—the positive effect of increases in output, on the one hand, and the negative effect of rises in unit cost, on the other—determine what the rate of profit will be at different levels of employment. At low levels of employment (high unemployment), each increase in employment brings about a sharp increase in output (shown in the middle panel) but only a modest increase in unit cost (shown in the top panel). As a result, the profit rate rises as employment increases. In this range of employment (where the line in the lower panel is rising), the contribution that each additional unit of output makes to profit outweighs the negative effect of the rising costs associated with increases in the amount of labor employed.

However, as employment continues to increase, additional hours of labor produce smaller and smaller increments of output, so the output curve levels off and the contribution of output to profit diminishes as more labor is hired. As additional hours of labor are hired, unit costs rise at an increasing rate (see the upward curving line in the top panel). At some point the negative effect of increases in cost (with both unit labor cost and unit materials cost rising) outweighs the (declining) positive effect on profit of more output—and at this point the profit rate itself (shown in the bottom panel) begins to decline. In the bottom panel the level of employment at which the profit rate is at its maximum is labeled N_{max}. At this level of employment the two influences on the profit rate just balance out, and any increases in employment beyond this point will only reduce the rate of profit.

The actual occurrence of the high-employment profit squeeze during the 1990s economic boom in the U.S. is shown in Figure 17.4. Like Figure 17.2, this figure shows the effects of a rising employment rate—only this time the focus is on the profit rate rather than on the wage. Starting in the lower left area of the figure, the data point for the third quarter (July–September) of 1992 shows that there was 7.6 percent unemployment (92.4 percent

---

is N^*, the *equilibrium level of employment*, and this will be located wherever the aggregate demand and aggregate supply curves happen to intersect (see Chapter 16). N^* can be at *any* point along the N axis, including N_{full}, N_{max}, or even a point such as the one where N^* is placed in this figure, at which there is a very high rate of unemployment. The level of aggregate demand determining the location of N^* will itself be influenced by consumer demand (*C*), government deficit spending (*B*), net exports (*X*), and the demand by businesses for investment goods (*I*), which in turn will be affected by the business climate, the rate of interest, the expected profit rate, and other factors.

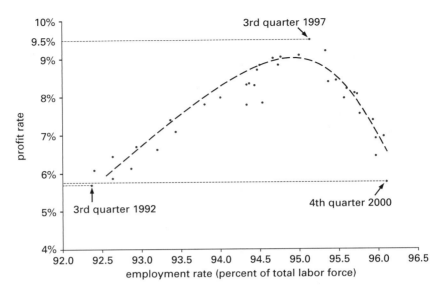

FIGURE 17.4   Employment and the profit rate during the 1990s boom in the U.S.   This figure charts the rise and fall of the rate of profit during the U.S. economic boom of the 1990s. It covers roughly the same period as—and is complementary to—Figure 17.2. Whereas that figure charted the relationship between real wages and the rate of employment, this figure focuses on the relationship between the rate of employment and the profit rate. Both figures use empirical data to show that the high-employment profit squeeze happened in the American economy during the 1990s. Moreover, the data presented in this figure follow the pattern shown and explained in Figure 17.3. Starting from a profit rate of 5.7 percent in the third quarter of 1992 (when the unemployment rate was still at its peak of 7.6 percent), the rising sales revenues and increasing capacity utilization that came with expanded employment led to increases in the rate of profit. This process continued for the first five years of the boom, but in the third quarter of 1997 the rate of profit peaked at 9.5 percent and began to decline as increases in labor and materials costs finally outweighed the positive effects of rising employment. Note that the profit rate peak occurred a full year *after* the real wage upturn shown in Figure 17.2 (the third quarter of 1997 as opposed to the third quarter of 1996); this is consistent with the analysis presented in Figure 17.3, which explains why the profit rate may continue to rise even as workers are bargaining for, and getting, higher real wages. It is only when the cost increases (including both labor and materials costs) overwhelm the positive effects of economic expansion that the profit rate begins to decline. In the U.S. economic expansion of the 1990s, the cost increases had pushed the profit rate down by the fourth quarter of 2000 to 5.8 percent, almost exactly to where it had been (5.7 percent) at the beginning of the expansion in the third quarter of 1992. It was no surprise, then, that by the end of the first quarter of 2001 the U.S. economy slowed down and went into a recession (the economy actually contracted). The profit data presented in this figure are for the nonfinancial business sector of the American economy; this excludes banks but represents more than 85 percent of the U.S. corporate business sector.

Source: U.S. Department of Commerce, Bureau of Economic Analysis, National Income and Product Accounts (NIPA), Table 1.14, available at http://www.bea.doc.gov/bea/dn/nipaweb/. Calculations by Arjun Jayadev, University of Massachusetts at Amherst.

employment) in that quarter, with the profit rate being 5.7 percent. As employment rose over the next 5 years, the profit rate rose with it, just as the bottom panel of Figure 17.3 suggests. The profit rate peaked at 9.5 percent in the third quarter of 1997 and then sank back to 5.8 percent as the employment rate continued to rise and the unemployment rate fell to 3.9 percent, again following the pattern laid out in Figure 17.3.

And so policy makers who seek to achieve full employment cannot escape the logic of a capitalist economy. Policies that succeed in increasing employment beyond a certain point will eventually drive the profit rate down. This will reduce investment and, as a result, reduce employment.

Beyond the economic logic of capitalism, there is a political obstacle to the achievement of full employment. People who receive most of their income from profits often have a considerable amount of political influence (money talks!), and many of them will resist the adoption or implementation of any policy that might have the effect of cutting into profits. (In Chapter 19 we consider how the government works in a capitalist economy, including the connection between money and politics.) If the stock market falls when the government reports higher employment, it should not be surprising that some business owners will openly state that in certain situations, at least, an increase in unemployment—even if brought on by a recession—may be a good thing (see box "One View: 'A Wholesome Recession'").

ONE VIEW: "A WHOLESOME RECESSION"

There is what I call a wholesome recession . . . [because] *with every adversity there is a seed of benefit.*

One thing most people don't have is the art of motivation. . . . A lot of people haven't realized you have to work for your money. They're a little more practical now. . . .

As for employees, with a fear of losing jobs they're really putting their heart into their work. Formerly, it was, "What's the difference?" They could quit and go elsewhere. If everything comes so doggone easy, they get into bad spending and living habits.

Anyone who wants a job can find a job. There's no doubt of it whatsoever. He may have to take a job that's honest and decent, though it may not really be the type of job he wants.

—W. Clement Stone, chairman of the Combined
Life Insurance Company of America;
billionaire; substantial contributor
to the Republican Party

Source: Interview with Studs Terkel, *New York Times Magazine,* Dec. 20, 1970, p. 50.

EXPORTS, IMPORTS, AND AGGREGATE DEMAND

The high-employment profit squeeze is not the only obstacle preventing the achievement of full employment. High-employment policies can also run into problems in the international economic arena. The main problem is that reducing domestic unemployment may conflict with the need to remain competitive in world markets. When domestic unemployment is low, prices will rise as employers attempt to hold on to their profit margins. As a result, buyers may find that goods produced in other countries are less expensive than domestically produced goods.

Unless all countries are pursuing full-employment policies, the higher costs and prices resulting from one nation's high-employment policies may mean that its goods and services will not be competitive in international markets. The result will be a fall-off of exports and a flood of imports as consumers and businesses shun high-priced domestically produced goods and buy cheaper imports.

Two problems then arise. First, as we will see shortly, falling exports and rising imports mean that there will be less aggregate demand for goods produced domestically. And second, there is the long-term reality that buying more from, while selling less to, the rest of the world cannot go on indefinitely. In the short run an excess of imports over exports can be paid for by borrowing, as the U.S. did on a massive scale during the late 1990s and early 2000s. But sooner or later the loans will have to be paid back. Here, we focus on the first problem, the short-term effect of trade deficits on aggregate demand.

We are interested in the demand for goods produced domestically, no matter whether such demand comes from inside or from outside the country. Only domestic goods production employs a particular nation's workers, and it is domestic employment that we are interested in. So, for example, the purchase of a U.S.-built drill press by a German firm and the sale of a pound of U.S.-grown wheat to a family in Bombay both contribute to U.S. aggregate demand and employment. By contrast, neither the purchase of a Japanese-built computer by an Atlanta business or the acquisition of a bottle of Italian Chianti by an inhabitant of Chicago will generate jobs in the U.S. Such purchases will contribute to aggregate demand, and hence increase employment, in other countries.

Once we take into account imports and exports, we can see that not all demand for consumer goods is part of aggregate demand in the home country—the U.S. in our example. As noted, an American's purchase of Italian wine is not. Neither is all demand for investment goods part of aggregate demand. The purchase of a Japanese-made computer by an American business is not. So when international trade is taken into account, the demand for *imports*—that is, demand that is not directed toward domestically produced goods—must be *subtracted* from aggregate demand. On the other hand, the demand for *exports*—the demand by foreigners for goods produced domestically—is *added* to aggregate demand.

A simple way to make the required adjustments is to use the term *net exports* to represent the difference between the total value of exports of goods and services and the total value of imports of goods and services. Net exports are positive—they increase aggregate demand—if a country exports more than it imports; conversely, net imports are negative—they decrease aggregate demand—if imports exceed exports. We use the letter X to represent net exports:

$$X = \text{net exports} = \text{total exports} - \text{total imports}$$

With this simplification, we can take into account both exports and imports by just adding *X* to the equation for aggregate demand (Equation 16.6) that was developed in the previous chapter:

$$\text{Aggregate demand} = AD = C + I + B + X \qquad (17.1)$$

As before, C = total demand for consumption goods, I = total demand for investment goods, and B = government deficit spending. From Equation 17.1 it can be seen that an increase in X, like an increase in B, C, or I, will increase aggregate demand and promote higher levels of employment (assuming nothing else changes), while a fall in net exports will have the opposite effect.

The Demand for Exports and Imports

As with investment and consumption, we need to know what determines the level of net exports. The short answer is that the level of net exports will be determined (a) by the level of incomes at home and abroad and (b) by the prices of foreign goods as compared with those of domestically produced ones. To achieve a fuller understanding of how the value of net exports is determined, we need to look at each of these relationships more closely.

First, consider the effect of rising incomes in a particular country on that country's net exports. As the incomes of U.S. families and businesses grow, more will be bought because there is more money to spend. Among the things that will be purchased are imported goods, including cars, machinery, and other items. For this reason imports tend to rise when incomes rise. Exports, however, do not grow as a result of incomes growing. If rising incomes cause imports to rise while exports remain at their existing level, net exports will fall.

Since incomes rise or fall with employment, the same conclusions can be arrived at looking only at changes in the rate of employment. At low levels of employment, incomes will also be low and hence spending by consumers and businesses—including spending on imports—will be restricted. But increases in employment will generate more income, and, as noted, some of the additional income will be spent on imports. Hence, imports will tend to rise with increases in employment and fall with contracting employment (rising unemployment). Unless the level of exports changes, then, rises in employment will reduce net exports, and less employment will have the opposite effect.

Just now we have been assuming that a country's exports are constant. But, of course, this is unrealistic. In fact, both exports and imports—and hence net exports—will change not only with changes in the country's own level of employment and income but also with changes in the levels of employment and income in other countries. Consider, for example, the situation of the U.S. If in the rest of the world unemployment is high and people are poor, the demand for U.S. exports will be low. If at the same time people in the U.S. are prosperous and buy a lot of imports, net exports will also be low, perhaps even negative. But if in some countries, at least, incomes are high, then the demand for U.S. goods and services will be higher, and net exports will also be higher.

The other main influence on the level of net exports is how high or low the prices of foreign goods are in comparison with the prices of goods made at home. If domestically produced goods are inexpensive compared to goods produced elsewhere, imports will be low and exports will be high (foreigners will find the lower-cost goods more attractive than their own). In this case net exports will most likely be positive. But if the prices of goods produced elsewhere are relatively low, or if the prices of domestically produced goods are relatively high, imports will be high in comparison with exports. This will be the case because buyers at home (be they individuals or firms) will prefer to spend their money on foreign-made goods (especially if their quality is good), so imports will be strong and net exports may even be negative. This has been the case with the U.S. in recent years: for several decades the U.S. has been running trade deficits with the rest of the world, and in 2003 its annual trade deficit was only slightly less than $500.

To make clear the influence of relative prices on the value of net exports, we can use (as we have in earlier chapters) P_z to refer to the price of goods produced domestically. Then we can represent the price of goods produced elsewhere by the term P_{im} (for price of imports). The ratio of the price of goods produced elsewhere to the price of domestically produced goods is the real price of imports:

$$\text{the real price of an import} = P_{im}/P_z \qquad (17.2)$$

Bringing back the example used in Chapter 5: Grainland exports grain and imports plows, while Plowland exports plows and imports grain. The exchange ratio on the international market is one plow for 10 bushels of grain. So the real price to Grainland of importing a plow from Plowland is 10 bushels of grain. Putting this same relationship in monetary terms, we could say that the price of a bushel of grain is $20 while the price of a plow is $200. Then P_{im}/P_z (again, from the standpoint of Grainland) will be $200 over $20, and the real price of importing a plow will be the 10 bushels of grain that Grainland must export in order to earn the $200 it needs to buy its plow.

In Chapter 5 we also explained how a change in the real price of an imported input would affect the size of the surplus product in the importing country. As the real price of the import goes up, the importing country will have to export more and more of its total output in order to be able to buy the same amount of its imported good. If nothing else changes, this will leave less and less of its total output to be garnered as surplus product by those who control the production process. The effect of an increase in the real price of an import, then, will be to reduce the surplus in the importing country.

That is how it works in our hypothetical Grainland. What about a real modern economy?

The foreign exchange rate.   Imagine that a farmer in the U.S. wants to import the plow in the previous example from, say, Germany. Buying the imported plow (a transaction that will most likely be accomplished by a U.S. agricultural equipment dealer) will have to be done in two steps. The first step will be to exchange dollars for euros, the euro being the currency now used in Germany, assuming that the German producer of the plow will want to be paid in the currency required for purchasing things made in Germany (or anywhere on the European continent). The second step will be the actual purchase of the plow, but this will require (ultimately) paying for it in Germany's currency, the euro, rather than in dollars. (It is unlikely that the purchaser of the plow in the U.S. will actually buy the necessary euros, but the agricultural equipment dealer he or she buys it from had to pay the

German plow manufacturer in euros, so the dealer or the dealer's bank had to buy euros to get the plow into the showroom). The cost of this step in the transaction will depend on how many euros each dollar will buy.

Thus, the price of the import (in dollars) depends on two things. It depends first on the price of the import in the currency of the country where it was produced. Second, it depends

> The **foreign exchange rate** is the amount of the foreign currency that a dollar will buy; it is also known as the **value of the dollar.**

on the *foreign exchange rate,* defined as the amount of a foreign currency that can be obtained in exchange for a certain amount of the currency of one's own country. The foreign exchange rate of the U.S. dollar is termed the *value of the dollar.* Of course, given the fact that the exchange values of currencies are allowed to fluctuate in global currency markets, the dollar exchanges for different amounts of the currencies of particular countries, and these amounts change daily. Thus, on February 10, 2004, a dollar exchanged for .79 euros, 105.6 Japanese yen, and 0.54 British pounds.

The price of an import in dollars (P_{im}) is the price of the import in its own currency (P_{imf}) divided by the foreign exchange rate (v). The "f" in "P_{imf}" signifies that this is the price of the import in its own "foreign currency," and the "v" here stands for "value of the dollar." Thus,

$$P_{im} = P_{imf}/v \tag{17.3}$$

If the plow in our example had been imported from Germany, knowledge of the exchange rate between dollars and euros on the day the plow was imported would enable us to figure out its original cost in euros. If the plow had been imported on February 10, 2004, when the value of the dollar (v) was .79 euros, the price of the plow ($200 in the U.S.) would have been 158 euros in Germany. (For the sake of simplicity here we make the following unrealistic assumptions: no transportation costs and no markup of the price by the agricultural equipment importer.) If the German price of the plow remained constant, a rise in the value of the dollar would have reduced the price of the plow as an import to the U.S. This result can be achieved using Equation 17.3, or it can be arrived at intuitively: a higher value of the dollar means that each dollar will purchase more in another country, so fewer dollars would be required to purchase the plow. When the value of the dollar rises, then, people in the U.S. will tend to buy more products made in other countries (more imports), and the opposite will be true when the value of the dollar falls.

What can we say in general about the effects of changes in the exchange rate between one country's currency and another's? If we substitute the exchange value of any country's currency for the v in Equation 17.3 (the v having stood for the value of the dollar), we can see that the effect of an *increase* in the exchange value of one country's currency will be to encourage imports by individuals or firms in that country. This is because a unit of their currency will buy more of another country's currency, thereby enabling them to purchase more imports for the same amount of their currency (in other words, making the imports cheaper). It will also discourage exports to other countries. This is because as the exchange value of the home country's currency increases, the prices of domestically produced goods will rise from the standpoint of buyers in other countries. A buyer in another country will have to pay more of that country's currency to buy the amount of the home country's currency needed to purchase the domestically produced goods.

We explain what determines the value of a particular country's currency in the following section. Summarizing what we have established so far, we can say that the demand for exports and imports—hence, the level of net exports—is determined by the following factors:

- household and business incomes at home and abroad
- prices at home and abroad
- the foreign exchange rate

With this information we can now consider the effect of exports and imports on employment and on high-employment policies.

INTERNATIONAL TRADE AND MACROECONOMIC POLICY

How do high-employment macroeconomic policies work when they are pursued in an economy with significant exposure to the global economy? Do the availability of imports and the existence of foreign markets for domestically produced goods place limits on the effectiveness of macroeconomic policies aimed at high employment? In considering the relationships between international trade and macroeconomic policy one is confronted by two basic questions: First, can policies deliberately aimed at promoting net exports be successful in achieving high levels of domestic employment? Second, does being competitive in a global economy require pursuing macroeconomic policies that keep unemployment high in order to maintain costs of production low enough to enable businesses to price their products competitively?

Promoting Net Exports

Promoting exports and discouraging imports (promoting net exports) would seem a promising way to promote domestic employment. If net exports could be promoted without bringing about changes in any other important economic variables, the result would certainly be an increase in jobs. But, in the real world, keeping variables constant is often difficult.

Imports can be discouraged by imposing taxes (tariffs) on them or by putting restrictions (quotas) on the quantity of goods that can be brought in from another country. The U.S. once did this successfully to hold down automobile imports from Japan. Such efforts as the "Buy American" campaigns that have been mounted in the U.S. may also reduce the demand for imported goods. The government of a particular country can promote exports by paying some of the costs of their production (as the U.S. does with farm products) or by persuading other countries to give favorable treatment to its exports (as various imperialist nations have done with their colonies).

Policies aimed at discouraging imports have worked at times in the past. In the 19th century both the United States and Germany used tariffs to protect domestic industry against lower-cost manufactured goods from Great Britain. By doing this they made possible the development of their own manufacturing industries while at the same time promoting employment and growth in their own economies. In recent decades the governments of

South Korea and Japan have actively promoted exports of their nations' products by subsidizing the export prices of them. Partly as a result of such policies, both of these countries achieved high employment rates and rapid economic growth.

However, export-promoting and import-restricting strategies will not work for everyone, much less for everyone at the same time. After all, more than one country can play the game, and the success of any one country will be limited by what other countries may do.

In the first place, other countries may retaliate. If the U.S. makes it difficult for Brazil, for example, to export shoes to the U.S., Brazil is likely to place obstacles to the exportation of farm equipment to Brazil. Any country attempting to create jobs by keeping out goods from other countries may find its own goods kept out of other countries' markets. The result may be a loss in jobs, rather than a gain.

Second, it is impossible for all countries to expand their net exports at the same time. This is true for the reason that the total amount of net exports in the world must always add up to zero. Imagine the case of a two-country world with one of the two countries enjoying positive net exports. In this case the second country would have to be experiencing negative net exports. With the first country exporting more than it is importing, the second country would have to be importing more than it is exporting, and the second country's negative net exports would have to balance exactly the first country's positive net exports. The logic is the same for a world of 200 countries, and what is involved here has nothing to do with retaliation; it is a matter of simple arithmetic.

Third, even if two countries manage to increase their exports to each other, it could happen that neither one experiences an increase in its net exports, in which case there would be no increase in aggregate demand and no increase in employment in either country. Again, there is no retaliation involved here, but in neither country will a successful export promotion strategy result in an increase in employment.

Imagine that the U.S. successfully promotes its exports of chemical products to Europe and that Europe successfully promotes its exports of automobiles to the U.S. The exporting industries of both countries will be booming and will be hiring more workers. Chemical workers in the U.S. will have no trouble finding work. Autoworkers in Europe will not worry about unemployment. But will there be a net gain in jobs in either country? Probably not. Europe's exports of automobiles will be automobile imports in the U.S., and U.S. autoworkers will be laid off. In Europe, it will be the chemical industry workers who will suffer unemployment. The increases in U.S. imports from Europe will count as a subtraction from U.S. net exports, and the increase in Europe's imports from the U.S. will be a drag on its net exports. If both double their exports, the *net* exports of both Europe and the U.S. will remain unchanged. (Note that *consumers* of automobiles and chemical products in Europe and the U.S. may benefit if Europe is better at producing automobiles and the U.S. is better at producing chemicals. In this case the increasing specialization of Europe in automobile production and the U.S. in chemical products will lead to greater total output of both types of products. Hence, there could be increases in total consumption of both automobiles and chemical products.)

While strategies to increase net exports cannot work for everyone, there are circumstances in which they may work. Promoting exports and discouraging imports can lead to an increase in the total number of jobs in a particular country if the country adopting such policies has one or both of two unusual advantages. First, the policies may work if the country is very powerful and can thus prevent retaliation. And second, net export promotion may succeed if a country can produce many goods much more cheaply than other countries at its prevailing wages and existing foreign exchange rate. A country that can claim either of these advantages will most likely be able to use net export promotion strategies successfully to improve its competitive position in the global economy.

Competing in Global Markets

Is it possible for a country to compete in global markets without maintaining a high rate of unemployment? To compete in global markets a country must be able to sell its products at prices that are competitive with the prices of other countries' products. But to preserve low prices, costs must be relatively low, including unit labor cost. As we know from the discussion of the high-employment wage push earlier in this chapter, however, unit labor cost rises when unemployment falls. So how does a country achieve high net exports while at the same time pursuing high-employment macroeconomic policies?

Here is the problem. With high unemployment, prices can be low, and a country's goods can be competitive on world markets. Exports will boom, and there will be little demand for imports since they cannot compete with domestically produced goods. In this situation net exports will be high. But high net exports will add to aggregate demand and thus generate higher employment.

As we have seen, an increase in employment will lead to falling unemployment and rising costs. As this happens businesses will raise their prices as much as they can to maintain their profit rates in the face of rising costs. But as prices go up, exports will fall off, imports will increase, and eventually imports will exceed exports so net exports will be negative. At this point international trade will be having the effect of reducing aggregate demand and placing a damper on further employment increases.

The impact of rising costs and prices on a country's net export position can be explained more precisely using Equation 17.2. With increasing prices the real price of imported goods will fall (as P_z rises, P_{im}/P_z falls). Responding to the more favorable price of goods produced elsewhere, buyers will buy fewer domestically produced goods and more imported goods. The result will be falling net exports, possibly even subtracting so much from aggregate demand that no further increases in employment will occur. So as imports rise and exports fall, the effect is not to create jobs at home but to create them elsewhere.

The independent macroeconomic policies of different countries have a distinct "after you" quality. Each country would like *the others* to adopt expansionary macroeconomic policies—for example, deficit spending and low interest rates—so that its exports will increase, generating more employment and income for its own people. The other countries' higher employment rates and incomes will increase the demand for the home country's exports, thus creating jobs in the home country. If all countries adopted deficit spending policies at the same time, their efforts would be mutually supportive. But any one country trying to expand employment alone could well face inflation, mounting imports, and little job creation to show for it.

The difficulties we have just identified arise from two sources: the high-employment profit squeeze and the lack of coordination among nations pursuing their own macroeconomic policies. Thus, the success of high-employment policies requires two things. First, a way must be found to reduce the cost pressures that develop with high employment. Second, the major governments of the world must adopt macroeconomic policies that are complementary rather than competitive and self-defeating. This would involve coordinating decisions to expand aggregate demand rather than discouraging imports or waiting for other countries to expand their aggregate demand. We consider some policies to achieve these objectives in our concluding section. Before considering those options, however, we examine a last major dilemma of macroeconomic policy.

MONETARY AND FISCAL POLICY AT ODDS

Both monetary policy, governmental influence on interest rates, and fiscal policy, changes in government spending and taxation, can be effective tools for increasing the amount of output and employment. But they often work at cross purposes, with the influence of one counteracting the influence of the other, so that the potentially beneficial effects of both are greatly reduced.

The main problem is that deficit spending designed to increase aggregate demand and generate more jobs requires the government to borrow money—often vast amounts of it—in order to make ends meet. When the government borrows large sums, it is more difficult for others to get credit (consumers wanting to finance a car purchase, for example, or businesses wanting to secure a loan to purchase some new machinery). The credit squeeze occurs because the government borrows money from the same sources (in the same markets) that businesses and families use; all potential borrowers are in competition with one another.

The result of such competition is that some businesses and families wanting to borrow money cannot get loans, and those who do obtain loans end up paying higher interest rates on them. This is just exactly what is *not* needed if there is a problem of insufficient aggregate demand, since, as we have seen, higher interest rates discourage both investment and consumer buying, thus reducing aggregate demand. This type of negative outcome will at least partially offset the positive effects of the increased spending.

Thus, spending and borrowing by the government may have the effect of reducing the spending and borrowing of families and businesses. This phenomenon is called "crowding out": the government's borrowing "crowds out" families and businesses from the markets where they all compete to borrow money, and this has the effect of reducing the spending of families and businesses. The positive effect of deficit spending on aggregate demand must therefore be measured taking into consideration its "crowding out" effects.

The extent of crowding out effects is hotly debated among economists. Clearly, the effects depend on how seriously government borrowing reduces the availability of credit to consumers and businesses and, in turn, on how much a reduction of credit availability affects consumer spending and investment spending. Unfortunately, there is not much agreement on these issues.

If, rather than borrowing, the government simply prints more money to finance its spending, it does not compete in credit markets against families and businesses. Still, crowding out may occur because the government will spend the money it has printed, and these dollars will then compete with the spending of families and businesses for the available supplies of goods and services. As we explain in the next chapter, when governments, families, and businesses spend beyond their means, either through borrowing or, in the case of the government, through printing additional money, inflation is likely to be the result. This is one reason why the government does not generally finance its spending by printing money.

What Determines the Interest Rate?

The interest rate (i) is simply the price of renting money. If the interest rate is 10 percent per year, the borrower who borrows $100 must pay back $110 at the end of the year. The $10 difference is the annual rent on $100.

There is no single interest rate. Interest rates vary depending on the length of the loan, its purpose, and the likelihood that the borrower will pay it back, among other things. But because all interest rates tend to go up and down together, we will discuss "the interest rate" as if there were an average of all interest rates.

Very simply put, the interest rate is determined by supply and demand, as are other prices. The relevant supply in this case is the supply of money available for lending, and this is called the *supply of loanable funds*. The demand in question is the *demand for loanable funds*. The interest rate is thus determined by how much money individuals, corporations, and the government want to borrow and how much individuals, businesses (especially banks), and the government want to lend.

Figure 17.5 shows how the demand for loanable funds and the supply of loanable funds interact to determine the interest rate. The demand-for-loanable-funds curve indicates how much money all the potential borrowers want to borrow at each interest rate. For example, if the interest rate is at the level "a" in the figure, borrowers will want to borrow a total of "Da" dollars. The demand for loanable funds stems from many different sources. These include consumers wanting to finance a car purchase or to get a mortgage to buy a house; businesses wanting to borrow money to make an investment (such as building a new plant); and governments (local, state, and federal) wanting to (deficit) spend more than they are collecting in taxes. Businesses must have enough money on hand to do business, and consumers must have enough money to keep up the flow between income and purchases. (These last two needs are called the "transactions" demand for money.) Businesses might also want to borrow money to buy another company or to buy land for speculative purposes (individuals might do this as well). And the list goes on. If the interest rate falls, the demand for loanable funds will increase, as is indicated by the fact that the demand curve slopes downward to the right.

The supply-of-loanable-funds curve is also indicated on the graph. It should be read the same way as the demand-for-loanable-funds curve. If the interest rate is at "a" percent, individuals, businesses (including banks), and the government will want to lend a total of "Sa" dollars. If the interest rate goes up, they will want to lend more, so the supply curve slopes upward to the right.

The borrowers and lenders need not be citizens, businesses, or governments within the same country; they may be from anywhere in the world. For example, the supply of loanable funds in the U.S. (as well as the demand for them) is not determined solely by what happens there. If the rate of interest is low in the U.S., many foreign borrowers may choose to borrow money there rather than in their own countries. This would increase the demand for loanable funds in the U.S. On the other hand, when the interest rate is high in

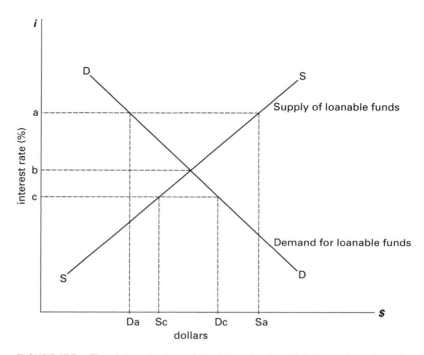

FIGURE 17.5   The determination of the interest rate.   This figure shows how the rate of interest (*i*) is determined by the interaction of supply and demand in the market for *loanable funds*. Like the supply curves for most goods and services, the loanable funds supply curve is upward sloping to the right, indicating that a rise in the interest rate will call forth a greater supply of loanable funds, while a fall in the interest rate will bring about a contraction in the supply of loanable funds. The supply of loanable funds depends on government policies regulating the lending practices of banks as well as on how much people at home want to save at various interest rates and how much people or governments abroad wish to lend in the American market, say, by buying U.S. government or corporate bonds. A change in any of these determinants will bring about a shift of the loanable funds supply curve. The loanable funds demand curve is downward sloping to the right, indicating that when the interest rate falls the demand for loanable funds will increase, and conversely, when the interest rate rises the demand for loanable funds will contract. The demand for loanable funds depends on how much the government needs to borrow to finance deficits or refinance existing debt, on how much consumers want to borrow in order to purchase goods on credit (cars and housing in particular), and on how much businesses want to borrow to make investments or finance their operations. As with the loanable funds supply curve, a change in any of these determinants will cause the loanable funds demand curve to shift inward or outward. Wherever the two curves happen to be on any given day, the rate of interest will move toward the market-clearing level—the level at which the two curves intersect and the supply of and the demand for loanable funds are equal to each other. In short, the interest rate is the price of borrowed money, and this particular price will be determined in the same way that prices are determined in most other markets. A change in any of the factors determining the location of either the supply or the demand curve—for example, people changing their consumption and saving habits or businesses deciding to increase or cut back on investment regardless of the interest rate—will cause the market-clearing interest rate to rise or fall.

the U.S., foreign banks and other lenders from outside the country will want to lend money to borrowers in the U.S., raising the supply of loanable funds there.

A very important determinant of the supply of loanable funds is the monetary policy conducted by a country's central bank, for example, the Bank of England in the United Kingdom and the Federal Reserve System ("the Fed") in the United States. (The monetary policy of the countries that have joined together in the European Union [EU] is conducted by the European Central Bank.) The U.S. central bank, like those of other countries, is an entirely independent and autonomous agency, its own board of governors having the power to decide, entirely on its own, what the monetary policy of the United States will be. And the Fed's board of governors is not an elected body. The only (indirectly) democratic aspect of this body is the fact that its chair is appointed every four years by the U.S. president (in the year preceding each presidential election year). All the other members of the board of governors are either representatives of regional branches of the Fed (themselves not popularly elected) or individuals (usually bankers) selected by the current members of the board.

A nation's central bank regulates its banks and has the power to affect the total amount of money (supply of money) available for lending and spending in an economy. In particular, the central bank can make it easier or more difficult for banks and other lending institutions to make loans, and this directly affects the supply of loanable funds. Thus, the position of the supply-of-loanable-funds curve on any particular day is strongly influenced by monetary policy.

As explained in the next chapter, the directors of a nation's central bank usually put a possible threat of inflation at the top of their list of concerns. They may come to believe that the elected leaders of the nation—for example, members of the Congress of the United States—are engaging in so much deficit spending (B) that the sum of the components of aggregate demand ($C + I + B + X$) exceed the economy's current capacity to supply goods and services. In this case the central bankers may try to head off inflation by curtailing the growth of the nation's supply of money. This would prevent the supply-of-loanable-funds curve from moving to the right, or it might even move it to the left. In any case, with the demand-for-loanable-funds curve moving to the right, as it will in a growing economy, the result will be a rise in the interest rate. And as explained earlier, a rise in the interest rate will tend to restrain the borrowing and spending decisions of consumers and businesses, thereby weakening aggregate demand and slowing or reversing the growth of employment. In this manner the Fed may influence the market for loanable funds in a way that intensifies its (already) counteracting effect on expansionary fiscal policy.

The supply of and demand for loanable funds determines the interest rate in the following way. Going back to Figure 17.5, imagine that the interest rate is at "c" and the demand for loanable funds is "Dc," while the supply is "Sc." Because "Dc" is greater than "Sc," some borrowers will not get to borrow the amount they want at that interest rate. Noticing this unsatisfied demand, banks and other lending institutions will reason that they could charge a higher rate. As banks raise their rates, the supply of loanable funds will increase, and the demand will decrease. In a way similar to the process of equilibration described in Chapter 8, the interest rate will tend to rise to "b" percent, the level at which the amount demanded and the amount supplied are equal. At this point the market for loanable funds will clear: there will be neither excess supply nor excess demand.

Many factors other than the interest rate influence the supply of and demand for loanable funds. The expectations of suppliers or demanders with regard to rates of employment, growth, inflation, and various other variables, including political stability and war or peace in the future, will affect their willingness to lend or their eagerness to borrow money. When suppliers' expectations about such matters change, the result will be a shift in the supply-of-loanable-funds curve; when demanders' expectations change, the result will be a shift in the demand-for-loanable-funds curve.

Borrowing and the Exchange Rate

Government borrowing can adversely affect spending even if it does not suppress the demand for consumer goods and investment goods. It can reduce net exports because it can push up a nation's foreign exchange rate (in the case of the U.S., the value of the dollar), thereby discouraging exports and encouraging imports. Net exports, as we have seen, will be reduced when the foreign exchange rate rises because such an increase makes a country's exports more expensive to buyers in the rest of the world while making imports from the rest of the world less expensive.

How does borrowing by a government in a particular country raise that country's foreign exchange rate? We have seen that government borrowing—at least when it takes place on a large scale—will tend to raise the interest rate in that country. When its interest rate rises, individuals and businesses in the rest of the world will want to invest their money in that country in order to cash in on the favorable rate of interest. But before they can invest their money in the high-interest-rate country, they will have to purchase a certain amount of its currency in the global currency market. In doing this they will shift the demand curve for this currency to the right. Unless there happens to be a simultaneous outward shift in the supply of this currency, the increased demand for it will drive up its value in relation to other nations' currencies, thereby increasing the foreign exchange rate of the country in question. For example, if the interest rate rises in the U.S. (say, as a result of an increase in government borrowing), foreign investors may want to purchase U.S. Treasury bonds since the rate of interest on them will now be relatively high. In order to do this they will increase their demand for dollars, offering to pay for them with their British pounds, Japanese yen, European euros, or whatever, and they will in the process bid up the value of the dollar (the foreign exchange rate for U.S. currency).

This brief look at the relationship between borrowing and the exchange rate brings us to another important conclusion. Because government borrowing raises interest rates in the country whose government is doing the borrowing, it also tends to raise that country's foreign exchange rate. This, in turn, will tend to increase imports, make exporting more difficult, depress net exports, and reduce aggregate demand (of which net exports is one component). The result is that the effects of the borrowing required to finance deficit spending will tend to counteract the employment-generating effects of it.

The Conflict between Monetary and Fiscal Policy

The conflict between the two arms of macroeconomic policy can be summarized as follows. When a government engages in deficit spending (fiscal policy) it must borrow in the market for loanable funds enough money to finance the deficit (assuming that it does not just print the money required). This borrowing competes with the borrowing of both consumers and businesses in the same market, raising the interest rate and "crowding out" at least some of the nongovernmental borrowers. The resulting increase in the interest rate will not only diminish aggregate demand by depressing spending by individuals and businesses on consumer and investment goods, it will also tend to raise the country's foreign exchange rate, encourage imports, and discourage exports—and the resulting decrease in net exports will also tend to reduce aggregate demand. Both of these negative effects on aggregate demand will tend to counteract the employment-generating effect of the original amount of deficit spending. Moreover, these counteracting effects will be amplified if the central bank (the Federal Reserve System in the U.S.) decides that the amount of deficit spending is threatening to cause inflation. In this case (this is often the case), the central bank will respond with a monetary policy that limits the supply of loanable funds by restricting the growth of the money supply. The lesson is clear: government borrowing can have a positive influence on the level of aggregate demand and employment, but the effectiveness of such a fiscal policy will be limited (counteracted) by its other effects. The positive effect of an expansionary fiscal policy on the rate of employment may be nullified if the Fed pursues a monetary policy that has the effect of raising the interest rate even further than it might otherwise be raised by the government's borrowing in the market for loanable funds.

INSTITUTIONS FOR ACHIEVING FULL EMPLOYMENT

The potential benefits to be gained from the use of macroeconomic policy—especially fiscal policy—were the focus of the previous chapter. In this chapter we have analyzed the difficulties such policies run into in practice. We now weigh both the benefits and the difficulties. There are many controversial issues in this area, but some points are clear.

First, in the absence of government policies to promote high employment, unemployment in a capitalist economy may at times reach unacceptable levels. And the negative human consequences of unemployment will be magnified by the uncertainties associated with the business cycle.

Second, government policies can affect the level of aggregate demand and thus reduce the amount of unemployment. Government policies can also smooth out at least some of the gyrations of the business cycle.

The third point on which there is general agreement is that fiscal and monetary policy *alone* cannot bring about lasting increases in employment (reductions in unemployment). Without institutional changes full-employment policies continue to face the obstacles outlined in this chapter:

- the high-employment profit squeeze
- the inflationary pressures that occur at high employment levels
- the negative effect of high employment on net exports
- the tensions between monetary and fiscal policy

All of the obstacles reviewed here will be present in a capitalist economy, but some countries have been able to achieve lower unemployment rates than the U.S. has in recent years. Figure 17.1 shows that both Sweden and Japan had significantly lower rates of unemployment than did the U.S., the U.K. and France, on average, during the period from 1959 to

2002. Comparisons with other countries remind us that unemployment is not, like the weather, something we simply have to accept and endure. Some countries have higher rates of unemployment over considerable periods of time because they have institutions and policies that produce that result. What changes are needed to achieve higher levels of employment?

Institutional Obstacles to Full Employment

To answer the question about institutional change we must understand exactly which institutional structures in U.S.-style capitalist economies are responsible for the persistence of high unemployment. There are two main ones.

The first is the *private and uncoordinated nature of economic decision making.* Each person's decision about how much to buy and each employer's decision about how much to produce and how many people to employ is made independently. There is no reason to expect that all of these independently made decisions will result in a level of aggregate demand that would require exactly the number of hours of employment equal to the number of hours workers would like to work.

However, the uncoordinated nature of economic decision making does not by itself mean that we must always have unemployment. It just means that the amount of labor demanded is usually not going to be equal to the amount of labor supplied. Excess supply (unemployment) is one possibility; excess demand is another, even though we have no term to describe it.

The distinct nature of the labor market is significant here. Other markets operate so that excess supply or excess demand tends to be eliminated by competition among the demanders and suppliers (recall the analysis of the beer market in Chapter 8). The ways in which the labor market is different from other markets help to explain why the uncoordinated decisions of economic actors are not likely to result in a clearing of this market. (See the analysis of the labor market in Chapter 12, in particular the discussion in that chapter of why businesses usually choose to offer wages that are above the market-clearing wage.)

The other important institutional structure that works against the achievement of full employment in a capitalist economy has to do with the fact that the capital goods used in production are privately owned (see Chapter 6). Since the ownership of capital goods is highly unequal (see Figure 6.2), the worker in a capitalist economy generally works for someone else rather than for herself or himself. Also, the goods or services produced are owned by the owners of the capital goods (the owners of firms) rather than by their employees. When workers do not own what they produce, they have little reason to do more than what is necessary for them to keep their jobs. Only the threat of unemployment keeps them on their toes.

If workers owned the tools of their trade and were thus able to work for themselves, each worker would enjoy the full benefits, in the form of higher income, of his or her own hard work. By the same token, each worker would pay the price of less income for slacking off at work. We can summarize these ideas by saying that unemployment exists because of the *class nature of the production process,* that is, unemployment is necessary to motivate and control workers who do not own the products of their labor.

In sum, there are two main reasons for the persistence of unemployment in a capitalist economy. First, the private and uncoordinated nature of economic decision making results in *a mismatch between supply and demand in the labor market*. Second, the class nature of the production process requires unemployment as a way of regulating *the conflict between capital and labor* on terms generally favorable to business.

The mismatch between supply and demand in the labor market seems at first to be just an accident (resulting from the lack of coordination). And there will be some situations in which increases in the rate of employment would be desirable from the standpoint of all involved. Employers would like to see increases in the rate of employment because such increases would mean operating at higher rates of capacity utilization (u) and hence would mean higher rates of profit (all other things being equal). From workers' and consumers' standpoints, increases in the rate of employment would mean more jobs and more consumer goods to enjoy.

As we have seen, however, increases in the rate of employment are not beneficial to all parties in all situations. This is because a decrease in the rate of employment—an increase in unemployment—is sometimes desired by business owners to tip the balance of power between labor and capital in favor of capital. In this case unemployment is not just a mistake: it serves the purpose of restraining wage increases and pressing employees to put forth the maximum amount of work effort for each dollar of wage paid. It thus benefits business at the expense of both workers and consumers.

Institutions for Achieving Full Employment

The two reasons for unemployment suggest quite different remedies. The remedy for the first is to coordinate economic decisions to eliminate the mismatch. Thus, when a mismatch occurs the government could intervene in some way to eliminate it. The remedy proposed by John Maynard Keynes and adopted by many governments since his time is to let economic decision making remain private but have the government adjust the overall level of aggregate demand with fiscal policy (deficit spending), thus correcting for mismatches that become too large.

The remedy for the second reason for unemployment—the class nature of production— is more difficult. Business owners are happy to let the government have a role in the economy as long as it means that macroeconomic policy will ensure a steady level of demand for their products. However, businesspeople tend to oppose a sustained reduction of unemployment, particularly if it involves a very low rate of unemployment. And, of course, they oppose changing the class nature of production because it is what gives them the right to hire and fire employees and own the products that they produce.

In the U.S., macroeconomic policy is quite effective in dealing with unemployment as a mismatch between supply and demand in the labor market. But it is not effective—nor is it intended to be effective—in eliminating unemployment, for if successful, this would tip the balance of power in favor of labor. Macroeconomic policy has succeeded in smoothing out the business cycle, but it has not succeeded in eliminating unemployment.

To summarize, unemployment is an economic problem, but its solution is in part political. When nothing is done about it, as the laissez-faire followers of Adam Smith would prefer, unemployment is a permanent and painful waste in a capitalist economy.

Where unemployment has been largely eliminated—whether in Nazi Germany or in modern-day Sweden—it has not been by means of Adam Smith's invisible hand. Rather, full employment has been brought about with a fist (as in Nazi Germany) or with a visible handshake (as in Sweden). The fist refers to the power of business to get workers to work on acceptable terms using the forcible power of the state rather than the threat of unemployment. The handshake refers to deals struck between business and labor to share the increased output associated with higher employment in ways that (a) are fair and (b) also allow for a high enough rate of profit to stimulate investment.

If the invisible hand approach does not solve the problem and the fist is unfair and undemocratic, the handshake is the only viable way to achieve full employment. But what would be the main elements of a handshake approach?

First, in order for high employment to be achieved, the high-employment profit squeeze and its associated inflationary consequences would have to be eliminated. But these two threats could be eliminated only if unemployment were no longer used to regulate the class conflict between workers and their employers.

One way to regulate class conflict is for employers and employees to find a way to determine both pay and work effort that does not rely on the worker's fear of job loss. In Sweden, for example, wages and work rules have been negotiated between the leaders of the major unions and the representatives of employers. During times of high employment the unions had the power to gain much higher wages, but they generally did not use it. Their reasoning was that if they did, they might price Swedish goods out of the world market, resulting in eventual income losses for themselves. Swedish unions were willing to exercise restraint in good times because they were powerful enough to insist that in bad times employers not use their authority to lay off workers and reduce wages. As a result, Sweden achieved very low levels of unemployment.

Another approach to regulating class conflict would be to change the class nature of the production process. This would mean going beyond the handshake approach, but it could be done keeping economic decision making decentralized and preserving market competition as a way to allocate resources. The difference would be that production would be organized in worker-owned and democratically run firms of the type described in the last section of Chapter 13. Since workers would be the owners of the products they and their coworkers produced, they would have no reason to work less hard or demand more pay when unemployment was reduced. If they shirked or demanded too much, they would be using their bargaining power against themselves; if they squeezed profits, they would be reducing their own income. If most workers in an economy worked for themselves in their own firms, the high-employment profit squeeze would be greatly attenuated.

Even in a democratic economy, however, macroeconomic policies would have to be used wisely. If deficit spending expanded aggregate demand to the point at which all workers were employed and all productive capacity was in use, inflation would most likely be the result. In this situation the demand for many products would be greater than the available supply of them, and worker-owned firms, like their capitalist counterparts, might well raise the prices of their products. This would most likely lead to a more generalized inflation. So workplace democracy is not a cure-all.

The second important element in the handshake approach to full employment is that an equitable solution must be found for the conflict of interests between employers and workers in the labor market. If workers are going to forgo using the bargaining power that high employment gives them, employers must also give up the bargaining power that high unemployment gives them. What labor agrees to do in the handshake must have its counterpart in a corresponding commitment on the part of business—otherwise it will be no deal. Employers must commit themselves to providing employment security both at the level of the firm (promising to refrain from laying off their employees) and as a macroeconomic strategy (supporting government policies to achieve high employment).

The third element in the handshake approach would be the expansion of built-in stabilizers, for example, unemployment insurance. This would not only strengthen income-support programs; such programs also have the effect of automatically dampening business cycle fluctuations because they pump more money into the hands of consumers when income from employment is shrinking, and they work the other way as well. More deliberate countercyclical (macroeconomic) policies, legislated changes in taxes or spending programs, for example, could also be used to maintain a stable level of aggregate demand. In the context of the whole bundle of "handshake" compromises, the effects of such policies would be beneficial to almost everyone, so both business and labor should be able to agree on them.

The fourth element of the handshake approach results from the fact that a handshake across the capitalist-labor bargaining table will not be enough: handshakes across national boundaries will also be necessary. Coordination among nations pursuing high employment policies must be secured through international agreements among the major countries.

To be effective, international macroeconomic policy agreements would have to discourage strategies whereby one country tries to export its unemployment problem to some other country by engaging in export promotion or import restriction to secure higher employment in its own economy. These agreements would have to enable countries to coordinate their policies of expanding aggregate demand so that each nation's expansionary policies would contribute to the success of similar policies in other nations.

The fifth and final element of the handshake involves policies that facilitate economic adjustment without imposing the costs of adjustment on particular workers or unemployed people. Some industries or sectors will be expanding while others are contracting. In responding to changing economic conditions, the economy must be flexible, but the costs of its flexibility must be distributed fairly.

To promote flexibility, a basic principle of a full-employment economy must be that everyone seeking work has a right to find employment but not to stay permanently in the job he or she currently holds. The economy must adapt to new technologies, to changes in consumer tastes, and to the new forms of international and other competition outlined in Chapter 15. This means that many workers will have to move from job to job and from industry to industry. But the government can ensure that any worker who loses a job will have income support during the transition from one job to another, will have access to adequate training for a new job, and will receive support, as necessary, for moving from one area of the country to another. The cost of such programs—in Sweden they are called "active labor market policies"—should be financed out of general tax revenues. Virtually all of a nation's individuals and businesses benefit from the continuous modernization of the economy, while the adverse effects of its modernization are felt only by particular workers. Thus, it is only fair that the beneficiaries of a flexible economy be required to support those who must pay the price of its flexibility in job loss, income loss, possible loss of self-respect, and severance of ties of friendship in the workplace and the neighborhood.

(Of course, care will have to be taken to make sure that such programs of support are limited and monitored in order to prevent their abuse.)

Handshakes do not mean the end of conflict, of course, either between nations or between classes. But they can be a way of regulating conflicts in a less wasteful and brutal manner than either the fist or the invisible hand.

CONCLUSION

With the exception of the fourth element of the handshake, international cooperation in the making of macroeconomic policies, the five institutional and political prerequisites for full employment are close to being achieved in some countries. Norway, Austria, and Sweden are examples. As a result, these countries have had very low unemployment rates. Unfortunately, the same cannot be said about many other countries.

The United States achieved relatively high levels of employment (low unemployment) during the decade beginning in 1994 not by the handshake but by a variant of the invisible hand. Figures 17.2 and 17.4 showed that during the business cycle expansion of the 1990s the high-employment wage push and the high-employment profit squeeze did not make their appearance until well into the expansion, when the unemployment rate had fallen below 5 percent. Thus, the economic expansion could proceed without interruption from these usual impediments to high employment.

Two aspects of U.S. economic institutions have made it more difficult for workers to push up wages when there is a low rate of unemployment. The first is the decline in union membership (see Chapter 7). This has weakened labor's ability to use the bargaining power that usually comes with low unemployment.

The second is the continued segmentation of labor markets and growing inequality of earnings among workers. Primary labor market workers—those in relatively well-paying jobs in manufacturing, for example—who are laid off or fired cannot realistically expect to find jobs with similar pay and benefits. These workers will most likely experience a period of unemployment, followed by reemployment in a position paying considerably less, possibly in the secondary labor market.

An important result is that the cost of losing a primary labor market job is now very high—*even when the unemployment rate is low*. Even at the peak of the business cycle, the threat of firing continues to be a powerful weapon in the hands of an employer in the core business sector. The loss of a machinist's job will probably be a financial disaster—even if the machinist knows that he or she can find work as a cashier at the supermarket.

Few governments have made long-lasting commitments to the goal of full employment. As we have seen, unemployment is not simply a mistake that can be corrected by government action: it is also a weapon in the conflict between workers and employers. Business owners do not want low unemployment to be used as a weapon against them, and they occasionally urge the government to adopt policies that will increase unemployment.

To understand how this happens, we must study the relationship between government and the economy. This is the topic of Chapter 19. Before we get there, however, we need to examine the causes and effects of inflation.

SUGGESTED READINGS

Roger Alcaly, *The New Economy* (New York: Farrar, Straus & Giroux, 2003).

Duncan Foley, *The Unholy Trinity: Labor, Capital and Land in the New Economy* (London: Routledge, 2003).

Doug Henwood, *After the New Economy* (New York: New Press, 2003).

Paul Krugman, *The Great Unraveling: Losing Our Way in the New Century* (New York: Norton, 2003).

Robert Pollin, *Contours of Descent: U.S. Economic Fractures and the Landscape of Global Austerity* (New York: Verso, 2003).

Joseph E. Stiglitz, *The Roaring Nineties: A New History of the World's Most Prosperous Decade* (New York: Norton, 2003).

CHAPTER 18

Inflation

D
uring the American War of Independence the familiar patterns of trade were disrupted, and the people of Philadelphia faced rapidly rising prices for coffee, tea, sugar, flour, and whiskey. A meeting to protest the price increases was addressed by Daniel Roberdeau, a leader of the Philadelphia militia:

> I have no doubt but combinations [monopolies] have been formed for raising the prices of goods and provisions, and therefore the community, in their own defense, have a natural right to counteract such combinations and to set limits to evils which affect themselves.[1]

And defend themselves they did. A committee of private citizens was formed to control the prices at which merchants sold their goods. Its members included Thomas Paine, author of *The Rights of Man* and one of the guiding spirits of the American Revolution. Even before the meeting at which Roberdeau spoke, men armed with clubs had visited shops and compelled merchants to rescind their price hikes.

At about the same time, bakers across the Atlantic in Paris took advantage of a shortage of bread to raise prices. There the citizens took advantage of the chaos of the French Revolution to break into the bakeries and seize loaves, in many cases leaving as payment exactly enough to cover the lower customary price of bread (and, incidentally, not touching the elegant pastries).

When prices go up, tempers rise, too. Paying more for something than you did last year is upsetting. It is also very common. Very few items cost less today than they did 10 or 20 years ago. The few exceptions are usually new products, such as DVD players,

---

[1] Quoted in Eric Foner, *Thomas Paine and Revolutionary America* (Oxford: Oxford University Press, 1976), p. 166.

whose prices tend to fall as more of them are produced and both competition and technical change reduce their costs of production. The prices of most other things generally go up.

It was not always so. A loaf of bread cost more—in dollars and cents per pound of bread—in Thomas Paine's Philadelphia than it did in the early 20th century. Wheat flour sold wholesale for about $10 per 100 pounds in Philadelphia in 1800. A century later the price had fallen to less than $2 per 100 pounds. Plain cotton cloth sold wholesale for about 17 cents a yard in Philadelphia in 1800; it sold for about 6 cents a yard in 1900. In the intervening years the price had gone as high as 50 cents a yard during the Civil War, when the high level of demand for uniforms and tents and the disruptions in the supply of cotton drove up the price.

Having fallen throughout most of the 19th century, the prices of both cotton cloth and flour have risen at least tenfold since the beginning of the 20th century. It is also a fact that prices in general have risen more rapidly since the end of the 1960s than in any comparable period since price increases have been systematically tracked.

Inflation is a general increase in prices, often measured by the CPI (Consumer Price Index).	When most prices are going up, *inflation* is taking place. Is inflation occurring right now? To determine whether inflation is occurring one must calculate an average of a large number of prices. Generally, this is done with something such as the *Consumer Price Index* (CPI) in the U.S. The CPI is a measure of the prices paid by a typical family for the goods they buy. When the CPI increases from year to year, inflation is occurring.
The **Consumer Price Index (CPI)** is a measure of the average prices a typical family pays for the goods and services it buys.	The "index" in the CPI refers to the fact that the average of prices at a certain time is set equal to 100, and then the price level at any other time, before or after, is compared with where it was then. Currently, the benchmark for the CPI is the average of prices over the period from 1982 to 1984. The CPI benchmark was set at 100 in July of 1983, and in January 2004 the CPI was at 185. This means that there was an annual rate of inflation of 2.9 percent in the U.S. during the intervening years.
Deflation refers to a general fall in prices as measured by the Consumer Price Index. It is the opposite of inflation.	When the CPI declines from one year to the next, it is called *deflation*. Deflation can be just as damaging as inflation because if prices are falling while costs are not falling—or not falling as fast—a lot of businesses will go under, people will lose their jobs, incomes will fall, aggregate demand will contract, and the whole economy may go into a tailspin.

Inflation means that the buying power of a family's dollar is falling. Each dollar buys less at the grocery store, at the gas pump, or wherever people make purchases. Other price indexes measure the prices of subcategories of goods. Examples include the medical care price index, the higher education price index, the used car price index, the raw materials price index, the index of food prices, and many more. In addition to the CPI there is also a wholesale (or "producer") price index. This measures the prices received by producers when they sell to stores or other intermediaries. Whichever index is used, inflation is measured by how fast an average of prices is rising.

This chapter focuses on *inflation as the result of unsettled conflicts over the distribution of income among employers, workers, raw material suppliers, governments, and others.* If one of these players were indisputably dominant, inflation could generally be kept under control. But if there is any question about who is dominant, the resulting conflicts are likely to result in inflation. This central idea is expressed in six key points:

1. The amount of inflation varies over the course of the business cycle and also between business cycles.

2. More rapid inflation, which typically takes place toward the end of a business-cycle expansion, is called *cyclical inflation*. It takes place because of the upward pressure on unit labor costs and unit materials costs that occur when unemployment is low.

3. *Structural inflation* occurs when the price level increases rapidly throughout the whole course of a business cycle. Structural inflation takes place because governments, businesses, and families are attempting to live beyond their means and are able to borrow so as to spend more than their incomes. Structural inflation is a relatively new phenomenon, dating back only a century.

4. The *unemployment-inflation trade-off* describes the tendency during a business cycle for inflation to rise when unemployment falls, and for inflation to fall when unemployment rises. *Stagflation* refers to a combination of slower economic growth (stagnation) and generally rising prices (inflation). The term was coined to characterize the hard times of the 1970s.

5. Inflation is costly because it makes economic outcomes unpredictable. It inflicts unforeseen costs and confers windfall benefits on people in arbitrary ways. Controlling inflation is costly also, since it often implies either high levels of unemployment and underutilization of productive capacities, or governmental controls on prices that may themselves produce arbitrary and unpredictable effects and inefficiencies.

6. The particular mix of unemployment and inflation experienced by a country affects its income distribution, with higher levels of unemployment implying greater inequality. For this reason people in various income groups and classes often have different interests concerning inflation and unemployment, with well-off people generally benefiting from lower inflation and more unemployment and the less well-off benefiting from more inflation and less unemployment.

The amount of inflation is called the *rate of inflation*. It is the percentage rate of change of prices. Suppose that two years ago a typical family bought their usual goods and services for $1,000 a month, on average, but last year it had to pay $1,060 a month to buy the same goods and services. The rise would show up as a 6 percent increase in the consumer price index, because 1,060 is 6 percent higher than 1,000. The rate of inflation would thus have been 6 percent between the two years.

As we have seen, inflation was not always a part of life in America. In the past, deflation was just as common. A consumer price index does not exist for the earlier years, but a wholesale price index exists for almost the whole of the history of the United States, relying on the data we have on the prices of cotton, flour, and many other goods.

We present a composite index in Figure 18.1 showing what one would expect from the prices of cotton cloth and flour mentioned above. Prices generally did not rise much before

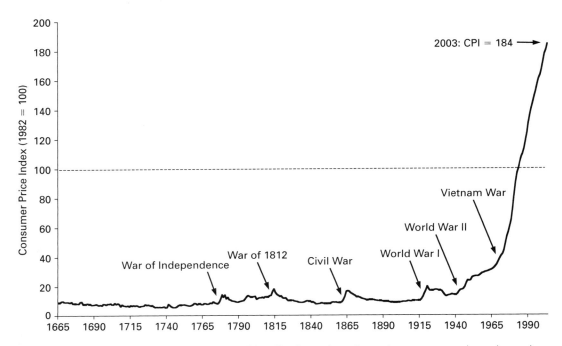

FIGURE 18.1 Inflation in the U.S., 1665 to 2003. This figure shows how prices, on average, have changed—most of the time rising—between the middle of the 17th century and the early years of the 20th century in the U.S. economy. The figure shows that the occurrence of a war, whether in the 18th century or the 20th, usually results in a significant rise in prices. Even the onset of World War II brought about a rise in prices in spite of the fact that prices were officially frozen and a government bureaucracy—the "Office of Price Administration"—was established to control prices.

Sources: John J. McCusker, "How Much Is That in Real Money?" *Proceedings of the American Antiquarian Society*, 2001, Table A-1, Column 6, for all data prior to 1912; Council of Economic Advisors, *Economic Report of the President 2003*, Tables B-60 to B-62; data-conversion calculations by Professor Robert Sahr, Political Science Department, Oregon State University, available at http://oregonstate.edu/dept/pol_sci/fac/sahr/sahr.htm#_Price_Levels.

World War I except during and just after wars. Over long periods prices fell. From 1665 to 1739, for example, prices fell by 40 percent, and from 1814 (just after the War of 1812) to 1845 prices fell by more than half. Prices again fell by half following the Civil War, with the result that in 1900 prices were actually lower than they had been 235 years earlier. In the 20th century, however, and particularly since the Great Depression of the 1930s, prices have risen steadily. At the end of the last century, prices were 20 times higher than they had been at its beginning!

TOO MUCH MONEY CHASING TOO FEW GOODS

Inflation occurs when, at the current or prevailing prices, demanders want to purchase more goods than suppliers have or are willing to sell at those prices. This is the grain of truth behind the popular explanation of inflation as "too much money chasing too few goods."

A dollar bill (or a credit card) in the hands of a potential spender represents a claim on some goods or services. Whether that dollar is in the hands of a family about to purchase groceries, a businessperson considering building a new plant, or a public school superintendent planning to buy additional textbooks makes no difference. In each case the person with the dollar is in a position to claim (by buying) the goods in question.

Whether demanders want to purchase more or less than suppliers have to sell at current prices depends, first, on the demanders' spending intentions and, second, on the availability of money and credit enabling them to carry out their intentions. Demanders' decisions regarding how much to spend will be limited, at least to some extent, by their present incomes, savings, wealth, and other circumstances. Of course, demanders—consumers, businesses, governments at all levels, and foreign buyers—can spend less than, exactly the same as, or more than their current incomes. To spend more than their current incomes they will have to borrow or, what is essentially the same thing, to buy on credit. In the U.S. consumer debt doubled in the decade between 1993 and 2003, going above $2 trillion for the first time at the end of 2003. Three out of five U.S. families have credit card debt, and the amount of credit card debt owed by the average American cardholder is approximately $9,000.

The second issue is whether demanders will be able to obtain enough money or credit to carry out their spending plans. Even for buyers to spend amounts equal to their current incomes, there will have to be a sufficient amount of money in circulation to support their transactions (this is called the "transactions" demand for money). We do not live in a barter economy! And, as noted, if demanders wish to spend more than their incomes, they will have to borrow, but they may not be able to obtain enough loans from banks or other lenders to make the purchases they want to make. This would be the case, also, if credit were available only on terms that are prohibitively expensive.

Even when people have sufficient resources to carry out their spending plans, there is no guarantee that, when all the claims are added, there will be enough goods to go around. When there are not enough goods to go around, inflation may be the result.

When the total claims of demanders exceed the total market value of the available supply of goods (valued at their current prices), there is no way that all the claims can be met. Unless prices rise, shelves will be bare before people can buy everything they want and can afford to pay for. In this situation some demanders will end up with unspent cash and nothing to buy with it. But if prices rise, as they tend to do when demand exceeds supply (see Chapter 8), the *market value* of the available supply will rise until it is equal to the value of all the claims.

Imagine a hypothetical economy (with dollars as its currency) made up of 10 farmers, each of whom grows a different kind of vegetable. One day each of the farmers sells his or her crop to a farm stand for $1,000. Thus, each farmer earns an income from vegetable sales of $1,000. Imagine, then, that the next day all the farmers go back to the farm stand to buy the other farmers' vegetables (they have no taste for the ones they themselves have grown).

But suppose now that on the way to the farm stand, the farmers recall that in the previous year (because of better weather conditions), they had each grown $1,200 worth of vegetables, sold them, and bought $1,200 worth of other vegetables. Hoping that this year's disappointing crop will not be repeated next year and determined to maintain their previous consumption of $1,200 worth of vegetables, they stop at the bank to get $200 loans, which, added to their $1,000 incomes, will allow them to buy $1,200 worth of vegetables. The farmers all go through the same thought process, and their friendly banker obliges. So the 10 farmers will now try to spend a total of $12,000 (each has an income of $1,000 plus a $200 loan). However, the amount of vegetables grown this year is worth only $10,000 at the current prices. Because the farmers' claims are now 20 percent larger than their incomes, their total demand ($12,000) exceeds the available supply ($10,000 at the current prices) by 20 percent.

If the farm stand owners do not raise their prices, they will end up with empty shelves, $10,000 in their pockets, and a line of unsatisfied customers wishing they could buy $2,000 worth of additional vegetables. Notice that up to this point we have conveniently assumed that the farm stand owners sold their vegetables for exactly what they paid the farmers for them. But now the farm stand owners see that they can raise their prices and end up with $2,000 more in their pockets (better in their pockets than as unspent money in the pockets of dissatisfied customers). The customers, the farmers, that is, will buy all the vegetables on the shelves. The only question is: how much will they pay for them? To meet all the money claims the farm stand owners will raise the prices of the vegetables. The same quantity of vegetables, which at the old prices was worth $10,000, will now, at the new prices, sell for $12,000. Thus, prices will have risen by 20 percent. When there are not enough goods to meet the demand for them, there will ensue a competition among would-be buyers that will allow those who own the goods to raise their prices.

TWO TYPES OF INFLATION

Economists often speak of two types of inflation, cyclical inflation and structural inflation.

Cyclical Inflation

Cyclical inflation occurs because of the high-employment materials cost push and the high-employment labor cost push described in the previous chapter. With regard to labor costs,

> **Cyclical inflation** refers to the price increases that typically accelerate toward the end of a business cycle expansion.

as employment rises and unemployment falls, the bargaining position of workers relative to their employers improves. The threat of job loss is now less intimidating because jobs are plentiful and workers are scarce. As a result, workers are able to bargain for higher wages.

Similarly, as the economy expands the demand for materials—both raw material inputs and capital goods—increases, creating excess demand over supply in the markets for these goods. Sellers of these goods are thus able to raise their prices, and the buyers face a materials cost push that, together with the labor cost push, leads them to raise prices.

When both unit labor costs and unit materials costs rise, the cost increases, as we saw in Chapter 17, will tend to reduce profits (the high-employment profit squeeze). Here we see that such cost increases also tend to create inflation.

Recall (from Chapter 12) that the price of the output, P_z, is equal to unit labor costs (*ulc*) plus unit materials costs (*umc*) plus unit profits (*up*). Thus,

$$P_z = ulc + umc + up \tag{18.1}$$

Unit costs ($uc = ulc + umc$) rise during a business cycle expansion (see previous chapter), and then two things can happen: either a firm will suffer a reduction in unit profit, or it will raise its price. In most cases both will happen.

Any increase in price will, of course, be limited by the amount of competition the firm faces. If the firm has many competitors, raising its price will probably result in a significant drop in its sales. In this case the firm would be better off not raising its price much and simply accepting a reduction in unit profit.

However, when the firm has few competitors or when most competitors are facing the same cost pressures and are therefore all eager to raise their prices, it may be possible for a firm to raise its price without losing market share. In this situation firms will try to maintain their unit profits by raising prices.

In either case some inflation will result during the expansionary phase of a business cycle. The opposite happens during a recession. With unemployment rising and demand for materials falling, unit costs begin to fall, or to rise less fast. This leads to less rapid inflation, or even (once in a while) to deflation.

The **inflation-unemployment trade-off** describes the tendency during a business cycle for inflation to rise when unemployment falls and for inflation to fall when unemployment rises.

The result is that the rate of inflation is correlated with the phase of the business cycle. The ups and downs of the economy result in ups and downs of the inflation rate. Moreover, there tends to be a *trade-off* between inflation and unemployment: when unemployment goes down (during the business cycle expansion), the rate of inflation tends to go up, and when unemployment goes up (during recessions), the rate of inflation tends to go down.

The *inflation-unemployment trade-off* is presented in Figure 18.2.

The downward slope of the line in this figure indicates that unemployment and inflation are negatively correlated: more of one is generally associated with less of the other.

In the 1970s and early 1980s, however, many countries, including the U.S., experienced more of *both* unemployment and inflation. This was due, mainly, to the formation of the Organization of Petroleum Exporting Countries (OPEC) and the success of this cartel in restricting the supply of oil and driving up its price. Because of the resulting rise in gasoline prices and cost increases for all enterprises using oil as an input, inflation took off. Because more inflation was occurring in the economy no matter what the rate of unemployment, the trade-off line shifted upward and to the right: all combinations of inflation and unemployment were worse than they had been before. In that period inflation was not "cyclical" inflation: the higher inflation rates could not be attributed to cost increases associated with a business cycle expansion.

The inflation-unemployment trade-off curve can also shift downward (or to the left) as indicated by the dotted line in Figure 18.2. Such a shift might occur as a result of the kind of "handshake" discussed in the previous chapter. If business and labor could come to an agreement whereby business pledged job security (or support for full-employment macroeconomic policies) in return for labor's willingness to accept relatively modest wage increases even in times of low unemployment, low inflation could be achieved without high unemployment. In this situation the economy could be at a point such as C in the figure, where there would be less inflation than at point A (with very low unemployment) and less unemployment than at point B (where the rate of inflation would be lower than at

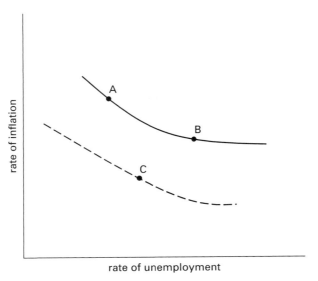

FIGURE 18.2   The inflation–unemployment trade-off.   The curves in this figure illustrate the process of cyclical inflation. Higher unemployment is associated with lower inflation, and vice versa. Hence, there is a *trade-off* between inflation and unemployment: having less of one requires having more of the other. Most people would like to have less of both, but we can have less of one only with more of the other. If the solid line in the figure represents the current inflation–unemployment trade-off, we are limited to moving up and down it between points such as A and B. The dashed line represents a *shift* of the inflation–unemployment trade-off curve itself. Such a shift might result, for example, from a drop in the price of oil, or it might be brought about by institutional changes such as the ones described in the "Institutions for Achieving Full Employment" section of Chapter 17. At least some of the points on the dashed line, such as point C, are unambiguously better than points A and B on the solid curve because they represent lower rates of *both* inflation and unemployment. A movement along the original trade-off curve may or may not be desirable, depending on how much one dislikes inflation or fears unemployment. But a movement to a point on a lower trade-off curve will usually be an improvement.

point A). Thus, the dotted inflation-unemployment trade-off curve in Figure 18.2 represents a set of choices more advantageous than those represented by the solid line.

Figure 18.3 shows how the inflation-unemployment trade-off worked in the U.S. between 1959 and 2002. Each point in the figure represents a particular combination of a rate of inflation and a rate of unemployment. The first panel in the upper-left corner shows the combinations of inflation and unemployment for each year between 1959 and 1969 (the 1960s). During these years inflation was clearly "cyclical": the economy moved up and down a very well-defined inflation-unemployment trade-off curve, with high inflation occurring when the unemployment rate was low, and vice versa.

The next panel in the upper-right corner shows what happened in the U.S. between 1969 and 1979 (the 1970s). In this period the inflation rate spiraled outward because, for reasons suggested earlier, the inflation-unemployment trade-off curve itself shifted upwards. Higher inflation and higher unemployment occurred together.

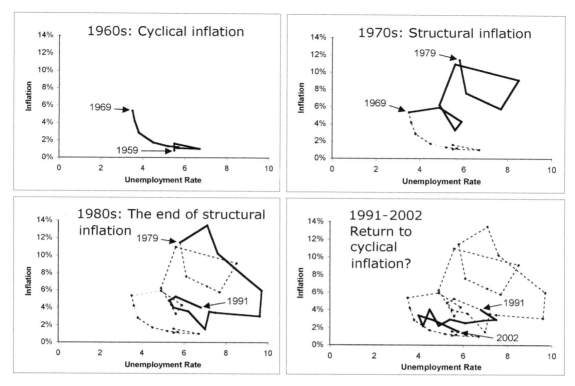

FIGURE 18.3   Cyclical and structural inflation in the U.S., 1959 to 2002.   As in Figure 18.2, rates of inflation are plotted on the vertical axis and rates of unemployment on the horizontal axis in each panel of this figure. The difference is that the panels in this figure present actual data from the U.S. economy for the last four decades of the 20th century and for the first two years of the present one. The lines in each panel connect a series of dots, each dot representing the rate of inflation and the rate of unemployment for a particular year. Although it is hard to see them all, the upper left panel has dots for each of the years from 1959 through 1969, with a line drawn from the dot for one year to the dot for the next year; the next panel has lines connecting the dots for the years from 1969 to 1979; and so on. The lines in each panel show the prevailing pattern of inflation and unemployment for the decade represented in the panel. Note how closely the shape of the line in the upper left panel resembles the shape of the lines in Figure 18.2; given this resemblance we can say that there was a particular inflation–unemployment trade-off in the 1960s. During this decade the economy seemed just to move up and down this trade-off curve. The decade of the 1960s can thus be categorized as a decade of "cyclical inflation" because the rates of inflation and unemployment seemed to vary in a predictable fashion over the course of the business cycle, with more inflation occurring when unemployment was low, and vice versa. The decade of the 1970s was just the opposite; this was a time of "structural inflation" (see text of this chapter). In this decade inflation and unemployment, far from moving up and down a discernable trade-off curve, seemed often to move in the same direction, with high inflation occurring at the same time as high unemployment. Indeed, the points in this panel for the second half of the decade lie generally above and to the right of the points representing its earlier years. The third panel, the one for the 1980s, shows that the combinations of inflation and unemployment recorded then, though not consistently moving along a particular trade-off line, did move back to the vicinity of the cyclical trade off curve of the 1960s, with the last five years of the decade seeming to move along a new trade-off curve. This suggests that in the 1980s we saw "the end of structural inflation." Finally, the last panel, the one for the years 1991 to 2002, provides evidence for the conjecture that the U.S. economy is returning to something like the cyclical inflation–unemployment trade-off pattern of the 1960s.

Source: Council of Economic Advisors, *Economic Report of the President* (Washington, D.C.: U.S. Government Printing Office, various years) available at http://www.whitehouse.gov/cea/pubs.html or at http://gpoacess.gov/eop/download.html.

> **Stagflation** refers to the combination of slower economic growth (stagnation) and generally rising prices (inflation) that characterized the hard times of the 1970s.

In the 1970s the U.S. economy was stagnating (that is, growing slowly), unemployment was high, and inflation was occurring nonetheless. So a new word entered our vocabulary: *stagflation,* referring to the combination of a stagnating economy and inflation. This term is generally used to describe the performance of the American economy during the 1970s.

As indicated in the next panel of Figure 18.3, the one in the lower-left corner, the 1980s saw the inflation-unemployment trade-off curve shift back downward. One explanation is that the conservative economic policies introduced after the election of Ronald Reagan as president strengthened business while weakening labor. (President Reagan's first act was to fire striking air traffic controllers, thereby sending a message to labor unions that they would not have a sympathetic ear in the White House.) In any case, whatever trade-off existed in 1979, it seems that a much lower trade-off came into effect during the 1980s.

Finally, in the period from 1991 to 2002, shown in the remaining panel of Figure 18.3, the inflation-unemployment trade-off curve seems to have flattened out, signaling perhaps a return to cyclical inflation.

Structural Inflation

It is clear from Figure 18.3 that the business cycle and the inflation-unemployment trade-off do not explain very much of the inflation that has occurred since 1970. Inflation rates were high at every stage of the business cycle. In fact, the highest rate of inflation in the 1970s occurred during the depths of a severe recession, in 1974 and 1975. What seems to have been at work, then, was *structural inflation.*

Structural inflation, like cyclical inflation, is a result of unresolved conflict over the distribution of income, and like cyclical inflation it occurs because claims on goods exceed sup-

> **Structural inflation** occurs when the price level increases rapidly throughout the course of a business cycle.

plies at the going prices. The fundamental difference between cyclical and structural inflation is that the conflicts that cause structural inflation are those arising not from the business cycle, but rather from more fundamental structural aspects of society. That is the reason we call the inflation *structural,* and it is also why the inflation happens over the course of a whole business cycle instead of only during the cycle's late expansion phase.

Structural inflation occurs typically when political conflict is high and no group has the upper hand. Structural inflation has erupted in the years prior to major revolutions, such as the French Revolution in the 18th century and the Russian Revolution in the early 20th century. During such periods traditional political structures are disrupted as new groups seek power.

> A **political stalemate** is a situation in which none of the major economic actors—banks, large corporations, labor unions, the major political parties, the government—has the power to impose its will on the others.

Structural inflation also happens under more normal circumstances. The presence of a *political stalemate* is crucial to structural inflation both in usual and in extraordinary times. A political stalemate is a situation in which none of the major economic actors—banks, large corporations, labor unions, the major political parties, or the government—has the power to impose its will on the others.

If a political stalemate coincides with a reduction or reversal in the growth of output over a period of many years, structural inflation is likely to result. The conditions for structural inflation can be summarized as follows:

Economic stagnation + political stalemate = structural inflation

Political stalemate and economic stagnation create the conditions for inflation, which, as explained above, occur when the total claims on goods and services in the form of money and credit in the hands of businesses, families, and governments exceeds the supply of available goods valued at their current market prices. The stalemate explains why the claims are excessive, and the stagnation explains why the supply of goods is limited.

Given the excess of claims over supplies at current prices, there are three possible outcomes. The prices of the goods could rise until the value of the existing supply of goods is equal to the total claims on the goods. This is the inflationary process we described in the example with the 10 farmers. But there are two other possibilities: first, the amount of claims in people's hands might be reduced, and second, the amount (rather than the prices) of goods might be increased. These last two possibilities are ways that inflation could be avoided, or at least moderated.

However, reducing the claims in the hands of governments, businesses, and families often is not easy to do. No group wants to give up its claim on the output, and often each party is powerful enough to prevent any reduction in either its income or in its access to credit.

Of course, if some group in the society is powerful enough, it can insist on keeping its claims and force the other groups to give up theirs. This could be done, for example, if very high interest rates discouraged families and businesses from borrowing while the government maintained a constant level of (deficit) spending. Before the 1940s very high rates of unemployment periodically resulted in major cuts in the incomes of workers and hence in reductions in the total claims on goods and services. But clearly such harsh outcomes are not popular. Under conditions of political stalemate, a reduction in claims is not likely to happen.

In the 1980s, with the growing political influence of business and the declining power of other groups, including workers (see Chapter 7), the political stalemate of the 1970s was broken. Much of the reduction in inflation since 1980 is the result of the wage stagnation brought about by the fall in the relative strength of labor unions and of workers in general.

Increasing the amount of goods available also would dampen inflation. And if the demand for many goods exceeds the supply, we would expect not only that prices would rise, but also that the amount produced would increase. This generally happens, but it may happen very slowly and not in sufficient quantity to meet the level of claims for goods. If businesses have a gloomy forecast for profits in the future, as they well might under conditions of political stalemate and economic stagnation, they may be reluctant to hire more workers and to produce more goods, even if there is excess demand. If output does not expand to meet the claims for goods, prices will rise. This is why economic stagnation is part of the explanation of structural inflation.

WHY WORRY ABOUT INFLATION?

The reason why people often worry about inflation is that a sustained rise in the price level erodes the buying power of a salary or wage. For this reason we need to have a way of thinking about the buying power of given amounts of income.

Economists use the term *real* to mean *corrected for inflation.* When we talk of an increase in the *real wage,* we mean an increase in the actual (money) wage large enough to more than keep pace with inflation.

> The **real wage**, or **real income,** refers to wages or income corrected to take account of the effects of inflation.

To understand what is wrong with inflation, we must ask two questions. First, what are the effects of inflation on the distribution of income? And second, does inflation affect real incomes?

Concerning the first question, inflation has an uneven and unpredictable effect on the distribution of income. Inflation distributes its costs (and sometimes benefits, too) very unevenly and arbitrarily. An elderly couple living on a pension with a fixed money income will find that the buying power of their income will fall as inflation takes its toll; their next-door neighbors who borrowed a large sum of money may benefit handsomely, because they can repay their debt with money worth less than the amount they initially borrowed. The distributional results of inflation often seem unfair because they are so uneven.

Concerning the second question, inflation clearly has negative effects on real incomes. Because inflation is unpredictable, it makes it very hard to plan for the future. It makes it difficult for families to plan for such things as retirement income and college expenses. Businesses will also have difficulty allocating funds for the purchase of equipment costing millions of dollars if they do not know how much their money will be worth in the future. Thus, inflation results in poor planning, mistaken planning, and sometimes no planning at all. The consequence of poor or inadequate planning is waste.

But inflation may also have positive effects. We can see the positive effects if we consider the negative effects that result from the methods usually deployed to fight inflation. We know from the inflation-unemployment trade-off that inflation can be reduced by macroeconomic policies that raise the rate of unemployment. Rising unemployment undercuts the bargaining power of labor and slows the rate of wage growth, thereby restraining business costs. And if costs are not rising—and aggregate demand is weak because of high unemployment—prices are not likely to rise, either.

Just the opposite series of events occurs during a period of expansion, whether brought on by a turn in the business cycle or as a result of deliberate expansionary monetary policies. Whatever the reason, people's incomes in expansionary periods typically rise faster than prices do. (It usually takes a while for businesses to decide that price increases will not just cause them to lose market share.) So real incomes tend to rise during periods when unemployment is falling and inflation is picking up.

However, if the cure for inflation is more unemployment (as it seems to have been in the U.S. in the early 1980s), fighting inflation will leave most people with less real income, at least in the short run. Thus, the overall cost to society of fighting inflation with more unemployment may be high. As an economy moves downward along the inflation-unemployment trade-off curve, more unemployment will result in less output, and less output will result in less real income.

MONEY WAGES AND REAL WAGES

oes a raise always improve your life? The answer hinges on, among other things, the distinction economists make between money wages and real wages. The actual dollar amount of a worker's wage, say, $8.50 an hour, is the *money wage*. The *real wage* is a measure of the buying power of a worker's hourly earnings in one year *relative to* the buying power of his or her hourly earnings in another year. As explained in the box "Measuring Total Output" in Chapter 16, pp. 412–413, the term *real* means *corrected for inflation*.

The distinction between money and real wages is made so that we can know whether increases in a worker's money wage keep up with, exceed, or fall behind the rate of inflation. This, in turn, enables us to know whether increases in the money wage represent actual improvements in a worker's standard of living.

If, for example, a worker's wage increased from $8.00 an hour in one year to $8.50 an hour the next year, can we say that this worker had a higher standard of living in the second year? Leaving aside the effect of taxes, the answer to the question depends on how much prices went up between the first year and the second. If prices went up by less than 6.25 percent (the increase in the money wage), then the $8.50 an hour enabled the worker to buy *more* in the second year than in the first year. If prices went up by more than 6.25 percent, however, the worker's buying power was *lower* in the second year than it had been in the first: less could be bought with the $8.50 than could be bought with the $8.00.

Economists calculate real wages by observing the general level of prices in a certain year—the "base" year—and then adjusting money wages by the amount of change in the price level using the *Consumer Price Index* (see the definition and discussion of the CPI elsewhere in this chapter). For the purpose of determining the real wage in a particular year, the index is set so that 1982 = 100. In the table below we provide data for certain years showing average money wages (per hour), the CPI, and average real wages (per hour) for U.S. private sector production workers (that is, excluding government and supervisory workers).

	Average Money Wage	CPI (1982 = 100)	Real Wage (1982 prices)
1972	$3.90	43.4	$8.99
1982	$7.86	100	$7.86
1992	$10.76	142.5	$7.55
2002	$14.95	181.4	$8.24

The data in the first row of this table show that in 1972 the average real wage for production workers in the private sector of the U.S. economy, calculated on

Continued . . .

the basis of 1982 prices, was nearly $9 per hour even though money wages were, on average, only $3.90 per hour. (This was the highest point for real wages between the mid-1960s and the 21st century.)

The decline in real wages between 1972 and 1982 is explained by the fact that in that decade prices went up by 130 percent while money wages rose only 102 percent. Relatively speaking, then, wage-earners could buy more with $3.40 in 1972 than they could with $7.86 in 1982.

The average real wage continued to fall until 1993, reaching its low point of $7.52 in that year. Although real wages have been rising since the mid-1990s, in terms of purchasing power they have not yet regained the ground lost since 1972. The average money wage in 2002 was $14.95 an hour, but the average real wage in that year, $8.24, was still 75 cents an hour less than the $8.99 an hour it had been in 1972 (both figures calculated in 1982 prices).

The importance of the real wage concept is that it allows us to see the *combined* effects of changes in money wages and changes in the general price level. Rising money wages are only as good as the difference between their rate of increase and the rate of increase in the consumer price index. If the former is not greater than the latter, you will be going backward while appearing to be going forward.

Source: Council of Economic Advisors, *Economic Report of the President 2004* (Washington, D.C.: U.S. Government Printing Office, 2004), Table B-47.

Is there another, less costly, way to fight inflation? For example, if we could somehow shift the inflation-unemployment curve inward, that would make possible both lower unemployment and lower inflation. If such a shift of the curve could be achieved, inflation could be reduced without lowering real income. Whether the trade-off curve can be shifted inward is a matter of debate, and the facts do not unambiguously support any one view of the issue.

In the early 1980s inflation was sharply reduced—from 13.5 percent per year in 1980 to 3.2 percent per year in 1983. A restrictive monetary policy sent the economy into a recession and thereby brought down the rate of inflation. The result, however, was a brutal bout of unemployment: in 1982 and 1983 the U.S experienced the highest unemployment rates since the Great Depression of the 1930s. The cost of reducing inflation in those years was huge: economists have estimated that the amount of output that could have been—but was not—produced was about $1.4 trillion worth of goods and services (in 2003 prices). This was greater than the entire money cost to the U.S. (in 2003 prices) of fighting World War II, and it came to about $14,000 per household (again, in 2003 prices). So, in effect, every American household gave up about $14,000 as its contribution to stopping inflation in the early 1980s. Between the mid-1980s and the early 2000s, however, inflation remained quite low despite unemployment rates below those that prevailed in the late 1970s.

Given the difficulties of containing price increases, it is clear that inflation should be added to the list of obstacles to full employment policies that was presented in Chapter 17. When employment is already high and unemployment is fairly low, any additional demand for goods—the result, say, of government deficit spending—will likely push up prices.

Thus, if high levels of employment actually are achieved, people may well be confronted with price increases resulting from the cyclical inflationary pressures identified earlier (rising costs). Although in the early 21st century such pressures are considerably lower than they were in the late 1970s, the pressures for cyclical inflation still exist.

Inflation poses a political challenge to full-employment policies because inflation, like unemployment, is unpopular. The costs of inflation and unemployment depend on who you are, of course. Workers suffer enormous losses from unemployment. Those who lose their jobs lose their incomes, while those who remain employed face insecurity and are forced to moderate their wage demands. Conversely, people with a lot of money tend to lose from inflation: inflation erodes the value of what they have. When prices rise rapidly, for example, banks and other lenders often find, to their dismay, that even with the interest payments they receive on their loans, the real value of the loan repayment is less than what was lent, so no real income is earned. In fact, income is lost.

For this reason movements along the inflation-unemployment trade-off curve are likely to redistribute income between the rich and those who are less well-off. In the U.S over the past three decades, increases in unemployment have typically led to a less equal distribution of income. This has been true even when high unemployment has brought a welcome reduction in inflation.

Debates concerning inflation often focus on issues such as the effects of government deficits, changes in interest rates, and rising or falling foreign exchange rates. But underlying the debates is the familiar question of how income will be distributed. Those who place primary emphasis on the need to fight inflation often advocate policies that will increase the amount of unemployment and redistribute income toward higher-income groups. Other people—not necessarily rich—often support anti-inflationary policies, even if the cost is higher unemployment. Workers with secure jobs and people living on fixed incomes (pensions, for example) often favor fighting inflation. For these reasons, the combination of inflation and unemployment each country actually experiences depends on the power of conflicting groups to bring about distributional outcomes that favor them or their allies.

The extent of the resulting inflation and unemployment depends both on the institutions that regulate the economy and on the economic policies followed by the government. There are really two issues here. The first is the position of the inflation-unemployment trade-off curve: does it allow low levels of both unemployment and inflation (like the dashed line in Figure 18.2), or does it permit only high levels of both (like the solid line in Figure 18.2)? The second issue is where on the inflation-unemployment trade-off curve the economy is located. Do we experience relatively high unemployment and relatively low inflation, or is the opposite true?

The actual levels of unemployment and inflation experienced in a particular country will, of course, depend both on the location of the inflation-unemployment trade-off curve and the position of the economy on it at any given time. In the 1960s and the late 1990s in the U.S., for example, both unemployment and inflation were low, while in the 1970s both were high. In the 1980s inflation was low and unemployment was high. Looking at differences among nations, Austria, Germany, and Japan have had low inflation rates and low unemployment, while Spain has had high levels of both. Sweden's relatively low level of unemployment has been accompanied by a rate of inflation somewhat higher than that in the U.S.

CONCLUSION

Economists do not agree on the reasons some countries do better than others when judged on their ability to maintain low levels of both unemployment and inflation. There is some agreement, however, that where the advocates of business interests are powerful, governments are likely to opt for higher unemployment and lower inflation. The United States and the United Kingdom in the 1980s are examples. And where advocates of working people's interests are more influential, government policies are likely to favor lower unemployment, even at the cost of higher inflation.

The government and its policies are obviously of major importance in determining macroeconomic outcomes, not only concerning unemployment and inflation but also affecting the rate of economic growth and the distribution of income. The government is no less important in influencing microeconomic outcomes, such as the prices at which goods sell and the way markets work. We explain the relationship between the government and the economy in the next chapter.

SUGGESTED READINGS

Peter Bernholz, *Monetary Regimes and Inflation: History, Economic and Political Relationships* (Northampton, Mass.: Edward Elgar, 2002).

Richard D. Duncan, *The Dollar Crisis: Causes, Consequences, Cures* (Hoboken, N.J.: Wiley, 2003).

Ellen Frank, *The Raw Deal: How Myths and Misinformation about the Deficit, Inflation, and Wealth Impoverish America* (Boston: Beacon Press, 2004).

Robert M. Solow and John B. Taylor, *Inflation, Unemployment, and Monetary Policy* (Cambridge, Mass.: MIT Press, 1999).

Joseph E. Stiglitz, *Globalization and Its Discontents* (New York: Norton, 2002), Chapter 4, "The East Asia Crisis: How IMF Policies Brought the World to the Verge of a Global Meltdown."

CHAPTER 19

Government and the Economy

In August 1963 more than 200,000 people came to Washington, D.C., and heard Dr. Martin Luther King, Jr., give a speech that marked the peak of the civil rights movement and is today as memorable as Lincoln's Gettysburg Address. "I have a dream that my four little children will one day live in a nation where they will not be judged by the color of their skin but by the content of their character," King told the crowd.

By mobilizing huge marches, challenging racial discrimination in the courts, provoking mass arrests by peacefully violating discriminatory laws and practices, and lobbying Congress for policies to rectify racial inequality and poverty, the civil rights movement transformed America. During the 1960s, new laws made the denial of equal voting rights and the barring of equal access to public accommodations and employment illegal. Deliberate policies to segregate schools by race came under attack by the U.S. Justice Department. Partly in response to the civil rights movement, President Lyndon Johnson inaugurated the "War on Poverty" in 1965.

Did the new policies make a difference? During the 1960s the pay gap between African Americans and others narrowed (see Figure 14.13). But it had narrowed in the 1950s, too, before the civil rights movement. And it is difficult to say how much of the improvement in the 1960s was due to new policies and how much resulted from the fact that the demand for labor was rapidly expanding during that decade (partly due to government spending on the war in Vietnam). The less well-off generally do better when the unemployment rate is very low.

In at least one area, however, the causal connection between civil rights activism and improvement of the lives of African Americans is clear. In 1964 African-American babies were twice as likely to die in infancy as were European-American babies. During the next 7 years the infant mortality rate among African Americans fell by more than a quarter (from

41 to 29 deaths per 1,000 live births). During the same period, the ratio of African-American to European-American infant mortality fell by a third, having risen during the 15 years before 1964.

The improvement in the health of black infants was especially great in the poorest parts of the South, where, prior to the civil rights movement, access to medical care had been segregated and the facilities open to blacks had been inferior. After passage of the 1964 Civil Rights Act, medical facilities were integrated, and this brought about a significant improvement in the quality of medical care for black citizens. Especially large improvements for black infants were made in reducing deaths from easily treatable causes such as diarrhea and pneumonia.

The connection between the civil rights movement and infant mortality makes it clear that government policies matter. Government can affect the way the economy works, and it is no less true that the economy has a big impact on how the government works. This chapter explores the relationship between the government and the economy.

As we have argued in earlier chapters, a capitalist economy operates on the basis of a set of principles, or "rules of the game," designed to organize commodity production for profit using wage labor and privately owned capital goods. Governments, on the other hand, are organized according to different principles, a different set of rules. These rules make possible collective action, and they involve a compulsory relationship between citizens and their government. Governments—or government leaders—act on behalf of the entire population of a nation, and their actions can be enforced on all of its residents.

BUSINESS AND GOVERNMENT

Business functions around one predominant organizing principle, profitability . . . Government, on the other hand, deals with a vast number of equally legitimate and often potentially competing objectives—for example, energy production versus environmental protection, or safety regulations versus productivity. . . . Thus, government and business will necessarily and properly function very differently.

—Robert E. Rubin, former U.S. Treasury Secretary
in a speech to the Economic Club of Chicago,
February 22, 2001

A democratic capitalist society will keep searching for better ways of drawing the boundary lines between the domain of rights and the domain of dollars. And it can make progress. To be sure, it will never solve the problem, for the conflict between equality and economic efficiency is inescapable. In that sense, capitalism and democracy are really a most improbable mixture. Maybe that is why they need each other— to put some rationality into equality and some humanity into efficiency.

—Arthur Okun, *Equality and Efficiency* (1975)

The main idea of this chapter is that *government, especially democratic government, operates on different principles from those of a capitalist economy, and each shapes how the other functions.* This central idea is expressed in five key points:

1. The *rules that determine how the government functions are different* from the rules that determine how the economy functions.

2. Because of its power and size, *the government affects the workings of the economy* in important ways. Government alters the horizontal, or market, relations among buyers and sellers, it affects the vertical relations of employers and workers, and it influences the time, or change, dimension of the economy.

3. *The government has grown* and become a more important part of the economy. The capitalist economy itself produced many of the tensions and pressures that led to the growing economic importance of the government.

4. Many of the most hotly debated conflicts over the government's economic policies arise from the effects that such policies have on the profit rate. We illustrate these conflicts by an analysis of what is called the *political business cycle.*

5. *The capitalist economy places certain limits on what the government can do.* The political power of the owners of large businesses derives in part from their ability to make large contributions to election campaigns and influence political agendas. Business leaders have tremendous indirect political power as well, since they control the process of investment, which in turn determines which states or even which nations will have jobs and economic growth and which ones will be faced with rising unemployment and economic stagnation.

THE RULES OF GOVERNMENT ORGANIZATION

Activities or relationships organized through the government tend to be compulsory, collective, and in the United States and many other countries, democratically determined. In using compulsion a government is quite different from other economic actors such as firms, workers, families, and unions. Some of these actors do, of course, have the power to structure the choices and limit the options of one or more of the others. Employers, as we have seen, can limit their employees' choices because they have the power to affect workers' livelihoods. An early 20th-century employer in the garment industry expressed this power succinctly in a notice to his employees: "If you don't come in on Sunday, don't come in on Monday."

However narrow the choices are, though, workers' relationships to their employers are ultimately voluntary because other employers exist. Even if other jobs are hard to find, it is, in fact, possible for workers to switch employers. The same is true with regard to consumers' relationships to particular sellers; the power to switch gives consumers a degree of sovereignty in product markets. In both labor markets and product

A **compulsory relationship** exists when a person cannot choose whether to enter the relationship but rather becomes subject to the relationship because of his or her status (such as being a citizen of a particular country).

markets—and other markets as well—the relationships between buyers and sellers involve exchanges and are based on contracts, whether written or unwritten. An exchange always involves a choice, even when the other options are not appealing, as when the alternatives to one's current job are unemployment, financial headaches, family disruption, and a difficult search for another job.

The citizen's relationship to his or her government, by contrast, is not voluntary, it is *compulsory*. Even in democratic political systems, where representatives of the people make the laws, the people are compelled to obey the laws. One can escape this compulsion only by changing one's nationality.

Consider taxes. Taxes are not paid in exchange for something, in the sense that one might exchange $20 for a shirt. They are sometimes paid willingly because people may appreciate the educational services, police protection, and other activities that may be supported by government tax revenues. But taxes are not paid voluntarily: they simply must be paid. If they are not paid, the "delinquent" taxpayer will have his or her property seized by the government. Only a government can legally take your money or your property without obtaining your individual agreement. Only a government can legally lock you up, draft you, or take your life.

Besides being compulsory, government activities are usually *collective,* in the sense that a government generally acts on behalf of all citizens. Taxes are supposed to be paid by all citizens. Goods and services provided by or distributed through the government are made available to all citizens, or to all citizens eligible for them. In the economic sphere money is paid in each particular transaction, and the individual buyer receives a product or service in return for the money. In contrast, government monies are usually collected from everyone (by means of taxes), and the benefits of government activities (potentially, at least) are available to all.

Collective activities are activities whose benefits or burdens extend, potentially at least, to all citizens.

A corollary of the compulsory and collective nature of government is that a citizen, at least ideally, can obtain benefits due to citizens by *right*. A citizen does not have to purchase police protection or the right to vote, nor do his or her children have to buy a place at the public school. When benefits are available only to part of the citizenry (such as food stamps for the poor), any citizen who meets the established criterion (in this case, being poor) gets the benefit by right. In the economic realm, on the other hand, benefits take the form of commodities that must be purchased. No commodities can be claimed as a right.

Citizen rights are the basis for a claim to share (some of) the benefits of society; this claim is based on one's citizenship instead of, for example, on possessing sufficient money to buy the benefits.

Finally, the rules of government organization preclude, in most cases, the exercise of arbitrary power. More than 100 nations, including the U.S., have political systems based on the principles of *democratic government.* These principles include popular accountability of government officials through elections with widespread and equal voting rights. Democratic government also requires a foundation of civil liberties—for example, freedoms of speech, thought, belief, action, assembly, and the press—established by law and widely respected.

Democratic government is a way of organizing a government based on (1) accountability of officials through elections with widespread and equal voting rights and (2) civil liberties and personal freedoms.

Of course, even democratic governments have often violated the rules of democracy. In U.S. history, for example, some citizens were

DEMOCRATIC GOVERNMENT: FAIR GAME OR STACKED DECK?

The rules of democratic government are a set of procedures to regulate how and by whom public decisions are made. Democratic procedures are like the rules of baseball or tennis—they determine only how the game of democratic government is to be played, not who wins.

The rules of democratic government do not ensure that each citizen will have a more or less equal say in the outcome of the governmental process. Whether the actual decisions made by a democratic government benefit all citizens equally or favor some special group—whether they are fair or biased—depends on more than the rules. It also depends on how much political influence each group has. People with more money or other resources to lobby, advertise, support candidates, and so on are likely to have more political influence, even when the democratic rules are faithfully followed.

legally denied the vote because they did not own enough property, were not white, or were not male. Until the 1970s the principle of "one person, one vote" was widely (if illegally) disregarded in those states that effectively excluded blacks from voting. Groups unpopular with the government, with business, or with other powerful institutions have often been harassed by the FBI or otherwise deprived of their civil liberties.

Equally problematic for democracy has been the fact that, particularly in the United States, many citizens who have the right to vote have not been exercising this right. Figure 19.1 shows that in the U.S. the proportion of the voting-age population actually voting in presidential elections fell from roughly three-quarters in the last half of the 19th century to barely one-half in much of the 20th century.

The same has not been true in other countries, however. As Figure 19.2 shows, nations as different as India, Argentina, Japan, and Sweden have all had higher voter participation rates since the end of World War II, on average, than has the United States.

Of course, the weakness of voter participation in the United States is not evenly distributed. As Figure 19.3 shows, the lower the family income the less likely it is that a voting-age member of the family will actually go to the polls—and vice versa. In families with more than $75,000 of income, 71.5 percent of their members voted in the 2000 presidential election, but among the poorest of the poor (families with less than $5,000 of income), the participation rate was only 28.2 percent. The smaller chart within Figure 19.3 shows that participation in the 2000 presidential election was higher for employed white people than it was for unemployed, black, or Hispanic people.

Nevertheless, the basic idea of democratic government is that a process of voting will determine who is to be a government leader. Voting will be democratic, however, only if it is conducted on a "one person, one vote" basis after there has been an open competition among at least two candidates with differing ideas.

FIGURE 19.1   The American voter: An endangered species?   In 1860, on the eve of the Civil War, 81 percent of those eligible to vote did so. In the 1896 election, when the agrarian populist William Jennings Bryan challenged the eastern establishment, 79 percent voted (Bryan lost). In this century, however, voter participation has sharply declined: only 57 percent voted for president in the 1936 election, considered to be a referendum on the New Deal and the presidency of Franklin Delano Roosevelt (FDR won by a landslide). The 1980 election saw the culmination of the conservative counterattack against policies that originated with the New Deal; only 53 percent thought it was worth the effort to vote for or against Ronald Reagan. Presidential voting declined to a historic low of 49.1 percent in 1996 (the first time it had fallen below 50 percent) and rose only slightly to 51.3 percent in 2000, when fewer than 26 percent of the voting-age population (18 years and older) elected George W. Bush. Although voter participation jumped to nearly 60 percent of the voting-age population in the hotly contested election of 2004, it remains to be seen whether this increase in participation will mark the beginning of a long-term trend. The voter participation percentages given in this figure are the ratios of the total vote cast for the highest office on the ballot (the presidency) to the total voting-age population (18 years and older). These figures may be inconsistent with other reported turnout figures—such as the ones given in the smaller chart within Figure 19.3—because some voters fail to vote for the highest office. Hence, total voter turnout percentages based on all ballots cast may be slightly higher than the ones in this figure.

Sources: U.S. Bureau of the Census, *Statistical Abstract of the United States: 2003* (Washington, D.C.: U.S. Government Printing Office, 2003), Table 421, available at http://www.census.gov/prod/www/statistical-abstract-03.html); U.S. Bureau of the Census, *Historical Statistics of the United States: Colonial Times to 1970* (Washington, D.C.: U.S. Government Printing Office, 1975); U.S. Federal Election Commission, available at http://www.fec.gov; Committee for the Study of the American Electorate, available at http://www.fairvote.org/reports/CSAE2004electionreport.pdf.

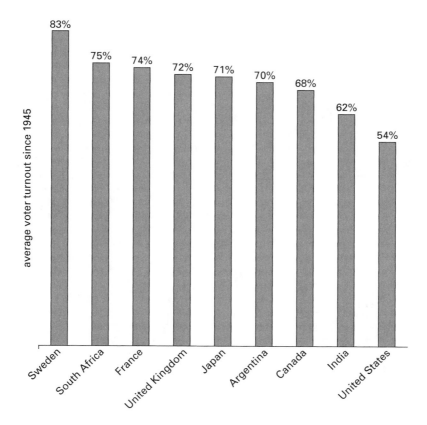

FIGURE 19.2 **Democracy around the world.** The average voter turnout figures provided in this figure are for Sweden from 1945 to 2001, for South Africa from 1994 to 2000, for France from 1965 to 2001, for the U.K. from 1945 to 2000, for Japan from 1945 to 2000, for Argentina from 1951 to 1999, for Canada from 1945 to 2000, for India from 1952 to 1999, and for the U.S. from 1948 to 2000. *Source:* International Institute for Democracy and Electoral Assistance, available at http://www.idea.int/.

The principles of democracy are very different from the principles that govern a capitalist economy. Generally, the employees of a corporation do not elect its leaders, the management, and neither does the community in which the corporation is located. In fact, corporate leaders are not elected at all in the sense that is usually attached to the word *election.* The people who own the corporation select them, with each owner having as many votes as the number of shares of stock he or she owns. Similarly, freedom of speech and other civil liberties guaranteed in the political sphere are often limited in the work-place. Many businesses enforce dress codes, and employees are generally not free to post information such as appeals from labor unions.

These two sets of rules—the rules of democratic government and the rules of a capital-ist economy—exist side by side in our society. Both affect the economy. They represent dif-ferent ways of coordinating labor processes and distributing products. For example, a person may purchase a ticket to go to a rock concert that has been arranged by a private company, or

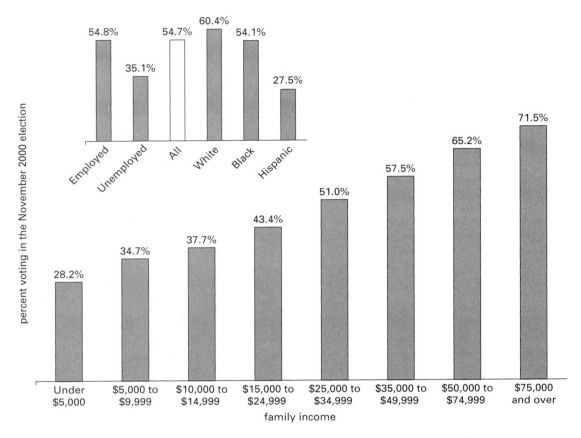

FIGURE 19.3 Who votes? U.S. voting patterns in the presidential election of 2000. This figure shows the fraction of various segments of the population, by family income, employment status, race, and ethnicity, reported to have voted in the November 2000 election.

Source: U.S. Bureau of the Census, *Current Population Reports,* P20-542, "Voting and Registration in the Election of November 2000" (Washington, D.C.: U.S. Government Printing Office, 2002), Table 8, available at http://www.census.gov/population/www/socdemo/voting/p20542.html.

the same person may attend a free rock concert sponsored by the local government and paid for out of tax revenues. In one case the concert is held because someone, the promoter, is hoping to make a profit; in the other it is held because the mayor, the city council, or some other government official thought it would be a fun—or a vote-getting—event to sponsor.

THE ECONOMIC ACTIVITIES OF THE GOVERNMENT

The government *enforces* the rules that regulate our social lives—the rules of the capitalist economy, the rules of democratic government, and other rules (for example, rules concerning relations among family members). The government also *makes* and *changes* the rules. Finally, the government is one of the major *actors* in the economy. We will discuss each of these roles in turn—the government as rule enforcer, as rule maker, and as economic actor.

Rule Enforcer

As the enforcer of rules, the government has the power to impose penalties on anyone who breaks the rules. Important activities of the government in this respect are the protection of civil rights—punishing acts of assault, rape, and homicide, for example—and the protection of property rights—in particular, punishing acts of theft and breach of contracts. National defense may be included as part of the enforcement of the rules, especially when it serves the purpose of preventing one government from imposing its rules on another. Also, the power of government to appropriate part of the surplus product by taxation supports its rule-enforcing function.

When the government acts to enforce rules, its activities often seem beneficial. We all certainly benefit from the prevention or punishment of thefts (crimes against our property) and assaults (crimes against our persons). But appearances can be deceptive. Sometimes the fair enforcement of rules works to the advantage of only some people. For example, it is usually illegal for both rich and poor to sleep in public spaces at night. But better-off people usually own (or rent) their own dwelling places, whereas a number of less-well-off people do not have access to housing. Therefore, the law, if it is enforced, prevents only poor people from sleeping in public spaces. There are generally both winners and losers when rules are enforced, even if they are enforced impartially.

It is also true that classes or other groups that benefit from existing rules may seek to have the government preserve and enforce those rules. As Adam Smith noted, one important function of government is to protect the property of the rich. "Civil government," he said, "is in reality instituted for the defense of the rich against the poor, or of those who have some property against those who have none at all."[1] Capitalist classes in many countries (including the United States) have benefited substantially from governmental enforcement of a set of "rules of the game" that enable them to organize production and distribution in ways beneficial to themselves.

> **Guard labor** refers to those who do not produce capital goods, materials, or consumption goods but who work to perpetuate the structure of the society including the power and economic advantages of the dominant class.

When labor is devoted not to the production of capital goods, materials, or consumption goods but is used instead to maintain the existing structure of power and ownership, it is termed *guard labor*. Examples of guard labor include soldiers, police, and security personnel (whether in the public or the private sector) as well as people in business firms whose role is (at least partly) to establish and preserve hierarchical relationships.

As we saw in Chapter 6, capitalism provides strong incentives for business owners to *invest* a substantial portion of the surplus product, and this makes the system inherently dynamic. However, when part of the surplus is used to employ guard labor, it is being used to maintain the status quo, not to change it.

---

[1] Adam Smith, *The Wealth of Nations* (New York: Random House, Modern Library, 1937 [1776]), Book 5, Chapter 1, Part 2.

GUARD LABOR: FORTRESS AMERICA

There are enough guns in private hands in the U.S. to provide every individual (including infants) with one. The U.S. produces and imports more than a million guns a year. A quarter of adults own at least one gun, and most of those own more than one gun. About half reported that they owned guns for self-protection. Why?

"The efforts of men are utilized in two different ways," wrote the great Italian economist Vilfredo Pareto a century ago. "They are directed to the production or transformation of economic goods, or else to the appropriation of goods produced by others." Adam Smith and the other classical economists termed the first "productive labor" and the second "unproductive labor." What we call *guard labor* is a kind of unproductive labor: its purpose is not to produce goods and services, but rather to influence the distribution of the goods and services produced, in important part by upholding the laws and maintaining the institutions of the economy.

The fact that guard labor is not involved directly in the production of goods and services does not mean that it is unnecessary. Guard labor exists in all societies for the simple reason that property rights and other institutions do not enforce themselves: they must be enforced and perpetuated by people.

Guard labor includes, of course, guards: private security personnel, corrections officials, and others who work in prisons. Also included are police officers, judges, and others who work in the judicial system because one of their main tasks is to prevent the illegal transfer of goods from one person to another. Less obvious but no less important are work supervisors who see to it that employees do not slack on the job. When employees slack, they receive wages without upholding their part of the (implicit) bargain: working hard for their employer. Also included are members of the armed forces, whose work protects the nation's boundaries and the international interests of its companies and others with global interests.

Finally, we include as guard labor two groups who do not work at all: prisoners and the unemployed. Prisoners do not (for the most part) engage in productive work; their "job" is to remind those on the outside that crime sometimes does not pay. Finally, the unemployed have a similar "job": they constantly remind employed workers that if they do not work hard and well, putting up with wages that allow for acceptable rates of profit, they could be replaced.

How much guard labor is there in the U.S economy? Using detailed information about occupations from the U.S. Bureau of Labor Statistics and other sources, we totaled up the numbers of workers in the categories defined above. We did not include all supervisors; we only counted those with direct labor disciplining functions. This meant excluding about half of all supervisors—those whose main job is to coordinate production or to train employees. We also excluded an estimate of what economists call *frictional* unemployment, people

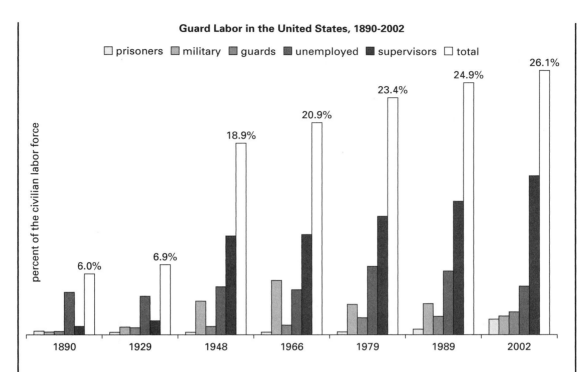

Guard Labor in the United States, 1890-2002

□ prisoners ■ military ■ guards ■ unemployed ■ supervisors □ total

percent of the civilian labor force

6.0%   6.9%   18.9%   20.9%   23.4%   24.9%   26.1%

1890   1929   1948   1966   1979   1989   2002

who are unemployed because they are switching jobs or just entering the labor force. We included workers producing military equipment for the Department of Defense, but we did not include those producing privately held handguns, sniper rifles, and other arms purchased by people reporting their purpose for owning a gun as self-defense. We did not include lawyers unless they held official positions (judges and the like). The precise procedures used in making the calculations are presented in the paper by Jayadev cited below.

In the figure above we represent guard labor as a fraction of the labor force. In 2002 the fraction of the labor force engaged in guard labor was larger than the fraction employed in goods-producing industries; of course, some of the people performing guard labor are employed in goods-producing industries, so the two categories overlap slightly—but the comparison is striking nevertheless. Notice the sharp decline in military employment since the Vietnam War, a decline that continued after the fall of Communism around 1989. Notice also the substantial rises in the prison population and number of work supervisors as a fraction of the total labor force.

Sources: Philip Cook and Jens Ludwig, "Guns in America: National Survey on Private Ownership and Use of Firearms" (Washington D.C.: U.S. Department of Justice, National Institute of Justice, 1997); Arjun Jayadev, "Guard Labor in the United States: 1890–2002" (Amherst, Mass.: University of Massachusetts at Amherst, Political Economy Research Institute, Working Paper, 2004); Vilfredo Pareto, *Manual of Political Economy* (New York: Augustus Kelley, 1971 [first Italian edition, 1905]), p. 341.

Since guard labor expenditures can be used neither for investment nor for capitalist consumption, the part of the surplus that is spent on guard labor does not directly benefit those who control the surplus. Although it serves to perpetuate the institutions that assure them their power and privilege, it is a deduction from the surplus. Hence, those who control the surplus will have an interest in minimizing the portion of it that has to be spent on guard labor.

The interest of the dominant class in holding down expenditures on guard labor may give it an incentive to avoid squeezing the producers' consumption too much and to refrain from working them to the limit of human endurance. Poor and overworked producers are not only likely to be unproductive, they are also likely to be angry and eager to change the institutions associated with their poverty and overwork. In such a situation the amount of guard labor required to keep the producers in line might soak up most of the surplus, leaving little for investment or luxury consumption.

Rule Maker

In making rules (a task that is shared among the legislative, judicial, and executive branches), the government can change the rules, make new rules, or alter old ones. The rules of free markets and private property are not timeless or everlasting. There have always been groups seeking to change these rules to make them more advantageous to themselves. For example, in the United States in the late 18th century, some people—Alexander Hamilton being the most famous of them—wanted the government to *prevent* certain markets from working. Hamilton and others advocated the imposition of heavy taxes (or *tariffs*) on imports of manufactured goods because they believed that free trade in such goods would prevent the U.S. from developing its own manufacturing capacity. Hamilton believed (correctly, it turned out) that discouraging or blocking the importation of manufactured products—thereby interfering with the free market—would make possible the development of manufacturing industries within the former British colonies.

> A **tariff** is a tax on goods or services coming into the country.

Later the owners of newly established textile factories wanted property rights changed so that they could divert rivers in order to use water power (or "water mills") to run the machinery in their factories. The existing property rights of farmers and others along the riverbanks were sacrificed so that textile mills could be more profitable. Still later, just before the Civil War, others pressed for yet another change in property rights, the abolition of slavery, which made it illegal to own, buy, or sell human beings.

In 1935 the National Labor Relations Act defined new rights for workers. This legislation, commonly referred to as the Wagner Act in honor of its proponent, Senator Robert Wagner, established for the first time the legal right of workers to come together in unions and bargain collectively with their employers. Before then most workers had to deal with their employers only as individuals in the labor market.

The process of legislative change has redefined property rights and altered the capitalist rules of the game. This process continued through the 20th century and is still occurring today. In 1964 the public accommodations section of the Civil Rights Act restricted the way owners of restaurants and hotels could use their property, making a particular form of racial discrimination illegal. More recently companies that manufacture and operate nuclear power plants obtained special laws limiting the amount they could be forced to pay in damages in case of a nuclear accident. Like the earlier changes in laws governing water rights, this law effectively limits the property rights of others whose property might be damaged by the plants. All these changes in the rules of the game have altered the way the economy works.

Economic Actor

The government can also act as a *producer* of goods or services, as a *microeconomic regulator,* as a *macroeconomic regulator,* and as a *distributor* of income or resources. As a *producer* the government employs people to produce goods or services intended to benefit society as a whole. The most important of these activities are schooling, health care, postal services, military defense, and police and fire protection. With the exception of the military and the post office, most government production in the U.S. takes place at the state and local levels.

As a *microeconomic regulator* the government uses its influence on the private economy to affect what goods and services will be produced, how they will be produced, and where they will be produced. To accomplish its tasks as a microeconomic regulator, the government can use various means. It may impose taxes on products, as it does on cigarettes to discourage the production and consumption of tobacco. It may also subsidize products to encourage their production. Since the 1940s the government's funding of research in nuclear weapons technology has had the effect of subsidizing the U.S. nuclear power industry, enabling it to expand much more rapidly than it would have without the research financed by the government. The government may also regulate industries directly, as it does when it imposes fuel economy standards on automobile manufacturers and safety requirements on mine operators. Local governments can affect where production is located by adopting zoning regulations.The government can act as a microeconomic regulator in other ways as well. It may set limits on prices, as it does when it establishes the minimum wage and sets public utility rates. It may influence the prices of goods such as farm products and oil by buying them up or releasing supplies of them (activities that the government might also undertake for other reasons). It may foster competition by implementing antitrust policies, as it attempted to do recently by taking Microsoft to court. It may also inhibit competition, as it does when it purchases military equipment only from large firms or prohibits doctors and taxi drivers from engaging in their professions without obtaining licenses from the government. The government also regulates banks, insurance companies, and other financial institutions.

As a *macroeconomic regulator,* the government uses monetary and fiscal policy to counteract the business cycle and reduce the instability of prices, profits, and employment resulting from its succession of booms and recessions (see Chapter 16). The government may engage in deficit spending—spending more than its tax revenues—to create jobs by boosting the total demand for goods and services. Alternatively, it may attempt to "cool" an "overheated" economy by raising taxes on families or businesses, thus discouraging spending on consumer products or capital goods and causing production cutbacks and increased unemployment. The government may also expand its own employment, say, to improve roads or clean up the debris left in national parks as more and more people use them; this would, of course, reduce unemployment. It may (through the Federal Reserve System) alter interest rates to make it easier or more difficult for businesses to borrow money to build new factories, thus encouraging or discouraging investment and expanding or contracting job opportunities. In its activities as macroeconomic regulator, the government can have major effects on the distribution of income, forcing wages down by increasing the rate of unemployment or squeezing profits by contracting the money supply.

As a *distributor* the government affects the distribution of income and resources between rich and poor, between one region and another, and among people of different ages, sexes, and races. It does this in part by maintaining a set of rules of the game that benefit one group over another, and in part through its activities as producer, as when it provides more adequate schooling to one group than to another. The average amount of money spent per pupil in public elementary and secondary schools in New Jersey in 2000–01 was $11,248; the comparable figure for Mississippi was $5,175. At the high end of the scale, Southampton, Long Island, a very wealthy town in New York, spends more than $15,000 per pupil.[2]

The federal government takes a certain amount of income from the residents of each state in taxes, and it also pays out money to finance numerous government programs in every state. For some states the amount of money paid in taxes to the federal government is greater than the amount of the federal expenditures in the state. In other states the amount of taxes paid is less than the amount of money spent on programs in the state. As a result, the federal government is constantly redistributing resources from some states to other states.

Moreover, the government affects the distribution of income and resources through its activities as a microeconomic regulator. When, for example, the government keeps agricultural prices high by buying up farm products whose presence in the market would have resulted in lower prices, it distributes income away from consumers, especially those who must spend a large portion of their income on food in order to survive, toward those who produce, process, and sell agricultural commodities.

The government also acts as a distributor more directly. It taxes some individuals at higher rates than others, and it gives out transfer payments to people who because of physical handicaps, old age, unemployment, or inability to work do not have much income from other sources.

THE EXPANSION OF GOVERNMENT ECONOMIC ACTIVITY

During the past century the economic importance of the government has grown dramatically. Because its role has expanded qualitatively as well as quantitatively, and because not all government activities are equally important in relation to the economy, there is no single measure by which the expansion of the government's role can be adequately gauged.

---

[2] U.S. Department of Education, National Center for Education Statistics, *Revenues and Expenditures for Public Elementary and Secondary Education: School Year 2000–01* (NCES 2003-362), May 2003, Table 5, available at http://nces.ed.gov; Josh Barbanel, "Charter Schools Grow in Suburbs, Uneasily," *New York Times,* May 3, 2003.

Measured in dollars, however, federal, state, and local government spending in the U.S. increased from 7.7 percent of the total output of the economy in 1902 to 31 percent in 2002.

In the United States, increases in military, Social Security, and health-related programs in the 20th century led to substantial growth of expenditures at the level of the federal government. Expansion of such direct services as public schools, municipal hospitals, and police and fire protection led to even more rapid growth of employment at the state and local levels. Although government expenditures at all levels in the U.S. increased greatly during the past century, the sum of such expenditures as a share of the nation's total output of goods and services is smaller than the comparable percentages of national output spent by governments in other advanced capitalist countries (see Figure 19.4).

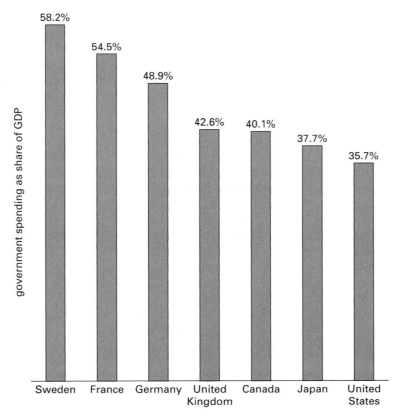

FIGURE 19.4   Government expenditures as percentage of total output, 2003.   This figure shows the amount of total government expenditures, at all levels of government, as a percentage of total output (GDP) in seven of the member nations of the Organization for Economic Co-operation and Development (OECD) in 2003. The average for the 28 nations in the OECD that year was 40.7 percent.

Source: Organization for Economic Co-operation and Development, *OECD Economic Outlook No. 75* (Paris: OECD, 2004), Annex Table 25, "General Government Total Outlays as Percent of Nominal GDP," available at www.oecd.org.

The reasons for the increased economic importance of the government are much debated. Some people see growing government as a triumph by the ordinary citizen over the self-serving interests of business. Others see the growth as the triumph of a bureaucratic mentality that assumes that if there is a problem, its solution must take the form of a government program.

But there is a more persuasive explanation for the increasing role of government in economic life: the survival and workability of capitalism as an economic system has required the government to grow. The ceaseless search for extra profits and the ensuing social, technical, and other changes outlined in earlier chapters have created conditions that have led to demands for a more active government. These demands have come as often from businesspeople as from workers, as often from chambers of commerce as from the AFL-CIO, and as often from Republicans as from Democrats. In addition, consumers and workers have supported the expansion of the economic role of the government, in part to protect themselves from the power of giant corporations. Passage of the Sherman Antitrust Act (1890), the Clean Air Act (1970), and the Consumer Product Safety Act (1973) are examples. The expansion of the role of government in the U.S. is not something that happened in *opposition* to capitalism. Rather, it is something that has happened in *response* to the development of capitalism. In what specific ways did this expansion occur?

Economic concentration.   Some of the growth of governmental economic activity can be explained by the growth of large corporations and the decline of small producers. The enormous power of modern U.S. corporations has allowed their owners to lobby the government for favors and to influence public opinion. Thus, big business is able to induce the government to do things that enhance profit making. Examples of this include subsidies for the nuclear power industry and exorbitant purchases of military hardware. U.S. corporate leaders have also supported the expansion of government regulation in the many situations in which they wanted protection from competitive pressures that might lower profits. Examples of such situations include regulation of the quality of meat and other food to prevent competition from companies that would lower the quality of such products.

International expansion.   The increasingly global reach of large American corporations has contributed to the development of a conception of "U.S. interests" around the world. As corporations expanded from national to international businesses, they changed from wanting the government to impose tariffs to keep out goods made abroad to insisting that the government protect U.S. investments around the world. They have promoted the development of an increasingly expensive military establishment to defend these interests. Preparations for war and the payment of interest on the national debt, much of which was borrowed to pay for past wars, have accounted for much of the growth in federal expenditures. Capitalism did not invent war, of course, but the degree of international economic interdependence and rivalry produced by the expansion of capitalism did make *world* wars more likely. After World War II a high level of military spending became a permanent feature of the U.S. economy.

The disintegration of the Soviet Union in the 1990s and the subsequent decline of Communism brought an end to the Cold War and with it a significant reduction in U.S. military expenditures. But even following this reduction, military spending absorbed

4.2 percent of the total output of the economy in 2002—nearly twice as much as all federal "nondefense" expenditures put together.

In the aftermath of the terrorist attack on the World Trade Center in 2001, there has been a more general expansion in the powers of the U.S. government. There is now a Department of Homeland Security, and the government has been empowered to monitor email communications and to bypass some of the rights of privacy that Americans have long taken for granted.

Economic instability.   The increasing instability of the economy, marked by periods of severe unemployment and dramatized by the worldwide Great Depression of the 1930s, has been another reason for the growing economic importance of the government. The stabilization of the U.S. economy was a major objective of the businesspeople who promoted the formation of the Federal Reserve System in 1913 and the Securities and Exchange Commission in 1935. An even more significant impetus for governmental intervention was the persistence of the Great Depression until military expenditures brought about full employment at the beginning of World War II. During the depressed 1930s radical political movements of both the left and the right spread around the world, generating political instability as people responded in different ways to the failure of capitalist economies to provide for their livelihoods.

In many countries broad coalitions of employers and workers pushed the government to take greater responsibility for maintaining economic growth, profits, and employment through its activities as a macroeconomic regulator. Immediately following World War II the Committee for Economic Development in the U.S. was successful in gaining congressional passage of the Employment Act of 1946. This legislation committed the U.S. federal government, at least in principle, to ensuring that there would be adequate job opportunities for everyone in the labor force.

The post–World War II growth of total government expenditures has increased the ability of the government to stabilize employment. As explained in Chapter 16, some government programs (such as unemployment insurance) act as built-in stabilizers that automatically raise government spending when the economy slows down, thus helping to maintain enough total demand to avoid severe recessions. Other more deliberate macroeconomic regulation such as new tax policies and changes in the rate of interest may also counteract the economy's tendency to provide too few jobs. Except during the Korean War, the Vietnam War, and the late 1990s, however, such policies have not succeeded in bringing about full employment in the U.S. In part this is because despite the Employment Act of 1946, the elimination of unemployment has never actually been the objective of the government's macroeconomic regulation. Alben Barkley, a U.S. senator at the time of its passage, drew attention to the inadequacy of the Employment Act by saying that the new law "promised anyone needing a job the right to go out and look for one."

Income support.   During the Great Depression many Americans became convinced that those unable to make an adequate living should be supported, at least at some minimal level, by the government. Government programs to support poor people replaced informal support systems and private charity, both because people who fell on hard times could no longer count on their families or neighbors to tide them over and because private charities did not have sufficient funds to take care of them. In the 1930s unemployment compensation, general relief, and Social Security were established. With the numerical growth and political mobilization of the aged population and of single-parent families during the 1960s and early 1970s, benefits and beneficiaries expanded.

In the last two decades of the 20th century, however, the idea of government support for those in need came under serious attack. From the early 1970s through the 1990s, the expansion of income support programs was halted and, in some cases, reversed. In 1998, for example, the average weekly unemployment insurance payment ($200.29) was more than 4 percent lower in real terms (corrected for inflation) than it had been 20 years earlier. The real value of the federal minimum wage also fell (see Figure 7.1).

Changing patterns of family life.   The combination in the early 1970s of a slowdown in the growth of real wages of men and an upsurge of women's demands for equality had the effect of altering relationships between women and men both in the household and in the economy as a whole. The two developments have made it less likely that men will be the sole "breadwinners" while their wives stay home to take care of the children, cook the meals, and clean the house. In 1900 only 20 percent of American women worked outside the home; by 2000 the percentage of women between the ages of 25 and 64 in the paid labor force had increased to 73.5 percent.[3]

In the face of wage stagnation from the early 1970s to the mid-1990s, more and more families found that they needed to have both husband and wife in the paid labor force in order to support their living standards. At the same time, the women's movement changed people's consciousness in ways that led at least some men to take more responsibility for household tasks and allowed many more women to take full-time jobs and have careers. Of course, these changes have been accompanied by the fact that more household tasks are now done for pay: more children are now taken care of in day care centers, more meals are eaten out or ordered in, and more housecleaning is done by paid "help."

Increases in the labor force participation of women and the broader changes in society's gender roles became yet another set of factors making for expansion of the government's role in the economy. To break down barriers to women's equality in the workplace, new laws and new enforcement activities were required. In the U.S. the Civil Rights Act of 1964 created the Equal Employment Opportunity Commission (EEOC) to secure the rights of women as well as members of minority groups to equal opportunities in the workplace. To help both women and men combine paid work with family responsibilities, Congress passed and President Clinton signed the 1993 Family and Medical Leave Act. Although compliance with these laws has been less than perfect, they are both significant in bringing U.S. policies closer to those in other advanced industrial nations.

Citizens in Japan and many Western nations have long had rights to government-funded child care, to health care for children as well as adults, to paid parental leave, and to generous required vacation time. In contrast, the U.S. government has been reluctant to

---

[3] U.S. Bureau of the Census, *Historical Statistics of the United States: Colonial Times to 1970* (Washington, D.C.: U.S. Government Printing Office, 1975); U.S. Bureau of the Census, *Statistical Abstract of the United States: 2001* (Washington, D.C., 2001), Table 571.

formulate comprehensive policies for the support of families, the only exception being for families at or below the poverty line.

The passage of the Family and Medical Leave Act in 1993 was at least a small step in the direction of governmental support for working families. The act requires that all workers in firms with more than 50 employees be allowed to take up to 12 weeks of unpaid leave at the time of the birth or adoption of a child or when an ill family member needs to be cared for. Both women and men are covered by the act. Although their leave is unpaid, employees retain their health benefits while they are on leave and are assured of an equivalent position within their firm when they return to work. What both the Equal Employment Opportunity Commission and the Family and Medical Leave Act do, then, is to assign greater responsibility to the U.S. government for regulating relationships between employers and their employees.

Environmental, consumer, and worker protection.   Many groups have demanded that government mediate the conflict between profitability and the protection of people and the environment. Over the past half century these conflicts created new demands for government action. Consumers have organized groups to lobby for product safety legislation. Workers—in mining, in textiles, in chemicals, and elsewhere—have organized for occupational health and safety regulation. In the last half century a number of protective laws have been enacted, the most important of which are the Mine Safety Act (1969), the Occupational Safety and Health Act (1970), and the Consumer Products Safety Act (1973).

Another issue that has aroused public demands for governmental intervention is the growing need to protect the natural environment from the effects of industrial production. Our natural surroundings—our land, freshwater, air, and oceans—are not only being used, they are being used up or contaminated as corporations compete to produce goods more cheaply. Historically, there have been no prices charged for the use—or misuse—of air and water, and the result has been the pollution of the elements that sustain life. In many cases the most profitable way of disposing of wastes, even very hazardous ones, has been simply to throw them away, using the natural environment as a free dumping ground. Incidents such as the burning of Ohio's Cuyahoga River in 1969, the poisoning of the Love Canal residential area outside Buffalo in the 1970s, and the 1989 *Exxon Valdez* oil spill off the coast of Alaska have dramatized the need for more adequate controls. The creation of the Environmental Protection Agency and the passage of the Clean Air Act and the Water Pollution Control Act in the early 1970s were important steps in this direction.

Discrimination.   Over the last three decades people have come to realize that the unrestricted exercise of individual rights can result in racial and sexual discrimination against both customers and workers. The lunch counter sit-ins that set off the civil rights movement in the early 1960s brought the issue into sharp relief: Should the owners of restaurants and lunch counters have the right to do whatever they please with their property, even if it involves the exclusion of black customers? Or do all people have a right to be treated equally in public places? Since 1964 the U.S. Civil Rights Commission has brought suits against companies, unions, and other institutions to force them to abandon discriminatory practices.

Many of the causes of expanded government economic activity discussed above may be understood as responses to particular aspects of the accumulation process of the capitalist

"ONE NATION . . . WITH . . . JUSTICE FOR ALL"?

The American "pledge of allegiance" expresses one of the highest ideals of modern democracy: one nation . . . with liberty and justice for all. But for most of American history U.S. laws have supported various types of discrimination. During the 19th century the right to vote was restricted in many states to people with substantial amounts of property. Women were denied the right to vote before the passage in 1920 of the 19th Amendment to the U.S. Constitution. Before a 1954 Supreme Court decision, African-American children in the South were assigned to legally segregated and inferior schools. And it was only with the passage of the 1965 Voting Rights Act that African Americans were guaranteed the right to vote.

Thanks to the victories of suffragists, labor unions, and civil rights activists, discrimination against less-well-off people, women, and African Americans is no longer written into the law. But discrimination—particularly racial discrimination—persists in the way the law is practiced. For example, the murder or rape of an African American is punished less harshly than the murder or rape of a person of European descent.

A 2002 study of the eventual sentencing of murderers convicted in 1988 found that a convicted "nonblack" murderer of a black victim was sentenced to seven years less prison time than was a black murderer of a "nonblack" victim. (*Nonblack* is the term the researchers used for all groups other than African Americans). If the victim was black and the murderer was white, the sentence was 3.7 years less than it would have been had the victim been white. If the victim was black and the murderer was also black, the sentence was 5 years less than it would have been had the victim been white. More remarkable still is the fact that in cases of vehicular homicide (in which the victim is generally not selected by the killer), those who kill African Americans get significantly shorter sentences than do those who kill whites, even though in (virtually all of) these cases the race of the victim is determined randomly. Another study found that men who rape black women receive shorter sentences than do men who rape white women.

The pattern is similar with capital punishment sentences. According to a recent study of sentencing in homicide cases in the state of Maryland, an African-American convicted killer whose victim was white was almost three times as likely to get the death sentence as was a white who had killed an African American. But the difference that matters is not so much the race of the defendant as the race of the victim. Looking at death-penalty-eligible cases and taking into account the nature of the crime and the county in which the case was heard, the study found that people of either race who killed whites were much more likely to be sentenced to death. But black defendants were not more likely than were whites to be sentenced to death. Part of the explanation for this is that most white victims are killed by whites. A study of all murders committed in the city of Chicago between 1870 and 1930 found similar differences in the racial patterns of death penalty sentencing.

It is difficult to escape the conclusion that, in *practice,* the life of an African American is valued less than the life of a European American in the legal system of the U.S.

Sources: Randall Kennedy, Race, *Crime and the Law* (New York: Pantheon Books, 1997); Edward Gaeser and Bruce Sacerdote, "Sentencing in Homicide Cases and the Role of Vengeance," *Journal of Legal Studies,* vol. 32, no. 2, June 2003, pp. 363–82. Raymond Paternoster, Robert Brame, Sarah Bacon, and Andrew Ditchfield, "Justice by Geography and Race: The Administration of the Death Penalty in Maryland, 1978–1999," *Margins: Maryland's Law Journal on Race, Religion, Gender and Class,* vol. 4, no. 1, 2004, pp. 1–97. Steven Raphael, "Anatomy of Racial Inequality," *Journal of Economic Literature,* vol. 60, December 2002, pp. 1202–1214.

economy. Thus, the growth of government regulation has been as much a part of capitalist economic development as has the growth of investment or the growth of technology.

But if government has had to grow to address the problems and hardships caused by the development of the economy, it does not follow that such growth has always succeeded in meeting human needs. It is debatable whether people are today more secure economically than they were 100 years ago, or better protected from the arbitrary power of giant corporations, or less susceptible to environmental or natural disaster, or less likely to encounter health hazards in their workplace or in their food. Many of the political battles during the last century have been about the extent to which the government can or should be called on to solve social problems caused by economic forces beyond the control of individuals.

Just as we should not overrate the impact of the government's economic activities, we should not exaggerate their extent. Government employment, including the military, is only 15 percent of the total labor force, and of greater significance is the fact that the most important determinant of the future course of the economy—investment—is still almost entirely in private hands.

GOVERNMENT AND THE PROFIT RATE

As is evident from the preceding discussion, there is much controversy over the appropriate amount of government participation in the economy. To understand this debate more fully, one must understand the effects of government economic activity on the profit rate and how these effects, in turn, give rise to complex patterns of conflict and coalition among different groups in society—business, labor, government, and citizens. We need to begin our discussion, then, with the question of how government taxation affects corporate profits.

After-tax Profits

As complicated as it was, our analysis in Chapter 10 of determinants of the profit rate only briefly discussed the effect of taxes on profits. But businesses are most interested in what is

> The **after-tax profit rate** is the profit rate made by firms after they have paid any required taxes.

left of profits *after* taxes have been paid: it is the *after-tax profit rate* (*atr*) that is of primary concern to a corporation. To simplify the discussion here, we make the assumption that businesses pay taxes to the government at a uniform rate, one that is a certain fraction of their total profits before tax. The after-tax profit rate, then, is a fixed proportion of the before-tax profit rate.

Suppose that the tax rate on corporate profits is 25 percent; in this case the government will receive tax revenues equal to a quarter of corporate profits. Looked at from the point of view of a business, a 25 percent tax rate on corporate profits means that three-quarters of before-tax profits will be left after taxes are paid. The after-tax profit rate (*atr*), then, will be three-quarters of the before-tax profit rate (*r*). If, for example, the before-tax profit rate is 16 percent, the after-tax profit rate will be 12 percent. In general, if *r* is the before-tax profit rate and *tax* is the corporate profits tax rate, the relationship between the after-tax profit rate (*atr*) and the before-tax profit rate (*r*) can be represented algebraically as follows:

$$atr = (1 - tax)r \qquad (19.1)$$

where atr = after-tax profit rate

tax = tax rate on profits

r = before-tax profit rate

The $(1 - tax)$ term in this equation is merely a convenient way of expressing the *fraction* of before-tax profits that businesses will have left after they have paid their taxes. Since 1 percent stands for one one-hundredth, or .01, we can say that a 25 percent tax rate is a 25 hundredths, or a .25, tax rate. Accordingly, we can restate our previous example as follows: if there is a .25 tax rate (*tax*) on corporate profits, the after-tax rate of profit (*atr*) will be $(1 - .25)$, or .75, of the before-tax rate (*r*). Thus, the $(1 - tax)$ term tells us how *atr* will be related to *r*.

The effect of taxes on corporate profits is easily understood: the higher the *tax* is, the lower will be the after-tax rate of profit (*atr*), and vice versa. Matters become considerably more complicated, however, when one brings into the picture all the other ways that government policies affect corporate profits.

At this point we pick up where we left off in Chapter 10, now taking into consideration how government policies may affect each of the profit rate determinants that were discussed there. (The reader may find it helpful at this point to review the analysis presented in Chapter 10, in particular, Equation 10.8 and Table 10.1.)

Government policies may affect the after-tax profits of companies, industries, or even whole economies. They can have such impacts by influencing one or more of the factors that determine after-tax profit rates. The number of ways in which the government might raise or lower profit rates is, of course, unlimited. But to illustrate some of the effects government policies can have, we offer some examples in Table 19.1. We can draw some important conclusions from the examples in this table.

First, there will be conflicts between employers and workers over many of the government's economic activities. While some activities, such as promoting research, may be

TABLE 19.1 Government Policies and the After-Tax Profit Rate

Profit Rate Determinant	How Government Policies Might Raise the Profit Rate
1. Price of output (P_z)	Use military and political power to expand foreign markets for output
2. Work effort per hour of labor (e)	Reduce budgets of agencies responsible for enforcing workplace safety standards
3. Output per unit of work effort (f)	Subsidize job training and investments in new capital goods
4. Materials used and wear and tear on capital goods per labor hour (m)	Support research designed to improve technology
5. Materials and capital goods prices (P_m)	Use military or political power to enable companies to have access to cheaper raw materials; make capital goods cheaper by allowing businesses to write off more of the cost of new equipment at the time it is purchased (depreciation allowances)
6. Hourly wages (w)	Increase unemployment enough to depress wages
7. Price of capital goods (P_c)	Grant tax credits for investment
8. Capital goods in use per hour of labor employed (g)	Repeal regulations requiring waste treatment equipment
9. Capacity utilization rate (u)	Maintain growing and predictable level of demand for goods through macroeconomic management
10. Tax rate on profits (tax)	Reduce corporate income tax rates

in the economic interest of most citizens, many other activities will benefit some groups and harm others. Consider the government policies listed in lines 2 and 6 of the table. These policies make possible a higher profit rate by cutting corners with safety and by causing higher levels of job insecurity, thus permitting employers to reduce wages, speed up work, and obtain other concessions from workers. As we have seen, these are contrary to what workers generally want—higher wages, safer and less stressful working conditions, and more job opportunities.

Second, one can see from looking at the table that some kinds of efforts on the part of government to raise profit rates will work at cross-purposes with others. For example, increasing the rate of unemployment (line 6) is also likely to cause more of the capital goods owned by businesses to be idle, thus lowering the capacity utilization rate (u), contrary to the policy suggested in line 9. Reducing the tax rate (lines 7 and 10) may make it more difficult to pay for the military (lines 1 and 5), research and training (lines 3 and 4), and other activities that favor businesses. Using military power (lines 1 and 5) may drive down the rate of unemployment (contrary to line 6). Thus, even if there were no conflicts with workers, business attempts to shape government policies to raise the profit rate might be contradictory and ineffective.

Third, businesses themselves may have contradictory goals for government. Each firm is not so concerned about the economywide profit rate as it is about its own profit rate. Thus, businesses are often ready to urge the government to adopt policies that will raise their own profit rates even though such policies may push down the profit rates of other businesses. Individual firms lobby the government to reduce their own taxes, to obtain subsidies, and to be allowed to set high prices for their output. Big oil companies benefit enormously from tax credits for foreign royalties paid. The Boeing Corporation has regularly obtained support through government-subsidized cheap credit for the company's foreign customers. Companies in the oil industry were quite happy when the government lifted its controls on oil prices, permitting the price of oil (a raw material input for most other companies) to go up, not down. The oil companies' support of decontrol seemed unaffected by the fact that this policy inflicted big losses on the auto industry, whose high-profit gas guzzlers fell from favor among consumers as gasoline prices rose. Most businesses would be happy to promote government policies that would allow them to pay their own workers less while forcing other firms to pay more. In all these ways, businesses lobby for special benefits that are often in conflict with policies to raise the general profit rate.

Workers, too, have divided interests concerning what the government should do, although often for quite different reasons. Workers in the automobile industry, for example, may want government policies to limit imports of cars produced elsewhere; other workers may want to save money by purchasing a cheaper automobile made in, say, Japan. To take another example, unions that have mainly white male members may be less enthusiastic about government programs designed to secure equal employment opportunities for women and minority workers than may unions with substantial minority and female memberships.

Our understanding of government policy is further complicated by the fact that employers and workers are not the only players in the game. Government leaders have their own objectives and face their own constraints. Most of all, they must find ways of getting reelected or reappointed. Such concerns may necessitate appealing to large numbers of voters, an objective that itself may require a combination of two strategies: adopting policies that are in the interest of a majority of voters, and instituting policies that appeal to individuals who can make substantial financial contributions to election campaigns. Only a combination of these strategies will improve one's chance of being reelected: politicians who faithfully serve the interests of the majority but cannot finance election campaigns are just as surely losers as those who too blatantly favor the few at the expense of the many.

Government leaders, like businesspeople, may thus find that their objectives work at cross-purposes. To gain favor with business, government leaders may want to cut taxes on profits or high incomes. But raising other taxes to maintain sufficient government revenues may incur the wrath of the broader electorate. And with lower taxes all around, it may be impossible for government leaders to offer public services that are considered essential by a majority of voters.

The three-way tug of war among government leaders, citizens (including workers), and business executives is illustrated in the following section focusing on macroeconomic regulation of the unemployment rate.

POCKETBOOK VOTING AND POLITICAL POLARIZATION

Do the two U.S. parties, Democrats and Republicans, represent different economic interests? The well-to-do have always feared that if economic conflicts—between employer and employee, between banker and borrower, between landlord and sharecropper—were to be carried over into the polity, the rich would be outnumbered. In the economy fewer is often better. Being a member of a small group—for example, the only restaurant or car repair outfit in town—is advantageous, as it limits competition. But in politics, numbers count.

The founders of the republic were concerned that in a democracy the haves can be outvoted by the have-nots. However, James Madison, one of the authors of the Constitution, argued (in a famous pamphlet written to persuade the well-off to support the ratification of the Constitution) that economic interests are not likely to determine the main battle lines in politics. Differences of religion, region, and national origin, he suggested, were likely to be more important.

Suitably updated to include matters of race and the family, Madison's assurances have for the most part been proven correct. There have been elections and issues that divided the electorate along lines of income and class, but these have been exceptional.

It is true that for most of the past half century high-income people have tended to be Republicans and lower-income people Democrats. But there have also been large numbers of poor Republicans and rich Democrats. In 1960, for example, people whose income placed them in the richest one-fifth of Americans were only 13 percent more likely to be Republicans than people in the poorest fifth. Income in the southern states was lower than the average for the nation as a whole, but among southerners, rich and poor alike tended to vote Democratic. By contrast, in rural areas outside the South, many lower-income people voted Republican.

But this is changing. Averaging the election results from 1992 to 2000, people in the top fifth of the income distribution were more than twice as likely (that is, 100 percent more likely) to vote for Republicans than were people in the bottom fifth. The difference between the voting patterns of rich and poor in these years, then, was seven times the difference of 13 percent recorded in 1960. Political scientists refer to this as political polarization. How did this come about?

Increasing polarization is partly explained by the fact that over the last half century two lower-income groups, women and African Americans, became more likely to support Democrats while a higher-income group, white men, became more likely to support Republicans. Another reason is that as the South grew richer, it became more Republican.

Some of the changes in voting patterns were unrelated to income. Women became more Democratic because they supported the positions Democrats took

Continued . . .

on abortion rights and affirmative action. Many southerners became Republicans not because their incomes rose, but because they preferred the Republicans' positions concerning race and the family. But polarization is also taking place because people are increasingly voting their pocketbook: income is an increasingly good predictor of party affiliation among people of the same sex, race, and region.

Source: Nolan McCarty, Keith Poole, and Howard Rosenthal, "Political Polarization and Economic Inequality," *Quarterly Journal of Economics,* forthcoming.

The Political Business Cycle

Imagine that the economy is in the midst of a strong expansion. Output is increasing rapidly, businesses find that new orders are rolling in, and companies therefore increase their hiring of workers. Consequently, the rate of unemployment is low.

As the expansion continues, workers realize that they have little to fear should they lose their jobs. With low unemployment, they know that they could probably find other work. In the language presented in Chapter 12, the workers' fallback wage increases. Accordingly, they may begin to ask for raises or improvements in their working conditions, and they may be more likely to resist "speed ups" or other efforts on the part of employers to push them beyond their limits.

Employers begin to worry. While growing demand will raise the capacity utilization rate (u) and thus tend to raise the profit rate (r), a long expansion may be too much of a good thing from their point of view. Why? Because the decline in unemployment that a long expansion brings will empower workers to push for higher wages (w) or allow them to reduce their work effort per hour (e), with the result that the profit rate (r) will be squeezed.

Business leaders then appeal to government leaders to pursue policies—cuts in government spending or increases in the interest rate, for example—that may bring on a recession and increase the rate of unemployment. In public the issue may be presented with reference to the threat of inflation or the danger of the economy "over-heating," and efforts will be made to convince the public that it is time to move along the inflation-unemployment trade-off line toward a higher level of unemployment. But in private the most important concern of business leaders is to discipline their employees, undercutting any effort to raise wages or reduce work effort (see box "One View: 'A Wholesome Recession'" on p. 457).

No capitalist can single-handedly create a recession, but government policies can. Thus, business lobby groups, the business-oriented press, and others with an interest in high profits use their influence to slow the economy down. Of course, no one can openly call for more unemployment, but the policies that might produce it can be billed as "fighting inflation," promoting "fiscal responsibility," or "keeping the money supply under control."

Government leaders may respond to business demands. If they wish to do so, they may choose to implement various policies, any one of which would tend to reduce total demand for output. They might use the tools of fiscal policy, cutting back on government expenditures and thus reducing government demand. Or they might raise personal or business taxes, thereby cutting into people's consumption expenditures or leaving businesses with less to spend and thus reducing the demand for capital goods as well as consumer goods.

The government can also use the tools of monetary policy to restrict credit and increase the cost of capital. These policies will make it more difficult or more costly for businesses to borrow money to finance their investment expenditures, thereby reducing demand for new capital goods. They will also make it more difficult for families to borrow in order to buy cars, houses, or other goods on credit, thus reducing the demand for consumer durable goods and housing.

With total demand down, new orders for goods and services start to dry up, production is cut back, and workers are laid off. Workers begin to hear about friends who were laid off or plants that were closed, and they begin to worry about holding on to their own jobs. The workers' fallback wage declines. Discipline becomes stricter in the workplace. If the contraction is short and is effective in lowering labor costs, businesses may consider the temporarily low capacity utilization ratio (u) and the brief fall in the profit rate (r) a price worth paying in order to regain the upper hand over labor. And when the economy begins expanding again, capacity utilization will rise, and the profit rate will recover.

Thus, the recession may be a success story from the employers' standpoint. But the politician knows there is an election around the corner. Unemployed workers and their families often (correctly) blame political leaders for being at least partly responsible for their distress, and they may vote for the opposition at the first available moment.

> A **political business cycle** occurs when recession and/or expansion are in part intentionally created by governmental economic policy, as officials attempt to generate a business cycle for their own or others' interests.

The result of these complicated interactions and reactions is what has been termed the *political business cycle*. The word *political* is added to the term *business cycle* to reflect the role of additional determinants affecting the usual ups and downs of prices, output, and employment. Taking into account these additional factors means that we can no longer assume that business cycles are determined solely by the millions of relatively uncoordinated spending decisions of investors and consumers. With this new perspective on macroeconomic regulation, the business cycle is seen to be determined, in part at least, by a political process whereby government leaders juggle the sometimes conflicting interests of workers, employers, and themselves.

THE LIMITS OF DEMOCRATIC CONTROL OF THE CAPITALIST ECONOMY

If recessions can be set in motion by public policy, might the economic powers of government be used instead to achieve economic growth that would benefit everyone? Can the citizens of a democratic society control the economy in ways that will promote their own well-being?

In the previous section we saw that because of the conflicting effects of government economic activity on the profit rate, contradictions and inconsistencies are built into the government's economic policy alternatives. In this section we see that the ability of voters, even large majorities of them, to alter the course of economic events is quite limited so long as the economy remains capitalist.

To understand the limits on government, recall that our economy may be thought of as a game in which there are two different sets of rules. One set of rules—the rules of a capitalist economy—confers power and privilege on those who own and control the capital

The **power of capital** refers to the ability of employers, especially the largest corporations, to influence governmental policy or to otherwise create conditions favorable to their own interests; this power grows out of their position as owners of capital goods.

goods used in production, particularly on the owners and managers of the largest corporations. The other set of rules—the rules of democratic government—confers substantial power on the electorate, that is, on the majority of adult citizens. Thus, our social system gives rise to two types of power: the *power of capital* and the *power of the citizenry*.

Those powers are often at loggerheads, as when citizens want to restrict the power of capitalists to sell dangerous or environmentally destructive products. In most such conflicts capitalists have immense and often overwhelming advantages, despite the fact that the owners of businesses (and particularly the owners of large businesses) are greatly outnumbered in the political arena. There are three explanations for their political power—one obvious, the other two not so obvious.

One reason capitalists have a significant amount of political power is that economic resources can often be translated *directly* into political power. Businesses or wealthy individuals can contribute to political campaigns; they can buy advertisements to alter public opinion; they can hire lawyers, expert witnesses, and others to influence the detailed drafting and implementation of legislation; and they can use their economic resources in other ways—engaging in outright bribery, for example—to influence the political system. In all these ways corporate control of economic resources makes it possible for businesspeople to influence government officials and economic policies.

The **power of the citizenry** refers to the ability of citizens to influence governmental policy or to otherwise create conditions favorable to their own interests; this power grows out of their position in democratic government.

A second reason for the disproportionate political power of business leaders is more indirect. The owners of today's media conglomerates control the TV stations, newspapers, publishing houses, and other capital goods used in the media that shape public opinion. Even "public" radio and TV now depend heavily on corporate contributions. The constitutional rights to freedom of speech and of the press (which include TV and radio) guarantee that people can say and journalists can write whatever they please. However, the private ownership of the capital goods used in the TV industry, for example, guarantees that what is broadcast is in the end controlled by corporate leaders, either the owners of the stations or the owners of the major corporations that buy the advertising for the programs. These are people who generally have little interest in promoting citizen power because increases in such power may jeopardize their profits.

A third way in which money brings power has to do with the fact that capitalists control investment and therefore can influence what happens in the economy of any particular area. If businesspeople see an area as having a bad *investment climate,* meaning that they may have difficulty making profits there, they will not invest in that area but will choose instead to invest somewhere else (if they invest at all). If they do not invest in a particular area, the result will be unemployment, economic stagnation, and probably a decline in living standards. This explains why political leaders in particular areas are apt to be easily influenced by the demands of business leaders. If the former do not go along with the wishes of the latter, the population of the area will suffer economic hardships and, placing at least part of the blame for their difficulties on their political leaders, will vote the incumbents out in the next election.

Something like the same process plays a role in the political business cycle. When there has been a long expansion, government leaders are usually willing to go along with the demands of business leaders to bring about a recession that will raise the rate of unemployment. Why is this? It is because in this situation government officials can anticipate that business leaders will blame them for any decline in profit rates that might result from increases in the power of workers. If the profit rate were, in fact, threatened, business leaders would not only withhold their investment, thereby causing economic hardships that would lead people to express their anger in the next election, they would also deny the current political leaders the financial support the latter would need in order to finance a re-election campaign.

When business leaders refuse to invest in a particular area, whether it is a locality, an area such as a state in the U.S., or an entire nation, the area will experience what is referred to as a *capital strike*. When workers strike they refuse to do their part in the economy: they do not work. When capitalists strike they also refuse to do their part: they do not invest. But here the similarity between the strikes of workers and those of capitalists ends. When workers strike they must organize themselves so that they all strike together. A single worker cannot go on strike (that would be called quitting). By contrast, when capital goes on strike, no coordination is needed. As we saw in Chapter 11, each corporation routinely studies the economic and other conditions relevant to its decision to invest. If the executives of the corporation do not like what they see, they will not invest. Nobody organizes a capital strike. Such strikes happen through the independent decisions of corporate leaders. If things look bad to a significant number of corporations, the effect of their combined withholding of investment will be large enough to change the economic conditions of a whole area.

> A **capital strike** occurs when, as a result of a negative business climate, many individual capitalists decide to reduce their investments or not to invest at all.

The potential for a capital strike severely limits what citizen power can accomplish when citizen power conflicts with the power of capital. A hypothetical scenario will make this clear. It is currently the policy in the United States that unemployed workers are entitled to receive unemployment insurance checks for 26 weeks after they lose their jobs. But imagine what would happen if the government of a particular state—let's call it "Anystate, USA"—were to decide to provide longer-lasting unemployment benefits so that workers could continue to receive unemployment insurance checks as long as they are unemployed. And suppose that these payments were financed by heavy taxes on the profits of firms that pollute the environment. If a majority of Anystate's citizens support these policies, the state government will adopt them, paying the additional benefits to unemployed workers and collecting the "pollution taxes" to pay for them.

Now imagine that you are the chief executive officer (CEO) of a large multinational corporation—let's call it "MNC Enterprises, Inc."—that employs large numbers of workers in Anystate. Assume that you are considering investing in Anystate, say, by building a new plant there. Not only will you worry about the potential taxes (applicable to any production process that pollutes the environment), you will also be uncertain, first, about how much power you will have over your employees and, second, about how hard they will work, knowing that they are entitled to receive unemployment insurance checks for a long period if you fire them.

You may even ask yourself what the citizenry will vote for next—and you will certainly think twice before investing in Anystate, not necessarily because you personally do not like the new policies, but because your profit rate, both before and after taxes, would most likely be lower in Anystate than it might be elsewhere. Not only would a low profit rate make it difficult for MNC Enterprises to maintain its competitive position relative to other corporations, it would also have additional consequences. Once it became known that the company's profit rate was falling, the price of the company's stock in the stock market would fall. This, in turn, might cause the stockholders to sell their shares, putting more downward pressure on the price of the stock. It is also possible that the board of directors of the company, in response to its poor "performance," would begin thinking about replacing you with a new CEO. Anticipating all this, you would probably put any new plant somewhere else, perhaps in a state that actively advertises its favorable investment climate.

Quite independently, other businesspeople will, no doubt, come to the same conclusion. Some may even close plants or offices in Anystate and move them elsewhere. The cumulative effect of these independently made decisions will be increasing unemployment and lower incomes for the people of Anystate.

The hard times may bring on a state financial crisis. As unemployment increases, state expenditures on unemployment insurance will rise, as will the costs of other income support programs. As people's incomes fall, the state's tax revenues will also fall, and a deficit will appear in the state's budget. (Most states are required by their state constitutions to balance their budgets.)

But the problems have only just begun. In order to spend more money than taxes are currently bringing in, the state government will be forced to raise taxes further or to borrow money from banks or individuals willing to make loans to the state or buy bonds issued by the state government. Because of the decline in Anystate's economy, the banks cannot be sure that their loans will be paid back promptly or that they will ever be paid back. If they agree to lend money to the state, they will do so only at high interest rates (to cover the risk of lending to the state). Similarly, investors will be willing to buy the state's newly issued bonds only if they are guaranteed high rates of interest. If the loans are granted and the bonds are bought, the state will have more money to finance its current expenditures, but its fundamental problems will only be put off. They will return with greater intensity when the high interest charges have to be paid, adding to the other demands on state revenues. The resulting vicious cycle, now evident in many U.S. states, is called a *state fiscal crisis*.

There are two likely outcomes. First, with repayment increasingly uncertain, the banks may refuse further loans until the state government changes its policy. If the state government is on the verge of bankruptcy—which means breaking contracts with state employees and not paying wages or bills—the bank's policy recommendations may be quite persuasive. Second, the sovereign citizens of Anystate may decide to elect a new government in order to change course. In either case the new policies will be reversed.

Sovereignty refers to the ability and right of a person or group to make a decision; democratic government confers sovereignty on the citizenry, whereas capitalist economy confers sovereignty, especially with respect to investment, on the owners of capital goods.

Our example was for a single state, but, in fact, the process we have outlined could well occur in any state or even in any nation. After all, MNC Enterprises did not have to locate any of its factories in the United States.

Let us go back over our Anystate example. Were the citizens' voting rights or civil liberties violated? No. Did capitalists collude to deliberately undermine citizen power? No, they acted independently and in competition with one another. Did they use campaign contributions or lobbyists to influence government officials or elections? They might have, but they did not need to do so.

Did the citizens exercise control over the economy? That is a much harder question to answer. The capitalist economy certainly imposed limits on what they could do. The citizens could vote for any policy they wanted, but they could not force businesses to invest in Anystate, and that fact severely limited the political options.

Where did they go wrong? The example could have turned out very differently.

One course the citizens of Anystate could have followed would have been to limit their expectations; they could have instructed their government to concentrate only on those programs that would benefit citizens but at the same time *raise*—or at least not lower—the profit rates of companies in the state. In other words, they might have accepted from the outset the fact that they were not "sovereign" in economic matters. This would have allowed them to make the best of a less-than-ideal situation.

Thus, for example, the citizens might have concentrated solely on eliminating the forms of air pollution that push down property values by reducing profits in recreation businesses. They might have designed programs to give economic security to the elderly but not to current workers. They might have tried to increase employment and equality of opportunity by giving all children more business-oriented schooling. And they might have voted to finance these programs by taxes that did not affect profits. If they had adopted any or all of these policies, many Anystate citizens would have benefited, and those who were adversely affected might not have been in a position to block the adoption of them. Specifically, capitalists might have looked favorably or at least indifferently at such policies and might not have brought about economic decline in the state by withholding or withdrawing their investments.

Again, our Anystate example is hypothetical, but it is, in fact, similar to a process that actually occurred in Wisconsin early in the 20th century. Wisconsin was a leader in trying out programs to make the most of citizen power while operating within the limits of a capitalist economy. Moreover, the federal government and a number of state and local governments now engage in many beneficial economic activities that also fit this description. Providing for social needs within the general framework of a capitalist economy has been the aim of European nations such as Sweden and Austria, where *social democratic* governments were in power during much of the last century. As beneficial as these programs have been, however, they are severely limited by the fact that many of the ways to improve living standards and the quality of life sooner or later also threaten the rate of profit.

There is yet another course that Anystate citizens could have followed, which, if not likely, is at least conceivable. When MNC Enterprises (or other companies) decided to close down their operations in Anystate, the plants could have been bought by their local communities, by their workers, or by the state government itself. When a business leaves a community, what it takes with it, usually, is just its money. The plant, equipment, and machinery—not to mention the workers—are left behind. If a way could be found to purchase the firm and sell its output, there is no reason why the workers who held jobs in the MNC Enterprises plant could not continue working there. They could do this by forming a community-owned enterprise, a worker-owned firm, or some other type of democratic organization.

We may conclude from our Anystate example that citizen power is severely limited in its ability to alter fundamental economic policies. These limits can be overcome only if citizens commit themselves to altering the rules of a capitalist economy. As argued in this chapter, the rules of a capitalist economy are not the same as those of democratic government.

SUGGESTED READINGS

Daniel Altman, *Neoconomy* (New York: Perseus Books, 2004).

Samuel Bowles and Herbert Gintis, *Democracy and Capitalism: Property, Community, and the Contradictions of Modern Social Thought* (New York: Basic Books, 1987).

Godfrey Hodgson, *More Equal Than Others: America from Nixon to the New Century* (Princeton: Princeton University Press, 2004).

Peter Lindert, *Growing Public: Social Spending and Economic Growth Since the 18th Century* (Cambridge: Cambridge University Press, 2004).

John Pencavel, *Worker Participation: Lessons from the Worker Co-ops of the Pacific Northwest* (New York: Russell Sage Foundation, 2002).

Adam Przeworski, *The State and the Economy under Capitalism* (New York: Harwood, 1990).

Adam Przeworski, Michael E. Alvarez, Jose Antonio Cheibub, and Fernando Limongi, *Democracy and Development: Political Institutions and Well-being in the World, 1950–1990* (Cambridge: Cambridge University Press, 2000).

PART 4

Conclusion

CHAPTER 20

The Future of Capitalism

We began our first chapter with the collapse of Communism and the tearing down of the Berlin Wall that divided Communist East Germany from West Germany, a historical surprise that few had expected. One of the few scholars who *had* anticipated the collapse of the Communist regimes was the Harvard sociologist Talcott Parsons. Three decades earlier, when Communist rule of the Soviet Union and its allies looked about as permanent as things get in history, he advanced a view that some types of institutions are built to last and others are likely to have a short life. Unsurprisingly, in view of his conservative political leanings, Parsons placed capitalism in the first category and Communism in the second.

Parsons called the institutions in his "built to last" category *evolutionary universals,* by which he meant ways of organizing society that had independently sprung up in many different environments and that, once born, had persisted over long periods and been diffused to other places (see box "Evolutionary Universals or Social Revolution?"). In Parson's view evolutionary universals are to society what such things as eyes are in the organic world—good things that have emerged independently many times and that have given the species possessing them advantages over other species. Parsons included religion, systems of kinship, money, markets, and democracy among the evolutionary universals. He noted that the economic and military successes of the Communist-ruled nations seemed to constitute an exception to his theory (the important role the Soviet Union had played in the defeat of Germany during World War II was still well remembered), but with regard to communism as a political system he predicted its eventual demise: "I do indeed predict that it will prove to be unstable and will either make adjustment . . . in the general direction of democracy or 'regress.'"

Will capitalism, as an economic system, also change? Is capitalism based on evolutionary universals in such a way that it, unlike communism, will last? We saw in Chapter 1,

"Capitalism Shakes the World," that capitalism itself has been the great lever of change in the history of the last 500 years. And we subtitled our book "Competition, Command, and Change" to emphasize the fact that at least since the beginning of capitalism, change has been the rule and lack of change the exception. Is capitalism itself, then, an exception to the rule? Or will it change in ways so fundamental that it will require a new name? Will it be replaced by some other economic system, as yet unknown? Will it be the end of history or the end of capitalism? Parsons had a clear answer to the question regarding the longevity of capitalism. His view was that capitalism, at least when coupled with democracy, will last. Its basic institutions are all among what he termed the evolutionary universals. In the early 1960s, when Parsons was advancing these views, his theory was an easy target for criticism. The evolutionary universals looked suspiciously like the things Parsons admired around him in Harvard Square. Wags dubbed it the "trolley car theory of history," since it appeared to be saying, "you know exactly where it is going; the only question is when will it get there." As soon as the world becomes like America, in this view, history will come to an end.

But Parsons did have a point. It *is* astonishing that many societies have come up with institutions such as money, markets, and private property, while very few have given up these institutions once they have caught on. The same goes for the almost universal practice of sharing food with people outside one's own family, whether it takes the form of prey being divided up after a hunt (see Chapter 2), lavish ceremonies and feasts given by tribal chiefs or high-status "big men," or, in the U.S. today, food stamps provided by the government for those in need. And democracy—universal suffrage, competitive elections, and individual liberties (see Chapters 3)—has expanded from its embryonic form in a few nations a century ago to a fully developed form of government in perhaps two-fifths of the world's 200 nations today. (We say "perhaps" because any count like this depends very much on exactly how one determines which countries are democratic and which ones are not.)

Parsons thought that history would end with capitalism and democracy. In contrast, Marx believed that since capitalism is inherently a system that brings about change, history will not end with capitalism. Indeed, capitalism is a system that, in his words, is headed for the "dustbin of history." He confidently predicted that, just like the other social and economic systems it had displaced, capitalism, too, will be displaced.

In Marx's materialist conception of history (see Chapter 4), improvements in knowledge, science, and technology (what he called the "productive forces" of the economy) propel society through a progression of different institutional configurations that he identified as the Asiatic, ancient (slave), feudal, and capitalist "modes of production," each with its own distinct set of class relations.

For example, when Europeans and Africans first came to the New World, from the 16th to the 18th centuries, cotton and sugar were grown by slaves on plantations rather than by wage laborers working for capitalist farmers. According to Marx's view, the slave mode of production prevailed not because the plantation owners had not yet figured out how to be capitalists (they had), but because, given existing technology, slavery was a profitable way of organizing agricultural production and thus could sustain a class system dominated by slaveholders. For the production of textiles and other manufactured goods, however, a system based on wage labor was more profitable.

With the development of machine technology in the 19th century, factory production in the northern states of the U.S. expanded more rapidly than did the production of raw

A CONQUISTADOR DISCOVERS
EVOLUTIONARY UNIVERSALS

H ernán Cortés's long letters to King Charles of Castile described the exotic and unusual customs he and his armed band encountered as they advanced toward Temixtitan in 1519. But in light of the 13 millennia that had passed since there could have been any sustained contact between the Old World and the New, what is striking about his account of Mexico is how familiar it all was. Upon reaching Temixtitan he wrote:

The city has many squares where trading is done and markets are held continuously. There is one square twice as big as that of Salamanca with arcades all around, where more than sixty thousand people come each day to buy and sell, and every kind of merchandise . . . is found. . . . It seems like the silk market at Granada, except that there is a much greater quantity. . . . Everything is sold by number and size . . . [and] there is in this great square a very large building like a courthouse where ten or twelve persons sit as judges. . . . There are in this square other persons who walk among the people to see what they are selling and the measures they are using; and they have been seen to break some that are false.

Likewise, the Aztec class structure presented no surprises for Cortés:

There are many chiefs, all of whom reside in this city, and the country towns contain peasants who are vassals of these lords and each of whom holds his land independently; some have more than others. . . And there are many poor people who beg from the rich in the streets as the poor do in Spain and in other civilized places.

The explorer went on with, among other things, a description of the "many temples or houses for their idols" and a comment saying that "the orderly manner in which, until now, these people have been governed is almost like that of the states of Venice or Genoa or Pisa."

Source: Hernán Cortés, *Letters from Mexico* (New Haven, Conn.: Yale University Press, 1986), as presented in Samuel Bowles, *Microeconomics: Behavior, Institutions and Evolution* (Princeton: Princeton University Press, 2004).

cotton and sugar under slavery in the South. Hence, the slave mode of production was eclipsed by the capitalist mode. In the U.S. this took place at first economically, with the growing prosperity of the northern states, and then militarily, with the defeat of the South in the Civil War.

Marx's idea is thus very different from that of Parsons. According to Marx, institutions emerge and persist as long as they are consistent with the current level of technology and class relations. Thus, during the early years of human history, capitalism was not just a better mousetrap waiting to be invented. Rather, it could not emerge until the development of technology had rendered earlier forms of society obsolete. This happened only with the

EVOLUTIONARY UNIVERSALS OR SOCIAL REVOLUTION?

[An] *evolutionary universal* [is] *any organizational development sufficiently important to further evolution that rather than emerging only once it is likely to be "hit upon" by various systems operating under different conditions.*

—Talcott Parsons, "Evolutionary Universals" (1964)

At a certain stage of their development, the material productive forces of society [its technologies] *come in conflict with . . . the property relations within which they have been at work before. From forms of development of the productive forces these relations turn into their fetters. Then begins an epoch of social revolution.*

—Karl Marx, "Preface" to *Critique of Political Economy* (1859)

development of modern science and factory production. Marx saw that capitalism had become the predominant mode of production in his time and place, but he believed that, with further developments in science and technology, capitalism would eventually be superseded by another economic system, just as slavery in America and feudalism in Europe had been undermined by the rise of factory production.

Although Marx and Parsons had very different perspectives, there is a "trolley car" aspect to Marx's theory, too. For Marx (unlike Parsons), the last stop is not capitalism. Rather, it is communism with a small "c"—a classless and participatory system very different from the one that existed in Russia (the Soviet Union) for most of the 20th century. Marx, as a democrat, would have detested Soviet-style Communism.

Many of Marx's predictions about capitalism proved to be remarkably accurate, but his prophecy that communism would replace capitalism missed the mark. He greatly underestimated the ability of capitalism to adapt, to change in response to new circumstances, and especially to address some of the most serious threats to its continuation. Among these was the remarkable ability of those capitalist countries that also became democratic to redress some of the inequalities between capitalists and workers with unemployment insurance, social security, public education, and other such policies. Another way in which capitalism has demonstrated its capacity for adaptation has been its ability to counteract the financial and other economic crises that Marx saw as the most likely causes of capitalism's demise.

As we come now to the last chapter of our book, what better way to end than to consider once again the long-term economic trends discussed in Chapter 1. Have they disappeared under capitalism? Or will such trends—and new forces as well—bring about fundamental modifications in the system or perhaps even usher in a new set of institutions? If something new is emerging, will the new institutions embody Parson's evolutionary universals? Or will the ideas of both Parsons and Marx be proven wrong? Any answer to such questions is bound to be speculative, but if our three-dimensional economics is to be of value, it should be able to illuminate some of the main possibilities that lie ahead.

The main idea of this chapter is that *changes in science and technology are likely either to bring about fundamental changes in the institutions of capitalism—extending its lifespan—or to lead to the emergence of a qualitatively different economic system.* This main idea is expressed in three key points:

1. Over the coming decades changes in technology, especially the information revolution, and the accelerating impact of humans on our natural environment, especially global warming, will confront us with challenges utterly without precedent in human history.

2. In response to these challenges, new institutions may emerge that will organize our economy in new ways and enable us to harness modern technology and improve human well-being.

3. Any new institutions may include some variants of Parsons's evolutionary universals, but, at the same time, they could well exhibit truly novel features.

The two challenges to existing economic institutions that we focus on in this chapter are, first, limits to the continuing expansion of capitalism such as global warming and other environmental effects of rapid economic growth and, second, the information revolution. In our view these two challenges, themselves the products of the development of capitalism as well as threats to the way it works presently, epitomize the kinds of issues human society faces today. Other possible developments—for example, the emergence of deadly viruses resistant to modern medicine and the proliferation of nuclear weapons—may pose challenges no less severe.

THE LIMITS TO GROWTH

The early 19th-century political economist David Ricardo, who, along with Adam Smith, was a founder of the classical school of political economy, thought that England's growth would be limited by its shortage of land. He believed that because the country was running out of land, its economic growth would grind to a halt. Ricardo's theory was that as the population grew, good land would become more and more scarce, and as a result the price of food would rise faster than the price of manufactured goods. To maintain a given nutritional level for workers, wages would have to rise, and this would squeeze the profits of manufacturers. This, in turn, would bring about a decline in investment and would thus choke off the growth process. Ricardo published his ideas in 1817. Two generations later William Jevons, a founder of the neoclassical school of economics, thought that England was running out of coal, and he also made dire predictions.

Both Ricardo and Jevons were proven wrong. Technical change in agriculture (see Figure 1.1) proceeded at such a rapid pace that, despite a seven-fold increase in the world's population since Ricardo's day (see Figure 1.6), the price of food did not rise faster than the prices of manufactured goods. Coal did become scarcer, but new sources of energy—petroleum and nuclear power—were harnessed to take its place. Temporary increases in the price of energy have occasionally depressed investment and growth, as they did in the 1970s, when the cartel of the oil producing countries (OPEC) raised the price of oil dramatically. However, in the periods directly following the dire predictions of Ricardo and Jevons, economic growth in the capitalist countries of the world did not slow down. On the contrary, economic growth accelerated. In the second half of the 20th century as well, the growth rates of the major capitalist economies were very robust (see Figure 1.3).

Does environmental pollution constitute a new kind of limit to growth today? Are those who warn of the consequences of global warming, of the reduction in biodiversity, and of other adverse impacts of humans on the natural environment just the most recent in a long line of doom freaks? Will they, too, be proven wrong by the march of technical change? In our view this will not happen unless technology gets a big push in the right direction.

Look again at Figure 1.8, which shows how our increasing use of fossil fuels such as coal and petroleum products has brought about dramatic climate change, and notice two things. First, far warmer temperatures have been recorded in recent decades than any that have occurred in the last 1,000 years or even, some think, in the time that humans have inhabited the earth. Even if the upward trend in temperature were miraculously to be checked, the likely consequences would still cause concern. The potential consequences include increased climatic variability with frequent disturbances in weather patterns; the destruction of rich agricultural areas; and the elimination, by rising sea levels, of coastal population centers. Nobody knows how severe such consequences of global warming might be. All we know is that humans have not experienced anything like such developments in at least 1,000 years and probably not since the beginning of human social life on earth.

Also, look at the insert in the lower half of Figure 1.8, which shows that most of the increase in CO_2 emissions, thought to be the primary cause of global warming, has occurred in the last 50 years or so. It is also the case that, as Figure 1.9 shows, the most rapid increases in such emissions have occurred in the richest regions of the world, especially North America, where most of the CO_2 emissions come from the United States. But since China and India, the world's two most populous nations, are experiencing rapid economic growth, the global rate of CO_2 and other "greenhouse gas" emissions will certainly increase further unless rich countries reduce their emissions and persuade (and aid) the poorer countries to adopt "cleaner" forms of production and transportation.

What would ecological preservation require? Could environmental impacts be reduced without diminishing the well-being of current generations in the rich countries? There are three ways in which environmental impacts might be reduced.

First, we could shift our consumption from goods produced in ways that adversely affect the environment—many agricultural and manufactured goods, second homes, air conditioning, and private automobile use, for example—to goods and services produced in ways less harmful to the environment—cultural goods, education, mass transportation, and many other types of services. The long-term shift away from agriculture and manufacturing to services that is now occurring in all the rich economies is positive in this respect.

Second, the technologies used to produce the goods and services we do consume might be made more environment-friendly. Improving the gas mileage of cars, SUVs, and trucks and adopting more energy-efficient appliances could certainly make a difference, as could shifts away from technologies that require CO_2-emitting sources of energy, such as coal, oil, and gas, toward technologies that can be powered by wind, solar, or hydroelectric energy.

Third, we could rethink what it means to have a good life, perhaps reducing our work hours, increasing our free time, and slowing, if not reversing, the ever-growing role of consumption in our lifestyles. In some countries this is already happening.

In 1960 German factory workers put in, on average, more than 2,100 hours of work per year, but 40 years later they worked less than two-thirds that number of hours. Norwegian and Dutch workers put in even fewer hours, averaging less than 27 work hours per week. This is the equivalent of a three-and-a-half-day workweek at eight hours a day. People in these countries actually work 35 or more hours most weeks but then take long vacations. In this respect Americans are the exception, working longer hours than workers do in any of the other rich countries. Moreover, U.S. workers in 2000 actually worked more hours than they did 20 years earlier.

Policies can readily be devised that would shift our consumption toward more environmentally benign goods and services, encourage the development of more environment-friendly technologies, and provide incentives to induce people to consume fewer goods and enjoy more free time. All such policies have the effect of making environmentally destructive activities more expensive or less attractive than environment-friendly ones. Policies designed to achieve this goal may include government prohibition—or direct regulation—of the use of environmentally polluting substances, such as gasoline containing lead. These types of policies are already in effect in many countries.

Alternatively, a government may reduce pollution of the environment by selling emissions permits and subsequently allowing them to be traded among current and prospective emitters (say, electric utilities), with the price of the permits then being determined by supply and demand. By making it either illegal or expensive to abuse the environment, such policies promote the three objectives listed above. In the long run they hasten the development of new resource-saving technologies and environment-friendly lifestyles. Putting a price on the use of the environment should work in exactly the same way that wage increases in the early period of capitalist growth provided a powerful impetus for the development of labor-saving technologies.

Both types of policies, direct regulation and the use of market-based incentives, can work under the right circumstances. Direct regulation is simpler to implement and is more likely to enable people to participate democratically in environmental policy decisions that affect their lives. The market-based approach, on the other hand, allows both producers and consumers (if they have the necessary information) to find the most cost-effective way to reduce emissions.

The obstacles to implementing policies that might halt the deterioration of the environment are not primarily economic or technical. Rather, they are political. In the U.S., at least, consumers and, even more so, businesses are unwilling to pay the extra costs resulting from the fact that our natural environment is scarce and endangered. Witness the fierce resistance put up by U.S. automobile companies against attempts by environmental activists and the U.S. Environmental Protection Agency (under some administrations) to improve the fuel efficiency of automotive products. Because of their different political values, some countries in Europe have made more progress than has the U.S. in this respect. (Recall the insert in Figure 1.9 showing that CO_2 emissions have leveled off in Europe during the past two decades.)

We have already noted one of the reasons why the U.S. has lagged behind Europe in protecting the environment: Europeans are choosing to consume fewer goods and enjoy more free time than Americans. But *why* do Europeans work less and consume less than Americans? One explanation is that "keeping up with the Joneses"—emulating the consumption standards of more affluent people—is more difficult to do in the U.S. than in most European countries. This is the case because high-income Americans have much more income compared with the average family than do high-income Europeans. As Figure 20.1 shows, the countries most unequal in the distribution of their income are also the ones with the longest work hours.

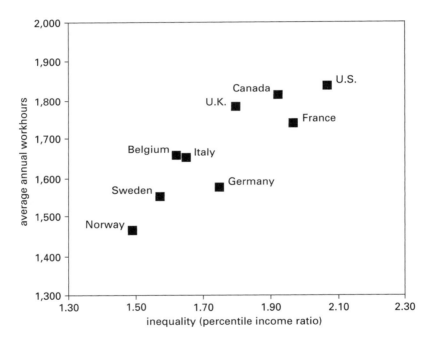

FIGURE 20.1   Inequality and work hours, 1963–1998.   This figure shows that among a number of European and North American countries, there is a positive relationship between the degree of inequality and the number of hours worked per year. Each square point represents the relationship between the average annual work hours for the country indicated (measured on the vertical axis) and the same country's degree of income inequality (measured statistically on the horizontal axis). The inequality measure is the ratio of the income of a person at the 90th percentile of the income distribution (only 9 percent of the population are richer) to the income of a person at the 50th percentile.

Source: Organisation for Economic Co-operation and Development (OECD) labor market statistics presented in Samuel Bowles and Yong-Jin Park, "Emulation, Inequality, and Work Hours: Was Veblen Right?" (Santa Fe Institute Working Paper 2001, #01-10-061), available at www.santafe.edu/~bowles.

Global warming and other forms of environmental degradation are examples of the "prisoner's dilemma" and "tragedy of the commons" types of situations described in Chapter 9, in which all parties would be better off if they cooperated but the individual interest of each is to not cooperate. Many environmental problems, such as global warming, are especially difficult because they are global. When the members of a single nation face a prisoner's dilemma, they often agree to pass a law (and to abide by it) making cooperation mandatory. Tax laws are one example, and laws protecting property rights another. But when the people interacting in a prisoner's dilemma type of situation are citizens of different countries—say, 200 different countries—the problem is much more difficult to solve. There is no world government able to impose environmental regulations on industrial enterprises throughout the world that are emitting greenhouse gases. The only other alternative, treaties among the nations to accomplish the same objective, has proven to be very ineffective when it comes to enforcing even the environmental regulations that already exist under international law.

For the reasons set forth above, the history of efforts to improve fuel efficiency and to limit overconsumption suggests that policies to adequately address global warming and other environmental challenges are not likely to be adopted as long as the distribution of income remains highly unequal and the distribution of political influence continues to be tilted toward business. Inequality among nations also contributes to the difficulty of finding solutions to environmental problems. The fact that some rich, high-emission countries (especially the U.S., which has refused to sign the Kyoto accord) have been unwilling to cut back their emission rates does not bode well for international agreement on effective global policies. The poor people of the world today are unlikely to settle for any arrangement by which their very low living standards would be held down by capping their industrial development to preserve the environment while the richest one-fifth of the world's population in North America, Japan, and Europe continues to enjoy their more affluent lifestyles.

FROM GRAIN AND STEEL TO INFORMATION AND IDEAS

The previous section on the limits to growth was about constraints. What follows is all about opportunities. Recent advances in our ability to create, store, and distribute information have changed the nature of work, consumption, and leisure. As Figure 20.2 shows, technical change has dramatically reduced the cost of storing and transferring information electronically. It is now much easier—and cheaper—to hold and transmit information than in any previous era of human history. And as the insert in Figure 20.2 shows, the last decade of the 20th century was when the internet suddenly enabled businesses and individuals to communicate with one another more rapidly, with the result that the number of messages traveling back and forth on the Web grew exponentially.

Of course, technical change does not just happen; it occurs as businesses invest part of their profit in new forms of capital goods, including computer hardware and software. In the last few decades, the "information revolution" has changed both the ways that businesses function and the ways in which businesses and consumers interact. The opportunities for cost reduction and the attendant competition for profits has called forth increasing amounts

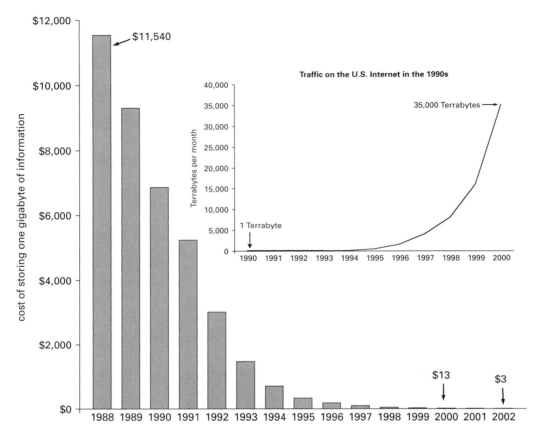

FIGURE 20.2 Information is cheaper to store, easier to access. With recent technical and infrastructural improvements relating to information technology, it is much easier to store and transmit information among individuals and businesses now than it has been previously in human history. For example, the cost of digitally storing one gigabyte of data (the equivalent of 30 feet of shelved books) fell from more than $11,000 in 1988 to approximately $3 in 2002. Also, the growth of the internet has made possible a dramatic increase in the amount of data that can be transferred in any given period of time. As shown in the inserted figure, approximately 1 terabyte (or 1,012 gigabytes) of data was transmitted through the U.S. internet in an average month in 1992. This is the equivalent of about half the printed material in a medium-sized academic research library. By 2000 the amount of data being transmitted monthly on the U.S. internet was about 35,000 terabytes, roughly 3,500 times the amount of information in all the printed documents in the Library of Congress.

Sources: P. Lyman, H. R. Varian, J. Dunn, A. Strygin, and K. Swearingen, "How Much Information?" (School of Information Management and Systems, University of California, Berkeley, 2000), available at: http://www.sims.berkeley.edu/how-much-info/summary.html; K. G. Coffman and A. M. Odlyzko, "Internet Growth: Is There a 'Moore's Law' for Data Traffic?" (AT&T Labs, Research Paper, 2001), available at: www.research.att.com/areas/transport_evolution/internet.moore.pdf.

of investment in information technology (IT). As Figure 20.3 shows, the percentage of private business investment going into information processing equipment and software grew steadily in the second half of the 20th century, surpassing in the early 1980s the portion being invested in goods-producing equipment.

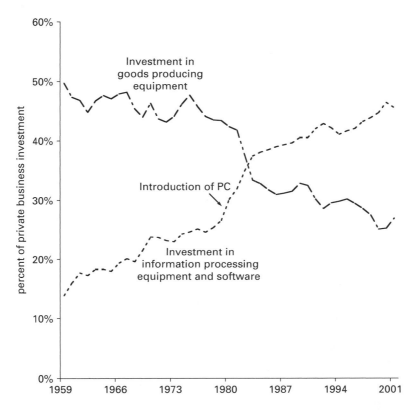

FIGURE 20.3   Information technology vs. goods–producing investment in the U.S., 1959 to 2001.   This figure charts the rate at which investment in information processing equipment and software has caught up with and surpassed investment in goods-producing equipment. Changes in the way business is done have made it imperative for companies to allocate more and more of their investment to information technology to keep pace with rapidly changing communications, computing, and accounting hardware and software. As shown in the figure, investment of this type amounted to only 13 percent of business investment expenditure in 1959; by 2001, however, it had risen to 45 percent. Moving in the opposite direction, the share of business investment allocated to goods-producing equipment (industrial and agricultural machinery, for example) fell from 50 percent in 1959 to 27 percent in 2001.

Source: U.S. Department of Commerce, Bureau of Economic Analysis, National Economic Accounts, Fixed Assets, Survey Tables, Table 3, "Current-Cost Net Stock of Private Fixed Assets, Equipment and Software, and Structures by Type" (Washington, D.C.: U.S. Department of Commerce, 2004), available at: http://www.bea.doc.gov/bea/dn1.htm.

As opportunities for cost savings stimulated businesses to invest more of their profits in IT, the predictable result was a substantial growth in the size of the IT sector itself, especially in the United States. IT-producing industries are involved in the production of the computer and communications hardware, software, and services that support electronic commerce (e-commerce), the latter term referring to business transactions on the Web or

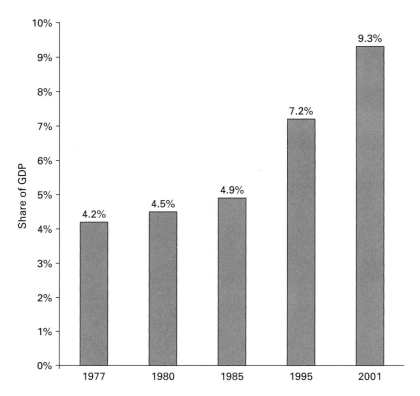

FIGURE 20.4   The growth of the information sector of the U.S. economy, 1977 to 2001.   This figure shows how the output of the information technology sector has grown as a share of total output (GDP) in the U.S. As noted in the text, the IT sector consists of the firms that produce the computer and communications hardware, software, and services that support business transactions on the Web (e-commerce). As shown in the figure, this sector grew from 4.2 percent of the economy in 1977 to 9.3 percent of it in 2001, with its rate of growth accelerating in the 1990s. Since these percentages are *shares* of the economy, they show that the IT sector has grown considerably faster than the economy as a whole.

Sources: U.S. Department of Commerce, *The Emerging Digital Economy,* Appendix 1, "Information Technology Industries—Of Growing Importance to the Economy and Jobs" (Washington, D.C.: U.S. Department of Commerce, 1998) available at http://www.technology.gov/digeconomy/emerging.htm; U.S. Bureau of the Census, *Statistical Abstract of the United States 2002* (Washington, D.C.: U.S. Government Printing Office, 2003) available at http://www.census.gov/prod/www/statistical-abstract-02.html.

Internet. As Figure 20.4 shows, the growth of the IT sector of the U.S. economy accelerated in the last few years of the 20th century, growing faster than the economy as a whole.

To put the growth of the U.S. information sector in an international perspective, we can think of investment in IT as bound up with the acquisition of new knowledge. Without the acquisition of new knowledge there could not have been an information revolution. Thus, we can consider the discovery of cheaper ways to store and transmit information

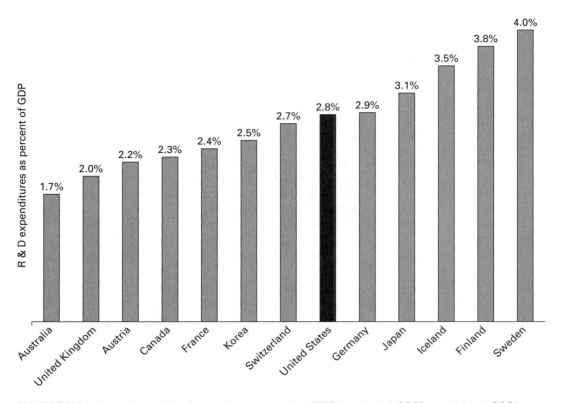

FIGURE 20.5   Research and development as a percent of GDP in selected OECD countries in 2001.
Research and Development (R & D) is an important part of the process of production, especially in a high-technology economy, since it provides the knowledge and technologies that can lead to advances in productivity—and hence profit-making—in the future. The United States spends more than any other country in the world on R & D. As this figure shows, however, U.S. expenditure on R & D is about in the middle of the spectrum when calculated as a percentage of GDP. In 2001, the U.S. allocated about 2.8 percent of its GDP to R & D, an amount corresponding roughly to its average over the last 40 years. By contrast, Japan spent more than 3 percent and Sweden spent 4 percent of GDP on investment in R & D.

Source: Organisation for Economic Co-operation and Development, Main Science and Technology Indicators, November 2002, OECD 9400003P, ISSN 1011-792X (Paris: Organisation for Economic Co-operation and Development, 2002).

(see Figure 20.2) as resulting from the more general business practice of "research and development" (R & D). Figure 20.5 shows the fraction of the total output (GDP) devoted to R & D in the countries belonging to the Organization for Economic Co-operation and Development (OECD).

Even before the information revolution, powerful trends were modifying the structure of economies in ways later accelerated by the development of computer technology. The most important of these trends in the rich countries has been the shift from an economy that mostly produced *goods*—things one could weigh, measure, or hold in one's hand—to one in which two-thirds of the labor in the economy (as conventionally defined, that is, excluding household labor) is engaged in producing *services*—teaching, waiting on tables, caring for the old, selling goods, caring for the sick and the young, providing security, guarding prisoners, designing computers, writing software, processing welfare cases, serving in the armed forces, and so on.

For the fifth of the world's population living in the rich countries, the 21st-century economy bears little resemblance to the economy of even a century ago. No longer an economy of grain and steel, of smokestacks and harvesters, today's economy is one of keyboards and classrooms, of retirement homes and checkout terminals. In the U.S., teachers and other educators outnumber all the people employed in manufacturing. Fewer than one in five Americans now work in agriculture, mining, and manufacturing combined. Today, more Americans sell cars than make them. In fact, there are more people employed in selling goods of every kind in the U.S. than in producing them. We exchange messages far more frequently than we exchange any of the usual goods that one can weigh and measure. In this regard the U.S. is similar to other rich countries. In an apt characterization, the Malaysian economist Danny Quah refers to the typical developed country today as having a "weightless economy."[1]

The economies of rich countries are becoming "weightless" for three reasons. One is that an increasing fraction of the world's output of material goods, such as steel, cars, and clothing, is now produced in poor countries and then shipped to rich countries. A second reason has to do the almost miraculous increase in output of material goods that has come with capitalism, but there is a limit to our capacity to derive pleasure from consuming more and more material things—more clothing, more cars, more food. Thus, as people become richer they seek out pleasures that are derived more from services than from goods.

A third reason for the growing weightlessness of advanced capitalist economies derives simply from the way economic activities are measured and presented in government statistics. In the past many of the activities that make up the weightless economy—caring for the old and the sick, preparing and serving food, educating the young, advising the troubled—were performed within the family (outside the market) and hence were not statistically counted as being part of the economy. As pointed out in Chapter 5 in our discussion of the reproduction sector, these activities are indispensable to the functioning of the economy. However, they are hard to measure and were thus left out of the national income accounts. But now more and more of these tasks are performed outside the family and are being paid for. This not only has made them easier to measure but also has led to their being counted as part of the economy's service sector, thus increasing the measured ratio of services to goods in the national income accounts.

Not only are the outputs of the new economy becoming more weightless, the inputs are increasingly weightless as well. Recall the grain model that we used to illustrate the concept of a technology in Chapter 5: the inputs were labor, materials, capital goods, and inputs from nature. Labor effort (e) and the contribution of inputs from nature are hard to measure, even when they can be directly observed, as in the growing of a crop. But the

---

[1] Danny Quah, "The Weightless Economy in Economic Development" (Discussion paper no. 0417, Centre for Economic Performance, London School of Economics, March 1999). Available at http://cep.lse.ac.uk/pubs/ or at http://ideas.repec.org/p/cep/cepdps/0417.html.

other inputs, materials and capital goods, are readily measured and hence are not difficult to contract for when buying or selling them. Now consider a typical technology of the modern economy: the relationship between the effort exerted by a software designer and the new application that results from her effort. In her productive effort she is using a lot of other software, information she picked up from other engineers, her training as a computer science major, and an idea she had while working out the previous weekend. The cost of physical inputs she is using—8 square feet of desk space, a 10-by-15-foot cubicle, some electricity, and a computer—is a tiny fraction of the income she will generate for her firm (if she is successful). Most of the inputs in the production process here are information and ideas.

For Adam Smith, David Ricardo, and the other classical political economists of the 18th and early 19th centuries, the "economic trinity" was Land, Labor, and Capital. Today we might better speak of Brains, Information, and Reputation.

THE NEW ECONOMY

Two novel aspects of the weightless economy make it different from the old economy of grain and steel. In the old economy (which continues in many industries), because grain, steel, shirts, and the like can be weighed and measured, contracts providing the legal basis for their exchange are easy to write. If you are a baker and you purchase a hundred bushels of Winter Red #2 wheat, you know what to expect, and if the seller fails to deliver, you have no difficulty establishing your claim to the wheat in court. Grain does not come in this form from nature. Rather, it has been consciously made into a standardized commodity by human beings (see box "Was Winter Red #2 a Gift of Nature?").

The software engineer referred to above is in a different situation. If either the information she obtains from other engineers or her own computer science training fails her, there is nobody she can sue. Moreover, when she (or her company) tries to sell the new application she has produced, its success in the market will depend primarily on the reputation of the firm and on how much advertising it does. Its success will not depend on customers' experience with the product, for the software application is entirely new, and the potential users therefore have no experience on which to base a guess as to how good it will be.

The second novel feature of the new economy is that, at least potentially, it is less competitive than the old economy. Competition prevailed in most industries in the old economy. By the last third of the 20th century, this was true even in the steel industry, in which the small number of U.S. steel companies had to compete with dozens of producers in other countries. Competition was never the "perfect" kind often described in economics textbooks. Firms did have some control over their prices and could use it to their advantage. Leaders in the steel and other industries sought tariff protection and tried to limit price-cutting by one or another form of collusion (see Chapter 11). But no firm could afford to ignore actual or potential competitors.

Competition among firms existed because in most industries the cost advantages that could be achieved by very large-scale producers relative to smaller ones were limited or nonexistent. That is, economies of scale were available in most industries, even to firms that were quite small relative to the size of their markets, and these economies of scale usually

WAS WINTER RED #2 A GIFT OF NATURE?

Whether a good's quality can be readily determined and contractually specified is in many respects an option, not a given: its measurability depends on specific human actions. For example, placing a Chiquita sticker on a banana has the effect of establishing for a buyer or a seller of it that the banana is likely to be of a certain quality. Similarly, the labeling of such items as Sugar Number 11, Corn Number 2 Yellow, or Light LA Sweet (oil) does not mean that they are pristine gifts of nature. Rather, it means that they were created with the help of a process of standardization, one intended to eliminate difficult-to-monitor changes in quality.

The human establishment of quality can be seen historically in the mid-19th-century transformation of Midwestern U.S. grain. From being a heterogeneous amalgam of countless different sizes, strains, and qualities, all of which differed from sack to sack, grain was transformed into a small number of homogeneous commodities. Newly created grades of white winter, red winter, and spring wheat came to be of such uniform quality that ownership of grain no longer pertained to any particular sack or lot of it; instead, such ownership could refer merely to a specified amount of a certain type of crop. Grain had become an abstract commodity, like a kilowatt-hour of electricity, and readily enforceable contracts could be written simply for specified amounts of it rather than for the products of particular farms. Remarkably, an entirely private body, the Chicago Board of Trade, accomplished the standardization of grain, and memberships in this organization themselves became marketable commodities before the end of the 19th century.

Source: Adapted from Samuel Bowles, *Microeconomics: Behavior, Institutions and Evolution* (Princeton: Princeton University Press, 2004); and William Cronon, *Nature's Metropolis: Chicago and the Great West* (New York: Norton, 1991).

did not increase much as firms grew beyond a certain size. Thus, many firms selling the same, or nearly the same, product could survive. As a result, the prices of many, perhaps most, goods were reasonably close to the marginal cost of producing them, at least on average and in the long run. Recall from the invisible hand argument discussed in Chapter 9 that when competition works to allocate resources efficiently, it does so because prices are equal to marginal cost.

That most goods could be specified in contracts and that most industries were reasonably competitive in the old economy did not mean that the market failures identified in Chapter 9 never occurred. But in comparison to what was to come, the market failures of the old economy were minor. Today, market failures occur in the new economy as a result of four phenomena.

The first is widespread *increasing returns to scale*. Where there are such increasing returns, prices will generally be higher than the marginal costs of production. Thus, the efficiency condition $P = MC$ will not prevail, and as a result the economy will not perform satisfactorily.

For many outputs of the new economy, the "first copy" costs are huge, while the costs of producing additional units may be very low or even zero. If firms producing such outputs are to make profits, they will have to charge prices that are higher than their marginal costs. Recall that with "increasing returns," average cost declines as a firm expands its output. Hence, marginal cost will, by definition, be less than average cost (see the discussion of this point in the last section of Chapter 9). If a firm in this situation were to charge only the marginal cost of production, so that P would equal MC (as would be the case in a competitive market and on which the theoretical "optimal allocation of resources" in a competitive market depends), the firm could not make a profit because even to make the average rate of profit (this being included in average cost), it would have to charge at least the average cost. In other words, if a firm with large "first copy" costs charges a price that covers only the marginal cost of additional units of its output, it will not be able to cover the costs of the "first copy."

First copy costs include such things as the costs of conception, design, and acquiring the necessary intellectual property rights (copyrights, patents, and the like). The first copy of the book you are reading, for example, required literally thousands of hours of the authors' time and thousands more labor hours of research assistants, editors, and others who contributed to the process. The costs of making additional copies of the book once the first copy is in existence are much lower. Anyone who photocopies the book will probably underestimate those costs, but they will certainly be lower than the book's "list price." What this means is that the marginal cost is below the price. Some other examples:

- A standard music CD costs less than a dollar to produce (its actual marginal cost is less than a dollar), but it sells for $14 or more (see Chapter 9). The difference pays for the "first copy" costs and allows the producer of the CD to make a profit.
- The first copy of Windows 97 is said to have cost Microsoft $50 million to develop. The second copy (fancy packaging included) cost the company $3, and the program itself can be copied on a computer for just a few cents.
- The software company Inktomi spent $20 million to produce the first copy of one of its products. However, its chief executive said (referring to the costs of producing additional copies): "You have no cost of [producing] goods. We don't even ship a physical diskette any more. Next to the federal government, this is the only business that's allowed to print money."
- Popular generic drugs in the U.S. sell for about half the price of the corresponding brand name drugs, and even the price of a typical generic exceeds the marginal cost of producing it. For some drugs the ratio of the brand name to the generic price is around 10 to one; one factor is that advertising costs drive up the prices of the brand name drugs.

In sum, if P is not equal to MC because of increasing returns to scale, there will be a "market failure," and the economy will not be allocating its resources efficiently.

The second feature of the new economy that results in market failure is the importance of what are called *network externalities,* namely, the fact that the value of computer programs, operating systems, online services, and many goods depends on how many other consumers are using them. Just as you would find it much more valuable to learn Spanish than Guarani (spoken by most people in Paraguay, but not elsewhere), one of the first things you want to know when buying a word processing program is: do most other people use this program? It sometimes takes many decades for goods and services that are technically feasible to become commercially viable. The underlying technology for fax machines was invented in 1853, and photo wire service was introduced in 1925 (by American Telephone and Telegraph), but fax machines remained a niche product until the 1980s, when they quickly became standard office equipment. Network externalities are sometimes referred to as *demand side increasing returns* because, in this case, the advantage of large scale comes not from falling average costs of production but rather from the fact that the good, once it catches on, will be demanded by large numbers of people.

> **Demand side increasing returns** exist when a rise in profitability results from the fact that a commodity becomes demanded (and purchased) by greater and greater numbers of people.

A third aspect of the new economy, *serial monopoly,* derives from the first two. Because of increasing returns on both the supply and the demand sides of the markets in which they operate, large firms have a decisive advantage over small firms. Consequently, it is difficult for competitors to dislodge a leading firm once it has been established, or even to survive competition with it. Because of this, firms may fail even if they have a better product than the leading firm in their industry. One example is the difficulty Apple Computer has always faced in a market dominated from the start by IBM and its clones.

A fourth aspect of the new economy leading to market failure has to do with the *incomplete contracts* that result when the cost of second and subsequent copies of a given product is very low. Stealing copies of the original product is easy, while enforcing contracts involving them is difficult, and even when such enforcement is successful it leads to inefficiencies. Of course, patents, copyrights, and other intellectual property rights are designed to prevent the use of computer programs, ideas, musical recordings, and other information without payment to the owners of them. Enforcing intellectual property rights is a relatively simple matter if it involves preventing a *firm* from producing a product or using a production process that was invented by someone else and for which permission has not been granted. It is a lot more difficult when such enforcement involves preventing *individuals* from sharing music on their hard drives or copying software. Even when enforcement is possible, it is often extremely unpopular, as when the U.S. and other governments attempt to prevent producers of generic low-cost drugs from making their products available to impoverished HIV-AIDS patients in the poor countries of the world.

The dilemma of intellectual property rights enforcement is that if they *are* enforced, the goods involved will sell at prices significantly higher than their marginal costs of production. When this happens there will be some people who would be willing to pay the marginal cost of a product but cannot afford to pay for it at its elevated price and who will therefore not be able to get the benefit of using it. Think of people with the HIV-AIDS virus in countries where the average income is less than $2 a day (which is the case in most of the world).

If intellectual property rights are *not* enforced, however, the firms that bear the first copy costs—including the research and development costs that were required to bring the first copy into existence—will lose out to firms that use the research but do not have to pay for it. This will effectively eliminate the profit motive as an incentive for investing in research in these products.

In all these ways, then, the new economy of ideas and information is quite unlike the old economy of grain and steel. A consequence is that Adam Smith's invisible hand—the idea that the pursuit of individual gain, constrained only by property rights and competition, will guide an economy to efficient use of its resources—is now an even worse guide to economic policy making than it was in the old economy. This, in turn, may lead people to question existing economic institutions, opening up possibilities for institutional innovation that would bring about more effective use of resources.

THE WEIGHTLESS ECONOMY AND THE INVISIBLE HAND

We concluded the section on the limits to growth with the idea that from a scientific standpoint we know (or could readily find out) how to halt or at least slow down the harmful effects of our economic activities on the environment, but that the political obstacles to implementing these solutions are substantial and, for the moment, decisive. Our conclusion concerning the weightless economy is different. It is hard to see how competition can make firms accountable to consumers when increasing returns and network externalities give such monumental advantages to larger firms. Nor are solutions to the dilemma of intellectual property rights enforcement easy to imagine. Thus, even if competition were to prevail, it would not bring the efficiency promised by the invisible hand. Rather, it would lead to gross distortions of resource use, for example, limiting the access of poor people to goods for which they would willingly pay the marginal costs of production.

The challenge of finding a reasonable way of pricing products in the new economy seems insurmountable. Surprisingly, however, humans have triumphed in the face of comparable challenges. During the first 100,000 years or so of human existence, that is, until agriculture was developed around 11,000 years ago, most of our ancestors lived by hunting animals and gathering fruits, nuts, roots, and other food, and some hunter-gatherer societies survive today. Indeed, the behavioral experiments described in Chapter 2 were carried out in societies of this type.

But what does hunting antelopes have to do with producing and marketing a product such as Windows XP? More than one might think at first glance. The hunting of the large game on which human diets depended during the preagricultural period involved three elements that are also characteristic of products in the weightless economy. First, antelopes and other large game, like a breakthrough idea by a software engineer, were hard to come by. Among the Hadza (mentioned in Chapter 2) the hit rate (the fraction of days on which a hunter was successful) averaged about 3 percent. Second, the animals being hunted were difficult to own. When a small group of Hadza hunters is stalking a giraffe, for example, no one of them "owns" it. Similarly with gathering, if a group is searching for a rich collection of fruit, they have no way of deciding that one member of the group will own it after it is discovered. Third, it was both wasteful and costly for any one hunter to keep others from sharing the prey. It was wasteful because after the hunter had eaten his fill, having an additional piece of the antelope was worth more to another member of the hunter's group than it was to the hunter. It was costly because to keep others from sharing the animal would take constant vigilance, diverting the hunter from other productive tasks.

Clearly, hunter-gatherers did not have a system of property rights like ours. Nor did they insist on "finders keepers." When early hunter-gatherers succeeded in catching a large animal, they divided and distributed it among large numbers of people using an agreed upon way of dividing it, just as the Lamalera in Indonesia (described in Chapter 2) do today with their whales (see box "Income Distribution among the Lamalera"). Other groups have had other rules. For example, in some groups the meat was distributed to relatives, but many of the "relatives" were just called that; they were not actually related by birth or marriage to the hunter. In still other groups the person whose arrow killed the animal distributed the meat, but it was very bad manners to use one's own arrows while hunting. The arrows used were often those of the elders or others who could not hunt, so the system was a kind of hunter-gatherer social insurance program.

The hunter-gatherer practices of sharing were maintained by elaborate social institutions. The anthropologist Christopher Boehm, one of the foremost scholars of hunter-gatherer societies, has observed that "in these [moral] communities, group sanction emerged as the most powerful instrument for regulation of individually assertive behaviors, particularly those which obviously disrupted cooperation or disturbed social equilibrium needed for group stability."[2]

Hunter-gatherers carefully monitored one another's contributions, lavishing praise and honor on the good and generous hunters and subjecting the stingy and boastful to gossip and ridicule. In many such groups eating in public was customary; it made the job of monitoring easier. Not only was food shared, so was valuable information about where game was plentiful, where water could be found, and the like.

We are not suggesting, of course, that the hunter-gatherers' methods would work for distributing software. But some of the basic ideas of hunter-gatherer economics might provide useful lessons. The first lesson is that competition for individual gain is not the only way to organize an economy. The second is that extreme inequalities among people may make cooperation difficult. If voluntary cooperation is essential to a group's success, the group should keep inequality to a minimum. Hunter-gatherer groups were (and are) harsh toward people who put themselves above others or failed to share. Because they needed to cooperate in order to survive, they did not tolerate much inequality between families. The third lesson we might learn from our hunter-gatherer ancestors is that contracts are but one way to facilitate mutually beneficial exchanges. Other ways, as Nobel Economics Laureate Kenneth Arrow has pointed out, include trust and moral norms. "In the absence of trust," he wrote, " . . . opportunities for mutually beneficial cooperation would have to be foregone . . . [N]orms of social behavior, including ethical and moral codes [may be] . . . reactions of society to compensate for market failures."[3]

---

[2] Christopher Boehm, "The Evolutionary Development of Morality as an Effect of Dominance Behavior and Conflict Interference," *Journal of Social and Biological Structures,* vol. 5, 1982, pp. 413–421.

[3] Kenneth J. Arrow, "Political and Economic Evaluation of Social Effects and Externalities," in M. D. Intriligator, ed., *Frontiers of Quantitative Economics* (Amsterdam: North Holland, 1971), p. 22.

INCOME DISTRIBUTION AMONG THE LAMALERA

The sperm whale shown illustrates the customary division of their prey by the Lamalera whale hunters in Indonesia, with each part customarily going to a particular individual or group—crew, sailmaker, blacksmith and boat builder, for example. The corporate group includes the members of the association whose boat was used (whether or not they participated in the hunt), and the "Lord of the land" is a group of families that, by custom, gets a share on the basis of its families' claims that their ancestors were the first inhabitants of the area.

Source: Michael Halbert.

Lamalera income distribution: customary shares

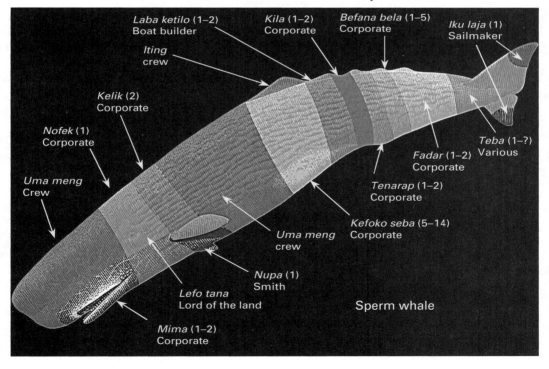

Sperm whale

It may be that hunter-gatherer economics is not completely irrelevant to the information economy after all. The highly successful Linux system of so-called open-source computer software is produced almost entirely by volunteers and is distributed freely. (*Open-source* means that the underlying code of the software is available to everyone, so anyone can have a go at fixing a bug or improving an application.) Virtually costless communication among literally thousands of participants allows easy monitoring of individual contributions. It also facilitates the process of reputation-building and makes it easy to ridicule people. Here is how Eric Raymond describes social life among open-source software participants:

> [T]he culture's "big men" and tribal elders are required to talk softly and humorously deprecate themselves at every turn in order to maintain their status . . . [a person in this culture] consciously distrusts and despises egotism and ego-based motivations; self-promotion tends to be mercilessly criticized.[4]

The resemblance between Raymond's description of the "open-source" culture and Boehm's description of hunter-gatherer norms (quoted above) is clear. We will not take our speculative analogy between hunter-gatherer society and the new economy too far, however. Hunter-gatherers faced (and, in some cases, still face) problems that are quite different from those we have to solve today. The tasks confronting us in the new economy include not only coordinating economic activities within small groups of close associates but, more problematically, regulating the economic relationships of hundreds of millions of actors across the globe, almost all of whom are strangers to one another. The population of the entire world during most of the time that foraging was the predominant mode of human economic life was less than the population of Mexico City today. Humans then, as now, had an impact on the environment (driving many large mammals to extinction, for example), but the environmental problems they faced were minor compared to ours.

Many economists see only two basic ways of coordinating economic activity—the invisible hand of market competition or direct regulation by a government or some other centralized body. Both methods are important and necessary: markets and governments can accomplish some of the tasks of coordination among large numbers of people that hunter-gatherer societies could not. But the invisible hand and centralized command are not just alternatives: they can be used in tandem with each other, as indeed they are in all modern economies.

What we may learn from hunter-gatherers (they had neither markets nor governments) is that some problems are best solved with the kinds of face-to-face cooperative interactions that one finds in many desirable residential communities, in happy families, and in successful firms. Thomas Hobbes, one of the greatest contributors to European political philosophy, wrote in 1651: "Where [there] is no trust, there can be no contract." This is a point that, as we have seen, has also been made more recently by Kenneth Arrow. In modern societies trust, a concern for others, and the esteem of one's fellows may be as important as the lure of individual gain or the fear of government sanction. The increasing importance of information in the economy and the growth of services at a faster rate than goods production are likely to make the first set of motives even more important.

We cannot predict what kinds of institutions would adequately address the challenges of the weightless economy. There may be none. However, it is doubtful that existing institutions can do the job. Arrow is most perceptive in his observation of what he calls the "tension" between the "economic fundamentals" of the information-based economy and

---

[4] Eric Raymond, *The Cathedral and the Bazaar* (Sebastopol, Calif.: O'Reilly, 2001), p. 88.

the "legal relations" of private property (see box "Fugitive Resources"). In this he is bringing up to date, in modern economic language and without the revolutionary prediction, a point that was made by Marx in the middle of the 19th century (see the quote from Marx in the box near the beginning of this chapter).

FUGITIVE RESOURCES

Economics Nobel Laureate Kenneth Arrow points out that it may not be possible or desirable to establish conventional property rights in information:

. . . information is a fugitive resource. . . . [W]e are just beginning to face the contradictions between the systems of private property and of information acquisition and dissemination. . . . [We may see] *an increasing tension between legal relations and fundamental economic determinants.*

—Kenneth Arrow, "Technical Information and Industrial Structure"
in Carroll Glenn and David Teece, eds., *Firms, Markets, and
Hierarchies* (Oxford: Oxford University Press, 1999), pp.156–163

CONCLUSION

At the beginning of this chapter we suggested that in response to technological and environmental challenges, new institutions might emerge that would organize our economy in new ways and enable us to harness modern technology and improve human well-being. As indicated by the tentative quality of our speculations in the chapter, however, they may not.

Today there are many people throughout the world who have done very well within capitalism as we know it. They appear to be reluctant to risk losing their privileged status by experimenting with new institutional structures that might be more suitable for dealing with the challenges of the information economy, controlling the encroachment of humans on our natural environment, and closing the gaps between rich and poor within and among nations. If established elites resist such institutional change, the next stop in our historical journey could well be a world plagued by economic irrationality, buffeted by environmental crisis, and divided into increasingly hostile camps of haves and have-nots.

Which outcome it will be may depend on what we do about it. An evening newscaster in Boston used to end his program with the words: "And that's the news, folks. If you don't like it, go out and make your own." Not bad advice for today. Our three-dimensional economics is certainly not all that you will need, but it may help.

DOMESTICATING A FUGITIVE RESOURCE

Music companies have tried in vain to find a way to prevent people from copying music without paying for it. Publishers and software companies are only slightly more successful at enforcing their copyrights, preventing photocopying of published material or pirating of programs. But nearly a century ago companies that sell agricultural seeds, facing a similar problem, came up with an ingenious solution: build an anticopy device into the design of the product.

A little background. Seed companies were in an even worse situation than producers of recorded music because seeds copy themselves; that is what seeds do. Thus, a farmer who bought a quantity of newly developed high-yielding seed from a seed company might never have had to go back again: he could have used the seed from the current year to plant next year's crop. This was bad news for the seed companies because, while the farmer would benefit from whatever research went into developing the better strain of the seed, the company was not able to share in the gains and make a profit.

Enter the solution: hybridization. A hybrid is a cross between two different strains or varieties; a mule, for example, is a hybrid resulting from a cross between a horse and a donkey. The key fact in what follows is that mules do not reproduce themselves; you need a horse and a donkey to do it. John Barton writing in *Science* explained:

[Because] *the seeds of the hybrid crop will not breed true to type, the farmer cannot effectively re-use the seeds. . . . [F]rom the viewpoint of the seed producer, this annual requirement for new seeds provides a form of economic protection that is more effective than a patent system.*

Donald Jones, whose research was critical to the development of hybrids, understood exactly what he was doing. In 1919 he and a coauthor compared the plight of the seed companies (called seedsmen) with other inventors:

The man who originates devices to open our boxes of shoe polish or autograph our camera negatives is able to patent his products and gain the full reward for his inventiveness. The man who originates a new plant . . . of incalculable benefit to the whole country gets nothing . . . for his pain, and the plant can be propagated by anyone.

Science to the rescue. Hybrids, they wrote, are

something that might easily be taken up by seedsmen; in fact it is the first time in agricultural history that a seedsman is enabled to gain the full benefit from [his research, because he can] *give out only the crossed seeds, which are less valuable for continued propagation.*

The seed companies concentrated their sales efforts on the hybrids, and lobbied publicly funded research to do the same, not because they were more productive (they were not initially) but because they were more profitable for the companies. The subsequent rapid spread of hybrid corn and other hybrids is not an example of science at the service of progress; rather, science had overcome an impediment to profit making that the companies faced.

Sources: John Barton, "The International Breeders Rights System and Crop Plant Innovation," *Science,* no. 216, June 4, 1982, pp. 1071–1075; Jean-Pierre Berlan and R. C. Lewontin, "The Political Economy of Hybrid Corn," *Monthly Review,* vol. 38, no. 3, 1986, pp. 35–47; Samuel Bowles, "Social Institutions and Technical Change," in *Technological and Social Factors in Long Term Fluctuations,* edited by M. Di Matteo, R. M. Goodwin, and A. Vercelli (New York: Springer-Verlag, 1989), pp. 67–87.

SUGGESTED READINGS

W. Brian Arthur, *Increasing Returns and Path Dependency in the Economy* (Ann Arbor, Mich.: University of Michigan Press, 1994).

Yochai Benkler, "Coase's Penguin, or Linux and the *Nature of the Firm*," *Yale Law Journal,* vol. 112, no. 3, 2002.

James Boyce, *The Political Economy of the Environment* (Cheltenham, U.K.: Edward Elgar, 2002).

Erik Brynjolfsson and Brian Kahin, *Understanding the Digital Economy* (Cambridge, Mass.: Massachusetts Institute of Technology Press, 2000).

William W. Fisher, *Promises to Keep: Technology, Law, and the Future of Entertainment* (Stanford: Stanford University Press, 2004).

Duncan Foley, *Unholy Trinity: Capital, Labor and Land in the New Economy* (London: Routledge, 2003).

Bill Gates, *The Road Ahead* (New York: Viking Penguin, 1995).

Eric Raymond, *The Cathedral and the Bazaar* (Sebastopol, Calif.: O'Reilly, 1999).

Carl Shapiro and Hal Varian, *Information Rules* (Boston: Harvard Business School Press, 1999).

Debora L. Spar, *Ruling the Waves: Cycles of Discovery, Chaos and Wealth from the Compass to the Internet* (New York: Harcourt, 2001).

LIST OF VARIABLES

(1) TOTALS

(a) Flows. These are physical or money totals for a firm or for the economy as a whole, for a given period of time, such as a year.

S = Money value of total *sales* during a year

Z = Money value of total *output* produced during a year

M = Money value of "machine" *depreciation* and *materials used* during a year

Y = Money value of *net output* produced in a year $= Z - M$; for a firm this is called *value added;* for the economy as a whole it is called *net national product*

N = Total *hours of labor employed* during a year

LS = *Labor supply* = total hours of labor workers would like to work during a year

W = Total *wages* and *salaries* paid during a year = the wage rate (w) times N

R = Total *profit* (money value) made during a year $= Y - W = Z - M - W$

AD = *Aggregate demand*

AS = *Aggregate supply*

C = Money value of *consumer goods and services* purchased during a year in the economy as a whole

I = Money value of business demand for *investment goods and services* during a year

G = Money value of total *government demand for goods and services* during a year

B = Money value of *government borrowing* from the public to finance government spending during a year

X = Money value of *net exports* = total exports minus total imports during a year

(b) Stocks. These are physical or money totals for a firm or for the economy as a whole that are in existence at some given moment in time (such as January 1, 2005).

CG = Amount of *capital goods owned,* or *capital stock*

$K =$ Money *value of capital stock* $= (P_c)(CG)$

CG in use $=$ Amount of *capital goods owned* that are actually *in use*

(c) Prices.

P_z = Price of a unit of output

P_m = Price of materials and machines

P_c = Price of capital goods (per "machine")

P_{im} = Price of an imported good in the currency of the importing country

P_{imf} = Price of an imported good in the currency of the country where it was produced

(2) RATIOS

These are totals divided by other totals; they can always be interpreted as "the amount of one thing per unit of something else" (for example, the ratio X/Y means "the amount of X per unit of Y").

z = Money value of output per hour of labor employed $= Z/N = ef$

m = "Machine" depreciation and materials used per labor hour $= M/N$

y = Money value of net output per hour of labor employed $= Y/N$

w = Wage rate = wage or salary per hour of labor $= W/N$

e = Work effort, or work done, in an hour of labor; intensity of work

f = Efficiency of labor = value of output produced per unit of work done

k = Money value of capital goods ("machines") owned per hour of labor employed $= K/N$

r = Rate of profit = amount of profit divided by the money value of capital goods owned $= R/K = (Y - W)/K = (y - w)/k$

r_u = Profit rate on capital goods in use

atr = After-tax profit rate

i = Rate of interest (in percent per year), which is the cost of borrowing money, say, for the purpose of investment = (interest paid)/("principal" of the loan)

u = Capacity utilization rate = percent of owned capital goods actually in use $= CG$ *in use*$/CG$

g = Capital goods in use per hour of labor $= CG$ *in use* $/N$

uc = Unit cost = cost of producing a unit of output

ulc = Unit labor cost = wage cost per unit of output $= W/Z = w/z = w/(ef)$

umc = Unit materials cost $= M/Z = m/z = m/(ef)$

up = Unit profit ("markup" on unit cost)

c = Fraction of wage and salary income spent on consumer goods and services $= C/W$

j = Profit effect on investment = how much total investment (I) increases (in units of a currency) when total profit (R) increases by one unit (measured in the same currency)

v = Value of the dollar = foreign exchange rate = the number of units of a foreign currency that can be obtained in the global currency market in exchange for \$1

(3) OTHER

ww = Weekly wage
ud = Unemployment duration (in weeks)
ui = Unemployment insurance paid per week
cjl = Cost of job loss

GLOSSARY

Accumulation is profit-driven investment, including the process of mobilizing, transforming, and exploiting the inputs required in capitalist production and then selling the output.

The **after-tax profit rate** is the profit rate made by firms after they have paid all required taxes.

Aggregate or **population-level outcomes** refer to the economic totals, averages, and relationships that are studied by economists.

Aggregate demand is the total demand for goods and services during some period, say, a year.

Aggregate supply is the total supply of goods and services produced during some period, say, a year.

Average cost is the total cost of producing a certain number of units of a good or service divided by the total number of units produced.

Barriers to entry are obstacles that make it more difficult or costly for new firms to enter a market; examples include technical secrets, initial investments that are very large, and exclusive marketing arrangements.

Beliefs are one's understandings of the actions necessary to bring about particular outcomes.

A **bond** is an "IOU" that contractually commits the issuer of the bond (the government or a corporation) not only to paying back the value of the bond but also to making regular payments, at a specified rate of interest, to the owner of the bond.

A **breakthrough** occurs when a firm discovers or develops a new method of doing business such as a new way of organizing work, a new product, or a new market.

Built-in stabilizers are automatic changes in government spending and taxation that dampen the business cycle without conscious policy decisions directed toward this end. Examples are unemployment insurance and income taxation.

Bureaucratic control is a system of control that uses job ladders, seniority rewards, and other organizational incentives in order to extract work from workers.

The **business cycle** is a periodic expansion and contraction of output and employment usually taking place over a period of 3 to 10 years.

Business cycle contractions (or **recessions**) are periods of increased unemployment and reduction in output and income.

Business cycle expansions are characterized by rapid increases in employment and income.

The **capacity utilization ratio** is the percentage of all owned capital goods currently being used.

Capital goods are goods used in production—machines, buildings, and the like—that are durable and will be used up only over the course of years.

Capital goods in use per hour of labor is the quantity of machines actually used in production divided by the total number of hours worked.

A **capital goods–saving technical change** is a new technology that reduces the capital goods and materials necessary to produce a given amount of total output.

A **capital strike** occurs when, as a result of a negative business climate, many individual capitalists decide to reduce their investments or not to invest at all.

Capitalism is an economic system in which employers, using privately owned capital goods, hire wage labor to produce commodities for the purpose of making a profit.

The **capitalist class,** or **capitalists,** are those who own capital goods used in production and exercise control over the labor of others; they receive their income in the form of profits or other payments (e.g., interest and rent) for the use of their capital goods.

The **capitalist epoch** began in some parts of Europe around AD 1500, when capitalist organization of labor processes first appeared. It continues to the present in most of the world.

Capitalist profits are profits that result from a labor process.

A **cartel** is a combination of states or business firms operating in concert to regulate the production, pricing, and marketing of goods by its members.

Change, or the time dimension in economics, refers to the historical evolution of people and economic systems.

Citizen rights are the basis for a claim to share (some of) the benefits of society; this claim is based on one's citizenship instead of, for example, on possessing sufficient money to buy the benefits.

A **class** is a group of people who share a common position in the economy with respect to the production and control of the surplus product.

A **class relationship** exists between the producers of the total product, including the surplus product, and those who command the use of the surplus product.

Collective activities are activities whose benefits or burdens extend, potentially, at least, to all citizens.

Collective bargaining occurs when, in negotiating wages and other employment conditions, all workers in a firm or occupation are represented collectively by a union; employers may also be collectively represented by an employers' association.

Command, or the vertical dimension in economics, refers to aspects of economic relationships in which power plays the predominant role.

Command relations are relationships between superiors and subordinates in which the superior exercises substantial power over the subordinate.

Commercial profits result from selling something for more than it cost to purchase ("buying cheap and selling dear"); no labor process is involved.

A **commodity** is any good or service that is produced with the intention of selling it in order to make a profit.

Competition, or the horizontal dimension in economics, refers to aspects of economic relationships in which voluntary exchange and choice among a large number of possible buyers and sellers play the predominant role.

Competition for profits is the struggle for survival and expansion among capitalists and firms seeking new ways of doing business, new markets, new products, and other possibilities for profitable investment.

Competitive markets are those with many potential demanders and suppliers.

A **complete contract** is one that fully specifies—in ways that the courts will enforce—everything that each party to the contract is to do as a result of the contract.

A **compulsory relationship** exists when a person cannot choose whether to enter the relationship but rather becomes subject to the relationship because of his or her status (such as being a citizen of a particular country).

The **consumer price index (CPI)** is a measure of the average prices a typical family pays for the goods and services it buys.

Constraints are the limits on the actions that an individual or a society can take.

A **contract** is an agreement, either written (explicit) or unwritten (implicit), that commits two or more parties to taking certain actions, such as making payments and delivering goods or services.

A **contract specifying work to be done** is an agreement between an employer and a worker that specifies payment for actual work activities instead of for work time.

Conventional economics. *See* **neoclassical economics.**

Coordination by command takes place when interactions are governed by orders specifying precise behavior.

Coordination by rules takes place when interactions are governed by general principles of behavior.

Coordination failure occurs when markets or other types of coordination by rules fail to coordinate an economy in such a way as to produce outcomes that are desirable.

The **cost of job loss** is the loss of income a worker experiences as a result of quitting or being laid off from a job.

Countercyclical policies are policies aimed at dampening the business cycle.

A **craft union** is a labor union whose membership is restricted to workers in the same craft, skill category, or occupation.

Crowding out occurs when spending by the government has the effect of reducing spending by families and businesses.

Cyclical inflation refers to the price increases that typically accelerate toward the end of a business cycle expansion.

Decreasing costs refers to a situation in which the average cost of producing something declines as the volume (scale) of production increases.

Deficit spending occurs when the government finances its purchases by borrowing from the public.

Deflation refers to a general fall in prices as measured by the consumer price index. It is the opposite of inflation.

A **demand curve** indicates, for each possible price, how much of the good or service demanders are willing and able to buy.

Demand side increasing returns exist when a rise in profitability results from the fact that a commodity becomes demanded (and purchased) by greater and greater numbers of people.

Democracy is a process with three characteristics: the exercise of power is accountable to those affected by it, civil rights and personal liberties are guaranteed, and citizens have relatively equal access to political resources and influence.

A **democratic firm** is one that is owned by its employees and run by people who are elected by the employees.

Democratic government is a way of organizing a government based on (1) accountability of officials through elections with widespread and equal voting rights and (2) civil liberties and personal freedoms.

Depreciation is the cost (due to wear and tear) of restoring the capital goods used up in producing last year's output.

Deskilling means changing a production process in such a way as to make it possible to employ workers with fewer skills.

The **determinants of the profit rate** are the things upon which the profit rate depends; they determine how high the profit rate will be.

Discrimination means treating someone differently simply because that person belongs to a certain group.

A **dividend** is a payment made by a corporation to an owner of a share of its stock.

Division of labor (or **economic specialization**) exists when people are not economically self-sufficient but instead produce things used by others and use things produced by others.

The **dual economy** is the industrial structure of contemporary American capitalism, consisting of core firms and periphery firms.

Economic concentration in the whole economy measures how much of the economic activity of the whole economy is accounted for by the largest firms in the economy.

Economic growth is defined as an increase in per capita income over a number of years.

Economic interdependence exists when the livelihood of a person depends on the activities of another person. *See also* **vertical economic interdependence** and **horizontal economic interdependence.**

Economic man (*Homo economicus*) refers to the assumption that human beings are calculating, amoral, and self-interested.

Economic specialization. *See* **division of labor.**

An **economic system** is a set of relationships among people that organizes the labor processes all societies need to sustain life.

Economics is the study of how people interact with one another and with their natural surroundings to produce their livelihoods.

Economies of scale exist when the average cost of producing something falls as more of it is produced.

An **economy** is a collection of labor processes.

The **efficiency of labor** refers to how much output can be produced as a result of a certain level of work effort.

The term **efficient** is applied to a labor process if the effort, time, intelligence, creativity, raw materials, natural environment, information, and machinery used in it are applied in a way that enhances people's well-being by equipping them with the things and the free time needed to lead a flourishing life.

Embedded economy is a description of the economy of the precapitalist epoch, which was so fully integrated into the whole society that it did not have a separate or specialized existence.

The **employment effect** is the change in the number of hours of labor employed that results from the direct and indirect effects of a change in business investment or government deficit spending.

The **employment multiplier** is the hours of new employment directly and indirectly created by an additional dollar of investment or other spending.

Equalization of profit rates refers to the process by which competitive pressures on firms in different industries, different geographical regions, and different markets push their profit rates toward a common, or average, level.

Equilibrium refers to a situation—a price and quantity exchanged—in which there are no forces internal to the situation pushing it to change.

The **equilibrium level of employment** is the amount of employment that corresponds to a particular macroeconomic equilibrium (when there is no excess demand or excess supply in product markets).

Excess demand exists when at a particular price more of some good or service is demanded than is supplied.

Excess supply exists when at a particular price more of some good or service is supplied than is demanded.

The **expected profit rate on investment** is a firm's estimate of the future profit rate that it thinks will be earned on its investment.

Externalities occur when some of the effects of a market exchange are not reflected in the price and are thus "external" to the participants in the exchange.

The **extraction of work from workers** is the process of transforming the labor time that an employer has purchased into work done.

Fairness means that people in an economic system suffer the burdens and enjoy the benefits of that economic system equitably.

The **fallback wage** is the wage at which an employee has no preference for keeping his or her current job as opposed to being fired or quitting; it varies with the employee's income prospects in the absence of the current job.

Feudalism was the dominant economic system in Europe in the Middle Ages; lords obtained the surplus product through rents and other customary obligations owed by the serfs.

Government **fiscal policy** uses taxes and spending to regulate the level of total output and employment.

The **foreign exchange rate** is the amount of the foreign currency that a dollar will buy; it is also known as the **value of the dollar.**

Full employment is a situation in which almost everyone seeking work readily finds it.

Guard labor refers to those who do not produce capital goods, materials, or consumption goods but who work to perpetuate the structure of the society, including the power and economic advantages of the dominant class.

Hegemony is the power to define, interpret, and enforce the rules of the game and thus to determine the range of possible alternatives for all the players.

A **hierarchy** is an organization of power in which superiors have command over subordinates.

The **high-employment profit squeeze** occurs when the high demand for labor creates both labor and materials cost increases, which in turn reduce profits.

Horizontal economic interdependence is based on specialization and is not necessarily based on unequal advantage or command.

An **incomplete contract** is an agreement between two parties that leaves out certain aspects of an exchange and requires or imposes, upon one party or the other, significant enforcement costs.

An **incomplete labor contract** is a contract (explicit or implicit) between an employer and a worker that is incomplete in the sense that it specifies the wage rate but does not specify the exact tasks to be performed or the amount of effort to be provided by the worker.

Increasing costs refers to a situation in which the average cost of producing something increases as the volume (scale) of production increases.

Increasing returns to scale exist when an increase in inputs—an increase in the *scale* of production—brings about a more than proportional increase in output.

The **independent primary labor market** includes those jobs with highly elaborate bureaucratic or professional career patterns; it contains mainly the jobs of craft, technical, professional, and lower-level supervisory workers.

Independent production of commodities is an economic system in which the producers own the capital goods needed in production and use (primarily) their own labor.

An **industrial union** is a labor union whose membership is open to all workers in a plant or industry, regardless of which specific occupations or jobs they work at.

An **inefficient technical change** is one that can bring about an increase in the output of a production process only by using proportionally more of at least one input.

Inflation is a general increase in prices, often measured by the CPI (consumer price index).

The **inflation-unemployment trade-off** describes the tendency during a business cycle for inflation to rise when unemployment falls and for inflation to fall when unemployment rises.

The **infrastructure** of an economy (sometimes called its "social overhead capital") consists of its roads, railways, airports, harbor facilities, bridges and tunnels, water and sewage systems, public utilities and electricity grids, and communications networks such as telephone lines and the internet backbone.

The **intensity of labor** is how much work effort producers must expend per hour of work, or more simply, how hard they work.

Interest is a contractual payment made by the government to owners of U.S. Treasury bonds, bills, or notes. Alternatively, it is a contractual payment made by a corporation to owners of its bonds or to banks that have provided loans to the corporation.

The **interest rate** is the cost of renting money; for a firm that borrows money, it is the percentage of the amount borrowed that must be repaid in addition to the amount borrowed.

Investment means spending money to repair, replace, improve, or add to a firm's productive equipment, software, facilities, or workforce skills in order to increase productive capacity and labor productivity.

Job ladders link together a series of related jobs, in which a worker over the years climbs from one job to another and gains access to jobs higher on the ladder only by first succeeding in the lower jobs.

Labor is any activity performed by people that contributes to production or reproduction.

The **labor extraction curve** describes for each wage rate the intensity of work that the worker chooses to perform.

A **labor market** is a market in which workers sell their labor time (not work itself) in return for a wage; employers are the demanders, and workers are the suppliers of labor time.

A **labor process** is any activity performed with the intention of producing something.

A **labor-saving technical change** is a new technology that increases the total output produced with a given amount of labor.

Labor time measures the number of hours worked; it does not measure how much work gets done, since there are many different levels of work effort (intensities of work) possible.

Laissez-faire is an approach to economic policy that advocates a very limited role for the government, confining its activities to national defense and the enforcement of laws and contracts.

A **layoff** refers to a firm's temporary or permanent dismissal of workers when the firm must reduce its workforce because of a shortage of customers.

A **lockout** occurs when an employer locks the workers out of the workplace and closes down production in order to force workers to accept the employer's terms for wages, work pace, or other working conditions.

A **long swing** occurs over a period of 30 to 50 years. The first part generally coincides with the "consolidation" phase of a particular social structure of accumulation (SSA) and is characterized by relatively high rates of investment and economic growth and relatively little unemployment. The remainder of a long swing is associated with the "decay" phase of an SSA; it is a period of stagnation of economic growth with relatively little investment and high unemployment.

The **Lorenz curve** is a measure of the distribution of income, indicating what percentage of the total income is earned by each percentage of the population.

A **macroeconomic equilibrium** exists when aggregate demand equals aggregate supply (no excess aggregate demand or excess aggregate supply exists) and there are no forces tending to change the situation other than accidental ones or ones coming from external sources.

Macroeconomics is about how the decisions of individuals, families, firms, and governments produce outcomes—such as economic progress or stagnation, inflation or unemployment—for society as a whole.

Marginal cost is the increase in the total cost incurred by a firm when it increases its total output of a commodity by one unit.

A **market** refers to all the buying and selling activities of those persons wishing to trade a good or service; it consists of suppliers wanting to sell and demanders wanting to buy.

The **market clearing price** is the price at which buyers want to purchase exactly the quantity that sellers want to sell.

A **market exchange** is a transfer of title to a piece of property (a good or a service) to another party in return for some form of payment at mutually acceptable terms.

A **market failure** is said to take place when the spontaneous interactions of buyers and sellers in markets each pursuing their own objectives results in outcomes that are generally undesirable.

A **market share** is one firm's sales as a percentage of the total sales in an industry.

Materials are goods used in production and used up during the process of production.

Microeconomics deals with what individuals, families, and firms do (and why).

Middle classes in capitalist society possess one but not both of the attributes of capitalists; therefore, they stand between capitalists and workers.

Monetary policy refers to government influences on the rate of interest intended to regulate the level of investment, output, employment, and other macroeconomic outcomes.

Monopoly power is the ability of one or a few firms in an industry to exercise substantial control over the market price and other aspects of competition, usually by excluding other firms.

A **multinational corporation** (MNC) is a firm earning profits throughout the world by locating its facilities wherever the combination of wages, materials costs, markets, government policies, and local markets for the relevant outputs yield the highest profit for the corporation as a whole.

The **necessary product** is the portion of the total product that is needed to maintain the inputs in the labor process—workers, materials, and tools—at their current level or in their current condition for the next round of the production process.

Neoclassical or **conventional economics** is an economic theory emphasizing the horizontal dimension of markets and voluntary exchange.

Net exports are equal to total exports of goods and services minus total imports of goods and services.

Net product is the total product minus materials and capital goods used up in the course of producing the total product.

Net worth, or **net assets,** is the sum of all of a person's assets minus all outstanding debts.

The **new middle class** consists of those who do not own the capital goods used in their own labor processes but who do regularly control the labor of others; it includes managers and supervisors.

Nonprice competition involves sales efforts, style changes, or other marketing strategies to increase the appeal of a product without lowering its prices.

The **old middle class** consists of those who do own the capital goods used in their own labor processes but who do not regularly control the labor of others; they are self-employed or are small business employers.

Oligopoly, or **shared monopoly,** is a market situation in which several firms together, but no one firm by itself, can exercise substantial monopoly power.

An **opportunity cost** is the value of the best opportunity given up (forgone) in order that whatever was chosen could be undertaken.

The **output multiplier** is the additional output generated directly and indirectly by a dollar of additional investment or other spending.

Parallel plants are plants owned by the same employer and producing the same product but located in different geographical regions in order to weaken the workers' ability to bargain collectively.

A **piece rate** is a form of wage payment in which a worker is paid for each unit of output produced instead of for work time.

A **political business cycle** occurs when recession and/or expansion are in part intentionally created by governmental economic policy, as officials attempt to generate a business cycle for their own or others' interests.

Political economy is a term we use for a theory that analyzes capitalism in terms of the three dimensions of competition, command, and change.

A **political stalemate** is a situation in which none of the major economic actors—banks, large corporations, labor unions, the major political parties, the government—has the power to impose its will on the others.

A has **power** over B if by imposing costs on B (or threatening to do so) A can cause B to act in a way that is to A's advantage.

The **power of capital** refers to the ability of employers, especially the largest corporations, to influence governmental policy or to otherwise create conditions favorable to their own interests; this power grows out of their position as owners of capital goods.

The **power of the citizenry** refers to the ability of citizens to influence governmental policy or to otherwise create conditions favorable to their own interests; this power grows out of their position in democratic government.

Preferences are the relative values one places on various outcomes that one's actions might bring about.

Price competition is a form of or strategy for competition in which firms attempt to attract customers primarily by offering lower prices.

Price leadership is an informal system for setting prices in which the biggest firm in an industry establishes an output price and the other firms in the industry tacitly agree to set the same price for their own outputs.

Private costs are the costs borne by the user of a good or service (a person or a company), while the total costs borne by all members of a society are termed *social costs*. At best, prices measure only private costs.

Private property is a social institution (or rule) that gives individuals or firms the right to use, lend, or sell things such as land, buildings, and artistic or intellectual creations of any kind; it means that one can have or use such things only if one has made, rented, purchased, or been given them.

Privately owned capital goods are machines, buildings, offices, tools, and other durable things needed in production and whose owner, because of a property right, determines how the property will be used.

Production is a labor process whose output is a good or a service.

Profit is the form of the surplus product in a capitalist economic system; it is what is left over, out of sales revenues, after wages, the costs of materials used up, and wear and tear on machines have been paid.

Profitability refers to how much profit is derived from a labor process.

The **profit effect on investment** is the amount by which investment will increase for each $1 increase in total profits.

A **profit-led employment** situation obtains when rising wages reduce employment.

Property income is income that is received in the form of profit, rent, interest, or dividends as a result of owning an asset such as a business, a piece of land, an existing structure, a bond, or a share of corporate stock.

Property rights establish the owner's right to control the property, to decide who uses it for what purpose, and to benefit from its use or sale.

The **rate of profit** is the total amount of profit divided by the value of the capital goods owned by the firm.

The **real price of an imported input** is the amount of domestically produced goods required to purchase one unit of the imported good. It is thus the price of the imported good divided by the price of the domestically produced goods, when both are measured in the same currency.

The **real wage,** or **real income,** refers to wages or income corrected to take account of the effects of inflation.

Rent refers to payments that firms are required make to the owners of land, office space, buildings, or other facilities in return for the right to use or occupy them.

Reproduction is a labor process whose output is people; it includes not only biological reproduction but also such activities as child rearing, training, feeding, and caregiving.

Retained earnings are the part of total profit that is set aside by corporations for future investment or other purposes.

A **runaway shop** is a workplace that an employer has moved from an area where workers are strong to an area where workers are weak in order to escape having to meet workers' demands.

The **sales effort** consists of all those activities by a firm that relate to the selling of the firm's product.

Saving is income minus consumption.

Scarcity is a relationship between a desire for something and how difficult it is to obtain. A highly desirable good that is difficult to obtain is said to be scarce.

The **secondary labor market** includes jobs in workplaces that lack the formal organization (such as collective bargaining agreements, bureaucratic control, or professional or craft patterns) of primary markets; it contains jobs such as those of service and retail workers, clerks, seasonal workers, and nonunionized employees of small businesses.

Segmented labor markets are labor markets that have been divided institutionally into distinct or separate markets (market segments); the separation of the segments is often maintained by racial, sexual, and other forms of discrimination.

Self-interest refers to a disposition to consider only how one's actions will affect oneself, not how they may affect others.

The **separation of conception from execution** is one method for deskilling work in which the workers who plan production are different from those who carry it out.

Shared monopoly. *See* **oligopoly.**

Simple control is a system of control that focuses on the supervisors' personal exercise of workplace rewards and sanctions to maintain the work pace.

Slavery was the dominant economic system in the U.S. South before the Civil War; slaveholders obtained the surplus product by owning all of the inputs (including slaves) and the output of slave production.

Social costs are the costs of producing a good or service that are borne by society as a whole. *See also* **private costs.**

Social democracy is a form of government intervention in the economy in which a democratic government obtains agreement between at least the most powerful groups of employers and workers on a "social contract."

The **social organization of work** refers to the way in which jobs are defined, work tasks assigned, supervisory power delegated, and other social aspects of the workplace organized.

A **social structure of accumulation (SSA)** is the institutional setting within which accumulation occurs; it structures relations among capitalists, between capitalists and workers, among workers, and between government and the economy. Two phases of an SSA can be distinguished: first, its "consolidation" and, second, its "decay."

Sovereignty refers to the ability and right of a person or group to make a decision; democratic government confers sovereignty on the citizenry, whereas capitalist economy confers sovereignty, especially with respect to investment, on the owners of capital goods.

Speedup is an effort by an employer to increase the pace of work.

Spillovers. *See* **externalities.**

The **stages of American capitalism** are distinct phases in the development of U.S. capitalism, with each being defined by a particular social structure of accumulation.

Stagflation refers to the combination of slower economic growth (stagnation) and generally rising prices (inflation) that characterized the hard times of the 1970s.

Stagnation refers to the hard-times phase of a long swing; it is characterized by slower economic growth or even economic decline.

A share of **stock** represents a share of ownership of a corporation and entitles its holder to receive a dividend—a specific amount of money per share—whenever a corporation decides to pay out a portion of its total profits in the form of dividends to its stockholders.

Structural inflation occurs when the price level increases rapidly throughout the course of a business cycle.

The **subordinate primary labor market** includes those jobs in workplaces organized according to the collective bargaining agreements of the labor accord; it contains mainly the jobs of the traditional, unionized, industrial working class.

A **supply curve** indicates, for each possible price, how much of the good or service suppliers wish to sell.

The **surplus product** is what remains out of the total product after the necessary product has been deleted.

A **system of control** is an employer's strategy or method for governing the workplace to facilitate the extraction of work from the workers.

A **tariff** is a tax on goods or services coming into a country.

Technical control is a system of control that incorporates a work pace designed into the machinery of production.

Technical progress is a change in the relationship between inputs and outputs that permits the same output to be produced with less of one or more of the inputs.

A production process is said to be **technically efficient** if the output of it cannot be increased without using more of at least one of the inputs.

Technology is the relationship between inputs and outputs in a labor process.

The **total cost of investment** consists of two parts, the cost of the capital goods purchased and the opportunity cost of the money used to purchase them.

The **total product** is the total amount of goods and services produced in an economy during a given period of time.

The **trade deficit** is the excess of the value of a country's imports of goods and services over its exports of goods and services.

A **trade-off** is a relationship between two or more things in which more of one thing can be obtained only at the cost of getting less of the other.

A **trade surplus** is the excess of the value of a country's exports of goods and services over its imports of goods and services.

Unemployment occurs when there are not enough jobs for all those who want jobs (an excess supply in the labor market).

Unemployment compensation consists of regular payments made to some unemployed workers from a government insurance fund to which employers contribute.

Uneven development is the process of rapid growth in some parts of the capitalist world and slow growth or even economic decline in others.

A **union** is an organization of workers established with the intention of providing a unified and stronger voice on behalf of the members' interests.

Unit labor cost is the labor portion of the average cost of producing each unit of output.

The **value of capital goods owned per hour of labor** is the value of the firm's total investment in capital goods divided by the total number of hours worked by employees.

The **value of net output per hour of labor** is the dollar value of the total output minus materials and machine costs divided by the total number of hours worked.

The **value of the dollar** is the amount of a foreign currency that a dollar will buy when exchanged in the foreign exchange market, also known as the foreign exchange rate.

Vertical economic interdependence exists when one person controls the labor and the products of another; it is based on a relationship of unequal advantage and command.

Wage labor is work performed under the direction of an employer in return for a wage or salary.

A **wage-led employment situation** obtains when rising wages increase employment.

The **wage rate** is the amount paid to a worker for each hour worked.

Wealth is the ownership of a stock of durable things or intangibles that yield income or other benefits over an extended period of time.

Work effort refers to a worker's level of exertion (intensity of work) on the job during a certain period of time, say, an hour.

The **working class,** or **workers,** are those who perform wage labor; they neither own the capital goods used in their labor processes nor command control over the labor of others.

INDEX